MW00992984

Global Supply Chains

About the Authors

Mandyam M. (Srini) Srinivasan, Ph.D., is the Pilot Corporation Chair of Excellence in Business in the Department of Statistics, Operations, and Management Science at the University of Tennessee, Knoxville. He won the Franz Edelman Award for Achievement in Operations Research in 2006. Dr. Srinivasan is the author of *Building Lean Supply Chains with the Theory of Constraints* and *Streamlined: 14 Principles for Building and Managing the Lean Supply Chain*, and coauthor of *Supply Chain Management for Competitive Advantage: Concepts and Cases.*

Theodore P. (Ted) Stank, Ph.D., is the Harry and Vivienne Bruce Chair of Excellence in Business in the Department of Marketing and Supply Chain Management at the University of Tennessee, Knoxville. He is the author of more than 90 articles in academic and professional journals and coauthor of *21st Century Logistics: Making Supply Chain Integration a Reality* and *Handbook of Global Supply Chain Management*. Dr. Stank was named a Logistics Rainmaker by *DC Velocity* magazine and serves as the Chair-Elect of the Board of Directors of the Council of Supply Chain Management Professionals.

Philippe-Pierre Dornier, Ph.D., is Professor of Operations Management at ESSEC Business School in Paris, France, where he teaches supply chain and operations management in the MBA, specialized masters, and executive education programs. He is Associate Dean of the executive program. Dr. Dornier is Managing Partner of Newton Vaureal Consulting and has been in charge of the re-engineering of global logistic networks for large companies.

Kenneth J. (Ken) Petersen, Ph.D., is the John H. "Red" Dove Professor of Supply Chain Management in the Department of Marketing and Supply Chain Management at the University of Tennessee, Knoxville, and Visiting Senior Fellow at Manchester Business School in Manchester, England. His research interests include buyer-supplier relationships, new product development, sustainability, global sourcing, and supply chain risk. Ken serves as an Associate Editor for the Journal of Operations Management, the Journal of Supply Chain Management, and the Journal of Business Logistics.

Global Supply Chains

Evaluating Regions on an EPIC Framework— Economy, Politics, Infrastructure, and Competence

Mandyam M. Srinivasan, Ph.D.

Theodore P. Stank, Ph.D.

Philippe-Pierre Dornier, Ph.D.

Kenneth J. Petersen, Ph.D.

New York   Chicago   San Francisco
Athens   London   Madrid
Mexico City   Milan   New Delhi
Singapore   Sydney   Toronto

1 2 3 4 5 6 7 8 9 0   DOC/DOC   1 9 8 7 6 5 4 3

ISBN   978-0-07-179231-8
MHID   0-07-179231-7

Sponsoring Editor Judy Bass	**Copy Editor** Kay Mikel
Editing Supervisor Stephen M. Smith	**Proofreader** Linda Leggio
Production Supervisor Lynn M. Messina	**Indexer** Robert Swanson
Acquisitions Coordinator Amy Stonebraker	**Art Director, Cover** Jeff Weeks
Project Manager Anupriya Tyagi, Cenveo® Publisher Services	**Composition** Cenveo Publisher Services

Printed and bound by RR Donnelley.

CONTENTS

PREFACE

The book you are holding is the outcome of a unique partnership between four coauthors who grew up in different parts of the world: the United States, France, and India. In late 2010, the four embarked on a journey to identify answers to key issues and questions about global supply chain management. Assume that you are the global supply chain manager of an organization and have been tasked by your chief executive officer with building partnerships with key suppliers and customers to enhance your organization's competitive position in the marketplace. To fulfill this key task, the scope of your decision making is global—you are not just focused on domestic partnerships but are contemplating collaboration with organizations in other regions of the world. What information would you need to help you decide with whom you would partner? On an even broader note, upon which region of the world would you focus?

The Promise and the Challenges for Global Supply Chains

From one perspective, global supply chains hold promise in two ways—to source cheaper goods and services, and to offer your products to a global marketplace thereby opening up your markets to a much larger population base. As global supply chain activity increases, organizations in one country increasingly depend on organizations from other countries, either to procure raw materials or to market their products. Organizations should, therefore, position themselves to take advantage of such codependencies to further their competitive position in the marketplace.

From another perspective, the complex interconnected nature of the activities in the global supply chain presents numerous challenges. Managing a global supply chain requires coordination of multiple inputs and outputs among several enterprises spread across several countries. Decisions surrounding supply chain strategies are often structural in nature, involving where to source material, where to locate a manufacturing facility, or where to open a retail center. For example, a decision to source material from a new location is often accompanied by a decision to close—or at least reduce the amount of material from—an existing source. Such decisions cannot be reversed easily if the new location does not meet expectations.

Building an efficient global supply chain poses other significant challenges. The manager has to juggle a multitude of often-conflicting objectives: changing consumer expectations of product features, quality and customer service, coordination between disparate supply chain partners to integrate supply and demand, the risk of supply chain disruptions, governmental rules and regulations in the countries involved in the supply chain, and environmental concerns. Managers of global supply chains can benefit from a framework that will help them assess their supply chain strategies. This book aims at providing the manager with such a framework.

The Purpose of This Book

The goal of this book is to provide information about supply chains in each region in the world, identifying their unique characteristics, to help the decision maker arrive at more informed decisions. Managers of global supply chains can use the framework developed in this book to help them assess their supply chain strategies, identifying the strengths, weaknesses, opportunities, and threats of the different regions in the world. This framework is termed the EPIC structure.

The EPIC Structure

The EPIC structure provides a framework for assessing 55 countries in 10 geographic regions around the globe on their supply chain readiness from four different perspectives: Economy (E), Politics (P), Infrastructure (I), and Competence (C). The purpose of the EPIC structure is to define and explain the conceptual dimensions of global supply chain management and to identify the characteristics of those dimensions in 10 distinct regions of the world. The structure is intended to help organizations that wish to invest in or manage supply chains in these regions or countries. Each of these dimensions evaluates a number of variables to arrive at a weighted score for that dimension. In turn, the scores on these dimensions are used to arrive at a weighted score for the country.

The majority of the variables in the EPIC structure are assessed using results from in-depth studies conducted by well-established organizations. These studies include the World Bank's Ease of Doing Business Index, Logistics Performance Index, and World Governance Indicators, the Central Intelligence Agency's CIA World Factbook, and the World Economic Forum's Global Competitive Index.

What Is Unique about This Book?

This book differs from the traditional perspective of global supply chain management in several ways. Global supply chain management has typically been defined and operationalized primarily from the perspective of academics and practitioners in either

North America or Western Europe, ignoring the potentially different perspectives native to other regions of the world. A major reason for such an ethnocentric North American and European perspective is historical, emerging from an economic history of the last 500 years that is weighted heavily toward the Western world. As we have been recently reminded, however, the world is becoming "flat," with increased interaction among different nations and regions around the world. At the same time, differences between countries are much larger than acknowledged. Thus organizations ignore regional uniqueness at their own peril.

Worse yet, organizations may not realize or be prepared for the regional differences—cultural and otherwise—that might jeopardize the success of their global strategies. For example, consider offshoring initiatives. Some organizations may not fully understand the rules of this new global playing field. They may not be prepared to manage the governmental rules and regulations of the country in which they are planning to conduct offshore activity. Even organizations that have significant experience in offshoring may find understanding this environment to be an ongoing process.

Most managers do not have the luxury of spending time "in country" to learn the nuances of such issues prior to making decisions. Having a handy reference to information critical to good global supply chain decision making can significantly help these executives manage supply chains in both emerging and mature markets. It is the pursuit of such knowledge that has driven the authors of this book to explore key elements of the Economy, Politics, Infrastructure, and Competence levels in 10 global regions and 55 nations.

How This Book Will Help You

The research conducted for this book reveals that key variables in the macro-environment can help managers better understand the framework for decision making and reduce uncertainty. For example, despite the dynamism and uncertainty of the global environment, there are longer and more consistent trends related to political stability, economic investment in capital, labor, and infrastructure, and cultural norms that either aid or hinder nations around the world from becoming viable options for supply chain operations. Such conditions may be analyzed to aid decision making. Other decisions are dictated by the location of relatively scarce materials such as energy, rare earth metals, or agricultural products. Similarly, the location of markets and infrastructure for final goods distribution can be determined with relative certainty.

Knowledge of the levels of these variables enables supply chain managers to choose the locations for value-added supply chain operations for their enterprise, including transportation hubs and modes for raw materials, location of parts and subcomponent suppliers, finished goods manufacturing and assembly locations, and transportation and distribution hubs for finished goods. In particular, the research results reveal interesting combinations of sourcing, manufacturing, and logistics options for different regional consumer markets.

This book supports the notion that global supply chains across the world will break into a series of demand and supply pods in which regional procurement and manufacturing operations will supply the major demand centers of the area, at least for a significant percentage of production requirements. Clearly some low-cost "commodity" items will continue to be procured from low-labor-cost regions across the globe. However, the trend appears to be toward more regional activity. The question then becomes one of identifying the most advantageous regional locations for such offshoring or outsourcing activity. Should organizations return to procuring from, and manufacturing at, their domestic locations? If so, is the talent and infrastructure still there? Are the total costs and tax environment competitive?

Although competing forces at play are "flattening" the world, there are also increasing differences among regions. Indeed, it appears that there will be a period of "semi-globalization" in business during which distance matters and different standards persist across regions. As a result, global supply chains will have to primarily deal with regional pods of demand that present unique supply challenges rather than working with one standard global supply chain footprint. Another consequence is that forward-looking supply chain managers must have the knowledge and information necessary to coordinate multiple inputs and outputs among several enterprises spread across several countries. These managers will have to learn how to mitigate the significant time delays and cost distortions that often accompany supply chains spread across the globe.

This book has taken shape over a three-year time period. During this time, the authors have traveled to more than 20 countries and experienced supply chain practices in these regions. These visits have helped reinforce some of the notions the authors had and led them to discard some other notions. For example, during a recent visit to China and Singapore, they found positive reinforcement for some of their beliefs on how the trading supply chains that existed among East, South, and Southeast Asian economies over the past two centuries have shaped some of the supply chain practices in these regions even in the 21st century. Many of these practices, deeply rooted in historic and cultural traditions, are significantly different from practices in the Western world, and they are unlikely to fade away even with increasing global supply chain activity.

Who Should Read the Book

When this book was conceived in 2010, the original intent was to develop material the four coauthors could present to students in the Global Supply Chain Executive MBA Program, launched in 2013 as a joint partnership between the University of Tennessee in

Knoxville, USA, and ESSEC in Paris, France. However, the book rapidly evolved into one that professionals can readily use. For example, it can be used as a guide for procurement, logistics, and operations professionals to help them better manage their activities within the broader context of the supply chain in which they operate. The book is also written in such a way that even full-time MBA students with relatively little experience will be able to understand the concepts and use them to enhance their knowledge of global supply chains. Furthermore, although the book was originally aimed at supply chain executive MBAs and professionals, it is valuable for students in any executive MBA or similar professional program that offers courses in operations, logistics, and supply chain management. The book is also a useful reference for educators, consultants, and practitioners who interact with any element in the supply chain.

Mandyam M. Srinivasan, Ph.D.
Theodore P. Stank, Ph.D.
Philippe-Pierre Dornier, Ph.D.
Kenneth J. Petersen, Ph.D.

ACKNOWLEDGMENTS

Generally speaking, business academics commit to write *after* they have developed considerable knowledge about a topic in the pursuit of other scholarly objectives. Once the original objective is achieved, they find that a book is the only appropriate outlet to disseminate the totality of the ideas bursting forth from that initiative. Such was not the case with this book. Our coauthor team has traveled the globe in pursuit of supply chain knowledge, but we are not trained in global economics or politics, nor are we experts in international tax law, trade law, or labor relations. Rather, we undertook to write this book because we recognized a need for a comprehensive treatment of the economic, political, infrastructural, and business competence complexities confronted by supply chain managers as they traverse the globe seeking efficient and effective solutions for supplying the products and services that make the world run. Thus, after agreeing to write the book, we first had to conduct the research needed to do so. The task was daunting, but we have managed to compile what we believe is a useful, although by no means exhaustive, guidebook for managers faced with the overwhelming task of making global supply chain location and management decisions.

As with any such undertaking, we benefited significantly from our support network, beginning with our wives, Kanchan, Lori, Valérie, and Sigrid, who all endured our absences as we traveled and locked ourselves in offices working on the research and the manuscript. In addition, a host of graduate students assisted us greatly, including Yuan Li, Tiffany Rosenbach, Corryn Mullins, Dan Pellathy, Erin Petersen, Ulrich Schmelzle, and Kendra Wills. We benefited considerably from the assistance of managers and colleagues all across the globe who took the time to help us better understand their worlds and improve our insights, including Jonathan Bader, Rob McIntosh, Karen Yan, Doug Grey, Leonard Alcala, Abdulrahman Al Husaini, Abdullah Al Hussaini, Marlon Catalano, Lisa Druesdow, Meghann Erhart, Hisham Khaki, Brad Liddie, Kim Miller, Mohamed Moustafa, Greg Salmonson, A. J. Schuchart, and Michael Weber.

A number of our colleagues helped us write some the chapters. Professor S. Viswanathan, Faculty of Information Technology and Operations Management, Nanyang Business School, Singapore, coauthored the chapter on Southeast Asia. Marina Razafindrazaka helped edit the chapter on Sub-Saharan Africa. Professor Sebastian Jarzebowski and

Professor Agnieszka Bezat-Jarzebowska, Faculty of Economic Sciences, Warsaw University of Life Sciences, Poland, coauthored the chapter on Central and Eastern Europe. Finally, we thank our editor Judy Bass and copy editor Kay Mikel. Without all of their assistance, this book would not have been possible. Of course, we take sole responsibility for all errors and misconceptions that may appear.

CHAPTER 1

The Global Supply Chain Landscape

"Global supply chains." These words can evoke widely contrasting emotions depending on your perspective. From one perspective, global supply chains offer significant benefits to consumers because the law of comparative advantage[a] promises the availability of cheaper goods and services to the multitude. Global supply chains also offer tremendous potential to producers, opening up their markets to a huge population base.

From another perspective global supply chains can hurt the economy in a number of ways. It can result in more jobs moving overseas to cheaper labor markets. An accompanying fear is that when these jobs move overseas, the skills associated with these jobs may also eventually disappear. Other concerns include a possible increase in supply chain risks and complexity because goods may now be procured from remote locations. The time delay in acquiring these goods is also a matter of concern.

Before weighing in on either perspective, let's define *global supply chain*: a worldwide network of suppliers, manufacturers, warehouses, distribution centers, and retailers through which raw materials are acquired, transformed, and delivered to customers. Whether global supply chains are seen in a positive or negative light, people across the world have come to accept the notion that globalization and global supply chains are here to stay. The British politician Clare Short aptly captured this notion, stating "People have accused me of being in favor of globalization. This is equivalent to accusing me of being in favor of the sun rising in the morning."

Assuming that global supply chains are here to stay, a logical conclusion is that organizations in one country will depend on organizations from other countries, either to supply material or to market their products. A natural question to ask is what are organizations doing to take advantage of such codependencies to build partnerships that will enhance their competitive position in the marketplace? What are the key issues on the

---

[a] In economics, the law of comparative advantage refers to the ability of a party to produce a product at a lower cost compared to another party.

mind of the *chief executive officer* (CEO) and her team, in particular, the global supply chain manager? Do these issues cover strategies for nurturing collaboration with organizations in other regions of the world? If so, which regions? Answers to these questions require an assessment of the key issues surrounding global supply chains.

One of these issues is that supply chains, and global supply chains in particular, have been defined and operationalized narrowly, primarily from the perspective of academics and practitioners in North America and Western Europe. Such a perspective ignores potentially differing perspectives from people in other regions of the world. The reasons for such ethnocentric North American and European perspectives are historical, emerging from the economic history of the last 500 years. However, the world is increasingly getting "flat," at least from a regional perspective. Thus organizations ignore regional uniqueness at their own peril.

The goal of this book is to provide information about supply chains in each region in the world, identify their unique characteristics, and help the decision maker arrive at more informed decisions. To this end, it is informative to discuss the evolution of supply chains over time to gain some insight into the nature of present-day global supply chains. These insights will facilitate subsequent discussions on strategies and tactics CEOs and their teams can adopt to enhance the competitive position of their organizations.

Supply Chain Evolution—Journey to the Past

Supply chains are not recent manifestations. They have been in existence for many centuries although the term *supply chain* was almost surely not commonplace until late into the 20th century. Supply chains have, however, undergone a series of phase transitions over the years, typically fueled by technological advances that made obsolete, or rendered ineffective, some supply chain practices in force at the time these technological advances took place. It is instructive to examine how leading organizations and even countries adapted to these advances to enhance their dominance in the marketplace.

Supply Chains through Circa 1750: Trading Supply Chains

Supply chains through about 1750 are best characterized as *trading supply chains*—networks of trading partners that engaged in moving goods from one location to another, usually without transforming the goods at intermediate locations. The Phoenicians, for example, traded actively with Egypt more than 4500 years ago. They established networks of trading partnerships with neighboring countries, exporting cedar, olive oil, and wine, and importing gold and other products from the Nile Valley. Initially, production was mostly localized, with individuals or very small groups producing the products from locally available materials. The products were originally sold only locally, but with improvements in transportation trade between more distant places emerged.

The Early Long-Distance Voyagers

Many historians believe that the earliest long-distance trade took place between the fourth and third millennium BC, between Mesopotamia (the region comprising Iraq and parts of Turkey, Iran, and Syria) and the Indus Valley in Pakistan. There is also evidence that maritime routes were already in place in India and China well before this time. In the absence of proper roads, goods were primarily transported by water. For example, the Egyptians had trade routes through the Red Sea, importing spices from East Africa and Arabia. Cities grew in fertile basins on the borders of rivers and expanded by using these water highways to import and export goods by sea to far-flung countries.

Around 1000 BC, trade routes over land emerged. Caravans using camels linked India and the East with the Mediterranean. Goods were now traded along routes that reached beyond the Mediterranean all the way to Scandinavia and Ireland.

The Silk Road and Incense and Spice Routes

The *Silk Road*, a term coined by German geographer Ferdinand von Richthofen in 1877, was a network of interlinking trade routes that extended over 4000 miles across the Afro-Eurasian landmass, connecting Asia with Europe. Trade on the Silk Road thrived during the Han Dynasty (206 BC to AD 220). The Silk Road lasted until well into the 15th century, and it played a significant role in the economic development of China, India, Persia, and Arabia.

The term *Silk Road* is somewhat misleading for a couple of reasons. First, it was not a single route but rather a network of routes passing through different oasis settlements across Central Asia. Second, although silk was the major commodity traded, many other commodities were also traded. Caravans heading toward the East carried gold and other precious stones, metals, and ivory. Traffic in the opposite direction contained furs, ceramics, jade, lacquer, and bronze objects. Goods often changed hands several times.

Even though the Silk Road was a network of routes, such trading supply chains were typically *linear supply chains* in the sense that goods and materials were moved directly from the production source to the customer destination.

Another important trade route, the *Incense Route*, was a network of major ancient land and sea trading routes stretching from Mediterranean ports to India and beyond, traversing the Levant-Mashriq region[b] and Egypt through eastern Africa and Arabia. The Incense Route flourished from around 600 BC to AD 100 and was mainly controlled by Arab merchants, who used camel caravans to transport frankincense and myrrh. These highly prized fragrances were obtained from trees growing in southern Arabia, Ethiopia, and

---

[b] The Levant and the Mashriq denote more or less the same geographic and cultural region. The Levant region includes modern Lebanon, Syria, Jordan, Israel, parts of Iraq, Cyprus, and parts of southern Turkey. The Mashriq region includes Lebanon, Syria, Jordan, Israel, Iraq, and Kuwait.

Somalia. These merchants also utilized the Incense Route to transport spices, gold, ivory, pearls, precious stones, and textiles from Africa, India, and the Far East.

The *Spice Route*, which refers to the trade between historic civilizations in Asia, northeast Africa and Europe, provides another example of a far-flung trading supply chain. This route flourished during the Middle Ages (AD 450 to 1500). Spices such as cinnamon, cassia, cardamom, ginger, and turmeric were traded on this route.

The Silk Road, Incense Route, and Spice Route connected the East with Europe, but there was little trade between the Americas and the rest of the world until the mid-1500s when the *Spanish Treasure Fleet* started operations. The Spanish Treasure Fleet, also known as the *Plate Fleet* due to the Spanish word for silver (*plata*), was a convoy system used by the Spanish Empire from the mid-1500s to around 1800 to transport silver, gold, wood, metal, precious stones, spices, silk, sugar, tobacco, and other goods from the Spanish colonies in the Americas to Spain. Tools and military personnel were transported on the reverse route.

Although the Incense Route and the Plate Fleet were mainly controlled by the Arabs and the Spanish, respectively, trading supply chains had no dominant organizations controlling them in general. A notable exception was the East India Company, which was established in 1600. This organization (the *Company*) started as a trading company, attracted by the Indian subcontinent's riches, in particular the wealth generated by the textile industry in the state of Bengal. However, in the 1700s it began to enforce its interests in textile trade and gradually started to assert territorial control of major portions of the Indian subcontinent. Until this time, India and China played dominant roles in trading supply chains. In 1700, these two countries were among the wealthiest in the world, with a combined *Gross Domestic Product* (GDP) that accounted for 46.74 percent of world GDP using an international dollar[c] as the basis for comparison (Table 1.1).

The trading practices of the Company combined with the Industrial Revolution in England to dramatically alter this situation. The Industrial Revolution, triggered by the growth of the textile industry in Manchester, England, in the 17th century, helped shift the center of supply chain activity from Asia to Europe. The Industrial Revolution also generated a phase transition from trading supply chains to *manufacturing supply chains*.

Supply Chains from 1750 to 1990: Manufacturing Supply Chains

Prior to the Industrial Revolution goods were produced manually or by using simple machinery. This was the *craft* method of production. Goods were usually made in rural areas from locally available raw materials. Individuals, or groups of individuals, typically worked on an item until it was complete and ready to deliver to a customer. For a while craft production continued to dominate and goods continued to be produced and consumed

---

[c] A hypothetical unit of currency used in economics, based on PPP and average international commodity prices.

Table 1.1 Share of World GDP, International Dollars, 1700 to 1973

Region	1700 (percent)	1870 (percent)	1950 (percent)	1973 (percent)
United Kingdom	2.88	9.10	6.52	4.21
France	5.70	6.55	4.13	4.26
Germany	3.61	6.49	4.97	5.88
Italy	3.94	3.80	3.09	3.63
United States	0.14	8.93	27.28	22.02
Japan	4.14	2.31	3.02	7.74
China	22.30	17.23	4.50	4.61
India	24.44	12.25	4.16	3.08
World (Total)	100.0	100.0	100.0	100.0

Source: Angus Maddison, The World Economy—A Millennial Perspective, Development Center of the Organization for Economic Cooperation & Development, p. 263, Table B-20, Paris, 2001.

within relatively small regions. Industrialization was, however, beginning to attract the same form of interest as was evoked by agricultural innovations developed by men like Jethro Tull (1674–1741), who is credited with the seed drill and the horse hoe.

Although it is difficult to pinpoint the beginning of the Industrial Revolution, historians generally agree that it originated in England in the 18th century, fueled by a series of technological and social innovations, and gradually spread to the rest of Europe. The Industrial Revolution, defined by the application of power-driven machinery to manufacturing, was enabled by the steam engine and its application to the creation of power-driven machines as well as to rapid advances in transportation.

By the middle of the 18th century, the tendency of craftsmen to resist industrialization was weakening even though supply chains in the early 1800s were still primarily trading supply chains, involving networks of trading partners. These trading partners did not operate on, or transform, the goods at intermediate locations. Manufacturing supply chains were still not prevalent at this time; they were awaiting a few key events that took place early in the 19th century. Notable among these events were the propagation of railroads and steamships and the harnessing of electric power.

Railroads, Steamboats, Rivers, and Canals

One reason the Industrial Revolution did not affect the United States as quickly as it did England and the rest of Europe was because the United States was a continental economy. Slow transportation was a formidable barrier to economic growth. The construction of turnpikes in the early 19th century helped, but only slightly, as wagons could only travel 20 miles per day. The Erie Canal, completed in 1825, improved transportation speeds.

The canal connected the Great Lakes with New York City and linked Midwestern farmers with the East Coast. But canal boats were relatively slow and could not operate when canals were iced up, so they offered an inadequate transportation solution. The introduction of railroads upgraded this state of affairs.

The railroads were the first "big business" in the United States, connecting the Atlantic coast with the Great Lakes in 1850, with Chicago in 1853, and with the western side of the Mississippi in 1856. Railroads cut transportation costs, expanded markets, and cut price differentials across distant markets. For example, in the late 1840s, Cincinnati wholesale flour prices were only 70 percent of the New York prices, but a decade later they were at 95 percent, as prices declined in New York. The convergence in pricing helped living standards on the East Coast, where the reduced prices made flour accessible to a larger population, and benefited Midwestern farmers, who could now supply that larger market.

The year 1869 was a significant year for U.S. railroad development because it signaled the completion of a continuous railroad line all the way from the Atlantic Ocean to the Pacific Ocean. Soon trains were carrying freight loaded with cargo such as tea, silk, and handiwork from Japan, India, and China as well as spices, fruits, cattle, sheep, and minerals all across the continental United States.

Just as the railroads were the first big business in the United States, they also played a significant role in the economy of the United Kingdom, albeit in a different way. Being a relatively small country, the United Kingdom did not gain the tremendous cuts in transportation costs the United States enjoyed from the introduction of railroads. However, railroads played a major role in its colony, India, where the British developed a huge railway infrastructure to transport the output from Britain's industrial revolution to the Indian hinterland, and to carry raw materials, troops, and agricultural products within the Indian subcontinent.

Steam-driven ships gained popularity at the turn of the 19th century. Unlike sailing vessels, steam-driven ships were not affected greatly by weather conditions and could travel faster across the seas. Steam-driven ships with paddlewheels began to replace sailing vessels in the U.S. Great Lakes and in the oceans, and the first steamship crossed the Atlantic in 1843. By the 1850s the North Atlantic was crossed regularly by steamship. Since steam-driven ships traveled much faster across the ocean, governments paid the ship owners large amounts of money to carry mail and freight. When Hans Christian Andersen published his first book of fairy tales in 1835, it took 43 days for news to reach the United States. Less than 20 years later, news from Europe was reaching U.S. residents in 14 days.

By the mid-1800s, industrialization was widespread in Europe and in the northeastern United States. As shown in Table 1.1, the U.S. GDP rose from 0.14 percent of world GDP to 8.93 percent in 1870, growing at a rapid pace even as manufacturing supply chains continued to develop in Europe and the United States. As new means of transportation and communication increased the pace of life, the world continued to shrink at a rapid rate.

The once-leading economies of the world, India and China, were now no longer the dominant economies, having a combined GDP of less than 30 percent in 1870. The Company hastened this shift, effectively transferring wealth from the British colonies to the United Kingdom, as discussed in Chapter 4 on South Asia. Thus, even as the GDPs for India and China were shrinking, the GDP of the United Kingdom rose sharply, from 2.88 percent in 1700 to 9.10 percent in 1870.

The Mass Production Era—Machines to Save Our Lives

Manufacturing supply chains gained momentum during the mass production era. Eli Whitney's discovery of interchangeability had a profound impact on mass production; it was now possible to produce components for a product at one location and transport them to another location for assembly. However, two events that took place in the early 1900s played key roles in the evolution of manufacturing supply chains. The first was the historic flight of the Wright brothers, which ushered in the age of air transportation, and the second was the moving assembly line introduced by Henry Ford.

As noted by Foster,[1] "the historic flight by the Wright brothers on December 17, 1903 covered all of 120 feet, less than half the length of a football field. Had they launched their aircraft at the back of the Boeing 747's economy section, they wouldn't have made it to first class." The Wright brothers were instrumental in changing the way people perceived transportation and travel times. Even Jules Verne, the well-known science-fiction author who wrote *Around the World in Eighty Days* in 1873, probably had no idea how much the world would advance in just 50 years.

Right around the time the Wright brothers were changing the way the world perceived travel, Henry Ford (1863–1947) was perfecting his manufacturing and assembly operations to change the way the world would perceive manufacturing. Henry Ford exploited mass production to the hilt, passing the benefits back to the customer. Before he established operations, automobiles cost more than $1000. Ford focused on removing waste from every step in the process, which allowed him to slash production costs. He passed much of the cost savings back to his customers. The price of the Model T dropped from $850 in 1909 to $260 in 1925. It is thus little wonder that *Fortune* magazine chose Henry Ford as the "businessman of the century" in its November 22, 1999, issue.

The U.S. manufacturing industry, in particular, the auto industry, flourished throughout the first half of the 20th century, well into the 1970s. It was a time when demand far outstripped supply, and customers were willing to buy anything the manufacturers had to sell. This period was perceived as a "golden era" for U.S. industry, but it was actually a problematic period in a number of ways. For instance, the big-three auto companies were effectively a cartel led by General Motors. But cartels, like their more integrated cousins, monopolies, tend to become inefficient and ineffective because they can afford to be.

Mass production methods compounded these problems, generating a large inventory of finished cars and *work-in-process* (WIP) inventory within the factories. The high WIP inventory buffered any production delays that might otherwise have resulted from quality problems, and diminished the sense of urgency to fix these problems so they did not occur again. Furthermore, quality problems often were not caught until after the product was sold. In short, the U.S. auto industry was badly in need of a shake-up. It got just this shake-up in the 1970s when the oil crisis opened the door for imports from Japan.

Japanese auto manufacturers produced about half a million vehicles in 1960, a year in which U.S. auto manufacturers built 8 million vehicles. Who could have predicted that in 1980, just 20 years later, the Japanese automakers would produce more than 11 million vehicles[2]—3 million vehicles more than the output from the U.S. automakers in that same year—and remain the world's leading auto producer for the next 10 years?

Lean Production—Domo Arigato, Mr. Ohno

The Japanese automobile manufacturers achieved this tremendous degree of success because they dedicated themselves, at least initially, to developing compact and subcompact cars with excellent fuel economy. The oil crisis provided the opportunity for them to penetrate the U.S. market with these smaller cars. Furthermore, these manufacturers succeeded in producing vehicles at a low cost by adopting *a just-in-time* (JIT) production management philosophy, led by pioneers such as Taiichi Ohno, who was largely instrumental in developing the well-known Toyota production system. These JIT production management techniques, often referred to as *lean production*, or simply *Lean*, became the model for manufacturing practices worldwide.

Lean was more flexible than traditional methods that manufactured products in large batches. Consequently, this flexibility was achieved with significantly less inventory in the system. The Japanese cars also found acceptance in the U.S. market because consumers found these cars were of much better quality than U.S. made cars.

A number of the Lean concepts embedded in Japanese manufacturing practices were inspired by Henry Ford's relentless attention to detail, but the Japanese automakers built on his ideas. For example, Henry Ford offered automobiles to his customers in only one color to reduce setup times when changing between paint colors. The Japanese adapted Ford's ideas to provide product variety in their offerings. By the end of the 1980s, Lean techniques were displacing traditional batch manufacturing techniques worldwide. Although initially applied only to the automobile manufacturing industry, other industries such as the electronics industry were soon adopting Lean to enhance productivity.

In general, Japan's manufacturing output grew at a remarkable pace. In 1970, its total annual manufacturing output was $71 billion, less than a third of the total U.S. annual

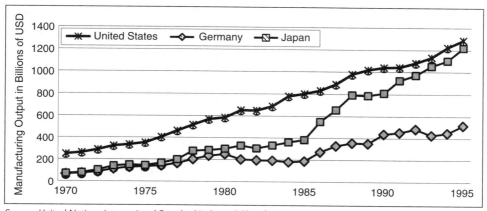

Source: United Nations International Standard Industrial Classification Data.

Figure 1.1 Manufacturing output for select countries, 1970 to 1995.

manufacturing output of $249 billion. By 1995, the manufacturing output for Japan was $1218 billion per annum, almost the same as the $1289 billion annual manufacturing output in the United States. Figure 1.1 provides the data on the three countries that had the highest manufacturing output in the world in 1995.

Until this time, communication between organizations located in different countries was typically limited to point-to-point communication between two end devices or users. Such communication took the form of either paper-based transactions, often delivered by snail mail, or via telephone, telegraph systems, or telex machines. Even email communication was relatively restricted. The introduction of the World Wide Web in 1990 removed these restrictions and dramatically enhanced global communication.

Supply Chains, 1990 to Present—Global IT-Enabled Supply Chains

In 1990, Sir Tim Berners-Lee, an employee of the European research firm CERN, and Belgian computer scientist Robert Cailliau proposed and developed a *hypertext* system to link and access various forms of documentation and information through "a web of nodes in which the user can browse at will".[3] This development, the World Wide Web, revolutionized information technology (IT). In particular, it unleashed the power of the Internet, which resulted in another phase transition, this time from manufacturing supply chains to global *IT-enabled supply chains*.

The Internet and the Web are often mistakenly understood to be synonymous, but the Internet predates the Web by several decades. The Internet was initially developed to facilitate point-to-point communication between mainframe computers and computer terminals in the 1960s. Shortly thereafter, the Internet was enhanced to handle point-to-point connections between computers, and eventually in the early 1980s it facilitated communication between networks of computers. Although originally conceived for use by the U.S. Department of Defense, the Internet was soon made available to research organizations and universities as well.

The development of the Web in 1990 allowed *Internet service providers* (ISPs) to provide commercial organizations access to the Internet. Commercial traffic initially faced some usage restrictions, but these restrictions were removed by 1995. With the removal of these restrictions, the cost of real-time international communications, barely affordable previously, became irrelevant.

The IT-enabled supply chain is now characterized by global reach between suppliers and customers—both within and across organizations. Enterprises in the supply chain now have the ability to determine the end user's actual demand and to plan their activities accordingly. Cutting-edge management techniques such as Lean have led to a quantum reduction in the time it takes organizations to fulfill customer demand. Advances in logistics have achieved similar reductions in the time products spend in storage and in transit. Supply chain members are more willing to set aside arms-length relationships to build long-term partnerships in industries as diverse as aerospace, grocery retailing, apparel manufacturing, automobile manufacturing, and health care.

Evolution or Devolution—Two Steps Forward, Two Steps Back?

Despite the promised benefits, the IT-enabled supply chain has not yet delivered to its full potential for a number of reasons. Unlike the *production-centric* era that prevailed for much of the 20th century, during which the demand for goods and services often outstripped production capacity, in the *customer-centric* business environment that characterizes the IT-enabled supply chain era, production capacity often exceeds customer demand. Managers in today's global business world are well aware of the fierce competitive environment in which they operate. Consumers are demanding better products, and they want them cheaper and faster. To remain competitive, organizations must respond to these customer demands in a world in which product life cycles are shrinking.

In many of these organizations, supply chain management has taken a step backward. These organizations are squandering some of the benefits that can be gained from improved technologies and techniques. Consider first the potential benefits provided by the Internet and advances in IT. The Internet has provided organizations with visibility of both customer demand and the movement of goods in the supply chain. However, the Internet has proved to be a double-edged sword for these organizations because it has also enabled price-sensitive customers to easily compare prices for any product or service. The majority of these products and services have thus become commoditized to some extent, resulting in some undesirable consequences, one of which is the manner in which organizations have responded to this commoditization.

Faced with increased global competition for their products and services, many organizations have resorted to cost-cutting efforts to meet Wall Street expectations on gross margins and quarterly profit and loss reports. No doubt costs must be controlled, but if cost considerations *dominate* decision making, the effectiveness of the supply chain or the product delivery system can deteriorate. It can lead to a paradoxical situation in which costs will, in fact, increase if all consequences are not carefully considered.

For example, to control costs, many organizations pursue labor and material arbitrage by *outsourcing* or *offshoring*[d] operations. The challenges faced by organizations in the 21st century that attempt to cut costs by offshoring are highlighted through a case study.

Homeward Bound—When Offshoring Goes Awry

Alpha Systems Corporation (ASC)[e] is a consumer electronics business headquartered in Knoxville, Tennessee. ASC's founder graduated from the University of Tennessee with a double major in business and agriculture. He combined his interests in business and animals to create a company focused on pet containment systems. His penchant was to create and sell innovative products; he left the sourcing, production, and logistics to outsourced providers.

In the early years he bought product from contract electronics manufacturers in the U.S. Southeast and Midwest and sold predominantly through regional sales outlets. As the business grew, his market area expanded and he began to use a national *third-party logistics* (3PL) organization to move his finished goods from the manufacturers to a distribution center in Indianapolis, Indiana. The 3PL also ran his customer order fulfillment from the Indianapolis facility.

As ASC continued to grow, it gradually added staff to plan and manage the increasingly complex supply chain. As this staff sought ways to reduce supply chain costs and boost profit margins, like many other electronics firms they began to consider sourcing product from contract electronics manufacturers in China. By the mid-2000s the firm had offshored virtually all product sourcing and manufacturing to Chinese suppliers.

---

[d] Both terms, *offshoring* and *outsourcing*, refer to the practice of contracting with another organization or person to perform a certain activity. Offshoring is a special case of outsourcing in which the activity is executed in another country.

[e] Actual name of the organization withheld.

Initially, ASC was enthralled by the dramatic reduction in its *cost of goods sold* (COGS) with this new purchasing arrangement. However, it soon found that this arrangement had a downside. There was a dramatic increase in average finished goods inventory, with an accompanying decrease in inventory turns. Cycle times from the Chinese manufacturers grew to an average of 140 days from order to delivery at the Indianapolis facility, and customer metrics such as product availability slipped. Worse, as fuel prices rose over the last several years, production labor rates in China steadily grew, and additional inventory was added to curb the risk of disruption or delay of orders, the COGS savings were greatly diminished. In sum, ASC discovered that there were a number of hidden costs and risks associated with offshoring. As a result of the changing cost and risk structure, the firm began considering other locations as alternatives to Chinese sourcing.

In general, when organizations pursue a cost-cutting strategy without giving much thought to enhancing customer service, they operate in a *cost world*. Such a world typically drives them toward incorrect decisions and strategies.

Where Have All the Savings Gone—When Will They Ever Learn?

Why do so many organizations find that the expected savings from offshoring and global sourcing initiatives do not materialize? An obvious answer is that these organizations simply did not do their homework, focusing on short-term cost reductions without considering all hidden costs while attempting to estimate the *total cost of ownership* (TCO) for offshoring decisions.

Clearly most organizations include transportation costs in TCO calculations. A number of organizations also consider port charges, customs duties, and tariffs; quality costs in the form of inspection costs and disposal costs per shipment; and schedule noncompliance costs that involve the costs of lost sales and expedited shipments. These organizations also typically consider the cost of additional pipeline inventory. A few organizations delve into the more complex costs involving supplier qualification costs and risk in the form of country risk, supply risk, currency risk, and intellectual property risks.

Only a very small percentage of these organizations, however, consider some of the hard-to-compute costs such as the cost of lead time and the cost of flexibility, two costs that can severely hurt an organization's competitive position. These two costs give a whole new meaning to the phrase "distance matters." Organizations that pay attention to these costs will tend to focus more on near-shoring, perhaps even in-shoring their procurement. In sum, the major costs that should go into the TCO calculations include:

- ▲ Transportation costs
  - ▼ Freight costs
  - ▼ Custom duties and tariffs
  - ▼ Brokerage fees

▲ Cost of additional inventory
  ▼ Pipeline inventory
  ▼ Safety stock
▲ Cost of quality and obsolescence
  ▼ Factor for warranty claims
  ▼ Scrap and obsolescence risk
  ▼ Inspection and disposal costs per shipment
▲ Cost of schedule noncompliance
  ▼ Expedite costs (air freight)
  ▼ Stockout and lost sales cost
▲ Risk costs
  ▼ Currency risk
  ▼ Country risk
  ▼ Competition (intellectual property) risk
  ▼ Job switching risk
▲ Payment terms
  ▼ Cash discounts
  ▼ Payment terms in days outstanding
▲ Cost of administration
  ▼ Offshore supplier qualification costs
  ▼ Cost of administration trips to offshore location
  ▼ Cost of communication
▲ Cost of responsiveness
  ▼ Lead time costs
  ▼ Flexibility costs
  ▼ Longer quality feedback loop costs
  ▼ Port congestion costs

In light of the TCO model, it seems clear that although fundamental changes are flattening the world, distance matters. It is likely that the boom in offshoring has passed. Organizations are a little more aware of the need to do a proper TCO analysis and to adopt a big-picture perspective with respect to their global supply chain.

Supply Chain Complexity—Does Anybody Really Care?

As the case study makes clear, offshoring typically increases the length of the supply chain both in terms of increased time delays and possibly an increased number of links in the supply chain. The result is increased supply chain complexity. Complex supply chains typically result in costs that are either hidden or, in the words of American statistician

Edwards Deming,[4] "unknown and unknowable." Some of the considerations are as follows:

▲ The decision process cannot ignore the impact of outsourcing on production costs for the products still manufactured in-house because these products will now bear the overhead costs that were previously absorbed by the outsourced product.

▲ Even if the organization carries some inventory of the outsourced product, there is a possible loss of responsiveness. The loss of responsiveness can result from the additional delays involved in transporting the product, not to mention possible delays in clearing customs if these products are offshored. This strategy also makes the organization more dependent on long-term forecasts and vulnerable to the inevitable demand cycles.

▲ Because the organization is no longer intimately involved in manufacturing the product, there is a real danger that the organization will be unable to manufacture it in-house at a later date if the situation requires it. This situation is analogous to the muscles in your body atrophying if they are not used.

▲ In addition, managers of such complex supply chains must now manage service providers more effectively to make these hidden costs as low as possible while, at the same time, making them more predictable.

Complex global supply chains with multiple links can result in some unintended consequences. For example, members in the supply chain may not know how their products are used by their downstream partners. In one instance a chip manufacturer thought its consignment was destined for DVD players, but the chip was instead diverted by the forwarding agent to be used in digital picture frames. Assuming that the chip worked well on the digital picture frame, the customers may have benefited from this error as they got a DVD chip for the price of a digital picture frame chip. However, the supply chain had to bear the difference in the production costs for the DVD player chips and the digital picture frame chips. Such a lack of clarity—and the accompanying costs—offset the increased visibility provided by the Internet, and lends support to the argument that some supply chains are undergoing a process of devolution.

The complex interconnected nature of the activities in the IT-enabled global supply chain presents numerous challenges. Managing a global supply chain requires coordination of multiple inputs and outputs among several enterprises spread across several countries. Simply passing orders up the supply chain and expecting upstream suppliers to execute these orders effectively is a mistake. The time delays and distortions are too great for this type of fulfillment. Vendors, brokers, *original equipment manufacturers* (OEMs), transportation providers, warehouses, and customers need the right kind of information to coordinate their activities to provide goods and services in timely and efficient ways. The need to manage such complex global supply chains cost effectively has also increased emphasis on the practice of *reverse logistics*.

Reverse Supply Chains—Return to Sender

Much managerial attention has been given to supply chain management in recent years, but most of that attention focuses on the forward supply chain—that is, managing the processes and activities related to getting products to customers. But sometimes goods move backward in the supply chain—from point of consumption or use, back toward the supplier. These reverse activities must be managed as well as the forward supply chain activities. Reverse supply chain activities include product recovery, reverse logistics, refurbishment/remanufacturing, product reuse and recycling, and remarketing into secondary markets.

Goods in the reverse supply chain can be categorized as consumer-generated returns or industrial returns, and can occur for a variety of reasons.[5] Consumer returns might represent buyer's remorse, Internet "try-on" returns (consumers order multiple sizes/colors and return the unsuitable items), product recalls, defective or warranty issues, or environmental returns (consumer recycling to keep products out of landfills). Industrial returns might include product recalls, defective or warranty issues, unsold retail items or leased items being returned to vendors, or reusable packaging being returned for reuse (pallets, drums, totes, cartons).

Recent attention on reverse supply chains may be attributed to a heightened focus on the environmental impact of products being sent to landfills. The European Union (EU), for example, has put increasing pressure on companies to recover and reuse products and to minimize hazardous substances in products.[6] There are also economic benefits deriving from reverse supply chain activities; for example, reducing costs by reusing products or by ensuring the latest styles occupy precious retail shelf space. Natural resource scarcity is also driving increased attention to the strategic importance of managing reverse supply chains. As both renewable and nonrenewable resources come under increasing pressure on a global basis, firms with supply chain capabilities geared toward recapturing and reprocessing components and materials from the marketplace are predicted to gain a significant competitive advantage.

A Spinning Wheel—What Goes Around . . . Comes Around

Regardless of whether the global IT-enabled supply chain has evolved or devolved, some countries that flourished during the trading supply chain era—but declined during the manufacturing supply chain era—are now reasserting themselves in this new era. The phase transition from trading to manufacturing supply chains was accompanied by a major shift in supply chain activity from Asia to Europe, eventually leading to the United States becoming the most dominant player in this arena by 1970. The phase transition from manufacturing supply chains to global IT-enabled supply chains is now providing compelling evidence

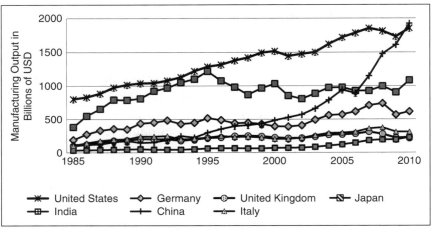

Source: United Nations International Standard Industrial Classification Data.

Figure 1.2 Manufacturing output for select countries, 1985 to 2010.

that the center of supply chain activity is moving full circle, from the United States and Europe back to Asia. Figure 1.2 presents data for 7 of the top 10 countries with the highest manufacturing output in 2010, measured in billions of dollars. This figure does not include the data on South Korea, France, and Brazil, the other three countries in the top 10.

As shown in Figure 1.2, China overtook the United States in manufacturing output in 2010. That same year, the manufacturing outputs of India and the United Kingdom converged. Although Japan threatened to overtake the United States in manufacturing output in 1995, it has since fallen back. However, in 2010 the combined manufacturing output of the three Asian countries exceeded the combined manufacturing output of the United States and Italy and Germany, the two European countries with the highest manufacturing output. A white paper published by the Australian Government predicts that "Asia is set to overtake the combined economic output of Europe and North America within the decade to 2020."[7]

Into the Great Wide Open—Adapting to the New World

There are several plausible explanations for the shift of power back to Asia. On one hand, there is little argument that advances in technology and events such as Y2K enabled developing countries such as India and China to become part of the global supply chain for services and manufacturing. For instance, when the Web was developed for commercial use in the 1990s, India had no resources to deploy for IT infrastructure and so could not afford to pay for the needed bandwidth. However, computers and computer communication were becoming more prevalent and affordable in the Western world and the developing world, the United States, in particular, was investing heavily in IT infrastructure, essentially creating broadband connectivity through satellites and undersea cables.

Organizations such as General Electric found that it was possible to outsource activities—essentially split up work and send individual pieces to far-flung locations like Bangalore and Beijing, enabling a situation in which activities could be performed virtually round the clock. Outsourcing activity also held the promise of tapping into intellectual capital all across the world. Such outsourcing was accelerated by fears of a Y2K meltdown, which essentially helped showcase Indian software capabilities to the developed world.

Thus, in a paradoxical turn of events, just as the UK's investment in rail infrastructure served to siphon wealth out of the Indian economy in the latter part of the 19th century, U.S. investment in IT infrastructure served to reenergize the Indian economy. Even as outsourcing gained momentum, the Chinese economy gained traction from the offshoring phenomenon. An increasing number of organizations in the Western world started to exploit labor cost arbitrage, accessing low-cost labor in China to produce their goods.

It is noted, however, that even though the most recent phase transition in supply chains—from manufacturing supply chains to IT-enabled supply chains—suggests that this transition might be accompanied by a shift in the balance of economic power back to Asia, it does not represent a threat to the developed world. On the contrary, it presents great opportunities as it has opened up the market to potentially 3 billion new customers globally, presenting an unparalleled opportunity for organizations all over the world.

Is the World Flat or Not?—A Planet with One Mind

The rapid ascent of the developing nations, China and India in particular, in the early part of the 21st century led Thomas L. Friedman,[8] author, reporter, and columnist for *The New York Times,* to write his bestselling book, *The World Is Flat.* The title of Friedman's book was inspired by a meeting he had with the CEO of the Indian software organization, Infosys, during which the CEO observed that the playing field was being leveled by such technological advances.

The main themes in Friedman's book are that a series of events such as deregulation and the development of the Internet have combined to "flatten" the world, presenting challenges and opportunities to developed nations such as the United States in the 21st century. Friedman presents a set of 10 "forces" that have flattened the world, which include breaking down various barriers to free-market capitalism such as the fall of the Berlin Wall in 1989, the events surrounding the introduction of Netscape Navigator in 1995, outsourcing, and offshoring.

Although Friedman's vision of the world in the 21st century was initially met with widespread support and acclaim, it has also been subject to some controversy and criticism. Critics argue that the world is far from flat, and that differences between countries are much larger than generally acknowledged.

The criticism surrounding the flatness of the world seems misdirected. Friedman arguably envisions an ongoing process in which the world is being increasingly flattened. Thus, although the title of his book is set in the present tense, he tacitly acknowledges the ambiguity surrounding the notion of whether the world is flat or is *getting flattened*. He writes, "The long-term opportunities and challenges that the flattening of the world puts before the United States are profound" (p. 276).

Globalization Adherents—A Band on the Run?

The real criticism surrounding Friedman's book seems to be that differences between countries are much larger than acknowledged. In a *Wall Street Journal* article, "The Retreat of Globalization,"[9] the authors claim that whereas "popular wisdom has it that trade and investment (both) continue apace across national borders," it has not quite panned out that way, and that "globalization is now showing signs of retreat." The article suggests that investors are also demonstrating "increasing home-country bias" in the light of global weaknesses.

One of the most vocal critics of Friedman's book is the author Pankaj Ghemawat, who argues that globalization is overhyped. In his book, *Redefining Global Strategy*, Ghemawat[10] states, "differences between countries are larger than generally acknowledged. . . . While it is, of course, important to take advantage of similarities across borders, it is also critical to address differences. In the near and medium term, effective cross-border strategies will reckon with both, that is, with the reality that I call semiglobalization."

In a follow-up book, *World 3.0*, Ghemawat[11] expands on the theme of semiglobalization. From a supply chain perspective, he underscores a point discussed at greater length subsequently in this chapter—that distance matters and will continue to matter. Ghemawat claims that the views of Friedman and his adherents represent "World 2.0"—a planet with one mind, in a manner of speaking, with global markets, global integration, and global standardization. In contrast, World 3.0 is a world that represents semiglobal markets, a world where distance matters, and different standards will persist across regions resulting in the development of strategies to overcome or harness differences.

To substantiate his arguments, Ghemawat presents a number of statistics aimed at showing how globalization is very limited, contrary to popular belief. Among the more dramatic statistics he presents: 1 percent of snail mail, 2 percent of phone traffic, and 17 to 18 percent of Internet traffic crosses international borders. He argues that "the globalization glass is more empty than full (i.e., the shortfall from levels predicted by World 2.0 is particularly large)" (p. 21). He summarizes his position by quoting the well-known economist, John Maynard Keynes, "Ideas, knowledge, art, hospitality, travel—these are the things which should, of their nature, be international. But let goods be homespun whenever it is reasonably and conventionally possible."

Additive Manufacturing—Get It On

The exhortation by Keynes to let goods be homespun may well be imposed on global supply chains by a recent development, *additive manufacturing*. Also frequently referred to as *3D printing*, additive manufacturing is a process for generating a three-dimensional object of virtually any shape from a digital model. As opposed to a conventional manufacturing process, a "subtractive" process that shapes objects by removing material from the object, additive manufacturing creates objects using a sequential layering process.

Few areas of technology have seen as much development in such a short period of time as additive manufacturing, a technique that promises a host of benefits. For example, it promises the ability to manufacture topologically optimized products that have a lower weight and fewer raw materials than traditional manufacturing techniques. Additive manufacturing could nullify many of the traditional economics of scale in manufacturing. Because designs can be quickly changed, the technology enables flexible manufacturing and true mass customization. Even though it is currently applied mainly for production of nonmetal products, and even though current technology causes it to be a relatively slow process, it is only a matter of time before additive manufacturing techniques enable more rapid production of metal parts. For example, NASA's Marshall Space Flight Center in Huntsville, Alabama, has "printed" nickel alloy rocket engine parts using a fabrication technique called selective laser melting.

The implications of additive manufacturing, however, reach far beyond manufacturing. Because there is little need for production tooling, additive manufacturing makes it possible for organizations to manufacture the same part at multiple locations that are very close to customers. Organizations that make customized goods would be more likely to move raw materials than finished products.

Additive manufacturing could thus dramatically affect global supply chain management, in particular, logistics and inventory management. Making products to order near the location where they are needed will reduce transportation and logistics costs. The reduced carbon footprint would also appeal to an ecologically minded consumer.

Whereas low-cost country sourcing has led to complex global supply chains, it is possible that global supply chains will rapidly transform to simpler regional supply chains if additive manufacturing gains traction at its current pace. Additive manufacturing could well be the catalyst for a potential "industrial revolution for the digital age."[12]

Economic Cold War or Global Reincarnation—Tomorrow Never Knows

In *The Last Economic Superpower,* Quinlan[13] traces the rise of globalization following the collapse of the Bretton Woods system[f] in 1971, when President Nixon severed the link between the dollar and gold. Kick-started by the liberalization of global capital markets, globalization in the form of increased cross-border trade and investment soared until the financial meltdown of 2008. Quinlan discusses the relative decline of the U.S. economy and its transition from a creditor nation in the mid-1980s to its status as the world's largest debtor nation, the fading appeal of Europe and Japan, the rise of China and India, and the new power brokers that include Brazil, China, Turkey, and India. Quinlan presents two scenarios for the United States and world economies.

In the first scenario, rather than adjust to a new global landscape and accept a diminished role in the world, rich developed nations cling to their old order, a situation unacceptable to the poorer developing nations, leading to increasing tensions. The result is increasing nationalism and xenophobia worldwide leading to an economic cold war between developed and developing nations, with global regulation replacing deregulation.

The second scenario recognizes the mutual interdependence between the "West and the Rest" leading to a path of mutual cooperation, not competition. It discusses joint global leadership with different characteristics representing the Chinese, Indians, Brazilians, Egyptians, and many others, leading to a global reincarnation. Although it is not clear whether scenario one or two, or a scenario somewhere in between, unfolds in the future, what is clear is that the opportunity exists for recasting and reenergizing globalization.

The question of which scenario—assuming that it is one of the two put forth—will prevail is unclear. What is clear is that regardless of how flat the world really is, and the extent to which it is flattening, Friedman's book and Ghemawat's books highlight some of the challenges faced by organizations that have to deal with globalization in the 21st century. These challenges take the form of increased supply chain complexity, a situation aggravated by an uninformed application of outsourcing and offshoring, two of the 10 "flattening" forces identified by Friedman.

The Path Forward—We Got to Get Out of This Place

The preceding discussion is not meant to suggest that outsourcing and offshoring are undesirable activities. Rather, it is meant to indicate that such activities must be considered from a more systematic, big-picture perspective. This book supports the notion that global

---

[f] The Bretton Woods system, established in July 1944, created an international basis for exchanging one currency with another. Member states agreed to fix their currency rates by tying their currencies to the U.S. dollar. The IMF was tasked with bridging temporary payment imbalances.

supply chains across the world will break into a series of demand and supply "pods" in which regional procurement and manufacturing operations will supply the major demand centers of the area, at least for a significant percentage of production requirements. Clearly some low-cost "commodity" items will continue to be procured from low-labor-cost regions across the globe. However, the trend appears to be toward more regional activity. The question then becomes one of identifying the regional locations for such offshoring or outsourcing activity. Should organizations return to procuring from, and manufacturing at, their domestic locations? If so, is the talent and infrastructure still there? Are the total costs and tax environment competitive? These questions are addressed in the following sections.

It is easier for organizations to acknowledge that they did not conduct a thorough TCO analysis than to accept a more profound problem—that they cannot execute a global supply chain well. The preceding discussion points out that going global increases cost, complexity, and risk. Managing these three aspects can be extremely challenging. Organizations might have estimated the total supply chain cost fairly well, but they may be unable to handle supply chain complexity very well.

Worse yet, these organizations may not realize or be prepared for the regional differences—cultural and otherwise—that exist in the location of the offshore activity. These organizations may not fully understand the rules of this new global playing field. They may not be prepared to manage the governmental rules and regulations of the country in which they are planning to conduct such offshore activity. Even those organizations that have significant experience in offshoring may find that this is an ongoing process. The story of the second decade in the 21st century is one of shifting cost curves that are rendering obsolete the procurement, manufacturing, and supply chain location decisions of the last 15 years.

Is near-shoring a solution for mitigating risk? Although this discussion supports the notion of the regionalization of supply chains, the answer to this question depends on whether the locations considered exhibit significant cultural or economic differences. Supply chain lead times and delays reduce significantly when distances are reduced, but some of the challenges that arise when products are offshored to far off locations may still exist when these products are near-shored or in-sourced. Thus, all organizations would benefit from a better understanding of regional differences, whether at near-shore locations or at far-flung offshore locations. One of the primary objectives of this book is to identify and explain such regional differences.

The next section discusses some of the issues that occupy the minds of global supply chain managers. In the process of doing so, some questions about identifying the regions where managers would benefit from mutual collaboration, partnerships, or investment are discussed. The concluding section presents a structure to help managers assess the regions across the world on their relative strengths, weaknesses, opportunities, and threats from a global supply chain perspective.

Leveraging Global Supply Chains—A Question of Balance

Gartner, Inc. is a leading IT research and advisory company that publishes an annual "supply chain top 25" list identifying the leading organizations that excel in global supply chain management and highlighting their best practices. In its 2012 report, Gartner identified three major trends based on the practices of these top 25 organizations: improved supply chain risk management and resilience, supply chain simplification, and a shift toward *multilocal* operations. The third trend, multilocal operations, relates to how these organizations are reassessing their sourcing and manufacturing network and rebalancing their supply network strategies. More specifically, "they are shifting from a centralized model, where these functions support global markets, to a regionalized approach, where capabilities are placed locally, but architected globally." This multilocal trend supports this book's position on regional procurement and manufacturing, as noted earlier at several places in this chapter.

The Gartner report identifies a number of factors driving this trend toward multilocal operations: tax and government incentives, wage increases in some of the developing countries such as China, and an ever-increasing demand to be responsive to local markets. With respect to wages, the report notes that manufacturers are shifting capacity based on regional wage and logistics expense differentials even within emerging markets.

Supply Chain Tradeoffs—We Can Work It Out

Supply chains exist to serve customers. Therefore, the primary tradeoff faced by the CEO and her team is the need to balance supply chain costs with customer service. Supply chain managers face significant challenges walking this tightrope, especially because quite often decisions affecting supply chain management are taken as part of corporate strategy without giving due attention to how such decisions can be implemented by the supply chain managers.

For instance, when formulating corporate strategies, the problem of managing global logistics is almost an afterthought, viewed as a matter of detail that can be accounted for eventually, based on the profit margins resulting from the strategic planning process. However, the fact is that logistics-driven costs are usually very significant and can severely erode profit margins. Logistics-driven costs accounted for 9.22 percent of the GDP for the United States, on average, from 2000 to 2009.[14] Assuming that this percentage is representative of the share of logistics costs for an enterprise, a 5 percent error in estimating logistics costs in a $3 billion organization can result in a profit margin erosion of more than $275 million—that is not small change. If other supply chain costs such as order processing, materials acquisition and inventory, supply chain planning, supply chain financing, and information management are considered, the potential erosion in profit margin would be much higher.

Decisions surrounding supply chain strategies are often structural in nature, involving decisions on where to source material, locate a manufacturing facility, or open a retail center. For example, a decision to source material from a new location is often accompanied by a decision to close—or at least reduce—the amount of material from an existing source. Such decisions cannot be reversed easily if the new location does not meet expectations. Fortunately, corporate strategies now tend to place much more emphasis on strategic importance of the supply chain management process.

Building an efficient supply chain, however, poses significant challenges, especially in the context of global supply chains. The manager attempting to implement an efficient supply chain has to juggle a multitude of often-conflicting objectives. The manager has to contend with

▲ Increasing consumer expectations on product quality and customer service
▲ Coordination between supply chain partners to integrate supply and demand
▲ The risk of supply chain disruptions
▲ Governmental rules and regulations in the countries involved in the supply chain
▲ Environmental concerns

The first three concerns are present even with domestic supply chains, but the last two are probably more relevant to global supply chains. In fact, environmental concerns are currently often overlooked, although a survey by McKinsey conducted in November 2010[15] on the challenges faced by supply chain managers indicates that environmental concerns pose a fast-growing challenge. More than 21 percent of the respondents indicated that environmental concerns were their top challenge—nearly double the percentage from a survey conducted three years earlier.

As noted earlier, decisions surrounding supply chain management are often structural in nature. Managers of global supply chains can benefit from a methodology that will help them assess their supply chain strategies, identifying the strengths, weaknesses, opportunities, and threats of the different regions in the world. Such a framework, termed the *EPIC framework*, is described in the following section. This framework provides a structure for assessing various regions around the globe for supply chain readiness from an Economy (E), Politics (P), Infrastructure (I), and Competence (C) perspective.

In Search of the Lost Chord: The EPIC Structure Revealed

The purpose of the EPIC framework is to define and explain the conceptual dimensions of the *global supply chain model* (GSCM) as well as to identify the characteristics of those dimensions in ten distinct regions of the world. The new framework measures and assesses the level of maturity of a geographic region with respect to its supply chain activities.

The Economy dimension assesses the wealth and resources of each region in terms of production and consumption of goods and services. The Politics dimension assesses the political landscape with respect to how well it nurtures supply chain activity. The Infrastructure dimension evaluates the existing and planned infrastructure in the form of transportation networks, the availability of electricity and power, and the IT infrastructure. The Competence dimension evaluates the competence of the workforce, the logistics competence, and the speed with which customs and security clearances take place.

The four dimensions (Economy, Politics, Infrastructure, and Competence) are, in turn, assessed using a set of variables associated with each dimension. Each one of these variables is assessed using a combination of quantitative and qualitative scores based on data drawn from a wide variety of data sources. The next chapter discusses the EPIC structure for assessing global supply chains in more detail.

Concluding Remarks

Charles Dickens begins his novel, *The Tale of Two Cities,* with the classic quote, "It was the best of times, it was the worst of times." In the context of global supply chains, this quote might sound too pessimistic. No doubt supply chain management has sometimes taken a step backward, typically as a consequence of some myopic cost-based decisions that needlessly moved jobs overseas, resulting in increased supply chain complexity. However, there is every reason to be optimistic about the future of global supply chains as new knowledge and methodologies develop for managing them. This book provides a systematic, structured approach to assessing global supply chains using the EPIC structure, which is explained in more detail in the next chapter.

The discussion thus far is summarized as follows:

▲ Supply chains have undergone a series of phase transitions over the ages, from trading supply chains to manufacturing supply chains to the current era of global IT-enabled supply chains. These transitions have been fueled by technical and technological innovations that include interchangeability, improved methods of transportation, mechanization, telecommunications, and the Internet.

▲ These technical and technological innovations have resulted in the global economic power moving from Asia to Europe beginning in the middle of the 18th century. However, recent trends suggest that the balance of economic power is either moving back to Asia or is being leveled across the Americas, Europe, and Asia.

▲ The world is becoming more flat as barriers to free-market capitalism are removed, the use of the Internet becomes more widespread, and there is an increased flow of goods across borders. However, the extent to which the playing field is being leveled can be questioned. Also, the question remains whether the flattening trend could reverse course.

▲ As global supply chains proliferate, organizations in one country will increasingly depend on organizations from other countries to either supply material or market their products. Organizations should therefore position themselves to take advantage of such codependencies to further their competitive position in the marketplace. The question is in which regions of the world should their attention focus on when developing such collaborations.

▲ This book supports the notion that global supply chains across the world will break into a series of demand and supply pods in which regional procurement and manufacturing operations will supply the major demand centers of the area, at least for a significant percentage of production requirements.

References

1. D. Foster, "From Wright Brothers to 'Right Stuff,' a Dream Took Wing," *The Advocate Online*, January 2000.
2. C. Berggren, *Alternatives to Lean Production: Work Organization in the Swedish Auto Industry* (Ithaca, NY: H.R. Press, Cornell University, 1992).
3. T. Berners-Lee and R. Cailliau, "WorldWideWeb: Proposal for a hypertexts Project," (n.d.). http://www.w3.org/Proposal.html.
4. W. E. Deming, *Out of the Crisis* (Cambridge, MA: MIT Center for Advanced Engineering Study, 1982).
5. L. N. van Wassenhove, "Closed-Loop Supply Chains: Practice and Potential," *Interfaces* 33, no. 6 (2003): 1–2.
6. See, for example, the *Water Electronic and Electrical Equipment (WEEE) Directive*, http://eur-lex.europa.eu/JOHtml.do?uri=OJ:L:2012:197:SOM:EN:HTML.
7. Australian Government, *Australia in the Asian Century*, White Paper, October 2012.
8. T. L. Friedman, *The World Is Flat: A Brief History of the Twenty-First Century* (New York: Farrar, Strauss and Giroux, 2005).
9. K. Warsh and S. Davis, "The Retreat of Globalization," *The Wall Street Journal*, October 14, 2012.
10. P. Ghemawat, *Redefining Global Strategy: Crossing Borders in a World Where Differences Still Matter* (Boston, MA: Harvard Business School Press, 2007).
11. P. Ghemawat, *World 3.0: Global Prosperity and How to Achieve It* (Boston, MA: Harvard Business Review Press, 2011).
12. N. Hopkinson, R. Hague, and P. Dickens, eds., *Rapid Manufacturing: An Industrial Revolution for the Digital Age* (Hoboken, NJ: John Wiley & Sons, 2006).

13. J. P. Quinlan, *The Last Economic Superpower: The Retreat of Globalization, the End of American Dominance, and What We Can Do about It* (New York: McGraw-Hill, 2011).
14. D. Gilmore, "State of the Logistics Union—2010: Not Good," *Supply Chain Digest*, June 10, 2010.
15. http://www.mckinseyquarterly.com/The_challenges_ahead_for_supply_chains _McKinsey_Global_Survey_results_2706.

CHAPTER 2

Understanding the EPIC Structure

Managing a complex global supply chain requires the manager to recognize and assess the quantitative and qualitative factors that can affect decisions on procurement, manufacturing, warehousing, logistics, distribution, and sales. The Economy, Politics, Infrastructure, and Competence (EPIC) structure assesses the maturity level of geographic regions around the world, in particular, select countries in these regions, with respect to their supply chain activities. The structure is intended to help organizations that wish to invest in or manage supply chains in these regions. The maturity level for each country is assessed along four dimensions that are represented by the EPIC acronym: Economy, Politics, Infrastructure, and Competence. Each of these dimensions is evaluated using a number of variables to arrive at a weighted score for that dimension. In turn, the scores on these dimensions are used to arrive at a weighted score for the country.

The *Economy dimension* assesses the economic output of the country, its potential for future growth, its ability to attract foreign direct investment, and how well it can generate a steady return on investments made in the country. The variables used to assess the Economy dimension are the *gross domestic product* (GDP) and its growth rate, the population, *foreign direct investment* (FDI), exchange rate stability, consumer price inflation, and the balance of trade. These variables represent the potential opportunity that exists for organizations wishing to engage in supply chain activity in the country. For instance, the GDP of a country is largely determined by its industrial activity, and the level of industrial activity significantly influences the level of supply chain activities.

The second dimension, the *Politics dimension*, assesses the political landscape with respect to how well it nurtures supply chain activity. The variables considered in the Politics dimension cover the ease of doing business (including bureaucracy and corruption), the legal and regulatory framework (including taxes and tariff barriers), the risk of political stability, and intellectual property rights.

The third dimension, the *Infrastructure dimension*, strongly influences how supply chains in the country are managed and operated and represents the potential for leveraging

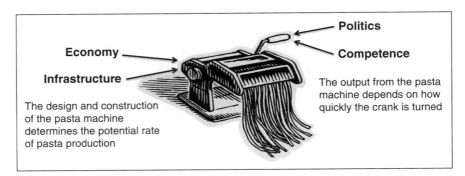

Figure 2.1 The EPIC structure: an analogy.

these activities. The variables considered in the Infrastructure dimension can be broadly classified into three categories: physical, energy, and telecommunications infrastructures. The physical infrastructure covers the roadways, the railway network, and air and water transportation. The energy infrastructure is responsible for the supply of electricity and fuel. The telecommunications infrastructure is captured by the extent of telephonic and Internet-based activity.

The fourth dimension, the *Competence dimension*, strongly influences the speed with which supply chain activities take place in the country. The variables used to assess the Competence dimension are labor productivity, labor relations, availability of skilled labor, education level of line staff and management, logistics competence, and the speed with which customs and security clearances take place.

An analogy drawn with a pasta machine may help illustrate the EPIC structure (Figure 2.1). Just as the design and construction of the pasta machine determines the potential rate at which pasta can be produced, the country's economy and infrastructure represent the potential for leveraging supply chains to generate profits. In this regard, the Economy dimension represents the potential for leveraging supply chains at a higher level—a macro level—whereas the Infrastructure dimension represents the potential for leveraging supply chains at a relatively more operational level.

Similarly, just as the actual production rate of the pasta machine depends on how quickly the crank is turned, the Politics and the Competence dimensions of the country play a major role in determining how effectively the supply chains can be leveraged to generate profits. As with the Economy and Infrastructure dimensions, the Politics dimension determines how effectively supply chains can be leveraged to generate profits at a more macro level whereas the Competence dimension determines how the supply chains can be leveraged at a relatively more operational level.

The following section presents the rationale for including each of the variables in the EPIC structure, discussing how they affect the assessment.

Assessing Countries with the EPIC Structure

The majority of the variables in the EPIC structure are assessed using results from in-depth studies conducted by established organizations. These studies include the World Bank's Ease of Doing Business Index (EDBI) and World Governance Indicators (WGI), the Central Intelligence Agency's CIA World Factbook, and the World Economic Forum's Global Competitive Index (GCI). These studies typically rank countries on various metrics using a combination of quantitative and qualitative survey data. In some cases, the studies categorize the countries into quartiles based on how they fare on these metrics.

Table 2.1 summarizes the EPIC variables and identifies the data sources used to assess these variables. The EPIC variables evaluated using these studies are identified with an asterisk (*). Although these variables are deemed to be assessed "quantitatively," it is noted that some of these assessments are based on rankings from survey data. In a few cases, the variables are evaluated using a combination of quantitative data blended with insights drawn from some qualitative studies and from interviews conducted by the authors. These variables are identified with the pound (#) sign.

Table 2.1 The EPIC Variables and Their Data Sources

Dimension	Variable	Data Source
Economy	GDP and GDP Growth Rate*	CIA World Factbook and WTO
	Population Size*	CIA World Factbook
	Foreign Direct Investment*	UNCTAD FDI Attraction/Potential Index
	Exchange Rate Stability and Consumer Price Index (CPI)#	CIA World Factbook
	Balance of Trade#	World Trade Organization
Politics	Ease of Doing Business*	World Bank EDBI and WGI
	Legal and Regulatory Framework*	World Bank WGI
	Risk of Political Stability*	Economist Political Instability Index
	Intellectual Property Rights*	International Property Rights Index
Infrastructure	Transportation Infrastructure*	World Economic Forum GCI
	Utility Infrastructure (Electricity)*	World Economic Forum GCI
	Telecommunications and Connectivity*	CIA World Factbook
Competence	Labor Relations*	World Economic Forum GCI
	Education Level*	World Economic Forum GCI
	Logistics Competence*	World Bank Logistics Performance Index
	Customs and Security*	World Bank Logistics Performance Index

A panel of supply chain managers assessed these variables for their ability to provide insight on various supply chain decisions. The supply chain decision areas in which each variable can be used, as determined by these managers, are included in Table 2.2.

Table 2.2 Supply Chain Decision Uses for EPIC Variables

Dimension	Variable	Supply Chain Decision Uses
Economy	GDP and GDP growth rate*	Retail store location
		Supply network—node location
	Population size*	Retail store location
		Sales channel—through direct sales store versus distributor
		Potential for use of e-commerce
	Foreign direct investment*	Manufacturing location
	Exchange rate stability and CPI#	Manufacturing location
	Balance of trade#	Sourcing and manufacturing location
Politics	Ease of doing business*	Retail store location
		Supply network—node location
		Sourcing and manufacturing location
	Legal and regulatory framework*	Retail store location
		Supply network—node location
		Sourcing and manufacturing location
	Risk of political stability*	Retail store location
		Supply network—node location
		Sourcing and manufacturing location
	Intellectual property rights*	R&D center
		Potential for use of e-commerce
Infrastructure	Transportation infrastructure*	Sourcing, manufacturing, and logistics location
		Modal choice for transportation
		Retail store location
	Utility infrastructure (electricity)*	Sourcing, manufacturing, and logistics location
	Telecommunications and connectivity*	Sourcing, manufacturing and logistics location
		Retail store location

(continued)

Table 2.2 Supply Chain Decision Uses for EPIC Variables (*Continued*)

Dimension	Variable	Supply Chain Decision Uses
Competence	Labor relations*	Sourcing, manufacturing, and logistics location
	Education level*	Research & Development (R&D) center
		Potential for use of e-commerce
		Sourcing, manufacturing, and logistics location
		Retail store location
	Logistics competence*	Sourcing, manufacturing, and logistics location
		Order fulfillment strategy (for example, just in time)
		Potential for use of e-commerce
	Customs and security*	Sourcing, manufacturing, and logistics location
		Order fulfillment strategy (for example, just in time)

Scoring the Quantitative Variables

The analyses provided by organizations such as the World Bank, the CIA, and the World Trade Organization (WTO) are based on comparative data gathered on countries in the world, typically resulting in a ranking of these countries on various measures. Such studies usually either cover all the countries, as is the case for the World Bank EDBI or the CIA World Factbook studies, or they cover countries that collectively represent more than 95 percent of the world GDP, as is the case for the World Economic Forum (WEF) data. The EPIC assessment assigns scores to countries by dividing the countries ranked by the study into equal segments, with each segment representing approximately one-twelfth of the total number of countries included in the study.

Thus the top three segments represent the first quartile of all the countries covered by a study, and the bottom three segments account for the fourth quartile of all the countries covered in the study. The three segments in the first quartile get grades of A, A⁻, or B⁺, depending on where they are positioned in the first quartile. Countries in the second quartile get grades of B, B⁻, and C⁺. Countries in the third quartile get grades of C, C⁻, and D⁺. Countries in the bottom quartile get grades of D, D⁻, and F.

Scoring the Qualitative Variables

Some variables in the EPIC structure do not lend themselves to a purely quantitative scoring approach. These variables are assessed using qualitative approaches combined with insights from interviews conducted by the authors.

Table 2.3 The EPIC Variables and Their Weights

Economy	Economic Output and Growth	Population Size	FDI	Exchange Rate Stability/CPI	Trade Imbalance
(30% of total EPIC score)	35%	25%	20%	15%	5%
Politics	Ease of Doing Business	Legal Framework	Political Stability	Intellectual Property Rights	
(20% of total EPIC score)	30%	30%	25%	15%	
Infrastructure	Physical Infrastructure	Energy Infrastructure		Connectivity	
(30% of total EPIC score)	50%	25%		25%	
Competence	Labor Relations	Education Levels	Logistics Competence	Customs and Security	
(20% of total EPIC score)	25%	25%	40%	10%	

Assimilating the Scores

The scores for the different variables are combined to form an aggregate weighted average score for each dimension. In turn, the weighted scores for each dimension are combined to provide an overall EPIC grade for each country. Table 2.3 shows how the individual scores are combined. The weight assigned to each variable within a dimension is shown directly below the variable, and similarly the weight assigned to each dimension appears directly below the dimension.

Interpreting the Scores

The scoring system outlined here provides a grade for each variable. However, it must be emphasized that although the EPIC assessment provides a score for a country it is *not an absolute measure* of the desirability or maturity level of that country from a supply chain perspective. It is essential to also understand other factors such as the history and the economic and the political background of each geographic region to appreciate its cultural roots and the implications for supply chain management in these different regions. These scores must therefore be considered in conjunction with a wide array of other factors that are discussed in subsequent chapters. The following sections are devoted to understanding the relevance of each variable to the overall EPIC assessment, and to presenting more details on how they are scored.

Examining the Dimensions in the EPIC Structure

This section examines the variables in the EPIC structure in more detail. Although the effect of many of these variables may seem quite apparent, it is useful to provide more specificity on why these variables are included in the assessment.

Economy

As noted earlier, the Economy dimension provides organizations with a macro-level indicator of a country's potential for leveraging supply chains to generate profits. Although the economy of a country may not be viewed as a major determinant of supply chain activity, it plays a key role in determining the level of investment in the country. The stability of the macroeconomic environment is vital for business and the overall competitiveness of a country. Macroeconomic stability cannot, in and of itself, increase a country's productivity, but an organization would be more inclined to invest in a country with a stable macro environment, especially if the stability is accompanied by a strong or growing economy. For this reason, the Economy dimension is assigned the highest weight (30 percent) for evaluating the overall EPIC score.

Economic Output and Growth Rate

The economic output of a country, measured by the GDP at *purchasing power parity* (PPP) is a good indicator of the overall potential for consumer sales, which in turn plays a role in determining supply chain activity. The data on GDP at PPP is obtained from the CIA World Factbook.[1] The GDP growth rate is another gauge of the potential for future investments, and a simple ranking of the countries based on both GDP at PPP and the GDP growth rate is used. The CIA World Factbook has data on the GDP growth rate. However, this metric is evaluated using WTO data because it directly provides the average GDP growth rate over the past five years.[2]

Population Size

Similar to the GDP and the GDP growth rate, the population of a country provides an indication of the potential for consumer sales. Arguably, the population size is a weaker measure than the GDP for inferring the current level of supply chain activity. However, it can be a strong predictor of existing sales potential, especially in developed economies. It can also be a good predictor of future potential for countries in which the population size is large and GDP is relatively small. The population data is drawn from the CIA World Factbook. In some cases, the Emerging Markets Logistics Index (EMLI)[3] is also used to help evaluate this variable. The EMLI ranks 41 emerging market countries for their attractiveness based on market size, compatibility, and attractiveness.

GDP per capita could also be considered as a variable for inclusion, in lieu of population size, but GPD per capita combines two variables: GDP and population size. Such a metric may be unable to distinguish between two countries with similar GDP per capita: one with a high GDP and a high population, and the other with a low GDP and a low population.

Foreign Direct Investment

Foreign direct investment (FDI) is a strong indicator of the global market's belief in the economic potential of a country. A country with a high FDI inflow suggests that the markets expect that country's economy to improve. Conversely, a high FDI outflow suggests that the country is facing, or will face, some problems in the future.

The United Nations Conference on Trade and Development (UNCTAD) publishes an annual "World Investment Report" dealing with issues related to investment and enterprise development within the United Nations system. The report includes an FDI Attraction Index[4] that ranks 182 countries in terms of their success in attracting FDI, using a measure that reflects a combination of total FDI inflows and inflows relative to GDP.

The UNCTAD report also presents a FDI Potential Index[5] that uses four key economic determinants of the attractiveness of an economy for foreign direct investors. These determinants are the attractiveness of the market, the availability of low-cost labor and skills, the presence of natural resources, and the presence of FDI-enabling infrastructure. Countries such as Afghanistan, Burundi, Gambia, Haiti, Nepal, Rwanda, and Togo fall into the fourth quartile in this index. The UNCTAD FDI Attraction Index and the FDI Potential Index are both used to evaluate the FDI variable.

Exchange Rate Stability and Consumer Price Inflation

Exchange rate stability plays an important role in determining the level of supply chain activity. A depreciation or devaluation of the domestic currency can be viewed as expansionary because it can stimulate economic activity by encouraging exports. Devaluation could help reduce a trade deficit, assuming the country is capable of meeting the expected additional demand by supplying more goods. However, evidence suggests that devaluation of the domestic currency often leads to contraction and negatively affects inflows of FDI into the country. Depreciation in the currency value results in more attractive export prices, but import costs also increase. For example, when the Pakistani rupee depreciated by about 28 percent relative to the U.S. dollar in 2008, it almost halted economic growth in the country, affecting both agriculture and industry.

Regardless of whether devaluation encourages exports or decreases FDI, the stability of the exchange rate for the country is an important factor. A stable exchange rate provides organizations with a higher comfort level when undertaking investment decisions.

Exchange rate fluctuations also affect procurement and logistics decisions. If the exchange rate for the country starts to weaken, there is an impetus for forward buying of imported products in larger quantities, resulting in increased inventories. The exchange rate stability is evaluated using data from the CIA World Factbook.

Consumer price inflation affects the procurement and logistics decisions of an organization in a manner similar to exchange rate fluctuations, albeit to a lesser extent. During periods of high inflation, the purchasing power of the local currency erodes, which tends to promote forward buying. The consumer price inflation variable is evaluated based on data drawn from the CIA World Factbook. Because exchange rate fluctuations and consumer price inflation affect supply chain activity in more or less the same manner, they are evaluated jointly in the EPIC analysis using the CIA World Factbook data.

Balance of Trade

Trade balance or imbalance measures the disequilibrium between the inflows and outflows of goods and services for the country. This variable affects procurement and transportation costs in complex ways. For example, suppose there is a high trade imbalance between two countries, with country X importing a lot of goods from country B without a corresponding procurement of goods from country Y by country X. In this situation, transportation costs per container for traffic headed from country X to Y could be higher than transportation costs per container for traffic headed in the reverse direction simply due to supply and demand imbalances. The balance of trade variable is evaluated using data drawn from the CIA World Factbook as well as data from the World Trade Organization.[6]

Politics

A 2013 report published by the World Economic Forum,[7] in collaboration with Bain & Company and World Bank, underscores the importance of the Politics and Infrastructure dimensions as they relate to supply chains. The report finds that supply chain barriers, in the form of complex regulations, inefficient customs and administrative services, and weaknesses in infrastructure services, to name a few, significantly affect GDP and world trade. The report states that if all countries were able to reduce supply chain barriers halfway to global best practice, global GDP could increase by 4.7 percent and world trade by 14.5 percent. The report urges governments to take a holistic approach, focusing on all policies that impact supply chain efficiency to improve national competitiveness.

Because the Politics dimension can significantly enhance or inhibit supply chain effectiveness, it is assigned a weight of 20 percent in the aggregate EPIC score. The Infrastructure dimension is assigned a relatively higher weight (30 percent).

Ease of Doing Business

The ease of doing business in a country strongly influences supply chain activity. It drives cost and time efficiencies on various activities such as land procurement, hiring, building construction, and cross-border logistics, and can therefore significantly influence decisions on offshoring or outsourcing activities to that country.

The "World Bank Doing Business" survey is a comprehensive survey that provides an Ease of Doing Business Index.[8] The 2012 index ranks 185 countries, with the highest rank awarded to the country with the most conducive environment. The survey covers 10 metrics: starting a business, dealing with construction permits, getting electricity, registering property, getting credit, protecting investors, paying taxes, trading across borders, enforcing contracts, and resolving insolvency. This index is used to evaluate the ease of doing business variable.

Bureaucracy and corruption hinder the ease of doing business because they present informal barriers to establishing and maintaining the business enterprise with associated implications for supply chain activity. For example, bureaucracy, corruption, and duplicity in dealing with applications for new business as well as for dealing with ongoing operations impose significant economic costs to businesses and slow the process of development. Bureaucracy and corruption can also hinder the smooth flow of goods and services, and thereby increase lead times, reducing the competitiveness of the country as a whole.

The World Bank World Governance Index (WGI)[9] maintains percentile rankings for 213 countries on a variety of metrics including Government Effectiveness and Control of Corruption, ranking them from zero (most inept government or most corrupt) to 100. These two metrics from the index are used to evaluate the bureaucracy and corruption variable.

Legal and Regulatory Framework

The legal and regulatory framework governs the level of government oversight and any accompanying restrictions on doing business and on supply chain investment. At a macro level, the quality of the legal and regulatory framework has a strong influence on competitiveness and growth. It influences decisions on, and the organization of, production in the country. For instance, businesses are unwilling to invest in a country if they perceive that their rights as owners or shareholders are not protected.

The legal and regulatory framework variable captures two related metrics. The first is the perception of the ability of the government to formulate and implement sound policies and regulations that permit and promote private sector development. This aspect is evaluated by the Regulatory Quality metric of the WGI. The second is a perception of the extent to which agents have confidence in and abide by the rules of society, in particular the quality of contract enforcement, property rights, the police, the courts, and the likelihood of crime and violence. This aspect is captured by the Rule of Law metric in the WGI.

It is noted that the Regulatory Quality metric captures the impact of taxes and tariffs. Managing local and foreign taxes effectively presents a big challenge, and a great opportunity, for a multinational organization. Strategies for managing foreign taxes affect initial overseas investments, financing international operations, and cross-border transactions.

Corporate tax rates and tariff barriers thus provide a measure of the cost of doing business and influence supply chain investments in manufacturing, warehousing, distribution, sales, and other supply chain activities. Nontariff barriers also exist, in the form of anti-dumping regulations and duties that restrict imports. Even though these regulations and duties are not present in the usual form of a tariff, they have the same effect as tariffs once they are enacted.

The Deloitte International Tax Source (DITS)[10] is sometimes used to help in evaluating the corporate tax rate. The DITS provides data on the corporate tax rate, measured by the amount of taxes and mandatory contributions payable by businesses after accounting for allowable deductions and exemptions as a share of commercial profits. Taxes withheld (such as personal income tax) or collected and remitted to tax authorities (such as value added taxes, sales taxes, or goods and service taxes) are excluded from these data.

Political Stability

Political stability affects the long-term viability of investments and the associated business model. Political stability, defined as the absence of a threat to government due to social protests, should be distinguished from the stability of a government although the two are closely related. The latter is characterized by the country having failed at some of the basic conditions and responsibilities of a sovereign government such as a loss of control of its territory, erosion of legitimate authority to make collective decisions, or an inability to provide public services.

Political stability, on the other hand, measures the economic distress and the underlying vulnerability of a country to social unrest in the region. Political stability drives diversification and risk management in global supply chains. The absence of political stability can potentially reduce the advantage a country offers for locating industrial activity in it because the investing organization either has to consider building in redundancy to cope with potential disasters or develop strategies to cope with such eventualities.

The Economist publishes a Political Instability Index.[11] The index scores are derived by combining measures of economic distress and underlying vulnerability to unrest. The 2009 index ranks 165 countries, with Zimbabwe at number 1 (most unstable) and Norway at number 165 (most stable). *The Economist* notes that the threat of social unrest has, overall, increased in most countries since 2007, when the index was previously compiled. This index is primarily used to evaluate the political stability metric.

Intellectual Property Rights

The presence or absence of *intellectual property* (IP) rights affects the long-term viability of an organization's efforts to capitalize on its core competencies when it competes overseas. An organization doing business in a country that has high piracy rates and poor enforcement of antipiracy laws is susceptible to imitations of its products that, in turn, could lead to a loss of brand image, especially when these imitations are of poor quality or are sold at significantly lower prices compared to the original.

The Property Rights Alliance, an international organization, developed an International Property Rights Index[12] report in 2012. As stated in that report, it "is the first international comparative study that measures the significance of both physical and intellectual property rights and their protection for economic well-being." The report provides a ranking of 130 countries that represent 97 percent of the world GDP, based on three areas: Legal and Political Environment, Physical Property Rights, and Intellectual Property Rights (IPR). The intellectual property rights rankings from this report are used to evaluate this variable.

Infrastructure

An extensive and efficient infrastructure is critical for safeguarding the smooth and effective functioning of the supply chain. It is an important factor in determining the location of economic activity and the kind of activities a country can promote. A well-developed infrastructure can also effectively reduce the distance between regions in the country, integrate the national market, and connect it at a low cost to markets in other countries and regions.

Effective modes of conveyance in the form of roads, railroads, ports, and air transportation enable businesses to get their goods and services to or from international markets in a secure and timely manner. The electricity supply and the network used to deliver the sources for generating energy—in the form of fossil or other fuels—allow these businesses to continue operations smoothly. Finally, an extensive telecommunications network provides a rapid and smooth flow of information vital for sustaining supply chain activities. For these reasons, the Infrastructure dimension is also assigned a relatively high weight in the EPIC analysis.

The 2013 report "Enabling Trade: Valuing Growth Opportunities," by the World Economic Forum, underscores the importance of the Infrastructure dimension as well as the Politics dimension. Specifically with respect to the variables considered in the Infrastructure dimension, the report finds that supply chain barriers, present in the form of inefficient customs and administrative services and weaknesses in infrastructure services, significantly affect GDP and world trade. These variables can also significantly affect lead times and supply chain costs.

Transportation Infrastructure

The transportation infrastructure is assigned the highest weight in determining the weighted score for the Infrastructure dimension, and is assessed on four components: the road network, the railroad network, water transportation, and air transportation. It is not easy to provide comparisons for these components uniformly across countries. For example,

Saudi Arabia, by the nature of its geography, has no inland waterways but has access to the Red Sea and the Persian Gulf. Some landlocked countries such as Niger in Africa have no waterways at all.

The four components of the physical infrastructure variable are assessed using data provided by the WEF. This organization publishes a Global Competitiveness Index (GCI)[13] that ranks countries along 12 "pillars." Each pillar evaluates a certain aspect of global competitiveness using a number of metrics. One such pillar, infrastructure, is evaluated using nine components. Only four of these—the quality of roads, railroads, ports, and air transport—are used to rank the physical infrastructure.

As noted earlier, the WEF GCI relies on survey data to a large extent. The quality of the roads component, for example, is evaluated based on how the survey respondents assess the roads in their respective country. A rank of 1 is assigned to a country for which the respondents view the quality of the roads to be extremely underdeveloped whereas a rank of 7 is assigned to a country in which the quality of the roads is deemed to be extensive and efficient by international standards. A similar ranking is made for the quality of railroads, the quality of ports, and the quality of air transportation. For landlocked countries, evaluating how accessible the port facilities are from that country assesses the quality of ports.

Utility Infrastructure

Utility infrastructure, as viewed here, primarily relates to the generation and transmission of electricity. No doubt the energy infrastructure in general also relates to the infrastructure for production (if any) and distribution of different types of sources for generating energy. Energy sources include fossil fuels such as oil, natural gas, and coal as well as other sources of energy such as wind power. However, eventually all these energy sources are drawn primarily to power transportation and/or electricity. The energy infrastructure variable is therefore evaluated using one of the metrics, quality of electricity supply, used by the WEF GCI to evaluate the infrastructure pillar. This metric is evaluated based on the presence or absence of interruptions to power supply and the presence or absence of voltage fluctuations.

Telecommunications and Connectivity Infrastructure

Connectivity in a supply chain context relates to how well information is communicated. Connectivity is measured by the number of telephone lines and the number of Internet subscribers. To measure the total number of telephone lines, only the number of mobile phones is considered simply because it provides a better comparison across countries. Although landlines are still widely used in developed countries, many of the developing countries have relatively few landlines on a per capita basis. The data on mobile phones and Internet users is obtained from the CIA World Factbook.[14]

Using absolute numbers can, however, be misleading because countries like India and China have very large populations. Therefore, these numbers are scaled by the population size.

Both the absolute number and the per capita values of mobile phones and Internet connections are considered when evaluating the connectivity of the region.

Competence

Competence can be described as the combination of knowledge, skills, and abilities that, when effectively applied, produce a successful performance in a defined function or activity. For the EPIC structure, the Competence dimension describes the mix of labor skills, management skills, the competence of the logistics functions, and the presence or absence of barriers from customs procedures and processes. The efficiency and flexibility of the labor market ensure that workers are used most effectively and provided with incentives to perform at their best levels. The implication is that labor markets must have the flexibility to shift workers from one trade to another quite rapidly. In addition, modern business practices emphasize improved productivity, and that implies the need to have skilled managerial staff conversant with sophisticated management techniques.

Labor Relations

From a supply chain perspective, the labor relations in a country serve to determine the attractiveness of a country for FDI investment. Poor labor relations can easily negate any perceived labor cost gains from offshoring. Factors to be considered when evaluating this variable include worker–employer relations, pay for productivity, employee turnover, labor laws, presence of strong unions, the ease of hiring or terminating employees, and the ease of closing down establishments.

For the EPIC assessment, labor relations is evaluated using three metrics from the WEF GCI's Labor Market Efficiency pillar. The first of these is the pay and productivity metric. This metric measures the extent to which the pay in the country is related to productivity. A country in which pay is unrelated to worker productivity is assigned a low rank of 1 whereas a country in which pay is strongly related to worker productivity is assigned a rank of 7. These rankings, as noted earlier, are based on survey data.

The second metric is cooperation in labor–employer relations. This metric evaluates a country based on how confrontational or cooperative the labor–employer relationship is. The third metric is hiring and firing practices. A country in which the hiring and firing of workers is impeded by regulations is assigned a lower rank, and a country in which the hiring and firing of workers is flexibly determined by employers is assigned a higher rank. As with the pay and productivity metric, a higher number is deemed to be a better rank.

Cheap labor is a major draw for industrial organizations wishing to invest in developing countries. Typically, these organizations tend to overestimate the availability of skilled labor. The reality is that the workforce in developing countries often has experience in an agricultural setting, and so the issue is whether this workforce can be retrained to work in an industrial setting, which requires an entirely different skill set.

Education Levels for Line Staff and Management

As distinguished from the type of skills required of labor, the line staff and management need to be familiar with continuous improvement methodologies. They should also be able to understand the cost of quality, be able to sustain initiatives, and generally be able to solve problems in real time.

The education levels variable is assessed using four metrics from the WEF GCI. These metrics are the quality of the educational system, the quality of management schools, the extent of staff training, and the reliance on professional management.

Logistics Operational Competence

An essential element of the Competence dimension is how well the various logistics functions perform along the supply chain within a country. These elements include the competence and quality of logistics services in the form of transport operators, customs brokers, and warehousing; the ability to track and trace consignments; and the ability to deliver shipments on time. The World Bank's Logistics Performance Index (LPI)[15] is used to assess logistics operational competence. Note that this index was used earlier to help assess the Infrastructure dimension.

Customs and Security

Customs and Security has two related facets. The first is the efficiency of clearance procedures used by customs authorities, measured in terms of speed, simplicity, and predictability of processes used to clear goods at the port of entry. The second facet relates to the existence of proper security controls for ensuring the protection of the internal market and the security of international supply chains. The World Bank LPI is used to assess customs procedures and processes.

Summary and Conclusions

It is often stated that the battleground has shifted—from competition between organizations to competition between supply chains. However, today there is an additional level of complexity introduced by the fact that these supply chains are increasingly global supply chains. Furthermore, these global supply chains operate in a complex multicountry environment that requires deep knowledge of the culture and operations in the different regions.

The EPIC structure provides managers of these global supply chains with an approach to evaluate the different regions, more specifically the countries within these regions, for their ability to manage their supply chains. This evaluation is made along four different dimensions based on the economy, the politics, the level of infrastructure, and the competence of the country or the region.

The following chapters identify 10 separate regions and analyze select countries in each region in depth using the EPIC structure. The countries covered in this analysis account for well over 80 percent of the world population and 90 percent of the world GDP.

References

1. https://www.cia.gov/library/publications/the-world-factbook/index.html.
2. http://stat.wto.org/CountryProfile/WSDBCountryPFReporter.aspx?Language=E.
3. http://www.agilitylogistics.com/EN/Documents/Agility_Downloads/2012_Emerging _Markets_Logistics_Index.pdf.
4. unctad.org/Sections/dite_dir/docs/WIR12_webtab31.xls.
5. unctad.org/Sections/dite_dir/docs/WIR12_webtab32a.xls.
6. http://stat.wto.org/CountryProfile/WSDBCountryPFView.aspx?Language.
7. "Enabling Trade: Valuing Growth Opportunities," report by the World Economic Forum, Geneva, Switzerland, January 2013. http://www.weforum.org/reports/enabling -trade-valuing-growth-opportunities.
8. http://www.doingbusiness.org/rankings.
9. http://info.worldbank.org/governance/wgi/sc_country.asp.
10. http://www.dits.deloitte.com/.
11. http://viewswire.eiu.com/site_info.asp?info_name=social_unrest_table&page =noads&rf=0.
12. http://www.internationalpropertyrightsindex.org/about.
13. http://www3.weforum.org/docs/WEF_GlobalCompetitivenessReport_2012-13.pdf.
14. www.cia.gov/library/publications/the-world-factbook.
15. lpisurvey.worldbank.org.

CHAPTER 3

East Asia

East Asia is a geographic region that encompasses the ancient cultural and economic centers of China, Japan, and the Koreas (Figure 3.1). This region includes the modern states of Japan, the Democratic People's Republic of Korea (North Korea), the Republic of Korea (South Korea), Mongolia, the People's Republic of China, the Chinese Special Administrative Regions (SARs) of Hong Kong and Macau, and the Republic of China (Taiwan). It is home to more than 1.6 billion people, accounting for 23 percent of the global population.[a]

Since rejoining the global economy in the 19th century after hundreds of years of isolation, East Asia has served as a key global source for both finished goods and raw materials. In the last 50 years, the region has developed as a hub for low-cost global manufacturing, beginning in Japan and Taiwan in the 1960s, continuing in South Korea in the 1970s and 1980s, and in China most recently. Each of these nations has been successful in leveraging low-cost manufacturing to boost economic development and evolve toward production of higher-value products and more mature, industrialized economies. The region, however, is not just a source of exports: the size and rising consumer wealth of the

---

[a] Secondary data and background information for this chapter and all subsequent regional assessment chapters were collected from a variety of sources, including the CIA World Factbook (www.cia.gov/library/publications/the-world-factbook); Deloitte International Tax Source (http://www.dits.deloitte.com/); Economist Intelligence Unit (viewswire.eiu.com/site); Europa World Plus (www.europaworld.com); IHS Global Insights (www.ihsglobalinsight.com); Passport GMIC (www.portal.euromonitor.com); Property Rights Alliance International Property Rights Index (www.internationalpropertyrightsindex.org/about); UNCTAD World Investment Report (www.unctad-docs.org/files/UNCTAD-WIR2012-Full-en.pdf); World Bank Doing Business Rankings, World Governance Index, Logistics Performance Index (www.doingbusiness.org/rankings; info.worldbank.org/governance/wgi; lpisurvey.worldbank.org); World Economic Forum Global Competitiveness Report and Networked Readiness Report (www.weforum.org); and World Trade Organization (stat.wto.org/CountryProfile).

Figure 3.1 East Asia.

region's population make it a highly attractive market for distribution and sale of finished goods from global manufacturers.

The sheer size of the region, coupled with the raw materials, industrial might, and increasing consumer power found in East Asia will ensure that it remains a central location for supply chain operations in the coming decades. Key facets of the region that supply chain managers should understand as they seek to develop or improve operations in the East Asian region are explored in this chapter.

Economic and Political Background

Supply chain managers should develop a sound understanding of the economic and political background in which their organization's supply chains operate. This section provides a brief insight into the economic and political history of the region as well as a summary of major external environmental characteristics that shape East Asian markets. The chapter focuses on the East Asian nations of Japan, the Republic of Korea (South Korea), the People's Republic of China (China), the Hong Kong Special Administrative Region (SAR) of China, and the Republic of China (Taiwan). These five nations represent 20 percent of the global *Gross Domestic Product* (GDP) and more than 30 percent of the global population, largely overshadowing the remaining nations in the region (Mongolia, SAR of Macau, and the People's Republic of North Korea).

Understanding the Region

East Asia is one of the great centers of human civilization, with a written history stretching back more than 5000 years. The history of East Asia is dominated by the influence that successive Chinese dynasties have had on the region for millennia in economics and politics as well culture and religion. Chinese civilization first developed along the major river systems of the Yellow River (Huang He), and then spread along the Yangzi (Chang Jiang) across southern and eastern China, where the population remains concentrated today in an area known as "China Proper." Ancient Chinese civilization eventually spread northward to influence civilizations in other areas of East Asia, first moving to the Korean peninsula and then onward to the islands of Japan, Taiwan, and Hong Kong, and southward to what is today northern Vietnam.[1]

As early as 200 BCE, Chinese commercial influence began to extend beyond the East Asian region as Chinese goods began to flow over the Silk Road through Central Asia and the Middle East and into Europe. Soon after, Chinese maritime traders were calling on ports across Asia and reaching as far as the African coast. Foreign trade was never a major economic activity for the Chinese, however, leading to its official discouragement until the 19th century when European nations used military force to initiate sustained trade with China to satisfy demand for Chinese tea, silks, and porcelain pottery. The lack of demand for Europe's manufactured goods and other trade items fostered a trade imbalance that led to the creation of the opium trade. From the mid-1800s until the founding of the People's Republic in 1949, various Western countries and Japan forced China into a series of treaties that established the basis of trade between China and the world.

Although China historically has been the dominant force in East Asian politics and economics, other civilizations in the region also have made substantial contributions to the development of both the East Asian and global economies. The Mongols gained fame in the early 12th century when Genghis Khan united the nomadic horse tribes of north Asia and established a Eurasian empire through a conquest that at its peak extended from Eastern Europe through the Caucasus across Asia to the Pacific Ocean. After Genghis Khan's death in the early 12th century, the empire gradually retired to their original steppe homelands and came under Chinese rule in the late 17th century. Although Mongolia won its independence from China in 1921 with Soviet backing, more ethnic Mongolians continue to live in the Inner Mongolia Autonomous Region in the People's Republic of China than in Mongolia. Although Mongolia is not subject to assessment in this chapter, the historical impact of the Mongols on the region is evident in the region's long and rich history.

Japan, whose history extends back to around 12,000 BCE, is home to a rich ecosystem ideal for the development of a thriving society. Initially influenced greatly by China, trade began with several European countries in the 1500s and lasted until the rulers of Japan decided to cut the country's ties with the rest of the world in the 1600s. Japan's isolation lasted until 1853 when U.S. warships sailed into Tokyo Bay, forcing Japan to open two ports to Western trade. As connections strengthened with the Western world, Chinese power began to diminish. Japan took the opportunity to begin conquering colonies. By the start of World War II, the Korean peninsula, Taiwan, and the northeastern part of China were all under Japanese control.

The post–World War II era was characterized by a heavy dependence of East Asian nations on trade with the West, in particular the USA and USSR, as regional industries recovered from the devastation of the war. The importance of trade in East Asia has continued and expanded, growing to include the nations of Western Europe as their own economies recovered from the war, and increasingly to other areas of the emerging world as first the East Asian democracies and eventually China focused their economic growth plans on becoming sourcing and manufacturing hubs for global demand.

Politics

Supply chain operations exist within the context of national legal systems, thus an understanding of political systems is imperative to supply chain success. This is particularly true in East Asia where the political systems vary greatly, ranging from the closed and centrally controlled government of the People's Republic of China to one of the world's most open and transparent governments in the SAR of Hong Kong. Taiwan and South Korea, both constitutional republics headed by popularly elected presidents, share some common political challenges and issues. Japan, with a constitutional monarchy and a parliamentary government, presents a relatively unique political environment.

The Japanese constitution, which went into force in 1947, guarantees freedom of religion, speech, and press. Japan's emperor is considered a symbol of the nation and has no real governing power. The highest lawmaking body is the national legislature (the Diet), which consists of the House of Representatives and the House of Councillors. South Korea, a constitutional republic whose national government leaders are elected by the people, guarantees freedom of the press and freedom of religion. The president of South Korea is the head of state and the country's most powerful official. The people elect the president to a five-year term and the president may not be reelected. The president appoints a prime minister, who carries out the operations of the government.

The People's Republic of China is a socialist republic ruled by the Communist Party of China. The Communist Party has four main administrative bodies, including the National Party Congress (NPC), the Central Committee, the Politburo, and the Secretariat.

The highest post in the Party is that of general secretary, who serves as head of the Secretariat. Power in the government is derived from the Communist Party, and the NPC serves as the single legislative branch of the government. Members of the NPC are elected by municipal, regional, and provincial people's congresses and the People's Liberation Army to serve five-year terms. The president, who is elected by the NPC to serve a five-year term (and is eligible for a second term), heads the executive branch of the government. The premier is selected by the NPC and serves as the head of the State Council.

As a SAR of China, Hong Kong comprises one of the 33 major political divisions of China. Hong Kong is governed by a unicameral Legislative Council, or LegCo, whose members serve four-year terms. Under the terms of the SAR agreement, Hong Kong is allowed to maintain its free-enterprise economy within China's government-controlled economic system for at least 50 years and is also allowed a high degree of autonomy in domestic matters. Hong Kong's foreign affairs and defense, however, are handled by China. The agreement, called the Basic Law of the Hong Kong SAR, became Hong Kong's constitution on July 1, 1997.

Taiwan's political status has been a subject of dispute since the mid-1900s when Chinese Communists and Chinese Nationalists clashed over the control of China. When the Chinese Communists seized power on the Chinese mainland in 1949, the Chinese Nationalists escaped to Taiwan. The Nationalists declared Taipei the capital of the Republic of China (ROC). Chiang Kai-shek, leader of the Nationalist Party, refused to recognize China's Communist government, which had established the People's Republic of China (PRC) on the mainland. Chiang's Nationalist government also established control over several groups of islands in the Taiwan Strait, including the Quemoy, Matsu, and Pescadores. Today, the People's Republic of China holds that Taiwan is a PRC province, but Taiwan remains effectively independent. Taiwan's constitution provides for five branches of government, including the executive, legislative, judicial, control, and examination branches, with each branch headed by a president. The head of state is the president of the Republic of China. Since 1996, Taiwanese voters have directly elected the president to a four-year term.

The Economies

The economies of the nations of East Asia are varied and complex. Japan emerged as one of the world's most technologically advanced economies in the years following World War II, enabled by government–industry cooperation, a strong work ethic, mastery of high technology, and comparatively low defense spending. As a result, Japan's total economic output is one of the largest in the world. In 2011, Japan ranked as the fourth-largest economy in the world. On average, the Japanese enjoy one of the highest income levels in the world, and their assets and savings are among the largest in the world. Japan lacks most of the natural resources necessary to support its industrialized economy, forcing it to import these resources from abroad.[2] Japanese firms manufacture a wide variety of products, including automobiles, computers, steel, televisions, and textiles. Manufacturing industries employ about 20 percent of the Japanese labor force and generate approximately 20 percent of the country's GDP. Economic growth slowed markedly in the 1990s as a result of bad investments and an asset pricing bubble that started in the late 1980s. Following these problems, it took years to reduce excess debt, capital, and labor.

From a supply chain perspective, Japan represents a sophisticated, although costly, supply chain source for high-value manufactured goods. It also provides a sizeable market for finished goods, although competition is fierce. The logistics infrastructure for market distribution is mature, with a high level of capabilities. Opportunities exist to export more product sourced in Japan to regional markets, although domestic economics, politics, and demographics cloud the future supply chain operating picture for Japan. The Economic, Politics, Infrastructure, and Competence (EPIC) assessment for each nation (see following section) expands on this theme and provides specific opportunities and challenges for supply chain operations.

South Korea has experienced incredible growth and global integration since the 1960s, rising from one of the poorer nations in the world to a high-tech industrialized economy, currently ranked among the world's 20 largest by GDP. This growth was fostered through close ties between government and business, including directed credit and import restrictions. The government promoted the import of raw materials and technology at the expense of consumer goods and encouraged savings and investment over consumption. The Asian financial crisis of 1997–1998 exposed weaknesses in South Korea's development model that included high debt to equity ratios as well as massive short-term foreign borrowing. The government adopted numerous economic reforms following the crisis, including greater openness to foreign investment and imports. Current challenges include a rapidly aging population, an inflexible labor market, and a heavy reliance on exports (which comprise half of its GDP).

South Korea's explosive economic growth since the 1960s has made the country an interesting option for supply chain operations. The manufacturing base is rapidly maturing and moving into more high-value industry sectors. The growing wealth of the middle class makes it attractive for finished goods distribution, and the logistics infrastructure is a strength, although metropolitan congestion poses a challenge. Increased trade with China and other Asian nations, as well as with emerging markets, is a likely future opportunity for supply chain focus.

Since the late 1970s, China has moved from a closed, centrally planned economy to a more market-oriented economy that plays a substantial global role. Reforms began with the phasing out of collectivized agriculture and expanded to include the gradual liberalization of pricing, fiscal policy, increased autonomy for state enterprises, the creation of a diversified banking system, the development of stock markets, the rapid growth of the private sector, and the opening of foreign trade and investment. As a result, China now has one of the world's largest economies in terms of its GDP (although it still ranks fairly low in terms of per capita GDP, falling in the lower half of the world's nations). Manufacturing and mining contribute more to China's GDP than any other category of economic activity. China produces more steel than any other country and is the world's largest producer and user of coal. China also outranks all other countries in the production of aluminum, lead, magnesium, tungsten, and zinc. In 1999, China signed a landmark trade agreement with the United States that lowered many barriers to trade. In 2001, China joined the World Trade Organization. China's chief trading partners include Germany, Japan, South Korea, and the United States.

China has resumed its historic role as the power player in the region. The presence of scarce raw materials, a growing middle class, its extensive manufacturing capacity, and the sophistication of its coastal logistics infrastructure make China an attractive option for supply chain operations focused on global export and increasingly for imports of high-value consumer goods.

After signing the Basic Law in 1997, economic cooperation between Hong Kong and China increased. Hong Kong industrialists moved more manufacturing activities to China to take advantage of inexpensive labor, and employment in Hong Kong itself shifted from low-cost manufacturing to service industries. Hong Kong is a free port, meaning that it collects no import duties on imported goods except for specific categories such as alcohol, tobacco, and perfume. The absence of import duties makes products bought and sold in Hong Kong less expensive than in most other parts of the world. The territory's economy is heavily dependent on gambling and tourism, but also includes manufacturing. Notably, much of China's international trade flows through the port of Hong Kong.

Hong Kong was founded as a trading hub for product moving into and out of mainland China. That role continues to provide the main focus of Hong Kong's economy. Organizations that seek a trading presence in East Asia, and particularly in China, must explore supply chain operations in Hong Kong.

Taiwan has a dynamic capitalist economy that has gradually decreased government control over investment and foreign trade, recently allowing privatization of some large, state-owned banks and industrial firms. Taiwan's economy relies heavily on manufacturing and foreign trade, serving as one of the world's largest producers of computers and electronics. Exports, led by electronics, machinery, and petrochemicals, have provided the primary impetus for economic development, exposing the economy to fluctuations in world demand. Taiwan's diplomatic isolation, low birth rate, and rapidly aging population are major long-term challenges. Although Taiwan has been excluded from much of the recent economic integration in East Asia because of its diplomatic status, it signed the Economic Cooperation Framework Agreement (ECFA) with China in June 2010. The ECFA is intended to serve as a stepping-stone toward trade pacts with other regional partners.

As a relatively small island nation, Taiwan's supply chain perspective is focused on providing a manufacturing location for goods destined for export. Increased trade with mainland China is a likely option for future supply chain operations.

The Markets

Asia's fast economic growth in recent decades has been, in part, fueled by favorable population demographics. In fact, it has been suggested that favorable population growth rates accounted for 20 to 25 percent of Asia's economic growth over the past decade. Following World War II, the introduction of new technologies and the rapid growth of a young labor force boosted productivity and overall economic growth in East Asia. Between the mid-1960s and the early 1990s, the working-age population of East Asia grew four times as fast as the population as a whole, significantly reducing the ratio of children and the elderly to the total population and causing labor output per capita to rise quickly. For example, in the 1960s and 1970s, Japan's economic growth was associated with entry of the postwar baby boom generation into the Japanese workforce. The high population growth rate that fostered this economic boom has reached its peak and is now in decline. East Asia grew by a little over 120 percent between 1950 and 2000 but is expected to grow by less than 10 percent between 2000 and 2050.[3] The growing consumer segment in East Asia still promises to be an appealing destination for finished goods, but supply chain managers must take the population decline into consideration as it will have significant implications on labor costs and availability in the coming decades.

Location of Markets

Key demographic characteristics, including geography, population, and culture, and major metropolitan areas within each of the East Asia nations are summarized next.

Japan

Japan is located between the North Pacific Ocean, the Sea of Japan, and the Korean Peninsula (Figure 3.2) and is comprised of four main islands and thousands of smaller islands. The four major islands (Honshu, Hokkaido, Kyushu, and Shikoku) form a curve that measures about 1931 km (1200 mi) from northeast to southwest. At their closest point, the main islands are only 193 km (120 mi) off the coast of Asia. Japan's close proximity to the Asian mainland has enabled it to borrow and adapt innovations from other Asian civilizations, yet still develop a very unique cultural identity. Mountains and hills cover most of Japan, making it a country of great beauty, but forcing the majority of its people to live on a small portion of land on the narrow coastal plains. Japan lies on an extremely unstable part of the earth's crust characterized by significant earthquake and volcano activity. Although most of the nearly 1500 earthquakes that occur each year in the islands are minor, severe earthquakes such as the one in March 2011 occur every few years. The Japanese islands also have more than 150 major volcanoes, of which 60 are active. Japan is the 10th most populous country in the world, with a land area (377,944 sq km or 145,925 sq mi) comparable to that of Italy or California, USA. The Japanese population of 127.6 million people (2012) has been shrinking

Figure 3.2 Japan.

since 2008. This negative population growth represents a significant threat to the Japanese economy. The median age of the Japanese population is 45.6 years, which is substantially higher than the East Asian regional median age. Furthermore, the marriage rate has fallen by a third from its peak in 1972, and the fertility rate is currently approximately 1.4 births per female, down from 1.9 in 1977. The government estimates that 40 percent of the population will be of retirement age by 2060. In an effort to spur population growth, the Japanese government has recently introduced a child benefit program, which provides parents with 13,000 yen per month per child less than 15 years of age.[b]

More than 67 percent of the Japanese population resides in cities (the primacy rate—the percent population living in Tokyo, the largest city—is 32), and this level is relatively stable.

_____

[b] See Kodomo Teate Law (introduced in 2010).

The largest cities include Tokyo (the nation's capital) with 36.5 million in the metropolitan region; Osaka-Kobe, with 11.3 million; Nagoya with 3.3 million; Fukuoka-Kitakyushu with 2.8 million; and Sapporo with 2.7 million people. The Tokyo metropolitan region, which includes the cities of Yokohama and Kawasaki, is situated in the middle of the Pacific coast on the island of Honshu and is the most populous urban area in the world. Tokyo has become extremely crowded, and its housing costs are among the highest in the world. It also faces such problems as pollution and some of the world's heaviest automotive traffic. Tokyo has a population density of about 15,500 people per sq km (40,000 people per sq mi), which is about one and a half times greater than New York City, although poverty and crime are not as severe as they are in many other large cities.

The vast majority of Japanese practice Shintoism (84 percent) and Buddhism (72 percent),[c] with 2 percent practicing Christianity. Ninety-eight and a half percent of the nation's population is ethnically Japanese, with a small number of ethnic Koreans and Chinese comprising the remainder.

South Korea

South Korea is the world's 25th largest nation, with a population of approximately 50 million people (Figure 3.3). Most South Koreans live in urban areas (83 percent, but increasing at only 0.6 percent per year), predominantly in the capital city of Seoul (with a primacy rate of 24) whose 24.5 million metropolitan National Capital Area inhabitants (including the city of Incheon and the surrounding Gyeonggi province) make it the world's second largest metropolitan area. Other major cities include Busan (3.5 million), Daegu (2.5 million), Daejeon (1.4 million), Gwangju (1.4 million), and Ulsan (1.1 million). The Capital City area of Seoul (as distinct from the broader metropolitan National Capital Area) hosts a population of more than 10 million people, making it the most densely populated city in the OECD,[d] with a density about twice that of New York City. Seoul is one of the world's top 10 financial and commercial centers and is home to major multinational conglomerates such as Samsung, LG, and Hyundai-Kia. Seoul is noted for its technologically advanced telecommunications and transportation infrastructure.

Incheon serves as the port city for the Seoul metropolitan area. Incheon had a population of only 4700 when it opened as a port to the outside world in 1883, but today it is host to approximately 2.7 million people. In 2003, the city was designated Korea's first free economic zone, attracting investment from many large multinational and Korean firms. Busan (formerly Pusan) is South Korea's second largest city. The Metropolitan area, which includes the adjacent cities of Gimhae and Yangsan, has a population of 4.4 million. Busan, located on the southeastern-most tip of the Korean peninsula, has Korea's largest beach

[c] The total exceeds 100 percent as many Japanese practice elements of both religions.
[d] The Organization for Economic Co-Operation and Development.

Figure 3.3 South Korea.

and longest river, and features both the largest port in the nation and the world's fifth busiest seaport (by cargo tonnage). Daegu, located in southeastern Korea about 80 km (50 mi) from the coast, near the Nakdong River, is the center of the central Yeongnam region's politics, economy, and culture. Daegu is the textile and fashion center of the nation. Daejeon is located in the center of the country and serves as the transportation hub for the main rail lines and highways. It is also the science and technology capital of Korea.

South Korea is one of the most ethnically homogeneous societies in the world, with more than 99 percent of its inhabitants having Korean ethnicity, including many ethnic Koreans with foreign citizenship. South Korea is experiencing population trends similar to those in the other developed economies of East Asia, with a birthrate that is among the world's lowest. Korean is the official language of South Korea, although the majority of

Koreans can understand six major dialects. Traditionally, many Koreans have been followers of Confucianism, but more than 26 percent of Koreans are Christian.

China

With a population of 1.34 billion people, China is host to the world's largest population and is the third largest country in landmass, surpassed in size only by Russia and Canada (Figure 3.4). Only 47 percent of the population lives in urban areas, although this number is growing by 2.3 percent annually; the primacy rate is only 2. China can be divided into eight major land regions, including the Tibetan Highlands, Xinjiang-Mongolian Uplands, Inner Mongolian Border Uplands, Eastern Highlands, Eastern Lowlands, Central Uplands, Sichuan Basin, and Southern Uplands.

China's largest population centers include Shanghai (the largest city, 16.8 million), Beijing (the capital, 12.2 million), Chongqing (9.4 million), Shenzhen (9 million), and Guangzhou (8.9 million). More than 90 percent of China's people live in the eastern half of the nation, which contains most of China's major cities and nearly all the land suitable for farming. Western China, by contrast, has far fewer people and resources and is home to many of the country's minority groups.

The fertility rate in China has plummeted to 1.4 births per woman in a lifetime since the implementation of the one-child law, which caused a dramatic change to China's age structure. The latest census data reveals that the absolute number of people between the ages of 15 and 59 (the core working age population) began to fall in 2010. It is projected that this age group will shrink by 29.3 million people by 2020.

Figure 3.4   China.

China's official language is Mandarin (Putonghua, based on the dialect of Beijing), with other languages and dialects including Yue (Cantonese), Wu (Shanghaise), Minbei (Fuzhou), Minnan (Hokkien-Taiwanese), Ziang, Gan, and Hakka. Ninety-two percent of the nation is Han Chinese, with Zhuang, Uygur, Hui, Yi, Tibetan, Miao, Manchu, Mongol, Buyi, Korean, and other nationalities comprising the remainder. The nation is officially atheist, although Taoism and Buddhism are commonly practiced.

Hong Kong

The territory of Hong Kong is comprised of two main islands (Hong Kong Island and Lantau Island) and a mainland strip along the coast that forms a natural geographic port for Guangdong province in southeast China (Figure 3.5). The entire northern coast of Hong Kong Island, the southern tip of the Kowloon Peninsula, and the satellite cities in the New Territories form the Hong Kong metropolitan area. Under British control

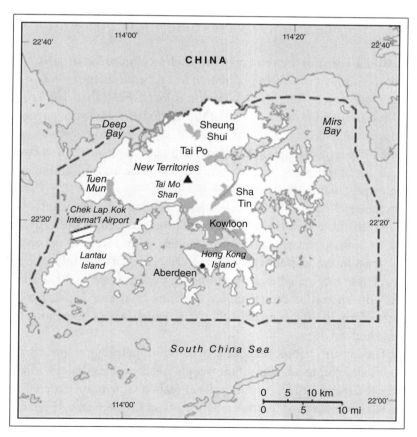

Figure 3.5 Hong Kong.

until 1997, Victoria (known now as "Central") continues to serve as Hong Kong's seat of government. Hong Kong originated as a commercial trading post for China's regional and global trade, a role it continues to play today. Macau, which lies across from Hong Kong to the east on the western side of the Pearl River Delta, was colonized by the Portuguese in the 16th century and became the first European settlement in the East Asia region. Both Hong Kong and Macau are Special Administrative Regions (SARs) of the People's Republic of China. Under an agreement that went into force on July 1, 1997, China promised that its political and economic system would not be imposed on either territory, allowing autonomy in all matters except foreign affairs and defense for the next 50 years.

Hong Kong's population of 7.2 million, all of whom live within the city-state (with a primacy rate of 100) is predominantly composed of ethnic Chinese who speak Cantonese, although English is also an official language and is spoken by nearly 3 percent of the population. From a relatively unpopulated territory at the beginning of the 19th century, Hong Kong grew to become one of the most important international financial centers of the world after undergoing rapid industrialization beginning in the 1950s.[4]

Taiwan

Taiwan (called Ilha Formosa by the Portuguese who colonized it in 1590) is a 180-mile long subtropical island nation with a population of 23.2 million, the majority of whom live in large population centers (Figure 3.6). Taiwan is located less than 161 km (100 mi) off the shore of China's Fujian province. Most of the island is covered with rugged mountains that rise to more than 3962 m (13,000 ft), with the large population centers located on the more habitable western coastal plain that faces China. East-west running rivers that have hindered north-south travel and severely limited economic and cultural integration cross these western coastal plains.[5]

Most Taiwanese people are of Chinese descent, including the descendants of the 2 million people who fled to the island from mainland China just before the Communists took power in 1949. About 80 percent of Taiwan's people live and work in urban areas. Taipei, the capital city and foremost political and financial center of Taiwan, is the island's most populous city. Taipei originated as a small trading port more than 200 years ago, before becoming the administrative capital under the Qing Dynasty. Taipei, New Taipei, and Keelung together form the Taipei metropolitan area, which hosts a population of 6.9 million people (primacy rate of 30).

About half of Taiwan's people practice a local traditional religion that involves the worship of folk gods and goddesses. Taiwanese people speak various dialects of Chinese, with most speaking Northern Chinese, or Mandarin (called Guoyu, or *national language*, on Taiwan). Taiwanese, a form of Southern Min spoken in the nearby Fujian province of China, is also widely spoken.

Figure 3.6 Taiwan.

Assessing the Maturity Level of East Asia Supply Chains

This section assesses the supply chain maturity of East Asia using the EPIC dimensions.

As stated previously, only Japan, the Republic of Korea (South Korea), the People's Republic of China, the special administrative region of Hong Kong, and the Republic of China (Taiwan) are covered as these areas represent the greatest percentage of GDP and population in the region. In each case, observations central to the decision to establish supply chain operations in an area are made, and the area is rated based on its attractiveness for supply chain operations.

Economy

An assessment of key elements of the Economy dimension follows, including economic output and growth rate; population; foreign direct investment; exchange rate stability and consumer price inflation; and balance of trade. A summary of Economy elements for each of the focal nations of East Asia is presented at the end of the section.

Economic Output and Growth Rate

Led by China, the manufacturing sector has exploded in the nations of East Asia, establishing the region as a major driver of the global economy. Supply chain managers would do well to understand the key economic growth drivers and industries in the region. The five East Asian nations considered in this analysis represent 22.8 percent of global GDP and, excluding Japan, have experienced continued strong growth over the last five years. The crisis in the eurozone in combination with weakened consumer spending in the USA slowed East Asia's growth, but recent increases in domestic spending on infrastructure and strengthening domestic consumer markets are expected to return the region to strong growth in the near term. Japan stands as the outlier to growth prospects in the region.

China, with the second largest economy in the world, leads the region with $11.3 trillion (US *purchasing power parity* [PPP]) in GDP in 2012, representing 14 percent of global GDP. Growth in 2012 was 7.4 percent, down from 9.3 percent in 2011 due to the economic downturn in the eurozone. Significant infrastructural investment projects and the strengthening of domestic and global consumer markets will likely increase growth prospects for China for the midterm. Household purchasing power and living standards in China are on the rise, which is helping to rebalance China's economy toward domestic consumption. The real value of private final consumption rose by 9.7 percent in 2011, and millions of new domestic consumers are created each year. Light and heavy manufacturing (dominated by state-owned firms) continue to lead Chinese industrial sectors. The Pearl River Delta (PRD) in Guangdong remains one of the biggest manufacturing hubs in China, on par with Shanghai, and Beijing and Shanghai are experiencing rapid growth in high-technology industries. Most recently, the Chinese government is encouraging firms to look to the east in Chongqing and Chengdu for manufacturing capacity. The hourly wage and manufacturing wage per hour, $2.9 (US) and $3.4 (US), respectively (2011), are among the lowest in the world. Both government and foreign investment have been made in chemicals and refining in hopes of taking advantage of the oil pipeline being built across China to link the energy fields of central Asia with the refining and industrial demand of the east coast. In addition to this industrial growth, the World Tourism Organization has predicted that China will become the world's top tourist destination by 2020.

Hong Kong's GDP in 2011 was $357 billion (US PPP) and 0.44 percent of global GDP; the economy grew by 4.9 percent in 2011, although growth slowed considerably in 2012 as global exports shrank. It has enjoyed strong growth over the last 20 years as its economy has been transformed from manufacturing to service, becoming Asia's leading financial services center and handling the vast amount of foreign investment that has flowed into the SAR to support Chinese operations. Trade drives Hong Kong's economy, and 95 percent of exports are re-exports moving between mainland China and the rest of world. Its container port is the third busiest in the world, and Hong Kong International Airport has one of the world's busiest air cargo operations. Despite a weakening in exports due to lower global demand, domestic spending has remained relatively resilient and continues to provide a current accounts buffer. Consumer expenditure per capita, disposable income, and real growth in consumer spending are all rising. The hourly wage and manufacturing wage per hour, $7.1 (US) and $8.4 (US), respectively (2011), are lower than Japan and Taiwan, although manufacturing has largely moved out of the territory in favor of locations in the PRD on the mainland in order to take advantage of cheaper labor, effectively making it the world's largest free trade zone. Hong Kong is also one of the world's most popular tourist destinations.

In 2011, Taiwan's GDP was $887 billion (US PPP) and 1.1 percent of global GDP. Growth is closely tied to the global export market, with more than two-thirds of GDP attributed to exports. As a result, growth in Taiwan slowed to 1.25 percent in 2012. Dominant industry sectors in Taiwan include semiconductors and other high-tech areas such as integrated circuits, LCD screens, optical electronic equipment, photoelectric chips, and dynamic random access memory technology. These sectors have been supported by excellent infrastructure, particularly in the industrial parks located in Hsinchu (northern Taiwan) and Tainan (southern Taiwan), as well as access to skilled workers and specialized suppliers. Producers, however, specialize in production and efficiency rather than innovation, subjecting Taiwan to growing competition from China and Singapore. Biotechnology, including specialty pharmaceuticals, represents a promising growth sector. From a domestic spending standpoint, consumer expenditures grew by only 0.4 percent, and disposable income (per capita) rose by 1.9 percent in real terms (2011). The country's rigid labor market and high labor costs make it less competitive when compared with other countries in the East Asia region. In 2011, the average hourly wage and average hourly wage in manufacturing stood at $8.2 (US) and $9.2 (US), respectively. A large swing in consumer spending is expected to occur as aging workers leave the workforce and move into a fixed or restricted income status.

Japan is an economic outlier in East Asia. As the first nation in the region to develop a modern industrialized economy, it has been mired in stagnant or negative growth since the Tokyo Stock Exchange crashed in 1990–1992 and real estate prices peaked in 1991. The 1.5 percent growth in Japan throughout the last two decades was slower than growth in other major developed economies. In 2011, Japan's GDP was $4.39 trillion (US PPP), and its economy was the fourth largest in the world (5.4 percent of global GDP), but it shrank an additional 0.7 percent during 2011, allowing it to be surpassed in size by India. Japan's economic development has always encouraged exports and discouraged imports, allowing it to develop a strong global position in heavy industries and high-technology equipment. Low interest rates, high levels of capital investment, and high educational attainment have allowed these industries to continually upgrade in order to improve efficiency and to gain an edge in terms of research and development. The current-account surpluses are also a result of a high savings rate in Japan, at nearly 25 percent of GDP. This high savings rate has fostered significant overseas investment to obtain higher yields. However, there are negative consequences associated with such high savings levels as consumer expenditure per capita and disposable income per capita both fell in 2011. In addition, labor costs are generally high in Japan when compared to other regional economies, with the 2011 average hourly wage and hourly wage in manufacturing at $22.6 (US) and $25.1 (US), respectively.

South Korea is the 12th largest economy in the world with a GDP of $1.51 trillion (US PPP) and a growth rate of 3.6 percent (2011). Major South Korean industry sectors include electronics, telecommunications, automobile production, chemicals, shipbuilding, and steel. Prominent exports are in semiconductors, wireless telecommunications equipment, motor vehicles, computers, steel, ships, and petrochemicals. South Korean households tend to carry large household savings (although it has been dropping, amounting to only 6.8 percent of GDP in 2011), but planned cuts in personal income taxes and sales taxes on automobiles and large electronics appliances could change this and increase spending. Consumer expenditure (per capita) and disposable income (per capita) grew at 3.7 percent and 3.2 percent, respectively, in 2011. However, growth in real wages lagged growth of GDP with a likelihood that this trend will continue into the future. The average wage per hour in manufacturing and overall wage per hour was $14.7 (US) and $14.9 (US), respectively, in South Korea, about midrange for the region of East Asia.

Population

Following World War II, East Asia experienced high rates of economic growth that resulted from its young, working-age population. However, each East Asian nation must now plan for the end of that boom in population and productivity as growth rates have fallen and the population has aged.[6] China remains the largest country in the world with 1.34 billion people (2012). However, the median age of China's population is 35.9 years, and the population is growing at only 0.481 percent per year, placing it 152nd in the world in terms of population growth. Hong Kong is home to 7.2 million, with a median age of 43.9 and a population growth rate of only 0.42 percent, placing it 155th in the world on population growth. Taiwan, with 23.2 million people and a median age of 38.1 years, has a population growth rate of only 0.29 percent (ranked 167th globally). Japan faces the most challenging population scenario as its population of 127.4 million is shrinking at the rate of 0.08 percent per year—the 198th lowest growth rate in the world. South Korea's 48.9 million people have a median age of 39 and a growth rate of 0.2 percent, or 176th in the world. The resultant decrease in the working age populations will have a dramatic impact on regional economies in terms of workforce availability, productivity, and domestic spending power. Supply chain managers will be faced with extreme competition for diminishing workforce talent, and wage rates may well increase significantly. In addition, regional economies could become even more dependent on exports for growth as shrinking populations begin to hamper domestic spending.

Foreign Direct Investment

China and Hong Kong have benefited greatly from foreign direct investment (FDI) over the past several decades. Significant amounts of FDI have flowed into China as cheap labor, a relatively skilled workforce, and large regional markets have attracted investment in economic sectors ranging from paper to chemicals, and heavy machinery to semiconductors. Initially targeted at the special economic zones along the eastern coast of China, FDI has been allowed in more diverse sectors and regions since China's acceptance into the World Trade Organization (WTO) in 2001. In fact, the Chinese government generally welcomes FDI and is bound under WTO rules to open its industries to foreign investors. However, there is a growing concern about the threat of continued economic protectionism and the lack of transparency in China's investment laws. Nonetheless, China was the second highest recipient of FDI inflows in the world, following the USA, with $106 billion (US) in 2010.

Hong Kong is consistently ranked as East Asia's second most popular FDI destination after China. Due to its position as the gateway between China and the rest of the world, the territory attracts regional headquarters and regional offices from companies around the world. Most investment is heavily weighted toward import/export trade, wholesale and retail, and finance and banking. It is an attractive destination for investors and exporters due to its strong regulatory environment, open trade policies, and simple and efficient system for conducting business. In addition, there are no restrictions on FDI; investors may bring capital into Hong Kong through the open exchange market and may remit it in the same way.

In recent years, the other nations in the East Asia region have not fared as well at gaining access to FDI. Taiwan is facing a considerable challenge with FDI as inflows have decreased dramatically while outflows increased during the 2006 to 2011 period, leaving the nation with a $2 billion (US) investment deficit (2011). The Taiwanese government has responded by making investments in technology development programs, land lease incentives, and low interest loans. However, many foreign companies still view Taiwan as unfavorable for investment. In addition, Taiwan is expected to sign two agreements with China (investment protection and customs cooperation) in order to provide more incentives for Taiwanese businesses that are operating in China. FDI in Japan is relatively low compared with that of other developed countries (1 percent of GDP), and there is a growing concern that the nation may be waning as an attractive investment target. Low FDI reflects a range of long-standing structural impediments that are commonly found in the country, including:

▲ The exclusive keiretsu networks that link manufacturers;
▲ Suppliers and banks that restrict investment from foreign investors;
▲ A high overall cost structure that makes market entry and expansion expensive for foreign investors;
▲ Weak independent regulatory bodies and bureaucratic red tape that can cause difficulties when setting up new businesses; and
▲ An inflexible labor market that inhibits mobility and negatively influences skills development.

Inflows of FDI into South Korea have eased over the past decade because the government has made little headway in its attempts to deregulate markets, enabling China to attract funds previously destined for South Korea. The government hopes to reverse this trend by establishing six free economic zones (FEZs), six foreign-exclusive industrial complexes, and four free-trade zones, all of which are designed to make the country much more attractive to foreign investment through reductions to and exemptions from corporate and local taxes as well as cash grants for investments that create jobs.

Exchange Rate Stability and Consumer Price Inflation

Exchange rate stability varies across the nations of East Asia. China's official currency, the renminbi (denominated into yuan), is considered to be relatively stable as it is pegged to the US dollar and several other currencies, (with daily deviations against the US dollar limited to 1.0 percent). The renminbi's prospects as a future global currency will likely be based on whether China is successful in developing financial markets, exchange rate flexibility, and liberalizing capital accounts. The Hong Kong dollar (HKD) is considered to be one of the most stable exchange currencies in the world. The HKD's target rate is set by the Hong Kong Monetary Authority and has been at 7.8 HKD/USD since 1983. The free market–oriented economies of the region have not enjoyed such stability, however, as the New Taiwan dollar, the Japanese yen, and the South Korean won have all experienced significant fluctuations in the last five years. The Taipei Foreign Exchange Market manages a flexible exchange rate system for the New Taiwan dollar with intervention by the Central Bank of China to smooth out excessive fluctuations. The Japanese yen has been free floating since 1973, with interventions by the Central Bank of Japan (BOJ) limited to easing excessive fluctuations in the market. The official South Korean currency is the won, which is allowed to fluctuate with supply and demand.

Regionally, consumer price inflation (CPI) in the region over the last five years has been below global averages. China's CPI rose only 1.7 percent in 2012, reflecting softening demand. Taiwan and South Korea's CPIs range from 1 to 4 percent and are attributed to both the worldwide decline in inflation and the central banks' handling of interest rates in these nations. Hong Kong is facing a problem of rising inflation, as a strong economy and inexpensive financing have attracted real estate investors from the eurozone and the United States, driving up property values. Japan again emerges as an outlier, as it has experienced long periods of deflation in the last 20 years as income inequality has worsened, the country has aged, and the income of its elderly has fallen relative to that of its wage earners. In addition, the small companies that represent the main source of new jobs have not maintained profitability, hurting income levels and employment. One result of these trends is that "irregular workers" make up one-third of the workforce and earn one-half the pay of regular workers for the same jobs.

Balance of Trade

Since China entered the WTO in 2001, its trade surplus with the European Union (EU) and the United States has ballooned, while its trade deficit with Asia has surged. China's exports are relatively well distributed across major importing markets. Nearly half of its exports are of machinery and transport equipment, with an additional 24 percent being miscellaneous manufactured goods. Sixty percent of exports come from foreign invested firms, and more than 90 percent are located in eastern coastal regions. Hong Kong is almost exclusively a trading nation whose economy depends on global demand for mainland Chinese export products. Overall trade (imports plus exports) substantially exceeds GDP because much of the export value consists of products that were imported from the mainland and then re-exported, causing a multiplier effect.[e] The value of Chinese products "passing through" the economy, when combined with the value of imports of commodities needed to support the population, gives Hong Kong a negative trade balance. Taiwan enjoys strong trade relations due to its high export dependence. Increasingly, Taiwan's economy is reliant on the Chinese market, as China and Hong Kong have surpassed the United States to become Taiwan's leading export destination. Singapore, Japan, and South Korea are also important trading partners. In addition to the WTO, Taiwan has free trade agreements with China, El Salvador, Guatemala, Honduras, Nicaragua, and Panama and is currently in negotiation with the Association of East Asian Nations (ASEAN), the Dominican Republic, the European Union (EU), India, Singapore, and the USA.

Japan enjoys a positive balance of trade, although exports have recently been lower than usual due to supply chain disruptions that have emerged from damage caused by the 2011 earthquake and tsunami, weak global demand, and an appreciation of the yen. China, the USA, and the EU are Japan's major trading partners, accounting for nearly half of all trade in 2011. Machinery, transport equipment, and basic manufactured goods make up nearly 75 percent of Japan's total exports. Very little of Japan's trade is covered by trade

---

[e] Multiplier effect—how much the money supply increases in response to a change in the monetary base.

agreements. However, Japan is currently negotiating with the EU, India, Australia, and Canada in an effort to develop more trade agreements. South Korean exports have been increasing, enabling it to maintain a large surplus on the merchandise balance as well as a surplus on the overall current account. Imports have also risen as the price of oil has increased. The nation is committed to trade liberalization policies with foreign trade agreements (FTA) in place with Chile, Singapore, the European Free Trade Association (EFTA), India, ASEAN, and the USA. Further FTAs with Canada, Mexico, Australia, Thailand, Colombia, and Turkey are under negotiation. High tariffs and nontariff barriers, however, are still applied to a number of sectors including agriculture and automobiles.

Table 3.1 presents the scores for the Economy dimension for each of the focal nations of the region and a summary of the strengths and weaknesses is shown in Table 3.2.

Table 3.1   Scores for the Economy Dimension

Economy	Economic Output and Growth Rate	Population Size	Foreign Direct Investment	Exchange Rate Stability/CPI	Balance of Trade	Overall Grade
30%	35%	25%	20%	15%	5%	100%
China	A	A	A⁻	A⁻	A	A
Hong Kong	B⁺	B⁻	A⁻	A⁻	A	B⁺
Japan	B⁻	A	B⁻	C⁺	B⁺	B
South Korea	B⁺	A⁻	B	B	B⁺	B⁺
Taiwan	A⁻	B⁺	B	A	B⁻	B⁺

Table 3.2   Strengths and Weaknesses Summary: Economy Dimension

Grade	Strengths	Weaknesses
China: A	Strong overall GDP and GDP growth; flexible and low cost labor; strength in diverse array of industries; rising consumer spending; largest population in the world; strong FDI, particularly in manufacturing and energy; low inflation; very strong balance of trade, although deficit with other Asian nations.	Aging population; currency exchange rate artificially pegged to international currencies.
Hong Kong: B⁺	Strong economy with good growth; positioned as "middleman" for trade to and from China; relatively low labor costs; rising consumer spending; extremely attractive environment for FDI in banking and logistics; stable currency; foreign trade is the basis of the economy.	Tightening labor market and aging population could constrain future growth; inflation a concern.

(continued)

Table 3.2 Strengths and Weaknesses Summary: Economy Dimension (*Continued*)

Grade	Strengths	Weaknesses
Japan: B	High overall GDP output led by export manufacturing of high-value goods; large population with strong spending power; generally strong absolute trade balance.	Dependence on global demand for high-value exports; high labor costs; consumer spending decreasing; rapidly aging and decreasing population; decreasing FDI inflows; danger of deflation; large fluctuations in trade balance based on the value of the yen.
South Korea: B⁺	Strong export growth; rising consumer expenditures; favorable conditions for FDI; relatively stable exchange rates; aggressive pursuit of trade agreements.	Rapidly aging population; midrange labor costs; losing FDI to China and Taiwan.
Taiwan: B⁺	GDP growth fueled by electronics exports; relatively low labor costs; market-based currency exchange; strong trade relations with China.	Susceptible to variation in export demand; increasing income disparity and flat consumer spending; rapidly aging population.

Politics

An assessment of key elements of the Politics dimension follows, including the ease of doing business, bureaucracy, and corruption; legal and regulatory framework (including tax codes and tariffs); political stability; and protection of intellectual property rights. A summary of Politics dimension elements for each of the focal nations of East Asia is presented at the end of the section.

Ease of Doing Business, Bureaucracy, and Corruption

The 2011 World Bank World Governance Index (WGI) ranks China in the bottom 46th percentile on regulatory quality (although it scores in the 61st percentile on effectiveness), and 29th percentile on control of corruption. In addition, Transparency International rates it a 3.6 out of 10 on the 2011 Corruption Perception Index (CPI). The massive Chinese bureaucracy is a formidable obstacle to conducting business in China, where foreign companies encounter rigid bureaucracy at every level of government. Corruption poses one of the most serious threats to the long-term political and economic viability of the country, as bureaucrats will often play one company against another in an attempt at self-enrichment. This is particularly true in the finance, banking, and construction industries as well as in government procurement contracts. The Chinese system of "guanxi,"[f] in which deals may not be done until the Chinese party has built a close relationship with potential

---

[f] Guanxi describes the basic dynamic in personalized networks of influence and is a central idea in Chinese society.

business partners through exchanges of gifts and favors as tokens of trust, creates many opportunities for abuse. Such challenges are more evident when operating outside of the traditional southeastern export hubs.

Hong Kong, on the other hand, prides itself on maintaining a highly stable and efficient business environment. It consistently scores as one of the top countries in the World Bank's Doing Business reports, with a ranking of second after Singapore out of 183 countries and territories (2012). Scores for the nation on the 2011 WGI include a 99 percent for regulatory quality, 94 percent for government effectiveness, 90 percent on rule of law, and 94 percent on control of corruption. In addition, the 2011 CPI score was an 8.4 out of 10. There are concerns, however, regarding spillover effects from the more corruption-prone Chinese mainland as the integration of Hong Kong into China continues. For example, increasing rates of cybercrime in the nation originate from the mainland, although this has not yet become a serious problem.

Taiwan has also worked to abolish obstacles facing foreign business. Regulations governing the establishment of business ventures have been simplified as a part of an effort to facilitate foreign investment, including the elimination of minimum capital requirements for establishing a company and reducing the workload for foreign companies seeking to enter the Taiwanese market. Previously, many firms experienced long delays in trying to establish operations in Taiwan. Corruption is not as widespread in Taiwan as in China but remains a problem (scoring a 6.1 out of 10 on CPI in 2011). Business is generally regarded as being conducted in a transparent manner, but the traditional system of "the granting of favors" can lead to corruption. Public procurement contracts are more likely to be affected by corruption than applications for private investments, although some local firms are known to have illegally paid to ensure favorable consideration of proposed investments. The 2011 WGI scores for Taiwan include an 83 percent on government effectiveness, 84 percent on regulatory quality, and 78 percent on control of corruption.

The large and cumbersome Japanese bureaucracy has come under public criticism for wielding unjustified levels of power over politicians. Power remains concentrated in 12 ministries and 10 agencies that determine all major policies before being passed down to governments for implementation. This gives the bureaucracy significant power over the Japanese economy through the thousands of licenses, permits, and approvals required to conduct business. In addition, informal but virtually compulsory edicts, called "administrative guidance," serve to tightly regulate business activity in Japan. Furthermore, the practice of "amakudari,"[g] placing retired government officials in prominent positions in private firms, places foreign companies at a disadvantage in their ability to understand laws, regulations, and ministerial guidance because they do not usually enjoy such connections to

---

[g] Amakudari is the institutionalized practice in which Japanese senior bureaucrats retire to high-profile positions in the private and public sectors. The practice is increasingly viewed as corrupt and a drag on unfastening the ties between private sector and state that prevent economic and political reforms.

the bureaucracy. The practice is particularly common in the financial, construction, transportation, and pharmaceutical industries, which have traditionally been heavily regulated. Pure corruption, however, rarely affects foreign companies in Japan. The 2011 WGI scores for Japan include an 88 percent on government effectiveness, 78 percent on regulatory quality, 91 percent on control of corruption, and 8 out of 10 on the CPI.

South Korean laws and regulations are not well developed in a codified system. The regular rotation of government officials who are tasked with interpreting the rules results in inconsistent interpretation and application that can cause bureaucratic problems, although government regulation in South Korea is generally effective. There are some instances of corruption in South Korea, owing to the overly close links between the government and "chaebols," or large conglomerates. Foreign companies encounter such direct corruption less frequently than do Korean companies, but they can suffer as a result of illegal collusion between Korean competitors and senior government officials. Further, corruption in bidding tenders is still common in some sectors. The 2011 WGI scores for South Korea include an 86 percent on government effectiveness, 79 percent on regulatory quality, and 70 percent on control of corruption. In addition, the 2011 CPI is a 5.4 out of 10.

Legal and Regulatory Framework: Tax Codes and Tariffs

China's legal tradition features deeply ingrained Confucian and Marxist-Leninist influences, in which social harmony and the collective good is prioritized over the Western notion of individual rights. Although the legal system has improved significantly and China is moving toward an established rule of law, the law is often politicized because the National People's Congress (NPC) has the power to both enact and interpret legislation. China's World Bank WGI score for rule of law was only 40 percent due to the presence of significant legal and tax risks. As compared to the East Asia average tax rate of 42.7 percent, China has a complicated tax system with a total tax rate of 63.5 percent. China's labor laws are well defined, with a mandatory 40-hour workweek that is based on an eight-hour working day and a five-day working week. Enterprises are allowed substantial autonomy in determining wage levels as long as they comply with the minimum wage requirements as determined by the local government. Minimum wage requirements, however, are set to increase by 40 percent by 2015 in an attempt to address disparities in the distribution of wealth. Employers must comply with health and safety measures and are obliged to pay old age and unemployment insurance to local governments or insurance firms. Employers may also dismiss workers with one month's notice, or one month's wages, if the worker is deemed incompetent. Apart from the national legislation, foreign investors are subject to the local labor regulations of the area in which they are located. The All-China Federation of Trade Unions (ACFTU) represents all unions, as independent trade unions are illegal.

Hong Kong is one of world's most free and open economies, and the role of the state in economic matters is limited. There are no investment restrictions, although some areas such as financial services and businesses related to the stock exchange are subject to the scrutiny and supervision of regulatory bodies. Laws governing the establishment of firms are straightforward, and the government makes no distinction between domestic and foreign investment nor does it require local participation. The WGI rule of law ranking for Hong Kong is above 90 percent, and the legal and tax risks are negligible. Similarly, Hong Kong has a low tax jurisdiction with a very simple tax system that is business friendly. In 2012, the corporate tax rate was 16.5 percent, with 23.0 percent of total profits taken. Employment is relatively unregulated in Hong Kong, with codes setting out certain basic rights and protections for all employees. There are no legal guidelines for maximum working hours or overtime payments, and labor markets and wage rates are flexible above a minimum wage requirement. Labor law applies to both local and foreign workers in Hong Kong.

Taiwan scored 88 percent on rule of law in the World Bank WGI, and is rated as a low to moderate legal and tax risk on the 2012 Economist Intelligence Unit Country Risk Rating (EIU CRR). Taiwan's legal system is based on a civil code with emphasis placed on statutes rather than case law; judicial decisions are based on code provisions rather than legal precedent. General contract and agency laws that are contained within the civil code govern business transactions. Under foreign investment law, applications to establish a foreign-owned company must be made to the Investment Commission of the Ministry of Economic Affairs; certain industrial sectors remain closed to foreign investment for environmental and security reasons. Taiwan may also restrict investment from mainland Chinese companies that have military shareholders or have a military purpose. Otherwise, restrictions on capital flows have been removed. The tax system in Taiwan is comprehensive and generally friendly toward business, with strong tax incentives for foreign investors and qualified enterprises. Taiwan has a corporate tax rate of 17.0 percent, with a total tax rate of 35.6 percent of total profits. Foreign companies sometimes complain about the arbitrary nature of tax imposition and of evasion by domestic firms; the government has been reforming the system to make it more transparent. Labor Standards Law establishes employers' minimum obligations for employment terms and conditions. Legal procedure means that strikes may only be called when 50 percent of union members endorse it and seven days advance notice is given to labor officials.

Japan scored 87 percent on rule of law in the World Bank WGI, and is rated as a negligible to low legal and tax risk on the 2012 EIU CRR. It is also a civil code country with a legal system based on codified laws that are a mixture of Western and Asian legal traditions. In particular, Western law has been adapted in areas such as copyright, antitrust, and unfair business practices. Judicial decisions are based directly on code provisions (not on case precedent), and criminal and civil trials do not employ juries. The civil courts enforce property and contractual rights without discriminating against investors, but they are not always suited to the needs of commercial litigation. It is common for cases to be settled out of court, as Japanese business owners tend to view a contract as one part of a long-term relationship, and lawsuits are deemed to disrupt social harmony. Under Japanese law, both foreign and domestic investors are assured of the right to establish and own businesses and to pursue all forms of profitable enterprise. There are no entry barriers for foreigners seeking to purchase property. Overseas investors may hold property in their own name, in joint ventures, in limited partnerships, or through limited liability firms. The tax system in Japan is well developed and transparent, although it is complex and is reflected in a large number of laws. The tax burden is moderately high as compared with other countries in the region, and foreign companies are generally subject to higher levels of taxation than domestic firms; the corporate tax rate is 25.5 percent with a tax rate at 49.1 percent of total profits. Labor regulations in Japan tend to be relatively flexible, with the law requiring only that conditions of employment are established in the employment agreement. Employment contracts may be unlimited or may function on a fixed-term basis, with the latter generally being limited to three-year terms. The right to unionize is constitutionally protected and is implemented by the Labor Standards Law, although unions are generally not very aggressive or political.

The legal system in South Korea is a statutory civil law system that is based on the continental European system, although commercial legislation has been influenced by the United States as well. South Korea scored 81 percent on rule of law in the World Bank WGI and is rated as a low to moderate legal and tax risk on the 2012 EIU CRR. Serious investment disputes involving foreign investors are rare in South Korea, but when they do occur, they often relate to the violation of intellectual property rights. Investment law categorizes businesses as either open, partly restricted, or closed to foreign investment. There are three specially designated areas for foreign investment including foreign economic zones, foreign investment zones, and tariff-free zones.

The tax system in South Korea is well regulated and its regulations are clearly articulated. However, the system is relatively complex and contains loopholes and generous allowances on the level of personal income taxes, reducing overall efficiency. The government has been moving toward lower effective tax rates for foreign investors through a comprehensive set of investment incentives. Currently, the maximum rate for corporate income tax (applicable for income over 200 MM won) is 22 percent, and the total tax rate was 29.7 percent in 2011 according to the World Bank. South Korea's organized labor movement, which is among the most active in the world's developed economies, wields much influence in labor law and makes the labor market very rigid as workers tend to stay with one employer.

Political Stability

The East Asia region features varying levels of stability and risk of political systems within the member nations. The EIU CRR ranked China at 124th out of 165 nations (where a higher ranking indicates greater stability), with significant risk to political instability on the EIU CRR (on a 9-point scale of insignificant to extreme risk), ranking. South Korea was considered a medium political instability risk, ranking 117th on the EIU CRR. All of the other East Asian nations are relatively stable. Hong Kong scored a negligible political instability risk rating, ranking 146th. Taiwan and Japan also had negligible risk, with rankings of 146 and 150, respectively.

Intellectual Property Rights

Within the East Asia region, China, Taiwan, and South Korea struggle most with intellectual property rights (IPR) enforcement. Incomplete enforcement of existing laws has obstructed progress in addressing widespread IPR infringement in China. Many foreign companies have experienced problems with joint venture partners that use the technology they have acquired in the partnership to directly compete with their former foreign partner. Piracy continues to be a serious issue for foreign companies operating in Taiwan, particularly in such fields as computer hardware and software, fashion items, films, and compact discs. However, the situation has improved significantly since the Ministry of Economic Affairs' IPR office implemented periodic crackdowns on violations, while at the same time strengthening cooperation with foreign enforcement agencies. South Korea has a history of IPR issues. However, the situation has improved as the Korean Intellectual Property Office (KIPO) has been given increasing powers to monitor the implementation of intellectual property legislation. Creating an effective response to Internet piracy of digital copyright material remains an ongoing challenge.

Japan is assessed as the best nation in the East Asia region with respect to IPR. Intellectual property is generally respected, protected, and enforced in Japan. The situation is also satisfactory in Hong Kong as the SARs system for protection of IPR, which has remained independent from that of the mainland, is comprehensive and largely effective. Also, both Japan and Hong Kong are signatories to international IPR treaties. Despite growing efforts to crack down on intellectual property rights violations, including raids and more severe jail penalties, counterfeit products remain available throughout Hong Kong on a small scale, mainly coming from the mainland.

Table 3.3 presents the scores for the Politics dimension for each of the focal nations of the region and a summary of the strengths and weaknesses is shown in Table 3.4.

Table 3.3   Scores for the Politics Dimension

Politics	Ease of Doing Business	Legal Framework	Political Stability	Intellectual Property Rights	Overall Grade
20%	30%	30%	25%	15%	100%
China	C	C	B	C⁺	C⁺
Hong Kong	A	A	A⁻	A⁻	A
Japan	A⁻	B⁺	A⁻	A⁻	A⁻
South Korea	B⁺	B⁺	B	B	B⁺
Taiwan	A⁻	B⁺	B⁺	A⁻	B⁺

Table 3.4   Strengths and Weaknesses Summary: Politics Dimension

Grade	Strengths	Weaknesses
China: C+	Labor laws and wage rates are predictable and favorable for business.	Highly bureaucratic and difficult to do business; corruption levels are very high; lack of transparency and predictability in the legal system; very high tax rates; significant risk in judicial and political institutions; property rights protections are in place but are largely unenforceable.
Hong Kong: A	One of most stable and efficient business environments in the world; high levels of corruption control; extremely open and free legal system with minimal control of business and investment; simple tax system with among the lowest tax rates in the region; very flexible labor system with low labor rates; stable political system.	Despite strong laws favoring IP protection, some small-scale counterfeiting still occurring.
Japan: A−	Relatively easy to do business with low corruption; stable political environment with comprehensive laws for tax, labor, and environment; strong IP protection.	Bureaucratic control of government policies and strong "favor" mentality; high taxes and complex tax code.
South Korea: B+	Moderately stable political environment with comprehensive and effective laws for tax, labor, and environment; relatively low tax rates.	Issues with government and legal transparency; corruption relatively high; complex tax code; rigid, difficult labor environment; issues with IPR protection remain.
Taiwan: B+	Relatively easy to do business; corruption largely controlled; stable political environment with comprehensive and effective laws for tax, labor, and environment; reasonable corporate tax rates.	"Favor" system remains strong in government organizations; IPR piracy a serious issue.

Infrastructure

An assessment of key elements of the Infrastructure dimension follows, including transportation, utilities, and telecommunications. A summary of Infrastructure elements for each of the focal nations of East Asia is presented at the end of the section.

Transportation

The Chinese government invests heavily in transportation infrastructure in order to improve competitiveness and reduce trading costs. The World Bank Logistics Performance Index (LPI) ranks China's transportation infrastructure at 3.61 out of 5, on par with such nations as Turkey, Spain, and Portugal. The nation features the second most paved highways in the world (Figure 3.7) and the third most rail lines, although this can be deceptive given the vast geographic size of China. Several infrastructure projects are planned over the next three years to further improve China's position as an export-oriented manufacturing base, including investment in urban transportation, railway construction, and rural infrastructure. Most population centers are accessible by road, particularly in the east and southeastern regions, but the road network is badly in need of improvement. Major cities, particularly Shanghai and Beijing, already face congestion and gridlock on substandard roadways, and the central and western regions lack appropriate road networks to support industry. In addition, most of the best intercity roadways are toll roads with tolls that are among the highest in the world.[7]

The rail system is the backbone of the Chinese transportation network, although increased demand has placed a strain on both passenger and cargo capacity (Figure 3.8). There are extensive north-south and east-west trunk lines in China. The north-south line, with Beijing as its hub, consists of the Beijing-Guangzhou Railway, Beijing-Shanghai Railway, Beijing-Kowloon Railway, and Beijing-Harbin Railway. The east-west line, with Zhengzhou as its hub, consists of the Lianyunggang-Lanzhou Railway and Lanzhou-Urumqi Railway. The latter has been extended westward to link up with the railways in Kazakhstan, with subsequent connections to Europe. In addition, new railway lines have been built in mountainous areas in southwestern China, mainly the Chendu-Chongqing Railway, Baoji-Chengdu Railway, Chengdu-Kunming Railway, and the Nanning-Kunming Railway. The Turpan-Kashi Railway has been newly built in the Xinjiang Uygur Autonomous Region.

China's extensive east coast features a number of deepwater ports that are suitable for trade. The coastal system is divided into two major navigation zones. Shanghai and Dalian form the centers of the northern zone, and Guangzhou serves as the center of the southern zone. Other major ports include Fuzhou, Haikou, Lianyungang, Nanjing, Nantong, Ningbo, Quingdao, Qinhuangdao, Shantou, Shenzhen, Tianjin, Xiamen, Yantian, and Zhanjiang. China leads the world in overall inland waterway capability, with extensive inland navigation on the Yangtze, Pearl, Heilongjiang, Huaihe, Qiantang, Minjiang, and Huangpu rivers, as well as the Grand Canal connecting Beijing and Hangzhou. An extensive air cargo network also serves the nation with major hubs in Beijing, Shanghai, and Guandong. Beijing Capital Airport is currently the second largest airfreight market in China, lagging only Shanghai. Shanghai is serviced by Pudong International Airport and Hongqiao International (eight miles from downtown). All international and regional flights operating through Shanghai were shifted to Pudong International Airport in 2002.

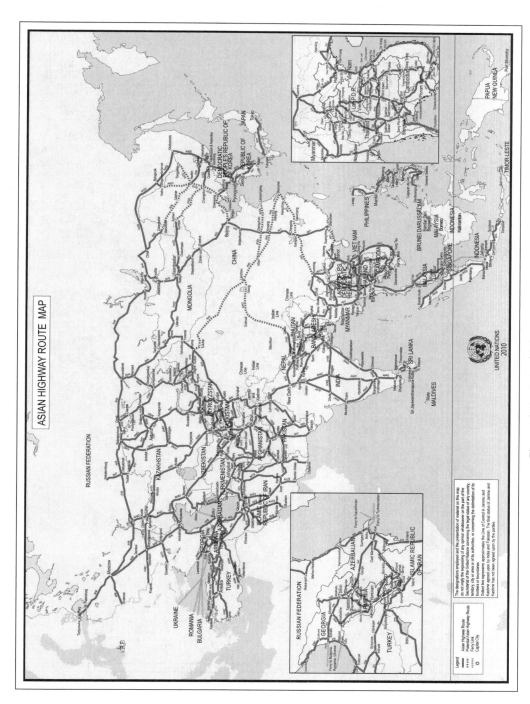

Figure 3.7 Asian highway route map.

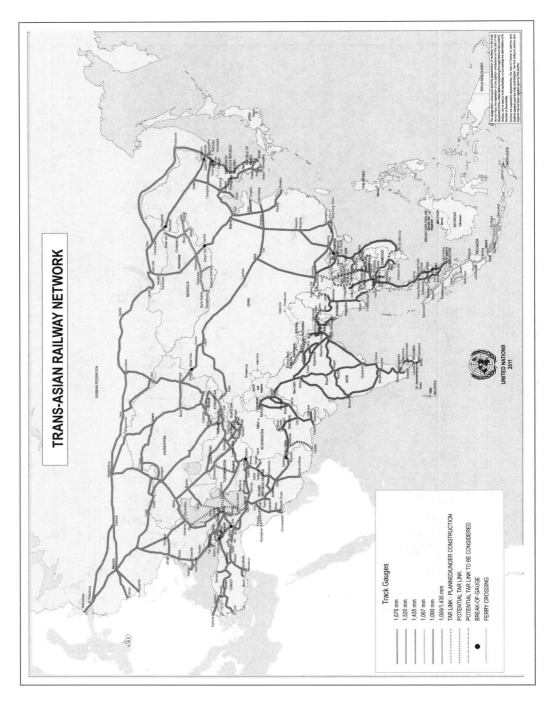

TRANS-ASIAN RAILWAY NETWORK

Track Gauges

———	1,676 mm
———	1,520 mm
———	1,435 mm
———	1,067 mm
———	1,000 mm
———	1,000/1,435 mm
··········	TAR LINK - PLANNED/UNDER CONSTRUCTION
··········	POTENTIAL TAR LINK
··········	POTENTIAL TAR LINK TO BE CONSIDERED
●	BREAK-OF-GAUGE
··········	FERRY CROSSING

UNITED NATIONS
2011

Figure 3.8 Trans-Asian railway network.

Hongqiao Airport is primarily a hub for domestic flights but has the capacity to handle international traffic. Baiyun International Airport in Guangdong has connections to more than 90 domestic and 25 international destinations and serves as the passenger and cargo hub airport for state carrier China Southern Airlines.

Hong Kong's natural deepwater port and trading history has made the city one of the world's major international sea and air cargo hubs. The island has a highly developed infrastructure with world-class facilities across all modes of transportation. Hong Kong infrastructure was ranked seventh in the world in the World Bank 2012 LPI. The Hong Kong SAR has one of the highest vehicle density rates in the world, and car congestion remains a problem. Ongoing investments in infrastructure projects, including road construction projects and taxes on vehicles purchased, are targeted at improving road transport. The rail system is excellent, with an underground mass transit system that is one of the most heavily used in the world and a light rail transit system that operates in the New Territories, with good connections to mainland China. Hong Kong features one of the most modern and fully developed deepwater harbors between Singapore and Shanghai and has the distinction of being one of the world's busiest container ports. Ferry systems connect Hong Kong passenger and freight traffic to Macau and other nearby destinations. Hong Kong International Airport is one of the busiest airports in the world and an important hub for China.

Taiwan has a well-developed transportation infrastructure that has enjoyed consistent government investment. Taiwan's infrastructure was ranked 21st in the world in the World Bank 2012 LPI, on par with developed nations such as Italy and Luxembourg. The infrastructure enables businesses in Taiwan to take advantage of its location at the center of air and sea transportation in East Asia. There is an extensive road network, but the system in general, and Taipei in particular, suffers from chronic traffic congestion. The first north-south freeway has been widened with additional lanes, and many sections of a second north-south freeway have been opened in an attempt to ease congestion. The state-owned Taiwan Railway Administration operates a modern, reliable rail network, which extends in a loop around the whole island and connects all major cities. The three main lines are Taipei-Kaohsiung, Taipei-Hualien, and Hualien-Taitung. Taiwan has seven large ports located at Anping, Hualien, Kaohsiung, Keelung, Suao, Taipei, and Taichung, with the main hubs at Kaohsiung and Keelung. The ongoing expansion of harbor facilities and the privatization of harbor operations have reduced waiting time into Kaohsiung, the fifth-busiest container port in the world (processing two-thirds of Taiwan's total import and export volume). Taiwan's air transport network is excellent. The island has three international airports including Taiwan Taoyuan International Airport near Taipei, Hsiaokang in Kaohsiung, and Taichung, in central Taiwan, which opened in March 2004.

Japan has an advanced infrastructure that undergoes constant upgrades. It ranked ninth on the World Bank 2012 LPI despite the earthquake that hit the northeastern Pacific coast in March 2011, which severely damaged the country's infrastructure. Massive reconstruction efforts have rapidly boosted the redevelopment of roads, railways, ports, and airports in the area. Japan has an extensively developed road and highway infrastructure that covers more than 1,177,278 km (731,526 mi). However, severe congestion constitutes a serious problem in major urban centers due to high population density in the major cities. In addition, high land prices constrain the ability to expand the road network, and unique regulations such as one restricting large stores, reduce the efficiency of the road transportation.

The Japanese rail network is extremely well developed and represents a prime means of transportation. The overall rail network spans more than 23,000 km (14,292 mi) of lines. Japan's fast-speed trains (shinkansen) can reach speeds of up to 300 kph (186 mph) and offer convenient high-speed travel between Japan's largest cities. Private and regional rail companies also provide efficient intercity passenger and cargo service. Japan has more than 1000 ports and harbors, of which 19 are designated as major ports for foreign trade and 11 are container-handling ports. Kobe, the second largest container port in the world, is the largest Japanese port with 37 berths, of which 28 are container berths. There are also major ports at Nagoya, Osaka, Yokohama, and Tokyo. Japan has more than 65 commercial airports, 14 of which handle international traffic. Japan's airports, however, are notoriously congested, expensive, and often inefficient, although competition between airlines is slowly helping to drive down prices. The largest and most important airport is New Japan Narita International, located 66 km (41 mi) from Tokyo. Narita has consistently been ranked as among the world's busiest airports. There are also major airports at Osaka, Nagoya, and Fukuoka.

South Korea's transportation infrastructure is ranked 22nd in the world in the World Bank 2012 LPI and, like Taiwan, compares favorably to developed nations in Europe such as Italy and Spain. South Korea's roads are paved, and freeways adequately connect all parts of the nation; all freeways, however, are toll ways. The rail network is excellent, with the backbone being the 444 km (276 mi) double-tracked Gyeongbu line that runs between the country's two principal cities, Busan on the southeast coast, and Seoul in the northwest. South Korea has 17 major ports, of which Busan is the largest. Inchon, the other main port, is located outside of Seoul. South Korea has an inland waterway network of 1600 km (994 mi) that permits navigation by small vessels. The country's major waterways are the Han, Kum, Naktong, and Somjin rivers, which move from the northeast to the southwest and carry significant volumes of internal commerce. Three international airports serve as the primary gateways into the country, including Incheon (52 km or 32 mi from Seoul), Kimhae (near Busan), and Cheju (on the island of that name).

Utilities

China is the second largest consumer of energy in the world. Although the nation is rich in energy resources (including coal, hydroelectrics, and natural gas), it has taken time for these to be developed enough to keep up with increasing demand, resulting in localized shortages in the industrial zones along the east coast. These shortages have now spread to adjacent provinces. Further complicating the matter is the fact that most energy resources are located well away from the fast-growing energy consumption centers of the east and south. The World Bank Doing Business report for 2012 ranked China 115th out of 183 nations for ease of getting electricity.

Hong Kong has no natural energy resources and depends on imports for supply. Still, the provision of utilities such as gas, electricity, and water is reliable, and obtaining service is a straightforward process. Hong Kong ranks 4th out of 183 on ease of getting electricity in the 2012 Doing Business report.

The rapid development of the Taiwanese economy in recent years has put considerable strain on the country's energy-producing capabilities. The leading provider of energy, the state-controlled Tai Power Company (Taipower), has been partly privatized, and the government is scrutinizing plans for full privatization. The country performs particularly well in ease of getting electricity, ranking 3rd out of 183 countries in the Doing Business 2012 report.

Japan's energy use per unit of GDP (energy intensity) is among the lowest in the developed world. The country's goal is to cut oil consumption to 40 percent of total energy consumption by 2030. In 2009, Japan produced 27 percent of its electricity from nuclear power. The government had previously planned to significantly increase the share of nuclear sources in total electricity; however, those plans have been scrapped since the 2011 earthquake and subsequent nuclear reactor disaster. Tokyo now plans to shut down all of its 50 reactors by 2040. The decision will have significant repercussions for global petroleum demand as Japan is already among the world's largest importers of crude oil, coal, and liquefied natural gas. The country has modest amounts of natural gas reserves, with more potentially located under the coastal seabed. Japan ranks 26th out of 183 countries in ease of getting electricity in the Doing Business 2012 report.

South Korea ranks 11th out of 183 countries in ease of getting electricity in the Doing Business 2012 report. South Korea has an adequate level of electricity-generating capacity and a well-developed infrastructure, making for adequate and reliable energy provision. The country has some of the largest and most advanced oil refineries in the world. However, because it has no domestic reserves, South Korea must import all of its crude oil. In the long term, the country is pursuing equity stakes in oil and gas exploration around the world, with 33 overseas exploration and production projects in 15 countries.

Telecommunications

In 2011, China had 500 million Internet subscribers and 986 million mobile phone users. Domestic and international telecommunications services are increasingly available for private use, and foreign investors do not have problems finding service. The unevenly distributed domestic system serves principal cities, industrial centers, and most townships. China has an estimated Internet penetration rate of 34.3 percent, although censorship remains problematic, and it can be difficult to obtain access to information that the

Table 3.5 Scores for the Infrastructure Dimension

Infrastructure	Transportation Infrastructure	Energy Infrastructure	Connectivity	Overall Grade
30%	50%	25%	25%	100%
China	C⁺	B⁻	C⁻	C⁺
Hong Kong	A	A	A⁻	A
Japan	B⁺	B⁺	B	B⁺
South Korea	A⁻	B⁺	B⁺	A⁻
Taiwan	B⁺	B⁺	B⁺	B⁺

Table 3.6 Strengths and Weaknesses Summary: Infrastructure Dimension

Grade	Strengths	Weaknesses
China: C⁺	Eastern region ports and airports; telecommunications is adequate and improving; significant investment is planned in transportation, power, and telecommunications infrastructure over the next five years.	Roads and rail are congested in the east, and infrastructure is insufficient in the central and west; congestion is rising in the east; insufficient electrical distribution capability.
Hong Kong: A	Infrastructure is world class with strong facilities across all modes of transportation; sophisticated telecommunications infrastructure.	One of the highest vehicle density rates in the world and car congestion remains a problem; energy generation all comes from the mainland.
Japan: B⁺	Excellent and sophisticated transportation infrastructure; excellent power generation and distribution capabilities; sophisticated telecommunications capability; some natural gas reserves.	Some transportation bottlenecks in major metropolitan areas; future of power generation unclear following nuclear disaster in 2011 that led to decision to close all nuclear reactors by 2040.
South Korea: A⁻	Excellent road and rail coverage; excellent sea and airports, plus significant inland water capability; power distribution is well developed and extensive, and water and sewage is improving; one of the best telecom services in Asia.	Congestion in major metropolitan areas; no internal energy resources.
Taiwan: B⁺	Well-developed transportation infrastructure across all modes; sea and airports are world class; power distribution and telecommunications capability are world class; strong nuclear power industry.	Significant congestion in Taipei; population growth has put strain on power production.

government deems to be of a sensitive nature. According to the World Economic Forum's 2012 Networked Readiness Index (NRI), China ranked 51st out of 142 countries, a better ranking than Brazil (65th) and India (69th). The NRI measures the propensity for countries to exploit the opportunities offered by information and communications technology. The Chinese government plans heavy investment in the development of the information and telecommunications infrastructure over the next five years.

Hong Kong is arguably the most liberalized market in the world for telecommunications services, and it has excellent fully digitized telecommunications capability. The telecommunications industry is highly competitive and has a sophisticated infrastructure. The penetration rates of mobile phone and broadband Internet reached 99.5 percent and 78.8 percent of total households, respectively, in 2011, among the highest rates in the world. Hong Kong is also a leading regional hub for cloud technology, offering local opportunities as well as potential for expansion into mainland China and international markets. In 2012, Hong Kong ranked 13th out of 139 countries in the Economic Forum's NRI.

Taiwan has a well-developed infrastructure and information, communications, and technology (ICT) sector. In 2012, the country ranked 11th out of 142 countries in the World Economic Forum's NRI. Taiwan's government invests heavily in the development of WiMAX, a wireless alternative that provides high-speed access links rather than using traditional copper lines. In 2011, the government invested $230 MM (US) in a WiMAX development project aimed at creating 20,000 jobs and attracting 2.2 million WiMAX wireless technology users by 2013.

In 2011, 95.4 percent of Japanese households possessed a mobile telephone, and 84.4 percent of households possessed an Internet-enabled computer. Japan's telephone system offers excellent domestic and international service, with data transmission–based modern technology. The Japanese population has also embraced mobile and Internet technology. In 2012, Japan ranked 18th out of 142 countries in the World Economic Forum's NRI.

South Korea has one of the better telecommunications services in Asia due to heavy government investment, particularly in the broadband sector. The country's broadband penetration rate stood at 97.8 percent of total households in 2009, the highest rate in the world. In 2012, South Korea ranked 12th out of 142 countries in the World Economic Forum's NRI.

Table 3.5 presents the scores for the Infrastructure dimension for each of the focal nations of the region and a summary of the strengths and weaknesses is shown in Table 3.6.

Competence

An assessment of key elements of the Competence dimension follows, including labor availability, productivity, and relations; education for line staff and management; and logistics, customs, and security. A summary of Competence elements for each of the focal nations of East Asia is presented at the end of the section.

Labor: Availability, Productivity, and Relations

China has a large labor pool that ranges from low-skilled workers to highly trained scientists and engineers. University-trained graduates are found in abundance and managerial skills are improving. The current labor pool in China is comprised of 795.5 million workers. There are significant concerns, however, related to the future of labor availability in China. There have been increasing reports of labor shortages in the country's southern coastal provinces including Guangdong, Fujian, Jiangsu, and Zhejiang. To some extent, the labor shortfall was the expected outcome of the changing balance of foreign investment in China, as it gradually moves from labor-intensive low-end manufacturing, requiring unskilled or semiskilled labor, to services industries and high-tech manufacturing, both of which need skilled specialist labor. The shortage is also partially the result of shifting demographics. China's birthrate has been in a state of gradual decline since the introduction of the "One Child" policy in 1977, meaning that fewer people are entering the labor force. A recent study by two economists at the International Monetary Fund suggests that by 2025 the country could face a shortfall of 28 million workers; as of 2010, China had a surplus of 150 million laborers.[8]

China has responded to the decreasing labor pool by attempting to improve labor productivity. Most of China's productivity gains have come from moving excess rural labor from low-productivity agricultural activities to higher-productivity manufacturing and service sectors. Productivity of labor grew by 20.1 percent per year in real terms between 2006 and 2011, reaching $8325 (US) per person employed in 2011. This compares favorably to peer economies like India ($4350 US per employee) and Indonesia ($7666 US) in 2011. A potential change in Chinese farming from the household-based small farms to large mechanized farms could affect the situation dramatically by reducing the demand for labor in the countryside and freeing workers for urban areas. This change will not be possible, however, without changing China's land ownership system in order to allow for the consolidation of land holdings in rural areas.

The Labor Contract Law of the People's Republic of China, enacted in 2008, permits collective bargaining, although only unions affiliated with the All-China Federation of Trade Unions, the Communist Party's official union organization, are allowed. The law has support from labor activists but was opposed by some foreign corporations, including the American Chamber of Commerce and the European Chamber of Commerce. A substantial increase in labor-related incidents have occurred in recent years, including notable cases at Honda, Toyota, and FoxConn.[9]

Hong Kong benefits from a well-educated and flexible workforce of 3.7 million people, which is highly computer literate and entrepreneurial. Historically, there has been a strong supply of immigrants from the mainland who provide relatively inexpensive manufacturing labor. However, the structural shift of the economy into value-added services has increased the demand for higher levels of skills and education and caused increased unemployment among low-skilled workers. Skilled labor shortages have also occurred in several industrial sectors (including telecommunications and financial services industries) owing partly to the aging population. Loosening regulations on the immigration of skilled labor from the mainland is one option to respond to the shortage. Productivity in Hong Kong is also improving. In 2011, productivity was around $66,151 (US) per employee, up from $54,988 (US) per employee in 2006. The Hong Kong government's refusal to guarantee the right of labor groups to engage in collective bargaining has meant that, on the whole, trade unions are not an influential force in Hong Kong.

Taiwan's labor force of 11.2 million is one of the best trained, educated, and entrepreneurial in Asia, but labor shortages remain in some sectors. Nearly 60 percent of the population is employed by the service sector, with industry and agriculture accounting for 37 percent and 5 percent, respectively; knowledge workers account for roughly 30 percent of total employment. As with other East Asian nations, labor shortages stemming from Taiwan's aging population will increasingly become an issue. Labor productivity has increased to $42,387 (US) per person employed in 2011, from $39,874 (US) in 2010, as the economy has regained momentum. Approximately 33 percent of the workforce is unionized, but organized labor has historically been weak in Taiwan and this trend continues despite rising levels of unionization.

Japan's workforce of 65.9 million people in 2011 is down from 66.6 million in 2006. The workforce is highly skilled and educated, with particular strengths in engineering and the sciences. However, the country is the most aged society in the world with an old-age dependency ratio (the share of population aged 65 and over to the working age population aged 15–64) of 36.6 percent in 2011. There is significant concern about the handover of skills from the increasing number of retirees to their younger counterparts, especially with regard to the problem of the knowledge gap that exists for production jobs requiring a complex set of skills. The situation could encourage Japan to loosen immigration laws directed at skilled workers. Productivity in Japan increased from $67,426 (US) per person employed in 2006 to $91,295 (US) per person employed in 2011. Labor relations have traditionally been harmonious, ruled by the principles of lifetime employment and seniority. These principles are being challenged by attempts to implement economic reforms, although there are no indications of a tangible worsening of labor relations.

The South Korean labor force of 25.1 million people has been characterized as of high quality, but somewhat rigid and inflexible. Labor shortages exist in sectors such as information technology, bioengineering, and telecommunications. Such labor shortages will intensify as the population ages and the workforce shrinks. South Korea increasingly relies on low-skilled laborers from the Philippines, Indonesia, and Vietnam. As the high-tech sector grows, importing skilled labor will become a necessity. Since 2007, the government has granted permanent residency to skilled workers from abroad in an effort to relieve skills shortages. Labor relations have worsened as the skills shortage has become more acute, and union activity has increased. Among the more common motivations for the unions' strike activities are efforts to increase wages, reduce work hours, prevent the usage of temporary labor, and safeguard the jobs of union members.

Education Levels for Line Staff and Management

The adult literacy rate in China was 94.6 percent of the economically active population in 2011, up from 93.0 percent in 2006. The Chinese government has been stressing the need for higher education and the importance of developing a human resources strategy for finding and nurturing human capital. Between 2006 and 2011, government spending on education rose 10 percent annually to 7.3 percent of government expenditure in 2011, a rate that surpasses other emerging economies like India. As a result of increased investment, the number of people in higher education increased from 23.4 million in 2006 (1.8 percent of the total population) to 32.9 million (2.5 percent of the total population) in 2011. The fields of engineering, manufacturing, and construction accounted for the highest proportion of graduates (37.7 percent); followed by humanities and the arts (23.6 percent); and social sciences, business, and law (12.5 percent).

Hong Kong has a well-educated workforce with an adult literacy rate of 96.2 percent of the population over age 15 (2011). Government expenditure on education in 2011 amounted for 2.7 percent of total GDP. There have been growing concerns over the declining rate of English spoken by locals in Hong Kong due to the influx of mainland Chinese and the ongoing exodus of expatriates. Language education is vital to Hong Kong's goal of becoming the region's leading value-added service sector. Surprisingly, Hong Kong's higher education rates are relatively low, despite government policy that has strived to promote a competitive, knowledge-based workforce by providing nine years of free compulsory education and contributing one-third of its overall education budget to tertiary education. The number of students engaged in higher education in the nation increased to 283,500 people by 2011, with the social sciences, business, and law accounting for 33.3 percent of total graduates.

Taiwan has a well-educated workforce that is supported by an excellent educational system. In 2011, the adult literacy rate was at 99.9 percent of the population over 15 years of age, up from 98.0 percent in 2006. Government expenditure on education remains high and reached 3.8 percent of total GDP in 2011. The number of people in higher education is increasing, but at a slow pace largely due to the decline in population growth. In 2011, Taiwan had 1.4 million people in higher education, only marginally higher than 1.3 million people in 2006.

The Japanese workforce is highly skilled and educated, with particular strengths in engineering and the sciences. In 2011, the adult literacy rate was 99.9 percent of the population aged 15 and over, and government expenditure on education was 3.5 percent of total GDP. Rates of university (or equivalent) attendance among Japan's workers are equivalent to, if not higher than, those in the United States and Western Europe. The number of students in higher education, however, has been declining each year due to the country's aging population. In 2011, 3.7 million students were engaged in higher education, down from 4.1 million in 2006. The disciplines of social science, business, and law had the highest number of graduates (2011) with 26.4 percent of total graduates, whereas the sciences had only 3.1 percent, the lowest number of graduates in the same year.

The South Korean workforce is highly educated and skilled, with particular strengths in science and technology. In addition to a 97.9 percent literacy rate, South Korea also has the second highest number of science and engineering graduates per capita in the world, with roughly 300,000 new graduates entering the workforce each year. The government spent 4.2 percent of GDP on education in 2011.

Logistics, Customs, and Security

China's overall logistics competence is ranked 26th in the world (out of 155 nations) by the World Bank 2012 LPI, similar to the nations of Ireland and Turkey. In particular, China earns high scores in timeliness, infrastructure, and international shipments. The logistics service industry, however, has traditionally been highly fragmented with most local firms engaged in basic transportation management and warehousing. The industry has also suffered from a lack of coordination among government oversight authorities for different services in different regions. International service providers that seek to provide a full range of logistics services face challenges, as they have to apply for a multitude of licenses from different government agencies. For example, different authorities regulate the trucking, shipping, aviation, customs brokering, and warehousing sectors. The Chinese government recently liberalized the regulatory structure to address this ambiguity. The lack of management knowledge in logistics and transportation remains one of the top problems faced by logistics service providers that operate in China. Although they are effective, logistics operations in China are relatively inefficient, consuming 18.1 percent of GDP. Corruption is widespread in the Chinese customs department, and in some cases customs departments have been directly involved in smuggling.

As befits the economic focus of Hong Kong, the nation's overall logistics competence is ranked second in the world (out of 155) by the World Bank 2012 LPI, with international shipping capability considered the best in the world and all other categories, including timeliness, infrastructure, tracking and tracing, logistics, and customs, among the global top 10. Hong Kong's customs authority is transparent and contributes to a ranking of second out of 183 in the World Bank's Doing Business 2012 report in the category of trading across borders. Hong Kong's strengths and achievements in the fields of logistics, shipping, and maritime service have been recognized by the Chinese government, and continued support for high-value goods, inventory management, regional distribution, and international maritime shipping are included in the most recent Five-Year Plan.

Taiwan's overall logistics competence is highly regarded, with a rank of 19th out of 155 in the world by the World Bank 2012 LPI, flanked by Australia and Spain in the global rankings. Although logistics is one of the most important industries to their economy, Taiwan has lost ground to regional competitors. As a result, the Taiwanese government has committed additional investment designed to improve customs efficiency and port infrastructure, strengthen logistics services, and promote cross-border cooperation and development in order to remain competitive for shipments bound to and from mainland Chinese markets.[10]

Japan enjoys one of the top logistics industries in the world, with an overall logistics competence ranked eighth in the world (out of 155) by the World Bank 2012 LPI. Compared with other industrial countries, Japan's logistics system is very complex, with most aspects of goods distribution tightly regulated by the government. Logistics service providers are not highly differentiated, although some offer highly specialized services. Joint distribution, in which competitors who make deliveries to the same businesses tend to use joint delivery capacities and trucks, is typical. As a result, a long and complicated network of relation-driven intermediaries who interact closely with wholesalers, brokers, manufacturers, importers, and retailers characterizes the Japanese system; it is not uncommon to include as many as four layers of wholesalers to reach a customer. The intricacy of the Japanese distribution channel is deeply rooted in the Japanese culture and socioeconomic setting that underlies Japanese business customs.[11] According to the 2012 World Bank Doing Business Report, Japan ranks 16th out of 183 countries in the Trading Across Borders section, which is measured according to costs, bureaucracy, and time spent when dealing with customs.

South Korea is one of the primary international logistics hubs for northeast Asia, owing to its strong economic connections with China, Japan, and Taiwan. Compared with any other area in East Asia, South Korea can connect to numerous cities faster and more frequently, providing world-class logistics services through its excellent transportation infrastructure of world-class airports and seaports, well-organized highway network, railroads, and inland logistics hub facilities. South Korea's overall logistics competence is ranked 21st in the world (out of 155) by the World Bank 2012 LPI, just behind Spain and ahead of Norway in the global rankings. South Korea has a well-functioning customs system that is not an obstacle to international business, ranking fourth out of 183 countries in the category of Trading Across Borders in the World Bank's Doing Business Report 2012.

Table 3.7 presents the scores for the Competence dimension for each of the focal nations of the region and a summary of their strengths and weaknesses is shown in Table 3.8.

Table 3.7 Scores for the Competence Dimension

Competence	Labor Relations	Education Levels	Logistics Competence	Customs and Security	Overall Grade
20%	25%	25%	40%	10%	100%
China	B	B⁻	A⁻	B⁺	B⁺
Hong Kong	A	A⁻	A	A	A
Japan	B⁻	B⁺	A	A	A⁻
South Korea	C	B	A⁻	A⁻	B
Taiwan	B⁺	B⁺	A⁻	A⁻	A⁻

Table 3.8 Strengths and Weaknesses Summary: Competence Dimension

Grade	Strengths	Weaknesses
China: B⁺	Huge pool of labor, ranging from cheap, low-skilled workers to highly trained scientists and engineers; favorable labor productivity and increasing education levels; logistics industry capabilities are basic.	Available skilled labor pool is shrinking due to population decline and increasing industrialization; significant congestion and corruption in customs and trade regime with high risk in operations and security; management skills not as strong as science, technology, and engineering; logistics services are inefficient.
Hong Kong: A	Well-educated and flexible workforce that is highly computer-literate and entrepreneurial; highly productive; world-class logistics service industry and capabilities and customs/trade apparatus.	Workforce is aging; unemployment has been generated by the ongoing reallocation of labor from manufacturing to the services sector; levels of higher education are shrinking; growing concerns over the declining standards of English spoken.
Japan: A⁻	Highly skilled and educated workforce; among top logistics services industries in the world; highly productive workforce; university attendance among highest in world; logistics service industry among world's best.	Rapidly aging population is leading to labor and skills shortages across industries; number of students in higher education has been declining each year owing to the country's aging and shrinking population.

(continued)

Table 3.8 Strengths and Weaknesses Summary: Competence Dimension (*Continued*)

Grade	Strengths	Weaknesses
South Korea: B	Workforce is highly educated and skilled with particular strengths in science and technology; second highest number of science and engineering graduates per capita in the world; moderate productivity; good logistics service quality, although higher levels of operational risk than in other nations in East Asia; strong customs system.	Rigid labor market; labor shortages exist in sectors such as information technology, bioengineering, and telecommunications.
Taiwan: A⁻	One of the most well-trained, educated, and entrepreneurial labor forces in Asia; well-educated workforce supported by an excellent educational system; good productivity; relatively high levels of management education; good logistics service industry.	Labor shortages remain in high-end product industries; number of people in higher education is increasing but at a slow pace.

Main Trends in East Asia

Table 3.9 presents a summary of the assessment scores on the EPIC dimensions for the selected nations of East Asia. This region as a whole, as well as each nation individually, represents an attractive opportunity for supply chain operations. All five nations possess features that make them attractive as a source of raw material or subcomponent supply, a location for manufacturing, a hub for logistics—or all three. This is not a surprising finding given the astonishing increase in trade between East Asia and the global marketplace in the

Table 3.9 Summary Assessment of EPIC Attractiveness for the Nations Represented in East Asia

	Economy	Politics	Infrastructure	Competence	Overall Grade
China	A	C⁺	C⁺	B⁺	B
Hong Kong	B⁺	A	A	A	A
Japan	B	A⁻	B⁺	A⁻	B⁺
South Korea	B⁺	B⁺	A⁻	B	B⁺
Taiwan	B⁺	B⁺	B⁺	A⁻	B⁺

past 20 years. The assessment does, however, highlight some areas of caution for supply chain managers challenged with managing high-performing supply chain operations in the region.

Supply Chain Challenges

Although there are significant opportunities in East Asia, significant challenges remain. The main trends revealed by the assessment are the focus of the following discussion.

Declining Population

Of great concern is the situation created by the aging and shrinking population across East Asia. Each nation in the region faces similar challenges, although the problem is most acute in Japan. With the fourth largest GDP in the world and a long-established middle class, there is no question that Japan will remain an economic power for the foreseeable future. The dire consequences of its shrinking population, however, cloud its long-term prospects. Consumer markets may well continue to shrink as the population contracts, unless immigration can be increased to sustain growth. Without significant economic policy changes, Japan may revert to becoming the location for low-cost manufacturing for the region. This scenario exists, although to a lesser degree, in each of the other nations of East Asia, including China. Supply chain managers must be fully aware of the talent management challenges that will increase in intensity over time in East Asia regional supply chain operations.

Transition in China

The Chinese eastern and southern provinces resemble the other nations of the region with respect to population, economic, and infrastructural development. China's challenge, and opportunity, lies with the central and western regions. The challenge for China will be to develop this vast area in terms of infrastructure and policy quickly enough to access the rich mineral reserves of the area and stem major economic breakdowns. This development will require immense investment of capital, political reform, and cultural change as the area has been largely agrarian for millennia.

A similar challenge lies in transitioning the Chinese economy from one based on export manufacturing to one fueled by internal consumption. As North American and European markets switch to regional manufacturing solutions, domestic consumers must make up the difference if China is to enjoy the GDP growth to which it has become accustomed. Again, this will require economic and policy reforms along multiple levels of government. These challenges are daunting; if China is able to create burgeoning industrial and manufacturing centers in the west and fuel growth in domestic consumption without permanent damage to culture and ecology, economic growth rates similar to those witnessed in the last 10 years might be sustained for many years to come. Supply chain managers must understand the risks and rewards associated with these twin challenges; the attractiveness of western resources will be challenged by poor infrastructure, and the need to support growing domestic consumption will require a heightened understanding of the Chinese market and channel opportunities.

Corruption

Widespread corruption and even piracy can be found across the region, although less so in Hong Kong and Japan. At best, such practices are a deterrent to business investment and development; at worst, such practices as theft of intellectual property and counterfeiting, ranging from high-tech engineering to fashion to pharmaceuticals, can negatively affect innovation and growth and drive out high-value-added industries, leaving much of the region saddled with low-cost, low-value manufacturing. Lack of trust in countries' IP laws is already causing some software, media, and entertainment firms to question the decision to operate in China.[12]

Supply Chain Opportunities

The most challenging task regarding the supply chain opportunities in the East Asia region lies in understanding which nation or nations to prioritize for pursuit.

Economies

From an economic standpoint, all of the East Asia nations have strong economies and, with the notable exception of Japan, will likely continue to grow. China remains by far the largest example, but Hong Kong, Taiwan, and South Korea all boast growth prospects. Wage rates in the region will continue to grow (for a variety of reasons, but primarily due to the increasingly unfavorable labor supply position as demand continues to grow), fostering a coming era of consumerism within the region. Firms interested in capitalizing on these developing consumer markets should consider acting soon. Wage increases across the region over the mid- to long-term, may make the region less attractive for manufacturing goods exports, but the loss of export volume may well be more than covered by increases in consumer purchasing power within the region. The vast raw material resources found in central and western China will also sustain export volumes.

Political Environment

The political environment in Hong Kong, Taiwan, Japan, and South Korea bode well for attracting manufacturing and finished goods distribution operations to serve both their own growing middle class and as a stable base of operations from which to access the huge and growing Chinese middle class. China has made some legal and policy progress in the last 10 years. However, concerns with respect to the Chinese political system may encourage the location of supply chain operations in more stable environments within the region.

Infrastructure

The region's infrastructure in transportation, utilities, and telecommunications all support the continued growth of consumer market size and power, although continued investment will be needed to deal with increasing population density and congestion in major metropolitan areas. Each East Asia nation, including China's eastern and southern provinces, is strong in this area, and continued government investment will only improve the situation. In addition, business competence in the workforce contributes to this attractive situation. Improved infrastructure, logistics capabilities, and a highly skilled workforce will all be increasingly needed to facilitate the high volumes of trade. Although the volume of trade to Europe and the Americas is likely to weaken over time, intraregional trade, as well as trade with South Asia, Southeast Asia, and Oceania, MENA, and sub-Saharan Africa will likely increase. This bodes well for Hong Kong, Taiwan, and South Korea because each boasts logistics service industries that are positioned to serve as intermediaries for such trade.

Key Takeaways for East Asia

The primary takeaway from the assessment of East Asia is that the region has a huge potential for supply chain operations in support of growth in domestic consumer spending. To a large extent, the infrastructure, logistics capability, and workforce already exist to support the new middle-class consumer base, but continued investment and policy change will be needed to generate the improvement and growth necessary to sustain such an economic conversion. The greatest challenge to success emerges from the aging population demographic, which will require innovation and change to avoid dramatic negative consequences. Based on this assessment, the key takeaways for supply chain managers regarding the East Asia region include the following:

1. Substantial increases in capacity for manufacturing and distribution of consumer goods will be needed as Chinese household purchasing power and living standards rebalance China's economy in favor of domestic consumption, with millions of people joining the middle classes each year.
2. Much of the manufacturing and distribution capacity will need to be established in the Chinese central and western regions as limits to space and workforce availability are already being felt in the east and south.
3. Manufacturing and distribution capacity in Japan will increasingly be directed toward Chinese consumers and away from Europe and the Americas as global trade costs move the world toward regional supply and demand.
4. In addition to Chinese sources, raw materials and subcomponents for East Asian manufacturing facilities will increasingly be imported from lower-cost regions such as South and Southeast Asia, Africa, and the Middle East and North Africa.
5. Hong Kong remains an attractive destination for logistics service providers, transportation companies, and exporters owing to its strong regulatory environment, open

trade policies, and simple business environment. This will continue as intraregional trade increases, as well as increases in trade with South Asia, Southeast Asia, MENA, and sub-Saharan Africa.

6. High-tech companies (such as Sony) may well find it profitable to locate research and parts supply facilities in Taiwan, even as bulk production shifts to cheaper markets.

7. South Korea and Taiwan will increasingly export subcomponent products into China as high-end manufacturing exploits the labor resources of the mainland.

8. Firms that are looking to establish supply chain operations in Japan, Taiwan, and South Korea may need to import skilled labor from abroad due to the declining populations in those nations.

9. Chinese operations should consider focusing on training and development of labor as unskilled laborers from western regions will increasingly need to be recruited to staff positions.

10. Firms operating in East Asia, in particular China and South Korea, must establish strong intellectual property protections to ward against piracy and counterfeiting.

References

1. John K. Fairbank, Edwin O. Reischauer, and Albert Craig, *East Asia: Tradition and Transformation* (Boston: Houghton Mifflin).

2. Fairbank, Reischauer, and Craig, *East Asia*.

3. Peter Drysdale, "China's Demographic Bombshell," *East Asia Forum*, September 10, 2012.

4. Catherine Schenk, "Economic History of Hong Kong," In Robert Whaples, ed., *EH.Net Encyclopedia*, March 16, 2008.

5. Kelly Olds, "The Economic History of Taiwan," In Robert Whaples, ed., *EH.Net Encyclopedia,* March 16, 2008.

6. G. Gordon Chang, "Ageing Asia's Demographic Dilemma," *World Affairs Journal*, November 27, 2012.

7. "Chinese Motorways: the Toll Factor," www.economist.com, October 24, 2012.

8. Minxin Pei, "How Can China Address Its Coming Labor Crisis?" http://management .fortune.cnn.com, February 6, 2013.

9. Edward Wong, "Global Crisis Adds to Surge of Labor Disputes in Chinese Courts," *The New York Times,* September 15, 2010.

10. Paul Lim, "Terms of Endearment," www.supplychainasia.org, October 24, 2012.

11. Logistics Industry Profile: Japan (2008).

12. Kevin O'Marah, "Why IP Pirates Are a Serious Threat to Our Supply Chains—and Prosperity," www.scmworld.com, February 8, 2013.

CHAPTER 4

South Asia

South Asia is a teeming, diverse region. The eight countries in South Asia—Afghanistan, Bangladesh, Bhutan, India, Maldives, Nepal, Pakistan, and Sri Lanka—accounted for 23.82 percent of global population in 2012. This chapter focuses on three of these countries, collectively referred to as the Indian subcontinent: India, Pakistan, and Bangladesh. These three countries accounted for 22.29 percent of the global population in 2012.

From a supply chain perspective, the Indian subcontinent demands significant attention if only due to the potential size of its market. The Central Intelligence Agency's (CIA) World Factbook for 2012 ranks India as the tenth largest economy in the world based on GDP at the official exchange rate and the third largest economy in terms of purchasing power parity (PPP). The 2012 GDP estimate for India was $4.76 trillion, or 5.6 percent of world GDP at PPP.

A wealthier India benefits the entire region in a number of ways. It will energize the economies of the other two countries in the subcontinent and provide regional stability. Furthermore, India can encourage organizations from industrialized nations to invest in the region, creating new markets and fostering existing supply chains within the region.

These three countries are in close proximity and share a distinct ethnic identity, but they have not functioned as a coherent geopolitical region since gaining independence from British rule in 1947. Events that unfolded around independence led to decades of mutual hostility and distrust, which significantly hampered economic and industrial growth in the region. These events also led to South Asia becoming one of the most highly trade-protected regions in the world, lagging the rest of the world in opening up to foreign competition and attracting foreign direct investment (FDI).

The economic climate and the prevailing mind-set of the subcontinent at the time of independence were a far cry from that prevailing a few centuries earlier. It is probably a little known fact that in 1700 the GDP for the Indian subcontinent, using an international

Table 4.1 Share of World GDP, International Dollars, 1700 to 1998

Region	1700 (percent)	1870 (percent)	1950 (percent)	1998 (percent)
Western Europe	22.46	33.61	26.27	20.64
U.S./North American Region	0.22	10.18	30.65	25.07
Japan	4.14	2.31	3.02	7.65
China	22.30	17.23	4.50	11.48
India	24.44	12.25	4.16	5.05
World (Total)	100.00	100.00	100.00	100.00

Source: Maddison, Angus, The World Economy—A Millennial Perspective (Paris: Development Center of the Organization for Economic Cooperation & Development, 2001), p. 261, Table B-18.

dollar[a] as the basis for comparison, was the highest in the world at 24.44 percent of the world GDP (Table 4.1).

Table 4.1 also shows that by 1950, three years after the subcontinent gained independence from British rule, India's share of world GDP had shrunk to 4.16 percent, again using an international dollar as the basis.[1] What is the explanation for this dramatic decline? How has that dramatic decline affected economic and political decision making in the region? And what does that portend for the future of foreign direct investment (FDI) and supply chain management in the subcontinent? The first two questions are addressed in the next section. The third question is addressed in subsequent sections.

Economic and Political Background

The Indian subcontinent flourished in the 1600s, combining skill with significantly low labor costs to produce textiles that were in high demand, especially in Europe. The subcontinent was known as the textile workshop for the world. Handwoven fabrics and cotton textiles (*muslin*) from the subcontinent were a household name in England. However, the landscape was dramatically altered by one organization, the British East India Company (the Company), which was established in 1600.

Trade in India was the primary charter for the Company for about 150 years after its establishment, but the Company started to assert territorial control of major portions of the subcontinent in the 1700s. The Company was attracted by the subcontinent's riches, in particular the wealth generated by Bengal's textile industry. At that time, Bengal's weavers were operating under favorable terms and conditions of sale in the face of a strong demand

---

[a] A hypothetical unit of currency used in economics, based on PPP and average international commodity prices.

from Europe.[2] When the Company army defeated the Nawab of Bengal in the Battle of Plassey in 1757, the Company began to enforce its interests in textile trade, and its agents began to dictate what the weavers could charge for their products.

The Indian subcontinent had led the world market in the production and export of textiles until then, but the tax structure enforced by the Company made these textiles less competitive. The first industrial revolution in England and the mechanization of textile manufacturing exacerbated this situation. Cheap, colorful products from the textile mills in Manchester, Lancashire, drove Indian handicrafts out of the European markets.

An Exporting Region Becomes an Importing Region

British-made products were now imported into India freely, and heavy duties were imposed on Indian goods, further discouraging their export. These machine-made products effectively caused rural artisan industries to go out of business. A self-sufficient village economy gradually morphed into a colonial economy, more specifically, an agricultural colony engaged in the production and supply of raw materials such as cotton and jute. Between 1814 and 1835, British cotton cloth imported into the Indian subcontinent rose 51 times, while exports from the subcontinent fell to a quarter of what they were at the start of this period.[3] By the time the First War of Indian Independence resulted in the dissolution of the Company and transferred political power from the Company directly to the British Crown in 1857, the transition of the subcontinent from an exporter to an importer was complete.

Independence and the Partition

The British Crown ruled the Indian subcontinent from 1857 until the subcontinent gained independence from British rule in August 1947. At the time of independence, the predominantly Hindu- and Sikh-occupied areas went to India, and the predominantly Muslim-occupied areas went to Pakistan. Independent Pakistan comprised two geographic regions—West Pakistan and East Pakistan—literally a thousand miles apart.

The partition of the subcontinent was chaotic and disruptive. More than 10 million people were displaced as they relocated to the country in which their religion was predominant. Most studies estimate that a million people died as a result of the partition, and India has since fought at least three wars with Pakistan over the state of Kashmir.

The partition promoted an intense lack of trust between the countries, which largely explains the significant decrease in intraregional trade in the region from 19 percent in 1948 down to a historic low of 2 percent by 1967. The three wars fought between India and Pakistan reinforced mistrust among the neighbors. In 1971, East Pakistan split from Pakistan to become the People's Republic of Bangladesh. Mistrust among the countries in the subcontinent still presents roadblocks to trade within the region.

Politics and Protectionism

The mutual distrust among the countries in the subcontinent certainly played a role in decreasing economic activity in the region. The protectionist leanings of postindependent India's leaders aggravated the situation and probably helped isolate the region from the rest of the world. Postindependence India started with a strong suspicion of the private sector and foreign investment. India's interactions with the Company and the years of colonialism played a large role in creating this stance.

Nehru's book, *The Discovery of India*, part of which was written in 1944 while he was imprisoned by the British, underscores his belief that two centuries of British rule had caused serious damage. Nehru is especially severe on the Company, stating, "The corruption, venality, nepotism, violence and greed of money of these early generations of British rule in India is something which passes comprehension."[4] Whether or not the Company's actions influenced his thoughts, Nehru felt capitalism created inequalities. Impressed by the Soviet Union's economic gains, Nehru steered the Indian government toward a socialist model, which resulted in protectionism and heavy regulations on foreign organizations wishing to conduct trade with India.

Thus, shortly after independence, India turned its focus inward, emphasizing import-substituting strategies even as the developed countries were opening their markets. Pakistan followed a similar inward-looking strategy as well, although the two countries followed diverging paths to industrialization—India focusing on the public sector and Pakistan encouraging private entrepreneurship. When Bangladesh became independent in 1971, it followed an import-substitution policy as well, emulating India's strategy of large-scale nationalization of economic activities. The subcontinent's inward-focused, import-substituting strategy slowed GDP growth in the region and created a bias against export-producing sectors, relegating exports to a secondary status.

Toward a Free Economy

The collapse of the Soviet Union convinced policymakers in the subcontinent that an inward focus does not lead to rapid growth. Indeed, by 1985 India was already facing a balance of payments problem that led to a financial crisis in 1990. In 1991, guided by finance minister Manmohan Singh, India initiated a program of economic liberalization, which ended many public sector monopolies, reduced tariffs and interest rates, and allowed automatic approval of foreign direct investment in many sectors.

Pakistan and Bangladesh had begun the process of liberalization around the same time. When increasing internal and external imbalances caused an economic crisis in Pakistan in 1988, a Structural Adjustment Program was initiated by the International

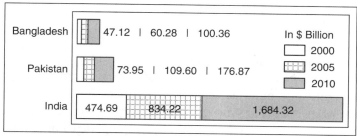

Source: World Bank data.

Figure 4.1 GDP growth in the subcontinent.

Monetary Fund (IMF) and the World Bank. Under this program, in 1990 Pakistan adopted a policy of market liberalization, privatization, and deregulation. A similar program was initiated in Bangladesh in 1987.

By the turn of the 21st century, the subcontinent had made considerable progress toward a free-market economy. Industries and services served as twin engines propelling growth in the subcontinent, attracting FDI from all over the world. The Indian economy surged at a rate comparable to those of many high-performing Southeast Asian and East Asian economies. It is not that the economies of Pakistan and Bangladesh stayed still, but rather that the Indian economy grew much faster.

Figure 4.1 shows that even as India's GDP attained a nearly fourfold growth in a decade, the economies of Pakistan and Bangladesh shrank relative to the Indian economy. Pakistan's economy shrank from less than a fifth of the Indian economy to a little more than a tenth in 2010. Similarly, the size of the Bangladesh economy shrank from about a tenth to about a sixteenth of the Indian economy in the decade. Thus, although India may only possess the potential to play a dominant role in the world economy, the transition to its role as the region's economic behemoth seems absolute.

On the flip side, when a region's economic growth is so closely linked to one country's progress, there are the inevitable negative consequences. For instance, South Asia's economic growth in 2011 was dragged down by a slowing Indian economy. In addition, such relatively rapid growth for India may fuel Pakistan's fear of Indian hegemony, presenting barriers to improving relations between these two countries.

In summary, despite significant progress made in recent years, South Asia is still not a well-integrated region. Intraregional trade is only 5 percent of the total merchandise traded in the region. South Asia is also one of the most highly protected regions in the world and lags behind most of the other parts of the world in opening up to FDI. However, the huge market size of the subcontinent demands a close look at investment opportunities.

The Markets

From a supply chain perspective, the geographical intensity of industrial activity in a given locality presents both opportunities and challenges for organizations considering investment. Having industrial activity concentrated in a specific locality increases that locality's visibility, making it more attractive for investment. Furthermore, it encourages the central and local governments to showcase that locality and promote it through strategies such as easing regulations and restrictions on investment, expanding tax incentives, and designating special investment zones.

The flip side is that concentrated activity in a locality tends to magnify any existing infrastructure issues such as traffic congestion, availability of electric power, water, and buildings and office space, issues that are even more pronounced in developing nations. Moreover, concentrating on specific localities will, by definition, detract from the goal of promoting development across the entire country. Smaller cities or zones, often located far away from their country capital, will be at a disadvantage, as they will not receive adequate resources for developing their region. Lacking direct access to ports, and sometimes badly connected to the country's road and rail networks, these localities are not well known to the global business community, which only serves to further isolate them from future development activities.

Location of Market Activity

Organizations considering FDI are increasingly assessing and comparing the attractiveness of cities, rather than countries, when evaluating locations for new projects. Coincidentally, as is the case with many other countries, industrial activity for the countries in the subcontinent is more pronounced around the urban areas. The *primacy*, which is the percentage of the urban population living in a country's largest metropolitan area, provides an indicator of the concentration of industrial activity. Table 4.2 presents the primacy values for the three countries in the subcontinent as well as for some select countries in Asia. The primacy for the United States is provided as a comparison.

The following discussion on market activity for each country in the subcontinent uses the primacy value as a surrogate for market concentration.

Table 4.2 Primacy Values for Select Countries

Country	Bangladesh	China	India	Indonesia	Japan	Malaysia	Pakistan	Philippines	USA
Primacy	35	3	6	7	43	7	20	19	8

Source: World Bank Urban Concentration Data, WDI and GDF, 2010.

Bangladesh

Bangladesh is situated on the delta of two of the largest rivers in the Indian subcontinent, the Ganges and the Jamuna (Figure 4.2). It is a country slightly greater is size than the state of New York, 56,249 square miles in area. It is divided into six administrative divisions (Dhaka, Chittagong, Khulna, Barisal, Rajshahi, and Sylhet), and four major municipal corporations (Dhaka, Chittagong, Khulna, and Rajshahi).

Bangladesh is a predominantly rural country, but it is urbanizing rapidly at a rate of 6 percent per annum since independence even as its population has only grown at a rate of 2.2 percent per annum during this period. As a result of this urbanization, the four municipal corporations now account for more than 10 percent of the country's population.

Bangladesh has a high primacy value of 35. More than a third of the country's urban population resides in Dhaka. To view this in perspective, consider for instance the textile industry, the mainstay of manufacturing activity in Bangladesh, accounting for more than

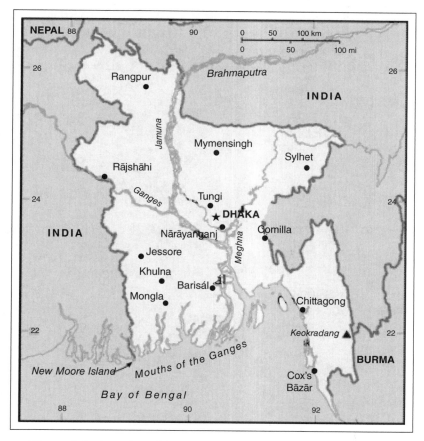

Figure 4.2 Location of the major cities and regions in Bangladesh.

10 percent of the country's GDP. More than 80 percent of the garment industry output is located around Dhaka. Overall, more than 65 percent of the manufacturing activity is concentrated in just four of the country's 64 districts: Dhaka, Gazipur, Narayanganj, and Chittagong.[5] The accompanying infrastructural and supply chain challenges arising from such concentrated activity are discussed in a subsequent section.

India

India is a country of 1.284 million square miles, slightly more than a third of the size of the United States, with 25 states and 7 union territories (Figure 4.3). The most populated states are Uttar Pradesh, Bihar, Maharashtra, West Bengal, and Andhra Pradesh.

As with Bangladesh, textile manufacturing is a major activity in India. The Indian textiles and clothing sector is the second largest employer after agriculture, contributing 4 percent of

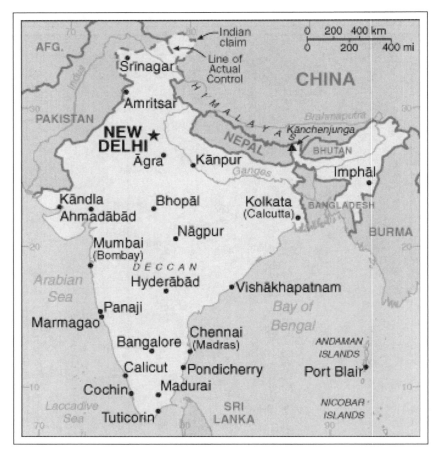

Figure 4.3 Location of the major cities and regions in India.

GDP, 14 percent of industrial production, and 12 percent of total exports for the country.[b] However, as seen from Table 4.2, India's primacy value of 6 suggests that industrial activity is not as intensely concentrated in specific localities as in Bangladesh. The relatively lower concentration of industry in India is also supported by the fact that textile manufacturing is spread across multiple locations, mainly in Madurai, Coimbatore, Chennai, Bengaluru, Nagpur, Ahmedabad, Kanpur, Kolkata, Srinagar, Guwahati, Indore, and Surat (see Figure 4.3). Figure 4.3 does not show the location of Guwahati (close to Imphal in the northeast part of India) or of Indore and Surat (cities near Ahmedabad in the western part of India).

Despite the low primacy, industrial development in India is still in imbalance. FDI activity is rather concentrated, going mainly to the country's southern and western states, where the administrations in power are generally more reform minded. A study by Columbia University concluded that over a third of FDI in India went to just three cities.[6] Six low-income northern and eastern states that are home to more than a third of India's population (Bihar, Chattisgarh, Jharkand, Madhya Pradesh, Orissa, and Uttar Pradesh) have relatively little industrial activity.

Pakistan

Pakistan covers an area of 310,963 square miles, almost twice the size of California. The country has four provinces, two autonomous territories, a federal capital territory, and a group of federally administered tribal areas. The four provinces—Balochistan, Khyber Pakhtunkhwa (Northwest Provinces), Punjab, and Sindh—cover 87 percent of the landmass and contain 94 percent of the population.

The primacy for Pakistan is 20, lower than that of Bangladesh, but still relatively high. The two cities, Karachi (Sindh province) and Lahore (Punjab province), account for more than 10 percent of the country's population of 190 million. The port city of Karachi, with a population of 13.2 million as of 2010, is the 13th largest metropolitan area in the world and is the hub of the financial and industrial activity in Pakistan. In contrast, the province of Balochistan in the southwestern part of Pakistan, which constitutes 44 percent of the landmass, has just a little over 5 percent of the population.

Pakistan has a semi-industrialized economy. Some of its major industries include textiles, chemicals, food processing, and leather goods. The major economic and industrial activity takes place around Karachi and the urban areas of the Punjab province including Lahore. Figure 4.4 shows the locations of these cities.

During the 1960s, Pakistan was viewed as a model of economic development, and some countries emulated its economic planning strategy. Since then Pakistan has faced numerous challenges including skill shortages, uneven distribution of economic growth,

---

[b] Working Group Report on "Boosting India's Manufacturing Exports," Ministry of Commerce and Industry, Department of Commerce, September 2011.

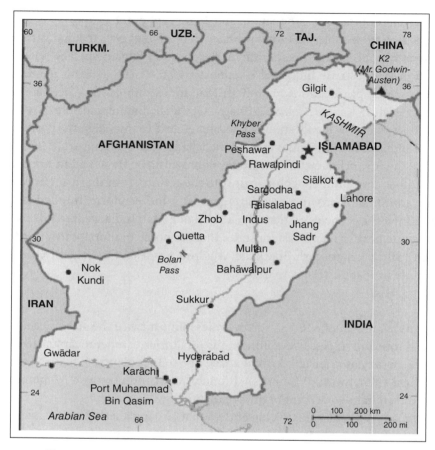

Figure 4.4   Location of the major cities and regions in Pakistan.

hostility toward its private sector model, and above all the threat of terror. The perceived political instability in Pakistan has hampered FDI inflows. Pakistan also faces some of the same infrastructural issues that trouble India.

Logistics Infrastructure

To some extent, Bangladesh and Pakistan may not face such formidable infrastructural challenges as India. These two countries have a relatively higher primacy value, suggesting that their infrastructure problems are more localized. From a supply chain perspective, the major infrastructural demands in Bangladesh are, arguably, restricted to the Dhaka region; similarly for Pakistan, the major infrastructural demands are felt in the Karachi, Lahore, and Peshawar regions, and around the capital city of Islamabad.

Bangladesh is a low-lying plain with fertile and mostly flat farmland. With the exception of the Chittagong Hill Tracts, it rarely exceeds 30 feet above sea level, making it very susceptible to a rise in sea level. The country gets flooded during the monsoon season, hindering progress in building modern transportation and communication networks.

Bangladesh has a network of about 150,000 miles of primary and secondary roads, but less than 10 percent of these roads were paved in 2010. The railway network in Bangladesh had about 1640 miles of track in 2010. Major railway links connect the largest port, Chittagong, with Dhaka and other regions in the northern part of the country, and other links connect major metropolitan centers such as Khulna and Rajshahi. Waterways are an important mode of transportation, especially to some remote areas of the country because no other mode of transportation is available to these locations during monsoon season. There are three major seaports at Chittagong, Dhaka, and Mongla, and several smaller ports.

Pakistan has a total of 162,975 miles of roads, of which about 113,000 miles are paved. Its railway network is 4869 miles long, almost all of which is broad gauge. It has 162,975 miles of road, of which about 112,500 miles are paved, but a large number of the paved roads are not wide enough for two lanes. That said, almost all of Pakistan's freight and passenger traffic travels by road. The major north-south link is from Lahore to Peshawar, and the major east-west link connects Rawalpindi with Peshawar.

The Karakoram Highway, probably the highest paved international road in the world, connects Pakistan with China across the Karakoram mountain range, through the Khunjerab Pass. The Silk Road, an extensive interconnected network of trade routes across Asia, connecting it with the Mediterranean countries, passes across the midsection of Pakistan through Peshawar. Over the years, there has been a marked shift in freight traffic from rail to road, a trend that the government has been trying to reverse. In general, Pakistan's logistics infrastructure suffers from decades of neglect. Roads and railways are insufficient and in poor condition. The administrative infrastructure is unable to enforce its tax policies, resulting in widespread tax evasion, and defense spending absorbs a high percentage of government resources. These problems have limited the public sector's ability to fund infrastructure development.

The three major ports in Pakistan are the Karachi Port, Port Muhammad bin Qasim, and the Gwadar Port in Balochistan. The Gwadar Port, a deep-sea port 300 miles west of Karachi and 45 miles east of Pakistan's border with Iran, is in a very strategic location, situated close to the Strait of Hormuz and its busy oil shipping lanes. This port has developed mainly with help from China, which is interested in turning the port into an energy transport hub by building an oil pipeline from Gwadar into China's Xinjiang region. The planned pipeline will carry crude oil sourced from Arab and African states.

Pakistan's major industrial activity takes place along the Indus River, but the waterway network is still in its infancy with Karachi being the only major water-accessible city, situated next to the Arabian Sea. However, plans are in place for development of waterways along the Indus River and through the Punjab.

Similar to Bangladesh and Pakistan, India's road, rail, and waterways networks are a legacy of British rule, historically developed to transport the output from Britain's industrial revolution to the hinterland and to carry raw materials, troops, and agricultural products. India's economic growth is placing a severe strain on its already strained logistics network. A report by McKinsey & Company[7] states that logistics infrastructure spending tripled in a period of seven years, from around $10 billion in 2003 to around $30 billion in 2010. The report states that despite this increase the country's network of roads, rail, and waterways will not be adequate to meet the demands by freight traffic that is expected to increase threefold in the coming decade, putting India's growth at risk.

As of 2010, India had more than 2 million miles of roads, placing it third in the world for roadway network miles. In 2010 it had nearly 40,000 miles of railroad, putting it in fourth place in the world for railway network miles, and more than 9000 miles of waterways, placing it ninth in the world for waterway miles. India has a long coastline of over 7500 kilometers, forming one of the biggest peninsulas in the world. There are 12 major seaports and 199 minor and intermediate ports, with the most recent port built at Port Blair in the Andaman Islands. All major ports except the Ennore port in the state of TamilNadu are government administered, although private sector participation is on the rise. Two ports handle more than 60 percent of India's container traffic: the Mumbai Port and the Jawaharlal Nehru Port Trust in Navi (new) Mumbai. The ports in Vishakhapatnam, Kochi, and Chennai in South India; the Paradip Port in the state of Orissa in the east; and the Kandla Port in the state of Gujarat in the west carry the greatest tonnage of cargo.

A major component of India's inland logistics network, accounting for about half of the total freight traffic, is a set of seven long-haul corridors, connecting 15 high-growth clusters that form the backbone of India's logistics network.[8] Six of these corridors connect the four cities—New Delhi, Mumbai, Kolkata, and Chennai—the well-known Golden Quadrilateral shown in Figure 4.5. The seventh corridor connects the ports of Kochi, Mumbai, and Kandla on the western peninsula.

The McKinsey report indicates that India's roads account for a higher share of freight traffic compared to other continental-sized countries such as the United States and China, and that India's reliance on roads is more than three times that of China. The report also suggests that a large part of India's freight traffic comprises bulk material moved across long distances, which could be more economically served by rail and waterways. Taking into consideration the geography of the country, the report proposes that resources should be deployed to strengthen a network with five dedicated freight corridors operated by rail and two coastal waterway corridors. The proposed rail freight corridors are New Delhi–Mumbai, New Delhi–Kolkata, Mumbai–Chennai, New Delhi–Chennai, and Mumbai–Kolkata. The two coastal corridors proposed are Kandla–Kochi and Kolkata–Chennai.

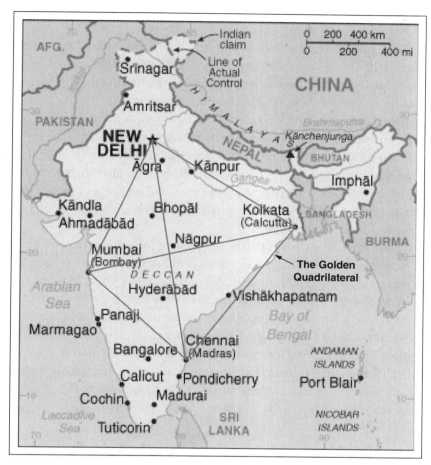

Figure 4.5 The golden quadrilateral.

The subcontinent relies on imports for a substantial portion of its energy use. Even India, whose domestic energy resource base is substantial, relies on imports. As an import-dependent country, India is constructing a strategic petroleum reserve to shield it from supply disruptions. Bangladesh and Pakistan are also working on similar efforts.

India is also improving its natural gas production, the bulk of which comes from the western offshore regions. Despite the increase in natural gas production, demand has out-stripped supply. India's net imports were estimated at 429 billion cubic feet in 2010.[9] To meet the anticipated increase in natural gas, a number of projects have either been imple-mented or considered. One of these is the Iran-Pakistan-India Pipeline, which has been the subject of discussion since 1994. Due to the political, economic, and security-related uncertainties, this project is currently on hold.

Regulatory Framework

The legal and regulatory framework in the subcontinent is influenced by 200 years of British rule as well as by Hindu and Muslim administrations that existed prior to British occupation. Since independence, the legal systems of the three countries have evolved to a structure modeled both on Indo-Mughal and British law.

The governments in the three countries monitor almost every aspect of business and the economy, and any move toward privatization still raises the fear of job reductions and layoffs with some local, state, or provincial governments. However, after the economic liberalization that took place in the early 1990s, the general attitude toward privatization has been much more relaxed. Licensing of industries and earlier governmental restrictions on increasing capacity and growth has been significantly reduced, although permission is still required to close down businesses.

A few sectors in India are now open to 100 percent foreign investment, although some important sectors such as banking, telecommunications, and aviation have a 49 percent cap. A few sectors such as agriculture and coal mining are off limits to foreign investment. Some sectors, such as postal services, are reserved only for the public sector.

The Indian government continues to liberalize cautiously by simplifying its FDI regime and raising some of the remaining caps. Current rules require single-brand retail organizations with more than 51 percent foreign holding to compulsorily source at least 30 percent of the total value of their products from Indian small industries, cottage industries, artisans, and craftsmen. Following protests to such rules by multinational corporations such as Nike, Ikea, and Apple, these local sourcing rules may be eased.

Assessing the Maturity Level of South Asian Supply Chains

This section assesses the supply chain maturity of the subcontinent using the Economic, Politics, Infrastructure, and Competence (EPIC) dimensions. The first dimension, the Economy dimension, assesses the wealth and resources of each region in terms of production and consumption of goods and services.

Economy

The major industries for Bangladesh are textiles, chemicals, steel, paper and pulp, and mining, but textiles is the major industry segment, accounting for 80 percent of Bangladesh's exports in 2011. The major industrial sectors for India are textiles, heavy and light engineering, steel, automotive, biotechnology, drugs and pharmaceuticals, food and food processing, and mines and minerals. The major industrial sectors for Pakistan are textiles and apparel, foods and beverages, tobacco, and petroleum products. The service sector, however, dominates the GDP in all three countries.

Economic Output and Growth Rate

The South Asian market, and in particular the Indian market, is huge. As noted earlier, the CIA World Factbook for 2011 ranks India as the ninth largest economy in the world based on GDP at the official exchange rate and the third largest economy in terms of PPP. The estimated GDP in 2011 for India was $1.68 trillion at the official exchange rate or $4.46 trillion at PPP. The GDP for Bangladesh was $113 billion at the official exchange rate or $285.8 billion at PPP. For Pakistan, the GDP was $210.6 billion at the official exchange rate or $494.8 billion at PPP.

The service sector dominates the GDP in all three countries. The 2011 CIA World Factbook notes that the services sector accounted for 49.7 percent of GDP in Bangladesh, with the industrial and the agricultural sectors accounting for 30.4 percent and 19.9 percent, respectively. In India, the service sector accounted for 55.6 percent of GDP in 2011, with the industry sector accounting for 26.3 percent, and the agricultural sector accounting for the remaining 18.1 percent. In Pakistan, the service sector accounted for 53.3 percent of GDP in 2011, with the industry sector accounting for 25.8 percent, and the agricultural sector accounting for the remaining 20.9 percent.

The Indian subcontinent has a higher growth rate than the global average. The global GDP growth rate estimated by the Economic Intelligence Unit (EIU) for 2012 was 3.2 percent, down from 3.7 percent in 2011. In contrast, the growth rates for Bangladesh, India, and Pakistan are at 6 percent, 6.4, percent, and 3.2 percent, respectively. Thus, despite the global economic downturn, the projected growth rates for India and Bangladesh are well above the average. The corresponding growth rates projected for 2013 are, however, lower. For example, India's projected growth rate for 2013 is less than 5 percent.

Population Size

Without question, the huge South Asian population, which accounts for more than 22 percent of the global population, influences the population size variable for all three countries. As expected, India scores high on this variable, coming in at second place behind China. Pakistan and Bangladesh are also ranked very high on this variable, placing sixth and eighth, respectively. Moreover, the population in this region is growing even though the growth rate is declining. India is expected to overtake China as the most populous country in the world within the next decade.

Foreign Direct Investment

The United Nations Conference on Trade and Development (UNCTAD) FDI Attraction Index ranks India 59th, placing it in the second quartile in the index. Pakistan is ranked

127th, placing it in the third quartile, and Bangladesh is ranked 144th, placing it near the top of the fourth quartile in the index. The FDI Potential Index places India in the first quartile, Pakistan in the second quartile, and Bangladesh in the third quartile ranking them 3rd, 50th, and 89th, respectively.

Issues such as stabilization in Afghanistan and ongoing security concerns in Pakistan present challenges to South Asian countries for building a favorable business environment and an attractive investment climate. Some political issues in India raise concern as well. However, recent developments promise new opportunities. For instance, India and Pakistan are looking for greater cooperation, with Pakistan granting India most-favored-nation status in 2011. In general, India, with strengths in diverse economic sectors such as information technology (IT), financial services, and automobile parts manufacturing, presents attractive investment options.

Exchange Rate Stability and Consumer Price Inflation

Exchange rate stability plays an important role in determining the level of supply chain activity, as noted in Chapter 2. For example, when the Pakistani rupee depreciated by about 28 percent relative to the U.S. dollar in 2008, it almost halted economic growth in the country, affecting all the important areas of the economy from agriculture to industry.

Bangladesh and India have enjoyed more stable exchange rates. The average exchange rate to the U.S. dollar for Bangladesh from 2008 to 2012 was 68.55 Bangladeshi Taka to the dollar, with a standard deviation of 5.74. The corresponding average and standard deviation for the Indian rupee relative to the U.S. dollar was 47.46 and 3.68, respectively. The exchange rate was not as stable for Pakistan during this period. The average and standard deviation for the Pakistan rupee relative to the U.S. dollar was 83.80 and 8.86, respectively.

Inflation has been relatively high over the past five years for all three countries although it is higher for Pakistan. The average inflation rate during the period from 2006 to 2010 was 7.66 percent for Bangladesh, 8.75 percent for India, and 12.67 percent for Pakistan. Correspondingly, interest rates have remained high for all three countries. The Reserve Bank of India is wary of cutting rates for fear of sparking inflation, despite calls for action from industry and government officials to try and revive growth in Asia's third-largest economy. The bank has also expressed concern over the widening current account deficit, saying that it "remains a constraint on monetary easing."

Balance of Trade

At the time of independence, the subcontinent's economy was predominantly agrarian, and it had to import heavy machinery and information technology products, creating a major imbalance in trade during the latter half of the 20th century. Although the subcontinent has reduced its dependency on foreign technology, it still faces a trade imbalance. FDI proposals that encourage exports are, therefore, welcomed. The outsourcing service sector

Table 4.3 Scores for the Economy Dimension

Economy	Economic Output and Growth Rate	Population Size	Foreign Direct Investment	Exchange Rate Stability /CPI	Balance of Trade	Overall Grade
30%	35%	25%	20%	15%	5%	100%
Bangladesh	B⁺	A	C⁻	C⁻	C	B
India	A⁻	A	B⁺	C	C	B⁺
Pakistan	B	A	C⁺	D	C	B⁻

Table 4.4 Strengths and Weaknesses Summary: Economy Dimension

Grade	Strengths	Weaknesses
Bangladesh: B	Growing population; stable exchange rates; leader in textile production; positive attitude to enhancing FDI despite very low FDI attractiveness.	One of the world's poorest nations; low real GDP growth; low FDI attractiveness; persistent inflation; high primacy; narrow tax base; low trade openness; poor balance of trade.
India: B⁺	Absolute volume and global percentage of GDP; high GDP growth; one of the most promising emerging markets; population and workforce growth; high FDI potential; diversification of economic sectors.	Negative balance of trade; negative budget surplus could cause exchange rate instability; high inflation; high tariffs; recurring fiscal deficits.
Pakistan: B⁻	Large market size; foreign investment actively encouraged.	Persistent double-digit inflation; poor balance of trade; unstable exchange rate; high primacy; low FDI attractiveness.

plays a major role in reducing the trade imbalance for the subcontinent, but in general the balance of trade is poor. India's trade deficit, for example, was $18 billion in December 2012, down from a peak of $21 billion in November 2012, but yet in line with a forecast made in May 2012[c] that India's trade deficit will reach $262 billion for the fiscal year 2012–2013, more than 15 percent of its GDP.

Table 4.3 presents the scores for the Economy dimension, and Table 4.4 summarizes the strengths and weaknesses for each country on the Economy dimension.

[c] www.assocham.org/prels/shownews-archive.php?id=3489, Associated Chamber of Commerce and Industry of India.

Politics

The Indian subcontinent does not fare well on the Politics dimension. India gets a low passing grade, and Bangladesh and Pakistan get a near-failing grade. Political stability influences these scores, but other factors do as well, as discussed next.

Ease of Doing Business, Bureaucracy, and Corruption

The 2012 World Bank Doing Business survey is not very positive for the Indian subcontinent. It ranks Bangladesh, India, and Pakistan at 129, 132, and 107, respectively. The most recent trend leading up 2012 is not very encouraging either. In 2009, the rankings for the three countries were either better or the same, coming in at 115, 132, and 85, respectively. For purposes of comparison, Singapore and the United States were consistently ranked number 1 and 4, respectively, during this period (2009–2012).

All three countries in the subcontinent have a high level of bureaucracy although efforts are in place to reduce it. Privatization has played a role in reducing this level, but it is difficult to dismantle decades of entrenched bureaucracy overnight. On the government effectiveness metric, Bangladesh, India, and Pakistan are at the 20th, 55th, and 22nd percentiles, respectively. Bribery and corruption are also present in these countries, and is especially severe in Pakistan and Bangladesh. On the control of corruption metric, Bangladesh, India, and Pakistan are at the 16th, 35th, and 16th percentiles, respectively. For comparison, China is at the 61st and 29th percentiles on these two metrics.

Tariffs in the Indian subcontinent are relatively high, but there is an increased interest in regional economic integration across South Asia since 1995 when the South Asian Preferential Trading Arrangements (SAPTA) came into force. There is a move to increase economic development by gradually removing tariff, nontariff,[d] and "para-tariff" barriers (border charges and fees) between the member countries.

Legal and Regulatory Framework

The World Governance Indicators (WGI) regulatory quality metric ranks Bangladesh, India, and Pakistan at the 22nd, 40th, and 30th percentiles, respectively. On the WGI rule of law metric, Bangladesh, India, and Pakistan are at the 29th, 53rd, and 21st percentiles, respectively. For comparison, China is at the 46th and 40th percentiles on these two metrics.

The Deloitte International Tax Source (DITS) pegged the corporate tax rates for Bangladesh, India, and Pakistan at 27.5 percent, 30 percent, and 35 percent, respectively, in 2012. For comparison purposes, the corporate tax rate for the United States that year was 35 percent, and the corporate tax rate for Singapore was 17 percent. In general, the

---

[d] As noted in Chapter 2, nontariff barriers are trade barriers such as antidumping regulations and duties that restrict imports. Although they are not in the usual form of a tariff, they have the same effect as tariffs once they are enacted.

countries in the Indian subcontinent have a relatively high corporate tax rate, coupled with enormous litigation on transfer pricing. However, the Indian tax system does offer some pricing agreements, providing some assurance of a stable tax regime in selected areas.

Political Stability

Pakistan fares poorly on political and economic stability. Pakistan has found the path to political and economic reform more slippery. Pakistan has taken steps toward economic liberalization since 2001, but the radical fringe has constrained its development. Furthermore, years of military rule have weakened some of its institutions, damaging the long-term political health of Pakistan.

Pakistan's political instability has an effect on its neighbor, India, as well. In addition, China, viewing India as a potential challenger in the strategic landscape of Asia, has tended to use Pakistan to counter Indian power in the region. China's presence in the Bay of Bengal via roads and ports in Burma, as well as in the Arabian Sea via the Gwadar port, has been a cause of concern for India.

The Political Instability Index published by *The Economist* ranks Bangladesh, India, and Pakistan at 19, 135, and 7, respectively, among 165 countries. As noted earlier, the country with a rank of 1 has the highest political instability. Based on this index, India's political stability seems relatively good despite the potentially detrimental influence of its neighbor Pakistan, and the alliance between Pakistan and China.

Intellectual Property Rights

The ranking on intellectual property rights (IPR) provided by the Property Rights Alliance organization is used to evaluate this variable. This ranking places Bangladesh, India, and Pakistan at 125th, 55th, and 112th, respectively, among 130 countries. For comparison, China is ranked 59th.

In general, India's IPR laws are strong, but the country has high piracy rates and importation of pirated material from neighboring countries, such as Pakistan and Malaysia, continues unchecked. Corruption, a lack of both resources and training for law enforcement officials, and an overburdened court system contribute to poor enforcement.

Pakistan has enacted laws on copyright, industrial designs, layout of integrated circuits, trademarks, and patents. However, protection of trademarks has typically been inadequate in Pakistan, with rights of prior use not recognized by the Trademarks Registry. Trademark names of many international products, including Barbie dolls, Shakey's Pizza, Burger King, and Maxim, have been appropriated. Although patents, trademarks, and copyrights are legally recognized, enforcement of IPR laws has improved very slowly. Piracy is common for books, video and audio cassettes, and textile designs.

Table 4.5 presents the scores for the Politics dimension. Table 4.6 presents the strengths and weakness on the Politics dimension and an attractiveness score for each country.

Table 4.5 Scores for the Politics Dimension

Politics	Ease of Doing Business	Legal Framework	Political Stability	Intellectual Property Rights	Overall Grade
20%	30%	30%	25%	15%	100%
Bangladesh	D⁺	D⁺	D⁻	F	D
India	C⁻	C	B⁺	C⁺	C⁺
Pakistan	C⁻	D⁺	F	D⁻	D

Table 4.6 Strengths and Weaknesses Summary: Politics Dimension

Grade	Strengths	Weaknesses
Bangladesh: D	Legal system is based on English law, giving it a strong basis; moves under way to regulate laws to increase FDI; few external threats; proactive stance against extremism; demand for increased energy and water needs from India will promote stronger ties.	Poor political stability; importance of military in political life is high with increased risk of military coups; police force widely seen as dysfunctional; legal system outdated and unevenly implemented; complex and obscure tax laws; many tax breaks; tax evasion; restrictive regulations; pervasive bureaucracy; strict employment and labor law in many industries.
India: C⁺	World's largest democracy; prognosis for reform, privatization, and deregulation is positive; relatively mature tax code; stable legal and regulatory framework; fair judicial process but large backlog of court cases; risk of political instability relatively low; demand for increased energy and water needs will promote stronger ties with neighbors.	Ease of Doing Business index below median; complex tax code but reforms under consideration; tax evasion; complex employment and labor laws; bureaucratic inefficiencies; bribery and corruption present; piracy enforcement relatively low; tariff barriers; historical tensions with Pakistan.
Pakistan: D	Simplified tariff structure; elimination of quotas; higher emphasis on private sector.	Fluctuates between weak civilian and strong military rule; severe security problems due to widespread militancy; poor relations with India and Afghanistan; bureaucratic inefficiencies; poor governance and corruption; ongoing insurgency in Balochistan; high levels of bribery and corruption; strong black market economy; high tariffs; legal system widely mistrusted; intellectual property rights a major concern.

Infrastructure

The growth in the subcontinent has put enormous demands on its infrastructure, be it the physical infrastructure (roads, railways, ports, water, power), the energy infrastructure, the digital infrastructure (networks, telecommunications), or the service infrastructure (logistics). All three countries face the same challenges in this regard in the sense that their infrastructures are being stretched to the limit and asked to perform beyond their capacities and capabilities.

Transportation Infrastructure

The World Economic Forum (WEF) rankings on the selected metrics from the Global Competitiveness Index (GCI) used to evaluate the roads, railroads, ports, and air transportation give Bangladesh, India, and Pakistan low grades. Bangladesh fares the worst with a grade of D⁺; India and Pakistan received a C⁺ grade each. Bangladesh receives a near-failing grade on all aspects of transportation except railroads. India fares well on its railway infrastructure, but the quality of its roads and port infrastructure hurt its performance. Pakistan's performance is raised a little by the quality of its port infrastructure.

Utilities Infrastructure

In 2009, India was the fourth largest consumer of energy, after the United States, China, and Russia. Despite a slowdown in growth worldwide, the energy demand continues to rise in the Indian subcontinent. The countries in the subcontinent often deal with a severe shortage of electricity generation capacity. The World Bank estimates that roughly 40 percent of residences in India are without electricity, and blackouts are a common occurrence throughout the country's main cities.

The situation is not very different in Bangladesh and Pakistan. The power generation system in Bangladesh depends on fossil fuels supplied by both private sector and state-owned plants. Bangladesh has the lowest per capita consumption of commercial energy in South Asia, but there is a significant gap between supply and demand. Furthermore, almost all power generation plants are dated and in need of upgrades.

Like Bangladesh, Pakistan has power supplied by private and public sector undertakings. Electricity shortages in the country have led to clashes and riots. *The Economist* reported in May 2012 that some private power producers curtailed production as the energy generation supply chain had a shortage of funds. The state-run power purchasing company could not pay these private power producers because their biggest consumers, the provincial and federal governments of Pakistan, had not paid their own electricity bills.

Telecommunications Connectivity

As noted in Chapter 2, connectivity can be measured by the number of mobile phones and Internet users in the country, as well as the per capita values for these numbers.

In terms of the absolute numbers of mobile phones and Internet users, the large population of the Indian subcontinent ranks all three countries very high. Based on information from the CIA World Factbook for 2011, India, with a little over 893 million mobile phones, had the second-highest number of mobile phones in the world, next to China, which had a little over 986 million mobile phones. Pakistan and Bangladesh placed 9th and 15th, respectively, on this metric. On a per capita basis, India, Pakistan, and Bangladesh placed 150th, 171st, and 181st, respectively, among 216 countries. Despite these relatively low scores on a per capita basis, the number of mobile phones per person was impressive when the large population sizes are taken into account. India had 0.74 mobile phones per capita, with the corresponding values for Pakistan and Bangladesh coming in at 0.58 and 0.52, respectively. Despite these low values, these numbers are still impressive given the large population sizes. For purposes of comparison, China was placed 151st on this metric with a value of 0.73 mobile phones per capita.

The total number of Internet users and the Internet users on a per capita basis convey a similar picture as far as India and Pakistan are concerned, but Bangladesh fares very poorly on these measures. In 2011, the number of Internet users for India, Pakistan, and Bangladesh were 61.3 million, 20.4 million, and 0.6 million, respectively, placing them 6th, 20th, and 112th among 213 countries. The corresponding per capita numbers for India, Pakistan, and Bangladesh, were 5.09 percent, 10.74 percent, and 0.38 percent, respectively, placing them 171st, 142nd, and 210th among the 213 countries. For purposes of comparison, China was placed 99th with a per capita number of 28.96 percent.

Table 4.7 presents the scores for the Infrastructure dimension, and Table 4.8 summarizes the strengths and weaknesses for each country on the Infrastructure dimension.

Competence

The subcontinent holds promise on the Competence dimension although the numbers may appear mixed at first glance.

Table 4.7   Scores for the Infrastructure Dimension

Infrastructure	Transportation Infrastructure	Energy Infrastructure	Connectivity	Overall Grade
30%	50%	25%	25%	100%
Bangladesh	D	F	D⁻	D⁻
India	C	D	D	C⁻
Pakistan	C⁺	D⁻	D⁺	C⁻

Table 4.8   Strengths and Weaknesses Summary: Infrastructure Dimension

Grade	Strengths	Weaknesses
Bangladesh: D⁻	Low lying basin allowing for water transportation to remote areas; number of steps taken to clamp down on corruption.	Serious energy shortages; significant natural hazards; very weak physical, energy, and telecommunications infrastructure; corruption is endemic.
India: C⁻	Extensive railroad and roadway networks although in need of upgrade; good access to commodities; low primacy; significant progress on airport and seaport infrastructure construction.	Significant need for expanded capacity and investment in road and rail infrastructure; port congestion to be addressed; power outages a major concern; telecommunications infrastructure needs improvement.
Pakistan: C⁻	Some areas are well industrialized; major cities connected by high-standard multilane, all-weather highways; good port access.	Poor infrastructure in many places; energy infrastructure a major concern.

Labor Relations

Absenteeism plagues businesses throughout India, particularly in the summer. The EIU reports that a combination of absenteeism, many holidays, and customary leave entitlements greatly reduces available working days although turnover rates are moderate in manufacturing, generally 1.2 percent a month. The labor laws in the subcontinent, a legacy of the British rule, are overlapping, potentially inconsistent and cumbersome, with more than 45 pieces of relevant legislation. Employers face particular difficulties in terminating employment and closing an industrial establishment.

Cheap labor is a major draw for industrial organizations wishing to invest in developing countries. Typically, these organizations tend to overestimate the availability of skilled labor. The reality is that the workforce in developing countries often has experience in an agricultural setting, and so the issue is whether this workforce can be retrained to work in an industrial setting.

The Indian workforce is easy to train, labor is abundant, and unskilled labor is relatively easy to find. There is a good pool of well-educated and competent staff, including technicians and engineers. However, high economic growth and increasing competition for these resources has caused labor shortages in manufacturing and service industries. Turnover rates are increasing as well, especially in service industries and in urban areas.

Education Levels for Line Staff and Management

The level of education and training for line staff is mixed. On one hand, the subcontinent enjoys a relative advantage in that a large percentage of the urban population is able to at least understand, if not converse fluently in, English. On the other hand, the lack of a skilled workforce is a significant constraint on business growth in many emerging market economies, and the subcontinent is no exception. Many studies reveal that the countries in the subcontinent do not have enough masons, carpenters, and machine operators to construct the roads, railways, and ports needed to improve the infrastructure. At the same time, the subcontinent, and India in particular, is facing a shortage of skilled labor in its back office outsourcing industry as well. The shortage is causing large job turnover as skilled operators are able to switch jobs quite easily, further aggravating the situation.

At the same time, the number of people with managerial and other white-collar skills is increasing as newly established management institutes begin to produce graduates. There are more than 5000 industrial training institutes as well, offering courses in engineering and nonengineering trades, although increased competition among organizations is making it more difficult to retain managers. In India, the demand for managers is particularly strong in financial services, information technology, telecommunications, infrastructure, and retailing.

Logistics Operational Competence

The World Bank Logistics Performance Index (LPI) rankings from 2012 are used to assess logistics operational competence. India is ranked 38th in the 2012 LPI Logistics Competence subindex, and Pakistan is ranked 72. Bangladesh is not ranked in the 2012 LPI although it ranked 96 in the 2007 LPI Logistics Competence subindex.

Despite the problems with infrastructure, the countries in the Indian subcontinent continue to find ways to overcome them. The following case study discusses a method for delivering home-cooked meals to commuters using the metropolitan railway network in the city of Mumbai that dates back to the late 1800s, a method that is still remarkably successful despite the tremendous increase in the city's population.

Logistics Competence and the *Dabbawalas*

In the late 1800s, the city of Bombay (Mumbai) was growing rapidly. Migrants from different communities and states came to Bombay looking for a job in the city. These migrants had different tastes and food preferences, but there were no restaurants or cafeterias in Bombay that catered to the multiple tastes at that time.

In a popular account of this time in history, these migrants, who were employed by the British, did not fancy the Western cuisine served in the British-managed cafeterias and sought alternatives for their lunch needs. These migrants traveled to the city from distant suburbs, and the lunch break did not give them enough time to go home for lunch. Enter the *dabbawalas*.

A dabbawala, literally meaning a person with a box, is a person who provides a lunch service to office workers in the city of Mumbai, India. The origin of the dabbawala lunch service dates back to 1890 when Mahadeo Havaji Bacche, a migrant to Bombay from the city of Poona (now known as Pune) in Maharashtra, India, started this service to cater to the needs of Bombay's migrant workers who wanted to eat home-cooked food for lunch.

The dabbawalas currently serve about 200,000 customers, office managers, workers, and students, charging a fee of just $6 per customer per month. There are 5000 dabbawalas; many of them can hardly read or write, and the average literacy rate is about eighth grade. They follow an intricate delivery system using Mumbai's metropolitan railway and bus transportation networks. Each lunch box carries a code that identifies the home address where the box originated, the train station where the box should be ultimately unloaded, and the building address where the box has to be delivered.

A *collecting* dabbawala, usually traveling on a bicycle, collects the lunch box from the worker's home at around 9:00 a.m. and takes it to a designated sorting place, typically the nearest train station, where he works with other *local* dabbawalas to sort and bundle the lunch boxes into pallets based on the code. The pallets are placed in a designated railcar.

The coding system is used by the local dabbawalas to move the boxes through the metropolitan railway and bus transport networks, often using hand-off points typically located at select train stations. At the train station, the lunch box could be taken out, placed on a different pallet, and possibly transported by a different dabbawala to another train station. The lunch box could thus conceivably change hands three or four times before reaching its final destination. At the train station closest to the destination, the boxes are handed over to a *local* dabbawala, who delivers them to the customers by around 12:30 p.m. The empty boxes are collected and sent back to the respective homes.

This intricate set of activities involving multiple splits and merges is strongly reminiscent of the cross-docking operation practiced by logistics providers today to transport goods across large distances. Unlike modern cross-docking systems that use sophisticated systems to track the progress of shipments in the supply chain, the dabbawalas use a simple coding system with colors and numbers to denote origin and destination points.

What is noteworthy about the dabbawala operation is that it has performed so well over the past 100 years with uninterrupted service even on days of extreme weather during Mumbai's monsoons. The delivery accuracy is also remarkable. In 1998, the *Forbes Global* magazine conducted a quality assurance study on the dabbawalas' operation and gave it a Six Sigma efficiency rating of 99.999999 percent accuracy, an error rate of less than 1 in 16 million deliveries. Remarkably, too, over the years the dabbawalas have transported lunch boxes from origin to destination without the use of any electronic communication device or advanced technology. The dabbawalas have created a win-win scenario. The customer gets a home-cooked meal for a nominal cost, and the dabbawala gets a comfortable salary with fringe benefits such as life and medical insurance.

Table 4.9   Scores for the Competence Dimension

Competence	Labor Relations	Education Levels	Logistics Competence	Customs and Security	Overall Grade
20%	25%	25%	40%	10%	100%
Bangladesh	C⁺	D	C	C	C⁻
India	B⁻	B	B	B	B
Pakistan	C⁺	C⁻	C⁺	B	C⁺

Customs and Security

The World Bank Logistics Performance Index (LPI) for 2012 also assesses the customs procedures and processes for the countries in the subcontinent. The performance of these countries is better than with the infrastructure subindex. India is ranked 52nd among the 155 countries in the customs subindex, with a score of 2.77. In contrast, the top performer in this subindex, Singapore, has a score of 4.10. Pakistan does slightly better with a rank of 46 and a score of 2.85, with a very significant improvement from the 2.05 score it received for this subindex in the previous LPI rankings published in 2007 (the top performer in that ranking was Luxembourg with a score of 4.04, with India coming in at 52 with a score of 2.70). As noted earlier, Bangladesh is not ranked in the 2012 LPI although it ranked 91 in the 2011 LPI customs subindex with a score of 2.33.

It is noted that the LPI rankings on customs is somewhat at odds with the Emerging Markets Logistics Index (EMLI) market connectedness subindex. For example, Bangladesh is placed 91st among 151 countries in the 2011 LPI customs subindex and 88th in the 2011 LPI infrastructure subindex. However, the EMLI market connectedness subindex places Bangladesh at the very bottom of all 41 countries for its "poor infrastructure and customs procedures."

Table 4.9 presents the scores for the Competence dimension, and Table 4.10 summarizes the strengths and weaknesses for each country on the Competence dimension.

Table 4.11 presents a summary of the assessment scores on the EPIC dimensions for the countries in the Indian subcontinent.

Main Trends in South Asia

The Indian subcontinent offers significant opportunities for global organizations wanting to enter newer markets. The vast middle class and the almost untapped retail industry are very attractive markets that continue to propel growth in the region. However, the subcontinent faces numerous supply chain challenges that must be overcome. To keep the discussion focused, the following treatment is restricted to India.

Table 4.10 Strengths and Weaknesses Summary: Competence Dimension

Grade	Strengths	Weaknesses
Bangladesh: C⁻	Cheap and flexible workforce; English-speaking management staff.	Frequent labor strikes and unrest; low literacy levels; absenteeism is a problem.
India: B	World-class information technology industry; working age population growing; good English language skills; productivity is improving but still far below world class; India fares well in management education and training; labor militancy has significantly diminished in recent years.	Difficulty in dismissing employees; complex labor laws; training of unskilled labor has to be improved; unions are strong but not strong enough to be a detriment; absenteeism is a problem.
Pakistan: C⁺	English-speaking management staff.	Low productivity; low literacy levels; absenteeism is a problem.

Table 4.11 Summary Assessment of EPIC Attractiveness for the Countries in the Indian Subcontinent

	Economy	Politics	Infrastructure	Competence	Overall Grade
Bangladesh	B	D	D⁻	C⁻	C⁻
India	B⁺	C⁺	C⁻	B	B⁻
Pakistan	B⁻	D	C⁻	C⁺	C

The Indian economy has had a varied and complex journey through the years. A globally dominant country in the 16th century, it became a minor player in the international arena and remained that way until the turn of the 21st century. The economy is now on an upturn, with some pundits predicting that India will be the largest economy in 30 years.

No doubt India's already large population will continue to grow, and as it grows the market will become bigger. However, from an EPIC perspective, the challenges are formidable. One concern is the high inflation rate, which has hovered around 10 percent for many years, threatening the country's macroeconomic stability. Another concern is external. Based on the EPIC scores presented in Table 4.11, Bangladesh receives a near-failing grade, and Pakistan receives a low grade as well. If the political situation in Pakistan continues to deteriorate, it could well drag the Indian economy down. The next section considers some of the internal challenges India faces.

Supply Chain Challenges

Two challenges faced by Indian supply chains are the poor logistics infrastructure and the presence of complex distribution networks. The logistics infrastructure is discussed first.

Logistics Infrastructure

As noted earlier, the logistics infrastructure is severely strained for all three countries in the subcontinent, and the countries get penalized on this dimension by several studies. For India it must be noted, however, that the situation has been slowly improving since 2006, even though that does not gain it a significant increase in infrastructure ranking as other countries have been improving at a faster rate.

The dominant mode of freight transportation in India is roads. The density of India's highway network, at 0.66 km of roads per square kilometer of land, is similar to that of the United States (0.65) and much greater than the density in China (0.16) or in Brazil (0.20). However, most roads in India are narrow and congested with poor surface quality, and 33 percent of India's villages do not have access to all-weather roads. Furthermore, the transportation and logistics sector in India is largely unorganized. About 90 percent of the trucks in the country belong to owners with less than five trucks. The unorganized truck industry results in unpredictable transportation lead times. Truck breakdowns are frequent, causing even more unpredictability in the supply chain. Goods flowing into and out of the country contend with customs delays, port congestion, and administrative bottlenecks. There is also a skill gap. One study estimates that at least 2 million new truck drivers will be needed in the next 10 years, and these drivers will have to be trained and licensed to operate the trucks.

To alleviate this problem, the McKinsey report proposes shifting a large percentage of the traffic to rail and water transportation. It proposes using five dedicated freight corridors operated by rail and two coastal waterway corridors. The proposed rail freight corridors are New Delhi–Mumbai, New Delhi–Kolkata, Mumbai–Chennai, New Delhi–Chennai, and Mumbai–Kolkata. The two coastal corridors proposed are Kandla–Kochi and Kolkata–Chennai. (Also see Figure 4.5 and the discussion surrounding the Golden Quadrilateral.)

Complex Distribution Networks

The distribution networks are mostly localized, and many large organizations manage their own distribution system. This situation presents a barrier to new entrants that wish to reach out quickly to a large segment of the population. Furthermore, the packaged goods sector uses a very complex distribution system with multiple layers of small retailers who serve as intermediaries between the manufacturer and end-customer. With the number of stock-keeping units (SKUs) increasing at a near exponential rate, it is an increasing challenge for organizations just to ensure availability at the last stage of distribution. A lack of stringent contract enforcement mechanisms between these stages of distribution has also led to counterfeit goods, a common problem with many developing nations.

As the supply chain evolves and more consumer-packaged goods are offered in a market dominated by unorganized retail, there will be challenges in warehousing and logistics. Warehousing managers of small-scale warehouses—*godowns* as they are called in India—will require a whole new set of skills and extensive training in modern warehouse operations including familiarity with the operation of modern equipment, IT systems, and material-handling practices. These have typically been poor-paying jobs due to the unorganized nature of the industry.

Despite these considerable challenges, India does possess a number of remarkable strengths in the more advanced and complex drivers of competitiveness. The country has a vast domestic market that allows for economies of scale and attracts investors. It has a well-developed and sophisticated financial market that can channel financial resources to good use, and it boasts reasonably sophisticated and innovative businesses.

The following sections discuss how leading organizations are developing supply chain solutions to meet these challenges. These solutions are not the standard solution approaches presented in supply chain textbooks but are uniquely home-brewed solutions.

Unique Solutions for Unique Supply Chain Challenges

The Indian retail sector is used to highlight how local organizations are overcoming their supply chain challenges. This sector is singled out because it is the second largest sector, next to agriculture, accounting for 22 percent of the GDP and for 8 percent of total employment. It is thus a bellwether for the Indian industry.

Catering to the Retail Market

A.T. Kearney, a global consultancy firm, has ranked India as the fourth most attractive nation for retail investment among 30 emerging markets. The Business Monitor International India Retail Report[e] has estimated that total retail sales in India will grow from US$411 billion in 2011 to US$804 billion by 2015. A robust economic growth and increased disposable income with the end-customer, combined with an increased emphasis on organized retail infrastructure, are key factors behind the forecast.

Consider how the average end-customer shops in India. A 2008 survey of the Indian retail industry by McKinsey & Company found that 64 percent of Indian shoppers prefer to travel no more than 15 minutes from their residence.[10] The survey also found that traditional retail stores, the "mom and pop" stores, were not going away, so large retail stores will have to find innovative ways to lure customers. For example, these large retail stores have

---

[e] http://www.businessmonitor.com/retail/bmiindia.html.

to work with the Indian shoppers preference for fresh produce over packaged food, a preference reinforced by low refrigerator penetration combined with frequent power outages. The survey also found that the typical Indian shopper is much less loyal to a single retailer; more than 60 percent of the shoppers covered in the survey indicated that they bought at more than one retailer, compared to 10 percent of Brazilian shoppers and 24 percent of Chinese shoppers.

A Focus on Rural India

The organized retail sector accounts for about 4 percent of the total retail business, which presents both opportunities for FDI as well as some of the threats to distribution mentioned earlier. A number of Fast-Moving Consumer Goods (FMCG) organizations such as Asian Paints, ITC, and Marico are focusing on rural India. These organizations expect growth in rural India as brand awareness spreads to rural regions and the government's rural development programs such as the National Rural Employment Guarantee Act continue to improve these regions. FMCGs are expected to gain from structural changes taking place in rural India that include rising income levels and increasing urbanization.

A 2012 study by the Boston Consulting Group identified four customer segments in India:

▲ *Affluent*: families with an annual household income greater than $18,500, accounting for 6 percent of the households in India.
▲ *Aspirers*: families with an annual household income between $7400 and $18,500, accounting for 14 percent of Indian households.
▲ *Next Billion*: families with an annual household income between $3300 and $7400, accounting for 30 percent of Indian households.
▲ *Strugglers*: families earning less than $3300 per year, accounting for nearly 50 percent of Indian households.

The FMCG organizations are convinced all four segments have a presence in rural India. In fact, over the past three years, consumer goods organizations have grown business in rural India at twice the rate of that seen in cities in spite of the fact that rural customers are more price conscious compared to urban customers. They have done so by introducing innovative ways to reach out to all customers. For instance, Marico's goal of "constant innovation" led to a focus on the introduction of a large number of newer brands in its supply chain through a vendor-managed inventory system.

The Bottom of the Pyramid

In his book, *The Fortune at the Bottom of the Pyramid*,[11] published in 2005, management guru C. K. Prahlad lays down the case for focusing attention on the poor people who earn less than $2 a day, a segment he terms the *bottom of the pyramid* (BOP). In today's context, the BOP would probably include more than 4 billion people with a total household income exceeding $5 trillion per annum.[12] Based on the Boston Consulting Group classification, the BOP would correspond to the Strugglers.

Prahlad's book contends that large firms and multinational corporations may have undermined the efforts of the poor to build their livelihoods, but the greatest harm they might have done to the poor is to ignore them altogether. Rather than relegating the BOP market to the realm of corporate social responsibility initiatives, Prahlad argues that they must become part of the organizations' core business, especially because the BOP represents a viable market.

The dominant assumption that the poor do not have money to spend and, therefore, are not a viable market is a traditional mind-set that misses a lot of opportunities. No doubt the buying power for those earning less than $2.50 per day cannot be compared with the purchasing power of individuals in developed nations. However, the BOP, with a total household income exceeding $5 trillion per annum, represents a significant latent purchasing power that must be unlocked. This latent market for goods and services provides a new growth opportunity for the private sector and a forum for innovations.

Traditional solutions cannot create markets at the BOP. Consider for instance, shampoo, a product used regularly in many households. The richer segments of the population can use cash to ensure inventory convenience, buying a large bottle of shampoo to avoid multiple trips to the store, but the poor have unpredictable income streams. Many subsist on daily wages and make purchases only for what they need that day. An innovative solution to include the BOP is the single-use packet of shampoo produced by organizations like Hindustan Unilever, allowing millions of Indians to purchase these products. Other examples of single-use packets include toothpaste, biscuits (cookies), jams, ketchup, coffee, and spices.

Consider cell phone usage. It is estimated that the poor in Bangladesh spend as much as 7 percent of their income on connectivity. Women entrepreneurs run a brisk business with cell phones, renting them out by the minute to other villagers.

Another example of innovation for the BOP is the *Grameen* Bank in Bangladesh, a microfinance organization and community development bank that makes small loans to the poor without requiring collateral. The *Grameen* Bank uses a group-based credit approach. In this model, instead of lending directly to individual borrowers, banks lend to groups of borrowers, who are jointly liable for a single loan. In the model as it was originally conceived, a group of five prospective borrowers is formed, with only two of them receiving a loan initially. The group is observed for a month to see if the members are conforming to the rules of the bank. If the first two borrowers repay the principal plus interest over a period of 50 weeks, other members of the group become eligible for a loan. This model imposes a substantial group pressure to keep individual records clear. Essentially, collective responsibility of the group serves as collateral on the loan. A distinctive feature of this approach is that about 98 percent of the borrowers are women.

Another example of innovative solutions that address the BOP is the *e-choupal* disintermediation scheme introduced by ITC. This scheme benefits farmers in remote rural villages who, otherwise, are compelled to sell their produce through an elaborate scheme involving traders and *mandis* (trading hubs). These market initiatives are described in the following sections.

Trading Hubs and *Mandis*

India's agricultural productivity has improved to the point that it is both self-sufficient and a net exporter of a variety of food grains. It is now the world's second largest grower of fresh produce. However, an estimated 40 percent of its fruits and vegetables are lost due to a hot climate, lack of refrigerated trucking, poor roads, and corruption in its supply chain. One problem with the supply chain is the distribution of the output from a huge number of small farmers, a problem exacerbated by a scarcity-era regulation.

The existing supply chain process for agricultural produce is a linear value chain. Farmers from small, fragmented farms produce crops sold to commission agents in a government-sanctioned *mandi* (a trading hub or market) at prices below market value. The agents resell the crops, either to organizations that process the crops such as Hindustan Unilever Limited (HUL) or to grocers. Next, the crops are processed and distributed to a reseller (generally open air markets). Finally, urban consumers purchase both the processed and unprocessed products. Figure 4.6 depicts the supply chain for agricultural products.

At the time of its establishment, the *mandi* was an innovation because it enabled the farmer to sell to the most competitive buyer. However, the *mandi* allows traders to act in collusion. Farmers have only an approximate idea of price trends and have to accept the price offered them at auctions on the day they bring their grain to the *mandi*. As a result, traders are well positioned to exploit both farmers and buyers, extracting higher trading profits by offering lower prices to farmers.

Farmers in most agrarian communities have no choice but the *mandi* to sell their produce. Without bearing the cost of transportation, most farmers would not be able to gather

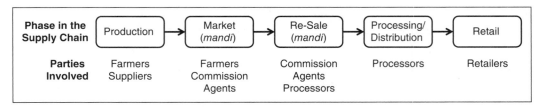

Figure 4.6 The supply chain for agricultural products in India.

price information and sell their produce. The process of transporting the produce to the *mandi* often results in considerable spoilage. Furthermore, after taking the produce to the *mandi*, the economic pressure to sell becomes intense, resulting in a loss of bargaining power for the farmers. In some cases, farmers sell their produce to intermediaries who then turn around and sell the produce in a *mandi*.

Each stage in the supply chain adds to the final price paid by the customer. It has been stated that the price markup for perishables such as vegetables and fruits at the various stages follows a 1:2:3:4 thumb rule. That is, a product sold by the farmer for 1 unit of price at the market is sold at the resale point for 2 price units, sold for 3 price units at the processing point, and eventually sold for 4 price units at the point of retail.

ITC, a large, multibusiness conglomerate, devised an initiative to mitigate some of the problems in the agricultural supply chain process. The name it gave to this initiative is *e-choupal*. *Choupal* is a Hindi word for a traditional village gathering place. So, the *e-choupal* was conceived as a virtual marketplace where farmers could transact directly with a processor and thereby could realize a better price for their produce.

Disintermediation and *E-choupals*

The *e-choupal* program serves to connect producers with users, eliminating the hierarchy of brokers. The program involves the installation of computers with Internet access in rural areas of India to offer farmers up-to-date marketing and agricultural information. Now geographical distances do not restrict participation in the *e-choupal*.

Following the introduction of *e-choupal* services, the bypassing of intermediaries has resulted in less spoilage as the produce is transported more quickly to retail outlets. The improvement in quality of output and a fall in transaction costs have led to a rise in income levels for the farmers.

The *e-choupal* has also enhanced quality for ITC. When ITC entered the branded *atta* (flour) market with the launch of Aashirvad Atta in 2002, its challenge was to offer consistency in quality. ITC decided to source wheat directly from farmers through its *e-choupal* initiative, unlike the competition that sourced wheat from *mandis*. In this case, ITC's supply chain successfully catered to the need to achieve consistent quality in its product offering—without overly focusing on sourcing cost. In 2012 the ITC website reported that there were 6500 *e-choupals* used by 4 million farmers spread across 40,000 villages.

Supply Chain Leadership in South Asia[13]

The leading organizations in India manage their supply chains with a different perspective compared to their competition. The average performing organizations agonize over the problems of catering to unorganized retail markets, poor infrastructure, port congestion, and inadequate warehousing, but the supply chain leaders think differently. For example, to market goods to the large segment of the population that lives in poverty, the consumer packaged goods sector is producing products with smaller pack sizes. To cope with the attendant transportation costs, as well as to reach out to the rural population, HUL uses a unique approach to deliver these goods to the end-customer in a cost-effective manner as described next.

Supply chain leadership in the Indian subcontinent comes in a variety of forms, producing unique supply chain solutions that overcome the region's unique challenges. An underlying theme in all of these solutions is an intimate understanding of the business terrain in the region. Consider how HUL, a leading Indian retailer, has reached out to customers in remote rural areas in a very cost-effective manner.

Accessing Remote Rural Areas: Hindustan Unilever Limited

HUL is India's largest fast-moving consumer goods organization. Founded in 1933 as Levers Brothers (India) Ltd., HUL is a $4 billion organization, with more than 400 brands spanning 14 product categories in home, personal care, and food products. HUL has a wide outreach in India through a network of 7000 redistribution centers covering more than 1 million retail outlets.

HUL has grown its business at a very impressive rate through a combination of excellent marketing, supply chain management and operations, and service. HUL strives to maintain a competitive advantage by continuously reengineering its supply chain. HUL has segmented its market based on the size and location of its retail outlets and provides tailor-made services through dedicated teams to each one of these segments. HUL's market segments are the *modern trade* segment (the organized retail sector), the *general trade* segment (the "mom and pop shops"), and the *rural market* segment.

The rural market segment is specifically targeted as a growth opportunity for HUL. The HUL strategy is to "create consumers out of non-users," which presented a challenge because HUL had to find an innovative way to reach the millions of potential consumers in small remote villages in India, where there was no retail distribution network, no advertising coverage, poor roads, and limited transportation. The solution was Project *Shakti* (a Sanskrit word meaning sacred force or empowerment), launched in the year 2000 in partnership with nongovernmental organizations, banks, and government.

The goal of Project Shakti is to penetrate rural markets by empowering underprivileged rural women to sell soaps, shampoos, and other personal care products. HUL has enlisted more than 45,000 Shakti entrepreneurs to cover more than 135,000 villages across 15 Indian states. These women are appointed as *Vanis,* or communicators, and are trained to communicate in social forums at schools and village meetings. The Vanis act as direct-to-home sales distributors for HUL products. These women access remote village locations, traveling from door to door on bicycles. HUL provides training in selling, commercial knowledge, and bookkeeping to help the women become micro-entrepreneurs.

Project Shakti is a successful low-cost business model that has enhanced HUL's direct rural reach. Currently, the rural market accounts for about 50 percent of HUL's revenues in India. Unilever (HUL's parent organization) is adapting the Shakti project for other rural markets in Sri Lanka, Vietnam, and Bangladesh. Unilever is also considering a similar model tailored to Latin American and African markets.

Addressing Infrastructure Problems: Safexpress, a Logistics Provider

Safexpress was founded in 1997 with the two core values of safety and speed, both of which were amalgamated into its name. It began operations with 9 offices and 12 vehicles, providing supply chain and logistics solutions to a number of large corporate organizations in India. Safexpress pioneered the concept of day-definite deliveries, taking this concept one step further to offer time-definite deliveries within the country.

Safexpress knew, at the outset, that guaranteeing time-definite service in a country with a poor logistics infrastructure would be a mammoth task. An additional problem was the multiplicity of checkpoints at state borders. Before it began operations, Safexpress mapped out all the routes and identified checkpoints and areas where its trucks may be delayed. To ensure low transit times, it operates around the clock, throughout the year.

In 2009, Safexpress introduced a new service, Stock2Shelf, an end-to-end time-definite service to address the supply chain requirements of major retailers across the country. The service uses professionally trained crews that manage stocks along with all the necessary paperwork needed to enter these malls in the face of increased security checks. The service allows retail stores inside malls to function seamlessly, especially during holidays, Sundays, and during sales periods when malls experience heavy traffic. In recognition of this service, Safexpress received the Innovative Retail Concept of the Year award from the Asia Retail Congress in 2010.

Today, Safexpress owns more than 3600 vehicles that cover 567 destinations to deliver more than 80 million packages a year. Its fleet is equipped with global positioning system (GPS) units so that any vehicle can be tracked with a precision of 50 meters. It owns 7 million square feet of warehousing space, and operates with 48 hubs and mega hubs, with over 1000 routes, and with its vehicles covering more than 600,000 kilometers every day. Safexpress's key strength is its understanding of the business terrain in India.

Understanding and Responding to Uncertain Demand: Asian Paints

Asian Paints is India's largest paint company, operating in 17 countries with 24 manufacturing facilities worldwide, serving customers in 65 countries, with an annual revenue of around $1.75 billion. One success factor for Asian Paints is its extensive distribution network in the rural market. Its products are priced low and have been very successful in other developing countries such as Nepal and Fiji.

Asian Paints has thus successfully addressed the BOP segment. It has developed an expertise in dealing with low-income, often illiterate consumers who only buy small quantities of paint that they later dilute to save money, and offers 50-mL and 100-mL packets of paint. Selling paints in these sizes might not always be remunerative, but it has given a tremendous boost to the organization's brand recall.

Asian Paints mines its data systematically to identify micro-patterns with a view toward reducing forecast errors over time. The analysis revealed that certain districts in the state of Maharashtra experienced a spike in demand for the 50- to 100-mL packs of the deep orange shade of paint during a specific period of the year. Further investigation revealed that these districts observe a local festival called *Pola*, and during this festival farmers paint the horns of bullocks with this deep orange shade of paint.

Such detailed analysis of past data enables Asian Paints to arrive at a more accurate demand forecast, allowing for better manufacturing and distribution plans. To ensure optimum raw material selection across its multisite manufacturing operations, Asian Paints uses an integrated IT system to manage demand and to determine which products are produced at its different plants. In February 2012, it won the Best Governed Company award from the Asian Center for Corporate Governance & Sustainability. Asian Paints has achieved this level of success by developing local knowledge and understanding cultural preferences in the country to identify customer demand and to develop production plans to meet the demand.

Using the Right Technology: E-Sourcing at Marico

Marico is one of the leading consumer products and services organizations in India, focusing on beauty and wellness. Founded in 1991, it has continually introduced new brands. Its consumer products business houses well-known brands such as Parachute, Saffola, Hair and Care, and Nihar. Every month, 70 million consumer packs from Marico reach 130 million consumers in 23 million households, through a widespread distribution network covering more than 2.5 million retail outlets in India and abroad.

Parachute is a coconut oil hair product and is Marico's flagship brand. The raw material for this product is *copra*, which is dried coconut albumen. Marico procures copra to the tune of 2 million coconuts a day. The annual procurement cost is about $60 million and accounts for 50 percent of Marico's total procurement costs. The copra is mainly sourced from the southern states of Kerala and Tamil Nadu.

The traditional procurement process took place in an unorganized market and involved long-drawn negotiations conducted over telephone. Marico's buyers had limited coverage of suppliers, and the majority of a buyer's time was spent on unproductive work and involved intermediaries. Marico also faced serious challenges in copra procurement due to the volatility in prices and an unpredictable supply process.

Between 2003 and 2005, Marico launched an e-sourcing initiative that transformed procurement into an automated electronic process. Marico initially faced huge resistance from the sellers with a one-month no-supply strike from the North Kerala suppliers. Copra sellers now send their quote through text messages and receive electronic confirmation within a half hour. Payments are also made electronically.

Marico has adeptly used mobile technology to reach out to a large number of small coconut farmers, bypassing intermediaries in the supply chain. Transactions are managed in a cost-effective way using the technology to quote and confirm orders. E-sourcing has significantly stabilized raw material prices and reduced variability in the supply process.

Capitalizing on the Capabilities of Multinationals: Bharti Airtel and IBM

Bharti Airtel is a leading telecommunications organization in India, operating in 19 countries across Asia and Africa. In 2004, it decided to outsource IT management to IBM. IBM's deep engagement with India firms resulted in a unique, on-demand business contract with Bharti Airtel. Under the terms of the contract, IBM provides all IT services for Bharti Airtel's business. Unlike a traditional client–customer contract, however, IBM is paid a portion of the client's revenue.

The partnership is a win-win and has resulted in higher revenues and profits for both parties. For IBM, this contract represents a high-profile example of its trademarked on-demand business model. For Bharti Airtel, the contract offers continuous access to state-of-the-art IT systems at a predictable cost.

Key Takeaways for South Asia

1. The countries in the Indian subcontinent share common geographic borders and a distinct ethnic identity. Logically it should follow that they work closely together to promote intraregional trade and grow their economies. This has not materialized. A history of conflict in the region led to a decrease in intraregional trade following independence from British rule.

2. A history of colonization and reprehensible practices by the British East India Company caused the subcontinent to morph from a net-exporting region into a net-importing region. It also generated a deep suspicion of the private sector and foreign ownership immediately following independence, especially in India, creating a protectionist mentality. The distrust has not fully dissipated despite a pronounced move toward liberalization put in place in the early 1990s.

3. The move from a rural economy to a more industrial and service-driven economy exacerbated the balance of trade. The move has also resulted in a high degree of urbanization,

especially in Bangladesh and Pakistan. Consequently, it has led to high congestion in these urban areas.

4. Poor infrastructure, excessive bureaucracy, and corruption will constrain FDI growth, but organizations across the world recognize that the huge market size presents a very compelling reason for foreign direct investment. In particular, the GDP for India at PPP places it near the very top in the Emerging Markets Logistics Index maintained by Agility. The huge market in the subcontinent, in general, makes it attractive for FDI, especially if the subcontinent can improve infrastructure and customs procedures.

5. The growth rate for the Indian subcontinent, in particular for India, is one of the highest in the world. Despite a recent slowdown in GDP growth, the EIU forecast for GDP growth in India for 2012 was 6.4 percent, well above the 3.2 percent forecast for world GDP. In general, on the Economy dimension, the subcontinent gets a passing grade.

6. The Indian subcontinent does not fare very well on a number of indices. Consider the Ease of Doing Business Index, which suffers because there are problems with closing a business in India. Overall, the subcontinent does not fare well on the Politics dimension.

7. The subcontinent does not fare very well on the Infrastructure dimension either. Aside from the physical infrastructure, the most pressing problem appears to be bureaucracy and corruption.

8. The Indian subcontinent fares well on the Competence dimension. In particular, despite the relatively rapid economic growth, the availability of skilled labor and competent senior managers remains high, especially in India.

9. The Indian subcontinent demonstrates an ability to create innovative solutions to its unique supply chain challenges. The case studies on the *dabbawalas* and Hindustan Unilever showcase these abilities. The *e-choupal* scheme to overcome some of the barriers in the agricultural supply chain provides another example of innovation. Another example of a cost-effective innovative solution to India's infrastructure problem is the case of Safexpress, a leading logistics provider in India that uses GPS data to manage a time-definite service in a very challenging situation caused by India's poor logistics infrastructure.

10. The bottom of the pyramid population presents huge opportunities for growth. At the same time, the BOP also presents challenges that require innovative solutions from private industries and multinational corporations.

References

1. A. Maddison, *The World Economy—A Millennial Perspective* (Paris: Organization for Economic Cooperation and Development, 2001).
2. N. Robins, *The Corporation That Changed the World: How the East India Company Shaped the Modern Multinational* (London, U.K. and Ann Arbor, MI: Pluto Press, 2006).

3. N. Robins, *Loot: In Search of the East India Company, the World's First Transnational Corporation*, Sage Publications, 2003. http://eau.sagepub.com/content/14/1/79.full.pdf+html.

4. J. Nehru, *The Discovery of India* (Bombay, India: Asia Publishing House, 1961), p. 297.

5. S.A. Mahmood, "The View from Outside Dhaka," *Forum*, a monthly publication of *The Daily Star*, vol. 2, issue 1, January 2007.

6. *Handbook for Promoting Foreign Direct Investment in Medium-Size, Low-Budget Cities in Emerging Markets* (Vale Columbia Center, A Joint Center of Columbia Law School and the Earth Institute at Columbia University, November 2009).

7. "Building India: Transforming the Nation's Logistics Infrastructure," McKinsey & Company Report on Infrastructure Practice, July 2010.

8. Ibid.

9. Energy Information Administration, "Country Analysis Brief on Power Generation in India."

10. "The Great Indian Bazaar: Organized Retailing Comes of Age in India," McKinsey & Company, Nariman Point, Mumbai, 2008.

11. C. K. Prahlad, *The Fortune at the Bottom of the Pyramid: Eradicating Poverty through Profits* (Upper Saddle River, NJ: Pearson Education Inc., 2005).

12. A. L. Hammond, W. J. Kramer, R. S. Katz, J. T. Tran, and C. Walker, "The Next 4 Billion: Market Size and Business Strategy at the Base of the Pyramid," World Resources Institute, International Finance Corporation, 2007.

13. Some of the material in this section is inspired by the cases presented in J. Shah, *Supply Chain Management: Text and Cases* (Upper Saddle River, NJ: Prentice Hall, 2009).

CHAPTER 5

Southeast Asia[a]

Southeast Asia is the region in Asia south of China and east of India. It comprises about 5 million square miles of land and sea, with the landmass covering a third of this area. From a supply chain perspective, this region is the most easily accessible tropical region in the world, conveniently located along the sea passage from the Middle Eastern/Mediterranean region to East Asia.

The countries in Southeast Asia are based in two geographical areas, Mainland and Maritime (or insular or archipelagic) Southeast Asia (Figure 5.1). Mainland Southeast Asia includes Cambodia, Laos, Myanmar, Thailand, Vietnam, West Malaysia (Peninsular Malaysia), and the city-state of Singapore. Maritime Southeast Asia includes Indonesia, the Philippines, Brunei, East Malaysia, and East Timor (Timor-Leste).

Southeast Asia presents a very convenient route for trade. Ever since the dawn of the trading supply chain era, merchant vessels traveling from Africa, Arabia, Persia, and India to the eastern seaboard of China traversed this region. In particular, the Strait of Malacca, the waterway between Malaysia and Sumatra in Indonesia, offered a long inhabited coastline that provided crews of these merchant vessels with accommodations and trading opportunities. To this day, the Strait of Malacca remains one of the most important shipping lanes in the world from an economic and strategic perspective.

Southeast Asia is arguably the most diverse region in the world, with an enormous number of ethnic groups and languages. For example, Myanmar (formerly, Burma) has 135 distinct ethnic groups officially recognized by its government as well as many unrecognized ethnic groups such as Burmese Chinese, Burmese Indians, and Panthay (Chinese Muslims). In view of such diversity, Southeast Asia is often treated as a miscellaneous collection of cultures, but paradoxically this region has been considered by its neighbors to be a region in its own right since ancient times. The Chinese called it Nanyang ("South Seas"). South Asians have referred to this region as Suvarnabhūmi (a Sanskrit word for "Golden Land").

---

[a] Professor S. Viswanathan, Nanyang Technological University, Singapore, coauthored this chapter.

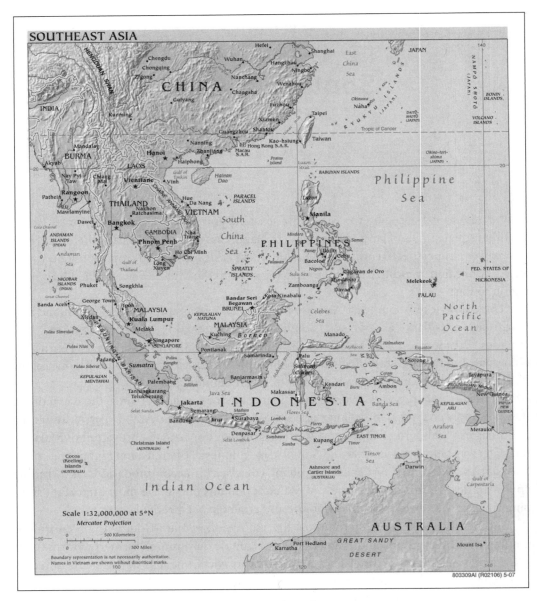

Figure 5.1 Map of Southeast Asia.

Incidentally, the king of Thailand, Bhumibol Adulyadej, gave the international airport in Bangkok that began operation in 2006 the name Suvarnabhūmi.

The diversity in Southeast Asia is reflected through a number of other measures. For example, the population of Indonesia, the most populous country in this region, is about

Table 5.1 GDP (PPP), Population, and Area for Southeast Asian Countries

Country	GDP at PPP	Population	GDP per capita	Total Area (sq km)
Indonesia	$1,212,000,000,000	251,160,124	$4,825.61	1,904,569
Thailand	$645,700,000,000	67,448,120	$9,573.28	513,120
Malaysia	$492,400,000,000	29,628,392	$16,619.19	329,847
Philippines	$423,700,000,000	105,720,644	$4007.73	300,000
Singapore	$325,100,000,000	5,460,302	$59,538.83	697
Vietnam	$320,100,000,000	92,477,857	$3461.37	331,210
Myanmar	$89,230,000,000	55,167,330	$1617.44	676,578
Cambodia	$36,640,000,000	15,205,539	$2409.65	181,035
Brunei	$21,940,000,000	415,717	$52,776.29	5765
Laos	$19,160,000,000	6,695,166	$2861.77	236,800
Timor-Leste	$11,230,000,000	1,172,390	$9,578.72	14,874

600 times that of the smallest country, Brunei, and almost 2.5 times the population of the second most populous country, the Philippines. The largest country is again Indonesia, with a landmass that is 2725 times that of the smallest country, Singapore. Indonesia has roughly 75 percent of the total population and 75 percent of the landmass of the remaining nine countries in the region. In terms of per capita income, the disparity is again extreme. The per capita income for Singapore is 45 times the per capita income of Myanmar. Table 5.1 presents data from the 2012 Central Intelligence Agency's (CIA) World Factbook on GDP, population, and area for the 11 Southeast Asian countries.

The cultural and religious views emanating from India and China have played significant roles in influencing the cultural development in this region. Merchants from India traded in this region as early as the 1st century AD and brought two religions to the region, Hinduism and Buddhism, both of which still considerably influence this entire region's culture. Around the 13th century, another religion, Islam, penetrated Southeast Asia, in particular the countries of Malaysia and Indonesia. Oddly enough, this religion was established by a group of people from the predominantly Hindu country of India. By the end of the 13th century merchants from the Indian state of Gujarat, trading through the Straits of Malacca, established Muslim settlements in northern Sumatra in Indonesia. The establishment of a Muslim sultanate in Malacca in 1445 cemented the presence of Islam along the Strait of Malacca. Christianity came with the Europeans in the 16th century. Currently, Buddhism, Islam, and Christianity are the three dominant religions among the Southeast Asian countries. The island of Bali in Indonesia is the only Hindu outpost in the region, although the practice of this religion has been modified over the years by animism and other influences.

Economic and Political Background

Until the turn of the 16th century, Southeast Asian kingdoms primarily engaged in commerce with China, India, and West Asia. The Indonesian archipelago, the largest group of islands in the world, consisting of approximately 17,500 islands in Indonesia and 7000 islands in the Philippines, has been an important trade region since at least the 7th century. In particular, the sultanates in north Molucca[b] dominated the spice trade and strove to maintain control. The most valuable crop was cloves, and there was intense competition between Muslims and the Chinese for control of the spice trade in Indonesia. Chinese, Arab, and Malay traders purchased cloves and nutmeg from what is now known as Indonesia and carried them in boats to the Persian Gulf or by camel and pack animals on the Silk Road. Clove trade was nonexistent in Europe until around the 11th century when Arab traders who controlled the trade of many spices introduced cloves to Europe.

In 1510, a Bolognese traveler, Ludovico di Varthema, published an account of his journey to this region in which he described the nutmeg trees growing in the Banda region of the Moluccas, the only place in the world where nutmeg grew at that time. The Republic of Venice was a major maritime power as well as a very important center of commerce, especially in the trade of silk, grain, and spices. By trading with Muslim states, Venice began to monopolize the spice trade in Europe between 1200 and 1500 through its dominance over the Mediterranean passage, which generated considerable interest in the region among other European countries.[c] In 1511, Portugal became the first European country to establish a presence in Southeast Asia, and with the conquest of the Sultanate of Malacca it started a flourishing trade with this region.

Portugal's success led to other European countries challenging Portuguese control over the islands. The Dutch wrested control of Malacca from the Portuguese in 1641. The Dutch also evicted another European power that was attempting to gain a foothold in the region; the British East India Company. In the 17th century, the island of Run in the Banda region had economic importance because the nutmeg tree, the source of the spices nutmeg and mace, were exclusive to the Banda Islands. The British East India Company landed on the island of Run in 1603 and fought with the Dutch East India Company for control of the island, eventually departing it in 1620. After the second Anglo-Dutch War of 1665–1667, Great Britain and the Netherlands entered a treaty in which Great Britain took formal possession of the island of Manhattan in North America and the island of Run was formally assigned to the Dutch. The Moluccas were now free of any significant British presence.

---

[b] Not to be confused with Malacca in Malaysia, the Moluccas, formerly known as the Spice Islands, are a group of islands in east Indonesia between Sulawesi and Papua New Guinea.

[c] The financial incentive to end Venice's dominance of the lucrative spice business was arguably the single most important factor precipitating the notorious Age of Exploration in Europe.

By expelling the British from the Moluccas, however, the Dutch unwittingly did them a favor. The British East India Company now concentrated its efforts on India.

The Dutch now had complete control of nutmeg production and trade, a control they exerted with ruthless efficiency. It is stated that during the 17th century clove trees were eradicated on all the Spice Islands except in Amboina and Ternate to limit production and keep prices high. The Dutch ruled the Dutch East Indies (Indonesia) from 1627 to 1942 with the exception of two brief periods of British rule during the turn of the 19th century.

While the Dutch were gaining control over the Indonesian archipelago, other European powers were establishing their presence in Southeast Asia. Spain colonized the Philippines in the 1560s, and Great Britain established a colony in Penang, Malaysia, in 1786. In 1819, Great Britain established trading posts in Singapore. Even the United States established its presence in the region. In June 1898, Philippine revolutionaries tried to declare independence from Spain, but instead this territory was handed over to the United States in December 1898 at the end of the Spanish-American War.

By 1913, the British also occupied Burma (Myanmar) and Brunei, in addition to Malaysia and Singapore. At this time, the French controlled Indochina (Vietnam, Cambodia, and Laos). Only Thailand remained relatively colonization-free, but it was affected by the power politics of the colonial powers and lost some of its territories to the Europeans. In the Anglo-Siamese Treaty of 1909, Thailand gave up the present states of Kedah, Kelantan, Perlis, and Terengganu in Malaysia to the British. Even Japan established a colonial presence in the region during World War II, although its presence was short-lived.

Colonization and Its Effects

As with most cases of colonization, the colonial powers profited tremendously from the region's vast resources and large market. British Malaya was the largest producer of tin and rubber in the world, and the Dutch East Indies was the economic engine for the Dutch. But colonial rule helped develop the region in two ways: by establishing modern institutions to operate the administrative machinery and by creating an infrastructure for its citizens. The colonial powers built ports, railways, and roads, which enabled people from remote villages to have easy access and communication with the urban population. However, the purpose of the network of roads and railways was to link up the various areas of commodity production and distribution, as with infrastructure development in South Asia during the colonial days, so the benefits were mixed. Infrastructure was developed mainly to facilitate production, distribution, and exports of commodities, which led to a pattern of selective development, a problem that still exists today.

A striking feature of colonization is its impact on the social fabric and racial composition of some of the colonized countries. The newly built plantations and mines required skilled and unskilled labor, labor that was readily available from China and the Indian subcontinent. In particular, tin mines were staffed by laborers drawn from China. Tamils from the southern part of India staffed the rubber plantations. Although the Tamils had established a presence in Malaysia much earlier, especially during the reign of the Chola dynasty in South India during the 11th century, the Tamil presence increased greatly under colonial rule.

It is probably coincidental, but the Southeast Asian regions in which newer immigrants, such as the Chinese and Tamils, reside are relatively stable and enjoy a high level of economic development according to Lim Chong Yah, the author of the book, *Southeast Asia: The Long Road Ahead.*[1] In this book, Lim Chong Yah also states, "most of the unstable parts of Southeast Asia today, such as Aceh in Indonesia, Pattani in Thailand and Mindanao in the Philippines have nothing to do with the new immigrants to Southeast Asia."

Colonization also introduced the modern legal system and the rule of law in the region. Among other long-lasting effects of colonization, the diversity of European languages and food stands out as an interesting remnant of the past. For instance, freshly baked French bread is a staple offering of Vietnamese roadside food vendors, an unexpected convergence of the European legacy in an otherwise very Asian country.

Although every country in Southeast Asia with the exception of Thailand was ruled by a colonial power until the end of World War II, these countries gained independence within a very short period of time. Indonesia, occupied at that time by Japan, declared independence in 1945, fending off attempts by the Dutch to regain control of parts of the country. The Philippines gained independence from the United States in 1946, and Myanmar gained independence from the British in 1948. The French were driven out of Indochina (Cambodia, Laos, and Vietnam) by the Viet Minh at the end of the First Indochina War in 1954.

The British gave independence to the Federation of Malaya (peninsular Malaysia) in 1957. In 1963 the Federation was extended to include Sabah, Sarawak, and Singapore and was reconstituted as Malaysia. However, tensions between the Singapore Chinese and the Malays led to Singapore withdrawing from Malaysia in 1965. The states that made up the Federation of Malaya is still referred to these days as Peninsular Malaysia. By now the entire region had gained independence from colonial rule, with the exception of Brunei and East Timor.

Association of Southeast Asian Nations (ASEAN)

On August 8, 1967, the foreign ministers of five countries—Thailand, Indonesia, Malaysia, Singapore, and the Philippines—met in the main hall of the building housing the Department of Foreign Affairs in Bangkok, Thailand, to sign a historic document.

This document created the Association of Southeast Asian Nations (ASEAN). The aim of ASEAN was to enhance cooperation among Southeast Asian communities and to establish a Free Trade Area to encourage greater trade among ASEAN members. Five other Southeast Asian countries—Brunei, Vietnam, Laos, Myanmar, and Cambodia—subsequently joined ASEAN, with Cambodia being the last among the 10 ASEAN countries to join on April 30, 1999.

East Timor applied for membership in ASEAN in March 2011. Indonesia, the country from which East Timor gained independence in 2002, supports East Timor's application, but other countries such as Singapore have not yet agreed to allow membership to East Timor, indicating that it is still not well developed economically.

ASEAN is now an integral part of the Asian economic miracle. In addition to benefiting from the growth of China and India, domestic markets in ASEAN are expanding, and the region is forging stronger links with other developing economies. Growth in the region will drive demand for sector-based supply chain solutions to address the needs of different industries. Overall, the future prospects appear bright for the region, and it is likely to play an increasingly dominant role in the global economy, extending much-needed leadership to drive multilateral and balanced growth.

ASEAN Economic Community

ASEAN is now actively working to create a single market—an ambitious European Union–like economic community that will compete with other economic communities in global and regional influence. The ASEAN Economic Community (AEC) was conceived in 2007 with a goal of regional economic integration with these key characteristics[d]:

- ▲ A single market and production base
- ▲ A highly competitive economic region
- ▲ A region of equitable economic development
- ▲ A region fully integrated into the global economy

The seeds of AEC were sown during the Asian financial crisis of 1997–1998, but it was arguably spurred by a need to counterbalance the Chinese and American presence and influence in the region. The bid to create a single market by 2015 has bogged down as a result of domestic political pressures and alternative trade initiatives vying for attention. Even though the 2015 date appears unlikely to be met, six ASEAN countries (Brunei, Indonesia, Malaysia, the Philippines, Singapore, and Thailand) have already made significant progress by virtually eliminating tariffs on goods they trade with one another.

---

[d] http://www.asean.org/communities/asean-economic-community.

The Markets

As noted at the outset, Southeast Asia is located very strategically from a supply chain perspective. In terms of world trade, it is the most easily accessible tropical region in the world, located along the sea passage from the Middle Eastern/Mediterranean region to East Asia. Furthermore, it is conveniently located relative to two of the world's biggest markets: China and India. The large Southeast Asian population, 629.38 million, combined with the populations of China and India, amounts to nearly 3.2 billion inhabitants, presenting a vast market that exceeds 45 percent of the world population.

This chapter focuses on 7 of the 11 countries in Southeast Asia: Indonesia, Malaysia, Myanmar, the Philippines, Singapore, Thailand, and Vietnam. In 2012, these seven countries accounted for 97.5 percent of the total GDP output (at PPP) for Southeast Asia, and for about 96.3 percent of its total population (see Table 5.1).

Location of Market Activity

Southeast Asia is a predominantly rural economy, with more than 75 percent of the people living in nonurban areas. As noted by the *Britannica Online Encyclopedia*, the population of Southeast Asia is heavily clustered in fertile river valleys, especially in delta areas such as those of the Mekong and Irrawaddy rivers. Agriculture is the primary source of livelihood in every country in Southeast Asia, with the exceptions of Singapore, Brunei, and arguably, Malaysia. However, employment in the agricultural sector is on the decline in Southeast Asia as a whole. Since the 1950s, the economic development strategies of the Southeast Asian countries have emphasized urban industrialization in general, with agricultural development viewed as secondary to industrial growth. As a consequence, many of the cities in the region have high urban populations. In particular, the capital cities of Jakarta, Manila, and Bangkok are among the 20 most populous urban areas in the world.[2]

Indonesia

Indonesia, the largest country in Southeast Asia, is an archipelagic country extending 5120 kilometers from east to west and 1760 kilometers from north to south (Figure 5.2). There are five main islands: Sumatra, Java, Borneo, Sulawesi, and New Guinea. The capital, Jakarta, is located in Java. Two of these five islands are shared with other nations. Borneo is shared with Malaysia, and New Guinea is shared with Papua New Guinea. In addition to these five main islands, there are numerous smaller islands including the Molucca Islands discussed earlier.

Indonesia is well endowed with natural resources, including natural gas, petroleum, tin, nickel, timber, bauxite, and copper. Its major exports are natural gas, mineral oils, electrical equipment, and machinery. Other exports include rubber and rubber articles, clothing,

Figure 5.2 Indonesia.

footwear, wood, and paper. In 2011 it was the world's third largest exporter of liquefied natural gas after Qatar and Malaysia, exporting 21.4 million tons.[3] Interestingly, Indonesia used to be the Organization of the Petroleum Exporting Countries (OPEC) only Asian member, but declining production meant the country became a net oil importer in 2005. It officially withdrew from OPEC in 2008.

Indonesia also has large reserves of precious metals including gold and silver. Since 2009 it has been the largest producer of palm oil in the world followed by Malaysia. An abundance of fish stocks and large coral reefs add to the country's natural resources. Industrial and agricultural activity has led to some problems, however. Air pollution from industrial and vehicular emissions is compounded by smoke/haze from Indonesian forest fires that result from clearing forests for agricultural purposes. Water pollution from raw sewage and deforestation poses an additional threat to the environment.

Malaysia

When it came under British rule in the 18th century, Malaysia was primarily a trading post for the British—a colonial backwater (Figure 5.3). Early in the 20th century the rubber trees in British Malaya triggered a major transformation, and by 1929 British Malaya had the highest per capita GDP of any country or territory in Asia.[4] This region gained prominence as a major supplier to the industrialized countries for primary products such as tin, rubber, palm oil, timber, and oil. Subsequent to the Federation of Malaya gaining independence from the British in 1957, it began to develop a range of export-oriented manufacturing industries such as textiles, electrical and electronic goods, and rubber products. By 1970,

Figure 5.3   Malaysia.

Malaysia had become the world's largest producer of palm oil. It has other natural resources in plenty, including tin, petroleum, timber, copper, iron ore, natural gas, and bauxite.

According to the Energy Information Administration,[e] Malaysia's oil reserves are the third highest in the Asia-Pacific region after China and India. In the 1970s and 1980s, the oil and natural gas industry was the most important source of Malaysian economic growth, enabling the country to become an export-oriented economy. Malaysia's main exports are electrical and electronics products, palm oil, petroleum products, liquefied natural gas, timber, and natural rubber. Malaysia also exports chemicals, machinery, and appliances. In 2011 it was the world's second largest exporter of liquefied natural gas after Qatar.

In line with its rapidly developing economy and status, the labor in Malaysia is increasingly engaged in the service sector. Currently, 13 percent of the labor is devoted to agriculture, 36 percent to industry, and 51 percent to the service sector.

Myanmar

Myanmar is a resource-rich country, but it suffers from pervasive government controls, inefficient economic policies, corruption, and rural poverty (Figure 5.4). It has rich reserves of petroleum, timber, tin, antimony, zinc, copper, tungsten, lead, coal, marble, limestone, precious stones, natural gas, and abundant hydropower.

---

[e] http://www.eia.gov/countries/analysisbriefs/cabs/Malaysia/pdf.pdf.

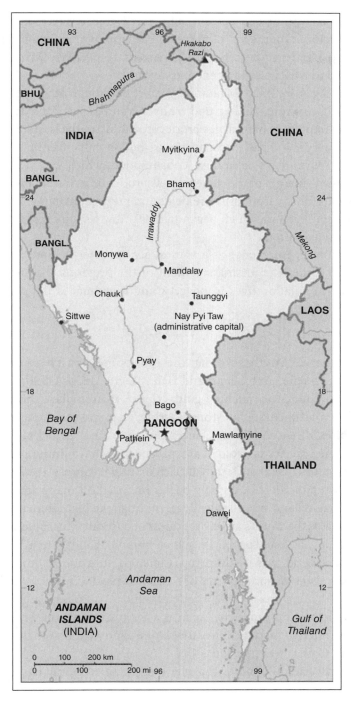

Figure 5.4 Myanmar.

Agriculture accounts for 39.3 percent of the GDP, industry accounts for 18.7 percent, and the service sector accounts for 42 percent. The employment in agriculture, industry, and services are 70 percent, 7 percent, and 23 percent, respectively. Myanmar is thus relatively very low in industrial employment and output.

Oil and natural gas dominate Myanmar's exports, although other exports include vegetables, wood, fish, clothing, rubber, and fruits. Myanmar has considerable natural gas reserves and is an important natural gas producer within Southeast Asia, with production rising substantially over the past decade from 61 billion cubic feet in 1999 to 420 billion cubic feet in 2011. Myanmar's natural gas consumption, which was 118 billion cubic feet in 2011, is increasing, but not at the same pace as production. The country's current natural gas output stems mostly from offshore fields and is expected to rise further due to new projects. Exports to Thailand, which began in 1999, now account for about 75 percent of Myanmar's natural gas output.

Despite Myanmar's emergence as a natural gas exporter, socioeconomic conditions have deteriorated under the mismanagement of the previous regime. Approximately 32 percent of the population lives in poverty, and Myanmar is the poorest country in Southeast Asia.

Philippines

Like most countries in Southeast Asia, the Philippines is rich in natural resources (Figure 5.5). It has fertile, arable land and rich mineral deposits. Some of the metallic minerals found in abundance include gold, copper, iron, nickel, chromite, and silver. Nonmetallic resources include limestone, marble, clay, and other quarry materials.

The Philippine Mines and Geo-Sciences Bureau estimates that about 30 percent of the land area of the country is geologically prospective, but mining permits only cover 1.5 percent of the country's land. Despite its rich natural resources, the Philippine government restricts its exploitation. A logging ban is imposed on many areas of the country, although illegal logging and small-scale illegal mining take place in many areas.

The Philippines is the world's largest producer of coconut, pineapple, and abaca. Abaca is a banana-like plant harvested primarily in the Philippines and is regarded as the strongest natural fiber in the world. It is used for ropes in ships, furniture, clothing, and currency. The Philippines is also a major exporter of electronic products such as processors, chips, and hard drives. Other exports include woodcrafts and furniture, apparel and clothing, and agricultural and petroleum products. Japan is a major destination for exports from the Philippines, accounting for about 28 percent of total exports, followed by the United States at 15 percent, and China at 12 percent.

The CIA World Factbook notes that the Philippine economy has weathered global economic and financial downturns better than its regional peers. This resilience is attributed to its minimal exposure to troubled international securities, low dependence on

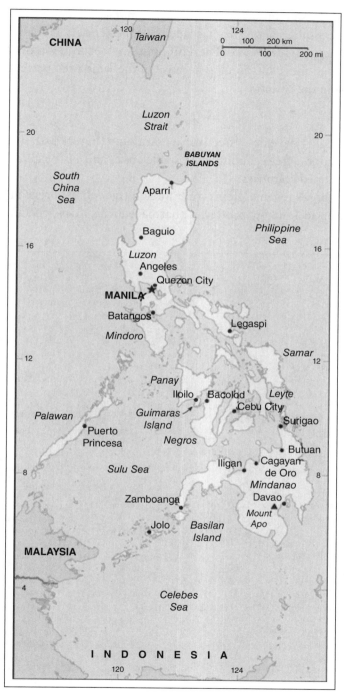

Figure 5.5 The Philippines.

exports, a robust domestic consumption, and large remittances from approximately 5 million Filipino workers. Another factor that has aided this resilience is a rapidly expanding business process outsourcing industry. The Philippines is becoming a major alternative to India for business process outsourcing because of the wide presence and practice of the English language in the country.

Singapore

Singapore has a highly developed free-market economy (Figure 5.6). In general, it enjoys an open and corruption-free economy, with stable prices and a per capita GDP higher than that of most developed countries.

Most of Singapore's revenue stems from foreign trade. It exports consumer electronic goods, information technology products, pharmaceuticals, fuels, chemicals, textiles, and

Figure 5.6 Singapore.

transport equipment. Its major export partners are China, Hong Kong, Malaysia, Indonesia, the United States, and Australia. With its easy access to the sea and a strategic location near the Strait of Malacca, Singapore is one of Asia's main energy and petrochemical hubs and is one of the world's top three oil trading and refining regions. Many global energy companies have regional headquarters in Singapore. Singapore has developed over the last two decades into a global financial center. It is now viewed as a private banking destination rivaling Switzerland. All of the world's leading banks now have a significant presence in Singapore.

Thailand

Thailand has a well-developed infrastructure (Figure 5.7). It is a free-enterprise economy that is generally pro-investment and has a strong export industry. In fact, Thailand's economy is very dependent on exports, with exports accounting for more than two-thirds of its GDP. It is the world's largest exporter of tapiocas and is a major exporter of shrimp and rice. It also exports corn, sugarcane, coconuts, and soybeans in the agricultural sector. Exports in the industry and technology sectors include high-technology products such as integrated circuit boards, electrical appliances, and vehicles. Thailand's main export partners are the European Union, the United States, Japan, and China.

Thailand enjoys a very low unemployment rate. Unemployment stands at less than 1 percent of the labor force, and Thailand also attracts nearly 2.5 million migrant workers from neighboring countries.

One supply chain risk factor for Thailand is the high population and industry concentration in metropolitan Bangkok. With a population of approximately 12 million, metropolitan Bangkok represents approximately 17 percent of the population of Thailand and accounts for the bulk of manufacturing activity in the country. The recent floods in Thailand caused widespread disruptions to supply chains for both the technology and automobile sectors. In response, the Thai government started flood mitigation projects in 2012 worth $11.7 billion and has pledged an additional $75 billion in infrastructure over the next seven years.

Vietnam

Vietnam is a densely populated country that is frequently viewed by the Western world as a viable alternative to China for offshoring activity (Figure 5.8). It is dominated by densely forested highlands. Vietnam's entire eastern border is coastline to the Gulf of Tonkin and the South China Sea. Its large presence in the South China Sea region has led to some disputes over territorial claims with China.

Vietnam has been transitioning from the rigidities of a centrally planned economy to a more capitalist economy since 1986. Progress in this direction has been a little slow. The CIA World Factbook reports that in February 2011, fearing that a high rate of economic growth was stoking inflation, the Vietnamese government shifted policy to stabilize the economy through tighter monetary and fiscal control. Although Vietnam unveiled a broad economic

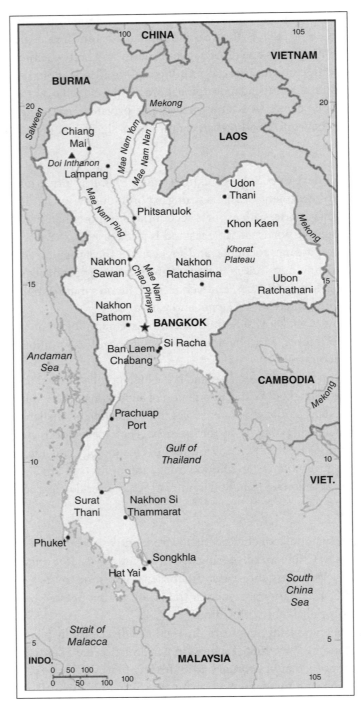

Figure 5.7 Thailand.

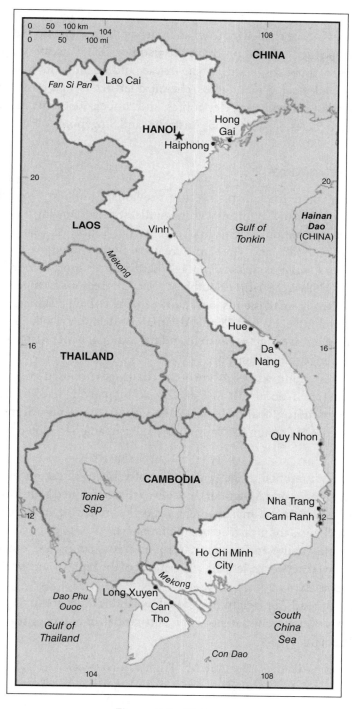

Figure 5.8 Vietnam.

program in early 2012, little perceptible progress had been made by early 2013, and Vietnam's economy continues to face challenges from an undercapitalized banking sector.

Vietnam's major agricultural products are paddy rice, fish, seafood, poultry, coffee, rubber, tea, pepper, soybeans, cashews, sugarcane, and peanuts. Its main industries are food processing, coal, steel, cement, glass, chemical fertilizers, and oils. Its major exports are crude oil, textiles, seafood, rice, electronics, and rubber. Vietnam's major export partners are the United States, Japan, China, Australia, and Singapore.

Logistics Infrastructure

The ports, railway, and road infrastructure previously built by the colonial powers deteriorated quickly in many countries within Southeast Asia following their independence. Consequently, transportation systems in a large part of Southeast Asia—in particular, in Myanmar, Laos, Cambodia, and Vietnam—are not well developed.

The *Britannica Online Encyclopedia* notes that road transport is more prevalent than rail transport, especially in Maritime Southeast Asia. This region's archipelagic nature, with a multitude of relatively small islands, only allows for short-haul distances, making railway transport less competitive. Even in Thailand, a mainland country with a high potential for rail transport, an extensive highway system and the availability of reliable vehicles provide a formidable challenge to rail transport.

The ASEAN community is well aware of the challenges imposed by global trade on the logistics infrastructure in Southeast Asia and the accompanying need to invest in logistics infrastructure to promote global trade. In a 2010 address, the Deputy Secretary General of ASEAN for the ASEAN Economic Community, S. Pushpanathan, noted four basic trends in road transportation[5]:

▲ Rapid rise in automobile usage (a doubling of vehicles in countries like Indonesia, Vietnam, Cambodia, and Myanmar), not always accompanied by infrastructure development or good demand management strategies, resulting in congestion in major cities and challenges to infrastructure maintenance.

▲ Highly variable quality and capacity of roads across countries. Whereas Singapore boasts fully paved networks, less than 10 percent of the highway networks in Cambodia and Laos are paved.

▲ Modal share of roads for freight movement by land is high, about 65 percent.

▲ New railway development has not been substantial in any country in recent years, except in Vietnam.

Pushpanathan indicated "the ASEAN Highway Network (AHN), which runs the length of 38,400 kilometres through all ten ASEAN countries, is a key flagship in ASEAN road transport connectivity." He also added, "A significant 97.4 percent of the desired

AHN length had been built by 2008 but missing links remain and road quality has not been as good."

Although considerable attention is being paid to the ASEAN Highway Network, the ASEAN community has not neglected rail transport. A flagship railroad project is the Singapore-Kunming Rail Link (SKRL) scheduled for completion by 2015, which will connect Singapore to Kunming in Southwest China. The SKRL line is built on existing national networks and will span seven ASEAN countries.

To many people the phrase "global supply chains" conjures the image of ships on the ocean, and indeed maritime transportation is crucial to the region's economic future. Southeast Asia has the largest coastline per unit area in the entire world. Table 5.2 presents the coast to land area ratio for the countries in Southeast Asia. This ratio measures how many meters of coastline correspond to every square kilometer of land area and is computed based on data provided in the CIA World Factbook. The ratio illustrates two aspects—the ease of accessibility to the country's coast from every point in its interior, and probably equally important from a global supply chain perspective, the importance of having a good port system for moving goods into and out of the country.

Table 5.2 shows that the overall coast/area ratio for the region is 2.43 meters of coastline for every square meter of land area. For purposes of comparison, the top 20 countries with the largest coastlines, excluding the Southeast Asian countries, had a combined

Table 5.2 Coastline Data for Southeast Asia

Country	Coastline (meters)	Land Area (sq km)*	Coast/Area Ratio (meters/sq km)
Indonesia	5,471,600	1,811,569	3.02
Philippines	3,628,900	298,170	12.17
Malaysia	467,500	328,657	1.42
Vietnam	344,400	310,070	1.11
Thailand	321,900	510,890	0.63
Myanmar	193,000	653,508	0.30
East Timor	70,600	14,874	4.75
Cambodia	44,300	176,515	0.25
Singapore	19,300	687	28.09
Brunei	16,100	5265	3.06
Laos	0	236,800	0.00
Total SE Asia	10,577,600	4,347,005	2.43

Note: *The Land Area in Table 5.2 is different from the area presented in Table 5.1, which includes Land + Water Area.

coast/area ratio of only 0.70 meters/sq km. In particular, Indonesia's unique geography enables most urban and manufacturing centers to have easy access to ports, and the quality of its ports can go a long way toward lowering transportation costs and improving export competitiveness.

Southeast Asia has close to 3000 domestic and international seaports that carry container traffic. The ships coming in and out of the Southeast Asian ports also carry oil, coal, and natural gas. As noted earlier, the Strait of Malacca is a major shipping channel for the Middle East, South Asia, Southeast Asia, the Far East, and Oceania. Vessels using this channel carry over half of the global annual merchant tonnage. Consequently, Southeast Asia has some of the busiest ports in the world. For example, the Port of Singapore, the second-busiest in the world, handles 130,000 vessels a year.

The S. Rajaratnam School of International Studies in Singapore reports that container ports in Southeast Asia accounted for about 30 percent of the world's transshipment traffic in 2008.[6] In particular, five ports—the Port of Singapore, Port Klang and Tanjung Pelepas in Malaysia, Laem Chabang in Thailand, and Tanjung Priokin Indonesia—are among the top 25 in terms of throughput in millions of *20-foot equivalent units* (TEUs). These five ports had a combined volume of over 58 million TEUs in 2011 with the Port of Singapore accounting for a total of 29.94 million TEUs.[7]

Vietnam is investing billions of dollars building ports for the world's largest container ships in a drive to draw export industries from China. Its port in Ho Chi Minh City carried 4530 million TEUs in 2011. The Port of Manila is the largest port in the Philippines and carried 3260 TEUs in 2011.

Many businesses are pursuing opportunities in Myanmar in hopes of securing access to previously closed markets and resources. Even though the coast/area ratio for Myanmar is only 0.30 meters per square kilometer, Myanmar is the second largest country in Southeast Asia, with a coastline of 467,500 meters. Furthermore, it is primed for massive port development. The country already has three large port development projects.

Sittwe Port on the northern coast, financed and constructed by India, is a key component of the Kaladan Multi-modal Transit Transport Project. It provides an alternative route to India's seven landlocked northeastern states. Absent this project, the only access to these seven states is through a narrow strip of Indian territory wedged between Nepal and Bangladesh. The Kaladan project connects the Sittwe Port in Myanmar with Indian ports on its eastern seaboard, and then through river and road to the state of Mizoram.

The second project, the Kyaukphyu Port, just 100 kilometers south of the Sittwe Port, is a key part of China's strategy in Myanmar and the region in general. As with the Chinese-controlled and administered Port of Gwadar in Pakistan, China views the Kyaukphyu Port as essential for land-based access to the Indian Ocean as well as providing an alternative route for its fuel shipments from the Middle East. The third project, the Daiwei deep-sea port and special economic zone project in southern Myanmar, is funded by the Thai and

Burmese governments and is scheduled for completion in 2020. The Italian-Thai Development Public Company Limited is the general contractor for the Daiwei Port.

Assessing the Maturity Level of Southeast Asian Supply Chains

This section assesses the supply chain maturity of the selected countries in Southeast Asia using the EPIC (Economy, Politics, Infrastructure, and Competence) dimensions.

Economy

The Southeast Asian countries account for almost 9 percent of the world population, and a little over 4 percent of the world GDP measured in purchasing power parity. The region's share of the world GDP is relatively low, but the GDP growth rate for the region is high. While advanced economies in the West struggle to recover from the effects of the recession, Southeast Asia is charging forward, led by the Asian Tiger,[f] Singapore, and the "tiger cub" economies of its five fastest growing countries: Indonesia, Malaysia, the Philippines, Thailand, and Vietnam. In particular, Indonesia, Malaysia, and the Philippines have had high growth in recent years.

Southeast Asia is relatively more agrarian compared to the rest of the world, but the five tiger cub economies have a higher percentage of GDP from industry compared to the corresponding average for the rest of the world. For example, in 2012 the average share of world GDP attributed to industry was 30.2 percent (CIA World Factbook), whereas the industry share of GDP for the Philippines (the country with the lowest percentage among the five tiger cub economies) was 31.1 percent.

Contrary to popular belief, the Singapore economy is not just based on trade and tourism. Manufacturing and other industrial activity accounts for about 27 percent of the country's GDP, a relatively high figure for an advanced economy. To place Singapore's high industry GDP percentage in perspective, it should be noted that manufacturing and industry in the United States account for about 19 percent of GDP and 24.6 percent of GDP for "industrial" Germany. It can be argued that the high share of GDP attributed to manufacturing and industry in Singapore is because Singapore has practically no agricultural activity. The CIA World Factbook reports that agriculture accounted for 0 percent of GDP, and for 0.10 percent of the workforce employment in Singapore in 2012.

Economic Output and Growth Rate

By virtue of its large population, Indonesia ranks at the top in terms of GDP although it only ranks in the middle of the ASEAN region in terms of per capita GDP. From a

---

[f] The term "Asian Tiger" refers to the highly developed economies of Hong Kong, S. Korea, Singapore, and Taiwan.

business perspective, the main story behind Indonesia has been the dramatic macroeconomic reforms of late that have led the mini-boom in its economy, registering a growth rate of 6 percent for 2012. Its large domestic market holds promise for foreign direct investment (FDI).

Malaysia's growth rate was estimated at a healthy 4.5 percent in 2012. However, there are concerns about the sustainability of growth. The economy seems to be mainly supported by the implementation of an Economic Transformation Plan, causing government-led investment programs to become a key driver of investment in the economy. This trend must be altered if Malaysia is to capture its pace of past growth and achieve its stated goal of becoming a high-income nation by 2020. It is important for Malaysia to move farther up the value-added production chain by attracting investments in high-technology industries, biotechnology, and services.

The administration is making serious efforts to boost domestic demand and to reduce dependence on exports. This task, however, has proved to be more difficult than expected. Export of electronics, oil and gas, and palm oil still form the mainstay of economic growth, with the oil and gas sector generating more than 40 percent of government revenue.

The Philippines and Singapore also score high on this variable, although Thailand is dragged down slightly on its grade because the GDP growth rate from 2005 to 2011 is somewhat low, averaging a little less than 3 percent. Thailand's relatively low score on GDP growth rate could be partly attributed to the supply chain disruptions caused by the floods in 2011, the Red Shirt protests in 2010 and early 2011, and the political uncertainties prior to those events. Vietnam receives an average grade on this variable due to a relatively low GDP and average GDP growth rate.

Myanmar is the most agrarian-based economy among the countries selected in this chapter, with 38.8 percent of its GDP coming from agriculture. About 70 percent of its labor is employed in this sector. The economy in Myanmar grew by a very impressive 6.2 percent in 2012. Although Myanmar scores high on this variable, primarily because of its high GDP growth rate from 2005 to 2011, the economy suffers from serious macroeconomic imbalances, multiple official exchange rates that overvalue the Burmese kyat, and fiscal deficits. The economy also faces a lack of commercial credit, a problem that is further distorted by a nonmarket interest rate regime, unpredictable inflation, unreliable economic data, and an inability to reconcile national accounts.

Population Size

With the exception of Singapore, almost all countries in Southeast Asia score high on this variable. As noted earlier, Indonesia is the most populated country in the ASEAN region by a wide margin. The CIA World Factbook estimates Indonesia's population at 251.16 million as of 2013. It also has the highest Muslim population in the world, but it is not an Islamic state and the constitution provides for religious freedom. The Philippines, the next most populous country in the region, is on track to double its current population of 105 million if population growth continues at its current pace.

Foreign Direct Investment

FDI has increased in Indonesia over the last few years, and this trend is expected to continue, at least in the near term. The Indonesian policy agenda remains focused on improving the investment and business environment. Consequently, it was named the most active Asian reformer in 2008–2009 by the World Bank. More important, even during the recession of 2009, Indonesia managed to grow at a very respectable rate of 4.5 percent, further boosting its credibility.

The United States is Malaysia's fourth largest trading partner. U.S. exports to Malaysia include machinery, aircraft, agricultural products, optic and medical instruments, and iron and steel. U.S. imports from Malaysia include machinery, agricultural products, and optic and medical instruments. The United States remains the largest foreign investor in Malaysia. U.S. FDI in Malaysia is led by the manufacturing, banking, and oil and gas sectors. Malaysian FDI in the United States is led by the real estate and wholesale trade sectors.

The Philippines lags behind some of its ASEAN neighbors in overall investment per capita levels.[8] However, strong economic growth and new anticorruption measures, combined with a recent credit rating upgrade from Fitch Ratings, have improved the Philippines' international reputation. FDI in the Philippines reached $2 billion in 2012. However, that is a relatively low number. In comparison, the Oxford Business Group reports that Vietnam and Thailand brought in $8.4 billion and $8.1 billion in FDI, respectively. The Oxford Business Group also reports that according to United Nations Conference on Trade and Development (UNCTAD), the Philippines attracted only $32.3 billion worth of FDI between 1970 and 2009, compared to a total of $285.8 billion for Singapore and $104.1 billion for Thailand.

Myanmar's poor investment climate hampers the inflow of foreign investment. In recent years, foreign investors have shied away from nearly every sector except natural gas, power generation, timber, and mining. In 2011 the Myanmar government took initial steps toward reforming and opening up the economy by lowering export taxes, easing restrictions on its financial sector, and reaching out to international organizations for assistance. Although the Myanmar government has good economic relations with its neighbors, significant improvements in economic governance, the business climate, and the political situation are needed to promote serious foreign investment.

Exchange Rate Stability and Consumer Price Inflation

Stability in exchange rates has been a major policy goal for a number of ASEAN countries in the aftermath of the 1997–1998 currency crises that, in particular, affected Thailand, Indonesia, Malaysia, and the Philippines. The Philippines appears to have a relatively stable exchange rate these days, at least, relative to the dollar, and receives a high grade. Singapore, an otherwise stellar economy, receives a relatively low grade on exchange rate stability due to its increasing strength against the U.S. dollar. During the financial crisis in 2008 and during other short-term market upheavals, the Singapore dollar was generally seen as a flight-to-quality currency. The cost of living in Singapore is the highest in the ASEAN countries, comparable to or higher than the cost of living in many developed economies.

Myanmar and Vietnam score poorly on the exchange rate stability/consumer price inflation (CPI) variable. Vietnam gets a near failing grade primarily due to its very high inflation, pegged at around 18 percent in 2012–2013. Myanmar gets a failing grade on its exchange rate stability.

Balance of Trade

The Southeast Asian countries were predominantly agrarian at the time of independence and depended on imports to drive their economies. The manufacturing and service sectors have played a major role in reducing the trade imbalance for the region. Singapore and Malaysia have led the transition, although Malaysia is still dependent on imports for heavy machinery and information technology products.

Thailand is an export-oriented nation. The Economist Intelligence Unit reports that Thai exports are expected to generate 80 percent of GDP by 2030[9] despite a blip caused by a drop in global demand. The score for Thailand, however, is affected by the fact that it is highly susceptible to external economic shocks, which could result in lower demand for its products. Myanmar has had modest trade surpluses for most of the past few years, but it trades mostly with neighboring countries due to its political climate and poor infrastructure, and that affects its score on balance of trade.

Table 5.3 presents the scores for the Economy dimension, and Table 5.4 summarizes the strengths and weaknesses for each country on the Economy dimension.

Table 5.3 Scores for the Economy Dimension

Economy	Economic Output and Growth Rate	Population Size	Foreign Direct Investment	Exchange Rate Stability/CPI	Balance of Trade	Overall Grade
30%	35%	25%	20%	15%	5%	100%
Indonesia	A⁻	A	B⁺	B⁻	B	A⁻
Malaysia	B⁺	B⁺	B⁺	B	C	B⁺
Myanmar	A⁻	A⁻	D⁺	C⁻	C	B⁻
Philippines	B⁺	A	C	A⁻	B	B⁺
Singapore	B⁺	C⁺	A	B⁻	B	B
Thailand	B	A⁻	B⁺	A⁻	C	B⁺
Vietnam	B⁺	A	A⁻	D	B	B⁺

Table 5.4 Strengths and Weaknesses Summary: Economy Dimension

Grade	Strengths	Weaknesses
Indonesia: A⁻	One of the largest economies in the world; more open and stable economy since the Asian crisis; rich in both natural and mineral resources.	As a archipelagic nation, with inadequate transport infrastructure; growth patterns are uneven, but close access to the Singapore port, alleviates this to some extent; corruption and bureaucracy can hinder economic growth.
Malaysia: B⁺	Third strongest economy in Southeast Asia after Singapore and Brunei; diversified economy with strong resource base, as well as strength in manufacturing, logistics, and services; stable currency since the Asian crisis; high savings rate.	Crony capitalism seen as drag to the economy; attracted less FDI than Thailand and Vietnam in the recent past; some of the government-led infrastructure development programs such as the multimedia corridor have not found success.
Myanmar: B⁻	Less isolated than before; resource rich and low labor cost economy; with recent political changes, strong prospects for increased economic growth; more open for FDI and economic reforms.	Weak macroeconomic management; insufficient domestic capital and market infrastructure.
Philippines: B⁺	Good growth rates; large English-speaking workforce; stable exchange rate and inflation level.	Low domestic savings; high levels of corruption; ineffective bureaucracy; less FDI compared to other ASEAN countries.
Singapore: B	Strong reserves that permit large investments in R&D; institutionalized approach to develop new industry clusters through Economic Development Board and other government institutions; strongly positioned as a regional headquarters city for Asian supply chain operations; stable exchange rates; global financial center; politically very stable.	High cost of labor and land; a city-state with no hinterland; dependent on imports for all resources including food; relatively increasing difficulty in employing foreign workers.
Thailand: B⁺	Open economy; strong international trade; large land area and population size; large domestic economy; high FDI.	High primacy; supply chain risk perceived to be higher after recent floods; higher taxation rates than neighboring countries; low R&D investment.
Vietnam: B⁺	Growing open economy with increasing GDP and FDI growth; lower labor costs; seen as an alternative to China as a manufacturing destination.	Exchange stability; low transparency; low efficiency of state-owned enterprises.

Politics

With the exception of Singapore and Malaysia, Southeast Asia scores relatively poorly on the Politics dimension. Myanmar gets a failing grade, the Philippines and Indonesia get barely passing grades, and Thailand and Vietnam each get a low passing grade.

Ease of Doing Business

All countries in the region have a high level of bureaucracy, but in some cases it does not hinder the attractiveness of the country for business. For instance, Singapore has a high level of bureaucratic control but otherwise provides the opportunity to conduct business with ease in terms of obtaining construction permits, getting electricity, getting credit, and so on.

In general, efforts are under way to reduce bureaucracy in every ASEAN country, albeit with mixed success. Corruption is a huge problem in most of the ASEAN countries due to a lack of resources, lack of training for law enforcement officials, and an overburdened court system. In particular, corruption, red tape, and contradictory legislation are among the most troublesome issues facing investors in Indonesia, placing the country at a disadvantage compared with regional competitors such as China, India, or Malaysia.

The business climate in Myanmar is widely perceived as opaque, corrupt, and highly inefficient. Wealth from the country's ample natural resources is concentrated in the hands of an elite group of military leaders and business associates. In 2010–2011, the transfer of state assets, especially real estate, to military families under the guise of a privatization policy further widened the gap between the economic elite and the public. Singapore, however, stands out as a model country that does not tolerate corruption.

With respect to tariff barriers, six ASEAN countries—Brunei, Indonesia, Malaysia, the Philippines, Singapore, and Thailand—have made significant progress by virtually eliminating tariffs on goods they trade with one another. Although formal tariffs have been significantly reduced, other barriers to trade exist. For example, Malaysia is reluctant to lower barriers in automobile trade in the face of fierce competition from its neighbor Thailand, a powerhouse in automobile manufacturing. Another form of protectionism is by placing restrictions on foreign investment as is the case with the Philippines. In an effort to boost its mining industry, Indonesia has capped foreign ownership of mines and has introduced a 20 percent export tax on metal ores.

Overall, all ASEAN countries have tended toward a socialistic mode of operation in the recent past, typically viewing privatization with some reservation. At present, the governments in most countries in the region are expected to be directly involved in all major economic and market decisions. In fact, leading companies in the region have significant ties to the government and enjoy a protectionist status, which has a negative impact on competition in the region. This perspective is being replaced by one in which a market-driven economy is looked at much more positively.

Legal and Regulatory Framework

The legal and regulatory framework of most countries in the region is influenced by hundreds of years of European rule, although it is also influenced by Indian and Chinese regulatory practices that were widely adopted before the colonial powers began to control the region. Since independence, the legal systems of all countries have evolved, albeit at different paces. Myanmar, for instance, follows a mixed legal system of English common law and customary law. Malaysia has enacted codes that borrow from English common law as well as Islamic law. The constitution of Malaysia provides for a unique dual justice system—secular laws (criminal and civil) and sharia laws. With the exception of Myanmar and Malaysia, the Southeast Asian countries tend to follow civil law as opposed to common law, although Thailand's legal framework is influenced by common law.

Indonesia's weak legal system and outdated regulatory environment is a burden on the new economy that is trying to establish itself after more than three decades of authoritarian rule. Fair and free elections have generated goodwill and faith in the system, but a lot more needs to be done quickly to maintain the momentum and lift a poverty stricken citizenry out of the economic morass and bring sustainable stability to the region.

With respect to the regulatory environment, the picture is mixed. Singapore is highly regulated in almost all aspects, but the regulatory environment is generally very favorable. Malaysia has very stringent rules and regulations, especially with respect to corporate governance, although enforcement is of very poor quality.[10] The legal framework in the rest of the Southeast Asian countries ranges from fair to poor. Indonesia, the Philippines, and Vietnam get barely passing grades, and Myanmar gets a failing grade. Private banks in Myanmar operate under tight domestic and international restrictions, limiting the private sector's access to credit. Myanmar's effort to boost its oil and natural gas production has been significantly impeded by an opaque regulatory policy and a lack of technical capacity. In the past, the United States, the European Union, and Canada had imposed financial and economic sanctions on Myanmar. These sanctions affected the country's garment industry, isolated a struggling banking sector, and raised the costs of doing business, particularly with firms tied to Burmese regime leaders. However, many U.S. and European Union sanctions were eased or suspended in 2012 in response to political and economic reforms.

Political Stability

As noted earlier, political stability refers to the relative absence of threat posed to governments by social protest. The Political Instability Index published by the Economist Intelligence Unit (EIU) rates most of the countries in Southeast Asia very poorly. The exceptions are Singapore and, surprisingly, Vietnam, with Vietnam being rated less

Table 5.5 Scores for the Politics Dimension

Politics	Ease of Doing Business	Legal Framework	Political Stability	Intellectual Property Rights	Overall Grade
20%	30%	30%	25%	15%	100%
Indonesia	C⁻	C⁻	D⁺	C⁻	C⁻
Malaysia	A⁻	B	C⁻	B	B
Myanmar	D	F	D	D	D⁻
Philippines	D⁺	C⁻	D⁺	C⁻	D⁺
Singapore	A	A	B⁺	A	A
Thailand	B⁺	C⁺	D	C	C⁺
Vietnam	C	C⁻	B⁺	C⁻	C⁺

politically unstable compared to Singapore. The Philippines, Thailand, and Indonesia get low ratings on the index because of extremist groups present in the region. In particular, the Red Shirt protests appear to have affected Thailand's rating.

Intellectual Property Rights

The countries in the region recognize the need for improved intellectual property rights. The ASEAN Project on Intellectual Property Rights (ECAP III), based on a financing agreement between the European Union and ASEAN signed in October 2009, began operation in January 2010. The project grew out of the recognition that strong intellectual property rights protection is crucial to fostering trade and investment flows. Although Singapore scores high on enforcement of intellectual property rights, most of the other Southeast Asian countries fare poorly on this metric. The subject of intellectual property rights continues to be a vexing issue, one that Southeast Asian countries find difficult to tackle effectively. These countries have been on watch lists in the past for infringement of intellectual property rights in the form of theft, piracy, and counterfeiting. The extent of violation is captured by a report prepared by the Directorate General for National Export Development in Indonesia,[g] which states that "appreciation towards intellectual property rights (in Indonesia) is still modest; therefore sometimes some people consider Intellectual Property Rights are not necessary."

Table 5.5 presents the scores for the Politics dimension, and Table 5.6 summarizes the strengths and weaknesses for each country on the Politics dimension.

---

[g] http://djpen.kemendag.go.id/contents/43-intellectual-property-rights.

Table 5.6 Strengths and Weaknesses Summary: Politics Dimension

Grade	Strengths	Weaknesses
Indonesia: C⁻	More politically stable and democratic since the Asian crisis.	Widespread corruption; high levels of poverty and bureaucracy.
Malaysia: B	Same ruling coalition since independence; relatively stable politically; relatively stronger regulatory environment and rule of law.	*Bumiputera* policy favoring indigenous Malays is hindering growth and race relations; election results are getting more polarized; ruling coalition has seen its mandate decrease in the past two elections.
Myanmar: D⁻	More reforms in the political process with recent elections, though the military is still in power.	Sanctions by Western nations due to its military regime, though some of the sanctions have been removed now; high corruption and low IP protection.
Philippines: D⁺	United States, Australia, and Japan are seen as strong allies.	High levels of corruption; ineffective bureaucracy; presence of extremist group and protests.
Singapore: A	Politically very stable; highly ranked for ease of doing business; strongest in ASEAN in terms of lack of corruption, IP protection, and legal and regulatory framework.	Recent election results have not been as strong for the ruling People's Action Party, though Singapore is still arguably the least populist of all governments; growing sentiment against foreign talent.
Thailand: C⁺	Relative ease of doing business as evidenced by the high FDI, the presence of Japanese multinationals in the automotive sector, and other multinational companies; the monarchy provides some political stability in spite of recent political events.	Low political stability since military coup in 2006 and the subsequent protests by the Red Shirts.
Vietnam: C⁺	A single Communist rule gives it political stability.	As a recently opened economy, legacies of a centrally planned Communist government still remain in terms of bureaucracy, legal and regulatory framework, and ease of doing business.

Infrastructure

While advanced economies in the West struggle to recover from the effects of the recession, Southeast Asia is charging forward with impressive GDP growth rates in most of the countries in the region. Infrastructure, no doubt, will play a huge role in determining the sustainability of such growth rates in the future. In that regard, Singapore is certainly well positioned and receives very high ratings. A December 2012 survey by Mercer ranked Singapore as the number one country in the world for infrastructure.[h] The ranking was based on a number of variables that included electricity supply, water availability, telephone and mail services, public transportation, traffic congestion, and the range of international flights from local airports.

Malaysia has a very good transportation and energy infrastructure, and Thailand receives good scores on its transportation, energy, and connectivity variables. The rest of the Southeast Asian countries, however, lag behind by a considerable extent.

Transportation Infrastructure

Singapore and Malaysia receive high scores for their transportation infrastructure. Thailand receives a B grade, but the Thai government is striving to foster Thailand's export-oriented economy by focusing on infrastructure development. Visitors to Thailand are typically surprised by the quality of its roads, especially in cities and developed tourist destinations. All major cities and regions are connected by a highway network consisting of two- and four-lane roads. The government is also focused on modernizing the rail network, improving water management systems, and expanding the Suvarnabhumi airport in Bangkok.

Indonesia receives a relatively poor grade for its transportation infrastructure. Although it has outpaced India's growth in the recent past, it shares some of the same infrastructural problems plaguing India. Major bottlenecks on the highways, ports, and airports are adding significantly to the cost of doing business in Southeast Asia's largest economy. Electronics giant Foxconn Technology Group, which is considering tapping into Indonesia's inexpensive labor pool to make iPads and other gadgets, is delaying the decision in view of Indonesia's poor infrastructure.

The Philippines faces some fundamental structural weaknesses in its infrastructure development and receives a D$^+$ grade. Decades of neglect and corruption have led to the Philippines lagging far behind Singapore, Malaysia, Thailand, and even Indonesia in infrastructure development. Only 23 percent of its roads are paved in its highway network. The country has nearly 8000 bridges, 35 percent of which are classified as being in poor or bad condition.

Vietnam's infrastructure is weak, partly as a result of years of war, although it has steadily improved since the war ended. Vietnam's rapid economic growth is, however, threatening to undo the improvement. The growth in Vietnam's economy has resulted in serious transportation bottlenecks and is demanding much more attention from the government for infrastructure investment.

Myanmar has had modest trade surpluses for most of the past few years, but it trades mostly with neighboring countries due to its political climate and poor infrastructure.

---

[h] http://www.mercer.com/qualityoflivingpr.

Manufacturing, tourism, and services in Myanmar struggle in the face of poor infrastructure and undeveloped human resources. Even though Myanmar has about the same landmass as its neighbor Thailand, its road network coverage is less than a tenth of its neighbor's.

Utilities Infrastructure

Global Infrastructure Monitor Private Limited[i] is a Singapore-based company dedicated to providing information, analysis, and insight on infrastructure sectors through magazines, research reports, websites, and conferences. It maintains a Southeast Asia Infrastructure website. An article published on its website in April 2013[j] stated that Southeast Asia's energy sector provides impressive statistics on the utilities infrastructure in this region, indicating that the region has more than 135 GW of power generation capacity. Furthermore, its onshore and offshore fields produce more than 200 billion cubic meters (bcm) of natural gas per annum and 5 million barrels of oil per day. The region is also a major exporter of coal and natural gas, and was, until recently, a net exporter of oil.

The critical role of an efficient, reliable, and resilient electricity infrastructure for stimulating growth has prompted ASEAN to undertake an ambitious project to build the ASEAN Power Grid (APG) as part of the master plan on ASEAN Connectivity. The APG is a 600 megawatt joint electricity network connecting Peninsular Malaysia and Sumatra, Indonesia, under the Indonesia-Malaysia-Thailand Growth Triangle arrangement. The Melaka-Pekanbaru interconnection was identified in October 2010 as one of the prioritized projects for APG. This project will connect Melaka (Malacca) in Peninsular Malaysia with Pekanbaru in Central Sumatra, Indonesia, through submarine cable that will cross the Straits of Malacca and Rupat.[11] Another priority project adopted in October 2010 was the West Kalimantan-Sarawak project, which will connect the electricity grids in the Malaysian and Indonesian parts of Borneo.

Myanmar relies on hydropower for its electricity, but the electricity sector has failed to meet the needs. Only 22 percent of the population had access to electricity in 2011. Traditional biomass accounts for two-thirds of the energy generated and consumed in Myanmar. There are efforts to invest in more hydroelectric, gas, and coal-fired electric capacity, and to improve grid reliability and demand management. The country suffers from electricity outages.

Telecommunications and Connectivity Infrastructure

Internet penetration and mobile phone usage is rapidly increasing in Southeast Asia, opening up new realms of communication and information sharing. The ASEAN Broadband Corridor is an effort by ASEAN to promote broadband penetration, affordability,

---

[i] http://southeastasiainfra.com/.
[j] http://southeastasiainfra.com/2013/04/.

Table 5.7   Scores for the Infrastructure Dimension

Infrastructure	Transportation Infrastructure	Energy Infrastructure	Connectivity	Overall Grade
30%	50%	25%	25%	100%
Indonesia	C⁻	C⁻	C⁻	C⁻
Malaysia	A⁻	B⁺	B	B⁺
Myanmar	D	D	F	D⁻
Philippines	D⁺	D⁺	C⁻	D⁺
Singapore	A	A	A⁻	A
Thailand	B	B	B⁻	B
Vietnam	D	D	B⁻	D⁺

and access across the countries in this region. The intent is to allow organizations to conduct e-business and e-commerce with ease. In general, Southeast Asia fares well on the connectivity variable.

Indonesia, the Philippines, and Myanmar are the laggards on the connectivity metric, earning scores of C⁻, C⁻, and F, respectively. An Open Technology Fund report[k] states that all Internet connections in Myanmar run through a single fiber optic cable, connections which have not been updated since 2008. Myanmar's domestic telephone system is barely capable of providing basic service, and the cellular phone system is grossly underdeveloped.

Table 5.7 presents the scores for the Infrastructure dimension, and Table 5.8 summarizes the strengths and weaknesses for each country on the Infrastructure dimension.

Competence

Southeast Asia's export-driven growth has been fueled to a large extent by multinationals seeking opportunities in countries with skilled, low-cost labor. In particular, rising production costs in China has resulted in shifting manufacturing and production momentum to Southeast Asia. In 2010, Vietnam overtook China to become the largest production venue for Nike, and Coach announced plans to shift half of its production activities from China to neighboring countries.[12] The Southeast Asian countries have adopted numerous initiatives to cope with the increased demand for high-skilled labor.

Labor Relations

As with many emerging market countries, labor relations in a number of Southeast Asian countries are characterized by a close relationship between the trade unions and

---

[k] https://www.opentechfund.org/files/reports/otf_myanmar_access_openness_public.pdf.

Table 5.8 Strengths and Weaknesses Summary: Infrastructure Dimension

Grade	Strengths	Weaknesses
Indonesia: C⁻	Proximity to Singapore Port and airport for port-based factories in Sumatra and other islands (Batam and Bintan) that are close to Singapore; infrastructure connectivity to Malaysia through the proposed ASEAN power grid and the natural gas pipeline to Singapore.	Weak land transport infrastructure; poor safety record for chartered flights and other intra-island domestic flights.
Malaysia: B⁺	Strong road transport infrastructure since the completion of the 772-km north-south highway in the 1990s; good port infrastructure that gives strong competition to Singapore.	Rail infrastructure has remained relatively stagnant since independence.
Myanmar: D⁻	Reliance on hydropower and biomass implies that it's CO_2 emissions due to energy generation are low.	Poor rail and road infrastructure and broadband connectivity; low grid reliability and frequent power outages.
Philippines: D⁺	Subic Bay was once a hub airport for logistics service providers in Asia; growing telecom and IT infrastructure.	Declining competitiveness in land transport, water, and energy infrastructure.
Singapore: A	World's second largest container port (largest until recently); top class transport, port, and airport infrastructure; stable and reliable electricity and water supply and telecom infrastructure.	High speed fiber-optic broadband connectivity is not as fast and strong as other East Asian nations such as Korea and Japan.
Thailand: B	New Bangkok airport is a strong competitor to Singapore as a hub airport; good quality of roads in cities, industrial hubs near Bangkok, and developed tourist destinations.	Road network not as strong as Singapore and Malaysia; high levels of traffic congestion in Bangkok.
Vietnam: D⁺	Growing FDI should pave way for improved infrastructure in the future.	Weak transport and energy infrastructure is not able to keep pace with rapid economic growth.

political parties. Even as the wealth in Southeast Asia grows, it increasingly has to deal with demands from trade unions for higher wages. Wages in Southeast Asia are among the lowest in the world. Although economists do not believe that rising wages will spoil the region's competitiveness or growth, manufacturers are warning that higher labor costs could trigger an exodus of investment.

The manufacturers' drive to contain costs by restricting wages has led to considerable unrest in some parts of Southeast Asia. Indonesia's 118 million workers participated in strikes in November and December 2012, protesting low wages and benefits. In response, the governor of Jakarta approved a 44 percent increase in the minimum monthly wage, much to the chagrin of the employers. Indonesian employers are typically reluctant to increase wages mainly because Indonesia is one of the most expensive places in the world to terminate employees. Dismissed employees are eligible for a severance pay equal to one month's salary for every year worked plus one month's salary, maxing out at nine months' salary if an employee has worked for eight years or more.[l] In addition, there is a service period recognition payment of up to 10 months' salary if the employee has worked for 24 years or more. Every time the minimum wage jumps, so does the severance payment. It is estimated that a 10 percent increase in Indonesia's minimum wage causes formal employment to drop by 1 percent.[13]

In general, however, the data provided by the World Economic Forum (WEF) Global Competitiveness Index (GCI) shows that labor relations are good in the region. Myanmar is not rated by the WEF, but among the other six countries considered in this chapter, the country with the lowest grade for labor relations, the Philippines, had a respectable C$^+$ grade. Singapore tops the list with an A grade, and Malaysia receives a grade of A$^-$.

Education Levels for Line Staff and Management

A weak link in the supply chains that underpin growth in Southeast Asia is a lack of trained and capable human capital. This problem is by no means unique to the region. However, Southeast Asia is starting from a lower base in that it lacks the education and research centers of excellence that are a feature of developed economies. A study by the Economist Intelligence Unit on the availability of skilled labor in Indonesia, the Philippines, Thailand, and Vietnam[14] finds that these countries often lack important skills such as English or other foreign language proficiency. The study found that employers were skeptical of the labor force's general problem-solving and behavioral skills and perceived shortfalls in computer and information technology proficiency.

Singapore once again tops the list on the education level variable, earning an A, and Malaysia receives an A$^-$. Vietnam receives a barely passing grade, scoring very poorly on three of the four metrics used to evaluate this variable: quality of management schools, extent of staff training, and reliance on professional management. As with the labor relations variable, Myanmar is not rated on the education level variable.

Logistics Competence

Despite the problems with infrastructure in some Southeast Asian countries, most of them display good logistics competence. The scores obtained from the LPI rankings grade all countries well with the exception of Myanmar, which receives a D grade. The next lowest

---

[l] http://www.mondaq.com/x/160956/Redundancy+Layoff/Termination+of+Employment+in+Indonesia.

Table 5.9 Scores for the Competence Dimension

Competence	Labor Relations	Education Levels	Logistics Competence	Customs and Security	Overall Grade
20%	25%	25%	40%	10%	100%
Indonesia	B⁻	B⁻	B⁻	C⁺	B⁻
Malaysia	A⁻	A⁻	B⁺	B⁺	A⁻
Myanmar	D	D	D	D	D
Philippines	C⁺	B	B	C⁺	B⁻
Singapore	A	A	A	A	A
Thailand	B⁺	C⁺	B⁺	B	B
Vietnam	B	D⁺	B⁻	B⁻	C⁺

grade goes to Vietnam, which gets a B⁻. Singapore was ranked best in the world for logistics performance in the LPI rankings for 2012. For the 2007 and 2010 LPI rankings, Singapore was ranked first and second, respectively.

Customs and Security

Four of the seven countries are rated well on customs and security. The rise in militancy in Indonesia and in the Philippines is partially instrumental in their receiving a relatively low score of C⁺ for this variable. Vietnam receives a B⁻ because its customs are considered slow, unresponsive, inconsistent, and vulnerable to corruption. Myanmar once again receives a D.

Table 5.9 presents the scores for the Competence dimension, and Table 5.10 summarizes the strengths and weaknesses for each country on the Competence dimension.

Logistics Competence and the Port of Singapore (PSA)

Apart from the high quality of labor relations and world-class universities, one of the reasons for Singapore's success in the Logistics Performance Index rankings is its superior port infrastructure.

The Port of Singapore (managed by the corporate entity PSA[m]) has been at the forefront in the use of technology to manage efficient operations. Singapore is the world's largest container transshipment port. Of the 31.65 million 20-foot equivalent units (TEUs) handled by PSA Singapore in 2012,[15] 85 percent were transshipped to another port.[16] As a major port of call, PSA is linked to 600 other ports in 123 countries over

---

[m] PSA Singapore is part of PSA International Pte Ltd., which owns/operates ports in 15 countries across the world. PSA International is fully owned by the Singapore Government linked to Temasek Holdings.

Table 5.10 Strengths and Weaknesses Summary: Competence Dimension

Grade	Strengths	Weaknesses
Indonesia: B⁻	Proximity to Singapore Port and airport to an extent counteracts it low LPI ranking for port-based factories in Sumatra and other islands that are close to Singapore.	Weak labor relations; no world-class universities; lack of English-speaking managerial and technical staff; weak logistics competence.
Malaysia: A⁻	Healthy labor relations; many overseas trained Malaysian graduates compensate for lack of world-class educational institutions.	Locally trained Malaysians weak in English, hence relative lack of English-speaking managerial and technical staff.
Myanmar: D	Labor costs lower than China for lower-end manufacturing.	Poor logistics competence; lack of English-speaking managerial and technical staff; lack world-class educational institutions.
Philippines: B⁻	English-speaking managerial and technical staff; decent quality of universities for technical and business education; seen as a growing center for outsourcing of services, IT, and knowledge work.	Rising militancy affects labor relations as well as customs and security; poor LPI ranking.
Singapore: A	Excellent labor relations managed through tripartite relationship between employers, government, and the labor unions; highest LPI ranking in the world; top logistics and port infrastructure; universities with engineering and business programs that are increasingly ranked among the top in the world.	No significant weaknesses.
Thailand: B	Reasonably low labor cost when compared to urban areas in China and India such as Shanghai or Bangalore; good quality technical manpower that helps it to be a regional powerhouse for automotive manufacturing; presence of universities that are regionally well known.	Lack of English-speaking managerial staff.
Vietnam: C⁺	Low labor cost compared to China.	Lack of quality universities; lack of English-speaking managerial and technical manpower; low competence levels in logistics, customs, and security.

200 shipping lines.[n] Ocean liners use transshipment as a strategy for improving the efficiency and capacity utilization of their shipping operations. A key performance measure for any transshipment port is how quickly it can move the arriving goods through the port to the departing vessel. Twenty-five percent of PSA's arriving containers in Singapore are transshipped within 24 hours, and the rest in an average of 4 days.[17] Although the term *cross docking* is used more in the context of distribution warehouses of Fast-Moving Consumer Goods (FMCG) retail chains such as TESCO or Walmart, what the port of Singapore achieves is essentially cross docking, albeit cross docking of 20-foot and 40-foot containers rather than pallets, packages, or tiffin boxes.

In the Dabbawala case in Mumbai discussed in Chapter 4, cross docking was achieved through a predominantly manual system with very little use of information technology (IT). At PSA Singapore, cross docking is achieved through a marriage of several IT systems and complex Operations Research–based algorithms.

The key components of the cross-docking system at the port of Singapore are Portnet, Computer Integrated Terminal Operations System (CITOS), and flow-through gate process. Twelve hours before the arrival of a ship, advance information about the vessel's capacity, sailing schedule, and number of containers is captured through the Portnet[o] system. The Portnet system enables arriving vessels to order berth and pilot services and to submit relevant documentation. The system thus provides advance information for planning for all the user groups—the port terminal operator PSA, tugboat operators, shipping lines and shippers, freight forwarders, and customs authorities.

Once the vessel arrives at the port, the quay cranes help unload the containers one at a time onto a prime mover, which moves the container to an assigned location in the port yard. The location of the prime movers within the yard are monitored through a global positioning system (GPS) and can be dynamically assigned to different vessels based on need. At the yard, the yard cranes lift the containers from the prime mover and stack them at least three-high to improve space utilization in the yard. The advance information along with the planning algorithms ensure that when the containers are removed from the yard for loading onto an outgoing vessel, the topmost container from the stack is the one that is removed first. This ensures superior material handling efficiency as well as reducing the turnaround time for the containers.

PSA has developed its own *computer integrated terminal operations system* (CITOS) for efficient management of all the container handling activities as well as resources such as prime movers, yard cranes, and quay cranes within the port. CITOS is essentially a custom-made enterprise resource planning (ERP) system that helps PSA direct its port operations for its berthing system, ship planning system, yard planning system, and

---

[n] http://www.edb.gov.sg/content/edb/en/industries/industries/logistics-and-supply-chain-management.html.
[o] www.portnet.com.

resource allocation system. CITOS also automatically generates the ship stowage plans for the containers as well as the yard layout plans. The yard layout plan ensures that space in the yard is used efficiently and the time spent on container handling is minimized. The CITOS also helps streamline the process for truckers who arrive at the port to pick up or deliver containers through a flow-through gate process.

The flow-through gate process uses advance information (obtained through the Portnet system), wireless technology, and visioning systems (for detecting the vehicle and container identity) to direct the arriving trucks to particular locations within the yard for the loading/unloading of containers. This ensures that the service time for the trucks (from arrival at the port gate to departure) is less than 30 minutes.

In addition to these systems that help PSA implement cross docking, the customs clearing and other performance measures for Singapore in the LPI ranking are facilitated by the TradeNet system. The TradeNet[p] portal is a web-based Electronic Data Interchange (EDI) platform provided by Singapore Customs for filing customs documents electronically. The system links various agencies such as customs, shipping agents, traders, freight forwarders, and the port and helps integrate the import, export, and transshipment documentation processing procedures. The TradeNet system reduces the cost and turnaround for import and export and customs clearance of cargo in Singapore from 2 days (manually) to just 15 minutes. Recently the TradeNet, Portnet, and several other online systems within the trade and logistics community within Singapore have been integrated into a single platform called Trade Xchange.

Singapore has thus been able to achieve the world's top ranking in logistics performance through its cross-docking system at PSA and through integration of various information systems for customs and security clearance.

Table 5.11 presents a summary of the assessment scores on the EPIC dimensions for the countries in Southeast Asia.

Supply Chain Challenges

ASEAN comprises a diverse set of countries that are very different in terms of their economies, per capita income levels, logistics infrastructure, and competence. Therefore, it is not easy to characterize a common set of challenges across all countries. However, some of the challenges faced by a majority of the countries are logistics infrastructure, domestic demand, human resources, and cost of doing business. In particular, building up a sound logistics infrastructure is a key challenge for Vietnam and Myanmar, and to a large extent for the Philippines and Indonesia as well.

---

[p] http://www.customs.gov.sg/leftNav/trad/TradeNet.htm.

Table 5.11   Summary Assessment of EPIC Attractiveness for Southeast Asia

	Economy	Politics	Infrastructure	Competence	Overall Grade
Indonesia	A⁻	C⁻	C⁻	B⁻	C⁺
Malaysia	B⁺	B	B⁺	A⁻	B⁺
Myanmar	B⁻	D⁻	D⁻	D	D⁺
Philippines	B⁺	D⁺	D⁺	B⁻	C⁺
Singapore	B	A	A	A	A⁻
Thailand	B⁺	C⁺	B	B	B
Vietnam	B⁺	C⁺	D⁺	C⁺	C⁺

Singapore, Malaysia, and Brunei have small populations, which limits the amount of domestic demand that a product can generate, making it harder to attract a multinational national company (MNC) to set up operations in the country. It is noted, though, that attracting such MNC investment is harder for some of these countries such as Singapore only if the main motivation for the MNC is to expand markets rather than to reduce their supply chain and manufacturing costs.

Building up a human talent pool is a challenge for all countries, including countries in ASEAN. As countries move up the production value chain and income levels, the economy has to diversify into higher valued-added and higher technology products and services, which requires human talent with new skill sets. For the less developed countries such as Vietnam and Myanmar, it is challenging to build up talent with even the basic skill sets.

Addressing the Supply Chain Challenges

Countries such as Singapore and Malaysia, with a relatively low domestic demand, can clearly gain a competitive advantage through a superior logistics infrastructure, which enables them to present a good business case as a vital supply chain node for an MNC. Singapore has succeeded in this regard due to its top ranked logistics infrastructure and the lower supply chain risk it presents.

As discussed earlier, the port of Singapore through its unique cross-docking system has emerged as the largest transshipment port in the world. Malaysia's north-south highway is another example of how building up the logistics infrastructure can significantly address supply chain challenges. Prior to the 1990s, the driving time from Singapore to the Malaysian capital, Kuala Lumpur, a distance of 350 kilometers, would have taken seven to eight hours. In the 1980s, Malaysia embarked on an ambitious project to connect the southern most point in Johor (with expressway links to Singapore) to the northern most point at Bukit Kayu Hitam in Kedah province. The 775-kilometer north-south highway was built on a Build-Operate-Transfer (BOT) model. Vehicles can travel at a maximum speed of 110 km per hour. Though not all of Malaysia's infrastructure projects (such as the multimedia corridor) can be defined as unqualified successes, the north-south highway substantially improved logistics connectivity within Malaysia.

In early 2013, the Singapore and Malaysian governments announced their intention to build a high-speed rail link between Singapore and Kuala Lumpur. With this proposed high-speed rail, the distance between the two cities will be covered in less than two hours. Such infrastructure projects, though very expensive, can significantly improve the attractiveness of the country/region for the supply chain of an MNC.

Thailand's effort to develop its automotive industry is a good example of how building up domestic demand can address some supply chain challenges. Thailand is popularly known today as the Detroit of the East.[18] In the 1960s, when countries such as Malaysia and Indonesia were very protective of their automotive industry, Thailand had the foresight to open the industry to Japanese and American car manufacturers. At the same time, to develop local competencies for parts manufacturing, Thailand imposed legal restrictions on the amount of imported content in vehicles. Combined with subsidies and tax rebates for the auto industry, that helped generate significant domestic demand. Thailand's automotive sector grew significantly between 1960 and 1997. Shortly after the Asian crisis, domestic demand dropped significantly, which prompted Thailand to open the automotive sector to foreign investment even further. Restrictions on foreign ownership in automobile companies as well as the percentage of imported parts content in vehicles were removed. Such initiatives spurred Japanese automakers such as Toyota to use Thailand as a global manufacturing base for some of their models. The open trade agreement with the ASEAN countries also helped boost regional demand for automotive manufacturers located in Thailand. The removal of the restriction on imported parts content was not an issue anymore as Thailand had already developed a healthy local auto parts industry by the 1990s.

Another way to boost domestic demand is to provide incentives to local companies to develop products to cater to the underserved bottom of the pyramid (BOP) market. One such example in the Philippines is the Hapinoy's chain[q] of Sari-Sari stores. Sari-Sari stores are small neighborhood stores in the Philippines that sell a wide variety of general merchandise. The largest percentage of the poor in the Philippines live in rural and remote locations that traditional retailing systems have ignored. Due to the inefficiencies in the supply chain, the poor often pay as much 20 percent more for staple goods[r] at a traditional store in rural areas. Hapinoy established its chain of Sari-Sari stores to address this issue. Hapinoy's stores are owned by female entrepreneurs who would otherwise not have a business opportunity or livelihood. Hapinoy provides these women entrepreneurs access to micro-financing, as

---

[q] http://www.partneringforglobalimpact.com/program/presentations/microventures_inc.
[r] http://www.synergysocialventures.org/featured-ventures/hapinoy/.

well as training to build their capacities to manage these stores. Hapinoy's eventual goal is to have 100,000 stores that bring quality-of-life goods and services to 5 million people in the base of the pyramid. Such efforts will also boost demand for large FMCG companies if they are able to develop products to serve these stores.

Building up human resources is a challenge that has not been well addressed by most of the ASEAN countries. Singapore with its rich economic reserves and wise spending on education has built up an excellent infrastructure of schools, polytechnics, institutes of technical education, and world-class universities. It has also managed to attract world-class business schools such as INSEAD and the University of Chicago to set up local campuses. Malaysia, with an open policy on foreign universities and the higher affordability level of their citizens, also has many branch campuses of British and Australian universities such as Monash.

Finally, managing the cost of doing business is a perennial challenge faced in all successful growth economies. With explosive growth in manufacturing in China and correspondingly increasing costs, many companies have moved their lower-end manufacturing to Vietnam and Myanmar. The only way to manage the cost of doing business is to ensure that the country is able to move up the value chain and go into more high-skilled and high-tech industries. In this respect Malaysia has been relatively less successful, but it has not had to address these issues seriously due to its significant natural resources in oil and gas and economic growth from government spending on huge infrastructure projects. Singapore, in constrast, has consistently moved up the manufacturing value chain, for instance, in the wafer fab and semiconductor industries. This requires conscious formulation of the right incentives and policies for firms as well as investments in retraining programs for workers. In the 1960s and 1970s, Singapore's shipping industry had focused on shipbreaking (ship demolition for recycling scrap, especially steel) and ship repair. Now shipyards of companies such as Keppel Offshore & Marine and Sembawang Shipyard are focusing on building offshore oil rigs and rig platforms using the latest available technology.

Key Takeaways for Southeast Asia

1. Southeast Asia is arguably the most diverse region in the world with an enormous number of ethnic groups and languages. This diversity poses some economic challenges to economic growth for some countries in the region, such as Myanmar.

2. Southeast Asia has, however, witnessed significant economic activity in the recent past, and the future appears to be quite bright for most countries in the region. The stage is set for Southeast Asia to take its place as a world-leading trading power.

3. Located very strategically from a supply chain perspective, in the heart of a vibrant economic zone, it is the most easily accessible tropical region in the world, located along the sea passage from the Middle Eastern/Mediterranean region to East Asia.

4. The ASEAN countries have a combined population of more than 600 million people and a GDP of $1.5 trillion. They generate $1.7 trillion worth of trade annually, a figure that is likely to increase significantly if Southeast Asian countries maintain projected growth rates of 5 to 6 percent over the next few years.

5. There are many reasons why the projected growth rates for Southeast Asia are likely to take place, least of which is the superpower status of neighboring China and India.

6. At the same time, however, risks and limitations to competitiveness due to their relatively smaller size pose a significant challenge.

7. Despite enjoying a favorable outlook, it is clear that the biggest opportunities for these countries lies in their coming together as a single entity, AEC, and compete in the global arena effectively.

8. Improving trade and openness of the ASEAN economies with the rest of Asia is also important, and this is perhaps the motivation for the East Asia Summit (EAS) and the Asia-Pacific Economic Cooperation (APEC). The EAS is traditionally held after the annual ASEAN meeting.

9. The effectiveness of the EAS and APEC to open the trade flow between and ASEAN and the rest of Asia is, however, still questionable. Domestic political pressures and alternative trade initiatives continue to vie for attention, threatening to undermine some of the effectiveness of the EAS and APEC.

10. Building up a human talent pool continues to be a challenge for all the ASEAN countries.

References

1. Lim Chong Yah, *Southeast Asia: The Long Road Ahead*, 2nd ed. (Singapore: World Scientific Publishing Company, 2004).
2. "Demographia World Urban Areas," 9th ed., March 2013, http://www.demographia.com/db-worldua.pdf.
3. World LNG Report, 2011, International Gas Union, sponsored by Petronas.
4. John H. Drabble, *An Economic History of Malaysia, c. 1800–1990: The Transition to Modern Economic Growth* (London: Macmillan Press and New York: St. Martin's Press, 2000).
5. S. Pushpanathan, "ASEAN Connectivity and the ASEAN Economic Community," Paper presented at the 24th Asia-Pacific Roundtable, Kuala Lumpur, June 7–9, 2010.
6. J. S. L. Lam, and W. Y. Yap, "Competition among Major Ports in Southeast Asia," S. Rajaratnam School of International Studies, September 3, 2008.
7. "The JOC Top 50 World Container Ports," *Journal of Commerce*, www.joc.com, August 20–27, 2012.
8. "The Philippines FDI on the Up," Report by the Oxford Business Group in *Business World Online*, May 2013.

9. *The Economist Intelligence Unit*: "Skilled Labour Shortfalls in Indonesia, the Philippines, Thailand, and Vietnam," A custom research report for the British Council, June 2012.

10. H. K. Leong, *Reforming Corporate Governance in Southeast Asia: Economics, Politics and Regulations* (Singapore: Institute of Southeast Asian Studies, 2005).

11. ASEAN Connectivity Project Information Sheets, Jakarta: ASEAN Secretariat, August 2012.

12. UNCTAD World Investment Report, 2011.

13. A. Gross, and C. Matacic, "Southeast Asia Responds to Worker Demands with Labor Reforms," *Society for Human Resources Management*, 2013, www.shrm.org.

14. *The Economist Intelligence Unit*: "Skilled Labour Shortfalls in Indonesia, the Philippines, Thailand, and Vietnam," A custom research report for the British Council, June 2012.

15. Daily Cargo.com. http://www.daily-cargo.com/english/2013/0221/.

16. Website of PSA Singapore, http://www.singaporepsa.com/transhipment.php.

17. "PSA: The World's Port of Call," Harvard Business School Case 9-802-003, 2004.

18. "Thailand's Booming Car Industry: Detroit of the East," *The Economist,* April 4, 2013, http://www.economist.com/blogs/schumpeter/2013/04/thailands-booming-car-industry.

CHAPTER 6

Australia

Australia is the world's largest island nation. The land area of Australia, 7.741 million square kilometers, is almost equal to the combined land area of India and all 11 Southeast Asian countries.[a] With a density of less than 3.4 people per square kilometer, Australia is one of the 11 least densely populated countries in the world. Its population is a little under 23 million, less than the combined population of two Indian cities, Mumbai and New Delhi.

The majority of Australia's population is located along the coastline, with more than 80 percent of the population living within 50 kilometers of the coast. Five cities along the coastline—Sydney, Melbourne, Brisbane, Perth, and Adelaide—have a combined population of more than 14 million. The majority of Australia's population is located in the eastern region, along the coastline from Adelaide to Cairns (Figure 6.1).

Australia is a geographically isolated country. The city of Perth in western Australia is one of the world's three most remote cities with a population greater than 1 million, the other two cities being Auckland, New Zealand, and Honolulu, Hawaii. The capitals of Australia and New Zealand, Canberra and Wellington, are the world's two most remote capital cities, as measured by the longest distance from the capital of a sovereign country to the capital closest to it. From a supply chain perspective, one clear implication of these statistics is that large distances must be covered to get products into or out of Australia, or from one location in Australia to another, presenting some logistical challenges.

Economic and Political Background

A little known fact is that the first authenticated European landing in Australia was from a ship led by the Dutch navigator Willem Janszoon. When this ship landed on the western shore of Cape York, in the northern end of Queensland, in 1606,[1] Willem Janszoon

---

[a] The 11 Southeast Asian countries are Brunei, Cambodia, Indonesia, Laos, Malaysia, Myanmar, the Philippines, Singapore, Thailand, Timor-Leste, and Vietnam.

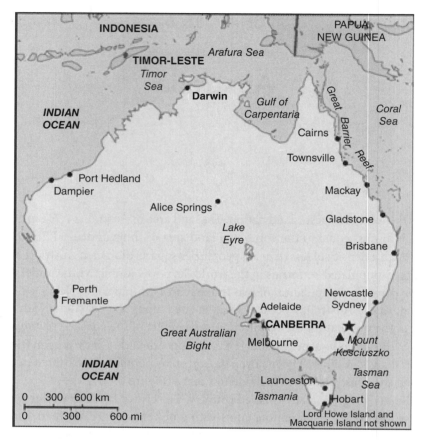

Figure 6.1 Map of Australia.

reportedly called the land he discovered "Nieu Zeland" after the Dutch province of Zeeland. Abel Janszoon Tasman, the Dutch explorer who subsequently visited and mapped the northern portion of the country in 1644 while under the service of the Dutch East India Company, called this land "New Holland" after the Dutch province of Holland. This name was associated with Australia until the early part of the 19th century.

Although the Dutch are generally recognized as being the first European visitors to this country, they did not colonize it. Willem Janszoon found the land inhospitable. Within four months, he returned to Bantam,[b] where his sailing expedition to Nieu Zeland had originated. And from the Dutch East India Company's perspective, Tasman's expedition was a disappointment because he had neither found a promising trade location nor a useful new

---

[b] Bantam (now known as Banten), near the western end of Java, was a major trading city with a secure harbor at the mouth of the Banten River, which provided a navigable passage for light craft into the island's interior.

shipping route. Although various proposals for colonization were made subsequently, none was officially attempted. Not finding anything to their liking from either a trading or shipping perspective, the Dutch soon lost interest in New Holland.

With the exception of further Dutch visits to the west, this country remained largely free of European visits for another hundred years. In 1769, a lieutenant of the Royal Navy commanding the HMS *Endeavour* decided to explore the east coast of New Holland, the only region that remained uncharted by the Dutch. He landed on the east coast at Botany Bay (now in Sydney), New South Wales. James Cook claimed the east coast for Britain without even conducting any negotiations with the local inhabitants.

At around the same time, in 1766, a proposal was made in Britain to establish a colony in the New Holland region for banished convicts. The proposal to establish a British colony was timely. Great Britain was losing the American colonies as a result of the 1775–1783 American Revolutionary War, and the region presented an attractive option for British colonization. In 1787, a fleet of 11 ships carrying more than 1500 people, about half of them convicts, set sail from Great Britain to New Holland. Rather than resorting to using slaves to build the infrastructure for the colony, convict labor presented a cheap and economically viable alternative. Colonization began in 1788. In 1817, Lachlan Macquarie, the Governor of New South Wales, recommended the adoption of the name Australia, which was officially approved by the British Admiralty in 1824.

It was not long before Australia's vast mineral wealth was discovered. One of the earliest metals discovered was gold, which was found in central Victoria and New South Wales in 1851. This discovery transformed Australia economically, politically, and demographically.

The Australian Gold Rush

A large number of people from the British colonies, as well of boatloads of prospectors from the United States, continental Europe, and China, soon entered the country, prospecting for gold. The Museum of Victoria states that immigrants leaving Britain in 1852 bought more tickets to Melbourne than to any other part of the world.[c] Interestingly, the flow of convicts to Australia's shores stopped around this time, presumably because it did not appear to be a good idea to give a free boat ride to criminals to enter Australia's rich gold fields.

Great Britain benefited considerably from the gold rush. Ships returned to Great Britain carrying huge quantities of gold, leading the *London Times* to declare in 1852 "this is California all over again, but, it would appear, California on a larger scale."[d] Although much

---

[c] http://museumvictoria.com.au/marvellous/gold/index.asp.
[d] http://www.goldoz.com.au/?id=358. The California gold rush took place between 1848 and 1855.

of the profit was sent back to Great Britain, the wealth generated allowed for substantial investments in industry and infrastructure within the country. In particular, a significant portion of these investments was directed toward the cities of Melbourne and Sydney. By the 1880s, these cities were flourishing. In 1861, Melbourne already had 125,000 inhabitants and was growing rapidly. Visitors to Melbourne in the 1880s were amazed by this city, larger than most European capitals, whose population had doubled in just a decade to half a million inhabitants.

Gold mines were also established at Mount Morgan, Rockhampton, in Queensland, and Coolgardie and Kalgoorlie in western Australia. Vast quantities of gold were discovered in the town of Coolgardie, but as with the other areas in Victoria and New South Wales, the gold deposits were largely exhausted in a relatively short time. The remoteness of that region did little to encourage sustained mining despite the arrival of the railways in 1896, and mining operations were already moving to nearby Kalgoorlie, where the gold deposits were much larger.

Australian Mining Activity and Economic Growth

In the 1870s, with the discovery of tin at Mount Bischoff in Tasmania, Australia also became an important producer of this metal. Mining in the country continued to flourish with the establishment of copper mines in Queensland; silver, lead, and zinc mines at Broken Hill in New South Wales; and iron ore mines at Iron Knob and Iron Baron in south Australia.

The value of mineral production continued to enjoy sustained growth during the first half of the 20th century. Although Australia has the world's largest economically demonstrated reserves of lead, rutile, zircon, nickel, gold, silver, and zinc, the only major new finds during this period were lead, zinc, copper, and silver deposits at Mount Isa in Queensland.

Australia ranks second in world reserves for iron ore, bauxite, tantalum, and tungsten and is in the top 10 for a number of other mineral reserves, including black coal.[2] In the early 1960s, following the removal of export controls on iron ore, the Pilbara region in western Australia stepped up production of iron ore. With the help of the Bureau of Mineral Resources, the pace of exploration increased and new metals were discovered. The discovery of some of these new metals, notably bauxite (the source of aluminum), nickel, tungsten, uranium, and titanium ore, led to a resurgence of interest in Australian mining. Mineral production continued to enjoy sustained growth during the first half of the 20th century even though the only major new finds during this period were lead, zinc, copper, and silver deposits at Mount Isa in Queensland.

By the end of the 1960s, Australia was a major raw materials exporter, especially to Japan and Europe, and the Australian economy was growing quickly with an accompanying rise in the standard of living. For example, the rate of home ownership rose from

40 percent in 1947 to more than 70 percent by the 1960s.[e] Oil and natural gas production activity also increased during this time period. The US Energy Information Administration reports that Australia is now the world's fourth largest exporter of liquefied natural gas.

The Markets

Australia is now one of the major mineral exporting regions in the world. The countries that receive a major share of these exports include Japan, China, South Korea, India, the United States, Taiwan, and New Zealand. Over the past decade, Asia's demand for Australia's natural resources has created an extraordinary boom in minerals and energy investment in the country. It has led to a substantial increase in Australia's GDP even though productivity growth has been modest during this period.[3] Other exports include agricultural products, mainly meat and animal skins, and some manufactured goods such as boats, cars, hats, clothing, and gaming machines.

Location of Market Activity

From a supply chain perspective, the geographical intensity of industrial activity in a given locality presents both opportunities and challenges for organizations considering investments in that activity. Having industrial activity concentrated in a specific locality increases that locality's visibility, making it more attractive for investment. The flip side is that concentrated activity in a locality magnifies existing infrastructural issues such as traffic congestion, availability of electric power, and water that are more pronounced in developing nations.

Primacy is used as a measure of the concentration of industrial activity. Primacy is the percentage of the urban population living in a country's largest metropolitan area. For Australia, a modification of this definition to include the four largest metropolitan areas in the country in this measure of concentration provides some revealing information. Based on data provided in the Central Intelligence Agency's (CIA) World Factbook, the combined population of Sydney, Melbourne, Brisbane, and Perth was 11.85 million in 2012. That accounts for more than 50 percent of Australia's population. Some of the logistical challenges that accompany such a concentration of population are examined next.

All logistics centers in Australia are located near the major coastal cities. Sydney, with 4.42 million residents, is the largest city in Australia and is a hub for the transport and storage sectors. Australia's agricultural processing industry, largely based around Melbourne,

---

[e] The Australian Bureau of Statistics reports that the rate of home ownership in Australia has ranged between 68 and 70 percent since that time.

supplies and delivers raw materials, intermediate products, and finished products to other parts of the country and to international markets. Melbourne has also evolved into a logistics center and hub for the southern Pacific region, especially for exports to New Zealand.

Much of the country's mineral and energy resources come from western Australia. Western Australia, which constitutes about a third of Australia in area, is not as temperate as the eastern part of the country. The eastern Pilbara region, 1200 kilometers north of Perth on the Great Northern Highway, is one of the most isolated and inhospitable regions in Australia. The inland districts of the Pilbara experience extreme ranges of temperature. The winter night temperatures drop below zero degrees Celsius, and temperatures in summer can exceed 45 degrees Celsius. The extreme temperatures partly explain why the population of western Australia, despite its large geographical area, is just a little over 2 million. Other reasons for the low habitation rate include lack of water and low levels of arable land.

The Trans-Australian Railway, which connected Port Augusta in south Australia to Kalgoorlie in western Australia in 1917, provided a physical link of major commercial and strategic importance. The Trans-Australian Railway significantly improved the country's logistics infrastructure, but Australia is an export-intensive island nation so a major share of freight is transported by sea.

Logistics Infrastructure

The railway system forms a critical part of Australia's transport network. Australia has more than 41,000 kilometers of rail track. Except for a small number of private railways, the Australian railway network is government-owned. Australia operates several long-distance and interstate train routes across different parts of the country. Two of the more famous long-distance routes are the Indian Pacific and the Ghan.

The Indian Pacific line is a passenger line that was formed by extending the Trans-Australian Railway eastward, from Port August to Sydney via Adelaide, and westward, from Kalgoorlie to Perth. This line, so named because it "connects" the Pacific Ocean and the Indian Ocean via the Australian continent, is one of the world's longest transcontinental railway journeys. It covers a distance of 4352 kilometers, takes about 65 hours to complete, and includes the world's longest straight stretch of railway track, a 478-kilometer section on the Nullarbor Plain.

The Ghan runs from Adelaide in the south to Darwin in the north, through Alice Springs in central Australia. It takes its name from the Afghans, or Ghans, who operated the caravans across the desert in Australia from the 1860s to the 1930s. The journey covers several diverse Australian landscapes, from temperate Adelaide to arid Alice Springs to the scenic Katherine region to tropical Darwin. The Ghan travels a distance of 2979 kilometers and takes 54 hours to complete, including a 4-hour stopover in Alice Springs.

Although the rail system forms a critical part of the transportation network, Australia relies heavily on road transport for its freight. Australia's reliance on road transportation for its freight has historic roots. The first railway lines built in Australia were built by private organizations that gave little or no thought to a nationwide network of railways, leading to at least three major railway gauges—Broad, Standard, and Narrow—with each state adopting its own gauge. The lack of a unified rail gauge led to problems connecting the different states in the country. Trains typically did not cross state boundaries, resulting in freight being transferred at each border.

Efforts at standardizing rail gauges began to gather momentum in the early 1960s although the conversion to the standard rail gauge has proceeded in fits and starts. In 1978 the Commonwealth Railways, South Australian Railways, and Tasmanian Government Railways were amalgamated to form Australian National Railways. The federal government's "One Nation" project, an Australian government program of infrastructure development carried out under the Keating government from 1991 to 1996, resulted in the broad gauge between Melbourne and Adelaide being connected by a standard gauge in June 1995. All mainland state capitals were now directly connected by a standard gauge. Although these developments made the railways a more practical means of transcontinental freight movement, by this time the road system had gathered momentum. With increased growth in interstate trade, roadways were increasingly being used for a range of freight tasks. Combined with easier regulations governing road freight carriage, *road trains* presented a compelling transportation alternative to the railroad industry.

A road train is a trucking concept used in remote areas in countries like Australia, the United States, and Canada to move freight efficiently. Australia has the largest and heaviest road-legal vehicles in the world, with some configurations topping out at close to 200 tons. Some road train configurations have as many as four trailers hooked together. The items carried on these road trains include livestock, minerals, fuel, and general freight. This cost-effective transport system has helped economic development in remote areas.

Waterways in Australia are managed by the Department of Environment and Conservation. The majority of the waterways are in the tropical savannas region and are generally divided into three broad categories: canal rivers, natural rivers, and artificial canals. Although waterways in Australia were used in the 19th century to transport produce such as wheat and wool, the water levels of the inland waterways are highly variable, making it difficult to navigate them for large parts of the year. Traffic on the inland waterways is therefore typically recreational craft.

Australia's energy sector is very reliable and low cost. Australia has significant reserves of petroleum, natural gas, and coal. It is one of a select few countries belonging to the Organization for Economic Cooperation and Development (OECD) that has a significant net hydrocarbon export, exporting about two-thirds of its total energy production. According to the US Energy Information Administration (EIA), Australia was the world's largest exporter of coal in 2010 and, as noted earlier, the world's fourth largest exporter of liquefied natural gas.

The stable political environment, substantial hydrocarbon reserves, and proximity to Asian markets make Australia an attractive place for foreign direct investment (FDI) in the energy market. The energy sector received a major investment in September 2009 when Chevron and joint venture partners ExxonMobil and Royal Dutch Shell announced the Gorgon project. This venture will drill fields about 130 kilometers offshore in western Australia to tap into an estimated 40 trillion cubic feet of gas and build pipelines and a liquefaction plant and port for about 43 billion Australian dollars, roughly the size of Guatemala's gross national product.

Overall, Australia is the world's ninth largest energy producer, accounting for 2.4 percent of the world's energy production, a relatively large number considering that the population of Australia accounts for less than 0.3 percent of the world population. Such a relatively large share of the world's per capita energy production does not come without cost. At 19 tons per capita, Australia remains the world's biggest emitter of carbon dioxide among major nations, followed by the United States at 17.3 tons and Saudi Arabia at 16.5 tons.

Efforts are under way to promote innovative and more efficient ways to supply and use energy. In July 2011, the prime minister of Australia, Ms. Julia Gillard, announced a carbon tax, reneging on her preelection promise not to do so. This was a politically charged announcement because the tax would put a substantial burden on energy consumers and producers. Australia introduced this highly controversial carbon tax in July 2012. The law requires about 300 of the worst-polluting firms to pay a levy of 23 Australian dollars for every ton of greenhouse gases produced.

Not all efforts are punitive. Most of the country enjoys many sunny days, and the government offers major incentives to households that install energy-saving devices such as solar panels for their electricity needs.

Assessing the Maturity Level of Supply Chains in Australia

Although Australia has historically been among the most remote countries in the world, the rise of Asia presents significant opportunities for reducing this remoteness. Australia, with its export-intensive status is now closer to the center of world economic activity. A white paper by the Australian government in October 2012[4] states, "The share of world output within 10,000 kilometers of Australia has more than doubled over the past 50 years to more than a third of global output today, and this share will rise to around half of global output in 2025." The report notes "reduction in transport and communication costs will support new opportunities for exporters to find new markets and integrate with cross-border value chains. . . . Australia's proximity to Asia is more of an advantage for goods with a higher freight component, like resource commodities. In absolute terms, exports in the mining, manufacturing, services, and agricultural sectors are all expected to increase between now and 2025."

Economy

The major industries for Australia are mining, agriculture (sheep, cattle, grain, and fruit crops), and tourism. Manufacturing is also gaining importance. Australia's major mineral exports are coal, iron ore, gold, and alumina, but a substantial percentage of Australia's exports are woolen textiles, wheat, machinery, and transport equipment. Until the 1960s, much of Australia's trade was with "Mother England." In 1960, Asia accounted for about 20 percent of Australia's trade, with Japan being the biggest regional trade partner. However, by 2010 more than two-thirds of Australia's trade was with Asia. Based on CIA World Factbook data, the countries receiving a major share of Australia's exports in 2011 were China (27.4 percent), Japan (19.2 percent), South Korea (8.9 percent), and India (5.8 percent). In 2010, Asia accounted for about 50 percent of Australia's imports.

The shift in Australia's focus on trading partners from the United Kingdom to Asia was driven to a large extent by the United Kingdom's entry into the European Common Market in the 1970s. Until that time, Australia was essentially considered "England's Farm," but the UK's shift in focus to trading with Europe for agricultural products meant that there was a sudden loss of markets for Australia, causing it to shift its trade focus to Asia. In essence, it spurred Australia's move to position itself as an "Australasian" nation.

Economic Output and Growth Rate

The CIA World Factbook for 2012 ranks Australia as the 19th largest economy in the world based on GDP in terms of purchasing power parity (PPP). The estimated GDP for Australia in 2012 was $1.542 trillion at the official exchange rate. The per capita GDP for Australia was estimated by the CIA World Factbook to be $43,300 in 2012.

The service sector dominates the GDP. The CIA World Factbook notes that the service sector accounted for 68.8 percent of GDP in 2012. Although Australia's economy is dominated by its service sector, its economic success is based on its abundant agricultural and mineral resources. Australia's comparative advantage in the export of these products reflects the natural wealth of the country and its small domestic market.

Looking ahead, in the medium term, the continued development of the economies of Asian countries, in particular China and India, will benefit the Australian economy. The Economic Intelligence Unit (EIU) forecasts an average growth rate of 3 percent a year for Australia for the 2013 to 2016 period, well above its average growth rate over the past 50 years.

Population Size

In absolute terms, Australia ranks 53rd in population across 239 countries in the world. From a supply chain perspective, Australia's low population, combined with the vast geographic distances that must be traveled to reach customers in the different parts of

Australia, results in a relatively lower score on this variable as compared to its scores on some of the other variables.

Foreign Direct Investment

The 2011 Inward FDI Attraction Index published by the United Nations Conference on Trade and Development (UNCTAD), which ranks 182 countries on their success in attracting FDI, ranks Australia 24th, placing it in the first quartile in the index. The FDI Potential Index published by UNCTAD ranks Australia 5th, placing it in the first quartile on this index as well. As noted in Chapter 2, this index uses four key economic determinants: the attractiveness of the market, the availability of low-cost labor and skills, the presence of natural resources, and the presence of FDI-enabling infrastructure.

Exchange Rate Stability and Consumer Price Inflation

The Australian dollar has had a slightly bumpy ride. In 2009, the exchange rate was 1.2822 Australian dollars to the U.S. dollar, and in 2012 it was 0.963 Australian dollars to the U.S. dollar. Although the U.S. dollar has weakened relative to the currency of many developed countries, the 33 percent move from 1.2822 to 0.963 is a relatively sharp swing upward for the Australian dollar. Most of the developed nations saw their currency move upward by about 15 to 20 percent relative to the U.S. dollar over this time period. Although the strength of the Australian dollar is a matter of some concern, consumer price inflation is relatively low, averaging about 3 percent over the last five years.

Balance of Trade

The Australian Bureau of Statistics reported a trade deficit of 427 million Australian dollars in 2012, in line with the average deficit of 396.04 million Australian dollars over the period from 1971 to 2012. Australia enjoyed trade surpluses in 2010 and 2011 due to the high price of commodities during these years, but the trade balance swung back to a deficit in 2012 due to a drop in the value of exports and an increase in imports of capital goods.

Despite the trade deficit, the overall outlook is bright. Australia's public finances are among the strongest in the world. Government debt is low, and Australia enjoys the highest possible sovereign credit rating. Table 6.1 presents the scores for the Economy

Table 6.1   Scores for the Economy Dimension

Economy	Economic Output and Growth Rate	Population Size	Foreign Direct Investment	Exchange Rate Stability/CPI	Balance of Trade	Overall Grade
30%	35%	25%	20%	15%	5%	100%
Australia	B	B+	A	C	A	B+

Table 6.2 Strengths and Weaknesses Summary: Economy Dimension

Grade	Strengths	Weaknesses
Australia: B⁺	Vast mineral wealth; high FDI potential; one of the world's most industrialized countries; low unemployment.	High dependence on its export economy; low population size; trade deficit despite strong export sales; strength of the Australian dollar has raised concerns about Australia's cost competitiveness and led to calls for its wage costs to be reduced.

dimension, and Table 6.2 summarizes the strengths and weaknesses for Australia on the Economy dimension.

Politics

Australia gets high marks on the Politics dimension. It scores well on all variables except for the one that captures tax rate and tariff barriers.

Ease of Doing Business

The 2012 World Bank doing business survey ranks Australia very high on this variable, placing it 10th among 185 countries. In particular, Australia scores high on the ease of starting a new business, placing second behind New Zealand, although it gets a relatively low score of 70 for protecting investors. For purposes of comparison, Singapore and the United States are ranked 1st and 4th, respectively. On government effectiveness and control of corruption metrics, Australia is at the 95th and 97th percentiles, respectively. For comparison, the United States is at the 89th and 86th percentiles on these metrics.

Legal and Regulatory Framework

Australia has one of the most transparent and efficient regulatory environments in the world. The 2011 World Competitiveness Yearbook published by the IMD Business School ranks it 10th in the world for encouraging enterprise competition. The World Bank World Governance Index (WGI) metrics on regulatory quality and rule of law are used to evaluate the legal and regulatory framework variable. Australia is at the 97th percentile on the regulatory quality metric, and at the 96th percentile on the rule of law metric. For comparison, the United States is at the 92nd percentile and 91st percentile, respectively, on these metrics.

The Deloitte International Tax Source pegged the corporate tax rates for Australia at 30 percent in 2012. For purposes of comparison, the corporate tax rate for the United States that year was 35 percent, and the corporate tax rate for Singapore was 17 percent. Although the tax rate is relatively high, it has remained steady over the years.

Political Stability

Australia ranks high on political stability. The Political Instability Index published by *The Economist* ranks Australia 154 among the 165 countries in the index. As noted earlier, a rank of 1 indicates the country with the highest political instability. Somewhat surprisingly, the United States is ranked 110th on this index, suggesting that the U.S. government is relatively vulnerable to economic distress and unrest caused by social protests.

Intellectual Property Rights

In general, Australia's intellectual property laws are very strong. The ranking on international property rights provided by the Property Rights Alliance organization puts Australia at 12th place among the 130 countries covered by the ranking. For comparison, the United States is ranked 18th.

Table 6.3 presents the scores for the Politics dimension, and Table 6.4 presents the strengths and weakness on the Politics dimension.

Infrastructure

Like with many countries, Australia's economic growth has stressed the country's infrastructure. The transport infrastructure is showing signs of strain with traffic congestion growing in the four major cities of Melbourne, Sydney, Perth, and Brisbane. Although the extent of congestion pales in comparison with congestion experienced in many developing countries, the problem is relatively high for a developed country. In 2010, the online journal thenewcityjournal.net reported that a one-way trip to work in Sydney

Table 6.3 Scores for the Politics Dimension

Politics	Ease of Doing Business	Legal Framework	Political Stability	Intellectual Property Rights	Overall Grade
20%	30%	30%	25%	15%	100%
Australia	A	A	A⁻	A⁻	A

Table 6.4 Strengths and Weaknesses Summary: Politics Dimension

Grade	Strengths	Weaknesses
Australia: A	Ease of starting business high; low bureaucracy; low corruption; legal framework provides a salubrious environment for encouraging investment.	Relatively high tax rates.

takes more time on average than the corresponding trip in all but one of 52 metropolitan areas in the United States with a population of 1 million or more.ʄ The only U.S. city that took more time was New York City, presumably because many commuters there use public transportation, an inherently slower method to get to work. A poll conducted by the National Roads and Motorists' Association (NRMA) showed that about 50 percent of businesses in Sydney have changed their operations to cope with traffic congestion.

Sydney's Kingsford Smith Airport typically experiences a lot of congestion, a problem that is expected to grow significantly by 2015. Infrastructure bottlenecks are emerging in some of Australia's major ports as well. The government is working hard to deliver both short- and long-term strategies to tackle the problem.

Transportation Infrastructure

The Logistics Performance Index (LPI) ranks Australia 19th on the infrastructure metric, which would give it a grade of A⁻. For comparison purposes, the United States is ranked 8th on this metric. Australia, however, receives a grade of B⁺ for the physical infrastructure variable, a notch below the LPI ranking on the infrastructure metric for two reasons, one of which is the large distances that have to be traveled to get from one location to another, which results in a relatively large carbon footprint. Traffic congestion in the major metropolitan cities is also a matter of concern.

Utility Infrastructure

Australia enjoys a stable electric supply with no major problems. The World Economic Forum Global Competitive Index (WEF GCI) ranks it 27th among 142 nations on the quality of electricity supply.

Telecommunications and Connectivity Infrastructure

As noted in Chapter 2, connectivity can be measured by the number of mobile phones and Internet users in the country, as well as by the per capita values for these numbers. Despite its small population, Australia ranks high in terms of the absolute numbers of mobile phones and Internet users. Australia, with about 25 million mobile phones, ranked 43rd in terms of the absolute number of mobile phones owned in a country, based on data from the 2011 CIA World Factbook. However, on a per capita basis, it places 79th with about 1.11 phones per capita. For purposes of comparison, the United States placed 118th on this metric with 0.93 mobile phones per capita.

The total number of Internet users and the Internet users on a per capita basis convey a similar picture. In 2011, the number of Internet users in Australia was 15.8 million, placing it 25th among 213 countries. The corresponding per capita number was 0.72, placing

---

ʄ http://www.thenewcityjournal.net/sydney_choking_in_its_own_density.htm.

Table 6.5 Scores for the Infrastructure Dimension

Infrastructure	Transportation Infrastructure	Utility Infrastructure	Telecommunications and Connectivity	Overall Grade
30%	50%	25%	25%	100%
Australia	B+	B+	B	B+

Table 6.6 Strengths and Weaknesses Summary: Infrastructure Dimension

Grade	Strengths	Weaknesses
Australia: B+	Road trains provide a more fuel-efficient mode of transportation compared to regular trucks; major reserves of natural gas; government committed to increase efficiency of energy generation and usage; connectivity is very good.	Large distances have to be covered to get from one metropolitan area to the next; world's worst emitter of carbon dioxide on a per capita basis.

it 31st among the 213 countries. For purposes of comparison, the United States placed 18th with a per capita number of 0.78. Table 6.5 presents the scores for the Infrastructure dimension, and Table 6.6 summarizes the strengths and weaknesses on the Infrastructure dimension.

Competence

Australia enjoys a multicultural, skilled, and creative population, with the know-how and technological ability to exploit its vast natural resources. It has a high-productivity economy, even though productivity growth has slowed over time. With respect to labor productivity, as measured by GDP per capita at purchasing power parity, Australia ranks 16th among 180 countries based on data compiled by the World Bank. However, Australia fares relatively poorly on productivity growth. An EIU study sponsored by the Australian Human Resources Institute placed Australia next to last among 51 countries included in the study, but the results announced in this report have been questioned in numerous discussions.

The CIA World Factbook provides data on productivity growth from one year to the next, based on which Australia, with a growth of 3.3 percent from 2011 to 2012, ranks 103rd among 217 countries. For comparison, the United States is ranked 138th with a productivity growth of 2.2 percent, and Singapore is ranked 140th with a productivity growth of 2.1 percent. This ranking can be questioned because some countries with a very low GDP show impressive productivity growth. For example, Sierra Leone places 2nd with a productivity growth of 21.3 percent, and Afghanistan places 6th with a productivity growth of 11 percent.

Labor Relations

On first glance, labor relations in Australia appear conducive to flexible and productive employment. Industrial disputes have, however, undercut the country's economic performance, and Australia has slipped in the rankings. Its rank on the labor–employer relations metric slumped from 39th in the 2011–2012 report to 67th in the 2012–2013 report. Between these two reports, Australia's rank on hiring and firing practices dropped from 97th to 120th, and its rank on pay and productivity dropped significantly from 40th to 80th. The WEF GCI report left Australia's overall competitiveness rating unchanged, but improvements in some areas were offset by the significant drop in the grade for the labor relations variable. In particular, restrictive labor regulations represented one of the principal problems in the report. Australia's grade for this variable is a C⁻.

Education Levels for Line Staff and Management

Australia scores high on the quality of its educational system and its management schools, but it does not score very high on the extent of staff training. Australia also scored very well on its reliance on professional management. Overall, it gets a grade of A⁻ on this variable.

Logistics Operational Competence

Australia is ranked 16th in the 2012 LPI logistics competence subindex, with a score 3.75, giving it a grade of A⁻. On the customs and security variable, Australia again ranks 16th and gets a grade of A⁻.

Table 6.7 presents the scores for the Competence dimension, and Table 6.8 summarizes the strengths and weaknesses on the Competence dimension.

Table 6.7 Scores for the Competence Dimension

Competence	Labor Relations	Education Levels	Logistics Competence	Customs and Security	Overall Grade
20%	25%	25%	40%	10%	100%
Australia	C⁻	A⁻	A⁻	A⁻	B⁺

Table 6.8 Strengths and Weaknesses Summary: 3-dimension

Grade	Strengths	Weaknesses
Australia: B⁺	Skilled English-speaking workforce; enjoys a competent logistics support system; absence of bureaucracy and corruption allows for efficient customs clearance and security.	Labor relations appear to be relatively poor and in danger of worsening.

Table 6.9 Summary Assessment of EPIC Attractiveness for Australia

	Economy	Politics	Infrastructure	Competence	Overall Grade
Australia	B+	A	B+	B+	B+

Table 6.9 summarizes the assessment scores on the Economic, Politics, Infrastructure, and Competence (EPIC) dimensions for Australia.

Key Takeaways for Australia

1. Australia enjoys a number of attributes that make it an attractive destination for FDI. It has vast mineral resources, a skilled workforce, and a sound legal framework.

2. Australia is a geographically isolated country. The city of Perth in western Australia is one of the world's three most remote cities with a population greater than 1 million.

3. Even though it is geographically isolated from almost every developed nation, its proximity to Asia—the continent that is becoming the economic powerhouse—presents an excellent opportunity for it to continue supporting the Asian economy.

4. The rise of Asia presents significant opportunities for reducing the remoteness. Australia has rapidly transitioned from a country that initially tried to align itself politically and economically with its colonizer, the United Kingdom. It is now more aligned with the Asian countries. According to the BBC news website,[g] Australia's politicians at first looked to Europe and the United Stated in foreign policy, but in the past 20 years or so they have made East Asia the priority, in particular Indonesia and China.

5. Australia enjoys vast mineral wealth. It is the world's leading producer of bauxite and iron ore. Australia is also among the top five countries in the world on the production of alumina, lead, manganese, coal, gold, silver, nickel, tin, zinc, and uranium.

6. The Economist Intelligence Unit notes that as a result of the small domestic market, FDI has traditionally focused on the services sector and primary-commodity industries. However, as one of the world's richest countries in income per capita, Australia is well positioned to attract FDI in the manufacturing sector as well.

7. Even though Australia is well positioned for growth, it faces some infrastructural challenges. One infrastructural challenge is the large distances that have to be traveled to get from one location to another, which results in a relatively large carbon footprint. Traffic congestion in the major metropolitan cities is also a matter of concern.

8. Although the rail system forms a critical part of the transportation network, Australia relies heavily on road transport for its freight due to historical reasons. With increased

[g] http://www.bbc.co.uk/news/world-asia-15674351.

growth in interstate trade, roadways are increasingly being used for a range of freight tasks. Combined with easier regulations governing road freight carriage, *road trains* now present a compelling transportation alternative to the railroad industry.

9. The Politics dimension is one of Australia's major strengths. Australia has one of the most transparent and efficient regulatory environments in the world. It also ranks very high on the political stability variable.

10. On first glance, labor relations in Australia appear conducive to flexible and productive employment. However, industrial disputes have undercut the country's economic performance, and Australia has slipped in the rankings on this variable.

References

1. J. P. Sigmond, and L. H. Zuiderbaan, *Dutch Discoveries of Australia* (Australia: Rigby Ltd, 1979), pp. 19–30.

2. Geoscience Australia, *Australia's Identified Mineral Resources 2011* (Canberra: Geoscience Australia, 2012). www.ga.gov.au.

3. "Australia in the Asian Century," White paper, Australian Government, October 2012. http://asiancentury.dpmc.gov.au/white-paper.

4. Ibid.

CHAPTER 7

The Middle East and North Africa

Throughout history, the Middle East and North Africa region (MENA) has been a strategic, economic, political, cultural, and religious center of the world, owing in part to its location at the north-south and east-west junctures of Asia, Africa, and Europe. The region is positioned at the confluence of the major waterways along whose banks early civilizations grew, including the Mediterranean, the Nile, the Tigris and Euphrates, the Persian Gulf, the Arabian Sea, and the Indian Ocean. In addition to waterways, the Spice Road was used to move highly valued spices, minerals, and other valued goods from Asia through the Middle East into Europe since before the Christian era, sparking both economic integration and cultural and political development that continued into the modern age.

Given this access to land and water trade routes, it is not surprising that the region has long been regarded as a crossroads of commerce. The historical importance of the area as a crossroads of trade continues today as the Suez Canal provides a function similar to that of the Spice Road for a broad array of goods. Infrastructural investment in nations throughout the region seeks to leverage this unique geographic positioning. From a supply chain perspective, MENA deserves attention due to its vast supplies of energy resources, but perhaps is equally important as a developing consumer marketplace and its aforementioned positioning astride major global trade routes that provide great potential as an intermediate trade hub that is very well suited to serve markets in Europe, China, and Africa. Figure 7.1 provides a map of the region.

MENA'S three distinct regions include the *Maghreb*, "the nations of the west" (Morocco, Algeria, and Tunisia), the *Levant*, "the rising" (Egypt, Lebanon, Syria, Jordan, Israel, Palestine, Cyprus, Hatay Province, some parts of southern Turkey, some regions of Iraq, and the Sinai Peninsula), and the *Arabian Peninsula* (Kuwait, Bahrain, Qatar, United Arab Emirates, Oman, Yemen, and Saudi Arabia). Iran is often included as part of the

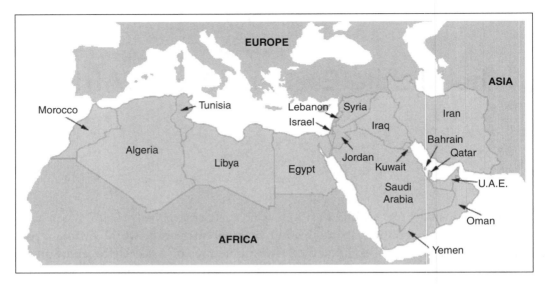

Figure 7.1 Middle East and North Africa region.

region although its Persian roots make it distinctly different from the rest of the region, tied mainly by its Islamic heritage. Given the current state of global relations with Iran, this book will not focus on supply chain opportunities in that country but rather will focus on key nations in the Maghreb, the Levant, and the Arabian Peninsula.

Although there are both significant similarities and significant differences between MENA's nations, the local geography helps to explain why MENA and its three distinct regions have come to exist. The Sahara Desert physically separates the North African nations from the rest of Africa, leading to the creation of stronger cultural ties between the North African and Middle Eastern nations than with the nations of sub-Saharan Africa (Figure 7.2). From a cultural standpoint, this regional grouping of nations has a clear Islamic influence that serves to create a significant cultural, although not always political, unifying force across MENA's nations and peoples.

In fact, MENA represents, perhaps, one of the two least economically and politically cohesive regions of the world. Of course, this lack of cohesion has negative implications for market integration, intraregional trade, financial flows, and standardized legal systems governing finance, technology, and taxes.[1] The region clearly remains in political transition. Not only does MENA have pressing social problems, it is situated in a region of the world that is associated with great political and economic risk, which hampers trade not only with other regions of the globe but also between nations within the region.

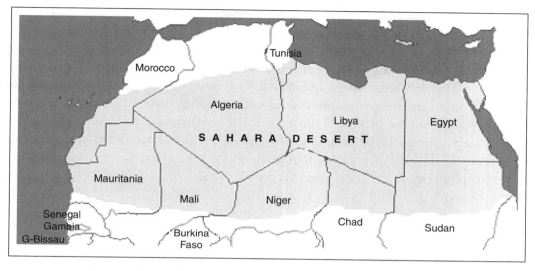

Figure 7.2 The Sahara Desert: A defining characteristic of MENA.

Economic and Political Background

Understanding the Region

Throughout history, the various regions of MENA have, at times, been unified under a variety of conquering civilizations. These conquerors started with the Neo-Assyrian Empire and were followed by a long line of other civilizations, including the Macedonian Empire under Alexander the Great, the Persian/Iranian empires, the Romans, and later the Byzantine Empire. The Arab Caliphates began a conquest of MENA in the 7th century AD that would, in some sense, unify the entire MENA region and create the dominant Islamic ethnic identity that largely permeates MENA today.

The modern MENA took shape after World War I. Having defeated the Ottoman Empire, the British partitioned MENA into a number of separate nations initially governed by the British and the French. Other defining moments in the modern transformation of MENA include the establishment of Israel in 1948 and the eventual departure of European powers by the end of the 1960s. Beginning in the early 20th century, MENA's significant stocks of crude oil put it back on the global economic and competitive landscape. Mass production of oil began around 1945, with the discovery of large oil reserves in Saudi Arabia, Iran, Kuwait, Iraq, and the United Arab Emirates (UAE). During the Cold War, MENA became a theater of ideological struggle between the Soviet Union (USSR) and the United States of America (USA). The USA (and North Atlantic Treaty Organization [NATO]) competed with the USSR (and Warsaw Pact) to influence MENA in an attempt to gain increased control of nearly two-thirds of the world's oil reserves. More recently, China has increased its influence in MENA, seeking to solidify the supply of petroleum necessary to fuel its substantial economic growth.

Economically, petroleum and petroleum-related products form the largest economic output of MENA and continue to be central to most of the economies of MENA. Israel is the notable exception, although the recent discovery of the large Leviathan natural gas field off Israel's coast may change that. Oil and natural gas exports dominate the balance sheets in Saudi Arabia and the UAE, in particular, but also are dominant in Algeria, Egypt, and other MENA countries. The economic dependency on global petroleum prices creates some economic fluctuation across MENA, although the general trend of increasing energy prices has given rise to favorable economic growth rates.

Politics

MENA's constituent nations are bound together by a very loosely shared political, socioeconomic, and cultural viewpoint that is rather distinct from other regions within the international system. The broadest MENA regional grouping of nations provides some benefits in terms of gaining an improved understanding of the region. However, this broad grouping only provides limited value in that it represents one of the least "regionalized" parts of the world. Certainly this is the case when considering the economic and political dimensions that affect market integration, intraregional trade and financial flows, and standardized legal systems governing finance, technology, and taxes.[2]

The political and economic backgrounds of the MENA nations are very diverse. Politically, the nations of the region range from presidential republics in Algeria and Egypt, a parliamentary democracy in Israel, to a Saudi Arabian monarchy that draws its institutional, legal, and political motivation and legitimacy from Islamic Shari'a Law, to the loosely federated sheikhdoms of the United Arab Emirates. The often violent upheavals experienced in Tunisia, Libya, Egypt, and Syria have had a dramatically destabilizing effect on the political environment of the Maghreb and the Levant, with the resulting forms of government in those nations still largely undetermined as of this writing. There is significant diversity in the political and economic background among the MENA nations, but the countries within each of the three distinct subregions identified earlier are relatively more homogenous along these dimensions.

The Algerian system of law is a mix of French civil and Islamic law. Algeria is a presidential republic, with the president serving as the head of state and the prime minister serving as the head of government. The Constitution of the Arab Republic of Egypt was adopted in 1971 and has its roots in English Common Law and the Napoleonic Code. The Egyptian head of state is the president, who is appointed by at least one-third of the Majlils ash-Sha'ab (the People's Assembly), approved by at least two-thirds, and elected by a popular referendum. The president serves a six-year term and may be reelected for subsequent terms.

The system of government in Israel is a parliamentary democracy. The prime minister is the head of government. Israel does not have a written constitution. The government of Saudi Arabia is a monarchy based on Islam and Islamic Law (Shari'ah). The king heads the government and appoints a crown prince to help in the administration of the nation. The government of the United Arab Emirates is a constitutional federation that is led by an elected president.[3]

Despite its wealth, the uncertainty emerging from political transition, pressing social demands, and an adverse external environment creates continued risk of political and economic instability in MENA. This has limited the industrial growth in the region in general, resulting in the need to import most manufactured goods from other regions. Further details on the political environment in MENA nations is provided in the Economy, Politics, Infrastructure, and Competence (EPIC) section.

The Economies

Algeria has varied natural resources. The coastal region features fertile plains and valleys that support the profitable growth of cereals, wine, olives, and fruit. The remainder of the nation supports very little agriculture, although grazing and forestry produce a small income in the mountainous region, and dates are cultivated in the oases of the Sahara. Mineral resources, in particular petroleum and natural gas, are abundant in the central and south, far from urban areas and infrastructure.[4] This location makes it difficult to supply food and other supplies needed to support operations. From a supply chain perspective, the northern coastal cities are accessible by ocean, but the bulk of the geography of the nation is difficult to reach.

Egypt's economy has been substantially influenced by its political circumstances since the 1950s. In particular, its relationship with Israel has had major repercussions on the nature of public expenditure and foreign aid, and the orientation of domestic policy has shifted from state socialism toward a market economy. Significant constraints on economic development have resulted from rapid population growth, a shortage of arable land for agriculture, and lack of water for irrigation.[5]

Israel has a technologically advanced market economy that features strong exports of cut diamonds, high-technology equipment, and agricultural products; Israel imports crude oil, raw materials, and military equipment. Israel frequently posts sizeable trade deficits, which are covered by tourism and other service exports, as well as significant foreign investment inflows. The Israeli economy has recovered better from the global recession than most advanced, comparably sized economies. Significant discoveries of natural gas fields off Israel's coast in 2010 are a positive factor for Israel's economic future. From a supply chain perspective, Israel is easily accessible through the major Mediterranean ports of Haifa and Tel Aviv, through the Red Sea/Gulf of Aqaba at Eilat, and through its land transportation infrastructure, which provides good connectivity to all population centers.

The economy of Saudi Arabia, the largest of the Arab nations, constitutes the power-house of the Arabian/Persian Gulf economy. It is a petroleum-dominated economy, and Saudi Arabia is by far the biggest producer within the Organization of the Petroleum Exporting Countries (OPEC).[a] Saudi Arabia has received massive revenue from petroleum exports (particularly since the dramatic increase in international petroleum prices in 1973–1974), some of which has been used to finance an ambitious program of infrastructural development and modernization, as well as far-reaching programs in the health, social, and educational sectors. From a supply chain perspective, Saudi Arabia is accessible by a number of ports on both the Persian Gulf and the Red Sea, and good highways and railways link the major population centers in the center and south of the nation. Significant infrastructure investment is under way to enhance the connectivity both within and across the nation.

Petroleum, the basis of the UAE's modern prosperity, was first discovered in 1958 beneath the coastal waters of Abu Dhabi. Onshore petroleum was found in Abu Dhabi in 1960, and commercial exploitation of petroleum began in 1962, providing the state with greatly increased revenue. The income from the petroleum industry was allocated for public works and the provision of welfare services. In 1966, petroleum was discovered in Dubai, which also underwent rapid development.[6] From a supply chain perspective, the UAE is a port nation with accessibility via the Persian Gulf and Arabian Sea; virtually all major population centers are on these two bodies of water.

The Markets

From a market perspective, MENA presents a compelling population demographic that resembles the high-growth populations of South and Southeast Asia. MENA has a substantial opportunity to improve education levels, employment levels, and health and gender parity of its population. In 2013, the MENA nation populations ranged from 0.8 million (Bahrain) to 83.7 million (Egypt). The two most populous nations in MENA (Iran and Egypt) have a population greater than those of Italy, the United Kingdom, and France. The youth dependency ratio (a ratio of the youngest to the oldest people living in a nation or region) is also very high in most of these nations, with the highest in the West Bank and Gaza and Yemen. The growth rates associated with the population and the labor force in these nations are much higher than the G8[b] average, with Qatar featuring the highest growth rates in both population and labor force over the last decade.[7]

Gender differences are substantial both in the structure of the population in MENA and in labor force participation rates and literacy rates. The country with the greatest

---

[a] The 12 member countries of OPEC include Algeria, Angola, Ecuador, Iran, Iraq, Kuwait, Libya, Nigeria, Qatar, Saudi Arabia, United Arab Emirates, and Venezuela.

[b] The Group of Eight (G8) is a forum for the governments of the world's eight wealthiest countries.

gap between male and female economic activity rates in 2010 was in Syria, followed closely by Saudi Arabia. MENA also features the highest youth unemployment rate in the world.

The effect of unemployment in some MENA nations, particularly in Egypt, Yemen, and Iran, is felt even more deeply due to very high rates of inflation. In MENA, life expectancy at birth is much lower than the G8 average due to relatively poor health conditions, with a substantial variance between MENA's constituent nations. For instance, very low life expectancy rates, high infant and child mortality rates, and poor health conditions characterize Djibouti, Egypt, Morocco, and Yemen, whereas Israel, UAE, and Qatar feature a relatively high quality of life.[8]

Location of Markets

This chapter focuses on five of the MENA nations: Algeria (*Maghreb*), Egypt and Israel (*Levant*), and Saudi Arabia and the United Arab Emirates (*Arabian/Persian Peninsula*). These five nations were chosen as they represent a cross section of the MENA subregions and feature among them the largest economy in MENA (Saudi Arabia), the largest population (Egypt), and the most stable government (Israel). For the remainder of this chapter the MENA abbreviation will be used to refer to these five nations. A summary of key demographic characteristics, including geography, population, and culture, and major metropolitan areas within each of the MENA nations follows.

Algeria

Algeria is the largest of the three nations in northwestern Africa that together comprise the *Maghreb* (the mountains, valleys, and plateau lying between the Mediterranean Sea and the Sahara Desert).[9] Algeria is situated between Morocco and Tunisia, with a Mediterranean coastline of nearly 1000 km (621 mi) and a total area of some 2,381,741 sq km (919,595 sq mi), over four-fifths of which lies south of the Maghreb and within the western Sahara (Figure 7.3). The vast majority of the 37.4 million Algerian residents live in the northern part of the nation, particularly along the Mediterranean coast, which is also home to the capital, Algiers, and the second and third largest cities, Oran and Constantine. The primacy rate (percent of the urban population living in a country's largest metropolitan area, providing an indicator of the concentration of industrial activity) for Algeria is 11,[10] and 66 percent of the population lives in urban areas of greater than 100,000 people. The rate of urbanization is increasing at 2.3 percent per year.[11]

The Algerian population is almost wholly Sunni Muslim (the state religion), with the vast majority of its citizens speaking Arabic and the remainder speaking Tamazight (the principal language of the Berber minority who were the original inhabitants of the Maghreb). Many Algerians also speak French. Ninety-nine percent of the population is of Arab-Berber descent, with the remaining 1 percent being of European descent.[12]

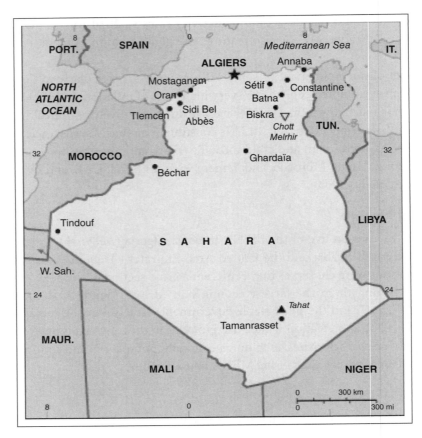

Figure 7.3 Algeria.

Egypt

The Arab Republic of Egypt occupies the northeastern corner of the African continent, with an extension across the Gulf of Suez into the Sinai region, which actually lies in Asia (Figure 7.4). Egypt comprises 1,009,450 sq km (389,751 sq mi), with only 5.5 percent of the country being permanently settled (or cultivated). The primacy rate for Egypt is 31 percent, and 43 percent of the population live in urban areas, a number that is increasing by 2.1 percent per year. Most of the population centers in Egypt are located in a narrow valley that is between 3 km (1.86 mi) and 115 km (71.5 mi) wide, through which the Nile River flows into the plateau of northeast Africa. The eastern border of the nation is formed by the Red Sea, which, together with the Suez Canal that connects the Red and Mediterranean seas, forms a critical part of the water route linking east-west and north-south global trade routes.

More than 90 percent of the Egyptian population (83.7 million) is Muslim, and most are of the Sunni sect. The remainder of the population of Egypt is largely Christian Copts (the Christians of Egypt). Arabic is the official language, although English and French are

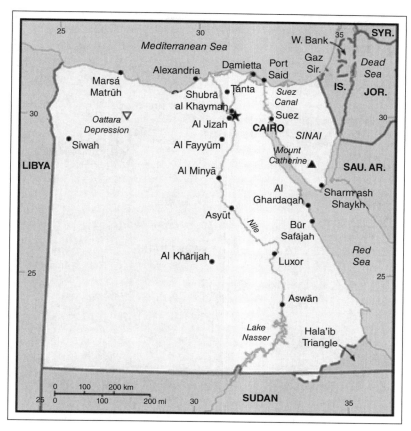

Figure 7.4 Egypt.

widely understood by the educated population. More than 90 percent of the nation is desert, and nearly 99 percent of the population lives in the valley and delta of the River Nile, most in the capital of Cairo. Ninety-nine percent of the population is of Egyptian, Bedouin, or Berber ethnicity, with Greek, Nubian, Armenian, and other European ethnicities (primarily Italian and French) comprising the remaining 1 percent.

Israel

The present State of Israel is bounded on the north by Lebanon, on the northeast by Syria, on the east by Jordan and the Palestinian Autonomous Area in the West Bank, and on the south and southwest by the Gulf of Aqaba and the Sinai Desert, occupied in 1967 and returned in April 1982 to Egyptian sovereignty (Figure 7.5). The Gaza Strip, a small piece of territory 40 km (25 mi) long, has been under the limited jurisdiction of the Palestinian (National) Authority (PA) since May 1994. The State of Israel has a population of approximately 7.6 million inhabitants, of which 75 percent are Jewish (32 percent European or American

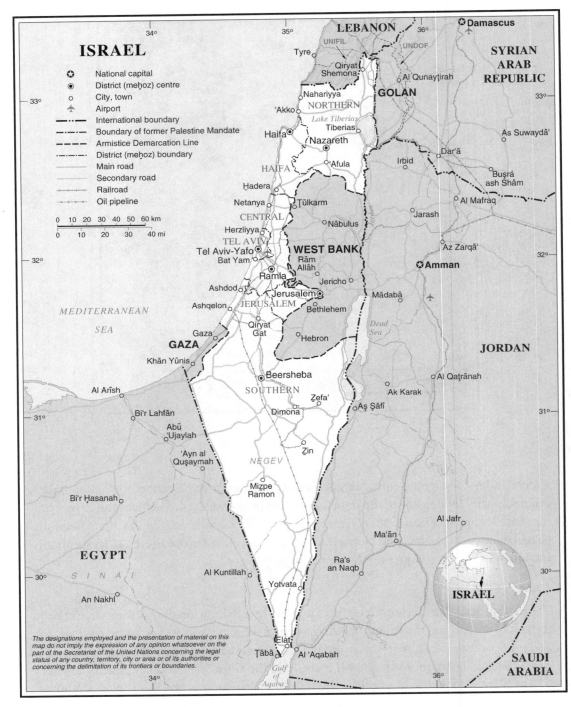

Figure 7.5 Israel.

born, 21 percent Israeli born, 15 percent African born, and 13 percent Asian born), 17 percent are Muslim, 2 percent are Christian, 1.6 percent are Druze, and the remaining 3.7 percent are classified as "others." Hebrew is the dominant language, followed by Arabic and English, which remains the first foreign language of many Israelis. The capital is Tel Aviv (Israel proclaimed Jerusalem as its capital in 1950, but this is not recognized under international law).[13] Forty-seven percent of Israelis live in Tel Aviv (the primacy rate), with 92 percent living in urban areas, increasing at a rate of 1.5 percent per year.

Saudi Arabia

The Arabian Peninsula is a distinct geographical unit, surrounded by water on three sides: on the east by the Persian (Arabian) Gulf and the Gulf of Oman, on the south by the Indian Ocean, and on the west by the Red Sea, and bordered in the north by the deserts of Jordan and Iraq (Figure 7.6). The Arabian/Persian Peninsula extends over 2.5 million sq km

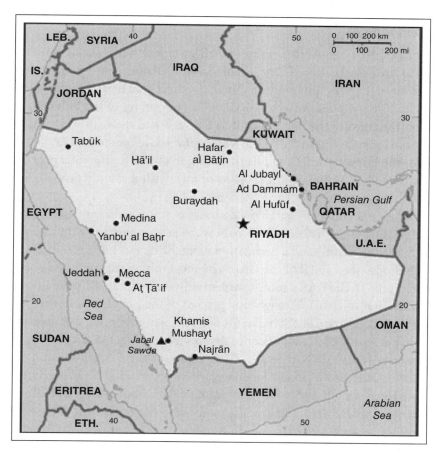

Figure 7.6 The Kingdom of Saudi Arabia.

(about 1 million sq mi), and is divided politically into several states. The largest of these is Saudi Arabia, which occupies 2,240,000 sq km (864,869 sq mi).

Nearly 85 percent of the 26.5 million inhabitants of Saudi Arabia belong to the Sunni sect of Islam, with most of the remaining 15 percent belonging to the Shi'ite sect of Islam. Nearly all the population speaks Arabic. The inhabitants of the center, north, and west parts of the nation are largely Mediterranean. There are two ethnically distinct regions within Saudi Arabia. One region includes a northern, central, and western area that is geographically arid and in isolation, with a relatively unmixed composition; the other area is found in the coastlands of the south, southwest, and east and hosts a multiethnic population. A recent result of the rapid economic growth in the petroleum-producing nations has been the influx of large numbers of expatriates from the developed nations of the world as well as laborers from the developing nations to the east. Twenty-one percent of Saudis live in Riyadh (the primacy rate), with a total of 82 percent living in urban areas, a number that is increasing at a rate of 2.2 percent per year.

United Arab Emirates

The coastline of the United Arab Emirates (UAE), a federation of seven emirates (states), extends along the eastern shore of the Arabian Peninsula for nearly 650 km (400 miles), from the frontier of the Sultanate of Oman to the Qatari peninsula in the Persian (Arabian) Gulf, interrupted only by an isolated outcropping of the Sultanate of Oman, which lies on the coast of the Persian Gulf to the west and the Gulf of Oman to the east at the Strait of Hormuz (Figure 7.7). The waters of the Gulf contain abundant quantities of fish, hence the importance of the role of fishing in local life. The total area of the UAE has been estimated at 77,700 sq km (30,000 sq mi), with a rapidly growing population totaling 5,474,000 in 2013.

The population is concentrated in the emirates of Abu Dhabi and Dubai, the principal commercial regions of the nation. Abu Dhabi is the largest emirate, with an area of about 67,350 sq km (26,004 sq mi) and a population of an estimated 1,967,659 in 2010. The city of Abu Dhabi is also the capital of the UAE. The most important city is the port of Dubai, which is the capital of the UAE's second largest emirate (with an estimated population of 1,905,476 at the end of 2010). Twenty-four percent of the population of the UAE lives in Dubai, with a total of 84 percent living in urban areas, a number that is increasing at a rate of 2.3 percent per year. Dubai's significance derives from the fact that it has one of the very few deepwater ports in MENA. In the UAE, many of the 5.3 million inhabitants are nomadic Arabs. Arabic is the official language, with Persian, English, Hindi, and Urdu also being spoken. Interestingly, non-Arab immigrant workers outnumber Arabs. In the coastal towns, there are many Iranians, Indians, Pakistanis, and Africans. Most of the native inhabitants are Muslims, mainly of the Sunni sect. As compared to Saudi Arabia, 96 percent of the people living in the UAE are Shi'ite Muslims.

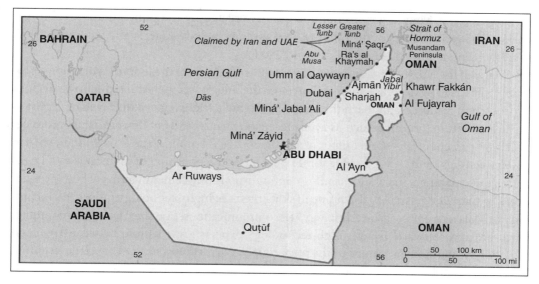

Figure 7.7 United Arab Emirates.

Assessing the Maturity Level of MENA Supply Chains

This section assesses the supply chain maturity of the five selected countries in MENA using the EPIC dimensions presented in detail in Chapter 2.

Economy

An assessment of key elements of the Economy dimension follows, including economic output and growth rate, population, foreign direct investment, exchange rate stability and consumer price inflation, and balance of trade. A summary of Economy elements for each of the focal nations of MENA is provided at the end of the section.

Economic Output and Growth Rate

Accounting for approximately 4 percent of the global GDP (purchasing power parity [PPP], 2011), MENA captures the attention of the world as the largest single global exporter of petroleum resources. For businesses seeking new consumer markets, the MENA region presents significant demographic interest due to its young and growing population. The GDP (PPP, 2011) of MENA varies from a low of US$216.2 billion in Israel to a high of US$686.2 billion in Saudi Arabia. MENA has continued to grow over the past five years, despite a very challenging global economic environment, achieving real growth in excess of 4 percent across MENA, led by Saudi Arabia, whose growth rate of 6.8 percent is substantially higher than the rest of the region. Egypt lagged the region with a growth rate of 1.8 percent, owing largely to the uncertainty created by the political upheaval in the nation. The growth rates of the other MENA nations include Algeria at 2.5 percent, Israel at 4.7 percent, and the UAE at 4.9 percent (2011).

Many of the MENA nations have attempted to diversify their economies into nonpetroleum industries to decrease their reliance on the energy sector. Israel, due to its lack of hydrocarbon resources, has been the leader in this area, featuring healthy levels of export in niche agricultural products such as avocados, exotic fruits, and cut flowers. Israel produces nearly 80 percent of the world output of small polished diamonds (those most often used in jewelry settings) and is responsible for 40 percent of the polishing of diamonds of all sizes and shapes, making it the world's leading diamond-polishing center in terms of both production and marketing. Israel is also home to skill-intensive high-technology industries, including medical electronics, agro-technology, telecommunications, fine chemicals,[c] and computer hardware and software. Israeli's high-technology exports grew tenfold between 1990 and 2010. Given the historic nature of the area, tourism contributes to the economic health of Israel but has not reached its potential due to the security concerns that dominate MENA.

Egypt has also attempted to diversify beyond hydrocarbon exports, growing telecommunications from near nonexistence to one of Egypt's fastest growing and larger economic sectors over the last 10 years. The telecommunication sector continues to grow, with the mobile sector providing the fastest rate of growth. The Internet market also continues to grow, but the infrastructure capacity combined with lower literacy levels tends to dampen expansion in this sector. Construction, steel, and tourism are other featured growth areas in the Egyptian economy, but the uncertainty of the political environment clouds near-term growth prospects.

Saudi Arabia has capitalized on its reserves of oil and gas, having developed a large petrochemical industry. Saudi oil production has largely been focused on methanol and ethylene, and the industry is largely managed by joint ventures between Saudi government firms and major international firms. As home to the holiest sites of Islam, Saudi Arabia hosts millions of religious pilgrims every year, generating significant economic value for the nation.

Besides petroleum production, the UAE is also investing heavily in tourism, which is generally centered in Abu Dhabi and Dubai. In addition, the UAE banking sector is one of the largest compared with other sectors in MENA. It is expected that the UAE will gradually open its banking sector to greater foreign competition in the coming years, but the government has presented no official timeframe for such regulatory change.

Algeria lags the other nations in terms of economic diversification. Agriculture is the largest employer after the oil sector, with 8 percent of total GDP output. Key agricultural products include wheat, barley, oats, grapes, olives, citrus fruits, sheep, and cattle. Light manufacturing and food processing are also present.

---

[c] Fine chemicals are complex, single, pure chemical substances. They are produced in limited volumes (< 1000 tons/year) and at relatively high prices (> $10/kg) according to exacting specifications, mainly by traditional organic synthesis in multipurpose plants.

Population

The MENA region represents 5.5 percent of the global population. Egypt's population of 83.7 million is the largest in MENA, followed by Algeria with 37.4 million, Saudi Arabia with 26.5 million, Israel with 7.6 million, and the UAE with 5.3 million. MENA has one of the youngest populations in the world, especially when compared to mature markets in North America and Europe. The median age in UAE is 20.2 years; Israelis represent the oldest population of the focal group with a median age of 29.5. Overall, the MENA population is growing at a rate of more than 4 percent per year. Of the five focal MENA nations, the UAE leads population growth with a growth rate of 3.01 percent per year (10th fastest in the world); Saudi Arabia, with the slowest growth of the five, maintains a population growth rate of 1.52 percent per year.

Foreign Direct Investment

Over the past decade, MENA nations have found it difficult to attract foreign direct investment (FDI), in large part due to the substantial unrest and political discord in the region, which often leads to outright armed conflict. Further aggravating the FDI inflow is a general tendency among MENA countries toward restrictive investment and ownership policies. Saudi Arabia and Israel lead the group in access to FDI. In Saudi Arabia this is in large part due to the prevalence of the hydrocarbon industry, aided by the recent relaxation of ownership laws in Saudi Arabia. FDI is attracted to Israel largely due to the open and democratic investment and ownership laws. The UAE has recently reformed its ownership laws, allowing foreign ownership in specific commercial zones. These reforms were enacted with the goal of increasing future access to FDI. On the other end of the FDI inflow spectrum, most investors fled Egypt, awaiting some sense of political stability, and Algeria has traditionally received relatively little FDI outside the energy sector.

Exchange Rate Stability and Consumer Price Inflation

Exchange rate stability varies widely across the MENA nations. The currencies of Saudi Arabia (riyal) and the UAE (dirham) are either directly or indirectly pegged to the US dollar, ensuring relative stability and helping those nations to control their money supply. Most currencies are allowed to float freely, providing heightened flexibility against the wild swings associated with volatile commodity prices. The Israeli shekel floats freely against other major currencies, with a strong balance-of-payments position and low market risk that results from its close association with the United States helping to prevent any currency crisis. The Egyptian pound also floats freely and has seen a recent slide against the dollar due to the nation's weakening economic prospects linked to sustained political volatility. The Algerian dinar is measured against a basket of euro and US dollars, balanced such that imports are cheap enough for the non–oil sector.

Inflation is a major problem for some nations in MENA, with Egypt experiencing inflation levels in excess of 10 percent as demand for food and energy have spiked relative to supply during its political crisis. Inflation in Algeria climbed to an annual average rate of 4.5 percent in 2011 due to increases in the food and housing components of the consumer price index and higher global commodity prices. Inflation in Israel was 3.5 percent in 2011 as housing prices surged, exposing banks to considerable risk in the housing and construction sectors, although it has stabilized at below 2% in 2012 and 2013. Saudi Arabia's level of inflation receded to 5.0 percent, down from 5.4 percent in 2010. This decrease was largely due to cost pressure in the food and housing sectors. The UAE enjoys the lowest inflation rate in MENA at 0.9 percent, which reflects a very healthy impact of lower commodity prices, a stronger dollar, and helpful real estate market value corrections.

Balance of Trade

Many of the MENA nations maintain positive trade balances, mainly as a result of their strong price position in the global energy market. Algeria, Saudi Arabia, and the UAE enjoy positive balances of trade, and as a result also enjoy strong government account balances. Saudi Arabia leads in this category, with a $245 billion positive trade balance in 2011 and $97 billion government budget surplus, followed by the UAE with $26 billion in trade and $2 billion in government surplus. Algeria has a positive trade balance of $73 billion, but a government deficit of $8 billion. This reflects the nation's larger population and the relative lack of capitalization to support that larger population, which then requires Algeria to seek higher levels of imports. Israel has a $9 billion negative trade balance and a $7 billion government deficit, reflecting the nation's lack of petroleum and mineral reserves and the subsequent need to import raw materials. Egypt lags behind the group with a $20 billion trade imbalance and a $50 billion government deficit.

Interestingly, trade among the MENA nations is relatively weak, with trade focused outside the region predominantly occurring with Europe, the USA, Russia, China, and India. Algeria's main trade partner is the European Union (EU); Egypt has various trade agreements, although the USA and Europe are their top trading partners, followed by growing trade with China. Israel's regional political situation tends to force it to predominantly trade with the USA and the EU. Although the USA is the largest Saudi trade partner, Japan is the largest buyer of Saudi oil, followed closely by China. Japan and India are the most important buyers of UAE oil. Such dependence on extraregional trade mandates the need for good sea and airport infrastructure. The notable exception to intraregion trade is the Gulf Cooperation Council (GCC), which includes the UAE, Saudi Arabia, Kuwait, Qatar, Oman, and Bahrain. The goal of the GCC is to serve as a common market by the end of 2014. Trade within the GCC is growing and represents the main source of non–oil trade for the UAE. Table 7.1 presents the scores for the Economy dimension for each of the focal nations of MENA and a summary of the strengths and weaknesses is shown in Table 7.2.

Table 7.1 Scores for the Economy Dimension

Economy	Economic Output and Growth Rate	Population Size	Foreign Direct Investment	Exchange Rate Stability/CPI	Balance of Trade	Overall Grade
30%	35%	25%	20%	15%	5%	100%
Algeria	B⁻	A⁻	C⁺	B⁻	C	B⁻
Egypt	A⁻	A	B⁻	B	C	B⁺
Israel	B	B⁻	B	A	A	B
Saudi Arabia	B	B⁺	A	A⁻	B	B⁺
UAE	B	C⁺	B	A	A	B

Table 7.2 Strengths and Weaknesses Summary: Economy Dimension

Grade	Strengths	Weaknesses
Algeria: B⁻	Young and growing population; strong demand for oil and gas; overall economic growth and positive trade balance; stable exchange rates.	FDI only evident in the energy sector; ownership laws are restrictive; inflation is high; government operates on a deficit; lack of diversification in the economy; not a member of the WTO.
Egypt: B⁺	Young and growing population; relatively large and diverse economy; positive trade balance and budget surplus.	Weak economic growth; political turmoil; decreasing economic growth in tourism; decreasing FDI; weak currency and high inflation.
Israel: B	Highly diversified economy; stable government; good investment and ownership laws; strong currency; low inflation; substantial FDI.	Small population; poor in natural resources.
Saudi Arabia: B⁺	Substantial petroleum reserves; strong economic growth; diversified economy with growth in tourism; positive trade balance; government budget surplus; member of the Gulf Cooperation Council.	Restrictive FDI laws; moderate inflation; lack of diversification in economic sectors.
United Arab Emirates: B	Young and growing population; relatively open economy; large banking sector; trade surplus; open ownership in free trade zones; strong FDI; stable exchange rates; low rates of inflation; government budget surplus.	Lack of diversification in economy; small population.

Politics

An assessment of key elements of the Politics dimension follows, including the ease of doing business, bureaucracy and corruption, legal and regulatory framework (including tax codes and tariffs), political stability, and protection of intellectual property rights. A summary of the Politics elements for each of the focal nations of MENA is presented at the end of the section.

Ease of Doing Business, Bureaucracy, and Corruption

Ranking 12th out of 183 nations, Saudi Arabia leads MENA in ease of doing business.[14] It is, for instance, relatively easy in Saudi Arabia to register property, pay taxes, start a business, and conduct trade across borders. Saudi Arabia has also made significant improvements regarding the protection of investors; for instance, it only takes three procedures and five days to start a business in Saudi Arabia as compared to the MENA average of five procedures and eight days.

Corruption is present in Saudi Arabia (63rd out of 180 nations,[15] and in the 48th percentile on control of corruption).[16] Corruption frequently arises from the fact that entire economic sectors are governed by members of the royal family and their partners (who are essentially above the law). Public procurement is an area that has been particularly affected by corruption because vested interests among individual family members is high and bribes are common. Anticorruption legislation was enacted in 2004, which has helped to dampen the effects of corruption on the practice of business in Saudi Arabia.

The UAE also provides a good environment for business, ranking 33rd out of 183.[17] By MENA standards, the business climate in the UAE is generally effective and mostly transparent (ranked 28th of 183 nations[18] and 82nd percentile on control of corruption[19]), particularly for businesses operating in the various free trade zones where special bylaws govern business activities and provide investment incentives that exempt enterprises from the constraints of federal commercial law and also allow 100 percent foreign ownership. Although oil wealth supports a high standard of living for Emirati nationals, which has a dampening effect on the economic incentive for corruption, a number of recent high-profile corruption and embezzlement cases among senior Emiratis in major domestic and government-owned firms have highlighted the existence of corruption.

Israel's business climate is regarded as relatively transparent and free of corruption, scoring well in various independent corruption indices, including a ranking in the 73rd percentile on control of corruption.[20] It ranked 34th on the World Bank Ease of Doing Business Index, with strengths in administration, but weaknesses in other areas such as obtaining permits for construction and electricity. In addition, enforcing a contract in Israel can be time consuming and expensive. Bureaucracy can be cumbersome, despite government reforms. It has been suggested that regulations are not always applied consistently in a number of areas and that the state run Israeli Investment Center, responsible for encouraging the development of industry and tourism, has rejected some applications for investment incentive grants in favor of less deserving applications. Sweeping reform of the bureaucracy is planned, but progress on this front has been slow.

Both Egypt and Algeria are difficult places to conduct business. Egypt ranked 110th out of 183 nations on the World Bank survey, receiving especially low scores on the broad topic of business administration. One of the biggest deterrents to conducting business in Egypt remains the large number of bureaucratic hurdles that must be cleared. The bureaucracy suffers from overstaffing and underemployment, a lack of funding and equipment, corruption, inefficiency, and frequently outdated methods. The concern over corruption is reflected in a score of 112 out of 183 on the Corruption Perception Index in 2011, and a rank of 28th percentile in the control of corruption on the World Governance Indicator (WGI) index. Algeria, ranking 148th out of the 183 nations in the World Bank Ease of Doing Business Index, suffers from widespread corruption and a business climate that is more hostile than in the rest of MENA. According to the Corruption Perceptions Index 2011 report, Algeria ranked 112th out of 183 nations (falling from 105th in 2010) and the 35th percentile in control of corruption on the WGI index. Algeria's judiciary is vulnerable to political interference and corruption, and the protection of property rights remains weak, undermining sustainable economic development.

Legal and Regulatory Framework: Tax Codes and Tariffs

The legal systems across the MENA region vary greatly from the Maghreb through the Levant and into the Arabian Peninsula, reflecting the varied histories and institutions from which those nations emerged. As a result, navigating business operations across MENA is a complex task that should not be taken lightly. Israel is an exception to this rule, regarded as having excellent legal and regulatory quality, dependence upon the rule of law, and governmental effectiveness. The Israeli legal system is an independent mechanism within the government, with written and consistent application of commercial law, and is based on the British Companies Act of 1948. Israel's commercial law contains standard provisions for governing company bankruptcy and liquidation. The Israeli government accepts binding international arbitration of investment disputes between foreign investors and the state. The Israeli tax system, however, can be complicated and expensive, although efforts are under way to simplify the system and also to lower tax rates. The corporate income tax rate has fallen from 29 percent in 2008 to 25 percent in 2010, with a plan for further reduction to 18 percent by 2016.

Saudi Arabia is an absolute monarchy with most senior government posts filled by members of the royal family. The legal system is based on Islamic Shari'a law and technically there is no constitution except for the Koran, reflecting the nation's role as "keeper of the shrines" of Mecca and Medina. Legal representation occurs through personal petitions to royal figures, and royal audiences are common. Traditionally, Saudi Arabia has been averse to the codification of laws. However, the nation's rapid economic development and acceptance into the World Trade Organization (WTO) in 2005 required an increase in the number of written regulations, especially in the commercial sphere, which has begun to bring the Saudi legal system more in line with WTO requirements. The lack of a written legal code remains a problem in transparency, and investors find that different government ministries can be unhelpful when project approval is being sought. In addition to its complexity, foreign firms find that nationals are generally given preferential treatment over foreigners. There is no personal income tax and no value-added tax (VAT). Corporate income tax is currently 20 percent, but gas and oil companies can be taxed upward of 85 percent, and labor taxes and contributions are low compared to Organization for Economic Co-Operation and Development (OECD)[21] nations.

As a federation of seven emirates, the UAE has a two-tier legal system: the first tier consists of the federal government, and the second consists of the Emirates' governments. The Emirati legal system is complicated by the fact that Islamic Shari'a courts exist alongside civil courts. Some legal issues are also decided on a regional basis, in line with the Gulf Cooperation Council (GCC). At present, customs regulations are being harmonized with other GCC member states following the creation of the GCC Customs Union in 2003. The total tax rate of the UAE was 14.1 percent of profits. However, the corporate tax rates are set by each of the seven emirates and taxes are typically only levied on foreign oil companies and banks. Under current business law, foreigners can hold a maximum of 49 percent ownership of companies outside the free zones where 100 percent ownership is permitted. The UAE Land Law restricts foreigners, both individual and corporate, from owning land. Only Emirati nationals may own land, although variations do occur between emirates, with Dubai leading the way toward allowing foreign interests to own land.

Until 2011, Egypt's legal system was dominated by the personality of President Hosni Mubarak, who was strongly supported by a corporatist elite of military, bureaucratic, and economic interests. Democratic institutions existed, such as the People's Assembly, but had limited power. Incidents of violence and fraud often surrounded elections, which were frequently boycotted by opposition parties and invariably returned overwhelming majorities for establishment candidates. As a consequence, the president's National Democratic Party (NDP) dominated parliament, providing very strong support for the government. The ultimate nature of the system that will result from the recent overthrow and subsequent democratic elections has yet to be seen. When allowed to function freely, Egypt does have one of the most highly developed legal systems in MENA. Its legal system is based on British Common Law, as well as aspects of both the French and Ottoman systems. A rapid increase in cases and legislation, combined with a shortage of judges and a general lack of resources, has mired the courts in delays and inefficiency. The laws governing foreign involvement in the Egyptian economy have been steadily reformed in recent years to open up the economy to outside investors. The environment is currently one of the most liberal in MENA, allowing 100 percent ownership by a foreign company and full repatriation of profits. Egypt also employs 41 industrial zones that provide tax breaks, and eight free trade Special Economic Zones (SEZs) that provide further incentives for export-oriented manufacturing by exempting investors from all income taxes and other direct taxes.

The president is a very important and central figure in the Algerian political system. However, the institutional role of the military is strong, and the head of state relies on the military's support to remain in his post, particularly since the Algerian Civil War in 1992. A bicameral[d] legislature was established under the 1996 revisions to the constitution. Algerian law is based on French and Islamic legal traditions, and legal proceedings are carried out in Arabic. Despite considerable bureaucracy within the system, Algeria is well served by a base of professional lawyers and legal officials, many of whom have studied and worked in France. However, the government is believed to influence the outcome of cases put before military courts. An experienced local lawyer is essential for a foreign company seeking to navigate Algeria's commercial laws and regulations. The system has also been criticized for being too sluggish with respect to the resolution of commercial issues, generally owing to a shortage of judges trained in commercial dispute matters. Algerian law provides incentives for direct investors and gives equal treatment to foreign and domestic investors. The effective corporate tax rate is 25 percent.

Political Stability

The MENA region features varying levels of stability and risk of political systems within the member nations. The Economist Intelligence Unit Country Risk Rating (EIU CRR) ranked Algeria as 61st out of 165 nations (where lower numbers indicate increased risk), with significant risk to political instability ranking (EIU CRR). Egypt was also considered to have significant political instability risk (EIU CRR) and ranked 106th out of 165 nations (EIU CRR). Israel, Saudi Arabia, and the United Arab Emirates were all considered to have medium risk, with EIU CRR country rankings of 99th (Israel), 83rd (Saudi Arabia), and 142nd (United Arab Emirates).

Intellectual Property Rights

The UAE is a regional leader in protecting intellectual property rights and is a member of the World Intellectual Property Organization (WIPO).[e] The emirate of Dubai has been particularly effective at fighting piracy. Intellectual property is also well protected in Israel, in keeping with a system that places a high value on property rights, although enforcement

---

[d] Bicameralism is an essential and defining feature of the classical notion of mixed government. Bicameral legislatures tend to require a concurrent majority to pass legislation.

[e] IHS Global Insight. The World Intellectual Property Organization (WIPO) is the United Nations agency dedicated to the use of intellectual property (patents, copyright, trademarks, designs, etc.) as a means of stimulating innovation and creativity.

of property rights laws is a weakness. Saudi Arabia is a member of the WIPO and has ratified the Paris Convention for the Protection of Industrial Property. Over the past decade, strides have been made to bring intellectual property rights in line with WTO standards. A Trademark Law was adopted in 2002, a Copyright Law in 2003, and a Patent Law in 2004. Although the authorities have stepped up efforts to tackle piracy, violations continue

Table 7.3 Scores for the Politics Dimension

Politics	Ease of Doing Business	Legal Framework	Political Stability	Intellectual Property Rights	Overall Grade
20%	30%	30%	25%	15%	100%
Algeria	D	D	C⁻	D⁻	D
Egypt	C⁻	C	B⁻	C	C
Israel	B⁺	B⁺	B⁻	B⁺	B⁺
Saudi Arabia	B⁺	C⁺	C	B⁺	B⁻
UAE	A⁻	B⁻	A⁻	B⁺	B⁺

Table 7.4 Strengths and Weaknesses Summary: Politics Dimension

Grade	Strengths	Weaknesses
Algeria: D	Open FDI laws; protection of intellectual property.	Widespread corruption; high levels of bureaucracy; sluggish legal system; high tax rates; unstable political system.
Egypt: C	Well-developed legal system; stronger FDI and tax laws; free trade zones.	Ineffective legal and regulatory system; unstable political environment; inadequate laws for protection of intellectual property.
Israel: B⁺	Transparent government and legal system; free of corruption; protection of intellectual property; low corporate tax rates.	Cumbersome bureaucracy; security/political risk.
Saudi Arabia: B⁻	Low corporate tax rates; ease of doing business; favorable FDI; improving protection of intellectual property.	Corruption; difficult to navigate legal system; political instability.
United Arab Emirates: B⁺	Ease of doing business; foreign trade zone; low corruption levels; low corporate tax rates; stable political system; strong protection of intellectual property.	Complex legal system; restrictive ownership laws.

to take place. Algeria has established the strongest protection of intellectual property rights among North African nations, although there are still reports of trademark counterfeiting and serious copyright infringement. The enforcement of intellectual property rights in Egypt is inadequate, but the regime improved in 2001 and 2002 with the passage of legislation bringing Egyptian law into 99 percent compliance, according to local officials, with the WTO's Trade-Related Aspects of Intellectual Property Rights (TRIPS)[f] principles. Table 7.3 presents the scores for the Politics dimension for each of the focal nations of MENA and a summary of the strengths and weaknesses is shown in Table 7.4.

Infrastructure

An assessment of key elements of the Infrastructure dimension follows, including transportation, utilities, and telecommunications. A summary of Infrastructure elements for each of the focal nations of MENA is provided at the end of the section.

Transportation

Algeria's roads are hazardous, suffering from underinvestment and maintenance that is well below standard. The nation has a total of 107,000 km (66,486 mi) of roads, of which around 72 percent are surfaced (including 640 km [398 mi] of expressways). All of these roads require massive investment to bring them up to industrial world standards. Major infrastructure programs are being implemented with the aim of improving traffic flow by reducing transportation costs, travel time, and road accidents. These programs include the 1216 km (756 mi) long east-west Mediterranean highway, which is near completion and links all of Algeria's major cities. Rail infrastructure is operated by the state-owned National Company for Rail Transport (Société Nationale des Transports Ferroviaires, or SNTF). The network primarily consists of two standard gauge coastal lines running east and west from Algiers and is 3973 km (2469 mi) in length. Extensive modernization is planned, including electrification of much of the line.

The Algerian seaport system, with 13 major container ports and two hydrocarbon terminals, has seen notable expansion. The most important port is at Algiers, which now handles 60 percent of the nation's external trade. Dubai-based DP World, one of the world's leading marine terminal companies, operates the Ports of Algiers and Djen Djen under a concession granted to a joint venture with the Algerian government. The company's priorities have been to reduce congestion and administrative port delays that have in the past seriously impeded Algeria's competitiveness. Djen Djen is positioned to become a main hub for eastern Algeria, as well as a major transshipment hub for the wider western

---

[f] The WTO's Agreement on Trade-Related Aspects of Intellectual Property Rights (TRIPS), negotiated in the 1986–1994 Uruguay Round, introduced intellectual property rules into the multilateral trading system for the first time.

Mediterranean area. There are 12 international airports, with the major airports located at Algiers, Oran, Annaba, and Constantine. A number of foreign airlines have begun offering scheduled services to Algeria, possibly as the result of decreasing levels of violence since the Algerian Civil War.

Egypt's infrastructure is well developed in comparison to its neighbors. The Egyptian government of Hosni Mubarak planned to invest billions of dollars in transport infrastructure to meet the demands of its growing economy and the creation of an operational environment conducive to private enterprise and foreign investment. Following the January 2011 uprising, however, the new administration has prioritized constitutional and economic reforms over transportation reforms. Despite this, there is an improved framework for foreign companies to bid for projects in Egypt, following the approval in 2010 of a new private–public partnership law. Egypt has invested considerably in the road network in recent years, although poor driving standards continue to prove hazardous. Plans to construct a new 900 km (559 mi) highway linking Egypt with Libya to the west and Israel and the Gaza Strip to the east are likely to be delayed as a consequence of national and regional political turmoil. Egypt has an extensive rail network (5015 km, 3116 mi), but the state of the nation's railways has come under increasing scrutiny following a number of train accidents that resulted in high numbers of casualties. Egypt has seaports on both the Mediterranean and the Red Sea at Alexandria, Port Said, Suez, Safaga, Marse Matruh, Damiette, and Ein al-Sokhna. State-of-the-art facilities are being built in some ports, including materials handling equipment upgrades. However, operations are still hindered by slow bureaucratic procedures, security measures, and inefficient operators, which include both public handling companies and small private sector companies. Egypt has 13 major airports, most of which provide adequate cargo handling capabilities.

The Suez Canal is the distinguishing characteristic of Egyptian transportation infrastructure and provides the nation with a commercial advantage. The canal, opened in 1869, connects the Mediterranean Sea with the Red Sea, allowing transportation by water between Europe and Asia without navigation around Africa. The northern terminus is Port Said, and the southern terminus is Port Tawfiq in the city of Suez. The canal is owned and maintained by the Suez Canal Authority of Egypt. Under international treaty, it may be used in both war and peace time by every vessel of commerce or of war without distinction of flag.[8]

Israel has an advanced infrastructure with comprehensive transportation and communication systems in place. The main roads are good, with most road signs displayed in English. Delays are frequent at the Rafah border crossing from the Gaza Strip into Egypt, and the security situation remains precarious. Travel to Amman (Jordan) is generally undertaken via the King Hussein (Allenby) Bridge or the Sheikh Hussein (Jordan River)

---

[8] Constantinople Convention of the Suez Canal of March 2, 1888.

Bridge further to the north. Israel has a small rail network that runs between Tel Aviv and Haifa, with one daily train running between Haifa and Jerusalem. The railway is undergoing a wide-ranging and comprehensive upgrade program that will see many of the lines electrified, the reopening of formerly closed lines, the construction of new lines, and the replacement of old rolling stock. A light railway project that will pass through Jaffa and Tel Aviv is planned for completion in 2017. A similar system began service in Jerusalem in late 2011. Israel's main seaports are located at Haifa, Eilat (Red Sea), and Ashdod, and a ferry service runs from Haifa to Greece, usually via Crete or Cyprus. The main airport is Ben Gurion International, situated 20 km (12.4 mi) from Tel Aviv. The national airline is El Al Israel. There are internal flights from Jerusalem, Tel Aviv, Haifa, Rosh Pina, and Eilat.

The transportation infrastructure in Saudi Arabia has improved significantly as a result of considerable investment, and the government is expected to continue to channel resources to it to keep up with rapid population growth. A good road system connects most towns, with the Trans-Arabian Highway linking the major cities of Dammam, Riyadh, Jeddah, Mecca, and Medina. In total, there are approximately 220,000 km (136,702 mi) of roads with 47,000 km (29,205 mi) being paved. There is also a causeway that links the kingdom with Bahrain. Saudi Railways Organization (SRO), a state-owned but independent public utility, operates about 1380 km (857 mi) of railroad network consisting of two main lines including a 450 km (280 mi) passenger line linking Dammam, Abqaiq, Hofuf, and Riyadh, and a 556 km (345 mi) freight line linking Dammam, Abqaiq, Hofuf, Haradh, Al Kharj, and Riyadh. There are also 373 km (232 mi) of branch lines that connect industrial and agricultural production sites with export ports. Extensions of rail lines are planned to connect the Riyadh refinery on the east coast to Jubail, and another track will link Saudi's east and west coasts. In addition, plans have moved forward to begin a Mecca-Medina railway that will significantly reduce travel time between the two holy cities. There are 21 modern ports in Saudi Arabia, with Jeddah, Dammam, Jizan, Al-Jubayl, and Yanbu representing the nation's main commercial ports. Ports are under the control of the Saudi Ports Authority, but all terminals are managed and operated by the private sector. Given Saudi Arabia's geography, air travel is the quickest way to link urban centers, and a growing number of airports offer local flight services. There are four main international airports, located in Jeddah, Riyadh, Dammam, and Medina. The airport at Medina is being expanded, with completion expected by the end of 2019.

The transportation infrastructure in the UAE is generally very good, and the government is continuing to invest in development projects to further increase the capacity of upstream activities in the petrochemicals sector, improve infrastructure in airports and ports, and develop new manufacturing plants in the metals sector. The road network links all cities via high-quality dual highways. Roads in the poorer northern emirates are of lower quality the further they are from urban areas. There are few public transportation services, but this has been designated as an area for expansion and investment.

Dubai's metro system was partially inaugurated in September 2009. In March 2009, the Ministerial Council for Services[h] endorsed a draft law for the creation of a government-owned rail company. This federal company is expected to facilitate the building of a national rail system that will eventually link the nation to a Gulf Cooperation Council-wide network. A monorail in Abu Dhabi is targeted for a 2015 completion date. Most of the emirates have well-equipped ports, with the largest being Port Rashed in Dubai. In combination with Jebel Ali, Port Rashed makes Dubai the 12th largest container-handling port authority in the world. The UAE currently has seven international airports, including Dubai's new Al Makhtum International Airport. Major investment continues to be made in existing airport infrastructure.

Utilities

The electricity infrastructure in Algeria is well developed, with 90 percent of the nation connected to the electrical distribution network, which has a capacity of nearly 5000 megawatts. Nearly 150,000 new homes are connected each year as rural electrification is completed. The World Bank has also helped Algeria develop its water supply and sewage-rehabilitation services. Due to recent major discoveries, natural gas is likely to be the primary growth engine of Egypt's energy sector for the foreseeable future. Egypt's estimated proven gas reserves stand at 2.2 trillion cubic meters, and the nation produced 56.9 million tons of oil equivalent in 2011. State-owned and regulated companies provide good energy services in Israel, with the entire nation on the electrical distribution network. Although the Israeli government favors privatization of the energy sector, it will likely remain nationalized for reasons of national security. One of Israel's major strategic concerns stems from the lack of an in-country source of energy; Israel has relied on Egypt for 40 percent of its natural gas needs. At this writing, however, this linkage is in jeopardy as the Egyptian partner in the joint venture that operated the pipeline threatened to terminate the contract. Discovery of huge natural gas reserves off the Israeli coast promises to dramatically change the energy situation in Israel, making it energy independent in the near future. Complications due to the fractious nature of relations between nations in the Levant, however, could slow progress.

---

[h] The Ministerial Council for Services was established in 2006 under the chairmanship of Sheikh/Mansour Bin Zayed Al Nahyan, Deputy Prime Minister and Minister of Presidential Affairs and member of the membership of ministers of service ministries. The council is to serve as an executive council for the cabinet. It follows up performance of the federal government authorities when implementing the general policy of the UAE government. It also studies reports on the business conduct of federal ministries and authorities and presents suitable solutions for improving the level of government services provided to UAE nationals, especially related to health, education, housing, roads, means of transportation, water, and electricity. Moreover, it takes the necessary action on the implementation process and progress.

Saudi Arabia faces a key challenge in improving utilities that are greatly strained due to high government subsidies and inadequate waste management. Electricity demand is growing at a rate of 5.5 percent per year, requiring extensive investment in new capacity, but subsidized prices have starved Saudi electric companies of investment capital. Domestic funding is being channeled into new power generation projects, but the Saudi government is also intent on increasing independent power projects. Shortages do occur, particularly in the hot summer months. The UAE faces a similar challenge, with demand for power rising at 10 percent annually, requiring substantial investment to raise capacity. The government has added electricity-generating capacity at an annual rate of 24 percent over the last 30 years and is planning to add a number of further projects. High water consumption is being met by increasing desalinization rates. Both the water and electricity sectors are heavily subsidized. In addition, the UAE is nearing completion of an oil pipeline through the mountainous sheikdom of Fujairah that will allow the bulk of its oil exports to be rerouted around the Strait of Hormuz, which Iran has repeatedly threatened to close.

Telecommunications

Algeria has a national information and communications technology (ICT) policy that aims to provide e-government and e-business solutions and nearly 300 online services for Internet users. Household Internet penetration rates remain among the lowest in MENA, however, with only 21.8 percent of households possessing an Internet-enabled computer in 2011. Alternatively, by 2011, 96.9 percent of households and 34.8 million subscribers possessed a mobile telephone, with the total number of mobile subscriptions increasing by 66.1 percent over the previous five years. The ICT industry is one of Egypt's fastest developing sectors, becoming the main target of the privatization program launched in 2004 that witnessed the opening of the mobile phone sector with operators Mobinil and Vodafone Egypt, which were joined by the UAE operator Emirates Telecommunications Corporation (Etisalat) in 2007. The liberalization of the mobile sector has not reached the fixed-line sector, which is completely monopolized by the state-owned Telecom Egypt. However, Egypt's National Telecommunications Regulatory Authority (NTRA) has recently opened telephone, Internet, and cable TV services to private licensing arrangements.

There are more than 3 million fixed telephone lines in Israel with an average 3 to 4 percent annual growth in services. The cellular market is highly competitive and has overtaken the fixed market in terms of subscribership. There are more than 40 Internet service providers (ISPs), with growth supported by a highly literate and technologically aware population. Broadband access is available from the former state operator Bezeq and cable operator HOT. The Saudi Arabian ICT sector is well developed, with 10 million Internet access users registered (32.1 Internet users for every 100 people), and 40.2 million mobile phone users. At the same time, the conservative Saudi government has attempted to ban and limit technologies such as camera phones. There are around 4 million fixed-line telephones in the nation.

The UAE has invested heavily in ICT infrastructure to attract foreign businesses and also as a means to diversify the economy. As a result, it is considered among the leading areas for ICT in the world. The primary provider, Etisalat, has created a modern and efficient telecom system and has established itself as a leader in the international telecommunications market. A second fixed-line operator, EITC ('du'), was licensed in February 2006 and is providing bundled packages that include broadband, TV, and fixed lines. The emirates had 1.46 million fixed lines in operation at the end of 2010 and 10.9 million mobile users. Table 7.5 presents the scores for the Infrastructure dimension for each of the focal nations of MENA and a summary of the strengths and weaknesses is shown in Table 7.6.

Table 7.5 Scores for the Infrastructure Dimension

Infrastructure	Transportation Infrastructure	Energy Infrastructure	Connectivity	Overall Grade
30%	50%	25%	25%	100%
Algeria	D⁺	C	C⁻	C⁻
Egypt	C	C	C	C
Israel	B⁻	B	B⁺	B
Saudi Arabia	B⁺	A⁻	B⁺	B⁺
UAE	A	A⁻	A⁻	A

Table 7.6 Strengths and Weaknesses Summary: Infrastructure Dimension

Grade	Strengths	Weaknesses
Algeria: C⁻	Adequate rail coverage; improving sea and airport capability; power distribution; water and sewage improving.	Hazardous roads; poor telecommunications capability.
Egypt: C	Extensive rail and road network; well-equipped sea and airports; Suez Canal; improving telecommunications; adequate power distribution.	Road and rail network aging and in need of repair; seaports hampered by inefficient and corrupt processes.
Israel: B	Advanced infrastructure; comprehensive transportation; excellent telecommunications; efficient sea and airports; adequate power distribution; discovery of large natural gas reserves.	Underdeveloped rail with improvements planned; current power generation dependent on imported oil (largely from Egypt).
Saudi Arabia: B⁺	Improving infrastructure with significant investment; good road connectivity between major cities and villages; rail is improving; seaports are modern and efficient; good and expanding air service.	Telecommunications services growth hampered by government restrictions; demand for electricity outstrips supply with shortages in the summer.

(continued)

Table 7.6 Strengths and Weaknesses Summary: Infrastructure Dimension (*Continued*)

Grade	Strengths	Weaknesses
United Arab Emirates: A	Well-developed infrastructure; good road connectivity between cities; well-equipped and efficient seaports; modern air facilities with continued investment; modern and efficient telecommunications; expanding water and power distribution infrastructure.	Minimal rail infrastructure.

Competence

An assessment of key elements of the Competence dimension follows, including labor availability, productivity, and relations; education for line staff and management; and logistics, customs, and security. A summary of Competence elements for each of the focal nations of MENA is provided at the end of the section.

Labor: Availability, Productivity, and Relations

Many of the nations in the MENA region (Israel is the notable exception) feature relatively low overall rates of labor participation due to low female participation. For example, in 2009 females accounted for only 16.2 percent of the total economically active population in Saudi Arabia and 25.5 percent of the total economically active population in Egypt. This feature biases most labor availability and productivity statistics in MENA.

Algeria has a youthful population, with more than 70 percent of workers under the age of 30, but suffers from a high rate of unemployment. As a result, labor is relatively inexpensive although the government retains tight control on salaries and minimum wages. The number of skilled and semiskilled workers is relatively low and will remain so until education levels and worker training improves. There are growing concerns that current skilled laborers do not have the skills necessary to meet the changing demands of the labor market. Partnerships between businesses and higher educational establishments have been introduced to address the skills shortfall, but the success of these programs has not been quantified. Labor productivity in Algeria is improving from its lowest levels during the Great Recession of 2007. It currently has the highest labor productivity in North Africa but is significantly behind the nations of the Saudi Peninsula. It is the lowest of the five MENA nations assessed here. Labor relations can be difficult in Algeria as the opening of the political system in the late 1980s led to an explosion of union activity. Dismissal of employees is often a costly affair that can take a substantial amount of time and is normally only possible when there has been a serious violation of an employee's contract. Dismissed employees can also bring their case to a labor tribunal.

Egypt's labor force has expanded at a rapid rate and ranks among the youngest in MENA. Rapid population growth and high rates of unemployment have continued to plague Egypt during the economic slump that followed the recent political upheaval. The majority of Egyptian workers are unskilled, with 32.1 percent of the population employed in the agriculture sector. Productivity in Egypt increased during the 21st century, but it is still among the lowest in MENA (surpassing only Algeria). The National Council for Wages[i] determines Egypt's minimum wage for both the government and private sector. Labor relations within the private sector are generally good, and workers are allowed to form trade unions, provided 50 employees in an enterprise wish to do so. All unions must belong to the Egyptian Trade Union Federation, which is the only legally recognized trade union and is closely tied to the government.

The Israeli workforce is made up of approximately 3 million people, with unemployment falling to 5 percent in 2011, largely improving as a direct result of a period of rapid economic growth. Israel's labor force is highly skilled and well educated, with particular strengths in the sciences, fueled by the rapid growth of Israel's high-tech industries during the 1990s. Labor productivity in Israel is by far the highest in MENA, approximating levels found in the developed nations of the OECD.[22] Organized labor has a strong history in Israel; unions are represented in almost all commercial and industrial enterprises. The main labor union federation, the Histadrut,[j] has maintained a powerful position since its inception in 1920 as a trade union body organizing the economic activities of Jewish workers. The Histadrut organizes approximately one-third of the Israeli workforce and is one of the largest employers in Israel.

Saudi Arabia relies heavily on foreign workers for manual and unskilled jobs as well as for a range of professional positions despite the fact that there is a large pool of unemployed nationals. Many Saudis do not have the educational background necessary to prepare them with the skills and knowledge that would enable them to be competitive for private sector jobs. The government has launched a program that seeks to reduce unemployment through a combination of tax cuts, subsidized pay, and other incentives and regulations designed to ensure that private firms hire a quota of Saudi nationals. Productivity levels in Saudi Arabia are the highest among the four Islamic nations in the MENA assessment, but lag Israel. Trade unions, strikes, and collective bargaining are banned, although a regional collective of taxi drivers has existed for several years and professional associations grouping computer experts, economists, and engineers also exist.

---

[i] The Egyptian National Council for Wages was formed to determine minimum wages at a level reflective of the cost of living and to balance between salaries and prices. The Council of Wages has set minimum annual raises at no less than 7 percent of an employee's base salary.

[j] The General Federation of Laborers in the Land of Israel (known as the Histadrut) is Israel's organization of trade unions. Established in December 1920 during the British Mandate for Palestine, it became one of the most powerful institutions of the State of Israel.

The UAE's labor market is highly flexible and dynamic, although more than 80 percent of the labor force is comprised of foreign workers, with foreign nationals holding 98 percent of private sector jobs. More than 60 percent of the workforce is employed in the burgeoning services sector, with around 30 percent in industry and only 6 percent in agriculture. With the indigenous population growing and an increasing number of national university graduates seeking employment, the government has stressed the need to provide job opportunities for its citizens. A new Emirates program requires specific sectors of the economy to employ a certain number of Emirati nationals. Nationals have traditionally worked in the public sector, where they are afforded large salaries by the Emirates' massive oil wealth. As the federal and Emirati governments prepare to diversify the nation's economy away from oil reliance, efforts to increase the participation of citizens in the private sector will continue. Still, the nation's dependence on expatriate workers is so extensive that the fundamental labor force structure is unlikely to change significantly in the near term.

Although among the highest in MENA, labor productivity in the UAE has been decreasing and is lower than that of Saudi Arabia. The fall in worker productivity has been attributed to the growth in construction that typically has lower levels of productivity compared to other sectors in the economy. Trade unions are banned, but the government has indicated that it may draft new regulations to recognize the rights of workers and allow collective bargaining.

Education Levels for Line Staff and Management

Algeria's adult literacy rate stood at 77.9 percent of the population over age 15 in 2011. Although literacy rates have risen since 2006, they still remain marginally lower than the MENA average. In real terms, government expenditure on education grew by 73 percent between 2006 and 2011. Unfortunately, many educated young people with a chance to emigrate to Europe or elsewhere often do so in order to seek opportunities outside of Algeria, thereby depriving the nation of a wider talent pool. The Algerian government continues to encourage foreign investors to recruit locally and to set up training programs. It is not uncommon for Western companies to recruit former Algerian émigrés who received a Western education for key roles in business in the country. Arabic is the official language of the nation, with French being the second language of many Algerians, although English is now beginning to overtake French.

Skills shortages are a persistent problem in Egypt, and public sector companies are routinely forced to recruit labor from overseas. Adult literacy is an added problem for foreign companies as only about 70 percent of the population above the age of 15 is literate. Government expenditure on education, in real terms, has steadily decreased over the last 10 years, although the number of Egyptians attending university has increased over that time. Despite the fact that many university graduates are bilingual, there remains a shortage of talent in the fields of management and information technology, necessitating the need for additional training.

Israel has a robust and well-supported education system with education being compulsory for 11 years and free for all children between 5 and 15 years of age. A high level of education is visible in the very high adult literacy rate, which stood at 96.8 percent in 2009. The workforce features one of the world's highest percentages of engineers and scientists, pushing Israel into the forefront of the high-tech industry and attracting many multinational high-tech firms. More than 30 percent of university students specialize in areas with high industrial research and development potential.

The Saudi government spends a high portion of its GDP on education, and nearly 90 percent of the population over the age of 15 is literate. The topical focus of education, however, tends to be on religious subjects at the expense of more applied areas (business, engineering, medicine, etc.), resulting in large numbers of Saudi students who enter the workforce with educational qualifications for which there are very few jobs. This has made it difficult for private sector businesses to employ nationals. The government is pushing gradual educational reform and boosting spending on programs to address the situation.

Literacy rates in the UAE are high, with more than 90 percent of the population over 15 (both male and female) literate thanks to state efforts dedicated to raising literacy rates. In addition, English is widely spoken in the business community and in the national and expatriate workforce. The government has been steadily increasing the amount of money spent on higher education, paying particular attention to scientific research and scholarships for UAE nationals. As a result, the number of students in higher education has increased significantly over the last decade. Despite progress, however, the UAE still suffers skill shortages in a number of sectors that include aviation, nuclear technology, banking, and information technology. In Dubai, the emirate with the largest population, 42 percent of university students studied business and 19 percent studied society, law, and religion. In contrast, only 9 percent of students in Dubai took courses in engineering, and 6 percent took courses in information technology in 2010. To improve these numbers, Dubai has set up free zones where higher education institutions from other nations can set up schools. The free zone schools also attract foreign students to Dubai, making up 57 percent of students in 2010.

Logistics, Customs, and Security

Algeria has the weakest logistics infrastructure in MENA according to the World Bank Logistics Performance Index (LPI) rankings from 2012. LPI ranked Algeria in the 45th percentile at 125 out of 155 nations that were ranked. Algeria scored relatively higher in the categories of timeliness and international shipments, although there was significant weakness in the areas of infrastructure, customs, and logistics competence. Despite this weakness, global logistics providers have indicated a willingness to continue to invest in the nation. Although the government is attempting to rid the customs system of corruption, customs officials have been reported to demand bribes to accelerate customs clearance for goods waiting in ports. In addition to these concerns, Algeria is considered a high risk for operations and security disruptions according the Economist Intelligence Unit's[23] Nation Risk Rating (CRR) for 2012.

Egypt's logistics competence is regarded as being significantly better than Algeria, with a ranking of 57th in the world and in the 63rd percentile. In particular, Egypt earns high scores in timeliness, infrastructure, and international shipments. Like Algeria, customs is a concern in Egypt, and businesses experience significant delays in clearing goods through the system. Moves have been made to simplify the system and to reduce the number of tariff bands, but the situation still proves frustrating. Customs duties are also extremely high. Modern customs centers are being established at Egypt's major ports, streamlining procedures between customs, port authorities, and freight forwarders. However, corruption is endemic throughout Egypt and is a major hindrance when importing or exporting goods, and the operational and security risk is considered significant. Despite these challenges, logistics professionals believe that Egypt continues to be an attractive business destination.

Israel did not participate in the 2012 World Bank LPI survey, but assessments are available from the 2010 LPI survey. In the 2010 assessment, Israel was ranked 31st in the world, scoring at the 77th percentile, with strengths in logistics competence and infrastructure; customs was considered a relative weakness, although scores were better than those for both Egypt and Algeria. EIU considers the risk to operations in Israel as moderate, although security risks are high.

Saudi Arabia was ranked 37th in the world, better than 70 percent of other nations ranked, on the overall LPI, with strong scores on timeliness, infrastructure, and tracking and tracing. Logistics competence and customs were considered weaknesses. The impressive performance of Saudi industries and their strong expansion plans, despite the global economic downturn, have opened up several prospects for logistics industry companies. An influx of global logistics companies is expected to facilitate the movement of a broad range of products as foreign firms expand their geographical reach and capture the highly lucrative Saudi Arabian consumer market. Since joining the WTO, Saudi Arabia has increasingly liberalized its customs policies, reducing tariffs and barriers to trade. More than 600 products, including some foodstuffs and basic goods, are duty free. Nontariff barriers to trade can be high, however. Problematic aspects include lack of transparency and lack of consistency in implementing regulations, and operational and security risks are considered significant.

The UAE received the highest LPI scores of all MENA nations, with an overall ranking of 17 (89th percentile). Timeliness, tracking and tracing capabilities, and infrastructure were noted strengths. The UAE is considered a premier logistics hub for the MENA region owing to its strategic location between the Eastern and Western hemispheres. It features the best logistics infrastructure in MENA and enjoys one of the lowest average logistics costs in the world. Opportunity for logistics service providers involved in freight forwarding and shipping services are particularly good, attracting such global players as DHL and Agility to compete with regional firms such as Aramex, GAC Logistics, and Al-Futtaim Logistics.

Customs regulations are generally liberal. A 5 percent import duty is charged on all products imported into the nation, excluding the many free trade zone areas, where no import duty is levied; tobacco products and alcohol are subject to a 50 percent import duty. Although each of the emirates has separate customs authorities, a Federal Customs Authority was set up in 2003.

Table 7.7 presents the scores for the Competence dimension for each of the focal nations of MENA and a summary of their strengths and weaknesses is included in Table 7.8.

Table 7.7 Scores for the Competence Dimension

Competence	Labor Relations	Education Levels	Logistics Competence	Customs and Security	Overall Grade
20%	25%	25%	40%	10%	100%
Algeria	F	F	D	D$^+$	D$^-$
Egypt	D	F	B$^-$	C$^+$	C$^-$
Israel	B	B	B$^+$	B$^+$	B$^+$
Saudi Arabia	A$^-$	B	B$^+$	B	B$^+$
UAE	A	A$^-$	A$^-$	A$^-$	A

Table 7.8 Strengths and Weaknesses Summary: Competence Dimension

Grade	Strengths	Weaknesses
Algeria: D$^-$	Low labor costs with plentiful low-skilled labor; relatively productive labor force; education levels improving in engineering, manufacturing, and services.	Limited skilled labor availability; restrictive labor environment with strong unions; relatively low education rates; weak logistics industry; significant bureaucracy and corruption in customs and trade with high risk in operations and security.
Egypt: C$^-$	Young and expanding workforce; increasing labor productivity; good labor relations; increasing number of educated workers.	Poor labor availability for skilled workers; inflexible hiring and firing procedures; education levels and literacy rates lag MENA; logistics capabilities barely adequate; significant bureaucracy and corruption in customs and trade; significant risk in operations and security.

(continued)

Table 7.8   Strengths and Weaknesses Summary: Competence Dimension (*Continued*)

Grade	Strengths	Weaknesses
Israel: B+	Highly educated and skilled workforce; labor productivity high; labor relations good; highest rate of scientists and engineers in the world; strong education system; strong logistics industry capabilities; customs bureaucracy low with few corruption problems.	Moderate to high risk to operations and security.
Saudi Arabia: B⁺	Large number of expatriate workers from unskilled labor to professional; labor relations good; education and training availability strong; management and engineering competence relatively strong; adequate logistics industry capabilities; customs infrastructure efficient.	Inadequately educated local workforce is more costly to employ than foreign nationals; focus on religious education has left many without qualifications for workforce; logistics cost high; moderate to significant risk to operations and security.
United Arab Emirates: A	Flexible and dynamic labor market led by foreign nationals; skilled labor; labor productivity high; high literacy and English competency levels; heavy investment in education and training; most highly competent logistics industry in MENA; liberal customs policies and tariffs.	Inadequately educated local workforce; insufficient level of technical education; moderate operational and security risk.

Table 7.9 presents a summary of the overall assessment scores on the EPIC dimensions for the nations in the MENA region. The scores for the five MENA nations reveal a differing pace of economic development that holds significant implications for supply chain management decision makers. Specifically, the UAE, Saudi Arabia, and Israel have established relatively high levels of EPIC performance, making them more attractive for

Table 7.9   Summary Assessment of EPIC Attractiveness for the Nations Represented in the Middle East and North Africa (MENA)

	Economy	Politics	Infrastructure	Competence	Overall Grade
Algeria	B⁻	D	C⁻	D⁻	C⁻
Egypt	B⁺	C	C	C⁻	C⁺
Israel	B	B⁺	B	B⁺	B
Saudi Arabia	B⁺	B⁻	B⁺	B⁺	B⁺
United Arab Emirates	B	B⁺	A	A	B⁺

supply chain investments. Egypt remains risky but is clearly moving upward in its trajectory toward becoming a much more attractive opportunity for supply chain investment. Algeria, is improving but remains far more risky when compared to other countries in MENA.

Main Trends in MENA

The MENA nations once hosted the global centers from which many human advances in politics, economics, science, and culture emerged. After centuries of conquest and turmoil, MENA was largely relegated to the margins of the global economy. Recent trends, however, indicate that some nations in MENA are poised to return to an influential position in global commerce, extending beyond that afforded by petroleum.

MENA Returns to the Global Marketplace

With the discovery of vast petroleum reserves in the early 20th century, MENA returned to the global limelight, but only in relationship to the supply of these natural resources to the global marketplace. During this time, MENA struggled with economic and political institutions that were not ideal for the growing 20th century global marketplace. In many instances, the establishment of modern states along artificial borders that did not support national identity exacerbated these challenges. Add to this the two world wars that raged across MENA as Western powers competed for access to MENA petroleum reserves, and the rancor caused by the establishment of a Jewish homeland nestled between what would become hostile neighbors, and the recipe for one of the world's most violent regions was born. As a result, the last century witnessed a chaotic struggle among the MENA nations to establish stable states that are capable of supporting consistent economic development and growth.

Movement toward Political and Economic Stability

The early 21st century witnessed the ascendance of a number of these states, including the UAE and Saudi Arabia, which have been able to stabilize political and economic institutions well enough to translate petroleum wealth into economic and social development. In addition, Israel, with a largely transplanted citizenry well versed in Western political and economic institutions, has established an enviable environment for growth and development despite the dangers of living among well-armed and sometimes hostile neighbors. Egypt, with its geographic position astride the Suez Canal and its large population, also offers promise for a brighter economic future, but only when concerns over political turmoil ease.

Lack of Uniform Economic Development in MENA

Unfortunately, economic growth has not been uniform across MENA. Other than Israel, the nations of the Levant are still struggling to establish an economic and political environment that invites sustained growth and development. The Maghreb nations of North Africa (including Egypt) were not blessed with the same petroleum reserves as those on the Saudi Arabian Peninsula. Finally, the political and military turmoil in MENA continues. As this turmoil has raged across MENA from Iran to Tunisia, and promises to explode from Syria to other nations in the Levant, significant strides in broad-scale economic development are a nearly impossible goal in the near term.

Supply Chain Challenges

The MENA region presents considerable economic challenges to developing high performing supply chain operations. From restrictive policies toward foreign direct investment (FDI), to economies that are tied too closely to global petroleum markets, to the generally small percentage of the population that has sufficient earnings to participate in the consumer market, many of the nations of MENA present economic obstacles that make the likelihood of a return on supply chain investment marginal at best. Although there is no uniformity around how these challenges present themselves across MENA, each of the five MENA nations have characteristics that give pause to any consideration for supply chain investment, whether for sourcing (outside of the obvious attractiveness of MENA for petroleum products), manufacturing, or market distribution.

Economic Challenges

Algeria and Egypt present the greatest economic challenges of the five nations considered. Even the UAE and Saudi Arabia, which generally enjoy favorable economic conditions, suffer restrictive FDI regulations in several sectors, and contend with moderate inflation as trade balances and revenues are susceptible to global oil prices. In addition, the UAE population enjoys high per capita income but is very small and thus not a major market demand point. Israel, which is dramatically different from other nations in MENA (as evidenced by the EPIC scores) including in their economy, also has a very small population, few native raw materials, and suffers from the constant threat of violent conflict with its neighbors.

Political Environment

The political environment of MENA represents perhaps the single biggest challenge to supply chain operational investment. In general, sluggish, nontransparent, ineffective, and autocratic legal and regulatory systems spawn widespread corruption and high levels of bureaucracy. In addition, many of the nations do not provide adequate protection for intellectual property rights. These conditions often are exacerbated by perceived instability in political systems. Of the five MENA nations considered here, these challenges again are most pronounced in Algeria followed closely by Egypt. Saudi Arabia, Israel, and the UAE present a far better picture with respect to political challenges, but issues remain. In Saudi Arabia, corruption emerges from the heavy involvement of multiple levels of the royal family in contractual decisions, and navigating the legal framework can be challenging due to the lack of codified, written laws. Israel currently features a cumbersome bureaucracy that supports relatively high corporate tax rates, but this may change in the near future. In the UAE, the challenge lies in traversing the complex legal infrastructure between federal, emirate, and Shari'a law, any one of which may apply in a given situation.

Infrastructure

Challenges in MENA also emerge from the lack of a fully developed transportation, telecommunications, and utility infrastructure in most nations. In general, there are weak or nonexistent rail systems, and in some areas road networks remain in need of significant investment. The political vestige of corruption expresses itself strongly in global trade, impeding the performance of seaports and airports. Additionally, existing telecommunications and utility systems capabilities and capacity lag behind demand and population growth. This is particularly true in Algeria, which features a large population dispersed over a relatively large land mass. Egypt, Israel, Saudi Arabia, and the UAE have all largely succeeded in overcoming these shortcomings, but unique challenges in each nation remain.

Business Competence

Business competence in MENA is challenged by a limited availability of skilled labor, resulting from education levels that are low and education systems that are poor. In addition, managerial, technical, and engineering skills in general are lacking. Of the five MENA nations considered in this work, Algeria and Egypt again suffered most from these challenges. Saudi Arabia and the UAE have both been able to overcome many of these challenges by attracting a very large and skilled foreign expatriate workforce, but the basic set of MENA challenges remains for native Saudi Arabian and Emirati citizens. Israel stands out as the lone nation in the assessment that has largely overcome this challenge, boasting one of the most highly skilled and educated workforces in the world. The corruption and bureaucracy mentioned earlier also manifests itself in challenges to global trade due to the inefficiency and corruption that is prevalent in customs and trade regimes. Both Algeria and

Egypt have significant shortcomings in their logistics industries, although global logistics service providers consider both nations attractive areas for investment and growth.

A Summary of MENA Supply Chain Challenges[k]

▲ Risk of facility ownership due to restrictive FDI laws, operational and security risks, and political instability.

▲ Risk of rapid swings in buying power among relatively weak government and consuming classes.

▲ Bureaucracy and corruption slows cycle times and make regulatory compliance onerous, especially in customs and seaports.

▲ Confusing legal systems make transparency and clarity of interpretation of laws difficult.

▲ Talent management at both skilled labor and management/technology levels will be very challenging.

▲ Information connectivity capacity and capabilities are underdeveloped.

▲ Accessibility to stable power and water utilities may be limited.

▲ Transportation lead times, reliability, and cost will be problematic as road networks can be weak and rail networks are almost nonexistent.

▲ Intraregional trade is challenged by a lack of road and rail infrastructure connecting the nations.

Supply Chain Opportunities

Although the MENA region presents significant challenges to establishing and maintaining supply chain operations, a number of trends within MENA present opportunities. Of the five nations assessed here, the economic opportunities are most prominent in the UAE and Saudi Arabia, with Egypt and Algeria lagging behind. Israel presents a different case, with a technologically advanced market economy, strong FDI and currency/low inflation, and strong extraregional trade links.

Wealth and Balance of Trade

From an economic standpoint, many nations in MENA boast favorable trade balances and government account balances, creating a good environment for infrastructure investment and capitalization. The wealth accumulated from petroleum is also driving diversification into related industries such as chemicals.

---

[k] These issues are present across MENA. Of the five nations assessed here, the challenges will be most pronounced in Algeria and Egypt, whereas conditions in Saudi Arabia, Israel, and the UAE will be more easily overcome. Legal clarity, however, is most pronounced in Saudi Arabia and the UAE.

Young and Growing Population

Some of the most favorable findings for the MENA region can be found in the area of competence. The young, expanding labor force generates low labor costs across MENA, albeit with low but improving productivity rates. Labor relations across MENA are generally good, although this may be attributed to the lack of organized labor unions in much of MENA. The oil rich states of the Persian Gulf have benefited from attracting a large number of expatriate workers, many of whom are highly skilled, as well as managers, engineers, and technicians. In addition, the competency of the logistics service industry in the five nations assessed for this research, developed over the last century to service the oil industry, ranged from on par with the global average (Egypt and Algeria) to much better in the cases of the UAE, Saudi Arabia, and Israel. Again, Israel is an outlier; with its highly skilled and well-educated workforce, high productivity rates, and the highest level of scientists and engineers in the world, Israel sets itself apart from other nations in the MENA region.

Developing Intraregional Trade

The region is also working to enhance its interconnectedness to facilitate greater levels of intraregional trade. This is particularly true in the Persian Gulf regions where the Gulf Cooperation Council is making inroads toward creating an effective regional trade bloc.

Abundant Natural Resources

Finally, nations such as Algeria, Egypt, and Israel, which were not blessed with oil deposits on the scale of the Gulf nations, have considerable deposits of natural gas. As natural gas increasingly becomes a viable and attractive energy source, these nations stand to benefit to the same degree that the UAE, Saudi Arabia, Kuwait, and Qatar have benefited from oil.

Institutions, Legal System, and Foreign Direct Investment

Although the state of political institutions in the MENA region generally presents a major problem, some noteworthy developments can be considered opportunities for supply chain development. In particular, FDI laws across MENA are being liberalized, and tax benefits, especially in foreign trade zones, are being extended to attract foreign investment. Additionally, many nations are working to streamline laws relating to business governance, licensing, and dispute resolution, as well as working to strengthen intellectual property rights protection. As has been the general trend, of the five nations in this assessment the

UAE and Saudi Arabia are leaders in this area, with Egypt and Algeria lagging behind. Again, Israel is somewhat of an outlier with a Western democratic political system that has been generally supportive of business.

Infrastructure

As the MENA region has gained wealth and stability, investments have clearly been made in infrastructure to support commercial development. Although much work remains, some opportunities are emerging with respect to infrastructure development. The region has long enjoyed the benefits of a large number of natural harbors and seaports. Many of the most densely populated cities are located near traditional harbors and seaports, and the basic infrastructure for global maritime trade has been in place for millennia. Although not all ports feature modern handling and information technology, accessibility to population and industrial centers via ocean transport is generally assured. The road networks are expanding, and some that connect major population centers are of good quality. Investment in road and rail connections between MENA nations is increasing, promising a land bridge between the Persian Gulf and the Mediterranean that could provide an alternative to complete water passage between Asia and the West. In addition, the region could become a major hub for distribution into sub-Saharan Africa.

There has also been significant improvement in telecommunications and power generation, as governments with positive account balances have sought to invest in infrastructural improvements. Of the five assessed nations, the UAE and Saudi Arabia have made the most progress. These nations enjoy the most positive cash flow from oil and feature well-developed infrastructure. Israel also enjoys a modern, well-developed infrastructure. Egypt and Algeria have benefited from their colonial histories, featuring adequate rail and road coverage, but investment is needed to modernize the systems. The telecommunications network in Egypt is among the fastest developing sectors in the nation.

A Summary of MENA Supply Chain Opportunities

▲ Petroleum wealth has fueled increasing levels of government investment and growth.
▲ Strengthening interest in trade associations is increasing levels of intraregional trade.
▲ Discoveries of large and as yet undeveloped deposits of natural gas promise to be a major source of future trade and wealth.
▲ Laws are changing to reflect a positive outlook toward FDI to attract investment.
▲ Seaports are located near population and industrial centers, providing inexpensive maritime transportation options for imports and exports.
▲ Governments are investing in road and rail improvement in wealthier nations.
▲ The generally young and growing population fosters low-cost labor availability.

▲ The logistics service industry in MENA is relatively well developed.

▲ Infrastructure, trade laws, and geography improvements return the region to its status as a global commercial crossroads, both for east-west trade as well as for the promise of future north-south trade.

MENA Best Practices

Some vignettes of best practices in global supply chain opportunities in the MENA region follow.

Barloworld and the Growth of Logistics in the UAE

Barloworld Logistics has recently focused on acquiring smaller logistics service providers in the United Arab Emirates with the goal of strengthening its logistics services in this region. Barloworld sees the MENA region as central to its growth initiatives and is expecting (largely from the UAE) to sustain an annual combined growth rate of 8 percent, reaching US$10.06 billion by 2015 (from US$6.35 billion in 2009).

Barloworld's CEO, Frank Courtney, was quoted as saying:

> Supply chain management plays a crucial role in the sustained economic growth of the UAE, as an increasing number of investors are taking advantage of the country's advanced logistics infrastructure and strategic location. Key international players are therefore keenly monitoring the UAE's capability to handle future demand and ultimately ensure the safe and efficient flow of goods in and out of the country. We are also witnessing similar developments happening in other GCC countries, which are likewise taking advantage of the region's strategic location to serve as a major logistics hub. In this regard, Barloworld Logistics is strongly positioned to support the continuing drive to bolster the status of the UAE and the rest of the GCC to serve key players in the global logistics industry, capitalizing on our experience and expanding international presence in Africa, Europe, the Middle East, Southeast Asia and the Far East.

- The supply chain and logistics sector now accounts for a significant percentage of the UAE's GDP, which is a strong indication of the possibilities and long-term growth opportunities emerging in this sector. Barloworld Logistics' strategic investments in recent years have certainly given us a strong head start as we enter a new era of growth and development in the supply chain and logistics sector.[24]

- The World Bank's Logistics Performance Index 2012 clearly positions UAE as the frontrunner in the entire GCC region with its superior logistics infrastructure and tightly integrated value-added services and amenities. The development of Dubai World Central, for instance, is a game-changing achievement that firmly establishes the UAE as a leading logistics hub, and a catalyst for the sustained growth of the regional logistics industry. Our strategy is to complement the government's proactive efforts to build world-class logistics infrastructure by focusing on delivering integrated smart supply chain solutions that empower businesses to move forward with their expansion plans in the region. The UAE continues to open exciting opportunities for logistics businesses to grow and expand, and we believe that Barloworld Logistics' strategic investments over the years have strongly positioned the company to capitalize on the favorable market conditions.[25]

High-Speed Rail in Saudi Arabia: Bombardier

Rail technology leader Bombardier is developing a high-speed rail network that will be serviced by 36 very high-speed trains. Bombardier has partnered with Talgo SA, who will develop the 450 km of high-speed rail lines that will connect the cities of Mecca and Medina (approximately US$367 million). The trains will be expected to operate at cruising speeds of 330 km/hr and will largely be manufactured at Bombardier's manufacturing facility located in Trápaga, Spain.

Prina Mello, Regional Sales Executive, Middle East and North Africa, Bombardier Transportation noted that:

> Saudi Arabia is presenting an excellent example of infrastructure development in order to meet expanding demand. This new agreement is another exciting step forward in our commitment to helping the Saudi market achieve its long-term urban transport goals, supplying crucial technology and components to this prestigious project is very important to us, and we are confident we can bring the same level of expertise to other ongoing projects in the Gulf region.[26]

DHL Breaks Ground on King Fahd International Airport Facility in Dammam

Ken Allen, CEO of DHL Express, commented:

> Since 1976, DHL has blazed the trail for express delivery in Saudi Arabia, and this investment is further proof that we have no intention of slowing down. The Saudi market offers vast opportunities for DHL's global customer base, and the multi-million dollar gateway we are opening today underscores the unwavering commitment of DHL and our longstanding partners at SNAS to driving further trade between businesses in the Kingdom and their partners around the world.

Nour Suliman, CEO of DHL Express MENA, noted:

The groundbreaking marks the beginning of construction of a 10,000 square meter facility. The new facility is expected to be operational by December, while other improvements will be completed by 2014. The new gateways will be linked to all major DHL Express distribution hubs around the world including the regional hub in Bahrain, as well as the new DHL Express North Asia Hub in Shanghai, China, which was launched in mid-July 2012, marks the largest hub in Asia with investment over $175m and further demonstrates DHL's commitment to providing fast, reliable and cost efficient logistics solutions.[27]

Key Takeaways for MENA

Breaking MENA up into its three constituent segments allows for the development of a more refined set of takeaways for this region. The *first segment*, consisting of the UAE, Saudi Arabia, and Israel (and likely Qatar and Kuwait, although they were not included in this work due to their relatively small populations and GDP), are poised for continued growth and modernization, thus presenting the most compelling opportunities for supply chain development and investment.

Egypt and Algeria represent a *second segment* of nations within MENA, with a need for considerable improvement in all areas of the EPIC assessment dimensions, yet featuring some opportunities for supply chain investment if trends continue.

The *third segment* includes all of the other nations in MENA, which vary greatly across size, population, history, and so forth, and suffer from substantial instability and turmoil. These nations present a risk profile that cautions against supply chain investment.

Based on this assessment, the key takeaways for supply chain managers regarding the MENA region include the following:

1. Expand use of the UAE as a gateway for distribution of imported finished goods into Middle East markets in anticipation of GCC expansion.
2. Establish relatively low-tech manufacturing facilities (e.g., finished goods electronics) in the free trade zone environment in the UAE to take advantage of its central location for subcomponent imports from Asia, Europe, and the Americas for redistribution in the MENA region.
3. Expand natural gas production and export opportunities in Egypt, Israel, and Algeria.
4. Utilize Egyptian and Algerian port facilities as an entry and redistribution point for consumer goods to population centers in North Africa.
5. Establish low-skilled manufacturing facilities in special economic zones in Egypt for export to the MENA region.

6. Establish R&D and high-tech manufacturing in Israel to take advantage of the availability of its skilled, highly educated labor force and high level and availability of engineering and technology skills.
7. Establish import facilities with distribution capability to penetrate the Israeli market with consumer goods.
8. Link Saudi Arabian transportation network and logistics capabilities to UAE import and manufacturing facilities for efficient and effective access to Saudi Arabian population centers, as well as for redistribution to Kuwait, Iraq, and the Levant.
9. Significant opportunities exist for logistics and transportation organizations to establish operations to support trade within MENA as well as to utilize the central location of MENA as a hub for global trade networks. With the centrality of MENA to population and industrial centers in Europe, Asia, Africa, and the Americas, MENA could continue to grow into the logistics and distribution hub for an increasingly connected global trade environment.
10. Opportunities for foreign firms to win government contracts to build transportation, telecommunications, and power utility infrastructures to support further supply chain capitalization are abundant given the strong account balance position of many nations in MENA.

References

1. Anoushiravan Ehteshami, *Globalization and Geopolitics in the Middle East: Old Games, New Rules* (New York: Routledge, 2007).
2. Ibid.
3. Europa World Plus.
4. Ibid.
5. Ibid.
6. Ibid.
7. Amlan Roy, Sonali Punhani, and Liyan Shi, "Middle East and North Africa: Demographic Highlights," *Credit Suisse*, February 25, 2011.
8. Ibid.
9. Europa World Plus.
10. CIA World Factbook.
11. CIA World Factbook.
12. Europa World Plus.
13. *Monthly Bulletin of Statistics*. Israel Central Bureau of Statistics, February 7, 2012.
14. World Bank's 2012 Doing Business Report.
15. 2011 Transparency International Corruption Perceptions Index (CPI).
16. World Bank World Government Index (WGI).

17. World Bank Ease of Doing Business Report.
18. WGI index.
19. CPI Index.
20. CPI Index.
21. http://www.oecd.org.
22. Ibid.
23. 2012 Economist Intelligence Unit Nation Risk Rating.
24. http://www.ameinfo.com/uae-logistics-market-exceed-10bn-2015-316305.
25. Ibid.
26. http://www.ameinfo.com/bombardier-signs-contracts-talgo-speed-rail-312716.
27. http://www.ameinfo.com/dhl-celebrates-groundbreaking-gateway-king-fahd-314502.

CHAPTER 8

Sub-Saharan Africa[a]

Sub-Saharan Africa (SSA) is a region of the world that holds substantial opportunity for supply chain operations—both now and in the future (Figure 8.1). In the 1980s, some used the word "dragons" to characterize the countries in Southeast Asia, reflecting a period of rapid economic development in those nations. Today we might similarly speak of several sub-Saharan Africa nations as "Lions," in recognition of the supply chain opportunity they present.

Over the course of many centuries, nearly constant conflict between the SSA kingdoms resulted in increased power for the victors and enslavement for the defeated. In the 14th century, Europeans (mainly the Portuguese) arrived in the eastern coastal regions of SSA. These Europeans traded for raw materials that had been transported to the coast by the indigenous peoples of SSA. During this period, the influence of the Europeans on SSA was largely limited to the port calls of European trade ships, with the one exception being South Africa, where the Dutch were welcomed and subsequently established permanent colonies. It wasn't until the end of the 14th century that Europeans began trading with the kingdoms located on the western coast of SSA. This period marks the beginning of both the colonization of SSA and the slave trade.[b] SSA comprises 50 nations[c] in an area that is larger than the United States, China, the European Union, and India combined, and represents 20.3 percent of the planet's landmass. SSA is home to approximately 1 billion inhabitants, although this number is somewhat speculative as there is a lack of good quality census data in the region. Even with this large population, SSA has a population density of less than 36 inhabitants per km^2.

---

[a] We would like to thank Marina Razafindrazaka for her invaluable assistance in editing this chapter.

[b] See http://www.understandingslavery.com/index.php?option=com_content&view=article&id=369&Itemid=145 for more details on the triangle made up of Africa, Western Europe, and the Antilles.

[c] There are 51 nations in accordance with the status given to the Western Sahara by the states.

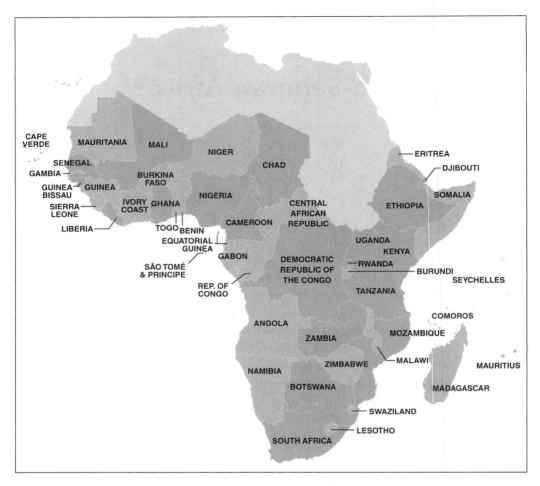

Figure 8.1   Sub-Saharan Africa.

Economic and Political Background

Understanding the Region

Despite similarities in culture across these regions, the economies within sub-Saharan Africa have developed in very different ways, resulting in a regional diversity that is often poorly understood. It is important to understand the heterogeneity and weak integration that creates barriers to effective trade within SSA. There are six different regions in SSA:

> **Western SSA:** Benin, Burkina Faso, Cape Verde, Ivory Coast, Gambia, Ghana, Guinea, Guinea-Bissau, Liberia, Mali, Mauritania, Niger, Nigeria, Senegal, Sierra Leone, and Togo

Central SSA: Burundi, Cameroon, Central African Republic, Congo (Brazzaville), Congo (Democratic Republic/Kinshasa), Gabon, Equatorial Guinea, Rwanda, Sao Tome and Principe, and Chad

Southern SSA: Angola, Botswana, Lesotho, Mozambique, Namibia, South Africa, Swaziland, Zambia, and Zimbabwe

Indian Ocean SSA: Comoros, Reunion, Madagascar, Malawi, Mauritius, and the Seychelles

Eastern SSA: Kenya, Uganda, and Tanzania

Horn of SSA: Djibouti, Eritrea, Ethiopia, Somalia, South Sudan, and Sudan

Across the many nations of SSA, more than 1000 languages are spoken. This cultural diversity not only exists between countries but also within countries. In Nigeria, for example, the official language is English, but at least 500 other indigenous languages are spoken by the more than 250 ethnic groups. Some countries have found ways to embrace this cultural diversity, but others have failed. A success story is that of Mauritius, which has been successful in establishing a climate of political, economic, and social stability favorable to business development. Mauritius is working toward becoming the Singapore of West Africa. Its stability has attracted investors to support economic development, especially around Port Louis.

The majority of SSA territory is comprised of large plateaus and plains, with very few mountain chains (with the exception of Ethiopia and Kenya). Rainfall is often heavy and violent, and the roads are so lightly paved that heavy rainfall can result in some territories being cut off entirely at times.

The principal dilemma in SSA rests in its vast distances, and more particularly for some countries, in the distance to the sea. In addition, SSA suffers from two enormous natural obstacles: (1) the Sahara Desert, which separates North Africa from SSA; and (2) a huge, nearly impenetrable equatorial forest. For this reason, SSA has very few natural trade routes. The best trade routes have historically been (1) the Nile, which offers an incredible opportunity as it opens onto the Mediterranean; (2) the coastline on the Red Sea, which is close to the Middle East; and (3) the caravan routes that connect North Africa to sub-Saharan Africa. Also, food supply remains a problem for numerous SSA nations, with many teetering on the brink of famine. In 2012 the exceptional drought in the United States, Russia, and Europe drove up the price of foodstuffs and substantially escalated the famine risk in SSA.

The combination of these natural barriers to trade, inadequate infrastructure, a sizeable black-market economy, and the disparity of wealth tends to hamper the development of supply chain operations in SSA. However, a new dynamic economy is in the process of being established, and opportunities in SSA are improving and will likely continue to do so. The annual average growth rate, sustained and propelled over the last decade through the export of raw materials to Asia and other geographic regions, bears testimony to this expansion.

Politics

Political stability continues to be volatile in a number of SSA nations. For a business, this volatility can bring with it risks that are difficult to surmount. For instance, in Madagascar, the textile industry collapsed as a result of ongoing political instability. In 2010, this instability resulted in the suspension of Madagascar from the AGOA (African Growth and Opportunity Act). American law favors those African countries that identify with U.S. markets, so textile businesses limited or removed their investment when they were no longer able to benefit from legal exemptions granted by the United States. Political instability has had a negative effect on the development of several nations, and some economies have been destroyed because the risk of operating businesses in these nations is simply too great to warrant the investment.

The Economies

There is a rich history of trade between SSA and the Middle East and North Africa (MENA). For all of history, the risks associated with crossing the trade routes between SSA and MENA have caused merchants and travelers to group together to support and defend each other. The historical caravans, often consisting of a hundred dromedaries (Arabian/Indian Camels), left North Africa to converge on the Sahel (a 1000 km [620 mi] belt that sits on the boundary of MENA and SSA) to barter, trade, and then return to MENA with the riches of central Africa. The principal crossroad for most of this trade was the town of Timbuktu, which is located in central Mali, south of Algeria (MENA). In this way, this part of sub-Saharan Africa was linked to Maghreb region of MENA, which then engaged in international trade with countries bordering the Mediterranean and the Red Sea.

Europeans, in particular the Portuguese, first appeared in sub-Saharan Africa around the 14th century although their presence was mostly confined to the coastal areas. The Europeans typically did not attempt to venture inland. Merchandise was transported to the coastal regions, which set in process trading and bartering activity. (It is observed that it wasn't until 1488 that Bartolomeu Dias first rounded the Cape of Good Hope.) The Europeans began trading with the kingdoms situated on the West-African coast, but their presence was restricted and often of short duration being linked to the arrivals of the boats. South Africa was a notable exception. It welcomed the Dutch colonies that settled there permanently, which significantly helped economic development in the country. It was not long before South Africa began to be viewed by the Western world as "the sole gateway to the continent."

China is a newcomer to SSA, arriving just about 10 years ago. The arrival of China in Africa has profoundly transformed the business environment in the region and promises to help the SSA region to develop its economy in a way that the European countries never could.

China sees Africa as a reservoir of raw materials (oil, minerals, etc.), while Africa perceives China as the ideal partner, imposing no special conditions or rules to their partnership. The partnership offers promise for both parties involved. China gets privileged access to raw materials. In exchange, China pays and finances huge infrastructure operations, which Africa's historic European partners had neither the desire nor the means to support. These nations include Zambia, Kenya, Ghana, and Nigeria. As a result, SSA has become the new "low-cost region" for China's manufacturing industry. China's presence in sub-Saharan Africa has also had some negative side effects. For example, the sub-Saharan African textile industry crashed after experiencing aggressive competition from imported Chinese products.

Much of the economic growth in SSA is along the west coast (Nigeria, Ghana, and Angola) and in east Africa (Ethiopia, Kenya). Meanwhile, other countries are working to improve their transportation infrastructures. A number of countries, such as Nigeria to the west and Mozambique to the east, are in full expansion mode and are developing the infrastructure to make them feasible access points to sub-Saharan Africa's economic zone. As a result South Africa may soon no longer be considered the sole gateway to the continent.

The Markets

Sub-Saharan Africa has an extremely young population, with half of its population being under 20 years of age, heralding opportunities for new markets that are associated with SSA's emerging middle class. Sudan and Angola have seen their trade buoyed up by the explosion in oil prices. The Democratic Republic of Congo has been directly affected by its exports of raw materials. Nigeria is one of five African countries in which China has invested heavily.

Seven SSA nations will be discussed in more detail in the rest of this chapter. These nations are Angola, the Democratic Republic of Congo, Ethiopia, Kenya, Nigeria, South Africa, and Sudan. These seven countries were selected because they offer the greatest potential for growth by virtue of their economic performance and size, and because they provide the best insight into the complexity of supply chain operations in sub-Saharan Africa.

Angola

Angola occupies a part of southwestern Africa and faces west along the South Atlantic Ocean (Figure 8.2). Angola shares borders with the Democratic Republic of Congo (2511 km, 1560 mi), Zambia (1110 km, 690 mi), and Namibia (1376 km, 855 mi), and faces the South Atlantic Ocean on its west coast (1600 km, 994 mi). Angola comprises 1,246,700 sq km (481,356 sq mi), which is approximately twice the land area of France. The primacy rate for Angola is 43 percent, and 59 percent of the population live in urban areas, a number that is increasing by 4 percent per year. Much of the population in Angola is located to the west and northwest. Since the early 2000s, Angola has rebuilt itself after 27 years of civil war. It is an oil

Figure 8.2 Angola.

rich country with profits from petroleum making up 40 percent of its GDP. Angola's income per capita is $5245 (USD). The country represents an enormous potential for development.

Democratic Republic of Congo

The Democratic Republic of Congo occupies central SSA, with a west coast that faces the South Atlantic Ocean (Figure 8.3). The Democratic Republic of Congo shares borders with the Angola (2511 km, 1560 mi), Burundi (233 km, 145 mi), the Central African Republic (1577 km, 980 mi), Republic of the Congo (2410 km, 1498 mi), Rwanda (217 km, 135 mi), South Sudan (628 km, 390 mi), Tanzania (459 km, 285 mi), Uganda (765 km, 475 mi), and Zambia (1199 km, 745 km) and has a small west coast along the South Atlantic Ocean (37 km, 23 mi). The Democratic Republic of Congo comprises 2,344,858 sq km (905,359 sq mi), which is approximately one-quarter the land area of the United States.

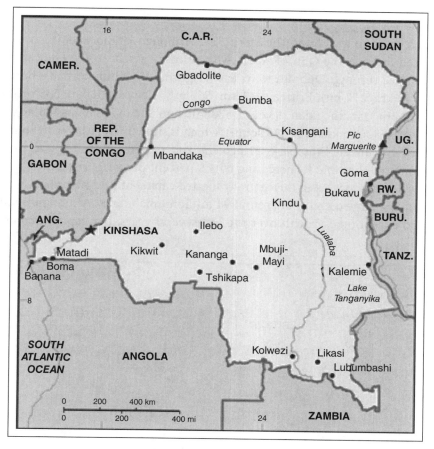

Figure 8.3 Democratic Republic of Congo.

The primacy rate for the Democratic Republic of Congo is 39 percent, and 35 percent of the population live in urban areas, a number that is increasing by 4.5 percent per year. The largest population center in the Democratic Republic of Congo is located to the west, in the capital of Kinshasa (8.4 million), with significant population centers also found in the cities of Lubumbashi (1.54 million) to the south, and the more centrally located Mbuji-Mayi (1.5 million).

The Democratic Republic of Congo is an immense country endowed with significant natural resources. With a population of 75.5 million, it is one of the largest French-speaking countries in the world (although its population also speaks the languages of Lingala, Kingwana, Kikongo, and Tshiluba). Its recent history of internal conflict has made it the poorest country in the world. Between 1997 and 2005, there were more than 5 million war victims. The income per capita in the Democratic Republic of Congo is $231 (USD).

Ethiopia

Ethiopia occupies an area of northeastern SSA. Although landlocked, it is very close to both the Red Sea and the Gulf of Aden, with primary access to the Gulf of Aden and the Arabian Sea through Djibouti to its east (Figure 8.4). Ethiopia shares borders with Djibouti (349 km, 217 mi), Eritrea (912 km, 567 mi), Kenya (861 km, 535 mi), Somalia (1600 km, 994 mi), south Sudan (837 km, 520 mi), and Sudan (769 km, 478 mi). Ethiopia comprises 1,104,300 sq km (426,375 sq mi), which is similar in land area to South Africa. The primacy rate for the Ethiopia is 21 percent, and 17 percent of the population live in urban areas, a number that is increasing by 3.8 percent per year. The largest population center in Ethiopia is located in the centrally located capital of Addis Ababa (2.9 million).

Ethiopia is a large country of around 94 million inhabitants. Although Ethiopia has experienced exceptional growth over the last several years, per capita income is only

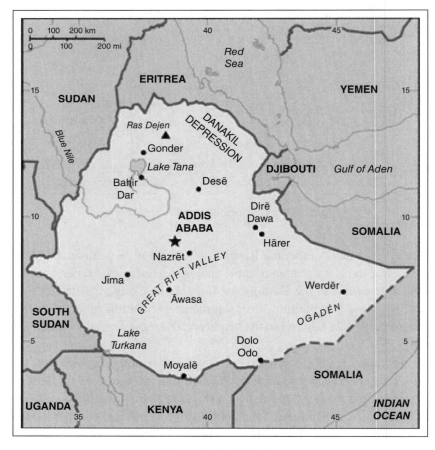

Figure 8.4 Ethiopia.

$374 (USD). Djibouti's Port of Djibouti was built to service the logistics needs of Ethiopia, which represents about 70 percent of the seaport's activity. The other strategically important seaport for Ethiopia is the Port of Berbera in Somalia. However, the road infrastructure linking Ethiopia to this seaport is poor, as is the infrastructure in the seaport itself. Further, political instability in Somalia has significantly degraded the usefulness of this port in serving SSA and Ethiopian supply chain operations.

Kenya

Kenya occupies an area of eastern SSA and has an east-facing coast on the Arabian Sea. Kenya shares borders with Ethiopia (861 km, 535 mi), Somalia (682 km, 424 mi), South Sudan (232 km, 144 mi), Tanzania (769 km, 478 mi), and Uganda (933 km, 580 mi). Kenya comprises 580,367 sq km (224,082 sq mi), which is slightly larger than Spain (Figure 8.5).

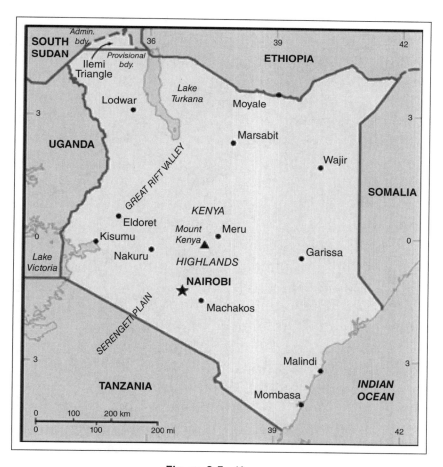

Figure 8.5 Kenya.

The primacy rate for Kenya is 37 percent, and 22 percent of the population live in urban areas, a number that is increasing by 4.2 percent per year. The largest population center in Kenya is located to the south of the nation around the capital of Nairobi (3.4 million), with Mombasa to the far south representing the next largest city (966,000). Kenya has a population of around 44 million. Kenya is one of the SSA countries that lacks natural resources and in which the geography hampers transportation. Kenya remains very poor, with a per capita income of $808 (USD). However, the country does have a developing middle class.

Nigeria

Nigeria occupies an area of northwestern SSA and has a west-facing coast on the South Atlantic Ocean (853 km, 530 mi). Nigeria shares borders with Benin (773 km, 480 mi), Cameroon (1690 km, 1050 mi), Chad (87 km, 54 mi), and Niger (1497 km, 930 mi). Nigeria comprises 923,768 sq km (356,670 sq mi), which is similar in size to Venezuela or Pakistan and is about twice the size of California (Figure 8.6). The primacy rate for Nigeria is

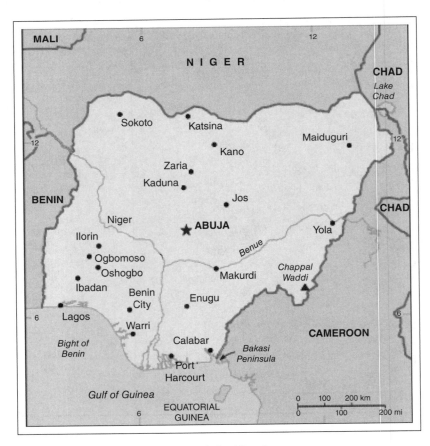

Figure 8.6 Nigeria.

14 percent, and 50 percent of the population live in urban areas, a number that is increasing by 3.5 percent per year. The largest population centers in Nigeria extend south along the coast from Lagos (10.2 million), with large inland cities including Kano (3.3 million), Ibadan (2.8 million), Abuja (capital, 1.9 million), and Kaduna (1.5 million). Nigeria has a population of around 174.5 million. Nigeria's wealth and large population make it a very important SSA nation with the possibility of large consumer markets. The income per capita is $1425 (USD), and its diverse economy is divided between industry (33.6 percent), agriculture (35.4 percent), and services (31 percent). Nigeria also relies heavily on its oil reserves. As with numerous other African economies, Nigeria has attracted the attention of the Chinese, who have invested heavily in the Lagos urban area (primarily around Ogun).

South Africa

South Africa occupies the southernmost tip of Africa and has both a west-facing coast on the South Atlantic Ocean and an east-facing coast on the Indian Ocean (Figure 8.7).

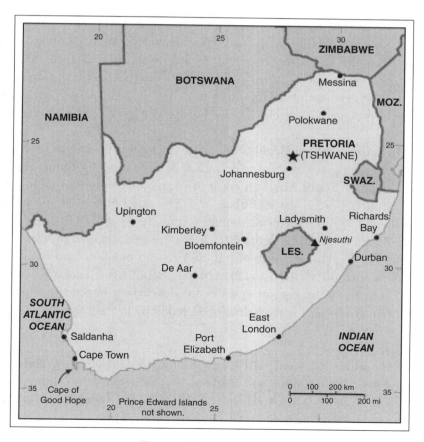

Figure 8.7 South Africa.

In total, South Africa has 2798 km (1738 mi) of coastline, with a relatively larger share of the coastline along the Indian Ocean than along the South Atlantic Ocean. South Africa shares borders with Botswana (1840 km, 1143 mi), Lesotho (909 km, 564 mi), Mozambique (491 km, 305 mi), Namibia (967 km, 601 mi), Swaziland (430 km, 267 mi), and Zimbabwe (225 km, 140 mi). Interestingly, both Lesotho and Swaziland are either entirely (in the case of Lesotho) or largely (in the case of Swaziland) inside the geographic boundaries of South Africa. South Africa comprises 1,219,090 sq km (470,695 sq mi), which is similar in size to Colombia or Peru (or about 20 percent larger than Alaska). The primacy rate for South Africa is 12 percent, and 62 percent of its population lives in urban areas, a number that is increasing by 1.2 percent per year. South Africa has a population of around 48.6 million. The largest population centers in South Africa are Johannesburg (3.6 million), Cape Town (3.4 million), Ekurhuleni (East Rand, 3.1 million), Durban (2.8 million), and the nation's capital, Pretoria (1.4 million).

South Africa represents a very different nation against the backdrop of the other nations of sub-Saharan Africa. For instance, South Africa represents 30 percent of SSA's GDP and 25 percent of Africa's GDP. South Africa has advanced levels of economic development, political stability, infrastructure, and logistics. With 50 million inhabitants, South Africa has the largest economy in Africa, boasting a GDP of $555.1 billion (USD, 2011), and per capita income of $8070 (USD). South Africa is the largest importer and second largest exporter of commodities in Africa. In 2010, 36 percent of its exports were destined for Asia, 27 percent for the European Union, and 18 percent for sub-Saharan Africa.

South Africa's industries are highly developed, and foreign businesses have always considered it as a landing point for expansion into SSA. Consequently, numerous businesses have set up centers in South Africa in order to access the rest of SSA. South Africa has 21 principal airports, a large port at Durban, and three other important ports: Cape Town, Port Elizabeth, and Ngqura. Its infrastructure is modern compared to other countries in sub-Saharan Africa. According to the 2012 Logistics Performance Index (LPI),[1] South Africa has the best logistics performance in SSA (ahead of China and Brazil). With the economic development in western and eastern SSA, South Africa is clearly losing its privileged position as the unique point of entry for developing businesses in sub-Saharan Africa, but it remains by far the most developed economy in this region.

Sudan

Sudan occupies northeast SSA and has a geographic footprint in both north and sub-Saharan Africa (Figure 8.8). Furthermore, Sudan has an east-facing coastline along the Red Sea, across from Saudi Arabia. In total, Sudan has 853 km (530 mi) of coastline along the Red Sea. Sudan shares borders with the Central African Republic (175 km, 108 mi), Chad (1360 km, 845 mi), Egypt (1275 km, 792 mi), Eritrea (605 km, 376 mi), Ethiopia (769 km, 478 mi),

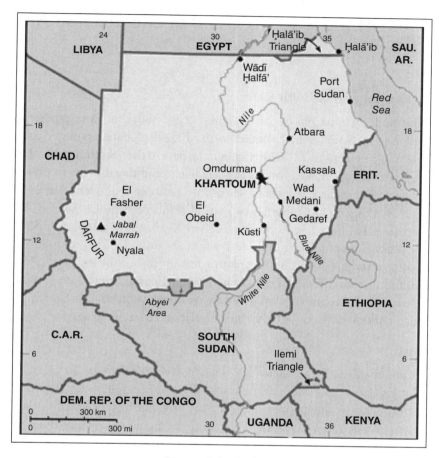

Figure 8.8 Sudan.

Libya (383 km, 238 mi), and South Sudan (2184 km, 1357 mi). Sudan comprises 1,861,484 sq km (718,725 sq mi), which is slightly smaller than Mexico. The primacy rate for Sudan is 40 percent, and 40 percent of the population live in urban areas, a number that is increasing by 3.7 percent per year. The population is more located to the south than the north, owing to the fact that north Sudan makes up the southern Sahara Desert, a much less hospitable region of SSA. The largest city in Sudan is the capital of Khartoum (5 million), which is situated along the Nile River. Sudan has a population of approximately 34.8 million. Recently, Sudan was partitioned into two countries. The southern portion of the country, South Sudan, gained independence from the north in July 2011, and it now relies heavily on its oil resources and on agriculture. The per capita income in Sudan is $1235 (USD).

Assessment of the Maturity Level of Sub-Saharan Africa Supply Chains

Economy

Economic Output and Growth Rate

Between 2001 and 2010, six out of the ten world economies that were experiencing rapid growth were found in SSA. Even in the context of the difficult global economy, SSA experienced a growth rate of 4.8 percent in 2011. Owing in large part to the vast mineral and oil deposits in several African nations, stable growth rates will likely continue into the future. However, it is important to note that there is substantial contrast between the SSA countries that benefit from oil reserves (Nigeria and Angola) or natural resources (the Democratic Republic of Africa), and those that have few resources (such as Kenya and Ethiopia). In SSA, it is also true that the proportion of GDP from industry remains poor. Instead, most SSA economies rely on agriculture and the export of their natural resources. In contrast, South Africa has the advantage of industry, and Kenya has a strong entrepreneurial orientation toward small- to medium-sized business ventures. Compared to Western countries, sub-Saharan Africa is a region of excellent growth, although the rate of inflation remains a cause for concern.

Population

The population of sub-Saharan Africa has quadrupled over the past 50 years. This region is notable for its ethnic diversity and its unusually young population. Depending on the nation, the number of young people in SSA is startling. For instance, half the sub-Saharan African population is under 20 years of age, and in Angola nearly half the population is less than 14 years of age. As a consequence, nearly 7 million people enter the workforce each year, resulting in an exceptionally high level of unemployment. The birthrate is likely to continue to remain high, at around seven children per woman.

SSA is unique in that 20 percent of the rural population represents a population density of less than 15 people per km². Furthermore, the population density, as also the wealth, is very unevenly distributed. As a result, not all of the nations of SSA are benefiting from the current period of intense regional economic growth. The poorest African countries continue to secure only a tiny fraction of the region's overall wealth. In 2008, 47 percent of the population of sub-Saharan Africa lived under the threshold of $1.25 (USD) per day. Although the poverty rate is below 50 percent for the first time in 30 years, it remains sizeable. To put it in perspective, only 2.7 percent of the population of MENA lives on less than $1.25 (USD) per day.

Foreign Direct Investment

Gifts and foreign direct investment (FDI) are two very important engines for economic development in Africa. In particular, China has made significant investment in SSA although the nature of this investment is such that only select nations and businesses can benefit from it. The development projects are decentralized and can depend on one or several ministries, provinces, and businesses, or a combination of all three. Overall investment in the region fell between 2011 and 2012, but FDI was constant, bolstered by investment in the extraction of raw materials. The FDI potential of the region appears strong, especially in light of the region's trend toward political stability. The World Bank is expecting the region to reach a record $48 billion (USD) in FDI by 2014. France and the United Kingdom are abandoning their SSA "privileged status," but China, India, and several emerging powers are investing massively and rapidly gaining this privileged status. For instance, China has more than 2000 businesses in Africa across a variety of industries, including agriculture, telecommunications, processing, and manufacturing.

Exchange Rate Stability and Consumer Price Inflation

African currencies have never been considered strong or stable, but three currencies are exceptions to this rule: (1) the West African CFA franc, (2) the Central African CFA franc, and (3) the South Africa rand. In west Africa, eight countries (Benin, Burkina Faso, the Ivory Coast, Guinea-Bissau, Mali, Niger, Senegal, and Togo) trade the Africa CFA franc (the Communauté Financière Africaine franc). Six countries of central Africa (Cameroon, the Central African Republic, the Republic of Congo, Gabon, Equatorial Guinea, and Chad) trade the CFA franc (the Central African CFA franc). These two currencies are indexed to the euro, giving them relatively good prospects for stability for the future. These two currencies are exchangeable in euros and are guaranteed by the French Treasury as part of the Treaty of Maastricht. The South African rand is somewhat volatile when compared to other currencies in the region. Finally, it is important to note that the large SSA black-market economy operates with both euros and U.S. dollars.

Inflation is a given in the majority of SSA, and regional inflation is higher than in other parts of the world. The SSA economies are not well positioned to resist external shocks (such as increases in oil prices) or internal shocks (such as a weak harvest and the resultant need to import). Ethiopia experienced inflation of 26.7 percent in 2011, 29.3 percent in 2012, and is anticipating a level of 14 percent in 2014. South Africa experienced a rate of inflation of 6.1 percent in 2011.

Balance of Trade

Trade in SSA has been transformed over several years. At the beginning of the century, more than 50 percent of SSA exports went to the European Union. Today, the European Union represents about 33 percent of SSA exports. This rebalancing of exports benefits the Chinese, who have absorbed nearly 15 percent of exports (25 percent of which are minerals and oil), and other emerging countries such as India. The balance of imported manufactured goods has also been readjusted. Europe accounts for just 13 percent of imports, while the United States accounts for 33 percent, and China accounts for 10 percent.

Table 8.1 presents the scores for the Economy dimension for each of the focal nations of the region. An overall assessment of the Economy dimension and a summary of the strengths and weaknesses is shown in Table 8.2.

Table 8.1 Scores for the Economy Dimension

Economy	Economic Output and Growth Rate	Population Size	Foreign Direct Investment	Exchange Rate Stability/CPI	Balance of Trade	Overall Grade
30%	35%	25%	20%	15%	5%	100%
Angola	A⁻	B⁺	D	D	B⁻	B⁻
Dem. Rep. Congo	B⁻	A	B⁻	F	D	B⁻
Ethiopia	A⁻	A	D	F	D	B⁻
Kenya	B⁻	A⁻	D⁺	D	C	C⁺
Nigeria	A⁻	A	B⁺	D	B	B⁺
South Africa	B	A⁻	B⁻	B⁻	A	B
Sudan	B	A⁻	C	F	F	C⁺

Table 8.2 Strengths and Weaknesses Summary: Economy Dimension

Grade	Strengths	Weaknesses
Angola: B⁻	The second largest producer of oil in Africa (after Nigeria); a GDP growth rate of between 7 and 8 percent; good political stability.	Inflation rate is more than 10 percent; 97 percent of exports are linked to oil; unemployment over 25 percent for several years; 50 percent of population is less than 14 years of age; difficult relations with the Democratic Republic of Congo have had a negative effect; a period of strong uncertainty followed President dos Santos taking office; cost of living in the capital, Luanda, is extraordinarily high.
Democratic Republic of Congo: B⁻	A growth rate between 5 and 6 percent; great potential thanks to its mineral resources; benefits from the mid-2009 price increase of mineral raw materials.	Seventy percent of those aged 15 to 24 are unemployed; no social welfare net; inflation level remains high even though it dropped from 23.5 percent in 2010 to 14.8 percent in 2011; black market and corruption dominate the economy.
Ethiopia: B⁻	Excellent and continuing growth rate (10th in the world by percentage) even though not an oil producer; 14 percent of GDP was industry-based in 2011.	Inflation rate of more than 10 percent that leapt to almost 30 percent in 2012; only 3.6 percent of GDP comes from manufacturing industries; economy mainly agricultural; has a trade balance deficit of more than 23 percent of GDP.
Kenya: C⁺	A diverse economy with a little more than 10 percent of GDP stemming from industry; network of small and medium enterprises that export to Tanzania and Uganda.	A moderate growth rate for the region of 4 to 6 percent but high unemployment in the younger population.

(continued)

Table 8.2 Strengths and Weaknesses Summary: Economy Dimension (*Continued*)

Grade	Strengths	Weaknesses
Nigeria: B⁺	A sustained growth rate of 6 to 7 percent per annum. The country is one of the most populated in Africa.	In 2011, 42 percent of GDP was linked to exports sustained by crude oil; two-thirds of the population lives on less than $1 (USD) per day; high inflation levels (close to 10 percent); between 20 and 25 percent of the population is unemployed; 40 percent of population is less than 25 years of age.
South Africa: B	A unique economy in sub-Saharan Africa; valuable industrial and service sectors; stock exchange in Johannesburg is the most important in Africa; benefits from a genuinely entrepreneurial spirit.	Unemployment rate is between 20 and 25 percent; in 2010, 50.5 percent of population was under 25 years of age; society is strained by serious strikes; social segregation continues; 30 percent of the population lives on less than $2 (USD) per day.
Sudan: C⁺	Rich in oil reserves; economy driven by exports of hydrocarbons since 1999; gold mines have attracted FDI.	In July 2011, South Sudan seceded splitting the country; growth is less than 3 percent; inflation is 20 percent; lacks a currency since the collapse of the Sudanese pound, which was introduced after secession.

Politics

Ease of Doing Business, Bureaucracy, and Corruption

According to the World Bank, sub-Saharan Africa remains the most expensive region in which to develop a new business. In its Doing Business Indicators report of 2012, the World Bank highlights 36 out of 50 countries in the region that have put into force important changes in their laws to ease business development.

Even though the overall ranking of SSA countries continues to be low, an evolution is taking place. Many SSA countries have placed their development in the hands of the private economy and have implemented important enabling changes. Among the highest ranked in Africa is Mauritius (in 19th place, ahead of Germany). South Africa is ranked 39th, and Rwanda and Zambia are in joint 100th place. South Africa is rated number 1 on getting credit and number 10 for protecting investors.

Legal and Regulatory Framework: Tax Codes and Tariffs

In sub-Saharan Africa, the implementation of laws often differs from the letter of the laws themselves. Governments are constantly looking for new and viable economic models, so the laws are continually evolving. The bureaucratic culture in this region inevitably results in the creation of rules (essentially laws) that exist in practice rather than being formally codified.

Laws, where they exist, frequently differ (disharmoniously) between countries. This inconsistency in legislation has negative consequences for the cross-border movement of goods. For example, in western Africa, member countries of the Economic Community of West African States (ECOWAS) do not have the same laws related to charges for axle and vehicle dimensions as do countries in the West African Economic and Monetary Union (WAEMU). In April 2011, application of identical laws was agreed upon (starting July 2012). However, many countries (especially those belonging to more than one organization) have never applied either law. Clearly, legal solutions to this problem are difficult to enforce. Therefore, it is not unusual to find an alternative solution that has been developed to circumvent the problem. As long as interpretation of the law is such that individuals and businesses can negotiate alternatives with the authorities, a profoundly corrupt system will tend to be the result. This is certainly a regional characteristic of SSA.

Political Stability

Sub-Saharan Africa is marked by endemic political instability as well as political unrest underscored by ethnic, religious, and political differences, both within and across nations. Developing supply chain operations in such an environment can be a risky proposition. For instance, the Global Peace Index[d] identifies SSA as a problematic world region. Many countries in SSA received bad ratings, and some were extremely bad. In the 2013 index, Somalia was ranked 161 (among 162 countries), Sudan 158, the Democratic Republic of Congo 156, and Nigeria 148.

Tensions within SSA are substantial. For instance, following the end of conflicts in the Democratic Republic of Congo, Ivory Coast, and Angola, other conflicts developed in Guinea Bissau, Sudan, and Mali. Ethiopia is experiencing heightened internal separatist disruptions along with severe tension with neighboring Eritrea. Several Nigerian states engaged in religious wars (Muslims vs. Christians), and there are severe terrorist clashes in the Niger delta (where there is oil exploration). Conflicts and civil wars in Somalia and Sudan are routine. Finally, foreign nationals in countries such as Mali, Niger, and Nigeria are regularly abducted.

Intellectual Property Rights

New product development in sub-Saharan Africa is nascent. Research centers are scarce, and sensitivity to intellectual property rights is poor. Industry is underdeveloped, so intellectual property violations are less numerous.

Table 8.3 presents the scores for the Politics dimension for each of the focal nations of the region and an overall assessment of the Politics dimension and a summary of the strengths and weaknesses is shown in Table 8.4.

---

[d] http://visionofhumanity.org/sites/default/files/2013_Global_Peace_Index_Report.pdf, pages 5 and 6.

Table 8.3 Scores for the Politics Dimension

Politics	Ease of Doing Business	Legal Framework	Political Stability	Intellectual Property Rights	Overall Grade
20%	30%	30%	25%	15%	100%
Angola	F	D⁻	D⁻	F	D⁻
Dem. Rep. Congo*	F	F	D⁻#	F#	F@
Ethiopia	C⁻	D	B	D⁺	C⁻
Kenya	D⁺	D⁺	D⁻	D⁺	D⁺
Nigeria	D⁺	D	D⁺	F	D
South Africa	B⁺	B⁻	D	B⁺	B⁻
Sudan*	D⁻	F	F	F#	F@

Note: *There is limited data on the Politics dimension for the Democratic Republic of Congo and Sudan. Grades presented in the table identified by the @ superscript are estimates based on partial numerical data, while grades identified by the # superscript are based on judgmental evaluation.

Table 8.4 Strengths and Weaknesses Summary: Politics Dimension

Grade	Strengths	Weaknesses
Angola: D⁻	Period of civil war has ended; country is enjoying a period of stability.	Political transition following the current presidency could be disruptive.
Democratic Republic of Congo: F	Incredibly rich in mineral resources.	Extremely low rating on the Global Peace Index.
Ethiopia: C⁻	Prepared to welcome and permit businesses to develop their activities.	Complicated relationships, especially with its neighbors (Eritrea); access to commercial licenses is growing more difficult.
Kenya: D⁺	Welcomes and supports businesses and business expansion.	Corruption scandal; postelection crisis of 2008 could destabilize the country.
Nigeria: D	President wants to implement political reform to achieve more transparency and better management.	Some of 36 states contest centralized authority; ethnic tensions and (especially) civil wars could destabilize the country.
South Africa: B⁻	Genuine talent for welcoming and protecting the interests of businesses.	President is head of the government and could act as a brake on real political reform and democracy.
Sudan: F	The largest African country (in terms of land); high-quality agriculture; rich mineral resources.	Security remains a serious problem; internal conflicts persist; extremely low rating on the Global Peace Index.

Infrastructure

Transportation

In such a large region, transportation infrastructure plays an important role in creating sustained economic growth. Most of SSA is characterized by inadequate transportation infrastructure. Consequently, movement between African regions remains difficult. Fifty years ago Africa had a level of infrastructure similar to that of many Asian countries. Today the gap has substantially widened as these Asian countries have pulled ahead, with SSA making relatively little progress. Without adequate infrastructure, it is difficult to build a local industry capable of manufacturing and distributing products. Other than in South Africa (where some freeways are operated under license), many existing state roads are in a dilapidated and often critically poor condition. These roads are used without consideration for their condition—mostly by overloaded trucks.

To resolve this situation, countries such as Ethiopia and Tanzania have designated special funds for the creation and upkeep of roads. Improvements in major transportation infrastructure have been achieved through privatization, including container-terminal concessions, several toll roads in South Africa, and 14 railroad concessions.

The road network is so limited that it is useful to know the main highways.[e] From the northern Africa region, three highways connect to an east-west highway running from Dakar to N'Djamena. The large interior regions are linked in the west to the Gulf of Guinea via Ghana (Accra), Benin (Cotonou), Nigeria (Lagos and Port Harcourt), the Ivory Coast (Abidjan), and Cameroon (Yoaunde and Douala), and in the east to the ports of the Red Sea. Also significant are the Khartoum to Port-Soudan and Addis-Ababa to Djibouti links. South Africa is the only country with a genuine road-transport network. It includes routes to Durban, Port Elisabeth, Richards Bay, and Maputo to Mozambique. The province of Gauteng is the economic heart of the country and contains its principal gold mines.

The Democratic Republic of Congo is an exceptional source of raw materials (for example, Kolwezi and Lubumbashi in the South Katanga province). Three possible routes exist for access to these raw materials: (1) via the capital Kinshasa, although transport faces numerous geographic obstacles, not least of which is crossing the vast rivers; (2) via Angola, although during the civil war (1975–2002) raw materials went via Luanda; and (3) via South Africa.

With many road networks still in an essentially unusable state, maritime transport plays an important role in international trade. Most SSA ports have low capacity. The most important port is Richards Bay in South Africa (90 million tons), followed by Durban in South Africa (more than 55 million tons), Lagos in Nigeria (38 million tons), and finally Abidjan in the Ivory Coast (20 million tons). Mombasa in Kenya has a large port on the

---

[e] Paragraph inspired by the site: http://www.xaviermartin.fr.

Indian Ocean that handled 21.92 million tons in 2011[f] but its capacity is inadequate to handle the demands of the interior part of the region (Kenya, the Democratic Republic of Congo, Uganda, Rwanda, and Burundi).

The terminals in the region have been massively subcontracted in order to improve their effectiveness, but there are still long delays unloading goods, among other significant obstacles. Once a vessel arrives, it is not unusual to waste time finding the right truck. After discharge, products pass individually through customs' procedures.

Rail should be the preferred mode of transport in Africa. If infrastructure and volumes existed to support this mode of transportation, the region's geography clearly favors it. However, there is little rail traffic; investment has dropped or is slow, and in many places rail networks have been abandoned altogether. Some countries such as Nigeria have only one rail line. In fact, rail transport in that nation dropped 91 percent in tons/km in the last 27 years (from 1,350,000 tons/km in 1981 to 57,000 tons/km in 2010). Some countries are pursuing railway infrastructure aggressively. Ethiopia, Africa's second-most populous nation, is negotiating with Brazil, Russia, and India to finance and build rail links after agreeing to terms with Chinese and Turkish companies for other routes. A report in Bloomberg.com[3] states that Ethiopia "is building 4,744 kilometers of electrified railway lines at a cost of 110.8 billion birr ($5.9 billion) as it seeks to reduce road-transport costs constraining the continent's fastest growing non-oil producing economy over the past decade." The World Bank has partnered with 14 SSA countries for construction, improved use, and maintenance of SSA rail networks. Nearly 70 percent of rail traffic in the region is now concessionary. These networks have made spectacular gains in productivity and productivity volume.

Telecommunications

SSA passed directly into the mobile phone era with nearly 500 million users in urban areas. The largest part of the remaining untapped market is in rural areas. Everyone agrees that good telecommunication coverage in this region is essential to its development.

Table 8.5 presents the scores for the Infrastructure dimension while Table 8.6 summarizes the strengths and weaknesses of the selected countries in sub-Saharan Africa.

Competence

Labor: Availability, Productivity, and Relations

In sub-Saharan Africa, labor productivity remains a significant concern. This is especially noticeable in agriculture as the majority of countries still use manual farming methods.

---

[f] http://africanbuilding.com/index.php/bim-2/26-transportation/263-construction-of-the-second-container-terminal-at-mombasa-port-is-on-course.

Table 8.5 Scores for the Infrastructure Dimension

Infrastructure	Transportation Infrastructure	Energy Infrastructure	Connectivity	Overall Grade
30%	50%	25%	25%	100%
Angola*	D#	D#	D−	D@
Dem. Rep. Congo*	D−#	D−#	D−#	D−#
Ethiopia	C	D	F	D+
Kenya	C	D+	D+	C−
Nigeria	D+	F	C−	D
South Africa	B+	C−	C+	B−
Sudan*	D−#	F#	D+	D−@

Note: *There is limited data for Angola, the Democratic Republic of Congo, and Sudan for the Infrastructure dimension. Grades presented in the table identified by the @ superscript are estimates based on partial numerical data combined with judgmental evaluation, while grades identified by the # superscript are solely based on judgmental evaluation.

Table 8.6 Strengths and Weaknesses Summary: Infrastructure Dimension

Grade	Strengths	Weaknesses
Angola: D	Busy with reconstruction; can create a "supply chain friendly" environment.	A high level of corruption.
Democratic Republic of Congo: D−	Built around mining; maintains a minimum level of infrastructure.	A high level of corruption and insecurity.
Ethiopia: D+	A low level of corruption compared to the majority of countries in the region; initial section of a hub is in place in Addis Ababa; significant attempts to improve railway infrastructure.	Aging rail and road infrastructures; 50 percent of the population is illiterate, the highest rate in Africa.
Kenya: C−	Significant state-led infrastructure development is under way; an important harbor in Nairobi.	A high level of corruption.
Nigeria: D	Benefits from a large harbor in Lagos.	Infrastructures are dilapidated; security is a preoccupation; and corruption and swindling are rampant.
South Africa: B−	A low level of corruption compared to other sub-Saharan Africa countries; respects the need for security; an extremely dense road network; quality harbors; heavily committed to the development of renewable energy.	Regular road congestion in some sections of its networks; infrastructure developed primarily for the transport of raw materials.
Sudan: D−	There are great expectations, although many obstacles need to be overcome to meet these expectations.	A high level of corruption; significant political unrest.

Bureaucracy also tends to dampen labor productivity as numerous time-consuming and obligatory procedures are imposed on workers.

Training is a major concern in sub-Saharan Africa. From the youngest age onward, children need to be educated to gain sufficient qualifications and subsequently make meaningful economic contributions and to eventually participate in the consumer marketplace. The number of children being educated is increasing, but the level of education is often mediocre, and students are frequently taught by people who are themselves poorly educated.

According to United Nations Educational, Scientific, and Cultural Organization (UNESCO), 38 percent of Africans (151 million people) are illiterate, two-thirds of which are women. In Ethiopia, less than half of the population is literate. In Sudan the literacy rate is 40 percent. However, in both Kenya and South Africa, rates of illiteracy are as low as 13 percent.

Education Levels for Line Staff and Management

South Africa contrasts greatly with the rest of SSA. South Africa is 24th in the LPI,[2] whereas the majority of the other SSA countries are below the 100th position. Of the 156 countries covered by the index, most of the last 50 places are held by countries in SSA, including Nigeria at 122nd, Kenya at 123rd, Angola at 139th, Ethiopia at 142nd, Democratic Republic of Congo at 144th, and Sudan in the 149th position.

The overall level of personnel training in Africa is low. Dedicated supply chain solutions that include training everyone involved need to be put in place. A major problem is that of training teachers; a third of primary school teachers in Africa have not received any formal training.

Logistics, Customs, and Security

Border controls pose a serious problem in Africa, unreasonably contributing to an increase in delays. A report on the African infrastructure[4] states that "a journey of 2,500 km from Lusaka in Zambia to Port Durban in South Africa takes around 8 days: 4 days travel (averaging 50 to 60 km per hour on the main highways), and 4 days to pass through the frontiers." The West Africa Trade Hub (USAID) is assisting countries of the ECOWAS and WAEMU. In its initiative for strengthening governance in road transport,[5] USAID compiled a register of roadblocks, merchandise–transport delays, and the "informal levying" of money. These controls are essentially directed at border police, local police, nationwide police, and others involved in "informal" activities.

Table 8.7 presents the scores for the Competence dimension while Table 8.8 presents a summary of the strengths and weaknesses of the selected countries in sub-Saharan Africa.

Table 8.7 Scores for the Competence Dimension

Competence	Labor Relations	Education Levels	Logistics Competence	Customs and Security	Overall Grade
20%	25%	25%	40%	10%	100%
Angola*	D#	D#	D⁻	C⁻	D@
Dem. Rep. Congo*	F#	D#	D⁻#	D⁻#	D⁻#
Ethiopia	C⁻	D	D⁻	D⁻	D
Kenya	B⁻	B⁻	D	D⁻	C⁻
Nigeria	C	C⁺	D	F	D⁺
South Africa	F	B	A⁻	A⁻	B⁻
Sudan*	F#	D#	F	D⁻	F@

Note: *There is limited data for Angola, the Democratic Republic of Congo, and Sudan. Grades presented in the table identified by the @ superscript are estimates based on a combination of partial numerical data and judgmental evaluation, while grades identified by the # superscript are solely based on judgmental evaluation.

Table 8.8 Strengths and Weaknesses Summary: Competence Dimension

Grade	Strengths	Weaknesses
Angola: D	Lack of skills compensated by a significantly large influx of Portuguese workers.	As a result of the long civil war, practically a whole generation is uneducated.
Democratic Republic of Congo: D⁻	A mining industry that has basic logistics abilities.	Few other logistics and supply chain abilities.
Ethiopia: D	Some notable improvements in the education sector could improve labor competence.	Logistics and supply chain abilities poor; illiteracy more than 57 percent.
Kenya: C⁻	A high rate of literacy; good levels of workmanship.	Few logistics and supply chain abilities.
Nigeria: D⁺	A hydrocarbon industry that has developed abilities specific to that sector.	Few logistics and supply chain abilities.
South Africa: B⁻	High literacy levels; training in supply chains and logistics take place at university and is well developed; the highest supply chain maturity in Africa.	Young people do not have adequate access to the employment market.
Sudan: F	A rate of literacy of 61 percent.	Few logistics and supply chain abilities.

Table 8.9 Summary Assessment of EPIC Attractiveness for the Nations Represented in Sub-Saharan Africa

	Economy	Politics	Infrastructure	Competence	Overall Grade
Angola*	B⁻	D⁻	D@	D@	D⁺
Dem. Republic of Congo*	B⁻	F@	D⁻#	D⁻#	D
Ethiopia	B⁻	C⁻	D⁺	D	C⁻
Kenya	C⁺	D⁺	C⁻	C⁻	C⁻
Nigeria	B⁺	D	D	D⁺	C⁻
South Africa	B	B⁻	B⁻	B⁻	B⁻
Sudan*	C⁺	F@	D⁻@	F@	D⁻

*Note: *There is limited data for Angola, the Democratic Republic of Congo, and Sudan. Grades presented in the table identified by the @ superscript are estimates based on a combination of partial numerical data and judgmental evaluation, while grades identified by the # superscript are solely based on judgmental evaluation.*

Table 8.9 presents a summary of the overall assessment scores on the Economic, Politics, Infrastructure, and Competence (EPIC) dimensions for the nations in the SSA region. The scores for the seven SSA nations reveal a differing pace of economic development, which holds significant implications for supply chain management decision makers. Specifically, South Africa has relatively high scores on the EPIC dimensions, making it a more attractive place for supply chain investments. In the middle group, Ethiopia, Kenya, and Nigeria may be considered for supply chain investments. Finally, Angola, the Democratic Republic of Congo, and Sudan should be cautiously watched for future developments that might improve their attractiveness for supply chain investment.

Main Trends in Sub-Saharan Africa

Improving Infrastructure

In sub-Saharan Africa, as in developed regions, quality of infrastructure is considered essential to economic development. The projects planned are numerous:

- ▲ Projects to connect the major cities of western Africa
- ▲ Construction of a huge harbor, "Port Lamu," a collaborative effort between Kenya, South Sudan, and Ethiopia (Launched in 2012, this project is expected to create 32 berths and rail and road infrastructures linking Ethiopia with South Sudan.)
- ▲ Several airports are under construction: Conakry in Guinea, Libreville in Gabon, Addis-Ababa in Ethiopia, Bamako in Mali, Accra in Ghana, and Dakar in Senegal

- ▲ Several railroad projects are under way
- ▲ Several high-speed passenger trains (TGVs) are under construction: Johannesburg to Pretoria TGV: 56 km in operation since 2011; Johannesburg to Durban TGV: 600 km financed by the Chinese rail group GCCF
- ▲ A railway link between Tanzania and Burundi (for completion in 2016, Isaka to Kigaliet, Keza in Tanzania to Gigeta, and Musongati to Burundi)
- ▲ A railway link of 2681 km is planned to link Cotonou and Abidjan via Niamey (Niger) and Ouagadougou (Burkina)
- ▲ A railway link connecting Dakar, N'Djamena, and Djibouti

Finally, a railroad between Mombasa and Kampala (930 km) has been under restoration since November 2010.

Structured Distribution

African economies are developing and diversifying. Those countries that depend too heavily on raw materials (Kenya, Angola, and Democratic Republic of Congo) have supply chains geared only to these specialized products. These supply chains do not fulfill the sophisticated and complex requirements of manufacturing and distributing consumer products. Nations diversifying into the industrial or service sectors (Kenya, eastern and southern countries, and South Africa) need sophisticated supply chain services: information systems, infrastructures, and capabilities. Limited availability of goods and their complex distribution networks mean that every African traveling abroad returns with goods (particularly automobile spare parts and electrical goods).

The more the African market remains fragmented and diffuse, the more difficult it is to access at a low cost. But urbanism is on the rise: in 1980, 28 percent of Africans lived in towns. Today this number is 40 percent, and by 2030 it is expected to be 50 percent.

Changing Cost Structure

Supply chain costs in sub-Saharan Africa are very different from those found elsewhere in the world. In many regions, the cost of transportation is high but product quality is poor. The main distribution and warehousing facilities tend to be situated close to ports, but it is difficult to find a facility that is both secure and in good condition. Cost of transport is calculated on very different variable cost to fixed cost ratios than the norm. In western and central Africa, the ratio is 60:40 (variable cost:fixed cost), and it is 60:40 in east Africa. In western European countries, it is closer to 45:55.[6]

Prices today are much higher in western and central Africa even though costs are not necessarily higher. The markets are essentially cartelized, so margins tend to be higher than free-market conditions would suggest. Prices are better in eastern Africa, where they are beginning to use southern Africa as a model for how to conduct business.

The initiatives taken in terms of progressive deregulation of markets and the disappearance of cartels that will follow suggest that logistics costs should be substantially reduced in the coming years, and the cost structure should move closer to developed market standards. The initial effects of the progressive deregulation of markets can already be seen in eastern Africa.

Lowering Customs Barriers and the War on Corruption

It is not just the deteriorated road infrastructure that slows down intra-SSA trade. High customs costs (customs rates can be 50 percent of the value of a product) and corruption are also part of the African business environment. Nevertheless, several African countries are fighting back against corruption by establishing specialist anticorruption bureaus and improved administrative oversight. The fact that progress toward reducing corruption is a criterion for obtaining debt relief from the World Bank, the Club of Paris, and the International Monetary Fund (IMF) has acted as a great incentive for several nations of SSA. U.S. businesses have also made considerable efforts to counteract corruption. Several initiatives have also been implemented to reduce or rescind customs duties and implement free trade zones.

Automating Procedures and Implementing Information Systems

In recent years, certain governments have set up offices to counteract bureaucracy, corruption, manual procedures, and procedural duplication. These offices have been set up with the sole purpose of helping foreign investors. Computer systems have been put in place in many services. IT systems connecting subsidiaries in Africa with the rest of the world are being developed for private companies.

Supply Chain Challenges

Logistics

Organizing logistics in Africa requires a good working knowledge of the country; expecting an expatriate to do this can be expensive and is generally not recommended. Working with a trustworthy local partner is preferable. In sub-Saharan Africa, you need to know if the region is safe, whether roads are in good condition, whether bridges are open, and the extent of the rainy and dry seasons.

Corruption

Corruption is everywhere in Africa. It is considered the norm, and it is part of the accepted way of conducting business. Even if by local law a service should take two days, the civil servant will probably tell you that it is not possible. In this case, it would be normal for that person to be offered something; if the civil servant is satisfied, the work will be done more rapidly (five minutes for a signature, for example).

Political Instability

Investors in Africa should bear in mind that political stability is often fragile. Therefore, actions should be measured against potential risk before they are undertaken. The risk of setting up unaided in a country should be weighed against that of going through an already established partner who understands the political situation. Political instability can destroy business and all of its assets in one fell stroke.

Logistic Hubs

European industry is talking about optimization, distribution, and regional hubs, but these are not priorities in Africa. Because of the region's political instability, there are no optimum solutions. Building a hub in a sub-Saharan Africa country can present several risky challenges: if the country is at war (internally or externally), you could find that all your goods are blocked; poor existing infrastructure creates distribution problems; and the level of crime, theft, loss, and damage is significant. Although South Africa is a successful African hub, it is not well connected to the rest of Africa. Companies in Africa generally do not seek to optimize or reduce transportation costs; instead, they add them to the cost of goods—in the Ivory Coast one tub of yogurt costs around €7.5 whereas in France it costs around €1. Lifestyle also has an impact on distribution. In Africa, a family buys staples as and when they need them; in Europe, a family buys and stores provisions in large quantities.

Conceptual Differences

Supply-chain managers should be aware of the differences in concept and terminology:

▲ When African people say, "The warehouse is very big," their concept of "very big" may well require further clarification. A "big warehouse" in Europe is 80,000 m², whereas in Africa a "big warehouse" could be 500 m².

▲ "The road is good," may mean that a person may need to cross the rivers on foot; not that the whole distance is paved road.

▲ "Delivery Monday morning," would mean 8 a.m. next Monday morning to a Singaporean, but in Africa it might mean any time next Monday.

▲ Deliveries in Europe are made with trucks or cars whereas in Africa they can be made by rickshaw or by camel.

▲ The notion of "near" and "far" are different; a five-year-old African boy may consider that walking for one hour to reach his school is "near," whereas in the United States that would be considered "far."

Furthermore, the notion of "best practices" has a different meaning in SSA. In Europe, a truck loaded with 22 tons is considered a full load. In Africa, if a truck can take a load of up to 30 or 33 tons, then that is the size of its "full" load. Quoting travel time by distance is unrealistic. In the United States and in general, road transport quotations are made per mile. In Africa, due to seasonal differences and road conditions, it might take 24 hours to travel 300 km to the north, whereas the same distance could be done in 6 hours traveling southward. Road conditions are not consistent.

General Infrastructure, Communication, and Technology

Although several sub-Saharan African countries are experiencing more than 5 percent economic growth, they are still weak in terms of infrastructure, communication, and technology. Inflation is generally higher than economic growth (for example, 14 percent in Kenya). Serious reforms need to be undertaken to ensure security in business. It will likely take 20 to 30 years for these reforms to reach the same standard as in Western Europe or the United States. Customs procedures are complex and shielded by governments. Public and private interests are often confused because politicians are frequently also business owners (for example, a Nigerian minister owns a radio station, and the former president of Madagascar was also CEO of a company).

Supply Chain Opportunities

The Social Network

An organization that does not have strong networking could be wasting its time and energy in Africa. The notion of being part of a family is very important in Africa, meaning that networking can be done through family, friends, tribe/ethnic group, or political party. If a person is introduced as someone's "brother," one could benefit from that person's reputation and network. It is helpful to have several different local tribal and political connections. Building a network alone is not sufficient; it is also necessary to identify an appropriate and ethical business partner. However, it is important to beware of charlatans who pretend to know everything and offer to introduce you into the highest level of the government.

Business Culture

In Africa, pushing a negotiation and "getting straight to the point" are strategies to avoid. Take your time; ask about your business partner's family and about his plans for the weekend. Offering a memento of your visit (which could be seen as corruption in Europe) is normal in Africa. Learn to speak a few words of the local dialect. This makes your African partner feel more comfortable and makes him or her more likely to trust you, and contracts will be concluded more quickly. Show your interest in becoming a friend or part of your African partner's "family." In Africa, this opens many doors. Even today, under many governments, the "daughter, son, best friend of" approach is still the best strategy for doing business.

SSA Is Diverse

SSA is enormous and diverse, and it should be considered as several regions. Many businesspeople make the error of considering SSA as a single region, treating all the countries in the region in the same way. In reality, each country should be viewed separately. In terms of language, there are both English-speaking regions and French-speaking regions. Each country has its own rules, business regulations, and currency (except the 14 countries that use the CFA francs).

International Interest in SSA

Former colonies played a central role in the African economy, but new players (such as China, India, Brazil, and Turkey) are entering the market and bringing a different approach to business. African leaders prefer to work with emerging countries rather than with historical partners. For example, China is actively building roads, hospitals, and infrastructure in exchange for rights to SSA's mineral resources and raw materials.

Sub-Saharan Africa Best Practices

The Example of Bolloré Logistics, Africa

The Bolloré Group is a French family business created in 1822. In 2011, the Group achieved a turnover of €8.5 billion, with 57 percent of its turnover (€4.9 billion) in transport and logistics. Its intensive development in African logistics dates from the beginning of the 1980s. It has the largest number of establishments in Africa, with a presence in 45 countries. The company has 250 offices and employs 23,000 personnel. The strength of the group lies in its control of vital transport resource nodes along with porthandling activities.

To ensure the smooth running of its activities, the Bolloré Group took control of some major African railroads.

Along with other businesses such as Getma (NCT Necotrans), Dubai World, DHL, and Maersk, the Bolloré Group has become a force in Africa. Having made successive gains over the past 20 years, it has become a major transport, storage, and port handling operator. To get a sense of its involvement in western and eastern Africa, 80 percent and 25 percent, respectively, of exports (excluding hydrocarbons) are handled by the Group. In the matter of rail transport, port handling, and river transport, it manages 13 concessions in eastern Africa and 28 concessions in the whole of Africa. For example, it has held the Sitarail concession since 1998. This company operates the Ouagadougou to Burkina Faso-Abidjan railroad in the Ivory Coast as well as the container terminals of Abidjan (Ivory Coast), Douala (Cameroon), Tema (Ghana), Lagos (Nigeria), and the entire port of Libreville (Gabon).

Key Takeaways for Sub-Saharan Africa

1. African supply chains are atypical and are often disintegrated and incoherent. These supply chains can be either dilapidated or undeveloped, and sometimes both. The continent sorely needs to set up statutory and political regulations governing interactions between countries.
2. With resource-hungry developing nations such as India and China having emerged on the global competitive stage, the competition for low-cost labor and inexpensive raw materials in SSA will continue to increase.
3. It is not unusual for sensitive networks (and, as such, many Africa networks) to require effective security solutions in the form of alliances or accompanying personnel. Good security results not only in the successful fulfillment of transport and storage contracts but also in the protection of goods.
4. New consumer markets are developing in SSA. Foreign companies looking to gain access to these new markets must begin to work in this region immediately to ensure future access.
5. It is only a matter of time before the remaining politically unstable nations stabilize. Once that happens, regions of SSA will develop quickly, especially moving inland from the west and east coasts of SSA.

References

1. Logistics Performance Index 2012. World Bank.
2. Ibid.
3. W. Davison, "Ethiopia Courts BRICS for Rail Projects to Spur Economic Growth," Bloomberg.com, May 13, 2013.

4. "African Infrastructure: An Imperative Transformation," French Agency for Development, World Bank, 2011.
5. http://www.watradehub.com/competitive-environment/transport-infrastructure
6. Supee Teravaninthorn and Gaël Raballand, "Transport Prices and Costs in Africa: A Review of the Main International Corridors," Africa Infrastructure Country Diagnostic (AICD), July 2008, p. 23.

CHAPTER 9

Western Europe

Western Europe might be considered an anomaly compared to most of the other regions explored in this book due to the difficulty in precisely defining its boundaries. The United Nations identifies the Western Europe countries as Austria, Belgium, France, Germany, Luxembourg, the Netherlands, Switzerland, and the Principalities of Liechtenstein and Monaco.[a] This demarcation, which notably excludes the United Kingdom, Spain, and Italy includes the original member countries of the European Economic Community (also known as the Common Market in the English-speaking world), which was formed when Germany, Belgium, France, Italy, Luxembourg, and the Netherlands signed the Treaty of Rome in 1957. The European Economic Community essentially formalized an earlier relationship called the European Coal and Steel Community that was formed shortly after the World War II to improve political cooperation among the member nations.

The *Encyclopedia Brittanica*[b] provides an alternate perspective, defining the boundaries of Western Europe as including 10 countries: Belgium, France, Germany, Greece, Italy, Luxembourg, the Netherlands, Portugal, Spain, and the United Kingdom. This demarcation is based upon the Western European Union, which took shape in 1948 when Belgium, France, Luxembourg, the Netherlands, and the United Kingdom signed the Brussels Treaty to provide for collective defense and to facilitate cooperation in economic, social, and cultural matters.[c] In 1954, West Germany and Italy were added to this group, which eventually led to the formal establishment of the Western European Union in 1955. Portugal and Spain joined the Union in 1988 and Greece joined in 1992.

Yet another popular but informal demarcation for Western Europe is influenced by geography, defining Western Europe as "the region comprising the westerly countries

---

[a] http://esa.un.org/unpd/wup/CD-ROM_2009/WPP2009_DEFINITION_OF_MAJOR_AREAS_AND_REGIONS.pdf.

[b] http://www.britannica.com/EBchecked/topic/640646/Western-European-Union-WEU.

[c] The Brussels Treaty of 1948 was the precursor to the North Atlantic Treaty Organization formed in 1949.

Figure 9.1 A demarcation of the countries in Western Europe.

of Europe."[d] Figure 9.1 provides yet another perspective on the boundaries of Western Europe.

This chapter's definition of Western Europe is more inclusive than any of the preceding demarcations, and includes the 10 nations of the Western European Union (Belgium, France, Germany, Greece, Italy, Luxembourg, the Netherlands, Portugal, Spain, and the United Kingdom) as well as Iceland, Ireland, Switzerland, Austria, Norway, Sweden, Denmark, Finland, Malta, San Marino, Vatican City, Cyprus, and the principalities of Andorra, Monaco, and Liechtenstein. Turkey,[e] a country that geographically belongs to both Europe and Asia, is included in Western Europe as well.

---

[d] en.wikipedia.org/wiki/Western_Europe.

[e] Although Turkey is located across two continents, it has been included in this chapter on Western Europe, rather than in the preceding Middle East and North Africa (MENA) chapter. The decision to include Turkey in this chapter was made strictly based on an observation that, economically, Turkey is a bit more closely tied to Western Europe and the European Union (EU) than to the Middle East and North Africa. This is not to suggest that Turkey is not also closely tied to the countries in Middle East and North Africa, as this is certainly also the case.

Economic and Political Background

Well positioned for international trade, Western Europe has a very high population density, high personal income levels, and a correspondingly high consumption of products and services. However, the Western European population is aging, and when combined with its relatively high population density, this creates some interesting "last mile" supply chain opportunities for the region in the future.

Any discussion of Western Europe inevitably includes a discussion of the European Union (EU), a union of nations that now encompasses practically every country in the western part of Europe except Norway, Switzerland, and Iceland. A discussion of the EU provides a good basis for understanding the western European region in general.

Understanding the Region: The European Union

The EU owes its origins to the six-nation European Economic Community, nations that would be classified as belonging to Western Europe by any definition. That said, the EU is rapidly growing to now include many nations that do not belong to Western Europe, no matter how broadly Western Europe may be defined. With the exception of Malta, which joined the EU in 2004, the 12 other nations that joined the EU in the 21st century belong to Central and Eastern Europe.

The EU is an economic region with a high population density. It is half the size of the United States but has almost 200 million more inhabitants, with a total population of 500 million and a population density of 116 people/km² as compared to 32.6 people/km² in the United States. Unlike the United States, which is relatively homogeneous, the countries in the EU vary greatly in terms of economic prosperity, language, and cultural identity. For example, as of 2013 there are 24 official and working languages recognized by the EU.^{f}

As an economic and political confederation of countries, the EU's borders have grown over time with the addition of new nations. This growth and the relatively constant transformation of the EU (addition of nations, the single currency, its ever-adapting regulatory system) makes operating supply chains in this region challenging in ways that are new to Europe and very different from how business was conducted in "old Europe."

The 28 countries in the EU have joined it over six major waves. The six-nation "founding group" (France, Germany, Italy, Belgium, Luxembourg, and the Netherlands) was joined by three countries in 1973 (the United Kingdom, Denmark, and Ireland), one in 1981 (Greece), two in 1986 (Portugal and Spain), three in 1995 (Austria, Sweden, and Finland), ten in 2004 (Estonia, Latvia, Lithuania, Poland, the Czech Republic, Slovakia, Hungary, Slovenia, Cyprus, and Malta), and two in 2007 (Bulgaria and Romania), with

^{f} http://ec.europa.eu/languages/languages-of-europe/eu-languages_en.htm.

Croatia joining the EU in July 2013. And the additions continue. Five other countries have officially applied to join (Macedonia, Montenegro, Turkey, Iceland, and Serbia). Among these, the EU has prioritized membership for the Balkan states, Macedonia, Montenegro, and Serbia, but Iceland and Turkey are also acknowledged candidates. Turkey's candidacy, which has been pending since the 1980s, is a contentious issue related to doubts regarding the nation's ability to meet the formal political, institutional, and economic conditions for membership. Albania has begun the application process to join the EU, and Bosnia and Kosovo are considered potential applicants.

Member nations have implemented fairly extensive EU directives into national laws as they moved toward integration, producing a common core of laws that exists across all member states. However, the implementation frameworks for these laws differ across nations. The general aims are the same, but their application can vary: labor legislation differs between countries, as do the rules on storage and transportation. The European Union's motto is *In varietate Concordia*, meaning "united in diversity," and diversity is indeed a defining characteristic in such a union, with its 24 official languages. Two EU nations have opted out of adopting the euro as their nation's currency (the United Kingdom and Denmark), and Sweden has yet to decide whether it will adopt the euro. Regardless, this common currency is likely the strongest bond between the EU member nations.

Understanding the Region: Western Europe

Western Europe is more homogeneous in terms of standard of living and infrastructure relative to the EU overall, but there are still substantial differences within the Western European nations. For instance, Figure 9.2 shows the importance of the five largest Western European countries in terms of population and GDP and demonstrates that these countries together represent 63 percent of the EU's population and 72 percent of the EU's GDP.

Country	Population (Millions–2013 Estimate)	Population as Percentage of EU	GDP (Billions of $ –2012 Estimate)	GDP as Percentage of EU
EU	503.89	100	16,360	100
Germany	81.15	16.10	3401	20.79
France	65.95	13.09	2609	15.95
United Kingdom	63.40	12.58	2441	14.92
Italy	61.48	12.20	2014	12.31
Spain	47.37	9.40	1352	8.26
Five-Nation Total	319.35	63.37	11,817	72.23

CIA World Factbook

Figure 9.2 Five nations' contribution to GDP.

The area's geography and population concentration partly explain why the main trade flows in Western Europe today are in the *blue banana*[g] or follow nearby parallel routes. Roughly speaking, trade in Europe follows a north-to-south direction.

This chapter focuses on eight EU countries and one non-EU country for further discussion. These focal countries, in alphabetical order, are Austria, France, Germany, Italy, the Netherlands, Spain, Sweden, Turkey, and the United Kingdom.

Politics

The political and economic backgrounds of the countries in Western Europe are diverse. Politically, the nations of the region range from parliamentary republics (Austria, France, Germany, Italy, and Turkey) to differing forms of mixed parliamentary republics and monarchies (the Netherlands, Spain, Sweden, and the United Kingdom).

The Economies

Austria is home to a developed market economy that is closely aligned with the EU, and Germany in particular. Austria has a very large and well-developed services sector, which is responsible for most of its GDP and is primarily focused on finance, banking, consulting, and tourism. Although representing a much smaller contribution to GDP, Austria also has major industry sectors in agriculture and iron and steel, electronics, paper, textiles, automobiles, and glass.

As the fifth largest economy in the world, France's economy is diverse and spans the full range of industry and service sectors. Areas of particular focus for the French economy are energy, agriculture, tourism, aerospace, and defense.

Germany, the fourth largest economy in the world, is relatively poor in natural resources but has a very large service sector and a smaller, but very well-developed industrial sector, with only a very small agricultural sector relative to the overall GDP. In the industrial sector, Germany produces automobiles, heavy machinery, metals, and chemicals. Germany is also a leading producer of wind turbines and solar power technology.

Italy has few natural resources but has a diversified industrial economy with important economic sectors in renewable/solar energy, agriculture, transportation, and finance. Italy's primary industries are tourism, machinery, iron and steel, textiles, motor vehicles, clothing, and footwear.

The Netherlands' economy is noted for stable industrial relations, moderate unemployment and inflation, a sizable trade surplus, and an important role as a European

---

[g] The blue banana, discussed in the following section on The Markets, is a corridor of concentrated urbanization in Western Europe that takes its name from the banana-shaped curvature of the corridor.

transportation hub. Industrial activity is predominantly in food processing, chemicals, petroleum refining, and electrical machinery. The agricultural sector employs only 2 percent of the labor force but provides large surpluses for the food-processing industry and for exports.[h]

Spain is a service-oriented economy that still lags behind most of Western Europe although it has made great progress in recent decades. The service sector accounts for 70 percent of Spain's GDP. The major industries in Spain are textiles and apparel, foods and beverages, metals and metal products, chemicals, ships, automobiles, and machine tools.

Sweden is largely export-oriented, with substantial natural resources in the areas of timber, hydropower, and iron ore. Sweden has substantial industrial sectors in automobiles, precision equipment, chemicals, telecommunications, pharmaceuticals, industrial equipment, forestry, consumer products, and steel.

Turkey has significant natural mineral resources (over 60 different mineral reserves). As an example, Turkey holds 72 percent of the world's supply of boron salts. Turkey's industrial economy is largely focused in the areas of agriculture, textiles, automobiles, shipbuilding, transportation equipment, construction materials, and consumer goods. In the services sector, Turkey is prominent in banking, transportation, tourism, and communications. Most of the industrial wealth of the nation is concentrated to the north and west (toward Western Europe).

The United Kingdom (UK) has one of the world's largest and most diversified economies, with substantial natural gas and oil reserves. As with other economically developed nations, the services sector is dominant in the United Kingdom, with the financial and telecommunications sectors representing the leading service sectors.

The Markets

The population distribution across Europe is concentrated in the blue banana (Figure 9.3), an oblong region of Western Europe that covers the southeast of England, the Netherlands, Belgium, the western part of Germany, and extends southward to the north of Italy. This narrow, yet highly populated region has 110 million residents. For example, the population density in the Netherlands is 450 people/km^2 as compared to 32.6 people/km^2 in the United States. As one might expect, this region has a high standard of living and is characterized by substantial consumption of goods and services. From a logistics perspective, this region is often the chosen location for warehouses to serve all of Europe and to handle regional distribution for major consumer markets. The result is that the blue banana is a region where truck traffic is heaviest, especially in north Germany heading toward the port of Hamburg and the Netherlands. In fact, at some times of year, these regions lack the trucks necessary to meet the demand for transportation.

---

[h] https://www.cia.gov/library/publications/the-world-factbook/geos/nl.html.

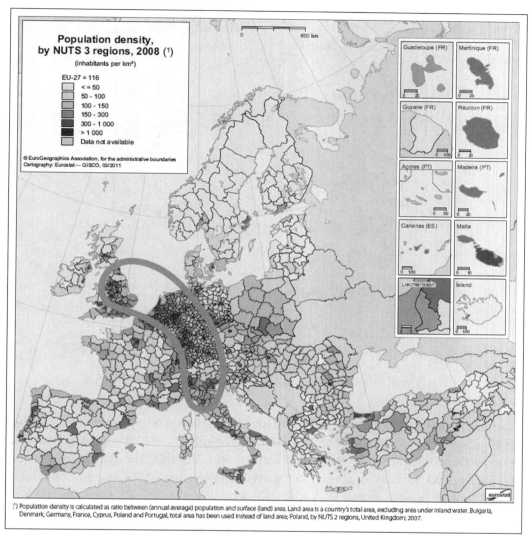

Figure 9.3 The blue banana.

Location of Markets

The following discussion uses the primacy rate[i] and the rate of urbanization to illustrate the growth and concentration of the markets, for the focal countries in Western Europe.

---

[i] The percentage of the urban population living in a country's largest metropolitan area; it provides an indicator of the concentration of industrial activity.

Figure 9.4 Austria.

Austria

Austria, a member of the EU since 1995, is home to a population of approximately 8.2 million people (Figure 9.4). With a total area of some 83,871 km² (32,383 mi²), Austria is situated between Germany, the Czech Republic, Liechtenstein, Slovenia, Slovakia, Hungary, Italy, and Switzerland, with its longest border shared with Germany (784 km, 487 mi) and its second longest border shared with Italy (430 km, 267 mi). The Alps, one of the great mountain ranges of Europe, crosses Austria from the southwest to the northeast, with the terrain of the northern, eastern, and southeastern parts of Austria reflective of lower and flatter terrain. The vast majority of the 8.2 million residents of Austria are located in these lower elevations toward its northern, southeastern, and southern borders. Austria's largest population centers are located in its capital Vienna (1.7 million), Linz (286,000), Graz (222,300), Salzburg (150,300), and Innsbruck (112,500). The primacy rate for Austria is 22,[j] and 68 percent of the population live in urban areas of greater than 100,000 people. The rate of urbanization is increasing at 0.6 percent per year.[k] The Austrian population

---

[j] The data on the primacy rates for all the countries mentioned in this chapter comes from the World Bank Urban Concentration Data, WDI & GDF 2010, Code: EN.URB.LCTY.UR.ZS.

[k] The data on the rate of urbanization is from the Central Intelligence Agency's (CIA) World Factbook.

is largely Roman Catholic (73.6 percent), with the vast majority of its citizens speaking German (88.6 percent), which is the national language.

France

France is a founding member of the EU (1952) and home to a population of approximately 66 million people (Figure 9.5). It has a total area (metropolitan France, French Guiana, Guadeloupe, La Réunion, Martinique, and Mayotte) of some 643,801 km² (248,573 mi²), which is about 80 percent of the size of the state of Texas (USA). France is situated between Andorra, Belgium, Germany, Italy, Luxembourg, Monaco, Spain, and Switzerland and shares its longest borders with Spain (623 km; 387 mi), Belgium (620 km; 385 mi), Switzerland (573 km; 356 mi), Italy (488 km; 303 mi), and Germany (451 km; 280 mi).

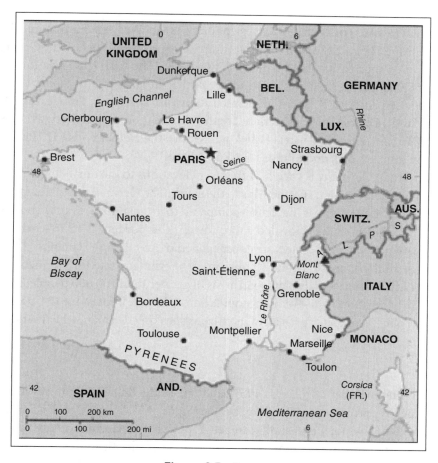

Figure 9.5 France.

The French terrain is varied, with plains and rolling hills to the north and west, the Pyrenees to the south, and the Alps to the east. French Guiana is located on the northeast coast of South America; Guadeloupe and Martinique are located in the Caribbean Sea midway between Puerto Rico and Trinidad, Venezuela; Mayotte is located off the east coast of Africa, and La Réunion is located off the east coast of Madagascar. The French population is dispersed more evenly across the nation, with its largest population centers in its capital Paris (2.2 million; 10.1 million in urban area), Marseille (795,000; 1.5 million in urban area), Lyon (472,000; 1.5 million in urban area), Lille (230,000; 1.2 million in urban area), Toulouse (433,000), and Nice (339,000). The primacy rate for France is 19, and 85 percent of the population live in urban areas of greater than 100,000 people. The rate of urbanization is increasing at 1 percent per year. The French population is largely Roman Catholic (85 percent), with all of citizens speaking French, the national language.

Germany

Germany is the country with the largest population in Western Europe and it is also home to Europe's largest economy. A founding member of the EU (1952), Germany has a population of approximately 81 million (Figure 9.6). The total land area for Germany is about 357,022 km² (137,847 mi²), which is similar in land area to Japan. Germany is situated between Austria, Belgium, the Czech Republic, Denmark, France, Luxembourg, the Netherlands, Poland, and Switzerland, with its longest borders shared with the Czech Republic (815 km; 506 mi), Austria (784 km; 489 mi), the Netherlands (577 km; 359 mi), Poland (456 km; 283 mi), and France (451 km; 280 mi).

The terrain in Germany is varied, with lower elevations to the north, higher elevations toward its geographic center, and the Alps to the south. The German population is relatively more evenly distributed across the nation compared to its neighbors, France and Italy, with its largest population centers located more toward the borders than toward its center. Germany's largest population centers are its capital Berlin (3.5 million), Hamburg (1.8 million), Munich (1.4 million), and Cologne (1 million). The primacy rate for Germany is 6, and 74 percent of the population live in urban areas of greater than 100,000 people. There is no growth in urbanization. The German population is largely Protestant (34 percent) and Roman Catholic (34 percent) with all of its citizens speaking German, which is the national language.

Italy

Italy, a founding member of the EU (1957) and one of the first EU countries to adopt the euro, is home to approximately 60 million people (Figure 9.7). With a total land area of some 301,340 km² (116,348 mi²) and similar in geographic size to Germany, Italy has 7600 km (4722 mi) of coastline falling along the Tyrrhenian Sea, Adriatic Sea, Mediterranean Sea, and Ionian Sea. Italy is situated between Austria, France, Vatican City, San Marino, Slovenia,

Figure 9.6 Germany.

and Switzerland, with its longest borders shared with Switzerland (740 km, 460 mi), France (488 km, 303 mi), Austria (430 km, 267 mi), and Slovenia (199 km, 124 mi).

The Italian terrain is largely rugged and mountainous with some plains and coastal lowlands. In northern Italy, one can find the east-west Alps, with the Apennines mountain range running most of the north-south length of the country. The Italian population is more concentrated in the north and south in Italy's lower elevations and coastal plains. Italy's largest population centers are in its capital Rome (3.4 million), Milan (2.9 million), Naples (2.3 million), and Turin (1.7 million). The primacy rate for Italy is 8, and 64 percent of the population live in urban areas of greater than 100,000 people. The rate of urbanization in Italy is approximately 0.5 percent on an annual basis. The Italian population is largely Roman Catholic (80 percent) with its citizens speaking Italian (the national language), German, French, and Slovene.

Figure 9.7 Italy.

The Netherlands

A founding member of the EU (1952), the Netherlands has a population of approximately 17 million and a total land area of some 41,543 km² (16,040 mi²). To the south the Netherlands is bordered by Belgium (450 km, 280 mi, of border), to the east by Germany (577 km, 359 mi, of border), and to the north by a coastline of 451 km (280 mi) that runs along the southern part of the North Sea (Figure 9.8). It is a very short trip across the North Sea from Netherlands to the southeastern region of the United Kingdom.

The terrain of the Netherlands is largely coastal lowland, with reclaimed land and hills to the southeast. The population of the Netherlands is somewhat evenly distributed across the nation, with its largest population centers located in the southern half of the nation and generally more toward the coast. The Netherland's largest population centers are its capital Amsterdam (1 million), Rotterdam (1 million), and The Hague

Figure 9.8 The Netherlands.

(seat of government, 629 thousand). The primacy rate for the Netherlands is 8, and 83 percent of the population live in urban areas of greater than 100,000 people. The rate of growth of urbanization is 0.8 percent. The population in the Netherlands is Roman Catholic (30 percent) and Protestant (20 percent), with the majority of the population being nonreligious (42 percent). The national languages in the Netherlands are Dutch and Frisian.

Spain

Spain joined the EU in 1986 and was among the first wave of nations to adopt the euro (1999). Spain is home to a population of approximately 47 million. With a total land area of some 505,370 km^2 (195,124 mi^2), Spain is situated between Andorra, France, Gibraltar, Portugal, and Morocco, with its longest borders shared with Portugal to the west

Figure 9.9   Spain.

(1214 km, 754 mi) and France to the north (623 km, 387 mi), and its shortest border shared with Gibraltar to the south (1.2 km, 0.75 mi).

The Spanish terrain is varied, with lower coastal plains, inland mountain chains, and the Pyrenees mountain chain on its border with France (Figure 9.9). The Spanish population is generally well distributed across the nation, but with greater density toward its borders. However, Madrid represents one of the most population dense locations in Spain, and it sits nearly in the geographic center of the country. Spain's largest population centers are its capital Madrid (5.7 million) and the cities of Barcelona (5 million) and Valencia (812,000). The primacy rate for Spain is 17, and 77 percent of the population live in urban areas of greater than 100,000 people. The rate of growth in urbanization is 1 percent per year. The Spanish population is largely Roman Catholic (94 percent), and its citizens speak Spanish (74 percent, official language), Catalan (17 percent), Galician (7 percent), and Basque (2 percent).

Sweden

Sweden joined the EU in 1995 but still maintains its own currency (krona). Sweden has a population of approximately 9 million and a total land area of some 450,295 km² (173,860 mi²). Sweden shares its borders with Norway (1619 km, 1006 mi) to the west, and Finland (614 km, 382 mi) and the Baltic Sea (3218 km, 2000 mi, of coastline) to the northeast and east (Figure 9.10).

The Swedish terrain is mostly flat, with mountains to the west. The southern regions of Sweden are much more densely populated, with the capital Stockholm representing the largest urban area (1.3 million), followed by Gothenburg (550,000) and Malmo (281,000). The primacy rate for Sweden is 16, and 85 percent of the population live in urban areas of greater than 100,000 people. There is 0.6 percent growth in urbanization on an annual basis. The Swedish population is largely Lutheran (87 percent), with most of its citizens speaking Swedish, the national language.

Turkey

Turkey is in the unique situation of being both a part of southeastern Europe and southwestern Asia (although it has more land area in Asia than Europe). The Straits of Bosporus (or Bosphorus) in the northwest region of Turkey runs through Istanbul and connects the Black Sea to the Sea of Marmara, which itself connects to the Aegean Sea and then connects into the Mediterranean Sea (Figure 9.11). The region of Turkey that is located to the west of the Straits of Bosporus lies in Europe, and the region to the east lies in Asia. Turkey has much less land area in Europe but it represents both a land bridge between Asia and continental Europe and is a major supplier to the interconnected set of nations that comprise the EU. Although Turkey is not a member of the EU, it is the largest exporter of many products to Europe (e.g., textiles, household equipment), with more than half of its exports being sent to the EU.

Turkey has a population of approximately 81 million, with a total area of some 783,562 km² (302,535 mi²), which is about the same size as Chile. Turkey shares borders with Armenia, Azerbaijan, Georgia, Iran, Iraq, and Syria to the east, Bulgaria and Greece to the south, and has 7200 km (4473 mi) of coastline along the Black Sea to the north, the Aegean Sea to the northwest, and the Mediterranean Sea to the south. Its longest borders are shared with Syria (822 km, 511 mi), Iran (499 km, 310 mi), and Iraq (352 km, 219 mi) to the south, and Bulgaria (240 km, 149 mi) and Georgia (252 km, 157 mi) to the north. The Turkish terrain is varied, with a high central plateau (Anatolia), a narrow coastal plain, and several mountain ranges, including the Taurus Mountains to the south and the Pontic Mountains to the north. The Turkish population is spread across the nation, with its largest population centers located away from its geographic center and more toward the west, south, and north. Turkey's largest population centers are its capital Ankara (3.8 million), Istanbul (10.4 million),

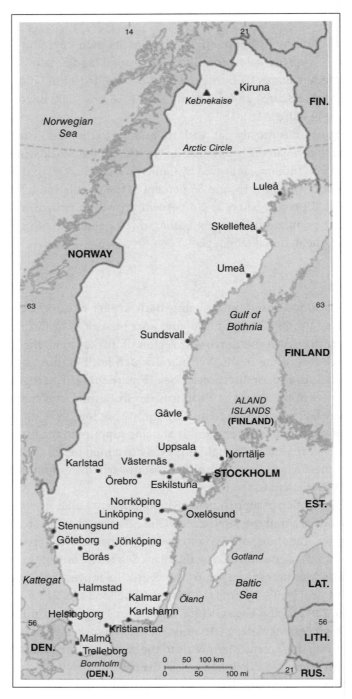

Figure 9.10 Sweden.

Figure 9.11   Turkey.

Izmir (2.7 million), Bursa (1.6 million), and Adana (1.3 million). The primacy rate for Turkey is 20, and 70 percent of the population lives in urban areas of greater than 100,000 people. Turkey is experiencing a growth in urbanization of about 1.7 percent per year. The Turkish population is nearly entirely Muslim (99.8 percent, mostly Sunni) with its citizens primarily speaking Turkish (75 percent) and Kurdish (18 percent).

United Kingdom (UK)

The United Kingdom has a long and somewhat tumultuous history that has shaped its borders. In 1707, The Kingdom of England (which included Wales) and the Kingdom of Scotland formed the United Kingdom of Great Britain. In 1800, the United Kingdom of Great Britain and Ireland joined together to form the United Kingdom of Great Britain and Ireland. In 1922, Ireland seceded from the United Kingdom of Great Britain and Ireland. Subsequently, Northern Ireland seceded from the newly formed Republic of Ireland and rejoined the United Kingdom, leaving the nation of the Republic of Ireland to the south and Northern Ireland a part of the United Kingdom (Figure 9.12).

Over the years, the Scottish and the Welsh have had concerns over the equality of their role in the United Kingdom. In 2007, the pro-independence Scottish National Party won the Scottish Parliament elections and has since formed a minority government with the goal of ultimately achieving independence for Scotland.

The United Kingdom joined the EU in 1973 and is home to a population of approximately 61.7 million people (Figure 9.13). With a total area of some 243,930 km² (94,058 mi²),

Figure 9.12 England, Ireland, Scotland, and Wales.

the United Kingdom has only one land border with the Republic of Ireland, which is 360 km (223 mi) in length. To the south of England, Scotland, and Wales is the English Channel, which connects the Celtic Sea with the North Sea. The Irish Sea is located to the east of Northern Ireland and to the west of England, Scotland, and Wales. The North Sea is to the east of England, Scotland, and Wales. Interestingly, Northern Ireland and the island that is home to England, Scotland, and Wales are not connected by land. The UK terrain is comprised of rugged hills, with some low mountains that level out to rolling plains to the east and southeast.

The UK population is somewhat evenly distributed across the nation, with its largest population centers located in England as well as population centers in the eastern region of Northern Ireland (Belfast) and southern Scotland (Glasgow). The UK's largest population centers are its capital London (8.6 million), Birmingham (2.3 million), Manchester (2.5 million), West Yorkshire (1.5 million), and Glasgow (1.2 million). The primacy rate for the United Kingdom is 17, and 80 percent of the population lives in urban areas of

Figure 9.13 The United Kingdom.

greater than 100,000 people. There is growth in urbanization at a rate of about 0.7 percent per year. The UK population is largely Christian (71.6 percent Anglican, Roman Catholic, Presbyterian, and Methodist) with a large portion of its population having no religion (23.1 percent). English is the official language of the United Kingdom, but it is important to note the other official languages include Scots (30 percent of the population of Scotland), Scottish Gaelic (60,000 people in Scotland), Welsh (20 percent of the population of Wales), Irish (about 10 percent of the population of Northern Ireland), and Cornish (2000 to 3000 people in Cornwall).

Assessing the Maturity Level of Western European Supply Chains

This section presents a summary of supply chain maturity in the zone, using an Economy, Politics, Infrastructure, and Competence (EPIC) analysis based on quantitative dimensions and the points covered in the previous sections of this chapter.

Economy

Despite the disparate growth rates and risks of recession in some Western European nations, the economic power of the region is still among the best in the world. Overall, the region's economy is very developed with large services sectors (70 percent of GDP). Industrial manufacturing generally accounts for much less (just over 20 percent of GDP).

Economic Output and Growth Rate

The economic situation in Western Europe has made headlines across the world in the last few years. Most of the region's countries have experienced the effects of the global economic crisis, which is associated with very significant increases in the levels of debt for some nations. Some Western European nations are carrying large deficits. For example, deficits are on the order of 15.4 percent of GDP for Greece, 11.4 percent for the United Kingdom, and 11.1 percent for Spain (2009). Overall, the EU's economic health has been seriously negatively affected, with substantial downturns in growth rates since 2011 and an unemployment rate of close to 25 percent in countries such as Spain.

Western Europe is a diverse region, and there is also great diversity within each Western European nation. For instance, Italy is economically divided with significant regional inequalities between the highly industrialized and dynamic regions of the north (Piedmont, Lombardy, Veneto, Tuscany) and the poor, rural regions of the south or Mezzogiorno (including Puglia, Calabria, and Sicily). Spain is in a similar situation, comprising 17 autonomous regions with economic development varying widely from Catalonia (around the city of Barcelona), which is very economically active, to the very poor region of Andalusia to the south. Similarly, since the reunification of East Germany and West Germany in 1989, Germany remains economically divided with a very rich west and a still-developing east.

Population

The region includes many small countries, but altogether it is home to 7.3 percent of the world's population. Observation of Europe's population indicates trends that are largely driven by the changing age profile of its citizens. First, Europe's population contains a very high proportion of people over age 40, which has been rising since 1990 and demonstrates substantial growth in the very senior age group (over 80 years of age). The population is getting inexorably older. The median age in the European Union was 35.2 in 1990, and 40.6 in 2009.[1] But this aging population in Western Europe masks disparities between countries. For instance, there is a projected decline in the German population, but France's population is growing. Studies project that by 2030 approximately one-third of the European population will be over age 65. New business models and supply chain designs will be needed to adapt to the aging consumer markets in this region.

This demographic change has consequences for consumer habits and ways of life. The proportion of people who are less mobile or even housebound will naturally focus concerns on supply chains designed for these population-dense urban regions, for example, the design of good distribution systems. As another example of the consequences of an aging population, health care costs are currently very high in Western European nations, and politicians have sought to rein them in. The European model is a solidarity-based model in which health care costs are mutualized and funded primarily by mandatory contributions withheld from salaries. To reduce costs, home health care solutions are in the works. This approach allows for the treatment of patients in their homes, greatly reducing the cost of dedicated hospital infrastructure. However, the challenges of designing supply chains to support at-home hospitalization and treatment are substantial.

Turkey represents a substantial departure from the population demographic described for most Western European countries. For instance, the world's population has doubled since 1960, but the Turkish population has almost tripled, with a high proportion of the population in the very young category. In the EU (2009), the ratio of those over 65 years of age to those between the ages of 15 and 64 was 26 percent. In comparison, the equivalent ratio for Turkey was only 8.8 percent. Hence, the issues associated with serving developing markets in Turkey will be very different from those of most of the other Western European nations.

Foreign Direct Investment

Western Europe remains one of the world's most active regions in terms of foreign direct investment (FDI). Inward flows of FDI were equivalent to around 1.8 percent of the EU's GDP in 2009, and outward flows were equivalent to 2.4 percent of GDP.[2] The United States is the main foreign direct investor in Western Europe, with the United Kingdom alone receiving more than a quarter of the European Union's FDI (primarily in its financial sector). Most of the EU's FDI stocks are in North America (more than €1000 billion), followed by Asia (nearly €500 million).

Exchange Rate Stability and Consumer Price Inflation

The euro, which has become the world's number two reserve currency, is currently on a somewhat bumpy road due to high national debt and the troubled economies of countries such as Greece, Spain, Portugal, and Italy. Control of inflation is the European Central Bank's prime objective, with inflation standing at around 2.5 percent in 2012. Inflation has been stable at comparable levels of around 2 percent for several years (apart from a spike to 3.7 percent in 2008).

The United Kingdom continues to use its own currency (the pound sterling), with inflation in 2011 above 5 percent, a number well above that of the rest of Western Europe. This inflation rate appears to be declining as the United Kingdom aims for a 2 percent inflation, in line with the other Western European countries.

Throughout the 1990s, Turkey experienced an inflation rate just short of being classified as hyperinflation. Even in 2002, the Turkish inflation rate was about 13 times the average rate of inflation in the world.[3] Since then the inflation rate has moved much lower and is now around 6 percent. The Turkish currency has, however, seen serious fluctuations recently. For instance, the Turkish lira fell by 21 percent against the U.S. dollar and 17 percent against the euro in 2011.

Balance of Trade

The European Union does not have a favorable balance of trade overall.[4] This is reflected in EU trade with China, which showed a deficit of €169 billion in 2010. The next largest trade deficit for the EU in that year was with Russia at €75 billion.[5] This deficit is partly attributable to energy costs.

Germany is the driving force for foreign trade in Western Europe. One-third of Germany's national output is for export, but most (60 percent) of that stays in Europe. In 2011, German exports outside the EU increased by 13.6 percent to €432.8 million. This growth in exports outside of the EU was achieved through an industrial sector renowned for its dynamism and a web of 300,000 highly proactive small and medium-sized businesses that do a good deal of export business. The same is true of Austria, which exports half of its GDP.

Turkey is a somewhat unique case with respect to Western Europe. Turkey is a country of entrepreneurs, with many multipolar groups. Geographically, it is very close to the countries of Western Europe and is home to suppliers that serve the industrial and consumer markets of Western Europe and the broader EU. Turkey is the EU's fifth-largest economic partner, and, as a result, Turkey felt the full brunt of the 2008 global financial crisis, registering a 4.8 percent contraction in GDP (2009). However, Turkey returned to significant growth rates in 2010 (8.9 percent) and maintained them in 2011 (8.5 percent), followed by a slowdown in 2012 (4 percent). The Turkish economy is driven by its young and growing population, but the largely imported domestic consumption of consumer goods adversely affects the balance of payments.

Table 9.1 presents the scores on the Economy dimension for the selected countries in Western Europe while Table 9.2 presents the strengths and weaknesses for each of these countries.

Table 9.1 Scores for the Economy Dimension

Economy	Economic Output and Growth Rate	Population Size	Foreign Direct Investment	Exchange Rate Stability/CPI	Balance of Trade	Overall Grade
30%	35%	25%	20%	15%	5%	100%
Austria	B⁻	B⁻	B	A⁻	B	B
France	B⁻	A⁻	B⁺	A⁻	B	B⁺
Germany	B	A	B	A⁻	A	B⁺
Italy	C	A⁻	B	A⁻	C	B
Netherlands	B⁻	B	B⁺	A⁻	A	B
Spain	B⁻	A⁻	B⁺	A⁻	C	B⁺
Sweden	B	B⁻	B⁻	B	B	B
Turkey	A⁻	A	B	C⁻	B	B⁺
United Kingdom	B⁻	A⁻	A⁻	B⁻	B	B⁺

Table 9.2 Strengths and Weaknesses Summary: Economy Dimension

Grade	Strengths	Weaknesses
Austria: B	A central position between the Western and Eastern zones of Europe, both geographically and in terms of culture and history; strong exporter, especially of machine tools.	No major leading companies at international level.
France: B⁺	Large companies that are world leaders; cultural influence on a certain number of countries (through language); active north-south axis; highest birthrate in Europe.	Constantly negative balance of trade; high labor costs.
Germany: B⁺	A powerful economy based on small and medium-sized businesses; well-controlled national deficit (1 percent); powerful export capacity; industrial products with high value added; centrally positioned between Western and Eastern Europe; structural reforms undertaken in the early 2000s are showing their full effects today.	Aging population; low birthrate; low consumption; high labor costs.

(continued)

Table 9.2   Strengths and Weaknesses Summary: Economy Dimension (*Continued*)

Grade	Strengths	Weaknesses
Italy: B	Very active small and medium-sized businesses (highest proportion in Europe), especially in the northeast of the country (e.g., Veneto); high level of exports by small and medium-sized businesses.	Traditionally strong competition from emerging countries undermining the district model.
Netherlands: B	Long-standing commercial activity, ranking the country fifth in the world for exports; significant logistics capacities; major gateway between Europe and the rest of the world; multilingual country.	Aging population.
Spain: B⁺	Some of the most economically successful regions of Europe (e.g., Catalonia); impressive expansion in the last 10 years; very strong development in renewable energies.	The national economy is in deep crisis; rarely seen high levels of unemployment; limited industrial development.
Sweden: B	Large companies specializing in powerful niches at international level; controlled public debt and balanced finances underpin good growth rates (5.6 percent in 2010 and 4.6 percent in 2011); positive balance of trade; strong export power (more than 50 percent of GDP); very strong commitment to sustainable development.	Has not adopted the euro; too far from the center of the EU to be part of the main flow of trade that reaches beyond the northern European countries.
Turkey: B⁺	Great expansion in industry; strong growth; inflation finally under control, from 40 percent a few years ago to a target 6 percent; large number of foreign investments; hub for trade between the Mediterranean Sea and the Black Sea, through the Bosphorus strait; young and fast-growing population and emerging consumer market potential.	Large-scale underground economy; currency fluctuations a matter of concern.
United Kingdom: B⁺	Powerful worldwide network (through language and former colonies); world's leading finance sector.	Underdeveloped industry in several sectors.

Politics

Western Europe fares very well on the Politics dimension with the exception of Turkey. In particular, the ease of doing business and the legal framework are strong for most countries.

Ease of Doing Business, Bureaucracy, and Corruption

In general, doing business in Europe is easy compared to several other regions of the world, and all the countries considered in this chapter, with the exception of Turkey and Italy, are in the top 25 percent worldwide with respect to ease of doing business. The region offers competent governments with low corruption, a large range of available services, and excellent infrastructure networks. Given the very diverse and multicultural nature of the EU, it is quite spontaneously open to, and accepting of, different cultures. In contrast to Asia, disputes relating to the World War II ceased long ago as a topic of debate. Life is genuinely peaceful in the region today. The ease of doing business in the EU varies broadly across its member nations. For instance, the United Kingdom is considered very user-friendly for businesses. As an example, in 2012, David Cameron (Prime Minister of the United Kingdom) invited French entrepreneurs to set up their business in the United Kingdom if they found it too difficult to do business under France's newly elected socialist government. The advantages of the United Kingdom are its simple company formation procedures, its attractive tax system, and its less restrictive labor regulations when compared with other European countries. Sweden is another country in which it is easy to do business, but its influence is limited by its relatively remote geographic position in Europe.

Legal and Regulatory Framework: Tax Codes and Tariffs

Most European nations have fairly sophisticated, and therefore complex, regulatory, tax, and tariff environments. These nations are governed by the rule of law, and laws are enforced. Much of the legislation in each nation is simply transposition into directives that are issued at the EU level. Most nations are "welfare states" and must levy high social security taxes/contributions to fund their social welfare programs.

In the current economic climate, taxes and welfare funding are being reviewed as a part of the search to balance budgets, or at least limit deficits. The overall economic situation and the accompanying unemployment are raising questions over how the EU will continue to compete, and European states are grappling with the thorny question of how to guard against competition that undermines employment stability while simultaneously increasing labor market flexibility. Tax rates are on the verge of change, and labor laws may well be amended, with adjustments to workforce legislation to decrease unemployment rates.

Political Stability

Political stability, as defined by the absence of a threat to government due to social protests, is generally good among the countries discussed in this chapter, with the exception of Turkey. With regard to governmental stability, Western Europe has lived in peace since the end of the World War II in the mid-20th century. There is no territorial conflict between countries, although significant differences in views remain. Economic and political integration in the European Union has united its peoples for the long term. The democratic tradition and application of common rules inside the European Union have made this part of the world a region of great governmental stability. Twenty-one of the EU's nations are republics, with seven being parliamentary monarchies. The inevitable consequence of democracy, however, is an alternation between right wing and left wing ruling parties, and economic policies are frequently reversed as governments change. This can generate a feeling of instability in the rules laid down, especially in times of economic crisis. But in most cases, the changes are only marginal and far from revolutionary as they relate to business.

Turkey stands apart from the rest of Western Europe and the EU in terms of geography, political stability, and governmental stability. Turkey lies in a very politically restless region at the junction of the East and the West and in very close proximity to Iraq and Iran. Turkey's attempts to establish a "zero problem" environment with neighboring countries have been shaken in recent years, particularly with respect to Israel. Turkey's recent history has involved highs and lows for the national political regime, including military coups, most recently in 1980. But today, with its moderate Islamic government, Turkey is considered a model for the region with respect to both economic affairs and democratic politics. However, Turkey's European future is complex. It has been involved in European history for centuries.

In the early days of European integration, Turkey was among the first partner countries, joining the OEEC (Organization for European Economic Co-Operation) as early as 1948. It is a member of the North Atlantic Treaty Organization (NATO) and the Council of Europe. Since 1995 it has been linked to the EU by a customs union. And it began negotiations to join the European Union in 2005, at a very difficult time when some Europeans had concerns about admitting a country that, although officially secular, is predominantly Islamic, lies close to the unstable Middle East and North African countries, and would, in terms of population, be the second-largest country in the EU.

Intellectual Property Rights

The technological tradition of Western European countries, their creativity, and their research potential has led them to protect the results of their research. Allowing free circulation of goods inside the European Union meant establishing a secure, harmonized system. Intellectual property is respected across all the countries, with only slight nuances. Also, the countries of Western Europe are home to firms with strong and internationally recognized brands. Western European nations have worked carefully to ensure that those brands are respected throughout the world, particularly in Asia. This protection is enforced in practice, mainly through lawsuits for forgery and counterfeiting. Turkey is being required to align its practices with EU member nation practices in view of its application to join the European Union. However, Turkey is still set apart by its highly active underground economy and the intensity of counterfeiting enterprises.

Table 9.3 presents the scores on the Politics dimension for the selected countries in Western Europe while Table 9.4 presents the strengths and weaknesses for each of these countries.

Table 9.3 Scores for the Politics Dimension

Politics	Ease of Doing Business	Legal Framework	Political Stability	Intellectual Property Rights	Overall Grade
20%	30%	30%	25%	15%	100%
Austria	A⁻	A	A⁻	A⁻	A
France	A⁻	A⁻	B⁻	A⁻	B⁺
Germany	A⁻	A⁻	A⁻	A⁻	A⁻
Italy	B⁻	B	B	B⁻	B
Netherlands	A⁻	A	A⁻	A	A⁻
Spain	B⁺	B⁺	B⁻	B	B
Sweden	A	A	A	A	A
Turkey	B⁻	B⁻	D⁺	C⁺	C⁺
United Kingdom	A	A	B⁺	A	A

Table 9.4 Strengths and Weaknesses Summary: Politics Dimension

Grade	Strengths	Weaknesses
Austria: A	Stable laws.	A strong rise by the political far right.
France: B⁺	The highest birthrate in Western Europe and natural population growth.	Frequent changes in tax rules particularly; labor relations can be tense.
Germany: A⁻	The most powerful country in the European Union, with an economically realistic political class; a federal system that makes some regions very dynamic (e.g., Bavaria, North Rhine–Westphalia, Baden-Württemberg); very good model for participative management and unions in companies (the Rhineland model).	Large and frequently changing body of standards and norms.
Italy: B	A flexible government; a culture of small businesses.	High levels of corruption; organized mafia in Sicily where the Camorra of Naples maintains a corrupt system for business; a political environment that raises the question of the north-south divide.
Netherlands: A⁻	Very good social model; has long been open to international business; country of tradesmen; lots of flexibility in support for businesses; high consensus in labor relations between companies, unions, and the state; constancy in decisions made.	High rate of economically inactive people.

(continued)

Table 9.4   Strengths and Weaknesses Summary: Politics Dimension (*Continued*)

Grade	Strengths	Weaknesses
Spain: B	Country divided into highly autonomous regions; naturally open to all Spanish-speaking countries and northern African countries.	A few regions are seeking independence.
Sweden: A	Excellent social model; very stable constitutional monarchy; highly egalitarian country with low poverty rates; high social protection; very safe country.	High tax pressure.
Turkey: C⁺	Striving to maintain a temperate, modern outlook.	High level of corruption; high level of counterfeiting activity; poor political stability; isolated position in its region.
United Kingdom: A	A very liberal system, which makes it hospitable for business; very open to international business; very liberal labor market; low levels of corruption.	Low consumer confidence in the future; a growing poor class.

Infrastructure

An assessment of key elements of the Infrastructure dimension, including transportation, utilities, and telecommunications, follows. A summary of Infrastructure elements for each of the focal nations in Western Europe is presented at the end of the section.

Transportation

The World Economic Forum (WEF) rankings on the selected metrics from the Global Competitiveness Index (GCI) used to evaluate the roads, railroads, ports, and air transportation give high grades to all the focal countries with the exception of Italy, which receives a C+ grade. The geography of Western Europe has some major features that influence transportation in this region. For example, transportation between many of the countries in continental Western Europe requires passage over the Pyrenees Mountains (between France and Spain), and the Alps (across France, Italy, Switzerland, and Austria). Although arguably not on the same scale as Southeast Asia, transportation within and into or out of Western Europe by any means other than air travel is characterized by extensive contact with the seas and oceans. Other than air travel, access to the United Kingdom is either by ferry or by the channel tunnel (the "Chunnel"), which carries rail shuttles under the English Channel.

The expansion of the EU in the early 2000s brought about a change in trade patterns. Austria's position as a central hub for trade flows with the new member states was strengthened. In the corridor along the Danube, merchandise transport routes increased 10-fold between 1990 and 2007. Austria's long-standing relations with countries such as Hungary and the Czech Republic facilitated this change. Cities like Linz became more important as logistics hubs.

On the edge of Europe, Turkey shares a border with Greece and has some of its territory on the European continent. It has a very determined economic focus toward the West. Being surrounded by the Black Sea and the Mediterranean Sea, it controls the strategic passage for a significant volume of maritime traffic via the Bosporus and Dardanelle straits.

This environment means it is theoretically easy to transport merchandise around Europe. Infrastructures across Western Europe are generally of good quality, up-to-date, and well maintained. Passengers and goods alike can travel from one end of Europe to the other in a maximum of two days, thanks to the dense road network. But much of Western Europe's infrastructure is congested. Most freight transport in the European Union is by road, carrying close to 80 percent of the total tons/kilometer (tkm). Rail transport accounts for just under 20 percent and waterways 6 percent. In the Netherlands, river transport reaches 35 percent of tkm transported.

Road transport laws, however, remain very diverse. For example, the permissible truck weight varies widely across countries, even though the maximum is set at 40 tons for international transport inside the European Union.[1]

Aside from a very dense road network and a number of large ports and airports, one unique characteristic of internal transport in the EU is that it is intensively covered by inland waterways. The system is organized around the Rhine and the principal tributaries and rivers, connected by canals: the Main, the Neckar, the Moselle, and the Meuse. The Rhine is navigable along an 800-km north-south axis (from Switzerland to the Netherlands), through the most densely populated and highly industrialized area of Europe. The delta has been developed and is connected to the port of Rotterdam, the largest in Europe and one of the largest in the world. The river traffic on the Rhine carries 100 million tons upstream and 50 million tons downstream each year. The world's largest river port is Duisburg, toward the downstream end of the Rhine.

The major points of access to Western Europe are via the seaports along the "Northern Range" that include the major ports of Rotterdam, Antwerp, Hamburg, and Le Havre. In 2011, Rotterdam was Europe's busiest port, with 11 million 20-foot equivalent units (TEUs), and the 10th busiest in the world, while Antwerp was in 14th place (8.5 million TEUs) with Hamburg in 15th place (8 million TEUs).

The Mediterranean Sea essentially carries traffic between its coastal countries, apart from the oil trade flows, which generate significant transit through the southern French port of Marseilles, for instance. Rail transport has long been a factor in European transport. But the systems have developed under national outlooks, and due to stiff competition from road transport the railways are particularly competitive today.

Airfreight transport is very active in three main countries: Germany (Frankfurt), the United Kingdom (London), and France (Paris). In addition to local business coverage

---

[1] European Directive 96/53, of July 25, 1996.

around the major centers (London, Paris, Milan, Turin, and others), there has been substantial development along the length of the blue banana, particularly in the Netherlands, Belgium, and north Germany. Two other high-concentration zones also exist in France, one around Paris and one around Lyon.

The physical transportation infrastructure is well integrated within much of Western Europe. However, transportation by road or rail between the northern European countries (the Scandinavian countries of Norway, Sweden, and Denmark, the United Kingdom, Ireland, Finland, Iceland, and the Baltic countries of Estonia, Latvia, and Lithunia) and the rest of Western Europe is limited by the geography of the region. It is not unusual to see Europe split into two zones, with northern Europe supplied by, for example, a warehouse located in the Netherlands, and the rest of continental Europe supplied by a warehouse in the south of France. Consider, for example, the case of Ikea, which aims to supply quality home furnishings to as broad a market as possible. The supply chain component is extensively integrated into its business model to help keep prices as low as possible. Ikea purchases close to 10,000 articles from 1075 suppliers: one-third of its products come from Northern Europe, one-third from the rest of Europe, and one-third from Southeast Asia. Distribution is currently organized not by country but on a pan-European scale. Spain and Portugal, for instance, receive most of their deliveries from a warehouse located in the south of France. As certain warehouses are specialized, the same sales outlet may receive deliveries from several different European warehouses, or directly from the suppliers, with or without cross-docking operations.[m] The Ikea case illustrates recent trends in physical distribution in this region:

▲ Increasingly integrated networks are being set up covering several European countries.
▲ Fairly complex networks are being rolled out, combining elements from different approaches to ensure supplies reach the final point of distribution.
▲ It is necessary to work with a large number of logistics service providers because integration of their services is still low.

Another problem slowly being overcome is inconsistencies in track gauges across the region. As an example, for a long time Spain and Portugal have operated with an *Iberian track gauge*,[n] a gauge that is different from the international standard gauge. The Iberian track gauge used in the Spanish railway network is spaced 1668 millimeters between the inner rail faces. In contrast, the normal or standard track gauge of most of the European and world rail network is spaced 1435 millimeters between the inner rail faces.

While new high-speed passenger lines in Spain have been built to the international standard gauge since the early 1990s, the points at which different track gauges still coexist

---

[m] Club Logistique Globale Rhône-Alpes 2012 © www.clubloglob.org.
[n] Track gauge is a technical term used to define the spacing of the rails on a railway track.

along the borders with France have resulted in the introduction of gauge-changing instal-lations at specified locations. These gauge-changing installations adjust the gauge of appro-priately designed wheel-sets for the railway cars on the fly, allowing trains to pass automatically from a line with an Iberian track gauge to another with the international track gauge, or vice versa, and without changing axles or bogies, as the train passes through the installation.[6]

Utilities

The WEF rankings from the Global Competitiveness Index (GCI) on the quality of electrical supply give high grades to all the focal countries with the exception of Turkey. In particular, the Netherlands receives a rank of 1 among the 144 countries included in the index. Austria, the United Kingdom, France, and Sweden also rank very high with a rank of 7, 8, 9, and 12, respectively. Germany is ranked 19 and Spain is ranked 30. Turkey is ranked 77 in this list. For comparison, the United States is ranked 33 and Mexico is ranked 79.

The GCI report indicates that the quality of electricity supply in Turkey requires addi-tional upgrading, as does Turkey's port infrastructure. The GCI report on Turkey is prob-ably influenced by the power generation rate not keeping pace with Turkey's economic expansion, which has caused demand for electricity to grow at an annualized rate of 6 percent in recent years. The International Energy Agency (IEA) estimates that Turkey will very likely see the fastest medium to long-term growth in energy demand among the IEA member countries.[o] The government has responded with plans to double generating capacity to 125 GW by 2023.[p] Overall, there appear to be no significant problems with the energy infrastructure for the focal countries in this region.

Telecommunications, Infrastructure, and Connectivity

As noted in Chapter 2, connectivity can be measured by the number of mobile phones and Internet users in the country, as well as the per capita values for these numbers. Based on the per capita values, the focal countries fare well with the exception of Turkey, which receives a C grade. In general, most of the other focal countries rank high on both mobile phone usage per capita and Internet usage per capita. In general, the telecommunications systems in most of these focal countries are highly sophisticated, with standards equivalent to or better than those in the United States.

To give the connectivity metric another perspective, Internet World Stats is an Interna-tional website that features up to date world Internet Usage, Population Statistics, Travel Stats and Internet Market Research Data, for over 233 individual countries and world regions.[q]

---

[o] http://www.mfa.gov.tr/turkeys-energy-strategy.en.mfa.

[p] http://www.toshiba.co.jp/about/press/2013_08/pr0501.htm.

[q] http://www.internetworldstats.com/.

In particular, this website lists the top 50 countries with the highest Internet penetration rate, where penetration rate is defined as over 65 percent of the population using the Internet. Sweden, the Netherlands, the United Kingdom, and Germany rank very high on this metric, coming in at ranks 3, 8, 14, and 16, respectively. France, Austria, and Spain also figure in the top 50 countries. The rankings provided by this website correlate well to the corresponding rankings on Internet usage provided by the Central Intelligence Agency's (CIA) World Factbook.

Table 9.5 presents the scores on the Infrastructure dimension for the selected countries in Western Europe while Table 9.6 presents the strengths and weaknesses for each of these countries.

Table 9.5   Scores for the Infrastructure Dimension

Infrastructure	Transportation Infrastructure	Energy Infrastructure	Connectivity	Overall Grade
30%	50%	25%	25%	100%
Austria	B⁺	A	A⁻	A⁻
France	A	A	B⁻	A⁻
Germany	A	A⁻	A⁻	A
Italy	C⁺	B	B⁺	B⁻
Netherlands	A	A	A⁻	A
Spain	A⁻	B⁺	B	B⁺
Sweden	A⁻	A	A⁻	A
Turkey	B	C	C	B⁻
United Kingdom	A⁻	A	A⁻	A

Table 9.6   Strengths and Weaknesses Summary: Infrastructure Dimension

Grade	Strengths	Weaknesses
Austria: A⁻	Important transit country for road transport; significant development of combined transport.	Challenging geography, with 80 percent of national territory covered by the Alps; extreme weather conditions; no coastline.
France: A⁻	The world's largest nuclear power producer; good quality road network.	The freight rail network is aging.
Germany: A	Low corruption; safety and security are highly respected; extremely dense road network; good quality ports; strong involvement in development of renewable energies.	Parts of the road network are regularly congested.

(continued)

Table 9.6 Strengths and Weaknesses Summary: Infrastructure Dimension (*Continued*)

Grade	Strengths	Weaknesses
Italy: B⁻	Country's railway system is highly developed.	Distribution made difficult by the country's geography; transport is saturated in certain regions; infrastructure is often insufficient even in some developed regions.
Netherlands: A	The transport system makes extensive use of waterways; very active logistics service sector; highly dynamic customs system due to the volumes processed by ports.	Very high traffic congestion in some places.
Spain: B⁺	Good transportation infrastructure; one of top 50 countries in Internet penetration.	Some parts of the national rail system still uses the nonstandard Iberian track gauge.
Sweden: A	Rail transport plays an important role (36 percent of tkm); maritime transport is particularly significant (2700 km of coast and islands); practically all international transactions and half of domestic trade are by sea.	Severe winter conditions can cause transportation difficulties.
Turkey: B⁻	Relatively well developed infrastructure with respect to roads and air transport.	Ports and electricity supply require additional upgrading; some of the country interfaces with less politically stable regions (Iraq, Syria).
United Kingdom: A	Energy infrastructure is very sound; efficient railway infrastructure even though it is overloaded.	Aging rail and road infrastructures; road and rail infrastructures are often saturated and underfunded.

Competence

Western Europe fares relatively well in the Competence dimension. In particular, it is particularly strong with respect to the logistics Competence variable. The education levels are also high among the countries considered in the region, with the exception of Italy and Turkey.

Labor: Availability, Productivity, and Relations

Western Europe is a region with good labor productivity. Despite the short official workweek in certain countries (35 hours in France, 48 hours in the UK, negotiated hours in Germany), international competition is inducing greater manufacturing production automation, which is leading to much improved levels of productivity. On an hours-worked basis, Germany is practically level with the United States, followed by France, Italy, and the United Kingdom. Productivity has improved in the EU overall, but productivity growth has been lower than in the United States and the gap is widening.

The competences required for skilled work are generally available in Western Europe. Almost all children attend school from the age of 3 or 4. There are considerable labor force differences between countries, with some labor forces aging especially in Germany, the European Union's leading economic power. As yet, this is not a major issue. Immigration is counterbalancing the situation, particularly since the labor market was opened up to nationals of all EU countries with the exception of the most recent members. But in the medium term, this may well become more problematic. In fact, by 2030, 25 percent of the working population is expected to be over age 55.

Finally, the development of in-service training has been an important concern in Europe, and opportunities for training throughout an employee's career provide further chances to improve professional work-related skills. Twenty years ago, this aspect of training was in fact the earliest channel for developing logistics and supply chain skills.

Education Levels for Line Staff and Management

Trade and logistics have long been associated in Europe through its economic history, and supply chain and logistics ideas and practices have been well established in Western European businesses for 15 years. The first managers in charge of supply chain functions learned their job through experience gained in the course of their professional duties, and they are over 45 years old today. The younger generations received training at higher education establishments. Because businesses need graduates who are specialized in these areas, business schools, universities, and engineering schools have all developed courses on these subjects at all levels from school-leaver to doctoral programs, so there are sizeable flows of trained students. Of course, the national vision of these questions can vary. Centers of excellence exist in many countries: Cranfield University in the United Kingdom, ESSEC business school in France, the Operations and Supply Chain Group TUM Business School and Fraunhofer Institut für Materialfluss und Logistik (IML) in Dortmund in Germany, the Università Bocconi in Italy, and the MIT Zaragoza Logistics Center in Spain. Although every European country has its own higher education system, the systems have been converging since the Bologna declaration was signed in 1999 to make courses and qualifications more homogeneous and to facilitate student exchanges. This homogenization process opened up opportunities for greater student mobility between countries, allowing them to spend a term, a semester, or a year in a university outside their own country. One striking feature in this context is the European students' ability to speak several languages.

Logistics Competence, Customs, and Security

The service levels expected by customers have generated truly sophisticated and necessary knowledge. The spread of cross-docking type solutions, which require complex synchronization of flows, leads to the use of very sophisticated information systems offering optimization models. There is a genuine capacity to design these solutions and roll them out, not only nationally but internationally. The World Bank report places Germany fourth worldwide for design capacity and the Netherlands is fifth. The United Kingdom is in 10th place, Austria is 11th, and France is 12th.

The earliest common interests shared by European countries concerned trade, which is reflected in creation of a customs union. This customs union was one of the first key steps toward construction of a united Europe, as it abolished customs duties at internal borders in the European Union. It also laid the foundation for a standardized taxation system for intra-EU merchandise imports. Western Europe is very safe, and a leading region with regard to security and safety of both goods and people. Turkey has specific geographical features. At its western end close to Europe, where almost 20 percent of the population is concentrated, the situation is very similar to Western Europe. But at the eastern end near Iraq and Syria, as might be expected, the situation is much more complex.

Western Europe has long had a large, active public sector that plays an important role vis-à-vis the state. Of course, the style of public sector involvement differs, from the highly centralized as in France and the United Kingdom, to the more decentralized as in Germany where the administration has grown from federal roots. Turkey, meanwhile, is a very bureaucratic state that is currently attempting reform. Transparency International's Corruption Perceptions Index (CPI) puts the countries examined here in very different positions. Italy, in 69th place, is among the countries with the highest perceived corruption, on an equal footing with Ghana, but not far from China (75th) and Turkey (61st). France is considered an intermediate country, ranking 25th. The United Kingdom and Austria score 7.8 and are among the leaders of the index. Germany with its score of 8, the Netherlands (8.9), and Sweden (9.3) are some of the most exemplary countries in Europe.

Table 9.7 presents the scores on the Competence dimension for the selected countries in Western Europe while Table 9.8 presents the strengths and weaknesses for each of these countries.

The following table (Table 9.9) summarizes the scores on the four EPIC dimensions for the countries observed.

Table 9.7 Scores for the Competence Dimension

Competence	Labor Relations	Education Levels	Logistics Competence	Customs and Security	Overall Grade
20%	25%	25%	40%	10%	100%
Austria	B⁻	A⁻	A	A	A⁻
France	D	B⁺	A	A⁻	B
Germany	C⁺	A⁻	A	A	A⁻
Italy	D⁻	C⁻	A⁻	B⁺	C⁺
Netherlands	C⁺	A	A	A	A⁻
Spain	D⁻	B⁻	A⁻	A⁻	B⁻
Sweden	C⁺	A	A	A	A⁻
Turkey	C⁺	C	B⁺	B⁺	B⁻
United Kingdom	A⁻	A	A	A	A

Table 9.8 Strengths and Weaknesses Summary: Competence Dimension

Grade	Strengths	Weaknesses
Austria: A⁻	Natural cultural openness to central European countries; good level of technical qualifications.	"Land-based" logistics culture due to the country's lack of coastline.
France: B	Internationally renowned higher education in engineering; well-trained labor force for logistics and supply chains; very good labor productivity.	High staff turnover in large warehouses; low percentage of staff on permanent contracts.
Germany: A⁻	Apprenticeship-based training system producing good-quality technicians; very good per-hour labor productivity.	Higher education system still lacks international openness beyond Europe.
Italy: C⁺	Good labor productivity; good logistics competencies; customs and security procedures functioning well.	No major well-known training centers for logistics and supply chains; logistics services and warehouses are of average quality; significant saturation in some zones (e.g., Veneto).
Netherlands: A⁻	Long-standing tradition in logistics and supply chains; good training bodies; renowned maritime and port management know-how; entrepreneurial spirit rooted in Dutch society.	Average levels of productivity.

(continued)

Table 9.8 Strengths and Weaknesses Summary: Competence Dimension (*Continued*)

Grade	Strengths	Weaknesses
Spain: B⁻	Genuine logistics competences in road transport; good levels of training.	The fabric of competences for large-scale logistics hubs still requires development.
Sweden: A⁻	Practical know-how in design and application of innovative logistics and supply chain solutions.	Average labor productivity.
Turkey: B⁻	Factories have some of the best productivity rates in Europe.	The education system needs to open up to specialist logistics subjects.
United Kingdom: A	Good supply chain culture; low labor costs; good service culture.	Low industrial productivity.

Table 9.9 Summary Assessment of EPIC Attractiveness for the Countries in Western Europe

	Economy	Politics	Infrastructure	Competence	Overall Grade
Austria	B	A	A⁻	A⁻	B⁺
France	B⁺	B⁺	A⁻	B	B⁺
Germany	B⁺	A⁻	A	A⁻	A⁻
Italy	B	B	B⁻	C⁺	B⁻
Netherlands	B	A⁻	A	A⁻	A⁻
Spain	B⁺	B	B⁺	B⁻	B⁺
Sweden	B	A	A	A⁻	A⁻
Turkey	B⁺	C⁺	B⁻	B⁻	B⁻
United Kingdom	B	A	A	A	A⁻

Supply Chain Challenges

Although Western Europe is a mature region with notable characteristics for supply chain operations, significant challenges exist. The following represent the most critical of these challenges.

To Import or Not to Import . . . That Is the Question

The main regions with which Western Europe trades are Asia and North America. Industry in Western Europe is, in fact, not very well integrated. There are exceptions to the rule, but most industries have remained national, leading to considerable overlapping of capabilities across Western Europe. The automobile industry, agriculture/food, the arms industry, and luxury goods are Europe's flagship export sectors.

Distribution: Brick and Mortar or e-Commerce?

Trade in Europe is basically subject to two constraints: very expensive real estate and very strong competition. The brick and mortar distribution model with its networks of physical sales outlets has pursued two main objectives for several years. The first of these objectives is to devote as much surface as possible to commercial activities. This leads to "logistical depollution" of sales outlets. Every surface that can be used for selling is used to sell. This makes it necessary to set up logistics networks capable of processing orders logically in a "push system" involving two types of infrastructure. The second objective is to refocus all sales outlet personnel on the act of advising and selling to customers, such that in-store staff devote all their time to sales. There is thus a trend toward remote management of sales outlet stock, either using the push system for resupply or restocking shelves under Vendor-Managed Inventory (VMI) processes. But in certain market segments, Internet sales are developing intensively in parallel to brick and mortar distribution. E-commerce growth rates and sales are higher in the European Union than in the United States.

Customer Expectations in Western Europe

It is possible to detect potential changes in patterns of consumer behavior by the population of European consumers in the next few years from early demographic trends, but it is interesting to see what service quality standards are already currently expected in different sectors. For consumer goods, the expectation for more than 99 percent of cases in Western Europe is delivered on time, at the right quality level, and so forth. Further, the newly emerging carbon footprint criterion and environmental supply chain is changing the nature of supply chains in Western Europe.

Aging Consumer Markets

The need to serve consumer markets that are aging and less mobile, when coupled with the very high population density in the blue banana, creates unique supply chain challenges. For instance, the last mile supply chain designs in Western Europe will need to become increasingly sophisticed to efficiently and effectively serve these unique markets. To some degree, success in serving these markets may well provide a first mover advantage with respect to other nations that will eventually also have the same problems of high urban population density in combination with aged and less mobile consumers.

The Challenges of Diversity

The challenges associated with so many traditionally independent nations are obvious. Currently, with the economic problems in Italy and Spain (national deficits, etc.), there is a large test of the cohesiveness of the entire EU. At a more micro level, the United Kindom has similar problems within its borders. For instance, Scotland has been attempting to secede from the United Kingdom for more than 10 years and has recently enacted a minority government that has secession as a platform agenda item. Beyond economic and political diversity, cultural diversity is also substantial across the EU. Finally, without a common currency that is adopted by all of the EU member nations, an integrated union may not be fully possible.

Supply Chain Opportunities

Despite a relatively flat growth rate over the past decade, Western Europe still offers significant opportunities for global organizations. The overall favorable political climate and the relatively high level of competence in the region provide a favorable business climate.

Aging Consumer Markets

The quickly aging population of Western Europe creates an opportunity for new business models and supply chain designs that are adapted to the needs of aging consumer markets in this region. For instance, a more aged population is less mobile, requiring businesses to interact with consumers much closer to where these consumers live, and potentially even at their residence.

Youthful Consumer Markets

Turkey represents a very different market opportunity when compared with other Western European nations. As its younger consumer markets develop, supply chains must be designed to bring appropriate goods and services into this economy, as opposed to the export-oriented economy that represents the current state of the Turkish economy. This change from supplier to consumer will mark a fundament change in the nature of how business models and supply chains must be designed.

A More Connected Blue Banana

The European Union is fostering development projects within Western Europe that are more integrated at the European level, setting up six corridors through which 20 percent

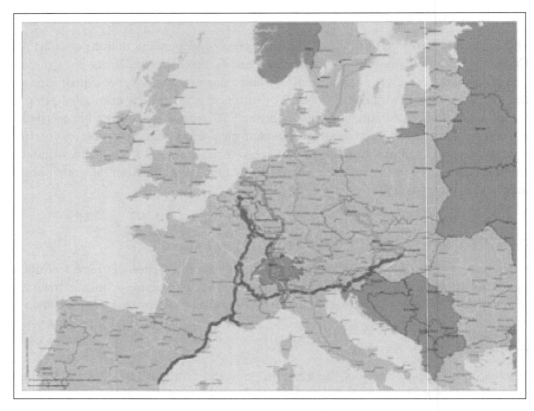

Figure 9.14 A more connected blue banana.

of total European freight passes even though they only cover 6 percent of the region's roads (Figure 9.14). These corridors reflect the general orientation of goods traffic in Europe along a major north-south axis, reflecting the position of the main ports, major industrial centers, and the region's population concentration (the blue banana). The six corridors are:

Rotterdam—Genoa
Stockholm—Naples
Antwerp—Basel—Lyon
Valencia—Lyon—Ljubljana—Budapest
Dresden—Prague—Budapest
Duisburg—Berlin—Warsaw

Extensive plans have already been drawn up, and projects are under way. For example, the Alps pose a real problem for circulation. Freight transport alone carries 130 million tons of merchandise through the area every year, and some of the countries concerned (Switzerland, Austria, France) are leading players on sustainable development and very vigilant on questions of pollution. This project is an opportunity for those countries to promote combined transport in which trucks complete part of their journey by train. The world's longest railway tunnel, the 57-km Gotthard tunnel, has been built under the Alps to connect northern and southern Europe. It is due to open in late 2016, with a final section to be completed by the end of 2019.

The idea of "sea highways" is also being investigated. In Italy, which has more than 150 merchandise ports along its coast, 20 percent of transport is by sea. Trials are under way in an attempt to develop joint solutions between countries.

In 2011, the European Union decided to launch its ambitious "Connecting Europe Facility" (CEF) to improve integration of national infrastructures. The transport section of the CEF is expected to have a budget of €31.7 billion to be spent by 2020.

A Sustainable European Supply Chain

Western Europe in particular has a long-term commitment to developing a sustainable economy. In fact, Western Europe views the move towards a sustainable economy as fostering a modern industrial revolution that will give a fresh impetus to the economy and set an example for the whole world. This is not going to be an easy task. A report on the attempts to nurture low carbon transportation in the European Union published in 2012 states[7] "Statistics indicate that the transport sector contributes 23 percent of all CO_2 emissions in the 27[r] EU Member States. Despite significant efforts to reduce emissions, transport has not achieved its decarbonizing targets. If this trend continues, transport is expected to contribute 50 percent of all CO_2 emissions in the EU by 2050, if not within the next two decades." The European Union has undertaken to cut greenhouse gas emissions from 1990 levels by 20 percent by 2020, and 85 percent by 2050. Sustainable development is deeply rooted in the modern European consciousness.

Supply chains will have to reckon with these newly emerging trends:

▲ Higher consumer sensitivity to suppliers' environmental credentials. The carbon footprint is part of the mix that will determine the choice of products in Western Europe.

▲ The emergence of shorter circuits closer to the production and consumption locations, particularly for agriculture/food products.

▲ New regulations are accompanying this trend, particularly through the introduction of ecotaxes. In a country like France, this will affect 800,000 trucks (600,000 French trucks and 200,000 foreign trucks). The French ecotax was planned to be introduced in 2013 and applied nationwide by the end of the year, raising approximately €1.24 billion annually for the state but has since been postponed to a date some time into the future.

---

[r] At the time the report was published, Croatia had not joined the EU. Hence only 27 EU countries were identified in the report.

Businesses are thus obliged to contribute to this movement. Logistics, which contribute to CO_2 emissions (storage, transport, etc.), are at the forefront of the associated initiatives. Half of European companies have decided to introduce criteria to assess their supply chain's "green" credentials; the proportion has already reached 77 percent in Scandinavian countries.

The results, however, are not yet convincing because the contribution of transports has been increasing over time. This is a real challenge for businesses, particularly as road freight transport is increasing: "by 2030, it is forecast to be 40 percent more than in 2005; 80 percent higher by 2050. Passenger traffic is set to grow too: 34 percent up on 2005 by 2030 and 51 percent up by 2050."[5]

Dramatic Cuts in Logistics Costs

Some economists are predicting a difficult future for Europe, and Western Europe in particular. There is even talk of a new poor class, which will need an entirely redesigned offering. Whether this is mere speculation or an inexorable trend, it must be prepared for. Certain companies are seeking not a moderate reduction in logistics costs, but a drastic cutback of 20 to 25 percent. How can such targets be achieved without in-depth change? Four principal vectors are being explored:

▲ Changing service specifications, with less value added for customers: longer delivery times, fewer deliveries, nonnegotiable delivery date set by the supplier.
▲ More intensive coordination, with economic actors sharing efforts and workload in a more coordinated way, not simply through a random grouping via a logistics service provider.
▲ Replacing on-demand transport management for certain deliveries, especially truck deliveries, with delivery following preestablished delivery schedules.
▲ Adapting urban goods deliveries with a focus on greater coordination of an organized or even regulated nature.

Key Takeaways for Western Europe

1. Although Western Europe gives the impression of homogeneity, it should not be considered homogeneous for supply chain purposes. Even Europeans can have difficulties understanding the specifics of supply chain solutions in a country other than their own.

---

[5] http://europa.eu/pol/trans/index_fr.htm.

2. Supply chains in Western Europe are currently being reassessed, either to make significant savings or to better incorporate sustainable development concerns. This is a political and operational fact of life in today's Western Europe. Solutions will have to evolve.

3. In Western Europe, road transport is dominant. It is highly integrated for the major companies, but much local transport is still handled by small companies that use traditional practices.

4. The population is aging in this region. Unless some unexpected event occurs, population development forecasts are fairly reliable. Real-life experience shows that people become less mobile as they get older. As a result, very intensive local logistics will need to be developed in many European countries.

5. The population density is high in Western Europe. Although infrastructure is generally of good quality, traffic congestion is an inescapable fact in certain regions and at certain times of year. Optimization models do not always take this into consideration. It may be better to be located further from the main routes but be able to travel or access transport capacities that become scarcer in peak periods.

6. Western Europe has good logistics service providers with genuinely high-level knowledge. They often follow their clients and set up establishments in other locations outside the home country.

7. There are many logistics and supply chain competences found in Western Europe. At the managerial level, Western Europe offers a high level of internationalization.

8. For logistics covering a worldwide scale or between major zones, there are not as many ways into Europe in practice as the maps might suggest. International trade involving Europe essentially transits through the northern area of Europe (the Northern Range seaports).

9. Storage infrastructures are generally of good quality and fairly modern. They are often owned by investors who tend to develop standardized warehouses.

10. Information and telecommunications systems are good, but it still takes long-term investment to develop a solution that operates effectively.

References

1. *Europe in Figures*, Eurostat Yearbook 2011, Population chapter.
2. *Europe in Figures*, Eurostat Yearbook 2011, Economy and finance chapter.
3. A. Kibritçioğlu, "A Short Review of the Long History of Turkish High Inflation," Ankara University, April 2004.
4. *Europe in Figures,* Eurostat Yearbook 2011, Economy and finance chapter.
5. Foreign trade by EU-27 with its main partners, INSEE (in French), http://www.insee.fr/fr/themes/tableau.asp?reg_id=98&ref_id=CMPTEF08458.

6. A. G. Álvarez, "Automatic Track Gauge Changeover for Trains in Spain," Fundación de los Ferrocarriles Españoles (the Spanish railways foundation), September 2010, http://www.vialibre-ffe.com/pdf/Track_gauge_changeover.pdf.

7. "Towards Low Carbon Transportation in Europe: Communicating Transport Research and Innovation," European Union, 2012.

CHAPTER 10

Central and Eastern Europe[a]

As with Western Europe, the borders of Central and Eastern Europe (CEE) are not easily defined. This chapter defines the countries in the Central and Eastern European region to be all the countries covered by the former Eastern bloc[b] as well as any other European country that was not included in the demarcation of Western Europe as defined in Chapter 9. With this definition, CEE would include 25 countries in three geographic regions covering Central and Southeast Europe, Northeast Europe, and Eastern Europe. Central and Southeast Europe accounts for 12 countries: Albania, Bosnia and Herzegovina, Croatia, the Czech Republic, Hungary, Kosovo, Macedonia, Montenegro, Poland, Serbia, Slovakia, and Slovenia. Three Baltic countries represent the Northeast European region: Estonia, Latvia, and Lithuania. Eastern Europe accounts for 10 countries: Armenia, Azerbaijan, Belarus, Bulgaria, Georgia, Kazakhstan, Moldova, Romania, Russia, and Ukraine. This definition includes Kazakhstan and Russia in Eastern Europe although the larger part of these two countries lies in Asia. It is also noted that although more than 100 UN members, the International Monetary Fund (IMF), and the World Bank recognize Kosovo as an independent country, the UN Security Council had not officially recognized this country as of 2013.

CEE has significant importance from a supply chain perspective. Under Communist rule, the countries in this region had practically no access to Western goods until the fall of the Berlin Wall in 1989, although the economies of the nations in CEE accounted for about 15 percent of the world GDP. Following the fall of the Berlin Wall, the relatively untapped markets and supply of low-cost labor in the region presented a compelling opportunity for Western multinational firms, with many seizing the opportunity to enter the CEE market. Today CEE continues to attract investment from organizations all over the world, not just from the United States and Western Europe but also from China and

---

[a] Prof. Sebastian Jarzebowski and Prof. Agnieszka Bezat-Jarzebowska, Faculty of Economic Sciences, Warsaw University of Life Sciences, coauthored this chapter.

[b] The Eastern bloc, or Communist bloc, refers to the former Communist states in Central and Eastern Europe that were either a part of, or were essentially controlled by, the Soviet Union following the end of World War II.

other countries in Asia. These developments have led to a corresponding increase in the demands placed on the region's supply networks, creating a need for a better understanding of the supply chain management practices in CEE.

The geographic proximity of CEE to Western Europe and the natural interaction between the two regions have led to the development of supply chain management infrastructures in CEE that compare well with similar systems in the West, particularly in large metropolitan areas where state-of-the-art information technology and sophisticated logistics providers enable access to international markets. However, in less populated areas options are restricted more toward simply transporting goods by any means available.

Historically the countries within CEE share close ties. Over time their borders have continually been redrawn, and many regions in these different countries once were part of the same nation. For instance, many CEE countries were a part of the Austro-Hungarian Empire during the period from 1867 until its collapse in 1918 at the end of World War I.

This chapter focuses on six countries in CEE: the Czech Republic, Hungary, Poland, Romania, Russia, and Ukraine. All six countries were members of the Warsaw Pact,[c] and the first four countries in the list are also currently members of the European Union (EU). To gain some insight on how the economies of these focal countries have been shaped, it is useful to journey back in time to briefly trace their often tumultuous political backgrounds and histories.

Economic and Political Background

The Czech Republic, which was a part of Czechoslovakia until 1993, was part of the Great Moravian Empire in the 9th century. Between the 9th century and the end of World War I in 1918, it was ruled by the Premysl Dynasty, the Luxembourg Dynasty, the Jagellon Dynasty, and finally the Habsburg Dynasty from 1526 to 1918.[1] Czechoslovakia remained an independent state from 1918 until it came under Communist rule from 1948 to 1989. On January 1, 1993, just a little over three years after its independence, Czechoslovakia separated into two countries, the Czech Republic and Slovakia.

The western part of Hungary was once a part of Pannonia, an ancient province of the Roman Empire. Following that period of Roman occupation, Hungary was ruled by the Huns and the Slavs. In 1541 the Turkish emperor, Suleiman the Magnificent, conquered Buda and much of Hungary remained under Ottoman rule for 145 years. Subsequently, the Habsburg monarchy ruled much of the country until it became a part of the Austro-Hungarian Empire from 1867 to 1918. Hungary was part of the Communist Eastern bloc from 1947 until 1989.

---

[c] The Warsaw Pact was a mutual defense treaty between eight Communist countries in Central and Eastern Europe that were in existence during the Cold War. Like the North Atlantic Treaty Organization, which was partially instrumental in shaping the boundaries of the Western European Union, the Warsaw Pact played a role in forming the Eastern bloc.

Poland experienced 50 years of destruction and raids from the Mongols in the 13th century. For most of the next three centuries, Poland was part of the Polish-Lithuanian Empire, one of the most powerful empires in Europe. Poland was controlled by the Austrians, Germans, and the Russians starting with the First Partition of the Polish-Lithuanian Commonwealth in 1772. After more than 150 years of foreign rule, Poland enjoyed a period of independence from 1918 to 1939 before it went under Communist rule from 1945 to 1989.

Romania's origins can be traced back to the medieval principalities of Wallachia, Dobrogea, Moldavia, Bessarabia, and Transylvania, which were formed in the 14th century. Transylvania subsequently became an Ottoman Empire vassal when the Turks conquered Hungary in the 16th century, paying tribute to the Ottoman rulers to retain autonomy. In the 17th century, Transylvania came under Habsburg rule. Wallachia and Moldavia became Russian protectorates following the Russo-Turkish War of 1828–1829 even though they remained in the Ottoman Empire. Romania was finally recognized as an independent state after the Russo-Turkish War of 1877–1878 during which it fought on the Russian side, and enjoyed freedom until World War II. From 1947 to 1989 Romania was under Communist rule.

The Principality of Muscovy, the predecessor of modern Russia, emerged from over 200 years of Mongol domination in the 13th to 15th centuries and gradually absorbed surrounding principalities. The Romanov Dynasty continued this policy of expansion across Siberia to the Pacific in the 1700s. Peter I (1682–1725) extended the empire to the Baltic Sea and renamed the state the Russian Empire. Repeated defeats of the Russian army in World War I led to widespread rioting in the major cities of the Russian Empire and to the overthrow in 1917 of the imperial family. The Communists under Vladimir Lenin seized power soon after and formed the Union of Soviet Socialist Republics (USSR), commonly referred to as the Soviet Union. Josef Stalin (1928–1953) strengthened Communist rule and Russian dominance of the Soviet Union. The Soviet economy and society stagnated in the following decades until General Secretary Mikhail Gorbachev (1985–1991) restructured the government in an attempt to modernize Communism, but his initiatives inadvertently brought about freedoms that splintered the USSR into Russia and 14 other independent republics from 1989 to 1991. After a brief trial with democracy, Russia has adopted a centralized semi-authoritarian state that has resulted in restrictions on freedoms but has fostered continued economic growth.[2]

Ukraine was ruled by the Kyvian-Rus Empire, a loose federation of Slavic tribes, from the 9th century until the middle of the 13th century. By the middle of the 14th century, Ukrainian territories were under the rule of three external powers: the Mongol Golden Horde, the Grand Duchy of Lithuania, and the Kingdom of Poland. In 1795, Ukraine was divided between Russia and Austria, wherein the greater part of Ukraine was integrated into the Russian Empire, with the rest of Ukraine ruled by the Austro-Hungarian Empire. Following a period of turbulence, Ukraine became one of the founding republics of the Soviet Union on December 30, 1922.

The Czech Republic, Hungary, Poland, Romania, and Ukraine have experienced periods during which they fell directly under Russian and/or Soviet control; however, this influence has been more prominent with Ukraine and to some extent with Romania. While many of the nations of Western Europe were experiencing economic growth in the 19th and 20th centuries with mixed capitalist economic systems and high levels of integration into the world economy,[3] Russia in the 19th century, and the Soviet Union in the 20th century experienced stagnant economic development and failed to develop strong capitalist institutions and international economic links. The countries in Central and Eastern Europe experienced a form of mixed development that lay somewhere between the development patterns experienced by Western Europe and by Russia.[4] Prior to falling under Soviet influence, Czechoslovakia adhered more closely to the mixed capitalist economic systems adopted by the Western European countries, which helps explain why the Czech Republic now has one of the most developed and industrialized economies among the emerging democracies in CEE. Countries such as Hungary and Poland fell somewhere in the middle in terms of economic development, and Romania and Ukraine adhered more closely to the Soviet pattern of development. The following section builds on this observation.

Understanding the Region

The Czech Republic is one of the most stable and prosperous countries in CEE and is classified by the World Bank as a high-income economy.[5] Even in 1945, following the end of World War II, Czechoslovakia ranked seventh in the world in GDP per capita.[6] The Czech Republic's strong industrial economy is also aided by history. Bohemia, a region in the west with rolling plains, hills, and plateaus surrounded by low mountains, and Moravia, a very hilly region on the eastern third of the country, formed the economic heartland of the Austro-Hungarian Empire.

Hungary is classified by the World Bank as an upper-middle-income economy. It is a nation that, for many centuries, helped arrest the expansion of the Ottoman Empire into Europe. Given its relatively short tenure under the shadow of Russian/Soviet influence, Hungary was able to transition from Communist rule to a more free-market economy with relative ease compared to some of its peers. Hungary, in fact, played a role in the collapse of Communism across Central and Eastern Europe in 1989 when it opened its border with Austria, which essentially allowed Germans living in the former East Germany to escape to the West. Hungary's terrain is mostly flat to rolling plains with hills and low mountains on the Slovakian border.

Poland is a country with a flat terrain and a lack of natural barriers, factors that have historically contributed to it being an area beset with conflict. Following the end of World War II, Poland engaged in heavy industry similar to other Eastern bloc countries. Poland was able to shake off the Communist influence much quicker than some of its CEE neighbors as the tenets of Soviet socialism were never well-accepted in Polish society; Stalin noted that introducing Communism to Poland was like putting a saddle on a cow.[7] Today Poland is one of the most stable and prosperous countries in CEE and is classified by the World Bank as a high-income economy.

Romania's terrain is distributed about equally between mountainous and plain regions with the Carpathian Mountains occupying the center of Romania. It is a country with a mixed economic history. Following the end of World War II, Romania became a Communist state. The Soviet Union depleted much of Romania's resources through the Soviet Union's SovRom agreements, which enabled the shipment of Romanian goods to the Soviet Union at nominal prices. The period under the rule of Communist Party leader Nicolae Ceauşescu and his economic policies worsened the situation. Consequently, following the fall of the Berlin Wall, Romania entered the 1990s as a relatively poor country. Romania's economy picked up in the 2000s, joining the EU in 2007. From 2006 to 2008, Romanian economic growth was among the fastest in the EU. However, GDP contracted by 7.1 percent in the third quarter of 2009 from the same period a year earlier, and by 2012 GDP growth was at 0.7 percent. The World Bank now classifies Romania as an upper-middle-income economy.

Russia's diversity is reflected by its terrain, ranging from steppes in the south, through humid weather in much of European Russia, to subarctic weather in Siberia, and the tundra climate in the polar north. Winters range from cool weather along the Black Sea coast to frigid weather in Siberia. Similarly, summers vary from warm in the steppes to cool along the Arctic coast. Russia has vast natural resources although a number of formidable obstacles with respect to climate, terrain, and distance inhibit its exploitation of these natural resources. The World Bank classifies Russia as a high-income economy.

Ukraine mostly has fertile plains and plateaus, with mountains found in the west and in the Crimean Peninsula. Ukraine has been ruled by several nations since the 13th century, mostly by Russia, until its independence in August 1991. The long domination by the Soviets has had an effect on Ukraine. As noted by the Central Intelligence Agency's (CIA) World Factbook, economic freedom continues to be severely repressed in Ukraine. Previous reforms, including implementation of competitive tax rates and minor regulatory changes, have failed to spur broad-based economic development, and Ukraine scores very poorly on the Ease of Doing Business Index. The World Bank classifies Ukraine as a lower-middle-income economy.

The Markets

Supply chain activity in the CEE region is increasing, heightening interactions both between the countries in the region and with external regions. As a result, many manufacturing plants have moved from Western Europe to locations in the region as the supply chain networks to support these increasing activities have evolved and become more sophisticated.

Location of Market Activity

The automotive industry is particularly important to the region and typifies the growth of manufacturing activity in CEE. A report published by the International Monetary Fund (IMF) in 2006 notes that the automobile sector represents almost 16 percent of output and 10 percent of value added in Central European manufacturing.[8] A number of automotive organizations in Western Europe have relocated their assembly facilities to CEE and are also sourcing their components from the region. These organizations are exploiting the skilled pool of low-cost labor in the CEE countries to reduce their costs in an increasingly competitive market. As noted by the IMF in its 2006 report, "The Automobile Industry is (literally) becoming a driving force of economic development in the Visegrad countries of Central Europe." The Visegrad countries referred to in the IMF report are the Czech Republic, Hungary, Poland, and Slovakia. In general, the major industries in CEE include automobiles, metallurgy, machinery and equipment, glass, textiles, footwear, chemicals, petroleum refining, and food processing.

Organizations considering foreign direct investment (FDI) typically assess and compare the attractiveness of cities rather than countries when evaluating locations for new projects. The primacy rate is a useful measure for such organizations because it provides an indicator of the concentration of industrial activity in these countries. As noted in earlier chapters, primacy is the percentage of the urban population living in a country's largest metropolitan area. Table 10.1 provides the primacy rates for the six focal countries covered in this chapter.

Table 10.1 suggests that the primacy rate may be a concern for just one of the countries, Hungary. The metropolitan area of Budapest accounts for about 28 percent of the urban population, but this large concentration does not appear to be a major concern for investment as Hungary offers a diverse range of industrial parks that enables investors to choose from more than 200 operating industrial sites, depending on their business requirements.[9] Similarly, although the Czech Republic, Poland, and Romania have relatively high primacy rates, the industrial activity does not appear to be as concentrated in these countries.

Table 10.1 Primacy Rates for the Six Focal Countries in CEE

Country	Urban Population (Percent of Total)	Population of Largest City (Percent of Urban Population)
Czech Republic	75	16
Hungary	65	28
Poland	63	14
Romania	55	16
Russia	73	8
Ukraine	68	7

The Czech Republic

The Czech Republic has a population of 10.16 million and a land area of 78,867 square kilometers (30,451 square miles). The Czech Republic is a landlocked country, spanning some of the oldest and most significant land routes in Europe (Figure 10.1). The Moravian Gate, a mountain pass that formed a traditional military corridor between the North European Plain and the Danube in Central Europe, represented one of the most important trade routes from southern Europe to the Baltic Sea. The geography of the Czech Republic is diverse and includes plateaus, highlands, and lowlands.

The Czech Republic has 13 regions and the capital city of Prague. Industrial activity in the Czech Republic is fairly widespread with major activity centers near Prague in the center of the country, Plzen in the west, Liberec in the north, Ostrava in the east, Brno in the southeast, and Ceske Budejovice in the southwest. The major industries in the Czech

Figure 10.1 The Czech Republic.

Republic are automobiles, metallurgy, machinery and equipment, glass, and armaments. In particular, the Czech Republic is the largest car manufacturer in CEE.[10]

Hungary

Hungary has a population of 9.94 million people and a land area of 93,028 square kilometers (35,918 square miles). Like the Czech Republic, Hungary is a landlocked nation located strategically between the Western European countries, the Balkan Peninsula, Slovakia, and Eastern Europe (Figure 10.2). The country is divided into seven regions: Northern Hungary, Central Transdanubia, Western Transdanubia, Northern Great Plain, Southern Great Plain, Central Hungary, and Southern Transdanubia. A large number of the more than 200 industrial parks are located in Central Hungary near the capital city of Budapest, but many industrial parks are spread throughout the country as noted earlier.

Hungary is one of nine countries through which the Danube flows, and it benefits from the Danube in a variety of ways: freight transport, hydroelectricity, water supplies, irrigation, and fishing. Hungary followed a traditionally agrarian economy model in the past but entered into a period of industrialization following the end of World War II, much of it focused on heavy manufacturing industries in the form of mining, metallurgy, and steel production. Industrial plants were nationalized by 1949, and the socialized sector accounted for about 98.5 percent of gross production in 1985.[11] Chemicals became the leading industry in the early 1990s, and the automobile industry grew in prominence in the 2000s.

The automotive sector is now one of Hungary's core industries, generating almost 21 percent of total exports in recent years. Although Hungary has been an important

Figure 10.2 Hungary.

producer of bauxite, and there is some mining activity for coal, copper, natural gas, oil, and uranium, it is poor in the natural resources essential for heavy industry and relies strongly on imports for its raw material needs in this industry.

Poland

Poland has a population of 38.38 million and a land area of 312,685 square kilometers (120,729 square miles). It is bordered on the west by Germany, in the north by the Baltic Sea, in the northeast by Russia and Lithuania, in the east by Belarus and Ukraine, and in the south by Slovakia and the Czech Republic (Figure 10.3).

Poland has 16 Voivodships (provinces) with the capital, Warsaw, located in the province of Mazovia. Poland enjoys a high-income economy. It is also one of the fastest growing economies in the EU. A report by *Forbes* published in September 2013[12] states that over the

Figure 10.3 Poland.

past two decades the Polish economy has grown at a record pace compared to its neighbors. The report notes that Poland is the only EU economy to avoid recession following the 2008 global financial crisis. The main industries in Poland are machinery, iron and steel, coal mining, textiles, glass, and food processing.

Romania

Romania has a population of 21.79 million and a land area of 238,391 square kilometers (92,043 square miles). Romania shares a border with Hungary and Serbia to the west, Ukraine and Moldova to the northeast and east, and Bulgaria to the south. It controls the most easily traversable land route between the Balkans, Moldova, and Ukraine (Figure 10.4).

Romania is divided into 41 counties and the principality of Bucharest. Romania has a wealth of natural resources and is ranked 10th in the world for its diversity of minerals.[13]

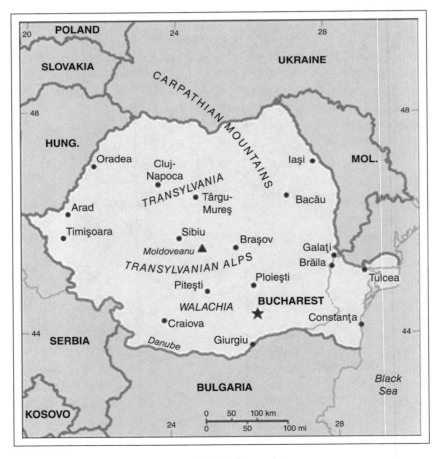

Figure 10.4 Romania.

As noted by the zetapetroleum.com website, Romania's production of metals (aluminium, copper, lead, zinc, and steel) and the quarrying and mining of industrial materials (salt, barite, and graphite) are of regional importance. The petroleum industry is the largest in the region and plays an important part in the country's energy balance. Romania is the largest natural gas producer in Eastern Europe, and it has the most significant oil and gas reserves in southeastern Europe. According to reuters.com,[14] Romania has estimated oil reserves of 1.4 billion barrels. Moreover, it has surplus refining capacity. Other industries include electrical machinery and equipment, textiles, footwear, construction materials, and automobile assembly.

Although the primacy rate for Romania is not very high, there is a significant difference between the population of the largest city, the capital Bucharest with 1.93 million residents, and the next two largest cities, Cluj-Napoca in the northwest and Timisoara in the west, each with populations of around 325,000. Indeed, the majority of industrial activity is focused in the urban areas of the southeast (where Bucharest is located) and the northwest (where Cluj-Napoca is located), with heavy industries generally located in the south.

Russia

Officially known as the Russian Federation, Russia is the largest country in the world in terms of area with a total land area of 17,098,242 square kilometers (6,601,668 square miles), with a population of 142.5 million. As Figure 10.5 shows, the major cities are concentrated in the western region of the country. Although the primacy rate for Russia is only 8 percent, four of the five most populated cities in Russia are also on the western end of the country: Moscow (10.52 million), Saint Petersburg (4.58 million), Yekaterinburg

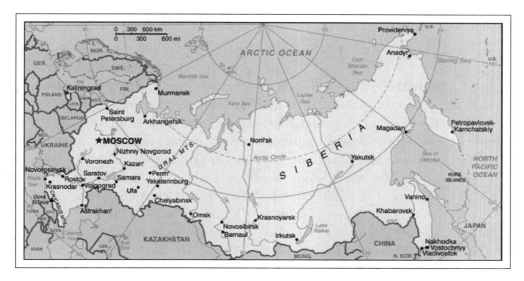

Figure 10.5 Russia.

(1.34 million), and Nizhniy-Novgorod (1.27 million). Only Novosibirsk (1.397 million), the third most populous city, lies further east.

Russia has abundant natural resources including timber, precious metals, and fossil fuels in the form of oil, natural gas, and coal. Furthermore, Russia enjoys the ability to develop its fossil fuels without the constraint of Organization of the Petroleum Exporting Countries (OPEC) production quotas. According to the United Nations Educational, Scientific, and Cultural Organization (UNESCO) World Heritage Center, Lake Baikal in the southern part of Siberia is estimated to hold a fifth of the world's total unfrozen freshwater reserve.[15] The World Heritage Center notes that Lake Baikal, also known as the "Galapagos of Russia," enjoys one of the world's richest and most unusual freshwater faunas. On the other hand, Russia has to contend with a hostile climate that is either too cold or too dry, at least as far as agriculture is concerned. A large portion of the region—especially Siberia—is basically uninhabitable. With a land area of 13.1 million square kilometers, Siberia constitutes about 77 percent of Russia but is home to only about 28 percent of the population, at a density of about three people per square kilometer.

The major markets for Russia span a very large range of products. The CIA World Factbook website notes that Russia has "a complete range of mining and extractive industries producing coal, oil, gas, chemicals, and metals." In addition, it is involved in "all forms of machine building from rolling mills to high-performance aircraft and space vehicles." The website goes on to note that Russia's defense industries include "radar, missile production, and advanced electronic components." Russia also has significant activity in shipbuilding, road and rail transport equipment production, medical and scientific instruments, and agricultural machinery.

Ukraine

Ukraine has a population of 44.57 million and a land area of 603,550 square kilometers (233,032 square miles) (Figure 10.6). Ukraine has rich farmlands with fertile plains, a well-developed industrial base, a highly trained labor force of 20 million, and a good education system. It enjoys a strategic position as it is located at the crossroads between Europe and Asia. Ukraine thus has the potential to become a major European economy, but it is hobbled by excessive government regulation, corruption, and a lack of law enforcement.

Ukraine is divided into 27 regions: 24 *oblasts* or primary administrative units, one autonomous republic (the Autonomous Republic of Crimea), and two cities with "special status" (the capital city of Kiev and Sevastopol in the south). The Autonomous Republic of Crimea occupies most of Crimea, a peninsula of Ukraine located on the northern coast of the Black Sea. The city of Sevastopol is located on the southern tip of Crimea and continues to be the home of the Russian Black Sea Fleet. This city also has a Ukrainian naval base. The major markets for Ukraine are coal, electric power generation, ferrous and nonferrous metals, machinery and transportation equipment, chemicals, and food processing.

Figure 10.6 Ukraine.

Assessing Supply Chain Maturity

This section assesses the supply chain maturity of the subcontinent using the Economy, Politics, Infrastructure, and Competence (EPIC) dimensions. The first dimension, the Economy dimension, assesses the wealth and resources of each region in terms of production and consumption of goods and services.

Economy

Data from the CIA World Factbook on the GDP composition by sector of origin shows that all focal countries in CEE have a relatively high industry component (as compared to services and agriculture, for example), ranging from a minimum of 28.5 percent of GDP for Hungary to a maximum of 38 percent for the Czech Republic. For comparison, the EU average for the industry component is 24.7 percent. The major industries for the six focal countries in CEE reflect a diverse set of capabilities. It includes heavy manufacturing, fossil fuel production, petroleum refining, food processing, automobile production, and the manufacture of consumer products such as textiles and footwear.

A majority of these countries engage in heavy manufacturing in the form of construction machinery, iron and steel, coal mining, and transportation equipment production—a reflection of the era of Soviet dominance—but each country has its own unique strengths. As noted earlier, the 2006 IMF report indicated that the automotive industry is now a driving force of economic development in the Czech Republic, Hungary, and Poland. Romania's economy is driven by its petroleum and natural gas industry, as well as by the production of metals, and Russia has the enviable position of developing its fossil fuels without the constraint of OPEC production quotas.

Economic Output and Growth Rate

The Czech Republic is the best performer among the focal countries as far as GDP per capita (at purchasing power parity, or PPP) is concerned, with a rank of 56 based on data from the CIA World Factbook for 2012. Extensive trade and financial linkages left some economies in CEE exposed to the global economic crisis[16] that took place in 2008, and the Czech Republic's recovery from this crisis has been in fits and spurts. Events that took place in 2013—devastating floods in the Bohemian region in the western part of the country, and the resignation of Prime Minister Petr Necas following the arrest of one of his trusted aides on charges of corruption and power abuse—have also presented some barriers to progress.

Hungary has managed to transition from a centrally planned economy to a market economy with a per capita income nearly two-thirds that of the EU-28 average. The private sector accounts for more than 80 percent of GDP. The global economic downturn, declining exports, and low domestic consumption resulted in an economic contraction of 6.8 percent in 2009. The economy recovered in 2010 with a boost from exports to Germany and achieved growth of approximately 1.7 percent in 2012.[17] Going forward, the economy is expected to recover, albeit at a modest pace.

Poland is the second largest of the focal countries in CEE. It is also a country whose economy has shown great resilience. In particular, when the economies in CEE were exposed to the 2008 global economic crisis, Poland was the only EU country not to fall into recession in 2009, although it narrowly avoided a contraction in 2013.[18] Private industry now accounts for two-thirds of GDP, making Poland one of the EU's strongest performers.

According to the CIA World Factbook, Romania had a GDP per capita (at purchasing power parity) of $13,000 in 2012, the lowest for a EU member state, placing it 101st among the 228 countries ranked in 2012. For comparison, Bulgaria, the EU state having the next lowest GDP per capita of $14,500, ranked 93rd that year. However, Romania was not the lowest ranked country among the CEE focal countries. Ukraine was ranked 140th in 2012, with a GDP per capita of $7500.

Since the breakup of the Soviet Union, Russia has gone through significant changes, moving from a centrally planned economy to a more market-based and globally integrated economy. In 2012 it was ranked eighth in terms of total GDP, and seventh in terms of total GDP at purchasing power parity. The once robust Russian economy is, however, slowing down. The World Bank noted that economic growth in Russia slowed significantly during the first half of 2013 due to a combination of external and domestic factors, some cyclical and others structural. A large part of the cyclical component is ascribed to Russia's high dependence on oil and gas exports.[19]

After a robust eight-year expansion beginning in 2000 that saw real GDP expand 75 percent, Ukraine has since slipped in its growth. It is the poorest among the focal countries studied in this chapter, with a GDP per capita rank of 140th as of 2012. In September 2013, the World Bank joined the IMF in deploring Ukraine's economic performance[20] and projected that Ukraine's growth in 2013 would be close to zero. The World Bank report on Ukraine followed a move by the IMF to place a multibillion euro loan to Ukraine on hold.

Population

Population is an issue for all the countries of this region. Eurostat, a Directorate-General of the European Commission located in Luxembourg, projects that the population of the focal countries will shrink steadily throughout the coming decades, with Romania projected to suffer the biggest population decline, almost 20 percent by 2060. For the Czech Republic, the population is projected to increase by 3.4 percent by 2030 and then decrease steadily to the same level in 2060 as in 2010. However, the most striking case is Russia, where the population is projected to fall from 140 million in 2010 to 108 million by 2050, a decline of 23 percent (that decline was temporarily interrupted in 2012 thanks to immigration).

In general, most of the countries in CEE have rapidly aging populations. By 2025, the median age is projected to be at least 10 years more than it is now for about half of the countries in the region. The number of elderly is already high in many countries and will continue to rise during the next two decades. The proportion of the population 65 years and older in Romania is projected to increase from 12 percent in 2010 to 35 percent in 2060. Similarly, in Poland, the proportion of the population 65 years and older is anticipated to go up by 21 percent to 34.5 percent. As with a number of other regions, the two primary contributing factors to the aging population are significant declines in fertility, and increased longevity resulting from advances in healthcare. The population is also becoming less and less rural and more and more urban. The effects of these changes on both the size and the structure of the population in the focal countries is substantial.

Foreign Direct Investment

In general, a significant portion of FDI into the region, in particular the Visegrad countries, has gone into the automotive industry, giving this region a special position in the automotive market for Europe. A majority of the automobiles assembled in CEE are destined for the Western Europe market, but many automotive organizations in Asia, particularly South Korea, are using plants set up in CEE as a springboard to export their products to the Western Europe region. A 2010 report by Ernst & Young[21] noted that despite the 2008 downturn, new capacity committed before the downturn hit full production in a number of CEE countries—notably the Czech Republic and Slovakia. Consequently, these countries are now major vehicle exporters although their domestic markets remain small by comparison, with the Czech Republic and Slovakia producing more than five times their levels of domestic demand.

The Czech Republic has benefited from open-market policies that have sustained global trade and investment flows into the country. These policies have also enabled the economy to capitalize on regulatory efficiencies achieved through earlier reforms. The Czech Republic has encouraged a competitive investment regime. Domestic and foreign investors are generally treated equally.

Hungary's investment regime is relatively efficient, but bureaucratic red tape and deficient transparency have impeded investment growth. Net FDI, which was €10.5 billion in 2012 was projected to go down to €3 billion in 2013, although it must be noted that net FDI was projected to decline almost everywhere across the world in 2013.

Poland enjoys high economic freedom but certain areas of investment require government approval. The regulatory system, in particular, is not efficient. Overall, however, Poland has done well with FDI.

Foreign investment in Romania is encouraged officially. However, it is discouraged in practice as a result of inconsistencies in regulatory practice and a lack of transparency. Ukraine's progress in attracting FDI has proceeded in fits and starts.

Russia performed well with FDI in the 2007–2009 period. In 2008 direct investment flows inward were equal to almost $80 billon, which was approximately eight times more than in the rest of the focal countries. However, in 2009 a major drop to just over $30 billion was recorded. The amounts invested were significantly affected by the crisis, and there were fewer mergers and acquisitions in Russia.

Similar to Romania, the Ukrainian government appears to encourage FDI, but there are institutional controls on capital and investment. A major obstacle to FDI in Ukraine appears to be due to corruption, which pervades all levels of the executive branch and all spheres of economic activity.

Exchange Rate Stability and Consumer Price Inflation

Although 17 countries in CEE use the euro as their official currency as of 2013 (Kosovo and Montenegro have also unilaterally adopted the euro as their currency, as have the principalities of Andorra and Monaco, San Marino, and the Vatican City), all the focal countries in CEE use their own individual currencies. The currency in the Czech Republic is the koruna, the currency in Hungary is the forint, the currency in Poland is the zloty, the currency in Romania is the leu, the currency in Russia is the rouble, and the currency in Ukraine is the hryvnia. Except for the Czech koruna, all the currencies have displayed considerable volatility during the period from 2008 to 2013, especially during the financial crisis of 2008.

With respect to Consumer Price Inflation (CPI), all the focal countries, with the exception of Russia, fare well based on data from 2011 and 2012. Both Russia and Ukraine were hard hit with inflation reaching upwards of 8 percent in 2011. However, the inflation rate was significantly reduced for Ukraine in 2012, reaching 0.6 percent. Inflation remained fairly high for Russia, at 5.1 percent in 2012.

Balance of Trade

The balance of trade grades for the focal countries may not reflect the strengths and weaknesses on this variable on an international level because most of the trading partners for three of these countries—Czech Republic, Hungary, and Poland—are within the continent of Europe. That said, five of the six focal countries enjoyed a trade surplus in 2011, with the sole exception of Ukraine. During all the years of its independence, Ukraine has tried to be an export-oriented country, but recently it has depended more and more on imports. In particular, although the Czech Republic lagged among the five countries with regard to trade surpluses in 2011, its year-on-year trade surplus in April 2013 exceeded expectations, fueled by rising automotive exports.

Table 10.2 presents the scores for the focal countries in CEE on the Economy dimension, and Table 10.3 presents their strengths and weaknesses for the Economy dimension.

Politics

The political environment in a country significantly affects supply chain operations. In particular, organizations planning to start supply chain operations in a foreign country should consider a variety of political factors. These factors include the ease with which organizations can conduct business, the level of bureaucracy and corruption, the regulatory framework to support entrepreneurial activity, the ability of the region to withstand social unrest, and protection of intellectual property.

Ease of Doing Business, Bureaucracy, and Corruption

The ease of doing business in a country strongly influences supply chain activity because it drives cost and time efficiencies on various activities such as land procurement, hiring, building construction, and cross-border logistics. All focal countries have attempted to improve the ease of doing business with mixed results. For instance, consider the effort involved in starting a new business. The International Finance Corporation (IFC), a subsidiary of the World Bank, maintains a website[22] that measures the number of process steps and the number of days required to start a new business. On these metrics, Hungary has had the best success, requiring just 4 steps and an average of 5 days to start a new business, but bureaucratic red tape and poor transparency could derail this success. Romania also fares well on these metrics (6 steps, 10 days). The Czech Republic (9 steps, 20 days),

Table 10.2 Scores for the Economy Dimension

Economy	Economic Output and Growth Rate	Population Size	Foreign Direct Investment	Exchange Rate Stability/CPI	Balance of Trade	Overall Grade
30%	35%	25%	20%	15%	5%	100%
Czech Republic	B⁻	B⁻	B	A⁻	B	B
Hungary	C	B⁻	B⁻	C	A	C⁺
Poland	B⁺	A⁻	A⁻	C⁺	B⁺	B⁺
Romania	B⁻	B⁺	B⁻	C⁺	C	B⁻
Russia	B⁺	A	A	C⁺	B	B⁺
Ukraine	B⁻	A⁻	A⁻	C⁺	B⁺	B

Table 10.3 Strengths and Weaknesses Summary: Economy Dimension

Grade	Strengths	Weaknesses
Czech Republic: B	Stable economy; good prospects for population growth; increasing balance of trade; relatively slower-aging population; stable exchange rate; stable inflation rate.	No major organizations at international level; small country.
Hungary: C⁺	Positive balance of trade; relatively efficient investment climate; close historical relationship with Austria.	Low birthrate; decreasing population; investment growth impeded by red tape.
Poland: B⁺	Structural reforms undertaken in early 1990s showing effects today; stable economy; positive GDP growth; stable inflation rate; centrally located in Europe; relatively high level of FDI; close relationship with Europe and the United States.	Low birthrate; decreasing population; aging population; negative balance of trade; certain areas of investment require government approval.
Romania: B⁻	Relatively stable consumer price inflation; a wealth of minerals; largest natural gas producer in Eastern Europe.	Negative balance of trade; aging population; inconsistencies in regulatory practices; lack of transparency.
Russia: B⁺	Positive balance of trade thanks to oil and gas; very high level of foreign direct investment (due to the size of the country); stable exchange rate.	Population projected to decrease 23 percent by 2050; high consumer price inflation.
Ukraine: B	Low labor costs.	Negative balance of trade; GDP growth slowing; unstable exchange rate; high consumer price inflation; corruption pervades all level of economic activity.

Poland (6 steps, 32 days), Russia (8 steps, 18 days), and Ukraine (7 steps, 22 days) fare relatively poorly on these metrics. To provide a set of reference points, the comparable numbers for China are 13 steps and 33 days. In the United States, 6 steps and 6 days are required to start a new business.

Governmental effectiveness and control of corruption remove two of the major obstacles to foreign investment. With regard to governmental effectiveness and control of corruption, the Czech Republic, Hungary, and Poland are slightly ahead of Romania and well ahead of Russia and Ukraine. Corruption still remains a cause for concern in the Czech Republic, but the government has taken steps to reduce it. The United States Department of State reports that the Czech parliament enacted legislation on corporate criminal liability effective January 1, 2012,[23] wherein the criminal code was amended to strengthen guidelines for sentencing persons found guilty of corruption. The criminal code also expanded the use of investigative tools such as wiretaps in corruption investigations. In Hungary, the government is making efforts to eradicate corruption although it does not seem to have been effective everywhere in this regard, especially in the case of government procurement contracts. In Poland, bribery and abuse of public office are punishable under the criminal code. Indeed, due to an overall decrease in corruption, the Polish chapter of Transparency International closed in 2011. Romania faces the threat posed by a slight increase in corruption, a threat worsened by a relatively inefficient judicial system.

While the four EU countries are combating corruption with varying degrees of success, Russia and Ukraine seem to have taken a step backward in this regard. As far as Russia is concerned, corruption appears to have increased to a point where it is now rampant. Corruption is also prevalent in Ukraine.

Legal and Regulatory Framework

The Czech Republic, Hungary, and Poland fare very well on the legal and regulatory framework variable whereas the other three focal countries do not. Romania gets a barely passing grade, and Russia and Ukraine fare poorly.

Among the three countries that fare well, the Czech Republic, in particular, follows a very streamlined regulatory process. In Hungary, laws governing commerce are well laid out, but enforcement could be improved. Poland has introduced regulatory reform that is very effective in encouraging entrepreneurship; commercial operations are aided by regulations that support open-market policies, but the judiciary process is slow and prone to political interference.

In Romania, regulatory inconsistency and a lack of transparency seem to be barriers to FDI. The judiciary system is prone to political interference.

Russia's economic progress is impeded by the lack of an efficiently functioning legal framework, a framework that has not been modernized. Furthermore, the Russian government exerts a lot of control in many sectors, a problem that is worsened by the fact that the state already owns many enterprises. Large state-owned institutions dominate the financial sector, outweighing private domestic and foreign banks. Such a restrictive regulatory regime can discourage private-sector growth that, in turn, can severely hamper meaningful economic development. As is the case with Romania, the judiciary system is vulnerable to political interference.

The Ukraine legal and regulatory framework has problems that are very similar to Russia's problems. The rule of law is uneven across the country, and laws are poorly administered. The judiciary is subject to political influence as well as corruption.

As far as tariff barriers are concerned, the four EU countries have very low trade-weighted average tariff rates as would be expected from EU countries. All four countries had an effective rate of 1.1 percent in 2011, a significant 45 percent reduction from the 1.5 percent trade-weighted average tariff rate in 2010. Ukraine, too has reduced its trade-weighted average tariff rate from 2.8 percent in 2010 to 1.9 percent in 2011. Although the 1.9 percent rate is low, some nontariff barriers constrain trade freedom. In sharp contrast to these countries, the trade-weighted average tariff rate for Russia in 2011 was 5.2 percent, which represented a 37 percent increase from the rate in 2010.

Political Stability

Corporations, investors, and governments have to deal with the risk of social unrest that may arise as a result of political decisions. Political stability, defined as the absence of threat posed to governments by social protest, is measured using the Political Instability Index published by the Economist Intelligence Unit. This index, last published in 2009–2010 derives its scores by combining measures of economic distress and underlying vulnerability to unrest. The higher the rank on this index, the greater is the absence of threats. The Czech Republic performs the best among the focal countries on this variable, ranking 153rd. Ukraine with a rank of 16th performs the poorest. Russia, ranked 66th on this index, has had its share of social unrest in recent times. The "Snow revolution" that took place in Russia in December 2011 first began as a response to the Russian legislative election process, which many Russians considered to be flawed, and continued for nearly two months despite statements from the Election Commission that the reports of fraud were greatly exaggerated.

Intellectual Property Rights

The Czech Republic, Hungary, and Poland earn a B grade on the intellectual property rights variable. Romania gets a C+ grade, but intellectual property rights are especially a problem in Russia and Ukraine. In general, property rights (real and intellectual) are relatively well protected by law through an independent judicial system in the Czech Republic, Hungary, and Poland. Similar laws exist in Romania, but the enforcement of legislation protecting patents, trademarks, and copyrights is very weak. Russia faces considerable infringements of intellectual property (IP) rights and receives a D⁺ grade. Ukraine has even more serious problems protecting IP rights and earns a D⁻ grade.

Table 10.4 presents the scores for the Politics dimension, and Table 10.5 presents a summary of the strengths and weaknesses for the focal countries.

Table 10.4 Scores for the Politics Dimension

Politics	Ease of Doing Business	Legal Framework	Political Stability	Intellectual Property Rights	Overall Grade
20%	30%	30%	25%	15%	100%
Czech Republic	B	B⁺	A⁻	B	B⁺
Hungary	B	B⁺	C	B	B⁻
Poland	B	B⁺	B⁺	B	B⁺
Romania	B⁻	B⁻	C⁻	C⁺	C⁺
Russia	C⁻	D⁺	C⁻	D⁺	C⁻
Ukraine	D	D⁺	D⁻	D⁻	D

Table 10.5 Strengths and Weaknesses Summary: Politics Dimension

Grade	Strengths	Weaknesses
Czech Republic: B⁺	Low tariff barriers; high political stability; good legal framework.	Corruption still remains a mild concern.
Hungary: B⁻	Good legal framework; ease of starting new businesses; low tariff barriers; intellectual property rights protected.	Some risk of political instability; corruption a mild concern; law enforcement could be improved.
Poland: B⁺	Good legal framework; low tariff barriers; good political stability.	Long time required to start a new business due to red tape.
Romania: C⁺	Low tariff barriers; ease of starting new businesses.	Relatively low political stability; intellectual property rights not well enforced.
Russia: C⁻	A large market for attracting foreign investors.	High tariff barriers; low rank on Ease of Doing Business Index; political instability concerns; poor intellectual property rights enforcement; rampant corruption.
Ukraine: D	Low tariff barriers although some nontariff barriers constrain freedom of trade.	Low ranking on Ease of Doing Business Index; high risk of political instability; poor intellectual property rights enforcement; corruption prevalent.

Infrastructure

The focal countries in CEE do not fare very well on the Infrastructure dimension, consisting of the transportation, utilities, and telecommunications infrastructures of each focal nation. Infrastructure is a decisive factor for attracting FDI. However, decisions in this regard are structural in nature and are both expensive and difficult to reverse. Either by accident or deliberately, infrastructure changes take place relatively slowly in this region. The following section presents an assessment of Infrastructure in each focal nation.

Transportation Infrastructure

The increased industrial demands placed on the complex distribution networks in countries like Russia, Poland, Hungary, and the Czech Republic have resulted in a significant focus on transportation in these areas. As demand for practices such as just-in-time deliveries to customers outside the region increases, the reliability of the transport network has become more important. Such demands for improved business practices to link CEE markets with those in Western Europe and Asia, however, often conflict with poor infrastructure. The increased demand for logistics services has made modernization of the transportation infrastructure and efficient integration of logistics networks all the more important, and the CEE countries are taking steps to meet these needs.

This is not going to be an easy task. For example, in the Czech Republic logistics centers have been built in a seemingly uncoordinated manner, causing traffic jams. A report on the *Financial Times* website in April 2013[24] states that in Central Europe, in particular in Poland, warehouses are being established "at the intersections of highways designed to service much of the region and occasionally parts of western Europe." Although the report goes on to suggest that "better roads mean logistics can be more centralized and shops can be smaller as they do not need to store as many goods," there is the question of whether it is desirable to let such warehouse building construction go unchecked because of the potential traffic congestion they can create. Another problem is the road density measured in kilometers of road per square kilometer of land area; the higher the road density, the greater the likelihood of traffic backups, especially with a poor road infrastructure. Hungary has the third highest road density in Europe, after Belgium and the Netherlands.

Regardless of these problems, the Czech Republic and Hungary are upgrading their transportation networks. The Czech Republic has experienced a sharp increase in road transport, especially international long-haul trucking. There is a need for greater involvement of other transport modes such as the railways. In general, road transport plays a large role in the transport of goods in western Hungary, whereas rail transport plays a leading role in eastern Hungary. In addition, Hungary will have four of the Trans-European Transport

Network (TEN-T)[d] corridors running through the country. These are Corridor No. IV, which runs from Northern Germany/North Sea to the Black Sea; Corridor No. V, which runs from the Adriatic ports to Kiev–Moscow; Corridor No. VII, which connects the Danube to the Rhine–Main canal from the North Sea; and Corridor No. X, the North-South corridor from the Baltic states to Turkey and Greece.

Poland and Romania are also attempting to improve their infrastructure by building national highway systems, although currently the quality of the roads in Poland and Romania are not very good. Poland benefits from its geographic position with access to the Baltic Sea. It has four major ports, located in Gdańsk, Gdynia, Świnoujście, and Szczecin, as well as several local ports supporting freight reloading processes. Poland's convenient location at the junction of the East-West and North-South trade, transport, and communication routes makes the country a perfect investment destination for enterprises targeting both western and eastern as well as northern and southern parts of Europe. From Warsaw a number of Europe's major capital cities (Berlin, Moscow, Vienna, Bratislava, Kiev, Vilnius, and Minsk) can be reached in just a few hours by car, train, or air. The international routes crossing Poland have been constantly developed and modernized, and Poland is part of four priority TEN-T corridors: the railway axis linking Gdansk–Warsaw–Brno/Bratislava–Vienna; the highway linking Gdansk–Brno/Bratislava–Vienna; the "Rail Baltica" railway axis linking Warsaw–Kaunas–Riga–Tallinn–Helsinki; and the sea highway on the Baltic Sea.

Despite these attempts at modernization, Poland's transportation infrastructure is poor, and development of the country's road infrastructure is one of the Polish administration's top priorities. Transport investments are possible largely thanks to cooperation between the national roads' directorates and governments of neighboring countries and substantial funds and subsidies from the EU.

Romania fares poorly in transportation infrastructure; the main roads are in disrepair, street names are incorrect in some cities, and the traffic is daunting, especially at night. There is a lack of adequate highways, and traffic jams are common near or in big cities. People do not respect traffic laws, and there have been reports of horse-drawn carts traveling without any lights at night on the wrong side of the road.[25]

A potential shift in the incentive structure to encourage rail traffic can especially be a beneficial outcome for Russia where very long distances need to be traveled. Existing train connections between Asia and Europe through Russia (Transsib Railway) are key to the Russian ambition to serve as a hub between Asia and Europe, facilitating the flow of Asian goods to European customers. A 2007 study by the global consulting company Capgemini[26] examined Russia's ambition to become a gateway to Europe for Asian products, the importance of rail

---

[d] TEN-T is a planned set of road, rail, air, and water transport networks in Europe. The TEN-T networks are part of a wider system of Trans-European Networks, including a telecommunications network (eTEN) and a proposed energy network (TEN-E or Ten-Energy). Plans are to have the core TEN-T network established by 2030.

transport in Russian logistics, and the underdevelopment of container freight. The study found that many investment projects are developing very slowly or are on hold due to a long investment decision process of the government, or issues with land or infrastructure owner-ship. More to the point, the study found that although the railway system offers a much better transport mode in Russia because of the large distances involved, the lack and the poor state of train rolling stock, together with the monopolistic position of the Russian rail network operator, makes many organizations still favor road transport even for such large distances.

Ukraine, which is strategically situated between the Russia and Western European markets, has access to the Black Sea and, hence, is one of the most important trade chan-nels connecting Asia and Europe. Being a transit country from Europe to the booming markets of East Asia and Russia, Ukraine requires a large transport and logistics capacity and a well-developed infrastructure. However, the Ukrainian logistics market is inferior to that of Western countries, both in the quality and comprehensiveness of services provided by the national transport and logistics providers.

Utilities

Based on the World Economic Forum Global Competitive Index (WEF GCI), which measures the quality of electricity supply, the Czech Republic performs the best among the focal countries, with Hungary and Poland also faring well. The proposed Trans-European Energy (TEN-E) Network may help these countries and Romania as well. The so-called North-South initiative in electricity, which is a part of this program, aims to strengthen regional networks in these four focal EU countries in the North-South and East-West power flow directions to solve infrastructure gaps, especially those gaps related to increasing generation from renewable energy sources.

Telecommunications and Connectivity

During the economic boom, the main problem of the logistics and transport industries in CEE was the lack of capacity. This was gradually resolved with heavy investments in infrastructure and vehicles. Nevertheless, there was a general lack of investment in information technology as well as other cutting-edge solutions that could have greatly enhanced the performance of existing capacity. Many of the CEE countries are now making remarkable progress in developing their telecommunications connectivity. The Czech Republic, Hungary, Poland, and Russia fare well on the connectivity variable. It is noted that Russia has one of the highest number of mobile phones and Internet users in the world. Even on a per capita basis, Russia has one of the highest number of mobile phone users, but it does not fare as well in terms of Internet users per capita.

Support of information and communications technologies (ICT) solutions for the logis-tics industry, however, remain insufficient in general.[27] The ICT market provides the logis-tics industry with very fragmented information solutions focused primarily on proprietary systems customized to individual requirements of large clients that can afford the high costs of implementation. The information gap between large and smaller organizations seems to be rising. The market lacks applications supporting cooperation between organizations operating as partners in supply chains as well as applications integrating transport modes or national transport networks.

Table 10.6 presents the scores for the Infrastructure dimension, and Table 10.7 presents a summary of the strengths and weaknesses for each of the focal countries.

Table 10.6 Scores for the Infrastructure Dimension

Infrastructure	Transportation Infrastructure	Energy Infrastructure	Connectivity	Overall Grade
30%	50%	25%	25%	100%
Czech Republic	B⁻	A⁻	B⁺	B
Hungary	C	B	B	B⁻
Poland	D	B	B⁺	C
Romania	F	C⁻	B⁻	D
Russia	D	C	B	C⁻
Ukraine	D⁺	C	C⁺	C⁻

Table 10.7 Strengths and Weaknesses Summary: Infrastructure Dimension

Grade	Strengths	Weaknesses
Czech Republic: B	Good air and railway infrastructure; well-developed energy infrastructure; developed communication technologies.	Traffic backups caused by logistics centers built in an uncoordinated manner.
Hungary: B⁻	Good energy infrastructure; developed communication technologies.	Air transport infrastructure could be improved; Danube offers excellent waterway connections, but infrastructure could be improved.
Poland: C	Important transit country for road transport; good connectivity.	Road infrastructure poor; low usage of water transportation; weak communication technologies.
Romania: D	Improving Internet and mobile phone connectivity.	Air transportation infrastructure weak; poor state of the roads; poor enforcement of traffic laws.
Russia: C⁻	Good Internet penetration; railway network and infrastructure is good.	Weak energy infrastructure; weather conditions can be extreme in winter.
Ukraine: C⁻	Railway network and infrastructure is good.	Weak energy infrastructure; poor air and water transportation; weather conditions can be difficult in winter.

Competence

An assessment of key elements of the Competence dimension follows, including labor relations, pay and productivity, and hiring and firing practices; education for line staff and management; logistics competence; and customs and security. A summary of Competence elements for each of the focal countries of CEE is provided at the end of the section.

Labor Relations

According to the WEF Global Competitiveness Index, the Czech Republic, Poland, and Ukraine are very good in paying for a skilled and productive labor workforce. The only country that does not fare very well in this dimension is Romania. Romania also has a problem in that logistics jobs are relatively new to the country, and there is a lack of trained workers in this profession. It is difficult to find experienced workers such as forklift drivers, quality operators, or pick and pack operators. Organizations in Romania seem to face exactly the same issue with lower management positions such as shift supervisors. The outmoded labor code continues to limit employment and productivity growth in Russia.

As far as hiring and firing practices are concerned, it is easier to fire workers in Ukraine than it is in any of the other focal countries, and that helps Ukraine's grade on labor relations. Ukraine is the only country among the six focal countries that gets a grade better than a C+ for the labor relations variable.

Education Levels for Line and Staff Management

The education levels variable is evaluated based on the quality of the educational system, the quality of management schools, the extent of staff training, and the reliance on professional management. All focal countries do poorly on this variable. The Czech Republic and Poland do relatively better than the other three focal countries based on their reliance on professional management, the quality of the educational system, and the extent of staff training. The Czech Republic has a well-educated population and a well-developed infrastructure, but its industrial plants and much of its industrial equipment are obsolete. The competence of senior managers is, however, changing in the focal countries. From 2006 to 2008, Hungary had competent senior managers, but this rate has been declining since then. Poland and Ukraine have seen increasing rates since 2008.

Romania does the poorest on this variable, earning a D. Logistics jobs are relatively new to Romania as noted earlier. Very few people are well prepared to be in a logistics or operations management positions at the level of quality expected by international organizations. It is difficult to find experienced workers such as forklift drivers, quality operators, or pick and pack operators. Organizations face exactly the same issue with lower management positions such as shift supervisors.

Looking ahead, the change in the demographic structure portends a shortage of skilled workers for all focal countries, which in turn would imply a shortage of workers in the transport and logistics sector, ultimately resulting in an inability to effectively meet the demand for these services effectively. From the perspective of employers, a labor shortage would result in a demand for higher wages and expenses.

Logistics Competence

The increased demand for logistics services and the complex distribution networks in countries like Russia, Poland, Hungary, and the Czech Republic have resulted in many organizations outsourcing their logistics activities to logistics providers in recent years. As these logistics providers develop their distribution networks to incorporate practices such as "just-in-time" deliveries for plants in Western Europe, the reliability of the transport network has become more important. Delivery lead-time is no longer the major factor by which these logistics providers are evaluated, but rather it is the ability to deliver per a schedule. Just-in-time delivery systems also mean that logistics providers are now part of the preassembly process.

The demand placed on the infrastructure by many organizations from different parts of the world when they entered CEE to either sell or source their products, or to take advantage of labor arbitrage, has affected supply chain activity in the region. In 2011, the European Region Development Fund sponsored a project aimed at providing small and medium enterprises (SMEs) in Central Europe with access to ICTs with the goal of helping them improve their competitiveness by optimizing their logistics expenses. This project, KASSETS (Knowledge-Enabled Access of Central Europe SMEs to Efficient Transnational Transport Solutions), resulted in a number of findings on the state of the logistics and telecommunications infrastructure that is documented in a report by the Technical University of Košice, Slovak Republic.[28] The report starts by identifying three distinct logistics markets in Europe using the GDP of a country as a measure of market potential, the Logistics Performance Index (LPI) as an indicator of logistics services quality in the country, and Internet usage as a measure of ICT sophistication:

▲ Developed logistics markets that use high-class logistics services and have adopted ICT solutions for logistics activities in large markets such as Germany, France, the United Kingdom, and Spain as well as in smaller markets in Scandinavia, Benelux, Austria, Switzerland, and Ireland.

▲ Developing logistics markets with relatively lower service quality and ICT support that include established EU members like Italy, Greece, and Portugal, EU members from emerging markets across all Central and East European countries, and EU candidates such as Turkey.

▲ Undeveloped logistics markets with relatively low rates of development of logistics and ICT in markets that are more peripherally located in Europe and not currently belonging to the EU. These include large markets like Russia and Ukraine and smaller markets like Belarus, Serbia, Croatia, Montenegro, Macedonia, Moldova, and Albania.

The World Bank LPI rankings from 2012 are used to assess logistics operational competence. Poland is ranked 30th in the 2012 LPI Logistics Competence subindex and earns a B⁺ grade. The other EU countries earn a B or a B⁻ grade. Russia is the worst performer on this variable, earning a C grade. Russia has to deal with a poor infrastructure that is exacerbated by numerous bureaucratic hurdles. In addition, a lack of competition, insufficient transparency, and limited logistics know-how make matters worse. Russia is, however, likely to do better going forward as it prepares to fulfill its ambition to become a hub between Europe and Asia.

The logistics sector in the Czech Republic is important to its national economy for a variety of reasons. Transportation and logistics accounts for approximately 10 percent of Czech GDP and for 8.2 percent of the employment in the private sector. In addition, the Czech Republic is geographically located in the middle of Europe, making it attractive for investment in logistics infrastructure. However, this sector has faced problems in recent times, notably due to the heavy traffic congestion mentioned earlier. Again, there is a need to integrate different modes of transport such as the railways into the overall logistics solution. Nevertheless, the logistics sector has good prospects in the Czech Republic, and its importance for the economy will continue to grow.

Hungary's geographical position is favorable from a logistics point of view for at least two reasons. One is its relative proximity to the developing neighboring countries such as Romania, Ukraine, and Serbia. More important, Hungary will have four of the Trans-European Transport Network (TEN-T) corridors running through the country, as mentioned earlier. From an environmental as well as an economic perspective, intermodal logistics centers that link various modes of transport should have high priority, and their development requires more intensive support.

The logistics activities in Romania are relatively new in many areas. They are linked mainly to the local development of mass-market businesses, with participation from international players such as Metro, Ikea, Carrefour, and Cora. The firms, coming mainly from the western part of Europe, have moved with their own supply chain solutions and often with their own third-party logistics (3PLs), such as FM Logistics. They have duplicated solutions they know very well because these solutions have been intensively developed in Western Europe. However, the local infrastructures were not ready to support such significant rapid growth, leading to heavy traffic jams, low speeds on the roads, security issues, and other complexities caused by a bureaucratic system.

In 2012, the Russian state-owned railway company, RZD, bought a 75 percent interest in a major European third-party logistics providers, Gefco (a €3.6 billion company), a former subsidiary of Peugeot. This purchase is symbolic of Russia's desire to become more involved in the European logistics network. Russia is unique in the sense that it is the largest country in the world with an area of 17 million square kilometers. It could be seen either as a European country or as an Asian country. Two-thirds of its territory is located in Asia. It has borders with China and North Korea and has territory issues with Japan too. Managing a supply chain is very different for organizations in the western part of the country, close to Western Europe with large cities, than it is in the middle part of the country (Siberia) with very few people, and in the eastern part of the country. The geography and the distribution of the population drive the logistics network in Russia.

Contract logistics and outsourcing in Russia are growing. This trend shows that people are more and more focused on complex operational activities and on engineering the supply chain and monitoring it. A report on contract logistics and outsourcing in Russia, exclusively focused on manufacturers, found that manufacturing managers were satisfied with their logistics outsourcing or contract logistics project.[29] According to this report, manufacturing managers indicated that their labor and capital equipment had been reduced as a result of these projects.

The Ukrainian logistics market is undergoing a period of rapid development, and the rate of growth of the logistics market is unlikely to decline in the coming years. The growth is accompanied by an increasing number of 3PLs and 4PLs actively being developed in Ukraine. Among Ukraine's large logistics providers are Europa-Trans-Logistic, Kamaz Trans Service, LAATrans, Rise, TNB Logistics Ukraine, and Ost West Express.[e] These providers have their own transportation facilities, customs bonded warehouses, and workshops that provide customers with a full range of services (forwarding, repairing, and technical service). However, many cost-conscious businesses, especially SMEs, tend not to use logistics providers because the cost of these services can be as high as 15 to 25 percent of the goods cost.[30] Although the number of providers specializing in a single service is large, it is also difficult for SMEs to find a provider that offers a variety of services (forwarding and warehouse storage).

Customs and Security

The World Bank LPI for 2012 also assesses the customs and security procedures for the focal countries in CEE. The performance of these countries is slightly worse than their performance on the Logistics Competence subindex. Poland once again performs the best with a rank of 28th. Ukraine does poorly due to a time-consuming customs clearance process. However, Russia is once again the worst performing country with a grade of D⁻.

---

[e] A large catalog of transportation and logistics providers in Ukraine is available at http://transport.ua-companies .com.

The real problem appears to be Russia's customs procedures and the poor customs infrastructure, which result in lengthy holdups. It is not uncommon to have waiting times of up to 40 hours for consignments waiting to cross the border. This presents another challenge to Russia's desire to serve as a hub between Europe and Asia.

Table 10.8 presents the scores for the Competence dimension, and Table 10.9 presents a summary of the strengths and weaknesses for each of the focal countries.

Table 10.8   Scores for the Competence Dimension

Competence	Labor Relations	Education Levels	Logistics Competence	Customs and Security	Overall Grade
20%	25%	25%	40%	10%	100%
Czech Republic	C⁺	C⁺	B	B	B⁻
Hungary	C	C⁻	B	B	C⁺
Poland	C	C⁺	B⁺	B⁺	B⁻
Romania	D⁺	D	B⁻	B⁻	C
Russia	C⁻	D⁺	C⁻	D⁻	C⁻
Ukraine	B⁻	D⁺	C⁺	C	C

Table 10.9   Strengths and Weaknesses Summary: Competence Dimension

Grade	Strengths	Weaknesses
Czech Republic: B⁻	Good pay for productivity; good reliance on professional management.	Poor labor relations; inflexible employment regulations.
Hungary: C⁺	Good labor productivity; availability of qualified engineers; good logistics competence.	Decreasing availability of competent senior managers.
Poland: B⁻	Good customs and security; good reliance on professional management; logistics competence good.	Relatively small pool of qualified labor.
Romania: C	Logistics competence improving.	Labor code limiting employment and productivity growth; lack of skilled logistics workers and overall lack of skilled managers.
Russia: C⁻	Well-qualified labor; presence of many western 3PLs.	Limited availability of skilled management; poor logistics competence; customs and security poor.
Ukraine: C	Flexible employment laws; good pay for productivity; low constraints on hiring and firing practices.	Lack of qualified engineers; few competent senior managers; time-consuming customs clearance process.

Table 10.10 Summary of Assessment of EPIC Attractiveness for the Countries in Central and Eastern Europe

	Economy	Politics	Infrastructure	Competence	Overall
Czech Republic	B	B$^+$	B	B$^-$	B
Hungary	C$^+$	B$^-$	B$^-$	C$^+$	B$^-$
Poland	B$^+$	B$^+$	C	B$^-$	B$^-$
Romania	B$^-$	C$^+$	D	C	C
Russia	B$^+$	C$^-$	C$^-$	C$^-$	C$^+$
Ukraine	B	D	C$^-$	C	C

Table 10.10 presents a summary of the assessment scores on the EPIC dimensions for the focal countries in CEE.

Supply Chain Challenges in CEE

The preceding discussion shows that a number of supply chain challenges need to be overcome, especially in Romania, Russia, and Ukraine. The challenges confronting Russia are well known, but similar situations exist in Romania and Ukraine.

In 1948, Romania started a national "collectivization" of lands, essentially a form of communalism in which the government confiscated land from their original owners. In 1997 the Romanian government started to return these properties to their original owners. For logistics investors such as Prologis, AMB, or Gazeley, who wanted to acquire land to build logistics centers, this created a difficult situation for they could not know with certainty who the owner was. Numerous cases have been opened, and several international groups have lost a lot of money despite the competence of their international legal experts.

Industrial organizations wishing to set up base in Romania faced other problems linked to the presence of unexpected pipelines that were not mentioned on the official maps, or with regard to heavy pollution of the soil. With the heritage of the Communist era still apparent in administrative matters, discussions are long, unclear, and complicated, without the absolute certainty that they will end in a positive way. In addition, administrative corruption is still possible and in some place usual.

Romania is located in a seismic area. Therefore, it is essential to check the quality of a facility to be sure of the structural integrity of the existing building with respect to local seismic norms. The same observation has to be taken into account when a new warehouse is built. Today Romania is building several industrial parks. Except in these specialized areas, it is very difficult to find a premium logistics warehouse.

A number of factors hinder the implementation of supply chain management principles at Ukrainian enterprises. Managers are skeptical regarding implementation of new managerial methods. There is an unwillingness to recognize fundamental changes that have taken place in the philosophy of shaping material, financial, and information flows. Ukraine also faces a shortage of staff specialists. There is a lack of comprehensive monitoring of business processes, a lack of a regulated legal framework, and a high level of corruption and bureaucracy.

Other problems faced in Ukraine include an underestimation of logistics costs. The share of logistics components in the value of output for Ukraine is 30 to 35 percent of GDP (for comparison, logistics costs in the USA are no more than 10 percent, in Europe they range from 9 to 11 percent, and are about 11 to 12 percent in Japan).[31] There is also a low level of logistics infrastructure maturity. Major drawbacks of the current Ukrainian transportation system include a time-consuming customs clearance process, corruption on all levels of cargo transportation, nontransparent tariffs for operations with seaports and railway stations, nonintegrated logistics system, duplication of some procedures concerning border crossings, and underdeveloped risk-management policies.

These negative factors notwithstanding, Ukraine promises several advantages for local entrepreneurs. Among them are a beneficial geographic location and the resources potential of the country. Ukraine has cheap resources (labor, material, natural, etc.). Recent developments in the maritime region of Odessa (south of Ukraine) have shown the potential for building a logistics cluster in that location. Odessa's share in the traffic of goods is 20 percent. The region is situated on the Pan-European Corridor, on the historic Silk Road, and Odessa is a member of the Black Sea Economic Cooperation (BSEC). Nearly 75 percent of the industrial potential of the country is situated in the Odessa region and is served by seven ports: Port of Odessa, Port of Yuzhniy, Port of Illichivsk, Port of Reni, Port of Izmai, Port of Ust-Dunay, and Port of Belgorod-Dnestrovsk.

Ukraine is a growing logistics market, especially for the Black Sea region. Growth and competitiveness of Ukraine can be increased in a number of ways: by using the Ukrainian Black Sea path as the shortest way from Asia to Europe; developing a river route on the Danube (VII Pan-European Corridor: one of the TEN-T priority projects); development, modernization, and specialization of ports; and establishing logistics zones in the hinterland.

Supply Chain Opportunities and Best Practices in the Region

The CEE chapter concludes with two case studies on best practices. The first is a best practices case concerning logistics and warehousing in the Wielkopolska region in Poland, and the second is a case study on the global medical technology organization, Becton Dickinson.

CASE STUDY

Case Study on Best Practices: Logistics Services in Wielkopolska

Wielkopolska, a historical region of west-central Poland, is one of the most important regions in CEE from a logistics point of view. It promises a well-developed market of logistics and transport services, a key factor for efficient movement of imported and exported goods.

The major business players in the region include Prologis, Parkridge, Librecht and Wood, Grontmij Real Estate International, and Centrum Logistyczno Inwesty-cyjne Poznań (CLIP). Logistics operators who have their own warehousing area include Raben, Kuehne and Nagel, PEKAES Multispedytor, Frans Maas, Wincanton, Maersk, Ponetex Logistic, Europegaz, Schenker, and TNT Logistics.

Road transport is the main means of transportation in Wielkopolska with more than 70 percent of the cargo in the area transported by road. A large number of road haulers are operating in Wielkopolska, creating a very competitive market and driving some haulers out of business. The Institute of Logistics and Warehousing (ILIM), widely recognized as the center of logistics competence in Wielkopolska, reports that some small and medium-sized enterprises keep their prices very low to win the competition. Such activities have resulted in a decrease in transport rates for the last three years. Although low transport rates may be attractive to manufacturers operating in the area, such cost cutting inhibits a focus on high-quality comprehensive logistics solutions.

CASE STUDY

Case Study on Becton Dickinson[32]

Becton, Dickinson and Company (BD) is a global medical technology company focused on improving drug delivery, enhancing the diagnosis of infectious diseases and cancers, and advancing drug discovery. BD develops, manufactures, and sells products across three segments: BD Medical, BD Diagnostics, and BD Biosciences. In 2009, it opened its first factory in Tatabánya, a city of 67,753 inhabitants in north-western Hungary in the Central Transdanubian region, 55 kilometers from the capital city of Budapest. According to Claude Dartiguelongue, President, BD Medical–Pharmaceutical Systems, "BD chose to establish this important production facility in Hungary because of the proximity to the important European customers it will serve. The availability of a highly skilled workforce, access to qualified subcontractors, and the support of local public officials were also key factors in our selection of this attractive location for BD's new manufacturing presence."

Factory director Csaba Vecsernyés stated that Becton Dickinson's expansion into Hungary was the result of a variety of factors. Global demand for prefillable syringes

---

CASE STUDY (*Continued*)

was increasing, and BD had to increase capacity. It chose to situate in Tatabánya after a survey that assessed 13 countries. Three locations, two in Europe and one in the Far East, were shortlisted from this search, and Hungary was selected in 2007. It chose to undertake a greenfield investment in 2008 and took over the plant in the Tatabánya Industrial Park in 2009. Since then it has continuously extended the facilities, even during the recession. Vecsernyés explained that the country's geographic position and its closeness to its European clients were important factors for the choice of location. The stable political environment in Hungary was another important factor, he added.

The capacity expansions undertaken between 2009 and 2013 were facilitated by the smooth, cost-effective, and quality implementation of the original project for manufacturing prefillable syringes. BD sees new opportunities for reinvestment or R&D capacity expansion in a variety of areas. One of them is to establish new technologies such as injection moldings in addition to the existing glassmaking operations in place at Tatabánya. BD, Tatabánya, is also looking to participate in self-administration of injectable systems.

Key Takeaways for Central and Eastern Europe

1. Increased demand for transregional trade carries the potential to increase demand for labor in the manufacturing, transport, and logistics sector.

2. Globalization necessitates improved education in transportation and particularly in logistics.

3. The region, like many other developed areas, is facing a large population decrease that will drive labor prices up in the midterm.

4. The aging population will put a strain on the tax base, limiting governmental ability to invest in supply chain infrastructure; more private investment will be required.

5. The decreasing population effect will be reflected in the composition of the workforce in the industrial sector, forcing it to explore new employee segments. Hiring older people and people from other sectors will compel the sector to look at new ways of training and lifelong learning initiatives.

6. Substantial differences in wages and working conditions between Western Europe and Central and Eastern Europe will create a need for a mobile workforce across member state borders as well as workers from outside of Europe; this mobility will require enhanced social skills for working in a multicultural environment.

7. More skills will be in demand. New technologies in infrastructure require that people be trained to use modern equipment and navigation systems. Technical skills will be

in demand. To a number of workers, this will be a challenge and require training not only in using the new equipment but also more basic IT skills or even reading and math skills. Increased international rail transport requires a solution to the language issue.

8. Language skills will be in demand. International standards increase the demand for cross-border traffic and thus also for workers with better language skills.

9. The least developed country in the region is Ukraine. Economic, political, infrastructural, and competence issues make Ukraine a high risk for supply chain investment.

10. Corruption, legal and regulatory inflexibility and complexity, and challenges to ease of doing business will limit opportunities in Romania, Russia, and Ukraine despite attractive markets and raw materials resources.

References

1. http://www.mzv.cz/tripoli/en/general_information_about_the_czech/history/index.html.
2. https://www.cia.gov/library/publications/the-world-factbook/geos/rs.html.
3. D. F. Good, "Economic Transformation in Central Europe: The View From History," Working paper 92-1, the University of Minnesota, January 1992.
4. Ibid.
5. http://data.worldbank.org/about/country-classifications/country-and-lending-groups.
6. http://www.czech-republic.net/economy/industry.html.
7. T. G. Ash, *The Polish Revolution: Solidarity*, Third Edition (Yale University Press, 2002).
8. "The Automobile Industry in Central Europe," www.imf.org/ external/cee/2006/1106.pdf.
9. http://www.mfa.gov.hu/kulkepviselet/UK/en/en_Bilateralis/hita_ip.htm.
10. http://www.miaeurope.com/en/news/75/the-automotive-industry-is-a-key-sector-in-central-and-east-european-economies-.html.
11. http://www.nationsencyclopedia.com/Europe/Hungary-INDUSTRY.html.
12. A. Storozynski, "The Lights Shine Brightly in Poland as a Former Basket Case Morphs Into a European Tiger," http://www.forbes.com/sites/realspin/2013/09/26/the-lights-shine-brightly-in-poland-as-a-former-basket-case-morphs-into-a-european-tiger/.
13. http://www.zetapetroleum.com/Our-Business/About-Romania.
14. http://www.reuters.com/article/2013/07/04/serbia-nis-oil-idUSL5N0FA1D920130704.
15. http://whc.unesco.org/en/list/754.
16. www.imf.org.
17. https://www.cia.gov/library/publications/the-world-factbook/geos/hu.html.
18. J. Cienski, "Exports Buoy Fragile Recovery in Eastern and Central Europe," FT.com, August 25, 2013.

19. http://www.worldbank.org/en/country/russia/overview.

20. http://www.euronews.com/2013/10/07/world-bank-slams-ukraine-s-economic-prospects/.

21. "The Central and Eastern European Automotive Market: Industry Overview." http://www.ey.com/Publication/vwLUAssets/CEE_automarkets_2010/$FILE/CEE_automarkets_2010.pdf.

22. http://www.doingbusiness.org/data/exploretopics/starting-a-business.

23. "Country Reports on Human Rights Practices for 2011: Czech Republic," U.S. Department of State, Bureau of Democracy, Human Rights and Labor, www.state.gov/documents/organization/186554.pdf.

24. J. Cienski, "Infrastructure: Road Schemes Help Drive Central European Logistics Deals," April 23, 2013. http://www.ft.com/intl/cms/s/0/69b2aad0-8667-11e2-ad73-00144feabdc0.html#axzz2hnN9wc3v.

25. http://blogs.telegraph.co.uk/news/harrydequetteville/3694421/Roadway_terror_in_Romania_/.

26. http://www.capgemini.com/.

27. http://www.kassetts.iff.fraunhofer.de/dateien/kassetts-project-mid-publication.pdf.

28. http://www.kassetts.iff.fraunhofer.de/dateien/kassetts-project-mid-publication.pdf.

29. G. Richard and G. Armin, "Contract Logistics and Outsourcing in Russia," *The Deutsche Bahn and Russian Railways Center for International Logistics and Supply Chain Management* (2012), p. 34.

30. http://www.taiwanservices.com.tw/org2/5/news_detail/en_US/35030/I.

31. T. I. Zharik, "Logistics in the Context of Stable Development of Ukraine," *Shaping Market Relations in Ukraine*, 11, no. 114 (2010): 19–22.

32. Hungarian Investment and Trade Agency, "Hungary Today 2013."

CHAPTER 11

North and Central America

Any discussion of business and economics in North and Central America over the last 100 years must acknowledge the disproportionate impact of the United States of America (USA), and to a lesser extent Canada and Mexico, on the world. The other countries of the region, including Belize, Guatemala, El Salvador, Honduras, Nicaragua, Costa Rica, and Panama, comprise a relatively small percentage of regional and global economic output and population. The region as a whole represents approximately 27 percent of global GDP, with the USA, Canada, and Mexico ranking as the 1st, 13th, and 11th largest economies in the world, respectively, based on percent of global GDP. The region represents just over 7 percent of global population, again with the USA, Canada, and Mexico forming the largest percentage of that total as the 1st, 35th, and 11th largest populations in the world, respectively.[1]

To a large degree, the geographic features of the USA and Canada form the primary reason for their ascendance to economic power in the 20th century. Their economic and political systems foster free trade, making them attractive for global companies seeking access to the abundant raw materials, manufactured goods, and wealthy markets they feature. In addition, the sophistication of the physical infrastructures, labor, and business competencies in the USA and Canada are among the world's best. For these reasons, much is known about supply chain management in the two nations, often to the exclusion of other important and emerging areas in the region that will be critical to business development today and in the near future. Mexico, in particular, has made dramatic strides in the last 30 years and represents one of the most intriguing opportunities for supply chain managers seeking alternatives to China as a manufacturing source for distribution to major consumer markets in the Western Hemisphere. Mexico, however, is not the only nation of potential interest in the region.

Although the importance of the USA and Canada to world commerce will not significantly diminish over the next 10 years, their economic and population growth will be limited. Rather, the story of business growth and profitability over the next 10 years likely will be written in the emerging nations in the region. This is not to say that the USA and Canada will not continue to be key drivers of regional commerce; it does say that the emerging nations of the region increasingly will be considered viable options for global supply chain solutions that seek to create value for the major regional markets and potentially for markets outside the region, notably the emerging markets of South America. In addition, as organizations from industrialized nations invest in supply chain operations in emerging nations, the resulting wealth will create new markets within the nations themselves.

Organizations seeking to establish regional supply chain operations to minimize *total cost of ownership* (TCO) for the USA/Canadian markets (and increasingly those of Mexico) as well as the burgeoning South American markets may well look to the emerging areas of Mexico and Central America as locations for low-cost sourcing and manufacturing. Thus, this chapter focuses on business conditions relevant to supply chain decision making in the USA, Canada, Mexico, Costa Rica, and Panama as the primary nations in the region that organizations may consider as they seek to optimize performance.

Economic and Political Background

Understanding the Region

The geography of North and Central America has had a significant influence on the societies of the continent, shaping the economic, political, and cultural development of the area. The triangle-shaped continent, centered in the temperate portions of the Northern Hemisphere, extends from Canada in the Arctic to Panama in the tropics (Figure 11.1). The Rocky Mountains dominate the western area of Canada and the USA, generating an arable zone east of the range known as the Great Plains. This zone comprises both the most productive and the largest contiguous acreage of arable land on the planet. East of this arable zone lies a second mountain chain known as the Appalachians. This chain is far lower and thinner than the Rockies, but it still constitutes a notable barrier to movement and economic development. The Canadian Shield, an area in which repeated glacial activity scraped off most of the topsoil, is located north of the Great Lakes. The lack of topsoil, combined with the area's colder climate, makes these lands unproductive compared to regions farther south or west and, as such, they remain largely unpopulated. In Mexico, the North American landmass narrows drastically from more than 5000 km (about 3100 mi) wide to less than 1000 km. This narrowing also occurs in the Rocky Mountain/Great Plains region of Mexico, generating a wide, dry area that lacks the agricultural potential of the Canadian and USA prairie regions.[2]

At the far south of the continent is the Central American isthmus. The wet climate and rugged environment of the area have largely prevented its economic development, resulting in a series of isolated city-states that to date have had a limited impact on continental

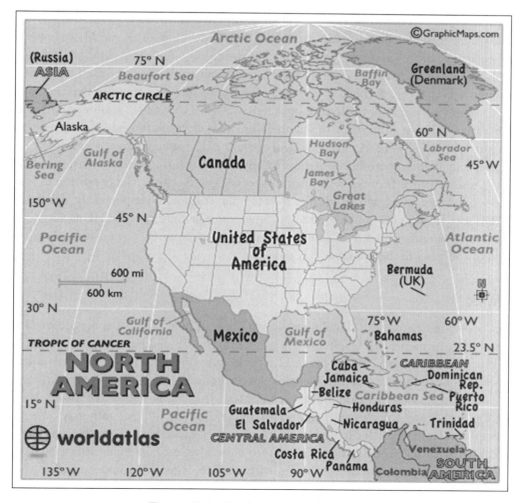

Figure 11.1 North and Central America.

affairs. In total, the nations of the Central American isthmus represent less than 0.3 percent of global GDP and only 0.6 percent of the world's population. Due to a series of swamps and mountains between North and South America, there still is no road network linking them, and the two Americas only indirectly affect each other's development.[3]

A number of maritime features define the continent, including Arctic, Atlantic, Pacific, Gulf of Mexico, and Caribbean coastlines, which feature a number of sheltered bays and natural, deepwater ports. The Great Lakes, situated in the middle of the upper continent, form a secondary water transport system that opens up lands for productive use and capital generation. The components of the river network in the USA are larger in both volume and length than most of the world's rivers and are easily navigable. The network consists of six distinct river systems: the Missouri, Arkansas, Red, Ohio, Tennessee, and Mississippi. The unified nature of this system greatly enhances the region's usefulness and potential economic and political power. A chain of barrier islands along the East and Gulf coasts of the USA allow river traffic to travel in a protected intracoastal waterway from the Rio Grande in the south all the way north to Chesapeake Bay. A final distinctive and important maritime feature of North America is the Panama Canal, which revolutionized global trade lanes upon its opening in 1914. A new canal will open in 2015 featuring greatly expanded shipping capacity that again promises to significantly affect the flow patterns of east-west trade. All of these maritime features make the transport of goods within a large portion of North America an order of magnitude cheaper than in other regions; in the petroleum age the cost of transport via water is roughly 10 to 30 times cheaper than overland. This simple fact makes regions with robust maritime transport options extremely capital-rich when compared to countries limited to land-only options.[4]

Politics

The USA is a federal constitutional republic, with powers held at the federal, state, and local levels of government. At the federal level, power is distributed between three branches; the executive, legislative, and judicial. The president is responsible for the execution of laws and is head of all executive agencies. As commander-in-chief of the armed forces, the president also controls the military. Congress, the seat of legislative power, is split into the Senate and the House of Representatives. Ultimate judicial authority rests with the Supreme Court, which can invalidate legislation or executive actions that are deemed in conflict with the Constitution. The nation is divided into 50 states and the District of Colombia (the capital); each has its own executive, legislature, and judiciary, and is theoretically sovereign.[5]

Canada's institutions reflect the country's colonial past, where France, England, and Holland fought for dominance in the 17th century. British preeminence was established after wars between the rival colonies in the 18th century. Canada became a self-governing dominion and adopted a constitution in 1867, retaining the British monarch as head of state.[6] Canada is a constitutional monarchy, parliamentary democracy, and federal state. In Canada's system of government, the provinces have considerable authority over major sectors, such as health care, education, and resources. The federal government is responsible for economic and monetary policy, currency, foreign affairs, and defense. Each of the federal and provincial governments maintains a judiciary and civil service. French is the working language in Québec; English is dominant in the rest of Canada, though one province, New Brunswick, is officially bilingual. Federal agencies and some provinces provide bilingual services.[7]

Mexico was a major administrative center for the Spanish for more than 300 years. Spanish rule ended when Napoleon Bonaparte seized Spain in 1808, and France accepted Mexican independence in 1821. Mexico's first president, Benito Juárez, was elected in 1861. The republic was short-lived, and after more than 30 years of dictatorship Mexico's society split in 1910, beginning a decade of revolution. Reformers and leftists eventually formed a coalition party, which ruled the nation for more than 70 years as the Institutional Revolutionary Party (PRI). Today Mexico is a federal, democratic republic governed by a federal constitution. The president's office combines the duties of head of the executive, head of state, and head of the armed forces. A bicameral Congress, consisting of a Senate and a Chamber of Deputies, legislates on all matters concerning the national government. The Mexican judiciary consists of federal and state court systems, with the Supreme Court representing the highest judicial power. The Mexican republic is made up of 31 states and a federal district (Mexico City).[8]

Costa Rica declared its independence from Spain in 1821, and became a state in the Federal Republic of Central America. The nation has avoided much of the violence that has plagued other nations in Latin America. Following the abolition of the army in 1949, Costa Rica became one of the most democratic countries in Latin America. Today Costa Rica is a democratic republic separated into executive, legislative, and judicial branches of power. The executive branch is headed by a president who is elected by the general vote for a term of four years. The president is assisted by two vice presidents and appoints a Cabinet. The executive is relatively weak in relation to the 57-member unicameral Legislative Assembly. A political system historically dominated by the social democratic Partido Liberación Nacional (PLN) and the right-wing Partido Unidad Social Cristiana (PUSC) has become fragmented in recent years, with other parties now wielding increased power, thereby compounding difficulties of governance. The highest judicial institution is the Supreme Court, supplemented by courts of appeal and trial courts. The country is divided up into seven provinces, headed by a governor who is appointed by the president.[9]

Panama became independent from Spain in 1821, originally as part of Colombia. It declared its separate independence in 1903 as part of the USA's efforts to build and control the Panama Canal. Panama is a multiparty democracy with an executive presidency. The president is both head of state and head of government and is assisted by two vice presidents. All three positions are elected by popular vote for a five-year term. Together with ministers appointed by the president, they make up the Cabinet Council. Legislative power is exercised by the National Assembly, a unicameral body with 78 members elected for a five-year term that runs concurrently with that of the president. The Supreme Court is the highest judicial body in Panama, currently made up of nine judges appointed for 10-year terms after nomination by the Cabinet Council and ratification by the National Assembly. The nation is divided into nine provinces and three provincial-level indigenous regions.

The Economies

The United States, the world's largest economy for nearly a century, has undergone a number of major transitions over the last 50 years, of which two stand out: the shift away from agriculture, extractive, and manufacturing industries and toward the services sector; and increasing interdependence with global economies. Following a sustained period of economic expansion during the last two decades of the 20th century, in 2007 the economy entered an acute crisis, led initially by the bursting of the housing market bubble. This in turn sparked a financial crisis as many lenders' overexposure to the subprime housing market became apparent. The crisis went on to hit all sectors, driving the economy into recession from December 2007. The economy took until June 2009 to emerge from recession and onto a very gradual recovery path. The federal government responded with increasingly dramatic policy measures, although government activity as a percentage of overall economic activity remains one of the lowest within the industrialized world. Current account and fiscal deficits remain formidable obstacles, and at the same time the U.S. economy faces growing challenges to its global dominance from emerging nations such as China and India. The currency is the U.S. dollar.[10]

Canada's economy was founded on the fur trade developed by the French and British. Thanks to its vast forestation, Canada also became a major source of raw timber needed for the burgeoning Industrial Revolution in Europe. Large-scale logging and paper industries still represent a significant part of the economy. Canada's natural energy resources are vast, forming the foundation of the country's massive primary resource industries. The country's oil and gas industry is primarily located in the Western Canada Sedimentary Basin, but production has recently been supplemented by offshore activity on the Grand Banks. Canada is the third largest producer of natural gas and the 10th largest producer of petroleum. Alberta's oil sands have become more commercially viable thanks to high oil prices, and massive investment continues to flow in. Canada's large Atlantic and Pacific coastlines present significant opportunities for fishing. The nonforested land, particularly the vast prairies of Alberta, supports a range of cattle and agriculture. Ready availability of labor and capital contributed to rapid industrialization in the late 19th century, encouraging the growth of urban centers and a shift of activity away from agriculture and fishing. The world wars increased Canadian production to help the war effort. During the late 20th century, the USA became an increasingly large economic partner, and huge amounts of American investment dollars flowed into Canada.

The Canadian economy has maintained relatively consistent growth for the last 20 years, stemming largely from increased exports fueled by a Canadian–U.S. Free Trade Agreement (CUFTA), which was introduced in January 1989. CUFTA was expanded into the North American Free Trade Agreement (NAFTA) when Mexico joined in January 1994. Today, Canada enjoys a significant level of export trade, predominantly with the USA but also with China, Japan, the European Union (EU), and increasingly the emerging markets of South America, India, and Russia. The currency is the Canadian dollar.[11]

Mexico is a semi-industrialized, upper-middle income country whose economy has developed and diversified significantly in the past couple of decades, largely on the back of an expanding network of free trade agreements and improved fiscal and monetary policies. Trade liberalization since the 1980s increased opportunities for private and foreign firms to take advantage of Mexico's relatively low labor costs and proximity to U.S. markets. This policy led to rapid growth of important economic sectors such as the *maquiladora* industry—literally "twin plants"—a system in which subcomponents are exported duty-free from the USA across the border into assembly plants located in Mexico to take advantage of low-cost labor, and finished goods are re-exported tariff free to the USA or foreign markets. Privatization also has helped generate significant growth in service sector industries such as telecoms and banking.[12]

Mexico is one of the world's largest oil producers, with oil and gas providing a third of the government's revenue. Agriculture is also an important employer as Mexico's system of communal farms, or *ejidos*, was reformed in the 1990s to promote private investment and large-scale agriculture. The nation is blessed with abundant minerals—notably silver, copper, sulfur, lead, and zinc—advanced technology, and a large workforce.[13] Mexico remains vulnerable, however, to fluctuations in the U.S. economy. The global economic downturn that began in the USA in 2008 adversely affected the Mexican economy toward the end of that year, and continued to undermine economic performance into 2009, leading to a significant contraction in output. Growth was restored in 2010, driven by the external sector, with domestic demand remaining subdued. The unit of currency is the New Mexican peso (100 centavos).[14]

From Costa Rica's colonial days, subsistence agriculture and smallholder farming was the economic norm until introduction of large-scale cultivation of first coffee and then bananas in the early 19th century. Since then, Costa Rica's development has outpaced the rest of Central America. It was first to export coffee (in 1832), to establish a commercial bank (in 1864), and to build a railway (in 1890). After a civil war in 1948, a welfare state was established and public utilities were nationalized and expanded.[15] Since the 1990s, the Costa Rican economy has been transformed into a diversified exporter with world-class companies through a mixture of government incentives and a network of free trade agreements. As a result, Costa Rica has become an attractive investment destination, its main assets being its traditionally good security record, skilled labor force, bilingual population, and long-standing tradition of democratic stability. These conditions have encouraged large corporations such as Hewlett-Packard, Intel, and Microsoft to establish operations in the country in the last 10 years. The currency in use is the Costa Rican colon.[16]

Panama's geographic location enabled it to develop into one of the most important shipping crossroads in the world. The country's most famous asset is the 82-km-long Panama

Canal, which traverses the Darién Isthmus, thus linking the Pacific Ocean with the Caribbean Sea and enabling shipping to avoid the lengthy Cape Horn route around the South American landmass. The canal diminished in importance with the advent of super-tankers and freighters, as the largest of the modern oil and bulk cargo tankers could not use it. However, with the major expansion of the canal's capacity, scheduled for completion in 2015, permitting the transit of significantly larger vessels, plus the rapid growth in cruise ship traffic in both the Caribbean and the Pacific, the canal has regained prominence in terms of income and strategic importance. Panama's continued role as a "land bridge" was also reinforced with the opening, in October 1982, of a transisthmian pipeline to carry petroleum deemed economically impractical for transit in the usual way.[17]

Panama possesses abundant natural resources, including high-quality fishing grounds, mineral deposits, forests, and a topography and climate ideal for the development of hydroelectric and thermo-electric power. Substantial reserves of gold, copper, and coal are underexploited. Apart from some manufacturing in the Colón Free Zone (CFZ—the second largest free trade zone in the world after Hong Kong), the primary and secondary sectors of the productive economy are also grossly underdeveloped. Panama has thus traditionally been a services-based economy, reliant on revenues from the canal, ship registration, free trade zone transactions, and contributions from "offshore" banking activities. Services account for nearly 80 percent of GDP; some of the largest individual subsectors are transport, storage and communications, renting, real estate, and business services. Agriculture (including hunting, forestry, and fishing) and manufacturing together account for only just over 20 percent of GDP. The Panamanian currency is the Balboa.[18]

The Markets

Location of Markets

United States of America (USA)

The USA is a nation of 312 million people living in a landmass of 9.8 million km^2 (3.8 million mi^2), with its capital in Washington, District of Columbia (Figure 11.2). It is the third largest country by size in the world. The official language is English, although a significant minority of the population speak Spanish. The ethnic diversity of the population includes those with European, African, Asian, and Amerindian roots.[19]

The United States may be divided into six large regions, each with a distinctive climate, culture, history, and geography: New England, the mid-Atlantic, the South, the Midwest, the Southwest, and the West. More than 50 percent of the nation's population live in less than 20 percent of the land area (excluding Alaska). Still, the USA has a much more disassociated population structure than most of the rest of the world. As wealth expanded along American rivers, small landholders banded together to form small towns. The capital they jointly

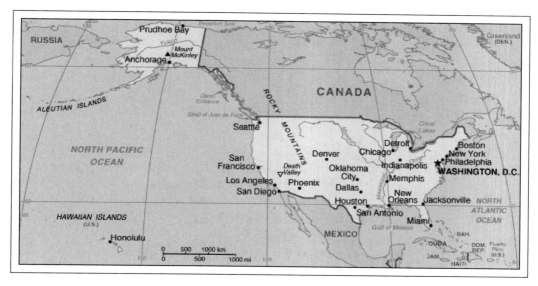

Figure 11.2 United States of America.

generated sped industrialization, typically on a local level. Population rapidly spread beyond the major port cities of the East Coast and developed multiple economic and political power centers throughout the country whose development was often funded with local capital, creating a broad distribution of wealth. Today, the United States has 20 metropolitan areas with an excess of 2.5 million people; in contrast, most major countries have a single, primary political and economic hub. These distributed economic centers connected by open transportation corridors led to a similarly distributed political system and the world's largest domestic consumer market with easy access to both the Atlantic and Pacific trading basins. The distributed nature of the USA is reflected in the *primacy rate*, a measure of the percent of total population living in the largest city in the nation, which is only 8 percent for the USA. Such broad distribution makes it difficult to reach the population, increasing supply chain costs and inventory and greatly adding to the complexity of supply chain network design in the USA.

Canada

Canada is a nation of 34 million people with a landmass of 3.9 million mi² (10 million km²), with its capital in Ottawa, Ontario (Figure 11.3). Canada recognizes two official languages, French and English, reflecting its colonial history. Citizens with British and French ancestry continue to be the largest population groups, although immigrants from southern and Eastern Europe, the Caribbean, the Indian subcontinent, and Southeast Asia have contributed to Canadian multiculturalism. Its major religious groups include a large Roman Catholic population, and a United Church and an Anglican church.

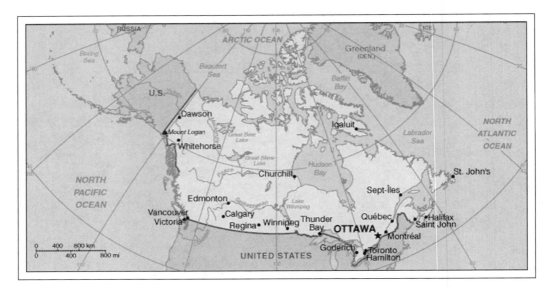

Figure 11.3   Canada.

The population is heavily concentrated in urban areas, with more than 25 million Canadians (80 percent) living in urban areas. Canada's primacy rate is 20 percent of the population who live in Toronto. The three largest urban areas in Canada (Toronto, Vancouver, and Montréal) make up 34 percent of Canada's population. The most heavily populated of Canada's 13 provinces and territories is Ontario, home to Toronto and the federal capital, Ottawa, and accounting for 38.8 percent of the total population, followed by Québec (23.2 percent) and British Columbia (13.3 percent). The Canadian population is also concentrated in the south of the nation, as 75 percent of Canadians live within 161 km (100 mi) of the U.S. border. This population distribution pattern makes it relatively simple to manage supply chain networks in Canada.

The second largest country in the world in physical area after Russia, Canada has coastlines on the Atlantic, Arctic, and Pacific oceans, giving it the longest coastline of any country. In area, Canada is slightly larger than the United States but has only 11 percent as many people. It is one of the least densely inhabited and most prosperous countries. Canada's maritime transport zones include the Great Lakes and the St. Lawrence Seaway, which together provide a navigable passage from the Atlantic Ocean to major population centers along the U.S. border. Canada has no naturally navigable rivers, often making it more attractive for Canada's provinces to integrate economic flows with the USA, where transport is cheaper, the climate supports a larger population, and markets are more readily accessible. The Canadian Shield, a region that covers more than half of Canada's landmass east of the prairie provinces, consists of a rocky, broken landscape that is unsuitable for agriculture or habitation, which greatly limits development opportunities. The Canadian Shield and the rugged Rocky Mountains in the west experience subarctic climates, resulting in a north that is nearly empty of population.[20]

Mexico

The United Mexican States is a nation of 113.4 million people living on a landmass of 1.96 million km^2 (0.76 mi^2), with its capital in Mexico City (Figure 11.4). Twenty-two percent of Mexicans live in the capital (the primacy rate), and 60 percent live in the center of the country, including the "Golden Triangle" comprising the cities of Veracruz, Mexico City, and Guadalajara. This area features 80 percent of the Mexican market, 70 percent of Mexico's international trade, and 70 percent of Mexico's automotive industry. Most Mexicans are of mixed Spanish and Native American descent, but about 30 percent are Native American, and many people speak native languages in the southeast. A 3115 km (1936 mi) common border, commerce, and tourism link the world's largest Spanish-speaking country to the USA to its north. The population is predominantly Roman Catholic, with 6 percent observing various Protestant faiths.[21]

Mexico features coastal plains along the Pacific and Atlantic coasts that rise to a central plateau. Northern Mexico is desert-like, and the south is mountainous jungle. Mexico lacks a single navigable river of any size. Its agricultural zones are disconnected, and it boasts few good natural ports. Mexico's north is extremely dry, its south extremely wet, and both are too mountainous to support robust agricultural activities. In addition, the terrain is rugged, making transport expensive, and it is difficult for the central government to enforce control.

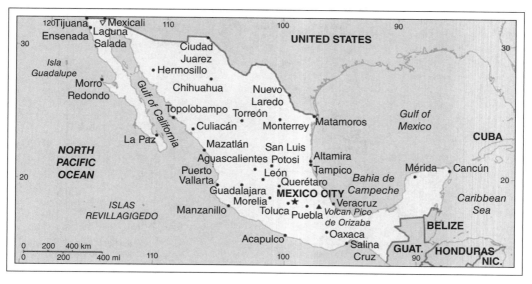

Figure 11.4 Mexico.

The result is the near lawlessness of the cartel lands in the north and irregular outbreaks of secessionist activity in the south.[22] Mexico is also exposed to a series of natural hazards, including earthquakes, hurricanes, and floods that occasionally create significant damage to the nation's infrastructure.

Costa Rica

The Republic of Costa Rica is the southernmost of the Central American countries, with Panama beyond the eastern border and Nicaragua to the north (309 km/192 mi). The country has coasts on both the Pacific (1015 km/630 mi) and the Caribbean/Atlantic (212 km/132 mi). Costa Rica has a total area of 51,100 km² (19,730 mi²). The San Juan River flows from Lake Nicaragua into the Pacific and forms much of the northeastern border (Figure 11.5). The capital city of San Juan is located in a fertile, upland basin,

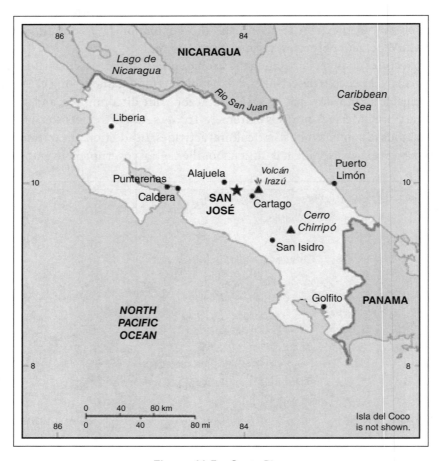

Figure 11.5   Costa Rica.

the Meseta Central Valley, at an altitude of about 1170 meters (3837.6 ft). On either side of the mountains are coastal plains, the Pacific coast being more irregular in outline and the Atlantic coast lower, swampier, and heavily forested (almost one-third of the country is wooded). The region is volcanic, with four volcanoes near San José, two of which are active, last erupting destructively in the mid-1960s.[23]

Costa Rica has a population of 4.63 million (2011), nearly half of whom live in the central plateau around San José. The primacy rate is 49 percent. The principal cities of the Pacific coast are Puntarenas, on the Gulf of Nicoya, in the northwest, and further north and inland, Liberia. The main city of the Atlantic coast is Limón. The white and Mestizo, or mixed-race population, mainly of Spanish descent, account for 94 percent of the total, with blacks at 3 percent, and Amerindians and Chinese at 1 percent each. Spanish is the official language, but some English is also spoken in the larger cities; numerous Amerindian languages are also spoken. Four-fifths of the population is Roman Catholic, and evangelical and other non-Catholic Christian groups represent more than one-sixth of the population.[24]

Panama

The Republic of Panama is often not included with Central America, its early history being related to Colombia rather than to the countries of the isthmus, but geographically it does occupy the narrowest part of the great land bridge connecting South and North America (Figure 11.6). The country covers 75,517 km² (29,157 mi²). Panama is an east-west land corridor, with the Caribbean to the north and the Pacific to the south. To the east is the

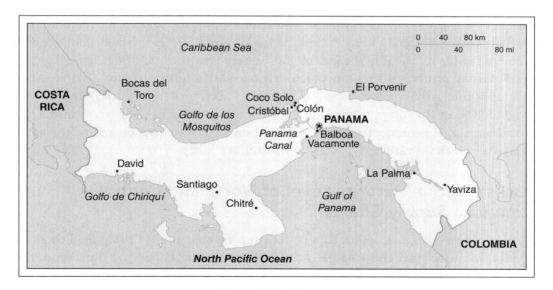

Figure 11.6 Panama.

South American country of Colombia, from which Panama was separated in 1903, and to the west Costa Rica. The country has a coastline of 2490 km (1547 mi). From 1903 the USA held "sovereign rights" over 1432 km² (553 mi²) of Panamanian territory, the Canal Zone that flanked the route of the transisthmian waterway for 8 km (5 mi) on either side. However, the lease was negotiated to an early end on December 31, 1999, when Panama assumed full sovereignty.[25]

The people of Panama are mainly of mixed Spanish and Amerindian race, the Mestizos; they constitute some 63 percent of the population. There are also large communities of predominantly black descent (14 percent) and Spanish descent (10 percent), as well as some of mixed-black descent (mulatto, 5 percent) and a number of Amerindian peoples (5 percent). There are also some of Middle Eastern and Asian descent. More recently, there has been a largely illegal influx of Colombians, either seeking employment or political refuge, particularly in the deserted borderlands. The official language, and the one in general use, is Spanish, but after long years of U.S. rule along the canal and immigration from North America and the West Indies, English is widely spoken (being the main language for up to 14 percent of the population), and many Panamanians are bilingual. English-based Creole is also in use, as well as indigenous Amerindian languages. The vast majority of people are still Roman Catholic, but in recent years membership in Protestant groups has increased. The largest non-Christian community is Muslim. There are also some Jews.[26]

The total population of Panama numbered 3.6 million in 2013, most of whom live in the region of the canal on the central isthmus. The largest city and national capital is Panama City (Panamá), where 53 percent of the population resides. Panamá lies at the southern end of the canal, on the gulf that bears its name, and was an early vice-regal capital for the Spanish in the Americas. The second city of the country, Colón, lies at the northern end of the canal and constitutes the world's second largest free zone for trade and industry. David, the capital of the agricultural, western province of Chiriquí, located on the Pacific coastal plains, is the most populous city outside the central isthmus. To the east of the transit zone is the sparsely populated and barely developed territory of Darién, covering one-third of Panama with the largest area of rainforest in the Americas outside the Amazon basin. The country is divided into nine provinces, with the more recent formation of three territories constituted for various Amerindian groups.[27]

Assessing the Maturity Level of North and Central American Supply Chains

This section assesses the supply chain maturity of the subcontinent using the Economy, Politics, Infrastructure, and Competence (EPIC) dimensions. The first dimension, the Economy dimension, assesses the wealth and resources of each region in terms of production and consumption of goods and services.

Economy

The economies of the five focal nations of North and Central America are diverse, ranging from natural resources and agricultural products to aerospace hardware. In addition, the USA, Canada, and Mexico all are major energy producers. Panama, with the pending opening in 2015 of the expanded Panama Canal, is positioned to grow its position as one of the major logistics and redistribution hubs in the world, mirroring the Middle East as the Western Hemisphere's east-west and north-south crossroads.

Economic Output and Growth Rate

The North and Central American market is among the world's largest. The Central Intelligence Agency's (CIA) World Factbook for 2012 ranks the USA as the largest economy in the world based on GDP in terms of purchasing power parity (PPP). The estimated GDP in 2012 for the USA was $15.66 trillion at PPP. The GDP for Canada, the 13th largest global economy, was $1.446 trillion at PPP. Mexico, the 11th largest global economy, had a GDP of $1.758 trillion at PPP. Costa Rica and Panama are much smaller, with GDP at PPP of $56.8 billion and $55.8 billion, respectively, in 2012.

Growth for the big three of North America has been slow, averaging 0.87 percent for the USA, 1.7 percent for Canada, and 2.1 percent for Mexico from 2005 to 2011. Growth is improving, however, as the USA had 2.2 percent growth in 2012, Canada had 1.8 percent, and Mexico had 3.9 percent. Both Costa Rica and Panama are experiencing significant growth, with Costa Rica at 5 percent in 2012 (4.5 percent from 2005 to 2011) and Panama enjoying 10.7 percent (8.8 percent from 2005 to 2011).

The USA is one of the most capital-intensive agricultural producers in the world, particularly of grain. The U.S. automotive industry is the largest in the world, and the U.S. energy market is the world's largest. It ranks first in the global production of coal and nuclear energy and continues to be a major oil-producing country, with new oil sand and natural gas fields promising sustained output in the future. The telecommunications, consumer goods, and industrial equipment industries are also major economic sectors. Canada's natural resources form the primary sectors of the economy, including agriculture, timber/pulp and paper, fishing, mining, and petroleum and gas extraction. The economy also features strength in services, including utilities and public administration, manufacturing (notably transportation, aerospace, and agricultural equipment), and construction (in addition to primary activities). The Mexican economy is primarily services based, followed by manufacturing (especially consumer durable goods, electronics, automotive, and aerospace) and agriculture; Mexico is also the world's ninth largest oil producer, and oil and gas provide a third of the government's revenue.

Costa Rica's primary agriculture products include tropical fruits and vegetables, coffee, beef, sugar, rice, dairy products, ornamental plants, and timber. Since 2000, technology companies (including Intel, Hewlett-Packard, and Microsoft) have been attracted to its free trade zones, transforming Costa Rica from a commodities-exporting economy to an IT hub, a manufacturing center for the region, and a back office and support services center to U.S. companies. In addition, tourism and services have expanded greatly since the 1970s. Panama's service sector represents the backbone of the economy, constituting more than 80 percent of GDP. The growth rate of the services sector is tied to activities in the Colón free trade zone (CFZ), the largest merchandise redistribution center in South and Central America where more than 1900 enterprises engage in re-exporting, repackaging, light assembly, and related activities. Mining, agriculture, manufacturing, and construction provide the remaining sectors of the economy.

Population

The 316 million population of the USA (2013) is growing slowly, mainly through immigration from Mexico. The median age is 36.9, and the birthrate is 2.06 children born per woman. The Canadian population of 35 million people is aging and shrinking rapidly, with a median age of 39.9 in 2011 (was 26.2 in 1971), and a birthrate of 1.58 children born per woman. Mexico's population of 118 million, however, is young and growing, with a median age of 27.2, and a birthrate of 2.27 children born per woman; 30 percent of Mexico's population is aged 14 or younger. Growth in the working-age population will continue to outpace overall population growth, adding to the available labor pool.

Costa Rica has experienced a population boom since 1980 that is expected to continue throughout this decade, with a 2013 population of 4.7 million. Costa Rica's potential workforce (those between 15 and 64 years of age) will be growing slightly faster than total population as a result of the prolonged population boom.[28] The median age is 28.8 years, with a birthrate of 2.1 children born per woman.[29] Panama, with a population of 3.6 million people, is in the midst of a demographic transition, characterized by steadily declining rates of fertility, mortality, and population growth. Although steadily declining, the birthrate of 2.4 children per woman still projects population growth; the median age of 28 years is also favorable from a workforce availability standpoint.

Foreign Direct Investment

The United Nations Conference on Trade and Development's (UNCTAD) Foreign Direct Investment (FDI) Attraction Index ranks 182 countries in terms of their success in attracting FDI based on a combination of total FDI inflows relative to GDP. In this index the USA ranked 62nd, Canada 57th, Mexico 61st, Costa Rica 51st, and Panama 18th. UNCTAD also presents an FDI Potential Index that uses four key economic determinants of the attractiveness of an economy for foreign direct investors, including the attractiveness of the market, the availability of low-cost labor and skills, the presence of natural resources, and the presence of FDI-enabling infrastructure. On this index, the

USA ranks number two in the world, Canada ranked 17th, Mexico 13th, Costa Rica 99th, and Panama 85th.

The USA is the largest host of FDI in the world. The Economist Intelligence Unit estimates that the value of the stock of FDI in the United States reached $2.6 trillion by the end of 2010, this is equivalent to only around 18 percent of U.S. GDP, compared with an average of around 30 percent of GDP in the other top industrialized countries. Canada enjoys strong foreign direct investment, with much of it originating in the United States. Mexico's large internal market and network of free trade agreements (FTAs) have placed Mexico among the more attractive investment locations in Latin America. The country's growing integration into the production and distribution systems of the USA since NAFTA implementation has been a major driver of FDI inflows to Mexico. The USA is the leading source of foreign investment in the country.[30]

FDI in Costa Rica continues to increase. Although much has come from the USA, FDI from China has been rising rapidly, totaling US$5.6 million in 2010, up from US$1.9 million in 2008. The relatively stable economic and security climate continues to be the most important feature encouraging foreign investment, and free access to foreign exchange, ease of purchasing United States dollars, and relatively painless procedures for repatriation of profits make investment attractive. Panama also has been experiencing dramatic increases in FDI, showing growth of 17 percent in 2011 over the same period in 2010. The modernization of the Panama Canal is largely responsible for increasing FDI, with inflows to the banking sector and the Colón Free Trade Zone enjoying the benefits. The free trade agreement (FTA) with the USA implemented in late 2012 will encourage significant increases of U.S. FDI into Panama.[31]

Exchange Rate Stability and Consumer Price Inflation

Exchange rate stability is important when projecting supply chain activity in a nation. Depreciation of domestic currency can encourage exports and reduce the trade deficit, although it often negatively affects inflows of FDI and increases the cost of imports. Strengthening currency attracts FDI, makes foreign imports more affordable, and encourages consumer spending, although exports tend to suffer.

The U.S. dollar is a free-floating currency and remains the most widely held reserve currency in the world. It is used in the vast majority of international trade transactions. Market prices for commodities such as petroleum, agricultural products, industrial goods, and precious metals are denominated in U.S. dollars. The dollar is freely convertible into other currencies at prevailing exchange rates. The dollar also serves as the sole or parallel currency in many other parts of the world. Some countries (such as Ecuador, El Salvador, and Panama) have adopted the dollar as their legal tender, and others (including Hong Kong and Saudi Arabia) peg their own currencies to it. Other countries aim to keep the value of their currencies in line with the dollar through the use of trading bands, central bank interventions, and other mechanisms.

The average exchange rate to the U.S. dollar for Canada from 2006 to 2011 was stable at one Canadian dollar to the U.S. dollar, with a standard deviation of 0.1 (an average fluctuation of 10 percent). Mexico also has had currency stability; the corresponding average and standard deviation for the Mexican peso relative to the U.S. dollar is 12.6 and 1, respectively, and an average fluctuation of only 8 percent. Similarly, Costa Rica has had a stable currency, with average and standard deviation values for the Costa Rican Colon relative to the U.S. dollar from 2006 to 2011 of 527.9 and 27.9, representing an average fluctuation of only 5.3 percent. The Panamanian economy has been dollarized since 1904, with one Panamanian Balboa equal to one U.S. dollar; most transactions are made in U.S. dollars. Therefore, the country is free of currency exchange risks.

Inflation has been in a band that is considered close to optimal over the past five years for the USA, Canada, and Mexico, although it has been slightly higher for Costa Rica and Panama. Correspondingly, interest rates have remained relatively low for all five countries. The average inflation rate during the period from 2006 to 2010 was 2.55 percent for the USA, 2.35 percent for Canada, 3.5 percent for Mexico, 4.7 percent for Costa Rica, and 6.0 percent for Panama.

Balance of Trade

The overall U.S. current-account deficit has increased in recent years, partly because higher oil prices increase the oil import bill. However, with long-term U.S. growth expected to be nearly twice as fast as European growth (thanks to more favorable demographic trends and productivity growth) and more than four times as strong as Japanese growth, the pressure on the dollar against the currencies of these economies will be upward. With the prospects of ample and relatively inexpensive energy supplies in North America and the promise of less dependence on imported energy, the current-account deficit of the United States may fall rapidly (petroleum imports are roughly 90 percent as big as the current-account deficit), resulting in upward pressure on the dollar.[32] The top 10 destinations for U.S. exports in 2010 were Canada, Mexico, China, Japan, the United Kingdom, Germany, South Korea, Brazil, the Netherlands, and Singapore. The top 10 sources of imports were China, Canada, Mexico, Japan, Germany, the United Kingdom, South Korea, France, Taiwan, and Venezuela.

The Canadian economy regularly has a surplus on merchandise trade, and export growth is expected to outpace import growth in the near future. In terms of trade balance, the largest surpluses are in product areas that have benefited from value-added processing, although in overall terms primary commodity resources still generate the largest volume of trade. The United States is by far Canada's largest trading partner, followed by the EU and Japan. Trade between Canada and the United States has doubled since NAFTA went into effect, and the two countries make up the largest bilateral trading partnership in the world. As a result, Canada will also rely more heavily on other large trade and export market opportunities, especially with Brazil, Russia, India, and China (BRIC countries).

Imports of goods and services represented about 29 percent of Mexican GDP, and exports of goods and services accounted for 28 percent. The USA was the destination for more than 70 percent of Mexico's exports and the origin of 48 percent of imports. The second largest single export market for Mexican goods was Canada, which received 7 percent of exports in 2010, followed by China at 2 percent. The largest source of imports was the USA, China, Japan, and the Republic of Korea. Mexico entered into free trade agreements with Bolivia, Chile, Colombia, Costa Rica, and Venezuela, and also sought to foster closer trading relations with countries outside Latin America to prevent excessive dependence on Canada and the USA.[33]

Costa Rica historically runs large trade deficits, fueled mainly by imports of oil. Tourism partially offsets the growing trade deficit. The nation is seeking to bolster manufacturing exports, particularly in the IT sector, through aggressive pursuit of FTAs. In particular, agreements that reduce or nearly eliminate tariffs on Costa Rican exports have recently been signed with China and the EU. In addition, Costa Rica is a member of the Central American Common Market (CACM), comprising all of the regional states except Panama (which has observer status), including the USA.

Table 11.1 presents the scores for the Economy dimension, and Table 11.2 summarizes the strengths and weaknesses for each country on the Economy dimension vis-à-vis the country's ability to support supply chain operations.

Politics

Supply chain operations are deeply affected by the political environment of the host country. The ease of interacting with governing bodies, level of bureaucracy and corruption, legal and regulatory framework, stability of the political system, and protection of intellectual property are all majors factors to be considered by organizations considering establishing supply chain operations in a nation. These elements of the political environment will be explored below for the focus nations of North and Central America.

Table 11.1 Scores for the Economy Dimension

Economy	Economic Output and Growth Rate	Population Size	Foreign Direct Investment	Exchange Rate Stability/CPI	Balance of Trade	Overall Grade
30%	35%	25%	20%	15%	5%	100%
USA	B⁻	A	B⁺	A	B	B⁺
Canada	B⁻	A⁻	B⁺	A⁻	A⁻	B⁺
Mexico	B	A	B⁺	B	B⁺	B⁺
Costa Rica	B⁻	C	B⁻	B	D	C⁺
Panama	B⁺	C	B	A⁻	C⁺	B

Table 11.2 Strengths and Weaknesses Summary: Economy Dimension

Grade	Strengths	Weaknesses
USA: B⁺	Absolute volume of GDP; global percent of GDP; absolute amount of exports; consumer price inflation low; stable exchange rates; large FDI; diversification of economic sectors; population and workforce growth (mainly due to immigration from Mexico).	High costs of taxes, land, labor, and capital; GDP growth low; negative balance of trade; negative budget surplus could cause instability; aging population.
Canada: B⁺	High percent of global GDP; absolute export volume; consumer price inflation low; strong FDI; significant amounts of raw commodities including energy, timber, and precious metals; cost of living relatively low compared to other industrialized nations; economic diversification; strong distribution of wealth.	High costs of land, labor, and capital; low real GDP growth; unstable exchange rate; workforce is aging and population is declining.
Mexico: B⁺	Real GDP growth; export volume; proximity, economic, and regulatory ties to the United States; low cost of living; low unit labor costs; low cost of capital; raw commodity energy reserves; relatively stable business environment and regulations for FDI.	High consumer price inflation; unstable exchange rate; low and risky capital markets; low FDI; high poverty and poor distribution of wealth; poor tax collection rates; strong "black market" economy; regional variation is high, with the south poor, underdeveloped, and uneducated, poor education system.
Costa Rica: C⁺	Trade ties within and beyond the Western Hemisphere; economic activity to expand long term; recent history of location of large electronics firms.	Economic growth tied to the United States; fiscal account deficit to continue based on needed expenditures on security and infrastructure.
Panama: B	One of the world's fastest growing economies; dollarized economy that removes exchange rate risk; Panama Canal and Colón free trade zone; privatization of the power generation system and telecomms, and the relative flexibility of the labor market; FTA with USA and other Central American nations, awaiting passage with Canada; commitment to fiscal prudence.	Poor income distribution; economy linked to health of USA and EU based on volume of freight traversing Panama Canal; fiscal debt.

Ease of Doing Business, Bureaucracy, and Corruption

The World Bank Doing Business survey provides an Ease of Doing Business Index that ranks 183 countries, with the rank indicating the relative ease of doing business based on the rules and regulations related to conducting business within the country. The survey covers 11 dimensions, including starting a business, dealing with construction permits, getting electricity, employing workers, registering property, getting credit, protecting investors, paying taxes, trading across borders, enforcing contracts, and closing a business. The nations of North and Central America have a wide disparity in rankings on the Ease of Doing Business Index. In 2012, the USA was ranked 4, Canada was ranked 17, Mexico was 48, Costa Rica was 110, and Panama was ranked 61. The most recent trend leading up to this year is not very encouraging either.

Two other World Bank rankings were evaluated to assess the nations in this area. The World Bank World Governance Indicators measure the quality of governance in 215 countries, based on 40 data sources produced by 30 organizations worldwide; the indicators have been updated since 1996 (annually since 2002). Six key dimensions of governance are captured, including Government Effectiveness (the quality of public and civil services, independence from political pressures, the quality of policy formulation and implementation, and the credibility of the government's commitment to these policies) and Control of Corruption (the extent to which public power is exercised for private gain, including both petty and grand forms of corruption, as well as the level of control of the state by elites and private interests). Scores on these variables are assessed as percentiles from 100 (highest score) to 1 (lowest score). While all the North and Central American nations scored in the top 50 percent in 2012, there remained a wide disparity. Canada scored at the 97th and 95th percentile in government effectiveness and control of corruption, respectively. The Canadian bureaucracy is regarded as one of the most transparent in the world, with several institutions safeguarding its credibility and efficiency, and corruption is not a threat to business interests. The USA scored 89th and 85th; business interest groups that lobby politicians to gain the measures they desire is an explicit feature of U.S. political life, although outright corruption is rare. Mexico, with effectiveness and corruption control scores at the 64th and 45th percentiles, has a large, cumbersome, and frustratingly slow bureaucratic infrastructure, and common practice has been to cut through this with irregular payments; corruption is endemic at every level in Mexico.

Costa Rica, with scores at the 64th and 72nd percentiles in effectiveness and control of corruption, suffers from bureaucratic inefficiencies that can result in administrative delays, although procedures are relatively fair and transparent when compared to the rest of the region; corruption is lower in Costa Rica than in other Central American countries. Panama scores at the 59th percentile in government effectiveness and 46th percentile in corruption control. Administrative procedures can be long, bureaucratic, and plagued by technicalities, although conditions have improved under President Martinelli's tenure as a result of Panama's investment-friendly legal framework. The judicial system is inefficient and thought to be corrupt, and there have been widespread charges of money laundering.

Legal and Regulatory Framework: Tax Codes and Tariffs

The U.S. legal system is clear and is pro-business. The tax system is attractive to businesses, and the burden on individuals is comparatively light, although it suffers from undue complexity. The federal, state, and local systems are confusing, and the statutory federal tax rate of 35 percent can be misleading as loopholes and tax-planning techniques can be exploited to reduce taxes. The U.S. Customs and Border Protection (CBP) agency is responsible for regulating and facilitating international trade, collecting import duties, and enforcing regulations. The USA provides fair, equitable, and nondiscriminatory treatment for foreign direct investors. The only limited exceptions are designed to protect national security.

The Canadian legal system is mature and well defined. The tax system is complex but also well defined, consisting of federal and provincial-level systems. The burden on individuals and corporations is traditionally high given the government's commitment to the welfare state, but has undergone a series of reductions to a 2012 nominal tax rate of 15 percent. Canada utilizes the international Harmonized Commodity Description and Coding System to classify goods to indicate whether prohibitions, quotas, or other preferential or punitive trade agreements apply. Foreign investment laws are generally straightforward, although the government has the power to block acquisitions in "sensitive" sectors, and incorporation processes are simple.

Mexico's Federal Constitution is at the apex of that country's legal system, governing both political and commercial procedures. The tax system is characterized by widespread evasion, a narrow base, burdensome reporting requirements, and an unsustainable dependence on revenues from the state-owned oil company. The standard corporate tax rate is 30 percent, but special rate applies to maquiladoras. Mexico also uses the Harmonized System for tariff classification. Besides duties, a VAT applies to all imports including those to the border region (although at a lower rate to encourage maquiladora operations). In most economic activities, foreign investors may participate freely and are allowed to own up to 100 percent of stocks in any company incorporated in Mexico. However, in practice monopolies and oligopolies continue to dominate key elements of Mexico's economy.

Costa Rica's legal environment is adequate and compares positively with the rest of Central America in terms of strength and transparency. Costa Rica's tax system is well defined, with a corporate tax rate of 30 percent. At present, corporations operating under the free trade zones law are granted substantial exemptions. As a member of the Central American Common Market, Costa Rica applies a harmonized external tariff on most items at a maximum of 15 percent with some exceptions. FDI licensing requirements have been reduced, but procedures for launching a business are still cumbersome and time-consuming. The judicial system can be slow and complicated, but contracts are upheld and investments are secure.

Panama's legal environment is business-friendly and oriented to attract foreign direct investment, allowing foreign investors to participate in almost all sectors of the economy. Investors may freely repatriate their profits and exchange local currency for any other. The country has modern procurement legislation and a competition and consumer protection system. The tax environment is stable and the fiscal burden moderate, with a nominal corporate tax rate of 25 percent. There are a number of tax incentives in most industrial sectors, aided by a large export free zone in Colón, as well as other smaller zones throughout the country. Panama's tariffs are relatively low at an average of 7 percent for industrial goods and 15 percent for agricultural products regardless of where the products are made.[34]

Political Stability

The U.S. political system is highly stable and remains a model for many other democracies around the world, although the two major parties are divided by genuine ideological differences that make consensus elusive. *The Economist* Political Instability Index that ranks 165 nations on the level of threat posed to governments by social unrest (a higher rank is a better, more stable score) ranks the USA at 110. Canada is among the most stable political environments in the world, with a political instability index score of 163, the third most stable in the world. Mexico is known for the traditional stability of its political system, particularly in comparison with those of its Latin American counterparts. Stability is not perceived to be under threat, but drug-related violence and activities are of real concern in terms institutional viability. This threat is reflected in *The Economist* Political Instability Index ranking of 79 (bottom half).

Costa Rica's attractiveness for investors hinges on its long-standing tradition for stable democracy, in sharp contrast with its Central American and South American peers. The decision to disband the armed forces in the 1940s has meant that the country has not suffered from military interference in politics, as has happened in almost all other countries in the Latin American region. Costa Rica's stability is reflected in the 2012 Economist Political Instability ranking of 158th, the most stable out of 165 nations ranked.

Corruption scandals in Panama President Martinelli's cabinet have raised tensions with the political opposition, with Martinelli claiming that the corruption claims against some of his ministers and former ministers are a strategy to destabilize the country. These issues have spurred concerns about the concentration of power in the hands of the president and the potential weakening of institutional checks and balances. Ongoing tensions with trade unions presents another issue that poses political risks to the current administration.[35] As a result, Panama ranks in the bottom quartile of nations on *The Economist* Political Instability Index at 33 out of 165 nations.

Intellectual Property Rights

Intellectual property rights (IPR) are well protected in North America, particularly in the USA and Canada. Private property rights are one of the fundamental elements of the U.S. Constitution and are well protected. IPR protection is compliant with World Trade Organization (WTO) standards, and enforcement is generally good. Canada has comprehensive intellectual property laws that offer protection for patents, copyrights, trademarks, industrial designs, and integrated circuit topographies. The Canadian legal system offers strong protection for personal property including land, although there is no constitutional protection for property rights. Although Mexico has a comprehensive legal framework for the protection of copyright, patents, trademarks, and industrial property, examples of enforcement, prosecution, and sanctions are rare. Piracy and counterfeiting are widespread, sparking concern over connections with criminal organizations.[36]

The situation in Central America is similar to Mexico's. Costa Rica is a signatory to the Central American Convention on Industrial Property and has enacted legislation to conform with World Trade Organization standards, including the Intellectual Property Rights Law 2000. Still, protection of intellectual property rights remains a concern, and the International Intellectual Property Alliance has identified serious enforcement problems created by the inefficiency of judicial proceedings; lack of an official administrative office, investigators, and public prosecutors; and budget restrictions on the judiciary. Panamanian laws similarly provide for the protection of intellectual property, but like Costa Rica piracy and counterfeited goods are problematic. Colombia has repeatedly complained to international organizations about counterfeited goods emerging from the Colón Free Trade Zone (CFZ).[37]

Table 11.3 presents the scores for the Politics dimension. Table 11.4 summarizes the strengths and weaknesses for each country on the Politics dimension as it relates to the country's ability to support supply chain operations, with an attractiveness score provided for each country.

Table 11.3 Scores for the Politics Dimension

Politics	Ease of Doing Business	Legal Framework	Political Stability	Intellectual Property Rights	Overall Grade
20%	30%	30%	25%	15%	100%
USA	A	A⁻	B⁻	A⁻	A⁻
Canada	A	A	A	A	A
Mexico	B	C	C	C	C⁺
Costa Rica	C⁺	B⁻	A	B⁻	B
Panama	B⁻	B⁻	D	C⁺	C⁺

Table 11.4 Strengths and Weaknesses Summary: Politics Dimension

Grade	Strengths	Weaknesses
USA: A⁻	Stable, fair, pro-business legal and regulatory framework; low bureaucracy; low bribery and corruption; low tariff barriers; low risk of political instability; fair treatment for FDI; absolute tax rate pro-business; strong intellectual property rights; strong expenditures on education.	Uncertainty over recent political gridlock; complex tax code; tax code varies by state; high border security regulations; complex employment and labor laws; some political corruption.
Canada: A	Stable, fair, pro-business legal and regulatory framework; low bureaucracy; low bribery and corruption; low tariff barriers on most business categories; low risk of political instability; fair treatment for FDI; strong intellectual property rights; strong expenditures on education.	Higher tax rates; complex tax code; tax code varies by province; strict employment and labor laws in many industries.
Mexico: C⁺	Stable political system; good laws on books for tax, IP, but enforcement an issue; good regulations for trade zones to protect import and re-export (related to maquiladora).	Complex legal and regulatory framework; high levels of bureaucracy with "irregular payments" often the norm; high levels of bribery and corruption; complex tax code and reporting requirements; relatively high tariff and protection barriers; FDI rules are open but significant monopoly and oligopoly prevents fair application of rules; some industries (energy, telecomm, freight, transportation) protected against FDI; good IP laws, but in practice much piracy and counterfeiting; stiff and complex labor laws.
Costa Rica: B	One of the most solid democracies in Latin America with peaceful and transparent election processes; pro-market and social policies; good security record; skilled labor force; legal regulations concerning business are generally straightforward; low levels of corruption; well-defined tax code.	Upsurge in drug trafficking and related violent crime; struggling to come to terms with the country's ailing financial situation; recent corruption scandals; regulatory environment can be complex for foreign ownership in industries with state-owned firms; bureaucratic inefficiency; IP rights a concern.
Panama: C⁺	Generally stable political environment; business-friendly president and legal system with pro-business agenda; modern procurement, business ownership, and consumer protection legislation; modern customs process; flexible labor laws in Canal Zone and FTZ.	High levels of corruption in judiciary; security issues and violence rising linked to drug organizations; pro-business agenda has stoked domestic tension, generating strong protests; lack of efficient protection of intellectual property, particularly when it comes to piracy and counterfeit items; restrictive labor laws limit hiring, compensation, firing, and flexibility.

Infrastructure

Infrastructure provides the backbone upon which supply chain operations rest. In particular, the cost and effectiveness of supply chain operations depends, to a large degree, on the ability to access transportation, utilities, and telecommunications services. An assessment of key elements of the Infrastructure dimension for North and Central America follows, including transportation, utilities, and telecommunications.

Transportation

With a population that is far more dissociated than most other industrialized nations, the physical infrastructure has been vital to the successful economic growth the United States experienced during the 20th century. The 100 largest metropolitan regions in the United States account for just 12 percent of the land area but contain 65 percent of the population, 69 percent of all jobs, and 70 percent of the nation's GDP. Urban congestion as a result of underinvestment in U.S. transportation infrastructure across all modes is causing a decrease in quality and an increase in transportation and logistics costs. The infrastructure in absolute terms, however, is extensive.[38]

The extensive road network in the United States includes 6.4 million km (3.98 million mi) of highways, of which 4.1 million km (2.55 million mi) are paved. Expressways account for around 75,000 km (46,600 mi) of the total, making it the largest controlled-access highway system in the world. In recent decades, congestion has become a huge problem in cities. There have been efforts to decrease car use, but public transport is often insufficiently available. Although the U.S. population is large, the country is not densely populated, meaning that public transport often fails to capture scale economies that would make it practical. The rail network is also extensive, although underutilized for passenger travel in comparison with Europe. There are a total of 228,000 km (141,700 mi) of track in use. The major concentration of routes are down the east and west coasts. U.S. freight railroads are the world's busiest, moving more freight than any rail system in any other country. Private companies that provide freight service own nearly all railroad corridors.[39]

The major seaports in the United States include New York, Baltimore, Charleston, Savannah, and Miami/Fort Lauderdale in the East; Houston and New Orleans on the Gulf Coast; and Long Beach, Los Angeles, San Francisco, and Seattle/Tacoma on the West Coast. The interior also has major shipping channels, via the St. Lawrence Seaway and the Mississippi River system. Freight on the Mississippi River system, one of the most extensive river systems in the world, is carried on barges and largely consists of bulk goods, such as petrochemicals, grain, and cement. An extensive domestic air network is made necessary by the vast U.S. geography. The United States has an advanced air transportation infrastructure that utilizes approximately 5000 paved runways. Many of the world's 30 busiest airports in terms of both passengers and cargo are in the USA. There is no single national flag airline; passenger airlines in the United States have always been privately owned. Airports suffer from ever-increasing congestion and inefficiency, and the 2001 terrorist attacks forced a major upgrade in security procedures.[40]

Canada boasts a physical infrastructure that ranks among the best in the world. The costs of using this infrastructure are also comparatively low. Canada has nearly 900,000 km (559,200 mi) of public road, with a Trans-Canada highway linking all 10 provinces. The provinces have jurisdiction over the road network, and shippers require operating authority from the relevant provincial Department of Transport or Highways. The road network includes a large number of crossing points with the United States and 18 major trade gateways. Canada has two major railways, Canadian National Railways (CNR) and the Canadian Pacific Railway (CPR). Both offer intermodal services to shippers between the Atlantic and Pacific oceans. Both are highly integrated with the U.S. railways.[41]

Canada has water access to the Pacific, Atlantic, and Arctic oceans and contains the world's longest inland waterway open to ocean ships, the Great Lakes/St Lawrence Seaway system. Vancouver is the largest port and the main terminal for shipments to the Asia-Pacific region. Major ports on the East Coast are Montreal, Halifax, St. John, and Quebec City. Foreign vessels need a license to operate commercially within Canadian waters. There are no designated free ports or zones in Canada, but the government has a variety of programs, such as the Duty Deferral Program, that postpones or refunds duties for re-exports. Canada has a highly developed air transport system, including eight airports that boast more than 1 million passengers per year. Despite increased competition from low-cost carriers, air transport remains dominated by the privatized former national carrier, Air Canada, which offers comprehensive international and domestic service. Connections with the United States are excellent and unrestricted.[42]

The Mexican infrastructure is one of the most extensive in Latin America, although it lags that of more industrialized nations. Road transport is the chief means of conveying passengers and freight in Mexico. In 2010 there were 366,905 km (227,984 mi) of roads in the total network, of which 37.1 percent were paved. The government granted private companies the right to build, maintain, and collect fees from toll roads in the 1990s to support the development of the export trade and spark economic growth. Still, 53-foot trailers common in the USA and Canada cannot legally travel on Mexican roads because they are too large and too heavy, limiting carriers' efficiency in cross-border shipments to Mexico. Either smaller trailers must be used from the start, or the freight must be loaded onto smaller trailers at the border for final delivery in Mexico.[43] The Mexican railway system, covering 26,715 km (16,600 mi) in 2010, was state-owned until 2001. Inadequate investment had resulted in deterioration of the service and a declining volume of freight traffic. The railway system was opened to private sector investment in preparation for NAFTA passage in 1993. Continued investment is needed to upgrade the country's railways.[44]

Mexico enjoys an extensive Pacific and Gulf of Mexico coastline. Veracruz, Altamira, Tampico, and Coatzacoalcos handle more than 80 percent of non–oil cargo that travels through Mexican ports on the Gulf of Mexico; Manzanillo and Lazaro Cardenas handle 75 percent of the non–oil traffic on the Pacific; and Lazaro Cardenas is growing as an alternative for shipments into the USA. There are plans to expand the capacity of all of Mexico's ports.[45]

Mexico boasts one of the largest networks of airports in the world, with nearly every town or city of over 50,000 inhabitants having its own airport. In 2010 there were 62 international airports. Aeroméxico, formerly state owned, is the dominant airline in the domestic market. Mexico has two types of trade zones: border zones (*franjas fronterizas*) and strategic bonded areas (*recintos fiscalizados estratégicos* or *refies*). The existing border zone regime establishes lower tariffs for 1735 products. Refies are bonded areas that allow for the temporary warehousing of goods, merchandise, and primary materials free of import taxes and normal import processing, for the purpose of storage, sale, transformation, repair, display, and export. Imported goods and materials can be stored in refies for up to two years.[46]

Figure 11.7 shows the North and Central America rail network; Figure 11.8 shows the North and Central America highway network.

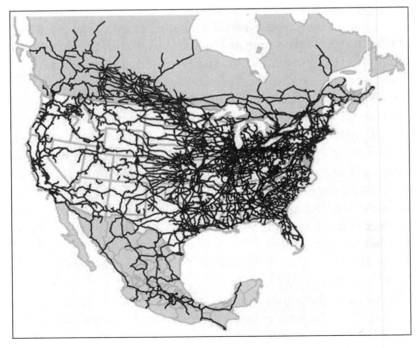

Figure 11.7 North and Central America rail network.

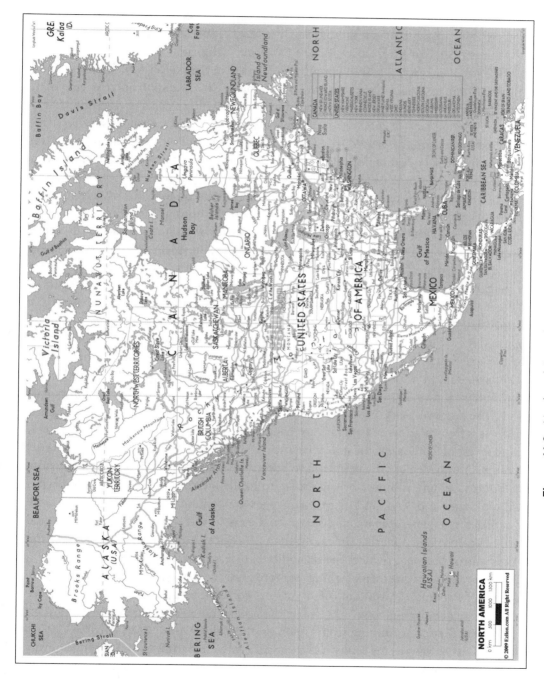

Figure 11.8 North and Central America highway network.

Lack of an adequate international land transportation infrastructure is one of the major obstacles to increasing trade among Central American countries. For example, it is far more expensive to ship tomatoes from San Jose, Costa Rica to Managua, Nicaragua than it is to ship it from San Jose, Costa Rica to San Jose, California (10 times the distance) mainly due to the increased cost of land transportation in the region, which can be up to four times as high as that in Organization for Economic Co-Operation and Development (OECD) nations. World Bank studies have shown that the high costs of domestic transport, caused by the lack of quality secondary roads, costly land transport services, and lengthy customs clearance procedures are the main hindrances to trade among Central American countries. For example, it should take 10 hours by truck move a product between Nueva Guinea in Nicaragua and Puerto Limón in Costa Rica. Instead, it can take more than 13 hours due to delays on the poor quality roads, detours to avoid bridges in poor condition, traffic in urban areas, and wait time to cross the border.[47]

In 2010, Costa Rica had 35,820 km (22,258 mi) of roadways of roads, of which 8083 km (5023 mi) were paved. Despite significant highway expansion since 2007, excessive delays remain. There also are frequent armed robberies on the highway, to the point that some truck freight is being shifted to air transport. In addition, there is minimum rail infrastructure. Puerto Limón-Moin is Costa Rica's main port on the Caribbean. Puerto Limón handles more cargo than any other port in Costa Rica, with most of its cargo destined for Europe and the USA. Puerto Limón handles petroleum and containers; growth in tourism led to the opening of the cruise terminal in Puerto Limón that offers a roll-on/roll-off ramp. Puerto Limón also offers storage areas for refrigerated cargoes. In 2007, Puerto Limón handled almost 20 million tons of cargo. Despite investment in structural improvements in the last five years, however, the port organization, operated by a state-owned utility, suffers from fragmented operations that greatly limit performance. Puerto Caldera, two hours west of San Jose, is the major Pacific coast port with trade relations worldwide. It contains an industrial complex meant to accommodate both cargo vessels and cruise liners. Puerto Caldera is linked by rail and road to the interior. Most of its trade is with the United States and Asia, and its major cargoes are containers, solid bulk, iron, fruit, tuna, vehicles, and general merchandise. Costa Rica is served by two major international airports, San José and Liberia, and more than 30 regional airports. Urban congestion increases transit time and reduces the reliability of receiving freight at the airport.[48]

Panama features world-class facilities for foreign trade, but its internal road structure is weaker. Of Panama's 11,100 km (6898 mi) network of roads, 3994 km (2482 mi) are paved. Every major city and town is linked by the system, but the two main paved highways of Panama are the roads running from Colón on the Caribbean coast to Panama City on the Pacific coast, known as the Transistmica, and the stretch of the Pan-American Highway (via Interamericana) connecting Panama City with the Costa Rican frontier. The region east of the Panama Canal, up to the Colombian frontier, consists mostly of jungle and mountains. Beyond Yaviza, in Darién province, the road ends, representing the only break in the continental span of the Pan-American Highway between Alaska and Argentina. The nations rail network features the Panama Canal Railway Company, which transports freight and passengers from Panama City on the Pacific coast to Colón on the Caribbean, offering a land bridge alternative to the canal.[49]

Panama's principal seaports are Balboa (near Panama City), which is being expanded by the private Panama Ports Company; Cristóbal (near Colón); two privately run container terminals at Coco Solo (Colón) and Evergreen (Colón Container Terminal); Manzanillo International Terminal; Bahia de las Minas; and Vacamonte. In addition to expanding the canal, Panama is investing in the modernization of the ports at Balboa, Cristóbal, Manzanillo, and Colón. Tocumen Airport, east of the capital, connecting the country with all major Latin American capitals, Europe, and the USA, is in the process of a major refurbishment that will include an expansion of the passenger terminal, runway repairs, improvement of the cargo terminals, and purchasing of equipment such as electric stairs, air conditioners, and elevators. Forty-three other airports in Panama have paved runways.[50]

Utilities

The World Economic Forum Global Competitiveness Index (GCI) provides an objective assessment of the quality of utility service for 144 nations. In 2012–2013, the utility quality for the USA was ranked 33rd out of the 144 nations (top quartile). U.S. utilities are run as natural monopolies because the infrastructure required to produce and deliver a product such as electricity or water is very expensive to build and maintain. As a result, they are often government monopolies. If privately owned, a public utility commission regulates them. The utilities sector in Canada is sophisticated and well run, ranking 14th in the GCI report. The sector is organized along provincial and territorial lines, and large government-owned public utilities play a leading role in the provision of electricity, water, and sanitation. Quality of utility provision varies widely across Mexico; the GCI report ranked Mexico at 79th out of 144. Along the industrialized northern border, where many businesses are based, distribution systems and infrastructure are well developed. Away from the U.S. frontier, major cities also enjoy good access to utilities, although water availability can fluctuate.[51]

Utility provision in both Costa Rica and Panama are considered to be at a high level. The GCI report ranked Costa Rica 42nd out of 144 nations, and Panama ranked 43rd; both are in the top quartile of nations. Both have solid utility infrastructure in major population areas, and particularly in industrial zones. Electric power generation and distribution is run by a combination of state and public entities. In addition, both nations are participating in the Puebla-Panama project, which seeks to unify Central American electricity grids to reduce costs and the frequency of power disruptions, as well as to attract private sector investment for the development of new power plants.[52]

Telecommunications

The World Economic Forum Global Competitiveness Index (GCI) provides an objective assessment of the level of telecommunications (mobile phone and Internet) connectivity for 144 nations. In 2012–2013, the utility quality for the USA was ranked 118th on mobile phone connectivity and 18th on Internet out of the 144 nations (top quartile). The United States boasts extremely advanced and extensive telecommunications infrastructure. The rather fragmented nature of the sector, however, has meant that systems are not always fully compatible, and there has been some lag in telecommunications technology adoption compared with Europe and Japan. The United States is the world leader in information technology (IT), with a highly developed computer and Internet infrastructure. U.S. companies have a dominant global role in manufacturing computers, developing computer software, and providing Internet access. The United States is also the largest market for electronic commerce and leads the world in the development of e-commerce. Similar to the transportation infrastructure, the U.S. electricity infrastructure is enormous but is also aged and vulnerable. There is a need for heavy investment, and inherent vulnerabilities in the system need to be addressed.[53]

The Canadian telecommunications system is highly sophisticated, with standards equivalent to those in the United States. The GCI connectivity for Canada is very low for mobile phones, however, due to the fact that services are concentrated in larger urban areas and in areas with greater transport links. Rural service is weak. The Internet ranking is 16th in the GCI report. Despite the mobile phone ranking, telecommunications service in the populated areas of Canada rivals that of the USA and Europe. Canada is integrated with the U.S. direct dial long-distance telephone system. Internet penetration is high in Canada, with a large majority of the population regularly accessing it. In terms of high-speed Internet penetration, Canada ranked 13th in the OECD, with a penetration rate of 78 subscribers per 100 households in 2010. Consumer- and business-orientated e-commerce has increased rapidly in recent years. The Internet is an increasingly important consumer sales channel. The state-owned Canadian Broadcasting Corporation is the dominant broadcaster, although services have expanded rapidly via cable and satellite platforms.[54]

The GCI connectivity for Mexico is poor, ranking at 134th for mobile phones and 11th for Internet in the GCI report. The Mexican state-owned telephone company, Telmex, was privatized in 1990. Further liberalization opened long-distance and cellular services to competition in 1996. In 1997, Telmex received a provisional license to provide services in the USA, in conjunction with the U.S. telecommunications company Sprint. In 2010 there were 77.3 mobile telephone users in Mexico per 100 inhabitants.[55]

Telecommunications connectivity for Costa Rica and Panama are also challenging, but improving. Costa Rica ranks 116th for mobile phone connectivity and 95th for Internet, and Panama is ranked 6th for mobile phones and 109th for the Internet. Costa Rica has invested in satellite and terrestrial microwave networks to meet demand in fixed, mobile, and Internet services and allowed multinational players to enter the market in 2009, providing private networks, Internet, and mobile phone service. The privatization of Panama's telecommunications market began in 1997 and was fully opened to competition in 2003. Panama has an extensive and relatively modern telephone system, served by a submarine cable, the Central American Microwave Network, and two Atlantic Ocean Intelsat earth stations.[56]

Table 11.5 presents the scores for the Infrastructure dimension. The strengths and weaknesses of the North and Central America nations on transportation, utilities, and telecommunications infrastructure that may aid to the attractiveness of supply chain operations are summarized in Table 11.6.

Competence

Elements associated with the business competencies needed to support supply chain operations in the region are assessed in the Competence dimension, including labor availability, productivity, and relations; education levels for line staff and management; and logistics customs and security support.

Labor: Availability, Productivity, and Relations

Labor availability in the USA has gone from limited in 2007 to plentiful in the years since the Global Recession. Forecasters who were predicting severe labor shortages due to the imminent retirement of waves of baby boomers have begun to reevaluate their predictions. There has not been a period in the United States over the past 30 years with as many qualified and experienced workers available in the labor market from blue collar to white collar, from skilled to unskilled, and from high school graduates to the highly educated.[57]

Table 11.5 Scores for the Infrastructure Dimension

Infrastructure	Transportation Infrastructure	Energy Infrastructure	Connectivity	Overall Grade
30%	50%	25%	25%	100%
USA	A⁻	B⁺	B	B⁺
Canada	A⁻	A⁻	B⁻	B⁺
Mexico	B⁻	C	C	C⁺
Costa Rica	D	B	C⁺	C⁻
Panama	A⁻	B	B	B⁺

Table 11.6 Strengths and Weaknesses Summary: Infrastructure Dimension

Grade	Strengths	Weaknesses
USA: B⁺	Good access to commodities; improving energy picture with Canadian shale oil and natural gas; excellent road, rail, water, and airport system; internal river system best in the world although underutilized for domestic transport; good telecomm capabilities, leading innovators; leader in e-commerce for Business-to-Business (B2B) and Business-to-Consumer (B2C).	Need for expanded capacity and investment in infrastructure a major challenge for coming years; air industry troubled, possibly in need of reregulation; power distribution extensive but outdated; high-speed telecommunications lags Europe and developed Asia; telecommunications industry fragmented.
Canada: B⁺	Net exporter of energy commodities; extensive road and rail network at low cost; ocean access on Atlantic and Pacific; extensive domestic water system with St. Lawrence Seaway and Great Lakes (although limited use due to seasonality); stable and effective air system; transportation system enjoys multiple connections with that of USA; extensive power distribution and telecomm/Internet system.	High air transport costs due to low competition; aging power distribution system.
Mexico: C⁺	One of best infrastructures in LATAM, but not up to par with USA or Canada; air network particularly good; significant investment in ports and rail to connect to USA, especially Manzanillo, Lazaro Cardenas, (both Pacific coast) and Veracruz (Gulf); quality of road, rail, water, and air transport improving with privatization.	Road, rail, water, air transport, power distribution, and telecomm still not at levels of industrialized world, with many challenges and barriers; availability and quality of infrastructure varies greatly across the country, being generally good in the central plain and north but poor in the south.
Costa Rica: C⁻	Strong air cargo system; Pacific and Caribbean/Atlantic port access; good power distribution, water access, and telecommunications.	Poor road and rail infrastructure; limited cargo capacity in seaports.
Panama: B⁺	Panama Canal; Colón Free Trade Zone; modern telecommunications and power distribution grid; sufficient road and rail connectivity between Pacific and Caribbean/Atlantic ports.	No continuous east-west highway to link North and South America.

The median age of the labor force continues to rise, however, high immigration levels means that the youth labor force (aged 16 to 24) will grow more rapidly than the overall labor force. The USA has been a leading innovator in productivity, and the U.S. workforce works longer hours and has fewer barriers to hiring and firing than any workforce among the industrialized nations. The USA ranks in the top quartile (12th out of 144) on pay and productivity in the World Economic Forum Global Competitive Index (WEF GCI).[58] Union membership in the private sector is relatively low (7.2 percent of workers), and strikes are relatively rare, with disruption kept to a minimum.

Canada faces a shortage of available labor that promises to worsen in coming years due to aging of the workforce and gaps in education for skilled jobs. Canada's labor productivity growth has been lower than that of the top industrial countries for many decades, although its relative performance improved in 2012 and it still compares favorably to non-industrialized nations (ranking 24th out of 144 on pay and productivity in the WEF GCI). Canada's productivity reflects low research & development (R&D) intensity, a weak innovation record, and the relatively small percentage of Canadians with advanced degrees in science and technology.[59] Organized labor plays a significant role in Canada, and unionized employees across the labor force was 26.1 percent in 2008. The political influence and militancy of the unions has decreased greatly since the 1970s, although union action is sometimes a problem for businesses in Canada, often staging wildcat strikes. Canadian firms rely to a large degree on centralized wage-setting processes and have relatively restrictive dismissal regulations.[60]

Growth in the working-age population in Mexico will continue to outpace overall population growth, adding to the available labor pool. A shortage of trained workers, however, has been a consistent challenge to the supply chain infrastructure of Mexico. Although a surplus of unskilled labor and international competition keep labor costs relatively low, businesses have complained about a shortage of technically skilled workers. Insufficient training of truck drivers, in particular, has been cited as a major reason for the long delay in full NAFTA implementation. Several large Mexican logistics companies reported difficulty in recruiting quality employees at every level from managers to line workers.[61] Mexican labor costs are low compared to those in highly industrialized countries, although they are still more than those in China. Low levels of automation and education hurt productivity, as reflected in a ranking of 83rd out of 144 on pay and productivity in the WEF GCI. Mexico's employment legislation is stiff, creating a burden on labor market flexibility and resulting in renewed efforts to reform labor laws. Unions tend to be strong in traditional sectors of the economy, but union membership in newer industries such as the maquiladora sector tends to be low.[62]

A skilled and high-quality workforce is readily available in Costa Rica and is undeniably an asset for investors. Costa Rica's productivity levels have been steadily increasing, as reflected in a ranking of 64th out of 144 on pay and productivity in the WEF GCI. Although the level of unionization in the private sector is relatively low, trade unions have a formal role in defining the minimum wage, which is decided twice annually by a tripartite council involving the government, business, and union representatives. Potential future protests should not be underestimated as the liberalization of state monopolies in the electricity, telecoms, and port sectors take place.

Panama features a young, growing population that will support economic growth in the next 20 to 25 years; a large pool of both skilled and unskilled workers is available. Job growth, however, has been highly labor-intensive, especially outside of agriculture, and as a result productivity has remained stagnant at best over the past decade. Policies of the current government have focused on changing this scenario. Panama would not gain much in terms of competitiveness by reducing its labor costs but rather needs to continue to invest in new technology, training, better health and working conditions, improved organization of work through greater cooperation and participation of workers, and reduced absenteeism. These productivity issues earned Panama a ranking of only 122nd out of 144 on the WEF GCI pay and productivity assessment. Union members represent around 13 percent of the workforce, but rates vary per sector. Labor organizations have proven to be able to mobilize to organize strikes and protests demanding an increase in wages and better labor conditions, especially with regard to the Panama Canal expansion project and the third set of locks.

Education Levels for Line Staff and Management

The U.S. education system is not as internationally competitive as it used to be, slipping 10 spots in both high school and college graduation rates over the past three decades according to Council on Foreign Relations' Renewing America initiative. Shortcomings among American workers threaten the country's ability to compete with other countries and set a compelling example internationally. The greatest weakness of the education system is the gap between socioeconomic groups. Although the United States spends the fourth most in the world on per-student primary and secondary education and by far the most on college education, funding is not distributed equitably. Still, more than 30 percent of Americans have college degrees, 20 million of the nation's 56 million bachelor's degree holders have a degree in science or engineering. The Obama Administration is renewing efforts to increase funding for vocational and skills training programs.[63] Despite these concerns, the USA continues to rank in the top quartile of nations on education statistics; the World Economic Forum GCI ranking for the USA on overall quality of education is 28th out of 144, and quality of management education is 12th out of 144; the ranking for extent of staff training is 15th out of 144.

Canada enjoys one of the best education systems in the world. According to the latest data from the Canadian Education Statistics Council, 49 percent of Canadians aged 25 to 64 had attained tertiary-level education in 2008, compared with the 28 percent average for members of OECD. The World Economic Forum GCI ranking for Canada on overall quality of education is 6th out of 144, and quality of management education is 5th out of 144. Apprentice programs are not as well established in Canada as in many European countries, but a record number of persons were in apprenticeship programs in 2007. Canada also has good technical schools, and the federal government is participating with union-employer groups to establish training centers.[64] The World Economic Forum GCI ranking for Canada for extent of staff training is 23rd out of 144.

The quality of education in Mexico is poor, impeding the development of a more highly skilled labor force and a rise in wages. The largely unskilled workforce is highly suitable for labor-intensive industries such as *maquilas*, but less competitive in more inno-vative, skill-intensive sectors. Companies typically invest in their own training programs. ProMéxico, the government's export and investment-promotion agency, is coordinating joint efforts between state and local governments, private industry, and universities to upgrade programs that train highly skilled professionals in complex manufacturing indus-tries. In the aerospace industry, for example, Honeywell and Gulfstream, as well as the Mexican Federation of Aerospace Industry, are directly participating in the design of the syllabus of aerospace engineering and related courses. The prospects of passing substantial educational and labor reforms to address both the weaknesses of the public educational system that restrict the availability of skilled labor and the rigid and cumbersome regula-tions that make hiring and firing employees costly for companies are unlikely to occur in the near term.[65] The World Economic Forum GCI ranking for Mexico on overall quality of education is 100th out of 144, and quality of management education is 51st out of 144; the ranking for extent of staff training is 67th out of 144.

Costa Rica enjoys one of the highest literacy rates in Latin America (96 percent accord-ing to government estimates), and English is commonly spoken amongst the middle class and university-educated workers. Primary education is free, barring a nominal charge of a few dollars. The government's approach to vocational training focuses on urban training centers that offer formal training in leading trades and technical occupations. Recently, the Ministry of Education introduced programs to guarantee widespread knowledge in com-puter sciences and English as a second language (ESL) to keep Costa Rican youth and the workforce on par with international standards.[66] The World Economic Forum GCI rank-ing for Costa Rica on overall quality of education is 21st out of 144, and quality of manage-ment education is 19th out of 144; the ranking for extent of staff training is 29th out of 144.

Panama's primary and higher education systems have shown marked improvement over the last 10 years, although they lag those of industrialized nations. Ninety-two percent of the population is literate. Retention has been one of the biggest challenges facing the Panamanian educational system because students often drop out after the primary grades when they are forced to pay tuition to register for higher studies. Ironically, robust growth and rising foreign investment has masked some problems associated with workforce edu-cation levels as business growth has attracted a large pool of foreign labor. There are instances when the lack of educated workers has caused companies to settle elsewhere. Notably, in 2009, General Electric opted for Chile over Panama for a project that local media said would have required up to 1500 English-speaking engineers and computer experts.[67] The World Economic Forum GCI ranking for Panama on overall quality of education is 112th out of 144, and quality of management education is 82nd out of 144; the ranking for extent of staff training is 43rd out of 144.

Logistics, Customs, and Security

According to the World Bank 2012 Logistics Performance Index (LPI), biannual ranking assesses the logistics efficiency of 155 nations. The U.S. logistics industry was ranked the 9th best in the world, on par with nations such as Japan and the United Kingdom but behind leaders Hong Kong, Singapore, and Germany. The USA's logistics network strengths were overall infrastructure, tracking and tracing capability, timeliness, and logistics quality and competence; customs and international shipments were ranked relatively lower, but were still in the top quartile globally. The U.S. Customs and Border Protection (CBP) agency is responsible for regulating and facilitating international trade, collecting import duties, and enforcing regulations. The agency has more than 20,000 officers screening passengers and cargo at over 300 points of entry into the United States. Security has been greatly stepped up since the terrorist attacks of September 11, 2001, and this has led to greater inconvenience for importers and exporters.[68]

Canada's logistics network ranked 14th in terms of performance on the 2012 LPI, relatively equal to leading industrialized countries such as France, Sweden, and Switzerland. Compared to top-performing countries, Canada's logistics network strengths lie in the area of timeliness with lower ranking in the areas of customs clearance, international shipments, and tracking and tracing processes; logistics quality and competence and infrastructure were on par with the overall ranking. Canada has a very advanced customs infrastructure, and commerce with the United States in particular is very straightforward. However, since the September 11, 2001, terrorist attacks, greater security has been introduced. Customs operations at land borders, seaports, mail centers, and international airports are all managed by the Canada Border Services Agency.[69]

Mexican firms lag behind world leaders in supply chain and logistics service levels. In recent years, many organizations in industrialized nations have delegated many or all of their logistics operations to third-party logistics providers (3PLs) to better focus on core competencies. As a result, 3PLs have expanded their service portfolio beyond traditional logistics operations to value-added activities such as kitting, light manufacturing, product labeling, and repair operations for warranty claims. A survey of Mexican manufacturers about their experiences with the 3PL industry found that fewer Mexican companies are using 3PLs than those in the United States and Europe; this difference is even more exaggerated among small and medium-sized companies. The study also found that Mexican companies that are using 3PLs are focusing on more routine activities such as customs clearance and freight bill auditing and payment. The relative underutilization of this expertise by Mexican firms as a whole leads to a less efficient logistics system.[70] According to the World Bank 2012 LPI, Mexico's logistics network ranked 47th in terms of performance, on par with such emerging market countries as Brazil, India, and Argentina but lagging most industrialized nations. Mexico's logistics industry strengths lie in the areas of international shipments, logistics quality and competence, infrastructure, and tracking and tracing, whereas customs and timeliness were considered areas of relative weakness.

The LPI ranks Costa Rica as 72nd out of a total of 150 countries. The most serious problems highlighted are linked to the organization of logistics services. The institutions responsible for infrastructure services are generally weak in terms of their human resources and are fragmented and lack coordination with each other. According to the World Bank 2012 LPI, Costa Rica's logistics industry ranked 82nd in terms of performance, below other emerging markets in Central and South America. Costa Rica scored well on international shipping and tracking and tracing, but scored poorly on overall logistics quality and competence. Customs was noted as another weakness, as the complexity of documentation needed for trading in Costa Rica extends the time traders spend exporting and importing goods; it takes an average of 18 days to export and 25 days to import, with more than 50 percent of this time spent on the preparation of documents.

Panama is rapidly becoming a regional logistics hub in which container consignments are broken down and reassembled to be sent as smaller loads to smaller ports elsewhere in the hemisphere. The government intends to build on that reputation with the creation of an urban center the size of London at a cost of US$10 billion. The project hopes to attract investors from neighboring countries that do not enjoy the political stability available in Panama. Not surprisingly, Panama's ranking on the LPI was the highest in Central America, ranked 61st globally out of 155 nations. Strengths included customs, international shipments, and logistics quality and competence, whereas infrastructure, tracking and tracing capability, and timeliness were relative areas for improvement. Panama enjoys a good reputation for its customs system, with few procedures and generally rapid processing. Customs authorities continuously seek to improve their services and are well equipped with X-ray units, scanners, and checkpoints equipped with nonintrusive check systems and other cutting-edge equipment, not only to improve detection of illegal trafficking but also to speed up the entry-exit process for imports and exports. Panama has specific customs regulations in place for companies operating in the Colón Free-Trade Zone (CFZ) providing a duty-free regime for both imports and re-exports. Special customs provisions are also included in the various bilateral free trade agreements to which Panama subscribes.[71]

Table 11.7 presents the scores for the Competence dimension. An assessment of the strengths and weaknesses for the selected nations of North and Central America are summarized in Table 11.8.

Table 11.7 Scores for the Competence Dimension

Competence	Labor Relations	Education Levels	Logistics Competence	Customs and Security	Overall Grade
20%	25%	25%	40%	10%	100%
USA	A⁻	A⁻	A	A	A
Canada	B	A	A⁻	A⁻	A⁻
Mexico	C	C⁺	B	C⁺	B⁻
Costa Rica	B	B⁺	C	C	B⁻
Panama	C⁻	C⁻	B⁻	C⁺	C⁺

Table 11.8 Strengths and Weaknesses Summary: Competence Dimension

Grade	Strengths	Weaknesses
USA: A	Workers are highly productive; working age population is growing due to Mexican immigration; education has its detractors, but in general fares well in education and training categories, both for labor and management; unions are weakening compared to other industrialized nations, although this varies by region; labor relations are good; logistics and transportation among the best in the world.	Overall skilled labor pool is shrinking; some big problems underlie the education system; training programs akin to apprentice programs in Europe are poor or nonexistent.
Canada: A⁻	Productivity is good, although at the bottom of OECD; outstanding education and training; labor relations good; very strong logistics network and industry.	Unions are strong and can be disruptive.
Mexico: B⁻	Productivity is improving (but still far below global standards); growing and young workforce; union membership in most industries low; government working to improve training and education.	Productivity lags global average; ensuring that workers show up has been a huge problem in the maquiladora industry; education, training, and managerial skills far below the global average; shortages of skilled workers in key industries; logistics industry lags industrial world.
Costa Rica: B⁻	Skilled labor is readily available; highly educated and literate; English commonly spoken; low levels of unionization and good labor relations; good productivity of labor and improving; overall logistics service industry satisfactory (but some issues).	Lack of integration in logistics services forces companies to deal with multiple parties, especially when utilizing seaports (lack of organization).
Panama: C⁺	Young and growing workforce; fairly well educated and skilled; Panama canal zone employees cannot strike; significant presence of global third-party logistics firms making integrated logistics a strength; strong customer and international shipping capability.	Organized labor relatively strong; limited skilled workforce capacity.

Main Trends in North and Central America

Table 11.9 presents a summary of the assessment scores on the EPIC dimensions for the selected nations of North and Central America.

The summary assessment reveals some attractive elements among the EPIC dimensions for Mexico, Costa Rica, and Panama that would support location of supply chain operations in these areas. In each case, however, there also is some uncertainty related to the Economy, Politics, Infrastructure, and Competence profiles of each nation. The big question, then, becomes whether the benefits of elements such as geographic location, access to global sea lanes of trade, low cost land, labor, and capital, and so forth, that are found in Mexico, Costa Rica, or Panama outweigh the costs of that uncertainty, particularly to serve the North and/or South American markets.

The summary also shows that the USA and Canada remain very attractive locations for supply chain operations provided issues related to cost and economic growth can be overcome. The movement toward a broader interpretation of total cost that includes exchange fluctuations, tariffs, transportation, pipeline inventory, risk, and responsiveness to the market has caused many firms to reconsider decisions to source manufacturing outside of U.S. and Canadian markets. The EPIC summary in Table 11.9 lends credence to this discussion.

Supply Chain Challenges and Opportunities

Establishing supply chain operations in select locations in North and Central America opens the possibility for developing more integrated Western Hemispheric supply chains that enable organizations to marry the benefits of low-cost sourcing with global or regional logistics and distribution capabilities. As suggested, this will require sophisticated total cost models that enable an organization to understand the overall value creation required for each product/customer pairing and then create the appropriate supply chain that enables them to deliver the required value with the lowest total cost and highest profit.

Table 11.9 Summary Assessment of EPIC Attractiveness of Key North and Central American Nations

	Economy	Politics	Infrastructure	Competence	Overall Grade
USA	B+	A−	B+	A	A−
Canada	B+	A	B+	A−	A−
Mexico	B+	C+	C+	B−	B−
Costa Rica	C+	B	C−	B−	C+
Panama	B	C+	B+	C+	B−

An understanding of the overriding challenges and opportunities in North and Central America will help organizations make those decisions.

Mexico, Costa Rica, and Panama represent interesting alternatives for organizations seeking to develop supply chain operations that facilitate low total cost solutions with good access to the large markets of both North and South America. There are interesting aspects of each nation that compare favorably to alternatives in the USA and Canada, South America nations, and even the popularly evoked low-cost areas of Asia. Each possesses strengths related to low costs of taxes, land, labor, and capital. There are also elements of each nation's politics, infrastructure, and business competence that make them interesting considerations for global supply chain solutions, although notable weaknesses for each must be acknowledged.

Mexico: Land of Opportunity or Violent Battleground?

Mexico features strong economic growth potential on a large and growing population base, plus it features close proximity to U.S. and Canadian markets without having to engage in multiple modes of transportation. The economic harmonization with the USA and Canada resulting from NAFTA makes export to those huge markets from Mexico relatively easy and attractive. Mexican politics provides a mixed bag, however. Although there has been a relatively long period of stability over the last 20-plus years, resulting in passage of pro-business policies, the increasing violence and corruption brought on by the strength of the drug cartels is of great concern to organizations considering locating supply chain operations in the country. In addition, Mexico suffers from weaknesses in competence, mainly poor education and training, low productivity, and poor logistics industry capabilities. The youth and availability of a large workforce, however, keeps costs low.

Although Mexico does not always compare favorably to industrialized nations, in comparison to many other Latin American nations the Mexican EPIC dimensions are promising. In particular, the infrastructural linkages that marry Mexican supply chain operations with transportation networks in the USA and Canada make Mexico an enticing alternative. The expansion of Mexican west coast ports (Manzanilla and Lazaro Cardenas), in combination with the rail lines that link them to the rest of North America, opens the prospect of transporting raw materials and subcomponents from Asia into Mexican facilities to take advantage of tax and tariff laws in the trade zones, finishing the goods with cheap labor and capital, and then distributing them to U.S. and Canadian markets without import taxes due to NAFTA regulations.

Panama: The New Crossroads

Panama is one of the world's fastest-growing economies, and enjoys a recently enacted free trade agreement with the United States, a "dollarized" economy that removes exchange-rate risks for U.S. firms, and one of the most well-developed transportation assets in the world, the Panama Canal and the accompanying Colón Free Trade Zone. With the opening of a new canal in 2015 that will be able to handle the largest ocean going merchant ships in the world, plus an advanced port and railway that can move containerized freight from Pacific to Atlantic ports in days or hours, Panama is poised to become a force in global supply chain operations. Although it has been prominent for a century as a transportation asset, recent political stabilization under a pro-business president has enabled it to pass policies that make it attractive for sourcing and manufacturing as well, including privatization of the power generation system and telecommunications, and laws that enhance the flexibility of the labor market. (Note: This is true in the Canal and Free Trade Zones only.) In addition, the workforce is young and growing and is fairly well educated and skilled. Panama canal zone employees cannot strike. Panama provides a compelling choice for the location of redistribution facilities for goods traveling from Asia to Atlantic markets in North and South America and Europe. In addition, and similar to Costa Rica, Panama should be considered for a location of sourcing and manufacturing operations.

Interestingly, a potential threat to Panama's status as the new crossroads has recently emerged. In June 2013, Nicaragua's National Assembly approved an ambitious plan to build a US$40 billion canal across the country, which would provide an alternate route to the Panama Canal. The assembly granted a 50-year concession to a Chinese company, HK Nicaragua Canal Development Investment Co., to build the canal. As yet, few details have been released about the plans for the new canal. Global engineering and shipping experts, however, question the commercial viability of the project as shipping is still suffering from an economic slowdown and vessel capacity exceeds demand. The Nicaraguan canal route would have to be three times the length of the Panama Canal, which is about 80 km (49.7 mi) long. At this point it is doubtful that there is sufficient return to justify the investment.[72]

Costa Rica: From Tourist Dream to High-Tech Capital?

Costa Rica benefits from participation in CAFTA, which includes the other nations of Central America and the United States, as well as a strong network of trade ties that extend beyond the Western Hemisphere. Politically, it has been one of the most solid democracies in Latin America, with peaceful and transparent election processes, low levels of corruption, a well-defined tax code, pro-business and social policies, and a good security record, although a recent upsurge in drug activity has increased the level of violent crime. This violence, in addition to a recent corruption scandal, has challenged the government, which is also struggling to improve a negative fiscal balance situation. The relative stability, however, has fostered a well-educated, literate (and largely bilingual Spanish/English), readily available skilled labor force that is productive and has low levels of unionization and good relations with management. There has also been investment in infrastructure, particularly the air cargo system, power distribution, water, and telecommunications, and geography has blessed the nation with both Pacific and Caribbean/Atlantic port access. However, port organization and overall integration across different logistics entities is a weakness that prevents seamless supply chain movements. In addition, poor road and rail infrastructure and limited cargo capacity in seaports require additional investment to overcome.

Although Costa Rica has some weaknesses, overall conditions are such that the economy is expected to expand in the long term. This combination of strengths and weaknesses indicate that the nation should be considered a source for manufacturing of consumer products for export. In addition to its labor, land, and capital cost benefits and stability, its central location and accessibility to both Pacific and Atlantic trading lanes are a major benefit. There has been a notable positioning of facilities here by large firms in the last 20 years, in particular information technology firms including Intel, Hewlett-Packard, and Microsoft.

The USA and Canada: Super into the Mid-21st Century?

The primary challenges associated with supply chain operations in the USA and Canada are the relatively high costs of land, labor, capital, and taxes, which may be prohibitive for some supply chain sourcing and manufacturing operations when compared to lower cost areas. Low GDP growth expectations, concerns about political stability and infighting in the USA, and a grave need for infrastructure investment for renewal and growth comprise other weaknesses. Finally, the domestic populations of each nation are aging and declining, although the high degree of Mexican immigration into the USA has helped forestall the overall trend in that nation.

Decisions to locate sourcing and manufacturing operations in either the USA or Canada should be considered risky due to the issues associated with land, labor, and capital costs. Careful attention should be paid to political decisions related to taxes, infrastructure, education investment, and immigration policies in the near future. Of course, the overall size of these markets, comprising by far the largest market and the 10th largest economies in the world, make supply chain distribution operations that ensure high-service access essential.

The infrastructure of the USA and Canada are also among the best in the world. The U.S. workforce is by far the most productive in the world, and Canadians are rated highly as well. There are, however, significant concerns about the future transport infrastructure in the USA without a dedicated and well-conceived investment policy. Similarly, the business support competencies in the USA and Canada are relatively well regarded, although concerns about education and training in the USA without significant investment are also frequently voiced; the Canadian education and training system is top rate.

Despite these concerns, locating sourcing and manufacturing operations in the USA or Canada should be carefully considered. These are appropriate only when the costs associated with transportation, compliance and security, pipeline inventory, risk reduction and redundancy, and delivery service levels required to distribute to U.S. and Canadian markets from offshore locations outweigh the additional costs of U.S. and Canadian taxes, land, labor, and capital. This is often the case when seeking highly skilled labor and the value of the finished product makes excessively long pipelines prohibitively expensive due to high inventory cost. In addition, industries that require very short customer response time and high levels of customization might incur pipeline costs that exceed the land, labor, and capital cost savings presented by offshoring sourcing and manufacturing. An intriguing possibility for optimizing this equation is to identify areas of relatively low tax, land, labor, and capital costs within the USA, predominantly in the Gulf coast states of Alabama, Mississippi, Louisiana, and Texas.

The notion of manufacturing returning to North America has been building for several years now. A February 2012 survey from the Boston Consulting Group (BCG) showed that 37 percent of U.S. manufacturers with sales above $1 billion said they were considering shifting some production from China to the United States. The factors they pointed to were not only that wages and benefits were rising in China, but that lower inventory costs, lower transportation costs, higher-quality production and technology, and proximity to markets all minimize the wage gap. In addition, China is also enacting stricter labor laws and experiencing more frequent labor disputes and strikes. American workers are becoming more attractive as worker productivity continues to rise, and as operations move to nonunion regions such as the U.S. South. Caterpillar and GE are notable examples of this; even European firms, including Ikea and Airbus, are making the move. Unions have also agreed to allow wages to fall in order to keep jobs in the United States. For example, Ford started bringing back production from China and Mexico after an agreement with the United Auto Workers let the company reduce labor wages. As a result, BCG suggests that some industries could slowly migrate back from China, including industries such as plastic and rubber, machinery, electrical equipment and computers, and electronics. Finally, the boom in energy production in the United States, both from the oil sands in the northwest as well as natural gas from shale-fracking, are reducing energy costs and adding to the attractiveness.[73]

Key Takeaways for North and Central America

The following 10 key takeaways are provided based on the EPIC analysis of the selected nations of North and Central America.

1. There is still a strong appeal for the political, infrastructure, and competence environments afforded in the USA. The major weakness of conducting supply chain operations in the USA relates to the costs of land, labor, and capital, as well as the complexity regarding the tax situation for organizations locating there. Firms will continue to

conduct distribution operations to reach the vast U.S. market, supported by the strong third-party logistics industry.

2. There are locations within the United States that may provide opportunity for manufacturing sourcing, especially in cases where inventory costs are high and customer markets require high levels of delivery service and customization. In these cases, organizations should explore the Gulf coast states of Mississippi, Alabama, Louisiana, and Texas. There have been recent announcements by firms such as Caterpillar, GE, Hyundai, and EADS. Other southern states, particularly Tennessee and South Carolina, have also enjoyed recent success with location of manufacturing facilities.

3. Similar to the USA, Canada provides a stable, safe, and noncorrupt political environment supported by strong infrastructure and business competence. Again, the predominant weakness associated with supply chain operations in Canada relates to the costs of doing business. Although the Canadian market is only a 10th of the size of the U.S. economy, it remains large on the world sphere. Organizations will continue to locate distribution facilities to access the Canadian market, especially if those enable them access to northern U.S. markets as well. In addition, Canada remains a source for high-end manufacturing to reduce pipeline inventory and transportation costs to Canadian and northern U.S. markets.

4. Due to its significant raw materials deposits, Canada will also increase its position as a prime location for sourcing of raw materials, in particular energy resources as the world—and the USA—looks for alternative locations for energy supplies. This decision is supported by both the strong Canadian infrastructure and favorable NAFTA trade regulations.

5. A compelling trend to follow in the near to mid-future is that of the thawing of the North Pole. Although this trend promises serious negative environmental consequences, Canada may become an attractive location for maritime trade movements between North America and Asia to take advantage of the great circle routes over the North Pole.

6. Mexico provides a compelling economy that is in a growth mode, with a young and growing population, and an infrastructure and business competence that is improving, although not yet on par with the industrial world. In addition, the violence and corruption associated with the increasing power of the drug cartels casts a significant uncertainty over the EPIC environment. Organizations should seek locations for manufacturing that enable them to benefit from the economic cost conditions while minimizing risks, particularly risks emerging from drug violence and corruption. Prime areas include Tijuana and Baja, California; Zacatecas and Monterrey in north central Mexico; and Laredo. The aerospace industry has already recognized this and has established a significant cluster of activity near Monterrey.

7. Mexican Pacific ports continue to emerge as an attractive option for inbound sub-components from Asian suppliers, with Mexican finished goods assembly and redistribution using the efficient rail lines that connect with U.S. rail hubs in Dallas and San Diego.

8. Costa Rica also presents an attractive mix of EPIC elements that make it a possible solution for low-skilled mass production and/or service operations. In combination with its improving politics, infrastructure, and business competence profile, the presence of both Pacific and Caribbean/Atlantic ports as well as the Panama Canal give it accessibility to major North and South American markets that makes Costa Rica an interesting option. The electronics industry has established a cluster in Costa Rica that enables firms to provide a hedge against the risk of disruption in supply chains from Chinese suppliers and a "foot in the door" in the event that Chinese labor costs and transportation and pipeline inventory costs render Asian operations less advantageous.

9. The singular presence of the new Panama Canal and the continued development of the logistics and light manufacturing infrastructure in the Colón Free Trade Zone, combined with the favorable trade policies emerging from a new government and passage of new free trade agreements, makes Panama a prime location for supply chain integration, assembly, and distribution operations. The opening of the expanded canal in 2015 will dramatically alter North/Central American regional supply chain flows, with a significant amount of trade from Asia to the USA/Canada flowing to Gulf or East coast ports for further distribution. In addition, the possibility of serving South American countries such as Brazil and Argentina as well as Western Europe through Panama arises with the opening of the new canal.

10. In all cases of operating in Mexico, Costa Rica, and Panama, organizations must ensure sensitivity to local culture and policy. Organizations should build solid relationships with reliable supply chain partners who can assist them. Similarly, they should ensure that foreign nationals operating in these nations are sensitive to cultural norms and traditions and provide training to prepare staff for these engagements. In addition, they should develop programs to identify top local talent and create incentives to retain them. Knowledge of supply chain management will have to be fostered because there is a general lack of this skill set in these countries.

References

1. CIA World Factbook, 2012.
2. George Friedman, *The Geopolitics of the United States, Part 1: The Inevitable Empire* (Austin, TX: Strategic Forecasting, Inc., 2011).

3. Ibid.

4. Ibid.

5. IHS Global Insights.

6. Ibid.

7. Ibid.

8. Ibid.

9. Economist Intelligence Unit; Passport GMID.

10. Europa World Plus; IHS Global Insights.

11. Ibid.

12. IHS Global Insights.

13. Europa World Plus; IHS Global Insights.

14. Ibid.

15. Europa World Plus.

16. Europa World Plus; IHS Global Insights.

17. Europa World Plus.

18. Ibid.

19. IHS Global Insights.

20. Friedman, *The Geopolitics of the United States*; IHS Global Insights.

21. IHS Global Insights.

22. Friedman, *The Geopolitics of the United States*.

23. Europa World Plus.

24. Ibid.

25. Ibid.

26. Ibid.

27. Ibid.

28. Passport GMID.

29. CIA World Factbook, 2012.

30. Europa World Plus.

31. Economist Intelligence Unit.

32. Europa World Plus.

33. Ibid.

34. IHS Global Insight.

35. Ibid.

36. Ibid.

37. Ibid.

38. Ibid.

39. Ibid.

40. Ibid.

41. Ibid.

42. Ibid.
43. Matthew J. Drake and Nelly Diaz Rojo, "The Current State of Mexican Logistics Operations," *The Journal of International Management Studies* 3, no. 2 (2008): 92–97.
44. Economist Intelligence Unit.
45. Drake and Rojo, "The Current State of Mexican Logistics Operations."
46. Europa World Plus.
47. "Logistics and Transport: A Long Road to Travel in Central America," February 8, 2013. www.worldbank.org.
48. World Bank, "Costa Rica Competitiveness Diagnostic and Recommendations," Vol. 1, July 1, 2009. http://siteresources.worldbank.org/INTCOSTARICA/Resources/CR_Competitiveness_Vol1.pdf.
49. IHS Global Insights.
50. Ibid.
51. Europa World Plus.
52. Passport GMID.
53. Europa World Plus.
54. Ibid.
55. Ibid.
56. IHS Global Insights.
57. C. R. Canup, "Labor Availability and Quality Peak in the United States," 2010, Canup & Associates, Inc. www.areadevelopment.com/LocationUSA.
58. Klaus Schwab, "Global Competitiveness Report 2012–2013," *World Economic Forum,* 2012. www.weforum.org/gcr.
59. The Conference Board of Canada, "Labour Productivity Growth," March 2013. www.conferenceboard.ca/hcp/details/economy/measuring-productivity-canada.aspx
60. IHS Global Insights.
61. Drake and Rojo, "The Current State of Mexican Logistics Operations." *The Journal of International Management Studies,* 3, no. 2 (2008): 92–97.
62. Economist Intelligence Unit.
63. "America's Misplaced Disdain for Vocational Education," *The Economist,* June 2010. www.economist.com/node/16380980.
64. Economist Intelligence Unit, 2011.
65. Ibid.
66. Elaine Ivey, "Education in Costa Rica: The Exception in Central America," 2004.
67. Sean Mattson and Abraham Teran, "Education Trap Threatens Panama's Economic Boom," Reuters, September 6, 2011.
68. Jean-François Arvis, Monica Alina Mustra, Lauri Ojala, Ben Shepherd, and Daniel Saslavsky, "Connecting to Compete 2012: Trade Logistics in the Global Economy," The World Bank, 2012.

69. Ibid.
70. Drake and Rojo, "The Current State of Mexican Logistics Operations." *The Journal of International Management Studies,* 3, no. 2 (2008): 92–97.
71. Passport GMID.
72. "Nicaragua Approves Trans-Oceanic Canal," *Breakbulk News,* June 14. 2013.
73. Brad Plumer, "U.S. Manufacturing Making a Comeback—Or Is It Just Hype?" *The Washington Post,* May 1, 2013.

CHAPTER 12

South America

The continent of South America is home to 399 million people (2013) living in 12 nations and three territories. South America contributes 5.6 percent to global GDP, is home to 6 percent of the world's population, and is the fourth largest continent (after Asia, Africa, and North America). From a supply chain perspective, South America is important due to its vast supplies of raw materials, for its position astride key trade lanes between Asia and the eastern coast of the USA and Europe, and for its emerging consumer markets. Seven countries have been chosen to represent the region: Argentina, Brazil, Chile, Colombia, Peru, Venezuela, and Uruguay. Together, these seven comprise 5.7 percent of global GDP and 5.8 percent of global population (2012), which is well over 90 percent of both the wealth and the population of South America. In addition, each of these nations demonstrates a level of development across key aspects of economics, politics, infrastructure, and business competence that makes it worthy of consideration for supply chain opportunities.

South America bears some similarity to North America, with high rugged mountains to the west and lower flatter mountains to the east, with lowlands and plains in between (Figure 12.1). South America's long coastline has relatively few prominent peninsulas or bays. The Pacific coast in particular has very few natural harbors, except in the extreme south. The Atlantic coast has more bays and inlets, but these are generally located well away from large cities, or are isolated from the interior by coastal mountains. The islands of South America generally lie near the extreme northern and southern ends of the continent, with the notable exceptions of Trinidad, the Falklands, the Galápagos, and the many islands of the southern Chile-Tierra del Fuego region. Most of the population of South America lies along the continent's eastern and western coasts, with the interior and southern portion of the continent only sparsely populated. This makes for an interesting supply chain challenge. The population centers on the continent tend to be isolated from each other due to geographic barriers, so traditional trade patterns have focused more on external regions rather than between nations in the region.

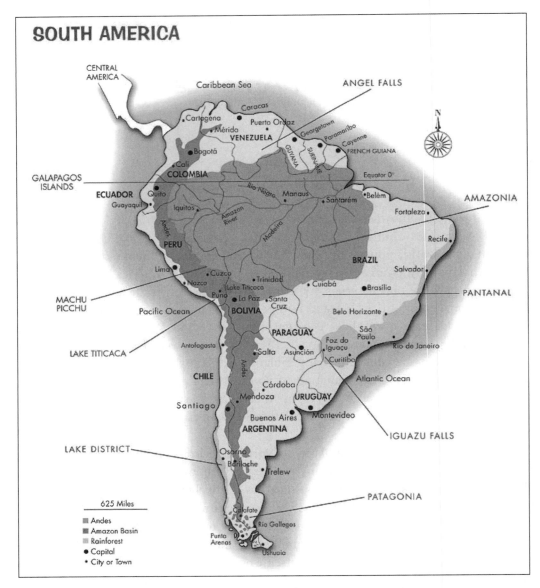

Figure 12.1   South America.

The Disintegrating Effect of Geography

The Andes, which extend more than 6400 km (4000 mi), constitute South America's most prominent geographic feature. Stretching along the west coast from the Caribbean Sea to Tierra del Fuego, the Andes form one of the world's longest continuous mountain chains and is a formidable barrier to economic commerce. For most of their length, the Andes consist of two and sometimes three cordilleras, or chains, with very deep valleys and high intermountain basins and plateaus spanning the gaps. Most of the populations of Colombia, Ecuador, Peru, and Bolivia live in these intermountain areas, where the altitude brings relief from the hot and humid equatorial climate of the lowlands. The ruggedness of the terrain and the lack of easy access through the Andes have long isolated various parts of each country and prevented building an adequate transportation system. The west coast of South America is essentially blocked from the interior by the Andes Mountains, and the southeast region of South America is additionally isolated to the north by the Amazon Basin.

All of the major rivers of South America flow to the Atlantic Ocean or the Caribbean Sea. On the western slopes of the Andes, the streams flowing to the Pacific are short and carry little water. Nearly one-third of the continent is drained by the huge Amazon River system, which has its headwaters high in the Andes and then flows across forest-covered lowlands to its mouth at the Equator. Rapids and waterfalls are common on South American rivers, largely preventing navigation. South America lacks an extensive lake system analogous to the Great Lakes of North America. Aside from reservoirs, nearly all the lakes are in or near the Andes. For instance, Lake Titicaca in the Andean Basin is 3810 meters (12,500 feet) above sea level and represents the continent's largest lake, but it is isolated from other population centers. The lakes feed the economies of the people living along their shores, but interconnections with other regions are limited.

Economic and Political Background

Understanding the Region

The pre-Colombian inhabitants of South America first developed agriculture along the coast of Peru and in the Amazon and Orinoco river basins. Agriculture and civilization advanced most rapidly in the valleys of the Andes, resulting in development of the sophisticated civilization of the Inca Empire in the 13th century. Beyond the Andes, most of the native peoples were still culturally primitive when the Europeans arrived at the end of the 15th century. The rapid Spanish colonization of South America occurred during the decades following Columbus's first landfall in 1498, while on his third voyage to the New World.

Spanish South America was ruled as the King of Spain's private property from the 16th to the early 19th centuries and was governed by a complex administrative system of Viceroys. The three primary vice-royalties were Peru, New Granada, and La Plata. Each was then divided into administrative districts presided over by Captains General, with a court of appeals established to exercise judicial authority. The Spanish colonial period was marked by a rigidly stratified society led by peninsulares (Spaniards born in Spain), followed by the creoles (persons of pure Spanish ancestry born in America). The peninsulares held all of the major offices. The mestizos (mixed Spanish and Indian ancestry) followed the creoles, and at the bottom of the social strata were Indians and Negroes.

Rivalry between Spain and Portugal caused Pope Alexander VI to draw the Line of Demarcation, which divided the known areas of the New World between Spain and Portugal. In 1500, the Portuguese explorer Pedro Alvares Cabral discovered coastal Brazil on the Portuguese side of the Line of Demarcation. Early settlement was limited to the coast, and few attempts were made to explore the interior. In Portuguese South America, the king granted large areas to nobles, who were responsible for colonization. In the mid-16th century, Brazil was united under a single colonial administration. During the 17th and 18th centuries, the interior was penetrated by missionaries and by farmers seeking land. A rigid class system did not develop in Brazil.

Mining, agriculture, and ranching were the main occupations of the South American colonists. The indigenous population was forced to work as slaves in the mines and on the haciendas (plantations). When much of the native workforce perished as a result of being overworked and of catching diseases introduced by the Europeans, African slaves were imported, especially along the northern and eastern coasts.

Roman Catholic missionaries were a powerful force in South America's colonial era, establishing many missions among the Indians. The Jesuits were one of the most influential orders; the La Plata basin was largely under their control for more than a century. The English, French, and Dutch were interested in South American trade and established settlements in the northeast.

Uprisings against the Spanish colonial governments became frequent toward the end of the 18th century. Most were led by creoles who resented Spain's tight control over their economy and politics. By 1810, revolutionary movements were under way in most of Spanish South America. Complete independence was finally achieved in 1825 after a series of bloody wars. The two great leaders of the revolution were Simón Bolívar and José de San Martín. Brazil achieved independence from Portugal in 1822, almost without bloodshed. Although Bolívar envisioned a confederation of all of Spanish South America, nine weak nations were carved out of the three Spanish vice-royalties. Many boundary disputes erupted among the new nations, leading to wars that lasted until as recently as 1942. Political instability plagued most South American countries throughout the 19th century and into the 20th century. Revolutions were frequent, and the constant turmoil led to the rise of dictatorships. Social inequalities dating from the colonial period continued. Growing pressure from the laboring and middle classes for social and political reform became widespread. Economic problems, especially inflation, were common in the period following World War II and added to the unrest.

South America's population increased rapidly in the 1950s and 1960s, and rural laborers migrated to cities in search of jobs. Land reforms were undertaken in several countries, and large estates were broken up to provide more of the rural population with land.

Economic difficulties and a heightened sense of nationalism led several countries to take control of foreign-owned industries. In the 1960s and 1970s, Communist-led revolutionaries were active in a number of countries, and most nations were at one time or another under military rule. During the 1980s, a number of countries replaced military rule with democratic rule, and by the mid-1990s all had some form of democratically elected governments. Economic problems, often caused by national debts owed to foreign banks and countries, continued into the 1990s. By the dawn of the 21st century, however, many nations in the region were recovering and experiencing strong economic growth.

Politics

The Argentine legal system is based in civil law, with the two primary pillars of its civil law system found in the Constitution of Argentina (1813) and the Civil Code of Argentina (1871). The president of Argentina serves as both the head of state and the head of government. The population of Argentina is overwhelmingly Roman Catholic, owing to the very large Spanish influence in Argentina's history. Brazil's system of law has its roots in Portuguese Civil law, with a Federal Constitution that has been in force since 1988. Brazil is a federal presidential representative democratic republic in which the president serves as both the head of state and the head of government. Chile is a presidential representative democratic republic, with a president who serves as both the head of state and the head of government. Chile's legal system is rooted in the tradition of Continental Law, and its constitution was enacted in 1980, with its most recent reformation in 2005. Colombia is a unitary constitutional republic, with a president who serves as both the head of state and the head of government. Peru is a presidential representative democratic republic, whose president serves as the head of state and the head of government and serves a five-year term. Venezuela is a federal presidential republic, with a president who serves as both the head of state and the head of government. Uruguay is a presidential representative democratic republic, in which the president serves as both the head of state and the head of government.

The Economies

The rugged South American geography has historically forced nations to rely heavily on exports destined for markets outside the continent. The fractious postcolonial political environment of the 19th century led to an economy that has traditionally been based on agriculture and exports of raw materials, with manufactured goods largely being imported. Industrialization and improvements in transportation infrastructure following World War II, combined with increasing populations, increased political stability, economic growth, and technological innovation have softened the hard geographic barriers and given rise to burgeoning domestic industries in several of the nations of South America by the 21st century.

Despite recent political turmoil, Argentina is South America's third largest economy and enjoys rich natural resources, a highly literate population, a relatively large consumer market, high levels of foreign direct investment, a diversified industrial base, and a strong export sector. Although historically dependent on livestock and grain exports, British and French investment (1875) marked the beginning of an era of economic expansion. Manufacturing surpassed agriculture in 1943, and accounted for more than 1 million employees by 1947. Juan Perón (President of Argentina from 1946 to 1955) nationalized strategic industries and services, sparking the growth of unions and the largest middle class in South America by the 1960s. Since then, however, Argentina's economic performance has been uneven; periods of both high economic growth and severe recession have resulted in uneven income distribution and increased poverty.

Argentina has a nascent mining industry, with a variety of natural mineral and energy resources, and is home to a variety of industrial sectors including automotive, chemicals, pharmaceuticals, and textiles. Interestingly, La Vaca Muerta in Argentina is now believed to be the world's third largest shale oil reserve, behind those of the United States and China. However, the challenging geography of South America has led to slower development of this sector. Argentina may well turn out to be one of the future world's largest energy providers; this would have very clear supply chain management implications, including the potential of increased economic growth in Argentina and the associated benefit for its Mercosur trading partners. More than 60 percent of Argentina's GDP comes from a diversified service sector, including substantial revenue from tourism.

Brazil is one of the 10 largest markets in the world and the largest in South America, producing steel, cement, consumer durables, petroleum, and petrochemicals. Brazil became one of the region's earliest industrial powers, as profits from the export of coffee, sugar, gold, and silver were invested in nascent industrial and commercial enterprises. These enterprises benefited further when the World Wars I and II interrupted trade, effectively providing protection to the domestic industrial sector. By the last quarter of the 20th century, exports had become increasingly sophisticated, and high-tech and heavy manufacturing, including telecommunications equipment, aircraft, and automobiles, increased. Several years of sustained economic growth, credible macroeconomic policies, and a rising middle class have positioned Brazil as a leading recipient of foreign investment and an emerging player in global commerce. In addition, Brazil has become the focus of the world's attention as the host to the World Cup in 2014 and the Olympics in 2016. These and other high-profile international events signal increased international attention on the consumer markets in Brazil. For instance, Nike recently partnered with DHL to better serve the quickly growing demand for its products in Brazil. This partnership is designed to support Nike's global and complex supply chain requirements while better meeting the needs of the Brazilian consumer. By 2025, Brazil and its Mercosur trade bloc are expected to become the world's third largest automobile producer behind the United States and China. On a global basis, automobile manufacturers are moving manufacturing into the region to support its burgeoning middle class. Volkswagen, Fiat, GM, and Ford have been manufacturing in Brazil for years, but new manufacturers such as Kia, Hyundai, Honda, Nissan, BMW, Chery, Geely, JAC, Hafei, Tata, and Mahindra are rushing into Brazil.[1]

With the fertile Central Valley, a long Pacific Ocean coastline, and abundant mineral wealth, Chilean exports traditionally focused on wheat and leather, fish, timber, and mining products. Today Chile is the world's largest copper producer and a significant producer of gold, silver, iron ore, precious metals, molybdenum, and nitrates. Increasingly open markets have encouraged development of newer commodities such as fruit, wine, and wood products as well as transport and other export services.

The natural resources of Colombia are varied and extensive with most of its territory and oceans still unexplored. Colombia has one of the largest open pit coal mines in the world in the region of Cerrejon in the Guajira Peninsula. It also has oil rigs and natural gas extraction in the eastern plains. Colombia is the main producer of emeralds and an important participant in gold, silver, iron, salt, platinum, and uranium extraction. During the 19th century, Medellín became the country's economic center, dominating coffee, gold mining, and the nascent textile industry. By the 1920s, Colombia had become the world's leading exporter of coffee, but the Great Depression ended a brief coffee-led period of prosperity in the 1930s. This led to a policy of import substitution, promoting local industry and fostering steady growth throughout the latter part of the 20th century. Colombia is a rare model of economic and financial stability in South America despite violent drug wars that began in the 1980s. Today Colombia has a free-market economy with major commercial and investment ties to the United States.

Important mineral resources are found in Peru's mountainous and coastal areas, and the coastal waters provide excellent fishing grounds. The Peruvian economy has been growing at an average rate of 6.4 percent per year since 2002, with a stable but slightly appreciating exchange rate and low inflation. Despite Peru's strong macroeconomic performance, dependence on minerals, metals exports, and imported foodstuffs subjects its economy to fluctuations in world prices. Poor infrastructure hinders the spread of growth to Peru's inland areas. A growing number of Peruvians are sharing in the benefits of growth, but inequality continues to pose a political challenge. Since 2006, Peru has signed trade deals with the USA, Canada, Singapore, China, Korea, Mexico, and Japan, concluded negotiations with the European Free Trade Association and Chile, and begun trade talks with Central American countries and others.

Formerly a major coffee exporter, the first commercial drilling of oil in Venezuela in 1917 and the oil boom of the 1920s brought the coffee era to an end and eventually transformed the nation from a relatively poor agrarian society into South America's wealthiest state. By 1928, Venezuela was the world's leading exporter of oil and second in total petroleum production. Venezuela remained the world's leading oil exporter until 1970, the year of its peak oil production. Reliance on petroleum export revenues rendered the country vulnerable to variations in global oil prices, which resulted in "boom and bust" cycles. High petroleum prices led to expansionary spending policies, which, in turn, led to severe fiscal problems when the petroleum price decreased. The strong rise in the international price for oil between 2003 and 2008 boosted economic performance, allowing the government to increase public sector spending and investment. Nationalization of industries by the Chavez government, together with increasingly restrictive business policies, has caused significant uncertainty in Venezuela's economic growth.

In Uruguay, beef, mutton, and wool exports sparked remarkable growth and a high standard of living from the 1800s until the 1950s. Advanced social welfare programs redistributed wealth from the livestock sector to the rest of the economy to raise the standard of living for a majority of the population and contributed to state-funded efforts to build new domestic industries in Uruguay. Export earnings faltered in the 1950s as livestock production reached its limits. Without a well-developed industrial sector, it became increasingly difficult for Uruguay to uphold the social welfare model it had adopted, resulting in a decades-long period of economic stagnation that did not recover until global commodity prices improved in the 1990s. Uruguay's economy remains characterized by an export-oriented agricultural sector, a well-educated workforce, and high levels of social spending. Economic growth for Uruguay averaged 8 percent annually during the period from 2004 to 2008. The country managed to avoid a recession during the recent global fiscal crisis and maintained positive growth rates through higher public expenditure and investment.

The Markets

South American markets have enjoyed considerable growth over the last 20 years, and they represent one of the more compelling emerging markets in the world. The nations of South America have established trading relationships to spur growth in regional markets and industries and to lessen reliance on global commodity prices. The biggest trade bloc in South America has been Mercosur, comprising Argentina, Brazil, Paraguay, Uruguay, and Venezuela. Associate states include Bolivia, Chile, Colombia, Ecuador, and Peru. The second biggest trade bloc is the Andean Community of Nations, comprised of Bolivia, Chile, Colombia, Ecuador, Peru, and Venezuela. A recent newcomer, the Pacific Alliance, was established in 2012 as a trade agreement between Chile, Colombia, Mexico, and Peru. Initially, it was unclear whether this trade agreement would lead to improved regional trade. However, in mid-2003 the leaders of Chile, Mexico, Colombia, and Peru decided to work together to move the Pacific Alliance forward. Interested in the economic opportunities that may be created by the Pacific Alliance, Panama, Guatemala, Costa Rica, Spain, and Canada are currently being considered for full membership. The Pacific

Alliance trade bloc represents 209 million people and 35 percent of total Latin American and Caribbean GDP.[2]

Location of Markets

Argentina

Argentina, the second largest country in South America and the eighth largest in the world, occupies approximately 2.7 million km² (1 million mi²). It is situated in the temperate zone of the Southern Hemisphere and has considerable variation in climate, topography, and natural resources (Figure 12.2). Its main geographic features include the Andes Mountains and surrounding areas, the fertile plains region known as the Pampas, and the nearly 5000 km (3107 mi) of coastline (including islands) along the Atlantic Ocean. The Paraná River forms Argentina's northern border with Paraguay, then winds its way through Argentina to the Atlantic Ocean, following the southern coast of Uruguay. Argentina claims a section of Antarctica and several South Atlantic islands that are administered by the United Kingdom.

Argentina is a nation of 40.8 million people (2011) with its capital in Buenos Aires. Although it was a Spanish colony, the country's population and culture were heavily shaped by immigrants from throughout Europe, most particularly Italy, which provided the largest percentage of newcomers from 1860 to 1930. Argentina is highly urbanized, with the 10 largest metropolitan areas accounting for half of the population and with fewer than 1 in 10 living in rural areas. About 3 million people live in Buenos Aires proper, and the metropolitan area is home to about 13 million people, making it one of the largest urban areas in the world. Other metropolitan areas with populations greater than 1 million include Córdoba and Rosario. Ninety-two percent of population lives in large urban areas, and this population is increasing at a rate of 1.1 percent annually. The primacy rate, the percent of the population living in the largest city (Buenos Aires), is 35.

Brazil

Brazil is the largest nation in South America in terms of both population and landmass (Figure 12.3). It occupies most of the eastern part of the South American continent and its geographic heartland, as well as various islands in the Atlantic Ocean. Much of the climate is tropical, although the south is relatively temperate. The Amazon River is the widest river in the world and is second in length only to the Nile. The rainforest that covers the Amazon Basin constitutes almost half of the rainforest on Earth. In addition, the Paraná has its source in Brazil. On Brazil's eastern border, the Atlantic coastline extends 7367 km (4578 mi).

Brazil is home to 196.7 million people (2011) living in 8,456,510 km² (3,265,077 mi²) with its capital in Brasilia. São Paulo and Rio de Janeiro are by far the largest Brazilian cities.

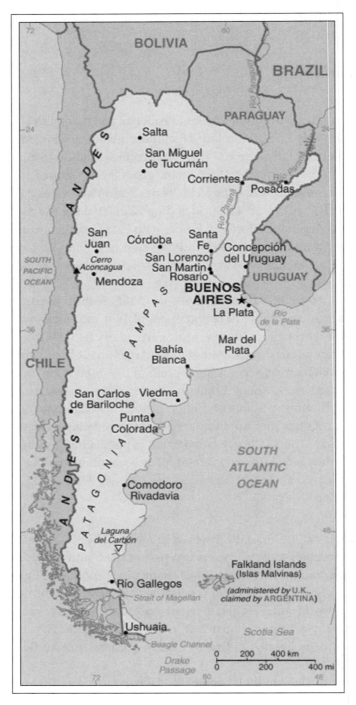

Figure 12.2   Argentina.

Figure 12.3 Brazil.

Eighty-seven percent of Brazilians live in urban areas, increasing at a rate of 1.1 percent per year, with a primacy rate in São Paulo of 12. Although its population growth has been trending lower as a result of falling birthrates, the age profile is extremely young, with 40 percent of the population under 24 years old. Brazil has the highest degree of intermarriage among different ethnic groups in the world. Fifty-five percent of the population is white (including Portuguese, German, Italian, Spanish, and Polish), 38 percent are mixed black and white, and 6 percent are black. Most of Brazil's population is Roman Catholic (74 percent), with about 18 percent Protestant.

Chile

Chile extends 4329 km (2690 mi) from the Atacama Desert, bordering Peru in the north and Patagonia in the south (Figure 12.4). Cape Horn, the southernmost point in the Americas,

Figure 12.4   Chile.

where the Pacific and Atlantic oceans meet, is Chilean territory. The breadth of the country does not exceed 180 km (112 mi) between the Pacific Ocean coastline to the west and the Andes to the east. Its length accounts for its mineral wealth and climate diversity; heavy rainfall in the south is distinct from the temperate Central Valley and the extremely arid north. Chile is located on a fault line rendering it prone to earthquakes. Twenty-eight major earthquakes, all with a force greater than 6.9 on the Richter scale, struck Chile in the 20th century, and the most recent occurred in February of 2010. Chile has an estimated population of 17.2 million people (2011), which is growing at a decreasing rate of about 1.0 percent per year. Chile's population is aging as a result of a slowing population growth rate and increases in life expectancy. Most Chileans live in urban areas (89 percent), a trend that is growing by 1.1 percent per year, of these, 39 percent live in San Jose. As with other nations of South America, the population is largely Roman Catholic (89 percent), with 11 percent Protestant. Over two-thirds of the population lives in the Central Valley region that includes Santiago and other main cities. In 2011, approximately 50 percent of the population lived in the greater Santiago area and in the neighboring Valparaíso region. The country has become increasingly urbanized, with 87.2 percent of the population estimated to live in cities and towns. In recent decades, a centralizing tendency has been slowed by a strong growth in mining concentrated in the north, and tourism and nontraditional exports, such as salmon farming and methanol production, in the south.

Colombia

Colombia is the only South American nation that has access to both the Atlantic (through the Caribbean Sea) and Pacific oceans (Figure 12.5). Colombia's population lives mostly in the mountainous western portion of the country in or near the capital city of Bogotá and along the northern coastline. The southern and eastern portions of the country are mostly sparsely inhabited tropical rainforest and inland tropical plains containing small farming communities and indigenous tribes. This geographic arrangement hampers connections and trade with the rest of the world.

Colombia, a country of 45,239,079 people with its capital in Bogotá, is the second most populous country in South America, behind Brazil. Although Colombia has one of the lowest urbanization levels in the region (75 percent), it is rapidly urbanizing at a rate of 1.7 percent annually; the primacy rate is 25. Although experiencing rapid population growth in the 20th century, four decades of civil war and urban violence, combined with mass poverty, have forced millions of Colombians to leave their country. Today the population growth rate in Colombia is 1.13 percent, with a median age of 28 years. Seventy-seven percent of the population lives in cities, including 30 cities with a population over 100,000. The nine eastern lowlands departments, constituting about 54 percent of Colombia's area, are home to less than 3 percent of the population and have a population density of less than one person per square kilometer. The vast majority (over 90 percent) of Colombians are Catholic.

Figure 12.5 Colombia.

Peru

Peru is divided into three distinct geographic regions (Figure 12.6). The best known of these is the central high sierra of the Andes. The second region is a narrow, lowland coastal region that is a northern extension of the Atacama Desert and is generally known as the most arid region on the planet. The climate along Peru's shores is made cooler and less dry by La Garuùa, a dense fog created by the collision of the frigid waters of the Humboldt Current with the heated sands of the Atacama. Lima, Trujillo, and Chiclayo, three of Peru's major population centers, are located along this coastal desert. Peru's third region is made up of the dense forest that surrounds the headwaters of the Amazon beneath the eastern slopes of the Andes. This part of the country, which represents 60 percent of the national territory and includes the Amazon, Marañón, Huallaga, and Ucayali rivers, is so

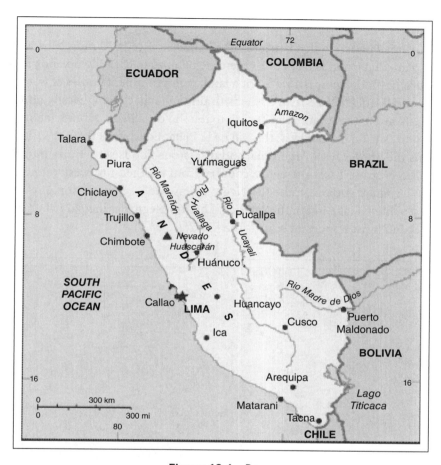

Figure 12.6 Peru.

inaccessible that the region's capital of Iquitos, a city of 400,000, is accessible only by air or by boat up the Amazon.

Peru, with its capital in Lima, is the third largest country in South America by geography (1.29 million km², or just under 500,000 mi²) and, with a population estimated at 29.4 million, the fourth most populous. Seventy-seven percent of Peruvians live in urban areas, growing at 1.6 percent annually; of these, 40 percent live in Lima. Peru is host to a very young population, with the median age just over 25 years of age. Peru is a multiethnic country that was formed by the amalgamation of different cultures and ethnicities, although Amerindian and mestizo form the largest ethnic groups. The languages spoken in Peru include Spanish (official), Quechua (official), and Aymara. Most Peruvians are Catholic, and the Catholic faith is closely aligned with the Peruvian government. In fact, Catholicism is the only religion taught in the public schools.

Uruguay

Uruguay is a small nation with a land area of 173,620 km² (67,035 mi²). Most of Uruguay is a rolling plain that extends from the Argentine pampas to the hilly uplands of southern Brazil (Figure 12.7). Uruguay is a water-rich land, with prominent bodies of water marking its borders on all sides. Three river systems drain the land, flowing westward to the Río Uruguay, eastward to the Atlantic, and south to the Río de la Plata. Montevideo, the capital and major port, sits on the banks of the Río de la Plata. Low banks flank the Río Uruguay, which forms the border with Argentina, and disastrous floods sometimes inundate large areas. The Río Negro crosses the entire country from northeast to west before emptying into the Río Uruguay. A dam on the Río Negro at Paso de los Toros forms a reservoir that is the largest artificial lake in South America. The Río Negro's principal tributary and the country's second most important river is the Río Yí.

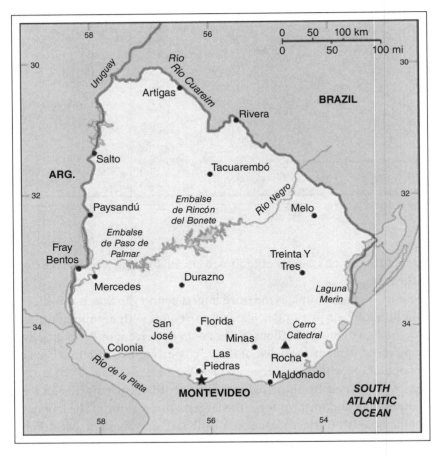

Figure 12.7   Uruguay.

The total population of Uruguay is 3,316,328 (2011), making it one of the least populated countries in the world. Montevideo, with about 1.5 million inhabitants, is the capital and largest city. Montevideo is only 200 km (124 mi) away from Buenos Aires in neighboring Argentina. The rest of the urban population primarily lives in 20 cities. In total, the urban population represents 92 percent of the population, although this level is relatively stable at 0.4 percent growth per year. Uruguay enjoys a high literacy rate (97.3 percent) and a large urban middle class. As a result of a low birthrate, high life expectancy, and a relatively high rate of emigration of younger people, Uruguay's population is mature, with a median age of 33.6 years. Unlike other South American countries, most of the population of Uruguay is white, with very few mestizos (about 8 percent) and no indigenous Amerindians. Uruguay is considered the most secular country in South America. About half of Uruguay's population is Roman Catholic, with about 11 percent Protestant, and the remaining with no religious affiliation.

Venezuela

Venezuela features a total land area of 882,050 km² (340,561 mi²) and 2800 km (1740 mi) of coastline (Figure 12.8). There are four well-defined regions in Venezuela, including the Maracaibo lowlands in the northwest; the northern mountains, which extend from the Colombian border along the coast; the wide Orinoco plains (llanos) in central Venezuela; and the Guiana Highlands to the southeast. Lake Maracaibo is the largest lake in South America; the low swampy shores and areas beneath the lake hold most of Venezuela's petroleum deposits. The lake is shallow and separated from the Caribbean by a series of islands and sandbars, although a channel has been cut through the sandbars to facilitate shipping between the lake and the Caribbean. The Orinoco is by far the most important of the more than 1000 rivers in the country. Flowing more than 2500 km (1553 mi) to the Atlantic from its source in the Guiana Highlands at the Brazilian border, the Orinoco is the world's eighth largest river and the largest in South America after the Amazon.

The Venezuelan population was estimated at about 28 million in 2011. As a result of a high birthrate, a comparatively low death rate, and significant immigration, Venezuela has a young population, with a median age of 26.1, with 20 percent of the population younger than 20 years old. Eighty-five percent of the population is concentrated in urban areas along Venezuela's northern coastal mountain strip, including Caracas (the capital), Maracay, Maracaibo, and Valencia. The primacy rate in Caracas is 11. Although nearly half of Venezuela's geographic area lies south of the Orinoco River, that area contains only 5 percent of the population. In total, 93 percent of Venezuelans live in urban areas, a number that is growing at 1.7 percent per year. Approximately half of the population is of racially mixed origin, including European/Amerindian, European/African, and Amerindian/African. Spanish is the official language, although numerous indigenous dialects are spoken. Venezuela is a predominantly Roman Catholic nation (92 percent).

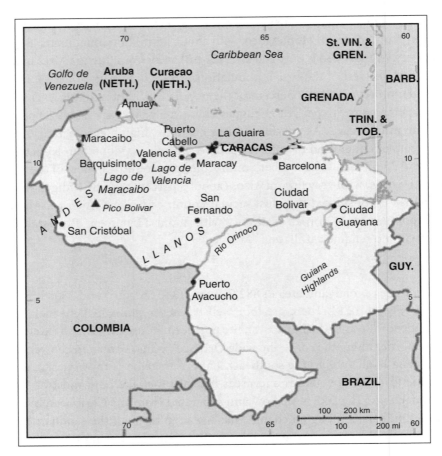

Figure 12.8   Venezuela.

Supply Chain Theme: A Region Divided

The dominant theme for South America that is relevant to supply chain managers who may be considering developing operations in this region are the barriers established by its geography. These natural barriers tend to delineate and separate nations and isolate South American population centers. The largest of these barriers are the Andes Mountains and its affiliated ranges. Where mountains do not interfere, the Amazon and its surrounding marshes act as a large sea, dividing the rest of the continent's major population centers.[3] Although this geography has dampened the scale of conflict between South American nations, the barriers have severely limited economic interaction between the peoples residing in different regions of the continent. As a result, supply chain managers interested in sourcing, manufacturing, or distribution in the region will need separate plans for each geographic area in which they plan to operate. Colombia and Venezuela are accessible via Atlantic or Caribbean ports; Colombia also has a Pacific coastline. Brazil, Uruguay, and Argentina are Atlantic seaboard nations, and Chile and Peru are only accessible via the Pacific Ocean. Flows of goods between the nations, and even between cities within individual nations, are difficult to achieve via land routes, although this may improve in coming years thanks to plans for massive infrastructure development projects.

Assessing the Maturity Level of South American Supply Chains

This section assesses the supply chain maturity of the seven selected countries of South America using the EPIC (Economy, Politics, Infrastructure, Competence) dimensions presented in detail in Chapter 2.

Economy

An assessment of the key elements of the Economy dimension follows, including economic output and growth rate, population, foreign direct investment, exchange rate stability and consumer price inflation, and balance of trade. A summary of Economy elements for each of the focal nations of South America is presented at the end of the section.

Economic Output and Growth Rate

South America, with 6 percent of the global GDP, has caught the attention of global businesses seeking locations for manufacturing as well as new markets for consumer products. The GDP (2012, purchasing power parity [PPP]) of the seven nations included in this research varies from a low of US$53.2 billion in Uruguay to a high of US$2393 billion for Brazil. It is significant that these nations have continued to grow during the most recent five-year period despite the challenging global economic environment, achieving real growth in excess of 3 percent across the region. GDP and growth rates for the last five years are shown in Table 12.1.

Table 12.1 GDP and Growth Rates

	Argentina	Brazil	Chile	Colombia	Peru	Uruguay	Venezuela
GDP (PPP (millions of USD)*	$746,900	$2,362,000	$319,400	$500,000	$325,400	$53,550	$402,100
Global Rank*	21	7	42	28	40	93	33
GDP Growth (2005–2011**)	7.09%	4.16%	3.96%	4.77%	7.1%	5.78%	3.78%

*CIA World Factbook 2012; **WTO 2012.

Agriculture and agricultural-related products comprise the traditional economic output of many South American nations and continue to be central to the economies of the region. The increasing sophistication of agribusiness has enabled the South American nations to produce and export a variety of agricultural products to the United States, Europe, and China, including beef and leather, cereals, cotton and wool (Argentina, Uruguay); and cane, cocoa, oranges, bananas, beef, corn, tobacco, and soybeans (Brazil, Colombia). In addition, trade arrangements within the region have made intraregional trade an increasingly important source of GDP for South American nations. Nontraditional agricultural exports such as cut flowers are developing significant overseas markets for Colombia, and the fishing industry continues to account for a significant portion of exports for both Chile and Peru. Chile is also a major source of hardwood. In many nations, farmland and forests are as yet underutilized and remain an important factor in the region's growing competitiveness.

Mineral and petroleum exports are another major source of income for certain South American nations. Chile and Peru are global leaders in copper production, and also export large amounts of iron, silver, molybdenum, gold, zinc, manganese, and lead. Colombia and Venezuela also enjoy considerable mineral resources, especially coal and natural gas reserves. Although these products are traditional exports of the region, state-of-the-art production technology in mining and petroleum exploration and production has increased competitiveness on the global market. Venezuela has the largest oil and gas reserves in the Western Hemisphere, and the discovery of potentially large oil fields in Brazil promises to boost the Brazilian petroleum industry for decades to come. Argentina also has large proven reserves of crude petroleum and is thought to have the world's third largest reserve of shale oil.

Many of the South American nations have diversified into other important economic sectors. For instance, the Brazilian telecommunications sector has often been cited as one of the largest and most attractive of all emerging telecommunications markets. In addition, Brazil has the largest vehicle market in South America, with the automotive sector accounting for nearly 10 percent of total exports. Textile manufacturing in Peru has been boosted by trade concessions with the United States, and the availability of low-cost energy in Venezuela has given that country's steel industry a comparative advantage.

Population

South America represents 5.8 percent of the global population, ranging from the fifth largest country in world (Brazil) to one of the smallest countries (Uruguay). The South American region is not the fastest growing region in the world, but it is definitely growing. Venezuela leads the growth at 1.67 percent per year, and Uruguay has the slowest growth of only 0.18 percent. Similarly, South America's population is not the youngest in the globe, but it is considerably younger than mature markets in North America and Europe.

The median age in Venezuela is 26.1 years; Uruguayans are the oldest population, with a median age of 33.6 years.

Foreign Direct Investment

Several nations of South America have been leaders in attracting foreign direct investment (FDI) over the last decade, with growing market and economic sectors that have overcome concerns about corruption and bureaucracy. Most have been able to achieve a sufficient level of political stability, and transparency has liberalized investment laws to improve foreign direct investment.

There are four identifiable segments of nations within the focal group with respect to attractiveness for FDI. At the top of the list, Chile and Uruguay, featuring stable democracies, respect for the rule of law, and favorable investment laws, represent the most favorable investment options. In particular, the mining industry in Chile has enjoyed significant FDI interest. Brazil stands alone in the second segment of the seven South American nations. Although property rights, corruption, and restrictive labor regulations continue to be a concern, vast market opportunities have made Brazil one of the most attractive destinations for FDI among emerging-market economies since 2007. Foreign companies are also using Brazil as a base for operations in South America. The third segment includes Argentina, Colombia, and Peru, where agriculture, automotive, tourism, mining, and petroleum have attracted investment from the United States, Europe, China, and even intraregion investment from Brazil. Finally, Venezuela's weakened economy and deteriorating business climate have created sharp disincentives for FDI as investors grow wary of the latest wave of nationalizations, poor contractual agreements and private property rights security, and the general aim of the late President Hugo Chavez's economic policies.

Exchange Rate Stability and Consumer Price Inflation

Exchange rate stability and inflation vary widely across the seven focal nations of South America. Most of the currencies are allowed to float freely, providing heightened flexibility against the wild swings associated with commodity prices. With the exception of Brazil and Venezuela, however, the nations of South America suffer exchange rate fluctuations that exceed those of most industrialized nations, although the rate of fluctuation is not nearly as high as it was in previous eras. Brazil uses a floating exchange rate for its currency, the real, to provide flexibility from exogenous shocks. The currency has steadily strengthened against the U.S. dollar since 2008. Venezuela has a fixed-exchange rate system with foreign-exchange controls. The unit of currency is the strong Bolívar, which is pegged to the U.S. dollar. Venezuela suffers from a second "parallel" foreign exchange market that exists to evade exchange controls. The stability of currencies in Chile, Colombia, and Peru lags behind those of the major industrial nations, but they are considered stable when compared to other countries in the region.

Chile (Chilean peso) and Colombia (Colombian peso) have adopted free-floating currency regimes, reflecting their confidence in the market to autonomously determine the value of their national currencies. Both currencies have appreciated strongly in recent years, reflecting robust capital inflows (including foreign direct investment, export earnings, and foreign debt) and strong reserve positions. In Peru, the Nuevo Sol is supposedly free floating, but monetary authorities keep a tight lid on liquidity in the markets, sharply reducing the currency's ability to fluctuate. Argentina and Uruguay have both struggled with exchange rate stability. Increased controls in Argentina (Argentine dollar) have fueled speculation that the Argentine dollar will stabilize. Argentina, however, also has a parallel market (called the "blue dollar") that impedes government control of the currency. Uruguay has experienced severe instability recently as the international financial community withdrew support for the Uruguayan peso in response to economic uncertainties regarding the sovereign risk turbulence in Europe. Tight monetary policies, however, prevented the peso from free falling against the U.S. dollar.

Brazil, Chile, and Colombia have experienced relatively low inflation, on par with the industrialized world, after their respective central banks adopted monetary policies to target inflation and abolish automatic indexing of wage increases to inflation. In Peru, monetary policy has set the targeted inflation rate at 2.0 percent plus or minus one percentage point, while the central bank publishes its open market operations on its website each day to improve transparency. Argentina and Uruguay have struggled with rampant inflation, although the central banks in both nations have intervened to help stabilize the local currency and maintain inflation at much tamer, lower rates than in the recent past. Similar to the concerns that have affected FDI in Venezuela, inflation in these nations far exceed global and regional averages as foreign investment flees the country for safer havens.

Balance of Trade

Five of the seven focal nations of South America enjoy positive trade balances, partly as a result of government attempts to limit import growth and partly due to demand for mineral, petroleum, and agricultural products in Europe, China, the United States, Korea, Japan, and India. In addition, an increased demand for manufactured goods fueled by the two predominant trading blocs—the Andean Community of Nations (Bolivia, Chile, Colombia, Ecuador, Peru, and Venezuela) and Mercosur (Argentina, Brazil, Paraguay, Uruguay, and Venezuela; associate states include Bolivia, Chile, Colombia, Ecuador, and Peru)—has increased intraregional export. The weakened economy in Europe, as well as fluctuations of minerals and petroleum prices on the global market, represent significant areas of uncertainty for South American exports. Concerns over the robustness of Mercosur are rising as political interests have begun to hold sway over economic ones. The addition of Venezuela has increased the politicization of the bloc. Also, the new Pacific Alliance trade bloc may well change the nature of several of the South American nations' regional and global trading partners as well as overall levels of trade.

Argentina, which has implemented one of the more restrictive trade regimes in the region, recently lifted controversial trade barriers that curbed economic growth and caused widespread claims that it was violating World Trade Organization rules. The new rules get rid of most nonautomatic licenses that required importers to get special approval to buy certain goods. The licenses severely limited trade with Brazil and other trade partners. Importing companies, however, still have to present sworn affidavits when permits are issued.[4]

Colombia and Uruguay have each experienced recent negative trade balances. Colombia's export earnings are dominated by primary commodities, making the country vulnerable to fluctuating commodity prices. Uruguay is highly dependent on foreign energy, meaning that volatile energy prices, and particularly oil prices, have a significant effect on the country's imports.

Table 12.2 presents the scores for the Economy dimension, and Table 12.3 presents a summary of the strengths and weaknesses of each of the focal nations of South America.

Politics

An assessment of key elements of the Politics dimension follows, including the ease of doing business, bureaucracy, and corruption; legal and regulatory framework (including tax codes and tariffs); political stability; and protection of intellectual property rights. A summary of the Politics elements for each of the focal nations of South America is presented at the end of the section.

Table 12.2   Scores for the Economy Dimension

Economy	Economic Output and Growth Rate	Population Size	Foreign Direct Investment	Exchange Rate Stability/CPI	Balance of Trade	Overall Grade
30%	35%	25%	20%	15%	5%	100%
Argentina	A⁻	A⁻	B	D⁻	C	B
Brazil	A⁻	A	A⁻	B⁻	C	A⁻
Chile	B	B	A⁻	A⁻	B	B⁺
Colombia	B⁺	A⁻	B⁺	B⁻	C	B⁺
Peru	B⁺	B⁺	A⁻	A⁻	B⁺	B⁺
Uruguay	B	C	B	B⁻	C	B⁻
Venezuela	B	B⁺	C	F	D	C⁺

Table 12.3 Strengths and Weaknesses Summary: Economic Dimension

Grade	Strengths	Weaknesses
Argentina: B	GDP and GDP growth strong; good economic strength in petroleum and agriculture; large consumer population; strong FDI environment; positive trade balance.	Exchange rate unstable; high inflation; stable and slowly aging population; very high tax rate; high cost of labor; some restrictive trade laws.
Brazil: A⁻	GDP size and growth strong; strong economic sectors in agriculture, petroleum, and increasingly manufactured goods; large population that is young and growing; strong FDI; high trade volumes; relatively low-cost labor.	Some exchange rate instability as real strengthens; moderate inflation; high tax rate.
Chile: B⁺	Significant GDP with slow but steady growth; strong mineral resources, forestry, and fishing sectors; relatively stable inflation; strong FDI; positive trade balance with many FTAs; low tax rate; moderate labor costs.	Small and relatively aging population.
Colombia: B⁺	Strong GDP with moderate growth; strong mineral, energy, and agricultural sectors; sizeable, young, and growing population; moderate FDI; low inflation rate.	Exchange rate becoming more unfavorable as peso strengthens; low trade balance.
Peru: B⁺	Significant GDP with strong growth; strong mineral and agricultural sectors; sizeable, young, and growing population; attractive FDI, especially in mining; sustainable inflation rate; stable exchange rate; good trade balance.	Low overall GDP; risk of commodity market price softening.
Uruguay: B⁻	Good GDP growth; strong agricultural and textile sectors; recent FDI growth.	Small GDP; high risk of commodity market price softening; small, aging, and slowly growing population; exchange rate instability and high inflation; low trade levels.
Venezuela: C⁺	Plentiful oil and gas resources; young and growing population; stable exchange rate; good trade balance.	Recent negative growth; economy and balance of trade based on global oil and gas prices; negative FDI due to fear of government intervention in business; rampant inflation; poor trade relations.

Ease of Doing Business, Bureaucracy, and Corruption

Argentina has a high level of bureaucracy. Privatization has gone some way toward reducing its burden, but a decade of economic reform has proved insufficient to completely change the frustratingly cumbersome bureaucracy. Argentina ranks in the 59th percentile of the World Bank World Government Index (WGI) control of corruption rating, and 47th in government effectiveness. Brazil has long been known for highly bureaucratic procedures, and corruption remains a problem. Brazil ranks 57th on the World Bank WGI government effectiveness rating, and only 40th for control of corruption. The Chilean trade regime has not faced the same severe corruption problems that have affected other Latin American countries. High levels of accountability and transparency may be found in Chile's government, and this, combined with low levels of bureaucracy, have ensured that cases of corruption are rare. Chile ranked 90th on the World Bank WGI control of corruption rating, and 84th in government effectiveness. Levels of corruption in Colombia are lower than in other major countries of the region, but corruption remains a well-entrenched practice in business, politics, and society. Colombia is ranked 43rd on the World Bank WGI control of corruption rating, and 61st in government effectiveness.[5]

Corruption is widespread in Peru due to largely poorly paid, low-ranking public officials. Bribery to secure favorable rulings is widely practiced, and political interference has not disappeared. Peru has signed the Inter-American Convention Against Corruption from the Organization of American States (OAS). It ranks in the 50th percentile of the World Bank WGI control of corruption rating, and 47th in government effectiveness. Corruption levels in Uruguay are perceived as low. Anticorruption legislation is strong and subject to continuous updates. It ranks in the 86th percentile of the World Bank WGI control of corruption rating, and 71st in government effectiveness. Drug trafficking and smuggling contraband have corrupted business, military, and political circles in Venezuela, although the level is hard to establish. According to the 2011 Transparency International Corruption Perceptions Index, the country has become the second most corrupt in the Latin American and Caribbean region, surpassed only by Haiti. Foreign companies must conduct due diligence checks if entering into partnership or joint ventures with Venezuelan businesses. Venezuela is ranked in the bottom 7th percentile of the World Bank WGI control of corruption rating, and the bottom 15th in government effectiveness.[6]

Chile leads the South American focal nations in ease of doing business, ranking 39th out of 183 surveyed countries for the ease of doing business according to the World Bank's 2012 Doing Business report, although trading across borders and enforcing contracts are more bureaucratic. All foreign firms are guaranteed free access to exchange markets. Capital repatriation can take place after one year has lapsed since the money was brought into the country. Peru is among the world economies making the most improvement in the World Bank report, ranking in 41st place out of 183. These changes were tied to easing procedures for foreign investors. Improvements in starting a business, registering a property, dealing with construction permits, and trading across borders, in particular, explain the upgrade in ranking. The Peruvian government actively encourages and tries to attract foreign and domestic investment, and there are no significant restrictions to investment in Peru. Colombia has tended to have a smaller bureaucracy than most of its regional peers, but bureaucratic procedures can still be cumbersome. Efforts have been made to decrease the level of bureaucratic hurdles in Colombia over the past few years. This has improved the efficiency of dealing with regulatory authorities for obtaining licenses and approvals. Colombia improved to 42nd in the World Bank ease of doing business ranking.

Uruguay ranked 90th out of 183 economies in the ease of doing business in 2012. Despite improvements in some areas, including business start-ups, the high levels of red tape prevalent in most areas of public administration continue to negatively affect the country's competitiveness. The legal environment for business is good, benefiting from Uruguay's high overall political stability. Argentina ranks 113th, reflecting a weakening across all measures of ease with the exception of closing a business. The government controls utilities prices and places limits on maximum foreign participation in some sectors. The government has also reasserted control over some privatized industries for failing to meet contractual obligations in terms of services or in investing and setting tariffs at levels approved by the state. Most controversially, the Argentine government effectively renationalized the pensions sector in late 2008.

Brazil ranks 126th out of 183 in the ease of doing business 2012 report, despite recent improvements to eliminate the distinction between foreign and domestic capital and to open certain protected industry sectors to foreign investment, including petroleum, telecommunications, mining, power generation, and internal transport. Legal and bureaucratic obstacles to setting up new businesses remain, including the rigidity of labor laws and excessive bureaucracy. Although Venezuela still has a full legal framework in place for international investment, and investment controversies can still be disputed through arbitration procedures, dealing with public officials is frustratingly slow. Low-paid officials often supplement their income by accepting payments to speed up administrative proceedings. As a result, Venezuela has the lowest ranking of the focal group, at 177th out of 183.

Legal and Regulatory Framework: Tax Codes and Tariffs

The legal system adopted by South American nations is modeled on the Roman civil law system and can be compared to the French, Italian, or Spanish legal structures. It is codified, and laws are issued by the federal government, the states, and the municipalities, with each level of government having a specific sphere of authority. Constitutionally, each nation is a variation of a democratic republic featuring a popularly elected president who heads the executive branch, bicameral legislatures with legal jurisdiction, and judiciary branches that rule on constitutional and legal questions.[7]

Chile and Uruguay represent the most advantageous tax environments in South America.[8] Chile features the most competitive tax rates among Latin American countries and a transparent tax administration that is generally favorable for business. The corporate income tax rate returned to 17 percent in 2013 after a temporary increase was needed to raise funds for the reconstruction efforts following the earthquake that struck the country in February 2010. Chile also offers a variety of tax incentives for investment, both at the industry and geographical levels, and there are two tax-free zones in Iquique and Punta Arenas. Uruguay's corporate income tax rate stands at 25 percent. Uruguay also offers an array of tax incentives as part of its investment promotions program, which includes tax benefits to some industries (e.g., tourism, development and exports of software and electronics manufacturing) and activities (e.g., research, technological development, and personnel training). The country offers a dozen free trade zones (FTZs), covering technology, services, and paper and pulp sectors, among others.

Argentina, Brazil, Colombia, Peru, and Venezuela offer far less attractive scenarios, frequently complicated by debilitating bureaucracy and inefficiency. The corporate income tax rate for Argentina in 2010 was 35 percent, and the standard VAT rate was 21 percent. In addition to these, companies have to face a tax on financial transactions, import and export taxes, and a turnover tax. Businesses operating in Argentina have to pay up to 27 percent of an employee's wages in payroll taxes. Argentina has comprehensive treaties for the avoidance of double taxation in force with 18 countries. Brazil has one of the highest corporate tax rates in Latin America, at 34 percent, as well as one of the most complex, featuring more than 15 different taxes plus dozens of surcharges and contributions applied discretionarily at federal, state, and municipal levels. Labor compensation and benefits are onerous, and it is estimated that they can add up to 80 percent of base wages of full-time employees on permanent contracts. Colombia's corporate income tax rate is 33 percent, and the standard VAT rate is 16 percent. A series of tax incentives for investment exist, the most important of which are a special tax regime for the dozens of Colombia's free trade zones, a 40 percent tax deduction for investments in fixed assets, and deductions for environmental and scientific investments.

The corporate income tax rate in Peru was 30 percent in 2010 and the VAT rate was 19 percent. Companies have to pay an equivalent of 10.2 percent of profits as social security contributions. In spite of a broad reform to the tax agency started in the early 1990s that eased procedures and improved collection, tax evasion levels in Peru are still high, with income tax evasion estimated at around 40 percent of potential tax income in 2006. The system is also extremely cumbersome. The top corporate income tax rate in Venezuela is 34 percent, and the VAT rate increased to 12 percent as part of the government's attempt to cope with mounting budgetary pressures. Companies had to pay up to 16 percent of a worker's salary as payroll taxes in 2009. Venezuela has a sizeable informal sector estimated at around 50 percent of the workforce. This results in high tax evasion levels, estimated at around 20 percent of potential tax income. As a result of the high evasion levels and of the enforcement program, the tax authority has shifted its attention primarily to the largest taxpayers, closely scrutinizing them and proceeding to closure even for minor tax-related infractions.

Political Stability

Chile enjoys low risk ratings on political stability and the rule of law according to the Economist Intelligence Unit Country Risk Rating (EIU CRR),[9] and it is in the top 67th percentile on World Bank World Government Index (WGI)[10] on political stability and violence, and 87th percentile on the rule of law. Uruguay has a moderate risk rating on politics, legal, and tax structure according to EIU CRR, and scores above the 70th percentile on the World Bank WGI political stability and violence and rule of law assessments. EIU CRR rates Brazil as a medium to significant risk on politics, legal, and tax structure, and Brazil scores only in the 48th percentile on World Bank WGI political stability and violence, and 55th on the rule of law. Argentina scores poorly on all accepted indices of political stability, including a rating of significant to high risk on politics and legal structure by the EIU CRR; it ranks 45th on the WGI for political stability and violence, and 33rd on the rule of law.

Colombia, Peru, and Venezuela rate as the poorest nations in the group for political stability. Colombia has a moderate to medium risk rating on politics, legal, and tax structure (EIU CRR), but scores in the bottom 10th percentile on the World Bank WGI political stability and violence and 45th on the rule of law. Peru is considered a high to very high risk in politics, legal, and tax structure (EIU CRR), and ranks in the bottom 20th percentile on the World Bank WGI political stability and violence index, and bottom 32nd percentile on the rule of law. Finally, Venezuela is regarded as a high to very high risk in politics, legal, and tax structure and scores among the lowest 10 percent on the World Bank WGI political stability and violence rating and the lowest 2 percent on the rule of law.

Intellectual Property Rights

Two distinct levels of performance characterize the protection of intellectual property (IP) rights in South America, with Chile and Uruguay leading the way amid concerns in all other nations of the region. Chilean laws and regulations protect trademarks, patents, utility models, industrial designs, and copyrights, with copyright protection covering a 70-year period. Uruguay has extensive and relatively long-standing legislation on intellectual and industrial property matters. International commitments include the ratification of the Berne and Paris Conventions, and membership in the World Intellectual Property Organization (WIPO).[11]

Threats by the United States not to renew duty-free exemptions for billions of dollars in Brazilian goods under the U.S. Generalized System of Preferences program because of insufficient protection of IP rights have encouraged the Brazilian government to take firmer action to deal with this problem. In Peru, the government and other sector-specific business organizations have successively launched campaigns to combat counterfeit, piracy, and contraband activities in the country. Still, enforcement of intellectual property laws remains weak despite improvements made to the legal framework. Important progress has been made in Colombia in recent years, including the creation of comprehensive legislation, but Colombian enforcement of IP rights remains spotty and infringements are common. The judicial process is slow and cumbersome, and it fails to imprison and adequately punish violators. In its 2010 report, the U.S. Trade Representative (USTR) retained Colombia on its Watch List of global intellectual property rights (IPR) offenders, although the USTR did note some improvement in enforcement.[12] IP rights are another area of concern in Argentina, with patent protection in particular still inadequate despite ongoing efforts by the government to improve performance. Venezuela's legislation relating to IP rights is fairly well defined, but enforcement is patchy at best.

Table 12.4 presents the scores for each nation on the Politics dimension. A summary of the strengths and weaknesses on the Politics dimension is included in Table 12.5.

Infrastructure

An assessment of key elements of the Infrastructure dimension follows, including transportation, utilities, and telecommunications. A summary of Infrastructure elements for each of the focal nations of South America is presented at the end of the section.

Transportation

Argentina has an extensive road system that carries the bulk of overland transport in the nation, although the road network is more comprehensive in wealthier urban centers.

Table 12.4 Scores for the Politics Dimension

Politics	Ease of Doing Business	Legal Framework	Political Stability	Intellectual Property Rights	Overall Grade
20%	30%	30%	25%	15%	100%
Argentina	C⁻	D⁺	D	C⁻	D⁺
Brazil	C	C⁺	B⁻	C⁺	C⁺
Chile	A⁻	A⁻	B	B⁺	B⁺
Colombia	B	C⁺	D	C	C
Peru	B	C⁺	D	C	C
Uruguay	B⁻	B	B	B	B
Venezuela	D⁻	F	D	F	D⁻

Table 12.5   Strengths and Weaknesses Summary: Politics Dimension

Grade	Strengths	Weaknesses
Argentina: D+	Comprehensive tax treaties with 18 nations.	Difficult to do business; high levels of bureaucracy; instances of corrupt business practices; high level of government control in key industries; very high tax rates; high risk in judicial and political institutions; inadequate protection of property rights.
Brazil: C+	Improving FDI legislation and culture; weak but improving IP environment.	Highly bureaucratic and difficult to do business; still concerns over political stability of democracy, although smooth transfers recently; high and complex tax rates.
Chile: B+	Easy to do business; bureaucracy low with few corruption problems; receptive to FDI; good labor laws; stable democracy with high accountability and visibility and negligible to low risk; lowest and simplest tax rates in South America; strong IP protection.	None noted.
Colombia: C	Relatively easy to do business; relatively low corruption; improving receptiveness to FDI; flexible labor market; good IP protection.	Remaining questions of political stability after decades of violence and corruption associated with drug lords; high tax rates.
Peru: C	Open FDI policy; overall trend of improvement, but still many issues.	High levels of bureaucracy challenge ease of business, but improving; widespread corruption makes it difficult to enforce contracts; high levels of government labor regulation; very high levels of political instability; weak IP laws.
Uruguay: B	Easy to start business; receptive to FDI; moderately stable democracy with low levels of bureaucracy and corruption; effective government; low and simple tax rates; strong IP protection.	Rising issues with Mercosur could affect trade with Argentina and Brazil.
Venezuela: D−	Receptive to FDI.	Highly bureaucratic, corrupt, and difficult to do business; restrictive labor laws; very high tax rates; highest risk in judicial and political institutions in the Western Hemisphere other than Haiti; drug trafficking and smuggling corrupting society and business; inadequate protection of property rights.

The rail system was privatized in the early 1990s and since then has experienced significant problems including strikes, passenger riots, fatal crashes, and strife among federal, provincial, and city governments and private operators. With numerous Atlantic ports including Buenos Aires, La Plata, and Bahía Blanca, water transport is one of Argentina's most important sectors, but the increased volume of international trade has stretched port capacities. Ezeiza, located in Buenos Aires, is Argentina's main international airport, with a new passenger terminal and good international connections.

The transport infrastructure of Brazil is generally well developed in the industrialized southern states of the country, but more investment is needed in the poorer northern states. Brazil's transport infrastructure still relies heavily on its road network, with approximately 2 million km (1.243 million mi) of highways, of which less than one-tenth are paved. The rail system is underdeveloped, although the privatization of freight rail networks has improved and modernized the rail infrastructure. A transcontinental railway project that would cover a total of 4100 km (2547 mi) and connect the Peruvian Pacific coast ports with Brazil's Cruceiro do Sul harbor on the Atlantic coast is under consideration. Brazil has 36 deepwater ports, including Belém, Fortaleza, Ilhéus, Imbituba, Manaus, Paranaguá, Porto Alegre, Recife, Rio de Janeiro, Rio Grande, Salvador, Santos, and Vitória, although the country requires large investments in port infrastructure to meet growing demand. The main international airports are Brasilia in the Federal District, Guarulhos in São Paulo, and Galeão in Rio de Janeiro. The most important domestic airports are Congonhas in São Paulo, Santos Dumont in Rio de Janeiro, and Pampulha in Belo Horizonte.

One-quarter of Chile's 80,000 km (49,710 mi) road network is paved. The Pan-American Highway is the only major north-south highway in Chile. Because the national rail network needs improvement, the government has confirmed large funding for several improvement projects, including a rail tunnel through the Andes to link Chile and Argentina. Chile has a world-class airport and seaport infrastructure. However, several new airport concessions are being looked at due to increasing demand for air travel from both international and domestic sources.

The mountainous and tropical terrain of Colombia generally means that overland travel by road is extremely time-consuming and vast areas of the country remain almost inaccessible, especially in the Amazon region and the northwestern department of Chocó. A major effort to upgrade the road network, aimed at linking key economic centers, has recently been launched. The railway system in Colombia is underdeveloped, although a modern 150-km (93-mi) track links the Cerrejón coal mines to the Atlantic/Caribbean port of Bahia Portete in the northern department of La Guajira. Colombia has major seaports on both the Atlantic/Caribbean and Pacific coasts, including Cartagena and Barranquilla on the Atlantic, and Buenaventura and Tumaco on the Pacific. In the more remote areas of the nation, waterways provide an important means of transport. Air services in Colombia are adequate, with frequent domestic flights linking major cities. The main international airport in Bogotá (El Dorado) has direct links to a number of U.S. and European cities.

Peru's infrastructure is not yet adequate in relation to the current economic growth that the country is experiencing. In particular, the coast's connection with the interior of the country is very underdeveloped. Remote areas and communities are failing to be integrated into the national economy because of infrastructure-related exclusion, compounded by a complex topography. Roads are currently under construction to link up with the highway system in Brazil; in particular, the planned Inter-Oceanic Highway constitutes the first ever fully paved east-west road crossing the Amazon. The rail system is in poor condition and is unlikely to show significant improvements over the next few years as a result of the government's prioritization of road and air services. Although Peru's port system was recently privatized, it remains generally inefficient. The country's main port is El Callao, located 14 km (8.7 mi) to the northwest of Lima. The aviation industry is liberalized, and air transport is commonly used to transport goods to and from remote areas where the road infrastructure is undeveloped.

Uruguay features an adequate overall infrastructure network with top port facilities. However, the quality of the railroad system is poor, and part of the road network lacks maintenance investment. In 2011, the government revamped efforts to finance large infrastructure projects, including rehabilitation of the railway system, port projects, and development of the energy matrix. The toll highways from Montevideo are of very good quality, with most of the other urban roads being of at least reasonable quality. Much of the remaining 8731 km (5425 mi) of national highways are narrow and of variable quality. There is more than 2000 km (1242 mi) of railway track, running mainly alongside the Uruguay River. Montevideo has a world-class seaport, and most of its services have recently been privatized. Approximately 5000 vessels and 400,000 20-foot equivalent unit (TEU) containers with a total cargo of 3.8 million tons are handled annually. The Carrasco International Airport, located 18 km (11.2 mi) outside of Montevideo, boasts a new passenger terminal that handles the bulk of passenger and freight traffic in the country.

An adequate and extensive road system provides the main means of transport in Venezuela. Of the estimated 100,000 km (62,137 mi) of roadway in Venezuela, 31,200 km (19,386 mi) are paved, 24,800 km (15,410 mi) are surfaced with gravel, and 25,000 km (15,534 mi) are unimproved dirt tracks. The transport infrastructure suffered from poor maintenance during the Chavez Administration and has not been able to keep up with increased demand. The railway system is limited, totaling 682 km (424 mi), with two main freight lines in the northern states that link the various seaports. Venezuela's Caribbean coast's main ports are Maracaibo, La Guaira, Puerto Cabello, and Guiria. There also are 7100 km (4412 mi) of waterways navigable by ocean-going vessels, including Lake Maracaibo and the Orinoco River. The country has four main airports, including Maiquetia/Caracas, Maracaibo, Valencia, and Barcelona.

Utilities

Argentina has the third largest power market in the region, relying mostly on thermal and hydroelectric power generation. Large projects have been commissioned in the generation and transmission sectors to keep up with a 6 percent annual increase in demand.[13] In Brazil, concerns over the reliability of power supplies emerged after a massive blackout in late 2009 that affected 18 Brazilian states and Paraguay. The outage was caused by a transmission line failure rather than a supply deficit. The dominance of hydropower (responsible for 91 percent of the total production) means that the vulnerability of energy supplies to droughts continues. Chile has limited energy resources, with the bulk of power coming from hydroelectric and natural gas sources. A drought that prompted the imposition of rationing measures highlighted the vulnerability of the power sector, which was threatened by the reduction of gas shipments from Argentina in 2004. The start-up of a second liquid natural gas (LNG) import terminal in 2010 has enabled Chile to reduce its dependence on just one gas supplier. However, the government predicts that the country's electricity generation capacity will have to double over the next decade, putting continued stress on available energy supplies.

Colombia's electricity infrastructure remains vastly dependent on hydropower, which accounts for 70 to 80 percent of total power generated, and Peru suffers from a shortage of electrical generating capacity and an overreliance on hydroelectric power, which has led to sporadic power outages in periods of drought. Uruguay has one of the highest electrification rates in South America (98 percent of urban households), although it is highly dependent on Argentina and Brazil for gas and hydrocarbon supply. In Venezuela, electricity generation, transmission, and distribution are conducted by public entities. Since former President Chavez came to power, private investment in the sector has been scarce, resulting in underinvestment that has made power failures more frequent in Venezuela.

Telecommunications

Internet services in Argentina range from traditional dial-up connections in rural areas to wireless broadband in Buenos Aires and other large cities. Although telecom service prices are high, Internet penetration was estimated at 66 percent in 2011. Telecommunications services in Brazil are well developed and provided by a number of privately held foreign capital companies, although service outages and slowdowns due to excessive demand remain prevalent. The telecommunications sector in Chile is one of the most modern and developed in the SouthAmerican region, with a highly competitive, liberalized environment. Both services and coverage of the telecommunications network have improved over recent years to bring Colombia in line with the regional average. Telephone usage in Peru is one of the lowest in South America. The telephone system is privatized, however, with plans to digitalize and increase the number of telephone lines beginning to make the system more efficient. Uruguay's telecommunications infrastructure is one of the best in the region. In addition to extensive landlines for telecommunications, a domestic satellite system with three earth stations provides coverage, and a national fiber optic network with capacity for digital and multimedia services is installed.

Table 12.6 presents the scores for the Infrastructure dimension. The strengths and weaknesses of the South American nations on transportation, utilities, and telecommunications infrastructure that may aid to the attractiveness of supply chain operations are summarized in Table 12.7.

Competence

An assessment of key elements of the Competence dimension follows, including labor availability, productivity, and relations; education for line staff and management; and logistics, customs, and security. A summary of Competence elements for each of the focal nations of South America is presented at the end of the section.

Labor Availability, Productivity, and Relations

The labor environment in Argentina is challenging at best. The global economic crisis intensified the need for highly skilled labor in engineering, management, and technician positions, putting a squeeze on the available skilled labor. Argentina also ranks poorly on pay and productivity, as the labor force is one of the most costly in the region.[14] Labor unrest is common and is often used as political leverage as organized labor remains a strong force. Since 2008, strikes and other protests have included oil workers, teachers, cattle ranchers, and subway staff. Hiring and firing practices are among the most restrictive in the world.

Table 12.6 Scores for the Infrastructure Dimension

Infrastructure	Transportation Infrastructure	Energy Infrastructure	Connectivity	Overall Grade
30%	50%	25%	25%	100%
Argentina	D⁺	D⁺	B	C⁻
Brazil	D⁻	C⁺	B	C⁻
Chile	B⁺	B⁻	B	B
Colombia	D	C⁺	B⁻	C⁻
Peru	C⁻	C	C⁺	C
Uruguay	C⁺	B	B⁺	B⁻
Venezuela	D⁻	D⁻	C⁺	D

Table 12.7 Strengths and Weaknesses Summary: Infrastructure Dimension

Grade	Strengths	Weaknesses
Argentina: C⁻	Good road, water, and air systems; rail better than in most of region, but decaying; high telecomm costs.	Infrastructure struggling to keep up with growth.
Brazil: C⁻	Infrastructure adequate in south; well-developed telecomm and utilities.	Infrastructure developed in some areas, but under capacity resulting in congestion; no national rail network; infrastructure needs investment to keep up with growth.
Chile: B	Adequate and improving transportation infrastructure; telecomm tops in the region.	Need to further develop rail; power distribution must grow and improve availability of energy sources.
Colombia: C⁻	Improving transportation infrastructure; telecomm and power distribution on par with rest of region, and well managed.	Weak rail infrastructure; road infrastructure weak.
Peru: C	Government working to improve infrastructure; efficient private management of infrastructure.	Currently inadequate infrastructure in transportation, telecomm, and power distribution.
Uruguay: B⁻	Overall good transportation infrastructure; telecomm and power among best in region.	Investment needed to upgrade infrastructure.
Venezuela: D	Adequate road, port, and air systems.	Rail system weak; ineffective infrastructure management.

Brazil has one of the highest labor force participation rates in the region, in part due to the high level of income inequality that prompts youth and women of lower-income classes to work. Labor availability, however, remains below the regional average. The World Economic Forum Global Competitive Index (WEF GCI) ranks Brazil's productivity below average for the region, although productivity has been growing at a double-digit rate since 2004, mainly as a result of increased investment in technology. Productivity growth, however, is threatened by significant increases in minimum wages compared to other emerging economies. Unions in Brazil are well organized and have the backing of legal commitments, such as the International Labor Organization (ILO) convention on workers' rights. Strikes often occur in private sector companies concerning profit sharing, which is a requirement under Brazilian law. Despite this, labor relations in Brazil are average for the region, although they are below the industrial world average. Restrictive hiring and firing practices, however, make labor issues a challenge.

Chile's labor force participation rate is one of the lowest in the region, mainly due to the low participation of Chilean women in the labor force due to cultural reasons. Despite this, the skilled labor availability in Chile ranks well above the regional average. As a result of increasing FDI inflows, productivity levels in Chile have been rising and are exceeding South American averages. The monthly minimum wage has increased on average by 4.5 percent per year in real terms since 2004, and high firing costs affect the country's competitiveness. Chilean labor unions have reemerged as powerful entities since the restoration of democracy in 1990. Periodic and short-lived strikes remain frequent in Chile, although they tend to be short-lived and nonviolent. Labor relations are the best in the region, and above the industrial world average.[15] Hiring and firing practices, as with other nations in the region, are relatively restrictive.

There is generally no shortage of either unskilled or skilled labor in Colombia, although technical positions, particularly in accounting and finance, production, and operations, were difficult for employers to fill. In general, availability of skilled labor is among the highest in the region. Productivity and pay levels lag the region, however. Colombia has a long history of violence against trade unions; only 10 percent of the workforce belongs to a union. Union action is concentrated in the public sector, with strikes by public school teachers accounting for the bulk of protests. Labor relations are about average for the region but below the industrial world average. Similarly, hiring and firing practices are less restrictive than in other nations in the region but lag the industrialized world.

Peru's high level of income inequality prompts women and youth to work, increasing labor force participation as a percentage of the economically active population. Although this suffices for unskilled labor, there is a shortage of highly skilled workers; availability of skilled labor remains among the lowest in the region. Peruvian labor productivity is very low, despite improvements since 2003 as a result of increasing FDI inflows. The minimum wage per month grew less than 1 percent in real terms during that period. The labor market is relatively rigid, which poses difficulties for hiring and firing personnel. The level of union organization in Peru declined during the 1990s, and it is estimated that no more than 6 percent of the labor force is organized. Strikes may only be called by gaining a majority of all workers, both union and nonunion.

Uruguay's labor market environment is among the most challenging in the world. The market has become increasingly rigid due to legislation introduced by the government since the mid-2000s that reduced flexibility in wage determination and hiring and firing practices, causing relatively high redundancy costs. The aging of the Uruguayan population further affects the tight labor environment, which is the oldest in South America. Productivity levels are at the South American average in most sectors, although tourism, real estate, and construction are significantly higher than average. Labor unions in Uruguay have strengthened since 2005, when the Broad Front (FA) government first took office. Unionization is particularly high in the public sector, with 80 percent of the workforce affiliated with a union. Labor conflicts have increased during the late 2000s, with subsequent productivity losses adding to other problems in the rigid labor market.

The Venezuelan labor market is among the worst in the world. There is an abundance of unskilled labor in Venezuela, but availability of highly skilled labor is the lowest in South America. Productivity in Venezuela is high, but this is largely due to windfall profits in oil and massive government expenditures. Monthly minimum wages in Venezuela are the highest in the region, with mandated large non–salary benefits to employees and restrictive laws regarding hiring, employing, and firing personnel.[16] The law allows strikes in Venezuela if they are announced five days beforehand and the grievances are presubmitted to the Labor Inspector's Office of the Ministry of Labor. Rates of unionization average 22 to 28 percent in Venezuela, with sharp disparities between the private and public sectors, the latter having almost 90 percent of its workforce unionized; labor relations in Venezuela are among the poorest in the world.

Education Levels for Line Staff and Management

The Argentinean education system is above average for the region, with 97 percent of the population literate and possessing strong English-language skills, but falls well below global standards. Management education and professionalism is regarded relatively highly in the region, although staff training levels are low. Despite advances to improve the quality of and access to education in Brazil, educational standards in the country are still deficient. Only 88 percent of the population is literate, and the education system falls below the regional average. Management education and staff training and professionalism, however, are above the regional average, approaching the industrial world average.

Chile offers an educated and trained workforce with low staff turnover and low absenteeism. Nearly 96 percent of the population is literate. Management education and professionalism meet the high standards common in the industrialized world. English is the most commonly spoken second language amongst executives.[17] Public education in Colombia has experienced significant improvement in urban areas such as Bogotá and Medellín, yet it continues to suffer under a lack of resources and poor quality in rural areas. Ninety percent of the population is literate. Vocational training is available through public and private technical educational institutions designed to equip individuals with the required skills for the workplace, although these are of varying quality. Management education and professionalism are above the regional average. The state education system in Peru is antiquated, lacks resources, and is of a low standard, although 92 percent of the population is literate. Management education and professionalism, however, are above average although staff training is poor.

Although the education system in Uruguay is weak, public investment in education has been growing over the past few years. Uruguay boasts one of the highest literacy rates in South America, and enrollment rates at all levels of education are also among the highest in the region; 98 percent of the population is literate. Uruguayan management education quality is high, with 10 percent of university graduates earning professional degrees in engineering, IT, and the physical sciences, fueling a growing software development sector.

Educational standards in Venezuela are low, and the government has consistently decreased its expenditures on education. As a result, there is an excess of semiskilled labor and a shortage of highly skilled labor. Although 93 percent of the population is literate, education and language levels are among the lowest in the region. In addition, there has been a marked emigration of young, educated professionals resulting from the unstable environment in Venezuela. As a result of this brain drain, talented personnel for managerial positions are among the most sought after in the country. Management education and professionalism are among the lowest in region.[18]

Logistics, Customs, and Security

The logistics infrastructures of the South American nations exceed global standards (with the exception of Venezuela), although they lag the standards experienced in mature industrial regions of the world. Chile and Brazil are in the top 10 logistics systems among upper-middle-income economies, and Argentina, Uruguay, Peru, and Colombia are in the second 10; Venezuela was ranked among the bottom third in the world.

Argentina enjoys relative strengths in international shipping, tracking and tracing, and timeliness, but customs procedures are bureaucratic, cumbersome, and lengthy.[19] Brazil's logistics system is strong in tracking and tracing and timeliness of deliveries. Brazil suffers from complex custom laws, multiple taxing authorities, and inconsistent enforcement of regulations that contribute to congestion throughout the supply chain. Chile's customs procedures, infrastructure, tracking and tracing, and timeliness are noted strengths. Chile's National Customs Service is working closely with the World Customs Organization (WCO) to establish international standards in the customs sector and boasts high levels of transparency by regional standards.

Colombia has strengths in logistics service competence and timeliness. Recent attempts have been made in Colombia to speed up customs procedures. The time needed to export goods has dipped below the regional average, but the costs for doing so remain significantly above the regional average, according to data from the World Bank. There have been renewed efforts to clamp down on corruption in customs authorities.

Peru shows strengths in tracking and tracing and timeliness. Peruvian authorities have been working on improving customs procedures since 2005 to cut down the entry and exit time of merchandise. Among other things, they are working to set up a one-stop procedure for both importers and exporters and an online invoice system, although as recently as 2010 Peru was evaluated as having more import and export documents than the regional average.

Uruguay has noted strengths in customs, tracking and tracing, and timeliness. Processes for both importing and exporting goods in Uruguay tend to be somewhat bureaucratic by regional standards, although the additional paperwork does not translate into higher costs or lengthier procedures. In fact, costs (per container) for both exports and imports are below the regional average, and the time taken to export or import is close to the regional average.

Venezuela has the worst logistics system in the region, although ease of international shipments and timeliness are noted strengths. Customs procedures in Venezuela are cumbersome, and the number and duration of procedures and the cost of both import and export activities lag the region despite government efforts to modernize processes and make them more transparent. The National Guard, a component of Venezuela's armed forces, holds strong influence in customs.[20]

Table 12.8 presents the scores for the Competence dimension. An assessment of the strengths and weaknesses for the selected nations of South America are summarized in Table 12.9.

Table 12.8 Scores for the Competence Dimension

Competence	Labor Relations	Education Levels	Logistics Competence	Customs and Security	Overall Grade
20%	25%	25%	40%	10%	100%
Argentina	F	C⁺	B	C	C
Brazil	C⁻	B⁻	B	C⁺	B⁻
Chile	B⁻	B	B⁺	B⁺	B
Colombia	C⁻	C	B⁻	B⁻	C⁺
Peru	C⁻	C	B⁻	B⁻	C⁺
Uruguay	F	C⁻	B-	B	C⁻
Venezuela	F	C⁻	D⁺	D⁻	D

Table 12.9 Strengths and Weaknesses Summary: Competence Dimension

Grade	Strengths	Weaknesses
Argentina: C	Educated and trained workforce; good management education; adequate logistics infrastructure.	Costly labor rates and getting more so; labor unrest is common, with frequent strikes; restrictive hiring and firing practices; below average availability of skilled labor.
Brazil: B⁻	Average labor unrest for region, although increasingly an issue; management education and professionalism and staff competence compares well to rest of region; one of the strongest logistics industries in the region.	Negative trend in labor productivity as costs rise; low labor availability for skilled positions; education levels lagging; significant bureaucracy and corruption in customs and trade.

(continued)

Table 12.9 Strengths and Weaknesses Summary: Competence Dimension (*Continued*)

Grade	Strengths	Weaknesses
Chile: B	Labor relations, management education, competence, and qualified engineering availability levels highest in region; availability of skilled labor and staff training and education above average; logistics industry capability strongest in region; customs bureaucracy low with few corruption problems.	Concern over rising labor costs that hurt productivity; increasingly rigid hiring and firing practices.
Colombia: C⁺	Labor relations average for region; staff education, training, and availability of skilled labor average for region; management education and professionalism adequate; logistics industry and customs capabilities average for emerging world (but costly).	Labor productivity and hiring and firing costs a concern; continued high risk to operational security due to drug violence; import and export compliance costly.
Peru: C⁺	High availability and low cost of low-skilled labor; managerial education and professionalism improving; logistics industry capabilities adequate across all dimensions.	Labor productivity, skilled labor, education, and staff training poor; bureaucratic customs authority; high-risk operations and security.
Uruguay: C⁻	Well-educated management; adequate overall logistics capability; good import and export administration; low-risk operations and security.	Extremely restrictive labor laws and high labor costs lead to low productivity; unionization leading to high levels of labor conflict; concerns over workforce availability; generally poor education system.
Venezuela: D	Productivity high, but mainly due to high oil prices.	Labor costs, relations, availability of skilled labor, training, and education lowest in region; management education and senior management competence among lowest in region; overall scope of logistics capabilities poor; highly bureaucratic and corrupt in customs; very high risk to operations and security.

Main Trends in South America

The 21st century could well represent the period when several nations in South America take their seats at the table with the major economic powers in the world. Although this statement was made about these same nations 100 years ago, the political environment today is far different than it was for much of the 20th century in the key nations of the region. In the past, political instability prevented the adoption of economic policies

Table 12.10 Summary Assessment of EPIC Attractiveness for the Nations Represented in South America

	Economy	Politics	Infrastructure	Competence	Overall Grade
Argentina	B	D⁺	C⁻	C	C
Brazil	A⁻	C⁺	C⁻	B⁻	B⁻
Chile	B⁺	B⁺	B	B	B⁺
Colombia	B⁺	C	C⁻	C⁺	C⁺
Peru	B⁺	C	C	C⁺	B⁻
Uruguay	B⁻	B	B⁻	C⁻	B⁻
Venezuela	C⁺	D⁻	D	D	D⁺

that were open to investment and the development of an infrastructure and business competence that facilitated growth. With a couple of notable exceptions among the seven selected nations of South America, the history of the last 30 years has witnessed increasing political stability and democratization of the region, permitting economic decisions that have favored development and growth. The exceptions are Venezuela, and to a lesser degree, Argentina. Each of the nations features certain strengths that make them worthy of consideration for supply chain operational development.

The EPIC scores for the seven South American nations in this assessment (presented in Table 12.10) reveal some interesting trends within the region that affect supply chain decision making. Six of the seven nations are moving in a positive direction with regard to the EPIC dimensions, albeit at different speeds, which will enhance the attractiveness of supply chain opportunities. The seventh nation, Venezuela, is moving in the opposite direction, and supply chain managers should be wary of investment in this nation. A brief summary of EPIC trends affecting supply chain management decision making for each of the selected nations of South America follows.

Supply Chain Challenges

Geography and Ground Transportation

The geography of South America presents a substantial challenge to the development of supply chain operations that require the overland movement of materials. With the Andes creating a formidable east-west barrier to transportation and the Amazon Basin creating a formidable north-south barrier to transportation, the region is effectively segmented into four main sections. With most of the landmass of South America to the south of the Amazon Basin and to the east of the Andes, developing supply chain operations that connect the eastern South American nations with western North America and Asia is challenging, typically requiring a longer ocean transit around Cape Horn (the southernmost part of South America). Connecting supply chains between western South American countries and Eastern North and Central America, the Middle East, North Africa, and Europe is equally challenging.

As an example of these "east-west" transit challenges, there are very few roads that connect Chile to Argentina (and the eastern South American nations). Between Argentina and Chile, some options for transiting the Andes are the Cardenal Antonio Samore Pass (Central Argentina/Chile with access to Osorno and the Pan-American Highway), Paso Los Libertadores (Central-Northern Argentina/Chile with access to Santiago, Chile), and Paso Pino Cachado (Central Argentina/Chile with access to Temuco, Chile). Figure 12.9 shows passes that have current and future commercial transportation applications. It is critical to note that none of these east-west South American passes and associated road systems are of a high standard, with most being largely gravel and subject to frequent closures in the winter months. For instance, Paso Los Libertadores was closed for more than a week in July of 2008, causing a backup of more than 5000 trucks on both sides of the pass.[21] On average, this pass is closed more than 40 days per year, and on a good day it may take well over 12 hours to cross the Andes using this pass. Furthermore, some sections of the roads leading through these mountain passes are, at very best, so far below a developed world standard for design and maintenance that they are among the most dangerous in the world. Firms considering establishing supply chain operations that will use motor freight to cross the Andes should do so with a realistic eye toward capacity and lead-time limitations—not to mention driver and product safety.

Corruption

Many South American nations still struggle with corruption and political instability, and many of the less stable nations create geographic gaps between the more stable nations. The three most attractive and mature locations for supply chain operations are Brazil, Chile, and Uruguay. Brazil and Uruguay share a common national border, but they do not share a common border with Chile, which is blocked from a seamless flow with those two nations by Argentina to the east, Bolivia to the northeast, and Peru to the north. Chile is politically stable and host to good standards of business and low levels of corruption, but its regional trading partners and over-ground access to the east coast of South America and to Brazil is limited. Similarly, Brazil and Uruguay are landlocked between Argentina, Paraguay, Bolivia, and Peru to the west, and Colombia and Venezuela to the north. Adding to that, the challenges of crossing the Amazon Basin to the north and the Andes to the west make connecting east-west continental trade in support of domestic and international markets extremely difficult. Thus it is likely that supply chain flows among the major growth nations of South America will continue to be by sea lanes. Similarly, import/export flows to and from these nations will continue to focus on trade partners external to the region.

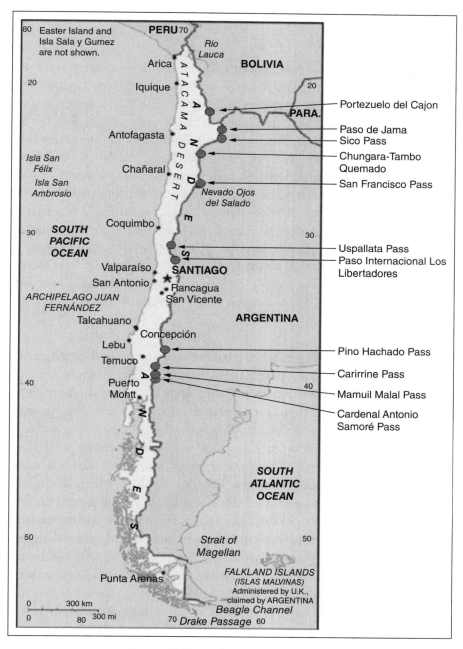

Figure 12.9 Andes Mountain passes.

Supply Chain Opportunities

A New "Low-Cost" Region

China and other important East Asian nations are continuing to invest in South America, in much the same way that the United States and prosperous Western European countries invested in East and South Asian countries as "low-cost regions." However, as these older low-cost regions of the world have developed their own economies, they too seek less expensive labor for sourcing options to serve both domestic and international markets. It seems clear that the much more prosperous East Asian nations have chosen South America as one of their preferred low-cost manufacturing regions. Brazil, in particular, presents a huge domestic market, cheap green energy, an existing manufacturing base, and a time-zone overlap with the United States. Global companies considering a supply chain strategy focused on the Americas, Europe, Middle East and North Africa (MENA), and the Asia Pacific might logically look at Brazil if they can overcome its political barriers to investment.[22] Given this, we expect to see improved supply chain management opportunities in this region in the coming years in the form of sourcing of subcomponent, assembly, repair parts, and low-value finished goods manufacturing for export.

Trading Blocs

One of the very interesting opportunities currently developing in South America is the advent of multiple competing trade blocs. Although traditionally split by bitter differences of opinion over trade policy, the nations of South America appear to be moving toward improved trade relations. Any firm considering developing or expanding supply chain operations in South America must consider the implications of the existing and developing trade blocs on the future value of their investment in specific countries in the region. With Mercosur (Argentina, Brazil, Paraguay, Uruguay, and Venezuela) and the Andean Community of Nations (Bolivia, Colombia, Ecuador, and Peru) representing the older of the trade blocs and the newer Pacific Alliance (Chile, Colombia, Mexico, and Peru) focusing specifically on promoting free trade between the countries and increasing exports to Asia, the fragmented and frequently fractious nature of international supply chain operations appears to be improving. Costa Rica, Panama, and Guatemala have already expressed a desire to become Pacific Alliance members. Challenges remain, however, as nations led by Venezuelan President Hugo Chavez spearheaded a move to reject free trade. His death may ease this unrest and pave the way to better trade harmony in the region.[23]

It will be important not only to evaluate specific countries but also the trade blocs to which they belong when establishing supply chain operations in South America. The choice of the country and paired trade bloc has significant implications for the ease of movement of labor, resources, and materials between these nations. This is a somewhat unique supply chain feature of South America that simply cannot be overlooked.

Investment in Infrastructure

As an emerging low-cost sourcing and manufacturing region for Asia, significant investment is being made to better connect Brazil and the nations to the east of the Andes with the seaports that serve most of South America's trade with Asia. As an example, a private railway is being considered (Aconcagua Bi-Oceanic Corridor) that would cross the Andes between Central Chile and Argentina at the Paso Internacional Los Libertradores. Approval of this project would have significant implications for the Mercosur trading bloc as the Argentina-Chile linkage is currently a significant weakness. Also, with ports on both the east and west coasts of South America, Colombia could well become an important land bridge that would connect the east and west nations of South America with the rest of the world.

Consumer Markets

The overall size and growth of the consumer markets in Brazil make it the most attractive market for the sale of finished goods in South America. Of course, significant and accessible consumer markets may be found in many South American nations, and Chile and Uruguay should certainly be considered, followed by Peru and Argentina. Firms tempted to enter this burgeoning consumer market must be well versed in the various trade laws of the market, encompassing import barriers, trade blocs, countertrade, and country of origin regulations that vary greatly from nation to nation. In addition, the multiple segments of South American culture present in nearly every South American nation will likely create a need for a high number of product variants.

Key Takeaways for South America

Key takeaways for supply chain managers from the assessment of South America include the following:

1. Establish a distribution presence in Brazil to sell to the domestic market. The growth of this large economy will continue as the population is young and growing. Demand for consumer goods within the country will continue. As the real strengthens, imports will become more affordable, and given the infrastructure capacity constraints, there is no time like the present to establish a distribution network. Be aware of the challenges presented by the bureaucracy, labor issues, and taxes by finding trustworthy and reliable Brazilian partners.
2. Source and produce in key industries in Brazil for both domestic as well as export product to other nations in South America and possibly out of the region. Specific sectors in which Brazil holds some global competitive advantages include chemicals, automotive, aerospace, pharmaceuticals, and textiles. Be aware of the challenges of operating in Brazil.

3. Chile is worth exploring for supply chain opportunities, particularly sourcing and producing products for export to other South American markets. Overall, Chile presents the strongest EPIC profile in the region. Chile is in a good position to provide goods for sale in Peru, Colombia, Ecuador, and even Brazil when the rail tunnel through the Andes is completed. Key sectors of strength in Chile include mining, iron and steel production, wood and wood products, transport equipment, and fishing.

4. The possibility of inbounding subcomponents from Asia into Chilean ports for assembly and redistribution in South America is particularly appealing.

5. Consider Uruguay as a potential location for production and export to Brazil and Argentina in key food and food processing segments. Uruguay is more stable and possesses a better environment for business than either Brazil or Argentina, and Uruguay has great port facilities to aid trade.

6. Similar to Brazil, but to a lesser degree, Colombia presents a large and expanding market with a young and growing population. Establish distribution networks in Colombia now to take advantage of what promises to be a period of sustained growth and wealth creation, particularly if the violence of the drug era is truly in the past.

7. Colombia may emerge as a viable east-west logistics hub, with ports on both the Atlantic and Pacific and proximity to the Panama Canal. Growing sectors for consideration for such trade in Colombia include chemicals, machinery and transport equipment, and textiles.

8. Argentina is the second largest market in South America, and it is experiencing strong growth. Many challenges remain, but future market opportunities should not be dismissed, and thus establishing a distribution footprint today could be prudent. Argentina has been on the brink of greatness several times in the past; one day they are certain to get it right.

9. Peru is still trying to establish its footing and move forward. Until then, regard it only as a source for basic commodities such as minerals, fish, and agricultural products.

10. Venezuela is a key source for petroleum. There are also some other industries that benefit from the ready availability of low-cost oil for power, and therefore provide low-cost sourcing options, including iron and steel, construction materials, and chemical and paper products. Beyond that, the country has far too many political and economic challenges to be worthy of consideration for investment in supply chain assets.

References

1. J. D. Power and Associates, *Forbes,* October 22, 2012.
2. http://alianzapacifico.net/wp-content/uploads/2013/07/ABC-ALIANZA-DEL -PACIFICO-PRENSA-INGLES.pdf.

3. George Friedmann, "Geopolitical Diary: Geography and Conflict in South America," www.StratFor.com, March 5, 2008.
4. Taos Turner, "Argentina Lifts Some Controversial Trade Barriers," *Wall Street Journal*, January 25, 2013.
5. World Bank WGI indices, 2012.
6. World Bank Logistics Performance Index, 2012.
7. IHS Global Insights.
8. Passport GMID.
9. Economist Intelligence Unit Country Risk Rating.
10. World Bank World Government Index.
11. IHS Global Insight.
12. Economist Intelligence Unit.
13. IHS Global Insights.
14. Klaus Schwab, "Global Competitiveness Report 2012–2013," *World Economic Forum*, 2012. www.weforum.org/gcr.
15. World Economic Forum Global Competitive Index; IHS Global Insight.
16. WEF GCI; IMD World Competitiveness Yearbook; Passport GMID.
17. Passport GMID; IMD World Competitiveness Yearbook; WEF GCI.
18. WCI GEF; IHS Global Insight; Passport GMID; IMD World Competitiveness Yearbook.
19. World Bank Logistics Performance Index, 2012.
20. IHS Global Insight; EIU Country Risk Ratings.
21. *New York Times*, August 8, 2006.
22. Kevin O'Maragh, "Brazil's Golden Opportunity," March 29, 2013. www.scmworld.com.
23. Eduardo Garcia, "Latin America's Free Trade Bloc Lifts Tariffs, Eyes Asian Markets," *Reuters*, May 24, 2013.

CHAPTER 13

Summary and Conclusions

The country "visits" in the earlier chapters—to established industrial nations, burgeoning growth economies, and countries struggling to establish viable economic structures—provide the reader with an intimate glimpse into the strengths and weaknesses associated with the broad macro environments within which global supply chains operate. An underlying premise of this book is that while competing forces at play are "flattening" the world they are also increasing differences among regions in many ways. One outcome of this premise, most forcibly supported by Penkaj Ghemawat in his books, *Redefining Global Strategy*[1] and *World 3.0*,[2] is that "differences between countries are larger than generally acknowledged." In other words, it is important to take advantage of similarities, but it is also critical to understand differences.

Indeed, it appears that there will be a period of "semi-globalization" in business, during which distance matters and different standards will persist across regions. As a result, global supply chains will have to primarily deal with regional pods of demand that present unique supply challenges rather than working with one standard global supply chain footprint. Another consequence is that forward-looking supply chain managers must have the knowledge and information necessary to coordinate multiple inputs and outputs among various enterprises spread across several countries. These managers will have to learn how to mitigate the significant time delays and cost distortions that often accompany supply chains spread across the globe.

Most supply chain managers, however, do not have the luxury of spending time "in country" to learn the nuances of these issues prior to making decisions. Failing to understand the complexity and nuances of a region and nation could have serious consequences, including:

▲ Market service failures
▲ Decreased efficiency and increased waste
▲ Higher purchase costs

▲ Labor challenges

▲ Loss of market competitiveness

Together these consequences add up to a loss of market competitiveness. Thus managers increasingly are pushed outside their comfort zones when making global supply chain decisions. Having a handy reference to information critical to good global supply chain decision making can significantly help these managers manage supply chains in both emerging and mature markets. It is the pursuit of such knowledge that has driven this book to explore key elements of the Economy, Politics, Infrastructure, and business Competence (EPIC) in nine global regions and 55 nations.

To help global supply chain managers improve their decision-making process, this chapter provides a summary of the lessons learned from this exploration of the world within which supply chains must live—a "slide show" of the book's long journey through space and time.

The Supply Chain Manager's Challenges: This Is the World We Live In

One truism of supply chain management is that supply chain managers do not typically influence highest-level strategic business decisions. Rather, they are required to manage the resulting supply chain structure with the set of constraints predicated by such strategic decisions. In this sense, supply chain managers tweak the knobs of the system to get the best performance, but others set the overall objectives. This may be changing in some leading-edge organizations, but for the most part strategic business decisions are made based on one or more dominant criteria, such as size and growth rate of consumer markets, or labor and capital costs of manufacturing, or cost of raw materials and subcomponents.

The research conducted for this book reveals that key variables in the macro environment can help supply chain managers better understand the framework for decision making and reduce uncertainty. For example, despite the dynamism and uncertainty of the global environment, there are also longer and more consistent trends related to political stability; economic investment in capital, labor, and infrastructure; and cultural norms that either aid or hinder nations around the world from becoming viable options for supply chain operations. Such conditions may be analyzed to aid decision making. Other decisions are dictated by the location of relatively scarce materials such as energy, rare earth metals, or agricultural products. Similarly, the location of markets for final goods distribution can be determined with relative certainty.

Knowledge of the levels of these variables enable supply chain managers to choose the locations for value-added supply chain operations, including transportation hubs and modes for raw materials, location of parts and subcomponent suppliers, finished goods manufacturing and assembly locations, and transportation and storage hubs for distribution of finished goods. In particular, the research results reveal interesting combinations of sourcing, manufacturing, and logistics options for different regional consumer markets.

It is not by accident that the concept of *total cost of ownership* (TCO) was born in the supply chain discipline. By the same token, the supply chain discipline has generated a renewed focus on considering the "economic profit" of sales and incorporating such cost and asset considerations as transportation, taxes and tariffs, exchange rates, risk issues, pipeline inventories, and responsiveness. The supply chain crosses all internal functions as well as the external supply and customer networks of an organization, so supply chain managers are often better versed in the service, cost, and asset issues associated with strategic decisions than are most of their functional colleagues in an organization. After all, managing the supply chain is their business! It should, therefore, not be surprising to find that operating a successful supply chain in the global environment is not a simple phenomenon, and there is far more to consider than meets the eye for the supply chain manager. We hope supply chain managers can increasingly use this knowledge to influence strategic business decisions as well as to improve supply chain performance.

The EPIC Dimensions: Revisiting the Fab Four

Elements within the Economy dimension certainly influence structural decisions on supply chains. For example, issues such as country size, GDP, GDP growth rate, foreign direct investment, and trade conditions can significantly influence the basic structure within which supply chains operate. All these variables affect the cost of land, labor, and capital and have important indirect influences on supply chain performance. Yet many of these variables fall outside the decision-making framework for supply chain managers in most organizations. Furthermore, the impact of other economic variables such as exchange rate stability, inflation, and trade balance are far more difficult to assess, yet also are influential on supply chain success. In particular, while conducting the research for this book, the authors, all of whom are operations management researchers, found to their surprise that there is no "good" or "bad" level of inflation or balance of trade. Rather, there are only different sets of pros and cons associated with different levels for these two variables.

Elements of the Politics dimension create the environment within which supply chains operate. Conditions related to the ease of doing business, bureaucracy, corruption, tax rates, stability of the political system, intellectual property rights, and hiring and firing laws significantly affect the day-to-day operations in a supply chain. Politics is particularly important in the initial implementation phase of a supply chain project. Costly delays can result from such issues as licensing, hiring, and environmental compliance. Furthermore, the encoding of cultural and historical norms in the laws of the nation forms the legal framework for operations. Issues related to taxes, wage rates, regard for intellectual property, and regulations related to hiring and firing are all issues that managers have mentioned as being among the most difficult when operating in a global setting.

Infrastructure has a direct impact on supply chain performance. The tangible characteristics of a region's or nation's transportation, utilities, and telecommunications infrastructure required to execute supply chain activities greatly affect supply chain performance. An effective ground transportation network greatly facilitates cost-effective movement of product between sourcing, manufacturing, and market areas. Air and seaport facilities are essential to support global trade by efficiently and effectively moving materials into and out of the region. Investment in infrastructure is an element that can be tracked and is a strong predictor of business growth in a nation or region. Decisions on infrastructure development also require a sound understanding of geography. Roads over high mountains, across vast deserts, and through jungles and marshes generally are not very effective or efficient. In addition, access to stable electricity, water, and telecommunications are essential. For example, many supply chain managers in emerging economies spend a significant time or money arranging for power generation. Even if a company does not operate in an emerging market, it is likely that one or more of its suppliers do. As a result, supply chain managers must be knowledgeable about the conditions in which those suppliers operate to ensure top overall supply chain performance; as the automotive industry has learned, the key to success is to go upstream in the supply chain.

Competence is another dimension with a huge direct impact on supply chain performance. Availability of labor, labor productivity, and the sophistication of supply chain support available through the logistics industry in a nation have a significant impact on the ability to run high-performing supply chains. Mastery of the tangible requirements for supply chain operations is a necessary but not sufficient condition for success. Supply chain managers must also explore the conditions related to "soft" issues that culture, history, population, and politics have on supply chain operations. Leading and managing a local workforce is a key success factor in designing and executing supply chain solutions. How people in a country, or a region in a country, regard work makes a difference. People do not have the same skills, the same references, the same education, or the same hope from one region to another, even in the same country, let alone across nations or regions. Such issues affect labor force management, attendance, attrition, skill levels, and so forth. Performance objectives are not the same across regions; in one region, level of service may be the requirement for success, in another efficient management of inventory may be key.

Takin' Care of Business in the 21st Century

The overall results of the global EPIC analysis and the accompanying research lead to some key rules to guide global supply chain decision making:

Rule 1: Supply chain solutions that work in one region cannot simply be duplicated in another without a high risk of failure. Each region has unique characteristics that require a unique solution dedicated to that region.

Rule 2: Expanding business into new geographic areas will have consequences on the entire existing supply chain. The addition of new regional or local solutions will deeply affect the design and operation of the former structure.

Rule 3: Supply chain leaders must acknowledge that no supply chain decision is static and permanent; rather, their job is to continuously reengineer the solutions they manage.

The Restless Consumer: Market Trends

Despite the fact that other regions of the world are closing the gap in economic activity, strong consumer markets for finished goods remain in the USA and Canada, the European Union (although at a lower level than pre-2009), Japan, South Korea, Taiwan, as well as in the large emerging markets of the BRIC (Brazil, Russia, India, and China) nations. Other nations to watch include Mexico, Turkey, Saudi Arabia, Colombia, South Africa, Indonesia, Malaysia, and Thailand.

Pull My Chain: Sourcing and Manufacturing

In line with previous predictions of dynamism in supply chain solutions to serve those emerging or transforming markets, significant reengineering of supply chain networks are currently under way. This is predominantly being driven by changes in the Chinese manufacturing arena, forcing a reconsideration of supply chain solutions for all of the aforementioned market areas as organizations struggle to reduce total supply chain costs to serve those markets. The top emerging areas of opportunity for supply chain sourcing, manufacturing, and logistics to support consumer markets include Vietnam, Malaysia, India, Chile, Colombia, Uruguay, Brazil, Mexico, Costa Rica, Poland, the Czech Republic, Slovakia, Nigeria, South Africa, Kenya, and—surprisingly—the southern and western regions of the USA. In addition, many opportunities are just beginning to emerge in Africa, largely supported by infrastructure investment from China.

Trading Places: Global Trade and Logistics Hubs

The many changes in market, sourcing, and manufacturing locations will require changing trade lanes among those business nodes. Emerging locations for establishing global trade and logistics hubs, as well as minor assembly, packaging, and redistribution facilities include Hong Kong, Singapore, United Arab Emirates (UAE), Panama, and Saudi Arabia (thanks to the developing trans-Arabian highway), as well as Egypt, Algeria, and Morocco, which serve as points of entry to sub-Saharan Africa. Even within regions, trade flows are shifting to highlight new areas of focus for assembly and logistics operations. In Europe, the center of gravity for trade flows is slowly moving, shifting from a Western-oriented logistics network to one that is more centrally focused on the continent. In North America, flows are slowly shifting from an east-west or west-east axis to a more south-north access as Mexican ports and manufacturing centers gain in prevalence. The opening of the new Panama Canal in 2015 also promises to increase trade volumes in the Gulf of Mexico and southeastern U.S. ports, further strengthening that trend.

As Time Goes By: Learning to Live in the Modern World

The passage of time continues to attest to the dynamic nature of the modern world. Supply chain managers are compelled to be closely in touch with cultural, historical, and political trends that can change the playing field virtually overnight. As testimony to this assertion, one need only consider some changes that have occurred since we first conceived the idea for this book in early January 2011. At that time, the social movement that would eventually overtake the Arab world and lead several nations in the Middle East and North Africa (MENA) toward violent revolution—a movement that continues today—was in its infancy.

Technology breakthroughs may also change the global playing field. For example, the breakthroughs in drilling technology that sparked oil production booms in the USA and Canada, as well as offshore oil production near Africa and South America, had only just begun to be reported. These breakthroughs have increased global oil output by nearly a third since 2008. In fact, less than five years ago major supply chain educational conferences were featuring keynote sessions focused on the end of affordable oil. Looking forward, emerging technologies such as three-dimensional printing and intelligent robotics promise to revolutionize concepts in sourcing, manufacturing, and logistics and to throw current supply chain wisdom topsy-turvy. Furthermore, the increasing sophistication of "big data" applications promises another technological impact on global supply chain management, potentially changing global network designs based on insights gleaned from massive amounts of operational data.

The changing dynamics of economics and politics could also abruptly shift the tectonic plates of global business, further changing today's accepted view of global supply chain wisdom. Lower salary growth in developed economies compared to those in emerging economies, combined with changes in energy prices, could change the sourcing and manufacturing attractiveness of a region in a very short period of time. The recent case of select manufacturing returning to the USA is a good example of this. Given the economic turmoil in the southern tier of Europe, this trend could emerge in Europe as well. Such trends could hasten the prediction of a less global and more regional supply chain focus.

A foundational change in global demographics is also under way. Every industrialized nation is experiencing population aging, some, particularly in East Asia, at alarming rates. Yet the emerging world is growing; in Africa, for example, the majority of the population is under 25 years old. In addition, populations are moving rapidly into large cities. Future supply chains will need to focus on the needs of this growing, urbanized population, yet their needs will not be the same from region to region. New variables will enter the supply chain puzzle: differentiating from, time and place value by population age, and level of urbanization.

Finally, the growing effect of sustainable development will impact supply chain decision making. For example, imagine the changes in consumer choice for products if the CO_2 footprint information was mandatory on packaging. If in certain regions this criterion became more important than the price, supply chains would have to adapt to find appropriate solutions, potentially altering the focus on short delivery time to instead optimize CO_2 consumption. Imagine how that would change the model being pursued by Amazon in the USA, for example, which is currently driving online consumer purchasing in a number of categories toward same day delivery.

Such unpredictable changes could discourage even the most experienced and confident global supply chain manager. Here is a final piece of advice to those managers: buckle up your seat belts and arm yourself with knowledge of the nuances among the nations and peoples of the world that affect supply chain decision making and operations. This isn't about operating in Kansas City or Paris or Stuttgart or Tokyo or Shanghai anymore—the picture is far more diverse and complex!

References

1. P. Ghemawat, *Redefining Global Strategy: Crossing Borders in a World Where Differences Still Matter* (Boston, MA: Harvard Business School Press, 2007).
2. P. Ghemawat, *World 3.0: Global Prosperity and How to Achieve It* (Boston, MA: Harvard Business Review Press, 2011).

INDEX

Note: Page numbers followed by *f* denote figures; page numbers followed by *t* denote tables.